Lecture Notes in Computer Science　9749

Commenced Publication in 1973
Founding and Former Series Editors:
Gerhard Goos, Juris Hartmanis, and Jan van Leeuwen

More information about this series at http://www.springer.com/series/7409

Norbert Streitz · Panos Markopoulos (Eds.)

Distributed, Ambient and Pervasive Interactions

4th International Conference, DAPI 2016
Held as Part of HCI International 2016
Toronto, ON, Canada, July 17–22, 2016
Proceedings

 Springer

Editors
Norbert Streitz
Smart Future Initiative
Frankfurt
Germany

Panos Markopoulos
Eindhoven University of Technology
Eindhoven
The Netherlands

ISSN 0302-9743   ISSN 1611-3349   (electronic)
Lecture Notes in Computer Science
ISBN 978-3-319-39861-7   ISBN 978-3-319-39862-4   (eBook)
DOI 10.1007/978-3-319-39862-4

Library of Congress Control Number: 2016940117

LNCS Sublibrary: SL3 – Information Systems and Applications, incl. Internet/Web, and HCI

This Springer imprint is published by Springer Nature
The registered company is Springer International Publishing AG Switzerland

Foreword

The 18th International Conference on Human-Computer Interaction, HCI International 2016, was held in Toronto, Canada, during July 17–22, 2016. The event incorporated the 15 conferences/thematic areas listed on the following page.

A total of 4,354 individuals from academia, research institutes, industry, and governmental agencies from 74 countries submitted contributions, and 1,287 papers and 186 posters have been included in the proceedings. These papers address the latest research and development efforts and highlight the human aspects of the design and use of computing systems. The papers thoroughly cover the entire field of human-computer interaction, addressing major advances in knowledge and effective use of computers in a variety of application areas. The volumes constituting the full 27-volume set of the conference proceedings are listed on pages IX and X.

I would like to thank the program board chairs and the members of the program boards of all thematic areas and affiliated conferences for their contribution to the highest scientific quality and the overall success of the HCI International 2016 conference.

This conference would not have been possible without the continuous and unwavering support and advice of the founder, Conference General Chair Emeritus and Conference Scientific Advisor Prof. Gavriel Salvendy. For his outstanding efforts, I would like to express my appreciation to the communications chair and editor of *HCI International News*, Dr. Abbas Moallem.

April 2016   Constantine Stephanidis

HCI International 2016 Thematic Areas and Affiliated Conferences

Thematic areas:

- Human-Computer Interaction (HCI 2016)
- Human Interface and the Management of Information (HIMI 2016)

Affiliated conferences:

- 13th International Conference on Engineering Psychology and Cognitive Ergonomics (EPCE 2016)
- 10th International Conference on Universal Access in Human-Computer Interaction (UAHCI 2016)
- 8th International Conference on Virtual, Augmented and Mixed Reality (VAMR 2016)
- 8th International Conference on Cross-Cultural Design (CCD 2016)
- 8th International Conference on Social Computing and Social Media (SCSM 2016)
- 10th International Conference on Augmented Cognition (AC 2016)
- 7th International Conference on Digital Human Modeling and Applications in Health, Safety, Ergonomics and Risk Management (DHM 2016)
- 5th International Conference on Design, User Experience and Usability (DUXU 2016)
- 4th International Conference on Distributed, Ambient and Pervasive Interactions (DAPI 2016)
- 4th International Conference on Human Aspects of Information Security, Privacy and Trust (HAS 2016)
- Third International Conference on HCI in Business, Government, and Organizations (HCIBGO 2016)
- Third International Conference on Learning and Collaboration Technologies (LCT 2016)
- Second International Conference on Human Aspects of IT for the Aged Population (ITAP 2016)

Conference Proceedings Volumes Full List

Distributed, Ambient and Pervasive Interactions

Program Board Chairs: **Norbert Streitz, Germany, and Panos Markopoulos, The Netherlands**

- Andreas Braun, Germany
- Willem Paul Brinkman, The Netherlands
- José Creissac Campos, Portugal
- Dimitris Charitos, Greece
- Adrian David Cheok, Malaysia
- Richard Chow, USA
- Dimitris Grammenos, Greece
- Nuno Guimarães, Portugal
- Dirk Heylen, The Netherlands
- Achilles Kameas, Greece
- Javed Vassilis Khan, The Netherlands
- Kristian Kloeckl, USA
- Shin'ichi Konomi, Japan
- Irene Mavrommati, Greece
- Ingrid Mulder, The Netherlands
- Anton Nijholt, The Netherlands
- Mike Phillips, UK
- Fabio Paternó, Italy
- Matt Ratto, Canada
- Carsten Röcker, Germany
- Victor Manuel Ruiz Penichet, Spain
- Jean Vanderdonckt, Belgium
- Reiner Wichert, Germany
- Woontack Woo, Korea
- Xenophon Zabulis, Greece

The full list with the program board chairs and the members of the program boards of all thematic areas and affiliated conferences is available online at:

http://www.hci.international/2016/

HCI International 2017

The 19th International Conference on Human-Computer Interaction, HCI International 2017, will be held jointly with the affiliated conferences in Vancouver, Canada, at the Vancouver Convention Centre, July 9–14, 2017. It will cover a broad spectrum of themes related to human-computer interaction, including theoretical issues, methods, tools, processes, and case studies in HCI design, as well as novel interaction techniques, interfaces, and applications. The proceedings will be published by Springer. More information will be available on the conference website: http://2017. hci.international/.

General Chair
Prof. Constantine Stephanidis
University of Crete and ICS-FORTH
Heraklion, Crete, Greece
E-mail: general_chair@hcii2017.org

http://2017.hci.international/

Contents

Tracking and Recognition Techniques in Ambient Intelligence

Human Behavior in Smart Environments

Emotions and Affect in Intelligent Environments

Smart Cities and Communities

Designing and Developing Smart Environments

Towards Ubiquitous Services Design and Development Approach

Aicha Azoui and Djilali Idoughi[✉]

Applied Mathematics Laboratory – LMA, University Abderrahmane Mira of Bejaia,
Bejaia, Algeria
aicha.azoui@gmail.com, djilali.idoughi@univ-bejaia.dz

Abstract. Today's evolution of mobile technologies, telecommunication infrastructures and service oriented paradigm is leading to the development of ubiquitous services. Ubiquitous services are software applications that have the capability
to run anytime, anywhere and on any device with minimal or no user attention.
However, the advancements and diversity in technologies, the dynamic and ubiquitous nature of these services increase the complexity of the underlying development
process. In this paper, we propose a design approach for developing service oriented
ubiquitous systems considering both business and ubiquitous requirements. The
approach is applied to a crisis management case study.

Keywords: Ubiquitous system · Service orientation · Ubiquitous service ·
Ubiquitous requirements · Design framework

1 Introduction

The Ubiquitous Computing or UbiComp [1] is currently used to describe a computing
environment in which computation is everywhere and computer functions are embedded
and connected with various entities so that anyone can access, communicate, exchange
and share information anywhere and anytime.

Broadly defined, the vision of ubiquitous computing environment considers the
environment which surrounds the user's everyday lives and activities, saturated with
computing devices and communication capabilities, which can be implemented in a
varied scale of spaces where information and services are provided to the users when
and where desired [2].

Figure 1 illustrates broadly the vision of ubiquitous computing environment. The
convergence of mobile technologies in terms of mobile devices and telecommunication
infrastructures and software engineering paradigms (i.e., especially the emergence of
service oriented paradigm (SOC)) has brought about a new service-oriented computing
paradigm known as ubiquitous services or context-aware services [3, 4].

However, these advancements and diversity in technologies and the highly dynamic
nature of ubiquitous services contribute to make ubiquitous services design a complex
and challenging software engineering task compared to conventional services. Thus, the
design and the development of ubiquitous services is a more complex task [3, 6]. In
conventional services input information can be managed in a common way since it is

© Springer International Publishing Switzerland 2016
N. Streitz and P. Markopoulos (Eds.): DAPI 2016, LNCS 9749, pp. 3–14, 2016.
DOI: 10.1007/978-3-319-39862-4_1

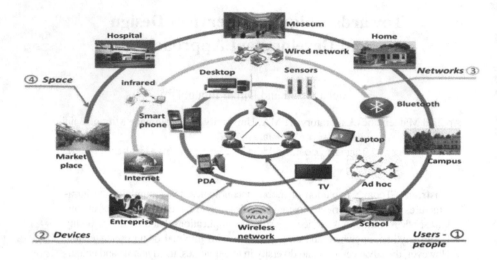

Fig. 1. Global ubiquitous computing environment vision [5]

mainly considered to be obtained principally from the user. In contrast, when developing ubiquitous services, input information needs to be managed differently since it is obtained from diverse sources [7]. This information, termed "context", affects both the behavior and the interaction of the service with the user in a variety of different ways, and enables the service to adapt its functionality accordingly.

In this paper, we aim to present an approach to develop ubiquitous systems based on the service-oriented paradigm providing the end-user with ubiquitous services that meet their current needs, and that adapt to their contexts.

The Remainder of this paper is organized as follows: Sect. 2 presents some related work to the development of service oriented ubiquitous systems. Section 3 presents the basic concepts of the proposed framework which is applied to a typical crisis management case study in Sect. 4. And finally, we conclude and give some further research work in the Sect. 5.

2 Related Work

The development of ubicomp services based systems has led to the emergence of different research works that have provided mainly design frameworks and systems architectures. The most proposed works concentrate mainly on one specific service design issue such as, discovery [8], composition [9] or adaptation [10]. In Chaari *et al.* [10] the focus is on the services adaptation to different contexts in a ubiquitous environment. This adaptation is achieved with a system containing management and storage of context and adaptation modules. Toninelli *et al.* [8], in a ubiquitous scenario, provide a middleware which adopts semantic techniques to perform the discovery of context-aware services based on the requirements and preferences expressed by mobile users. The middleware exploits the users' devices and service profiles metadata to provide personalized and customized services. Meanwhile, Tili *et al.* [9] propose an architecture model for the service composition which is based on an assembly of lightweight components. The model relies on a software and hardware execution environment evolving dynamically. It is based on a web service for the device infrastructure using events, and dynamically discoverable in a distributed way.

Moreover, some other research work [7, 11, 12, 4, 13] suggest the employment of a model driven engineering process which is an approach for using models at various levels of abstraction in software development. The key idea is to automatically transform highly abstract models into more concrete models from which an implementation can be generated in a straightforward way. Therefore, Achilleos *et al.* [7] propose a model-driven development process that facilitates the creation of a context modeling framework simplifying the design and implementation of ubiquitous services. In this process, functional and ubiquitous requirements analyses are lacking and adaptation mechanism of the created services is not addressed. Vale and Hammoudi [11] propose the use of the model driven engineering approach to develop context-aware services by the separation of concerns in different models. However, the requirements analysis is not taken into consideration, as well as the proposed context meta-model is not generic and the adaptation strategy is not described. Sheng and Benatallah in [12] present a UML based modeling language for the model driven development of context-aware services and a generic meta-model of context is presented. The proposed approach does not provide guides and instructions for context modeling and requirements analysis. Moreover, the authors do not specify the mechanism used to fulfill context aware services adaptation. In [4] the authors propose an architecture for the development of context-aware services. The development work is based also on the aspect oriented paradigm. The aim of this architecture is to address fundamental challenges for the design of services in context-aware service-oriented systems. This architecture allows the creation of generic context meta-models and adaptation strategy. However, the functional specification of the system and identification of services are not addressed. Moreover, it does not provide guides for identifying context information. Finally, Abeywickrama and Ramakrishnan [13] propose an engineering approach for context-aware services that models and verifies these services at the architectural level. The approach benefits from several software engineering principles such as the model driven architecture, the separation of concerns through aspect-oriented modeling and formal verification using model checking to facilitate context aware-services engineering. The approach development process is incomplete because it does not take into account the analysis phase and a context model is not given.

The most approaches highlighted above have focused on the context modeling and adaptation to context changing as dominant and unique aspects of ubiquitous systems. However, the functional aspect of the system is neglected, this makes these approaches incomplete. In addition, the requirements analysis phase identifying business and ubiquitous requirements yielding to necessary services and context models is absent in all the approaches presented. Therefore, the aim of this paper is to present a service based ubicomp system design framework which overcomes these lacks and provides a richer engineering process as it is described in the next section.

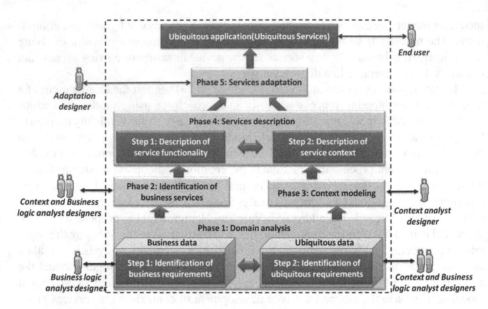

Fig. 2. The global view of the design framework along with the involved design roles

3   Our Proposal

3.1   The Framework Basic Concepts

The proposed framework is based on a set of founding concepts and principles such as facilitating separation of the developer's tasks and specification of ubiquitous models. It considers ubiquitous services as a central concept resulting from building both service oriented business and ubiquitous views. Thus, we separate the development process into business and ubiquitous views. The business view focuses on the business logic of the system and its functionalities. Whereas, the ubiquitous view is responsible for the definition of a context, acquisition, interpretation, modeling and exploitation by the application. Moreover, four different actors (roles) may be involved in the development process of ubiquitous services (Fig. 2) as follows:

1. **The Business logic analyst designer,** focuses on the business logic of the application model without ubiquitous and technological considerations.
2. **The Context analyst designer**, responsible for the identification of ubiquitous functionalities supported by the system. These functionalities involve context data specific to the users and their environment.
3. **The Adaptation designer,** defines a set of mechanisms and rules necessary for the dynamic adaptation of business logic to the context of the application at runtime.
4. **The End user**, the human actor who invokes services anywhere, anytime. The system, transparently, provides the appropriate services using the context.

3.2 The Proposed Framework

The proposed approach is a methodological framework (Fig. 2) which consists of five phases. Each phase includes one or more steps that can be performed by different actors involved (business, ubiquitous). It is an iterative process aimed to achieve user satisfaction and monitor requirements evolution.

Phase 1: Domain analysis. This phase is a preliminary study of the business domain by analyzing both business and ubiquitous issues to elicit and identify business and ubiquitous requirements. It identifies the business processes through different domain scenarios. The ubiquitous requirements are linked to business processes. The outcome of this phase is a domain model and a business use case model enriched with ubiquitous requirements which expresses the potential functionalities of the ubiquitous system.

Step 1: Identification of business requirements. The aim is to identify what the system performs or does; it is performed by the business logic analyst-designer who proceeds to an overall identification of the various business processes described in the functional requirements of the system. As a consequence, a list of business processes relevant to the domain is obtained.

Step 2: Identification of ubiquitous requirements. This step is performed by the context analyst-designer in collaboration with the business logic analyst-designer. It consists in analyzing the business requirements to extract and identify ubiquitous requirements. The context analyst-designer analyzes these requirements and places them in the business scope. The result of this step is a use case diagram model highlighting the overall business processes, their interdependences along with actors and the associated ubiquitous requirements.

Phase 2: Identification of business services. This phase is realized by the business logic analyst-designer collaborating with the context analyst-designer. The purpose is to identify a set of candidate business services from business processes identified in the previous phase. Our approach is based on the concept of goals underlying the business services. Each business process strategic goals are elicited. Thus, the strategic goal is decomposed into one or more functional and sub functional goals. This detailed goals decomposition enables to identify the goals of fine granularity (operational goals) as business services. Afterwards, a goals hierarchical structure is obtained. The realization of this hierarchy takes into account both the ubiquitous and functional goals.

Phase 3: Context modeling. This phase is the first ubiquitous phase. The context analyst designer formalizes the context by analyzing the different ubiquitous goals identified in the previous phase as well as the definition of the context model relative to the ubiquitous functionalities.

Step 1: Definition of ubiquitous rules. The different ubiquitous goals identified in the previous phase should be detailed by transforming them into ubiquitous rules. The generated rules are written in the following form: **If** condition **then** consequence.

Step 2: Generation of the Context model. The set of ubiquitous rules defined in the previous step allows the generation of context data to be considered in the system and to be modeled. The generated conceptual context model includes the entities, their profiles and their interdependences with the environment (Fig. 3). It contains only the needed pertinent elements to model the context and eliminates details that could affect its generic character.

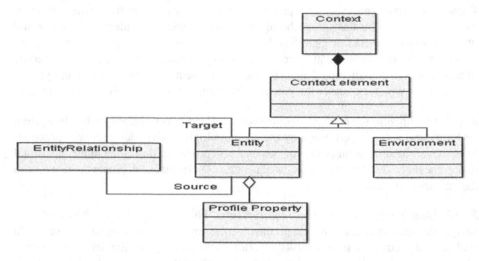

Fig. 3. Context meta-model

Phase 4: Services description. For each identified service, both its functionality that meets user's needs and the context in which the service is valid and executed will be described.

Step1: Description of the service functionality. This description contains information about the functionality that this service can provide. All this information is grouped into an interface.

Step2: Description of the service context. This description contains the information about the context of the service such as the type of device, network, the time required to deliver to the user the service final response, cost of service, etc. This context presents additional information about the service in order to determine whether or not, this service is relevant to the current context of the user, and improve the quality of the response returned to the user.

Phase 5: Services adaptation. The adaptation designer defines a strategy for a dynamic service adaptation to new contexts of use. Aspect-oriented programming [14] is used to adapt the service behavior according to contextual changes, without modifying its business logic. The separation between business services considerations and contextual considerations remains fundamental to the adaptation of services. Therefore, modification of the adaptation actions should not cause changes in the business logic of the service. These aspects will be dynamically woven into the core service to be adapted (Fig. 4).

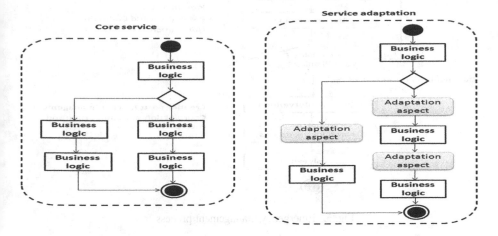

Fig. 4. Service adaptation strategy

The following section describes broadly the application of the framework on a concrete case study relative to the crisis management field.

4   Case Study - Crisis Management Field

4.1   Scenario Description

Crisis management is a special type of human and complex organization [15] in which, various actors belonging to different authorities need to collaborate and work together with the shared aim to solve, or at least reduce, a crisis situation. Each actor may be equipped with different devices and communication technologies to carry on specific tasks. In this paper, a crisis can be defined as a disruption in the normal functioning of an organization or society, resulting from a brutal and sudden event. The main crisis management activities can be grouped into four phases: (1) prevention, (2) preparation, (3) emergency management (response) and (4) recovery.

Hereafter, we focus on the emergency management phase where the underlying response process is divided into two main steps (Fig. 5): (1) Alert and (2) Intervention.

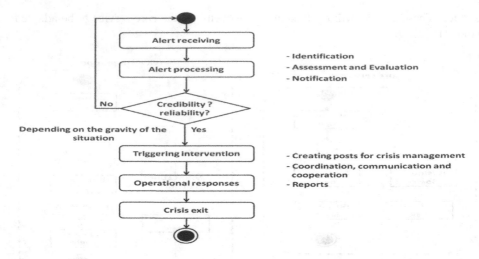

Fig. 5. Emergency management process

The Alert step represents a significant level of emergency that informs required people depending on the scope and gravity of the situation. It is triggered by the detection of an event or upon a receipt of an incident report. Afterwards, an evaluation of relevance of the emergency is determined, taking into account various types of data (affected people number, number of responders required in a short lapse of time, intervention of one or several governmental departments, etc.). Hence, a series of preplanned strategic tasks such as quickly mobilizing resources and required of various concerned organizations are carried out.

4.2   Application of the Framework

Phase 1: Domain analysis. A set of business processes have been identified. Two business processes are identified for emergency management: (1) *Alert Processing* and (2) *Intervention Order*.

Phase 2: Identification of business services. A hierarchy of functional, operational and ubiquitous goals corresponding to "*Alert processing*" process is obtained. The *Alert* process must satisfy the strategic goal "*Improve the time of detection and response*". The ubiquitous goals "*Consider personal information and context*" and "*Adjust the display*" are directly linked with the strategic goal which means that context information should be considered in all sub-functional and operational goals.

After the decomposition of the *Alert Processing* business process, four business services are identified: *Monitoring, Receiving Alert, Evaluating Alert*, and *Notifying Alert*.

Phase 3: Context modeling. The ubiquitous goal defined in the hierarchy is used to derive ubiquitous rules to identify the necessary context information which facilitates context modeling. Table 1 illustrates the derived ubiquitous rules that are applied to the *Alert processing* business process.

Table 1. A driven set of ubiquitous rules

Ubiquitous rules	Conditions	Consequences
The location must be considered before sending an alert	Detection of a disturbance	Send an alert
The surrounding disturbances have to be considered	Damage on infrastructure (roads)	Inform rescuer
during the movement of the rescuers	A traffic alert	Inform rescuer
The context of the rescuer (location, device and environment) must be considered before notifying	The crisis is large-scale	Send notification
The display must consider the context of the rescuer and his preferences	Preference of display	Interact by respecting the preferences

Figure 6, illustrates a context model for the crisis response obtained by instantiating the context meta-model (Fig. 3) and considering the set of ubiquitous rules above.

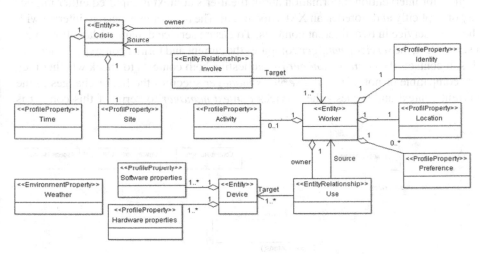

Fig. 6. A context model for crisis response

Phase 4: Services description. The Fig. 7 shows an extract of the WSDL (Web Service description Language) document describing a hardware resource allocation service invoked by an intervener on the crisis site. This service has a list of material resources which are available during the crisis. When this service is invoked by the intervener, the service enables the selection of the desired equipment to validate the allocation in this latter. The WSDL description presents only information about service functionalities. Moreover, we take into account the context of the service. This context is defined by three XML elements: "device", "service" and "network".

```
<definitions targetNamespace="http://ws/"
name="ressource_allocation_serviceService">
<types>
    <xsd:schema>
<xsd:import namespace="http://ws/"
schemaLocation="http://localhost:8080/ressource_allocation/ress
ource_allocation_serviceService?xsd=1"/>
    </xsd:schema>
</types>
<message name="Allouerressource"> .... </message>
<message name="AllouerressourceResponse"> .... </message>
<portType name="ressource_allocation_service"> .... </portType>
<binding
name="ressource_allocation_servicePortBinding"type="tns:resso
urce_allocation_service"> .... </binding>
<service name="ressource_allocation_serviceService">
    <port name="ressource_allocation_servicePort"
binding="tns:ressource_allocation_servicePortBinding">
        <soap:address
location="http://localhost:8080/ressource_allocation/ressource_a
llocation_
    serviceService"/>
    </port>
</service>
</definitions>
```

Fig. 7. WSDL document of the service hardware resource allocation

Phase 5: Services adaptation. A crisis management scenario is used to illustrate the service adaptation process. A rescuer on the disaster site makes a resource allocation request for intervention. Information about the user's context is captured either implicitly or explicitly and stored in an XML document. The rescuer may need to interact with the same service in two different contexts. To ensure service dynamic adaptation to the user context, the *services manager* compares the current and former contexts. To achieve this, it contacts the *context manager* by requesting both contexts to check whether they are compatible or not. If not, the *services manager* specifies the list of changes in the current context and requests the services *context manager* to verify if this context is

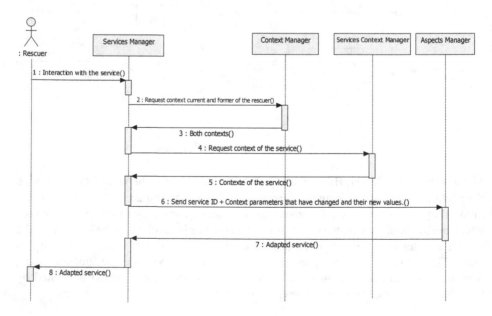

Fig. 8. Sequence diagram for the dynamic adaptation process

compatible with the list of changes in the current context or not. Similarly, it compares the value of each element in this list with the context of the service. If they are not compatible, the *services manager* returns the identifier of the service (service ID) as well as context parameters that have been changed to the *aspects manager*. The *aspects manager* selects appropriate aspect for adapting the service. The selected aspect must contain the adaptation action corresponding to the change of context. Thereafter, this aspect is woven within the core service to be adapted and provides a relevant response to the end user as illustrated by the sequence diagram in Fig. 8.

5 Conclusion

In this paper, a design framework for developing ubiquitous system based on the service-oriented paradigm is proposed. This provides a high level of abstraction and has several advantages. In addition to the benefits of productivity and quality improvement of context and ubiquitous services development, the framework has also the advantage of considering ubiquitous requirements to extract ubiquitous rules and provide formal procedures. This is to identify context information needed to build easily the context model using a predefined context meta-model. The context meta-model is generic and open to allow its extension to various domains depending on needs. Ubiquitous requirements are developed in a separated way from system functionalities (i.e., business requirements), which is useful to enhance flexibility and facilitate system reuse and modifications. The framework is applied on a real case study related to the crisis management field.

Acknowledgments. The authors gratefully acknowledge and express their warm thanks to the Direction Générale de la Protection Civile de la wilaya de Bejaia, Algeria and the University A. Mira of Bejaia.

References

1. Dhingra, V., Arora, A.: Pervasive computing: paradigm for new era computing. In: First International Conference on Emerging Trends in Engineering and Technology, 2008, ICETET 2008, pp. 349–354. IEEE (2008)
2. Weiser, M.: The computer for the 21st century. Sci. Am. **165**(3), 94–104 (1991)
3. Abeywickrama, D.B.: Pervasive services engineering for SOAs. In: ICSOC Ph.D. Symposium (2008)
4. Hafiddi, H., Baidouri, H., Nassar, M., Kriouile, A.: Context-awareness for service oriented systems. Int. J. Comput. Sci. Issues (IJCSI) **9**(5), 95–104 (2012)
5. Idoughi, D., Azoui, A.: SOA based ubiquitous computing system design framework. In: Proceedings of the 12th ACM International Symposium on Mobility Management and Wireless Access, pp. 71–75 (2014)
6. Preuveneers, D., Berbers, Y.: Semantic and syntactic modeling of component-based services for context-aware pervasive systems using OWL-s. In: First International Workshop on Managing Context Information in Mobile and Pervasive Environments, pp. 30–39 (2005)

7. Achilleos, A., Yang, K., Georgalas, N.: Context modelling and a context aware framework for pervasive service creation: a model driven approach. Pervasive Mobile Comput. **6**, 281–296 (2010). Elsevier

8. Toninelli, A., Corradi, A., Montanari, R.: Semantic-based discovery to support mobile context-aware service access. Comput. Commun. **31**(5), 935–949 (2008)

9. Tigli, J.Y., Lavirotte, S., Rey, G., Hourdin, V., Riveill, M.: Lightweight service oriented architecture for pervasive computing. Int. J. Comput. Sci. Issues (IJCSI) **7**(4), 1–9 (2010)

10. Chaari, T., La forest, F., Celentano, A.: Adaptation in context-aware pervasive information systems: the SECAS project. Int. J. Pervasive Comput. Commun. **3**(4), 400–425 (2007)

11. Vale, S., Hammoudi, S.: Model driven development of context-aware service oriented architecture. In: International Conference on Computational Science and Engineering - Workshops (2008)

12. Sheng, Q.Z., Benatallah, B.: ContextUML: a UML based modeling language for model-driven development of context-aware web services. In: 4th International Conference on Mobile Business (ICMB 2005), pp. 206–212 (2005)

13. Abeywickrama, D.B., Ramakrishnan, S.: Context-aware services engineering: models, transformations, and verification. ACM Trans. Internet Technol. (TOIT) **11**(3), 10 (2012)

14. Kiczales, G., Lamping, J., Mendhekar, A., Maeda, C., Lopes, C.V., Loingtier, J.M., Irwin, J.: Aspect-oriented programming. In: Akşit, M., Matsuoka, S. (eds.) Object-Oriented Programming, ECOOP 1997. Lecture Notes in Computer Science, LNCS, vol. 1241, pp. 220–242. Springer, Heidelberg (1997)

15. Aitabdelouhab, K., Idoughi, D., Kolski, C.: Agile & user centric SOA based service design framework applied in disaster management. In: ICT-DM 2014, 1st IEEE International Conference on Information and Communication Technologies for Disaster Management (2014)

Exploring Design for Multi-device, Multi-environment and Multimodal Connected Experiences

Himanshu Bansal[✉], Sai Shruthi Chivukula, and Sanjay Ghosh

Samsung R&D Institute Bangalore, Bangalore, India
himanshubansal99@gmail.com,
{ch.shruthi,sanjay.ghosh}@samsung.com

Abstract. Increasing user encounters with connected devices, IoT, Smart Home and Connected Cars have been motivating designers and HCI researchers need to craft interaction solutions for such scenarios of the future. Designing solutions for scenarios, which we named M3 that involves multiple contexts (Multi-Environment) with users using connected devices (Multi-Device), using natural interactions (Multimodal) is complex. In this research, we employed visual stimuli and activity based methodology to explore such scenarios for connected home infotainment and connected car contexts. We explored the interrelationships among these M3 aspects and identified user preferences to evolve design direction for designing effective interaction, user workflows and tasks for such encounters. This helped us evolve the M3 Design framework which describes cause-effect relationships among various themes of a sample scenario of connected cars. We also present the applicability of the framework as a reference tool for brainstorming, comparative evaluation of design alternatives and solution detailing.

Keywords: Multimodal interaction · Connected devices · Internet of things · Smart home · Connected car · User centred design

1 Introduction

Users of today are well surrounded with many connected devices providing easy things and more than 5 billion people will be connected by 2020 [9]. Internet of Things is reshaping the connected experiences of user's lives. With the evolution of natural mechanisms of interaction in future, users are expected to switch to these interaction methods to interact with the connected environments and devices. User's choice of interaction is likely to depend upon the kind of environment, the task situation, the devices and the available interaction modalities and relationships among these factors. Therefore, in order to design solutions for such connected experiences of future, one has to consider the user's preferences and interrelationship among these three components named as M3(Multi-Environment, Multi-Device and Multimodal).

The key challenge is to take holistic approach towards understanding interdependencies among these components and designing solutions for such complex scenarios. There have been lot of research in the past focused on multimodal interaction for particular task context and evaluation of certain modalities [2, 4]. Moreover, considering that

© Springer International Publishing Switzerland 2016
N. Streitz and P. Markopoulos (Eds.): DAPI 2016, LNCS 9749, pp. 15–25, 2016.
DOI: 10.1007/978-3-319-39862-4_2

these scenarios being futuristic, it is also difficult to design for such scenarios by adopting conventional user centred design approach. In [6], authors proposed a methodology to ideate for IoT services by placing probes in daily environments or bodystorming and Nieminen [7] described user-centered concept development process for emerging technologies in four phases while giving emphasis on technology findings.

Other than these methodologies, researchers have proposed frameworks based on meta-design approach [3] and analysis of relationship among services, spaces, and users [10] for smart home like scenarios. We applied activity based user-centred design methodology through use of visual stimuli to understand the relationships between M3 factors and task types using modality and device switching patterns of the participants. Also this helped us identify fundamental themes responsible for these relationships and dependencies. Through systematic analysis of qualitative data, we evolved the M3 design framework for Connected Car context. Our choice to explore Connected Car as a sample domain for our exploration is motivated out of its great potential. A forecast predicts more than 92 million vehicles with Internet connectivity by 2016 [1]. This framework can help designers contemplate holistically and come up with solutions without losing user's concerns.

2 Methodology

We conducted interactive user sessions for two contexts: Home and Car. For these activity based sessions, we involved a total of 21 participants; 11 participants (6M, 5F) were involved for Smart TV viewing (Home) context and 10 (7M, 3F) connected car context. All participants were in the age group of 21–35 yrs (Mean $= 27$, SD $= 2.36$) and they were screened on the basis of their prior experience of the contexts.

Contextual scenarios were created for both Smart TV viewing and connected car situations. We gave the following scenario of Smart TV viewing in home context to participants: "You are watching a movie on TV and along with that you are following a Cricket match. During commercial, you switch to Sports channel. You find that one of the players is leading the team to win the match. You post about this on Facebook to show your happiness." The scenario involved four unit tasks: T1- Changing the channel, T2- Specify action of posting on Facebook, T3- Add text to the post and T4- Confirmation of posting. Similarly, in car context, we presented the following scenario to the participants: "While driving the car to your Home, you receive the message a friend that your common friend is in the town. You reply back her saying that you will reach there in 15 min. Then, you change the navigator destination to your friend's place." Here again, the scenario consisted of four unit tasks: T1- Giving command to open/read the message, T2- Replying to the message, T3- Opening navigator and T4- Changing route in the Car navigator.

In order to maintain consistency between both contexts and ensure the exhaustive variability in the nature of the tasks, all the four tasks in both contexts were categorized under three categories:

(i) T_a: Tasks that involved changing the value through multiple similar interactions-
  T1 in home context and T4 in car context

(ii) T_b: one touch/command tasks- T2, T4 in home context and T1, T3 in car context
(iii) T_c: composing task- T3 in home context and T2, T4 in car context.

Participants were familiarized with the scenarios using Wizard of Oz with the help of interactive prototype. During this familiarization phase, they were asked to complete the four tasks of the context. During this process, participants were encouraged to discuss their expected usage style and response from the systems and also how according to them, these expectations depend on various factors.

Later on, respondents were inquired about their order of priority of modalities and devices for each of the tasks by means of cards. Each card graphically represented a choice of combination of a device and a modality. The choices given in both contexts and the devices made available to the users are shown in Table 1. Participants were asked to arrange the cards in the order of priority for each of the four tasks one by one. In order to observe the effect of change in the devices on modality preference, each user session was conducted in two parts where additional device(s) were given to the participant in the second part. Participants were asked to think aloud during the activity and the entire user session was audio-recorded. Post each of the tasks we involved them in a qualitative interaction to understand the reasons for their choices.

Table 1. Devices and modality choices for both contexts

Context	Device[(parts)]	Modality
Home	Smartphone[(1, 2)]	Touch, Voice, Phone motion
	Smartwatch[(2)]	Touch, Voice, Air gestures
Car	Car dashboard[(1,2)]	Touch, Voice, Steering/Dashboard buttons
	Smartphone[(2)]	Touch, Voice, Phone motion
	Smartwatch[(2)]	Touch, Voice, Air gestures

3 Quantitative Analysis

Preference score for a particular device-modality combination was generated by summing reverse of the ranks given by user. Task wise preference scores for all device-modality pairs (only in part 2) have been shown in Fig. 1. From the analysis of these scores, following patterns were observed:

1. In home context, unlike other tasks, smartwatch gesture was preferred most for T1 task (changing channels) because of the task features: high frequency and quickness. As changing channel is relatively frequent while watching TV (other 3 tasks were related to posting on Facebook), participants were fine with defining gestures for it.

2. In T4 task in Home (confirm posting on Facebook), touch was preferred relatively more than the other tasks because participants reported as it is the last step, they wanted to be sure of the action and unintentional mistake would bring back to the initial step or something wrong would be posted.

3. In car context, touch was preferred relatively more in the T4 task (change destination in the navigator) when compared to other tasks because there are lots of possibilities

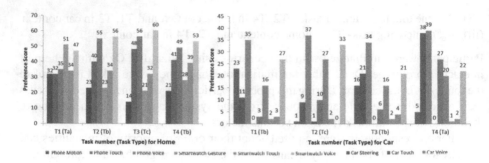

Fig. 1. Task wise preference scores for all device-modality pairs in home and car environments

in terms of outcomes of a task which may lead to mismatch between result and intention of the users. Therefore, participants wanted to look at the screen and use touch (zoom and pan) for verification and preparation before driving the car.

4. Smartwatch and Car-Dashboard were most preferred devices in Home and Car respectively. This shows that users are more likely to choose devices most accessible to them in order to minimize the distraction from primary task (even if other devices have advantages like larger screen size and more familiarity).

4   Interrelationships Among M3 Aspects

We converted participants' individual device and modality preferences into switching patterns and created Fig. 2. These switching patterns led us to our initial explorations in establishing the relationships among M3 aspects and task which is summarized pictorially in Fig. 3. Following paragraphs explain how these relationships were evolved:

Environment: It was observed that changing environment from Home to Car resulted in device preference change (watch to car dashboard) for all three types of tasks. At the same time, environment change resulted in change in modality preference for only one type of task (one step task). This suggests that environment is more crucial for device selection than modality selection (a > c in Fig. 3). It is also clear from Fig. 2 that participants showed more modality and device switching in home context compared to car.

Modality: It is evident from Fig. 2 that modality-switching occurred lot more because of task change than device change i.e. for modality selection, task is more important factor than device (d > e). In [5] also, authors showed the dependence of modality on task type. As mentioned earlier, change in environment resulted in change in modality preference for one of the three types of tasks whereas modality was switched only 4 times out of total 84 (44 + 40) cases for device addition. It means environment is more important than device for modality preference (c > e).

Device and Task Type: Moreover, device switching was observed for all 3 types of tasks with the change of environment. On the contrary, out of total 63 (33 + 30) cases of task change, only seven resulted in device-switching. This indicates environment as

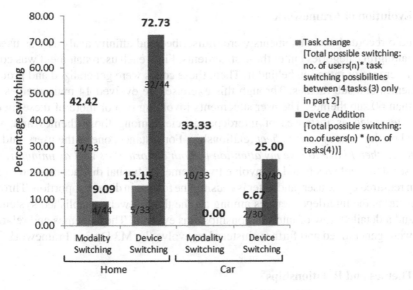

Fig. 2. Modality and device switching patterns

more influential factor for device preference than task (a > b). Lastly, it can be seen in Fig. 2 that in case of task change, frequency of modality switching is higher than device switching for both contexts i.e. task type affects modality preference more than the device preference (d > b).

5 M3 Design Framework

Further qualitative analysis was done to identify intermediary factors behind the relationships described in previous section. This analysis resulted into M3 design framework.

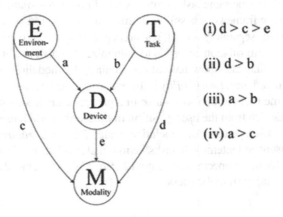

Fig. 3. Inter-relationship among M3 and task

5.1   Evolution of Framework

The audio recorded user statements were transcribed and affinity analysis was used to get meaningful categories out of these statements. First, each user-statement was coded by its inference or intention behind it. Then, these codes were generalized and grouped into themes and sub-themes. Through this exercise, we evolved 14 main themes and more than 60 sub themes. The user statements involving two or more of these themes were interpreted as instances of interdependencies among those themes and were inferred on the basis *of cause-effect* relationship. For instance, one of the users said, *"if I use touch then I have to give my attention to both important as well as unimportant"* This user statement was found to involve two themes of 'visual distraction' and 'information required by the user' and latter is causing the former in direct proportion. Through such patterns the interdependencies among all the themes were established systematically and a detailed flow of interrelationships was evolved. These themes and relationships were generalized and further clustered to evolve the M3 Design Framework.

5.2   Themes and Relationships

We here describe the M3 Design Framework through its 14 main themes. *Characteristics of a task* as a theme include the importance, urgency and frequency of a certain task. *Continuity* is about continuing a certain modality or device throughout an activity or while task-switching and how it had an effect on the remaining factors or themes. *Distraction* has different kinds of visual, audio or task switching disturbances or case of user's attention requirement. *Ease of Use* refers to the convenience of a choice, number of steps and total time involved in performing a task with certain choices of devices and interaction modalities. *Effort* refers to any kind of pain or strain the user goes through in terms of physical, cognitive load or due to too many actions expected from the user in a short time. *Familiarity* refers to the user's prior experience in using various available options like devices, interaction modalities in various tasks involved in different environments. The kind and amount of feedback from the device in terms of information and modality is considered in the theme of *Feedback*. *Flexibility* is about having a choice of device and modality for a certain task and of doing the same task in many ways. Flow of *information* among various themes included in the framework is split into information required by the user and those required by the system separately. In [8], researchers highlighted the hierarchy input and output modality and information in order to minimize distraction while driving a car. Further, *Intuitiveness* indicates how natural and similar, the modalities and the expected user actions are in affordance. *Learnability* is the extent to which certain modality or device is remembered by the users to perform a task in a particular environment. Device screen size, proximity of device from the user, position of device for certain user input, environmental factors and user patterns are included under *Physical features*. *User Control* includes user's consent and intention in tasks/actions that involves user commands or decision. Additionally, for the connected car context *Safety* was also included as one of the key themes based on the input from the users.

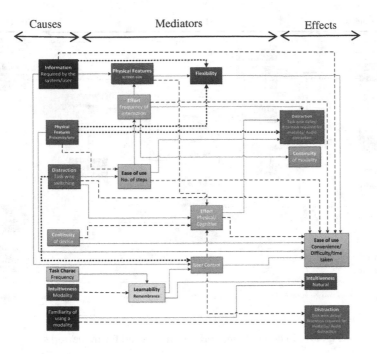

Fig. 4. M3 design framework-home

All the themes in the framework were categorized as Cause, Effect and Mediators or Influencers as shown in Figs. 4 and 5. There exist direct and inverse proportionality relationships between Causes-Effects pairs. Direct proportionality refers to relationship where Effects show similar changes to the Cause while inverse proportionality refers to the Effect showing opposite changes to the Cause. This relationship was used to understand the effect from the initial Causes through the Mediators. This kind of proportionality was not applicable for few non quantifiable themes such as type of environment, type of feedback, etc.

6   Application of M3 Design Framework

6.1   Design Ideation

In this approach, framework is used to come up with multiple ideas for a pre-decided domain. Out of the 14 themes, the themes which would play role in forming the ideas particular to that domain are discussed and identified. Then, each of these themes is separately branched out to come up with their detailed aspects through mind-mapping. Different aspects are connected across and within themes in such a way that a series of links result in one category of ideas and through multiple such links, many categories of ideas can be generated.

For example, when goal is to come up with multiple ideas on 'proactivity in car' as a domain, appropriate themes are 'information required/received by system and user',

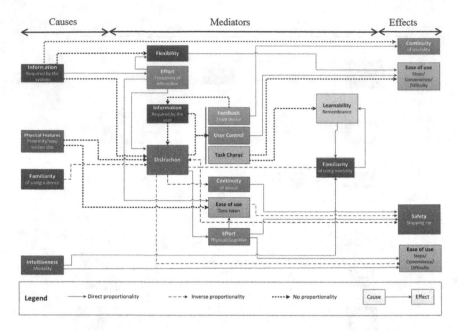

Fig. 5. M3 design framework-car and legend for frameworks

'user control', 'feedback', 'task characteristics' and 'environmental factors'. All six themes are branched out to details through mind mapping (see Fig. 6(a)). Time or place for providing a particular type of info required by a user can be connected to a particular task characteristic. One example of such information can be petrol level which should be proactively informed to driver when its low (urgency as a task characteristic) and a petrol pump are nearby.

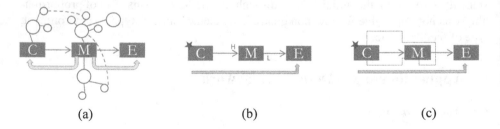

| (a) | (b) | (c) |

Fig. 6. Flow in frameworks of the Applications: (a) design ideation, (b) comparing design alternatives, (c) solution detailing [C- Cause, M- Mediators, and E- Effect]

6.2   Comparing Design Alternatives

This approach is used when designers have to choose which idea works better keeping user's considerations in mind. In this case, flow goes from the cause side of the framework towards the effect side. First, the causes which are relevant for a particular idea are discussed and identified by the designers and each one is marked with one of the four values: High (H)/Medium (M)/Low (L)/User-dependent. Cause- effect and proportionality relationships are used to carry forward these values to mediators and effects (from mediators). If a mediator theme is affected by multiple causal themes, average of the values received from the causal themes is passed to the effect theme. This procedure is followed for all the ideas to be compared. Finally, different values received by an effect is compared across ideas to know which idea is better for that effect because these effects are the goals to be achieved through the idea.

For example, let's take an example of comparison between movie ticket booking and e-booking in home context. The activity includes the primary task as watching television and doing the above two tasks when a movie trailer or product advertisement comes on TV. Take Fig. 4, for movie ticket booking, physical features and task characteristics act as user dependent factors, information required(H/M), frequency of interactions(M), number of steps(H), continuity of device(M) (these values are given on comparing both the examples) act as inputs or initial causes. These values have an effect on 'physical/cognitive effort' which has values of H/M, M and M, so the average value is taken and the final effect of ease of use is given a value M. Similarly, when it was applied for E-Booking, the final effect 'ease of use' had a value L and distraction had a value of H. So comparing these two shows that achieving Movie ticket booking is better and solutions should be detailed for E-Booking under ideation application (which is explained in the next section).

6.3 Solution Detailing

This happens when you have certain goal to achieve. This includes flowing from the effect to the cause side in the framework, marking the important and controllable mediators and causes according to how they should be tweaked for the necessary effects or goals. The designer jots down few questions first according to how the mediators should be and ideates at every theme solving these questions.

For example, let's take an example of detailed ideation on travel blogging in car context while the user is driving. Take Fig. 5, our main goal is to increase safety and ease of use while blogging in a drive. Few important and controllable mediators/causes can be information and flexibility etc. among others. Questions like *"how to lower the information required by the system/user?"*, *"How to increase the flexibility in the way of using a modality?"* etc. have to be jotted down. The ideas in terms of modalities, devices and information should be provided to answer these questions e.g. giving predefined or auto-detected hashtags for a photo though voice to reduce the information input by the user. Similarly, ideas can be jotted at every theme for the required effect.

6.4 M3 Design Framework Used in a Design Iteration

We have applied this framework, in case of 'information on the go' for context of 'Watching TV'. After generating a number of ideas on this domain, all of them were compared (shown in Sect. 6.2) and 'movie ticket booking while watching TV' was chosen for idea detailing part. Ideas like 'Introducing contextual icon in the mobile for booing app w.r.t the movie trailer on the TV', 'Using voice input or biometric inputs for entering card details to reduce the number of steps', 'auto selection and introducing one step confirmation steps for the user to reduce distraction' and related things were finalized while detailing for prototyping the movie ticket booking idea.

7 Conclusion and Future Work

The M3 Design Framework presented in this paper can be used as a reference tool to design user's connected experience encounters for futuristic domains like connected cars, smart homes, IoT. In this paper, we presented an activity based qualitative research methodology which we used in two contexts of 'Smart TV viewing' and 'Connected Car'. As the activity involves a structure flow and visual stimuli, it provides the participants with ground to divulge their choices in such scenarios and more importantly, reasons behind the choices. Through device and modality switching patterns, we established relationships among M3 aspects and task type. We have also explored relative dependencies of one factor on another compared to third factor. In order to inform design decisions, it was essential to dive deeper and to identify intermediary factors behind the relationships. Affinity analysis of the qualitative data helped us to obtain 14 such intermediary themes and evolve M3 design Framework by making cause-effect relationships among these themes.

The M3 design Framework can be used as a reference (1) to aid brainstorming to generate multiple ideas, (2) to comparatively evaluate various design alternatives on the basis of user's preferences, and (3) for solution detailing till the level of designing interactions and features. Additional application of the M3 design Framework can be formulation of questionnaires for usability testing of a prototype in which relevant effects and mediators can be considered as factors to be evaluated. The methodology can be used to generate frameworks for other contexts like office, public spaces etc. by providing context relevant tasks and visual stimuli during user-sessions. Therefore, along with M3 design framework for 'Connected Car' to produce design solutions for it, we propose the method to create similar frameworks for other contexts.

In future, we plan to extend the framework to include multi-user as fourth parameter. We will continue to generate these frameworks for smart home and other IoT contexts by incorporating quantitative approach as well.

References

1. Connected Cars-Consumer & Commercial Telematics and Infotainment 2014–2018: Juniper Research, 1 Jun 2014. http://www.juniperresearch.com/researchstore/key-vertical-markets/connected-cars/consumer-commercial-telematics-infotainment
2. Cohen, P.R., Johnston, M., McGee, D., Oviatt, S., Pittman, J., Smith, I., Chen, L., Clow, J.: QuickSet: multimodal interaction for distributed applications. In: Proceedings of the 5th ACM International Conference on Multimedia, pp. 31–40 (1997)
3. Fischer, G., Giaccardi, E.: Meta-design: a framework for the future of end-user development. In: Lieberman, H., Paternò, F., Wulf, V. (eds.) End User Development, pp. 427–457. Springer, Netherlands (2006)

4. Metze, F., Wechsung, I., Schaffer, S., Seebode, J., Möller, S.: Reliable evaluation of multimodal dialogue systems. In: Jacko, J.A. (ed.) HCI International 2009, Part II. LNCS, vol. 5611, pp. 75–83. Springer, Heidelberg (2009)
5. Naumann, A.B., Wechsung, I., Möller, S.: Factors influencing modality choice in multimodal applications. In: André, E., Dybkjær, L., Minker, W., Neumann, H., Pieraccini, R., Weber, M. (eds.) PIT 2008. LNCS (LNAI), vol. 5078, pp. 37–43. Springer, Heidelberg (2008)
6. Negri, A.L., Trousse, B., Senach, B.: Ideation of IoT services with citizen: coupling GenIoT and AloHa! methods. In: ServDes 2012-Service Design and Innovation Conference (2012)
7. Nieminen, M.P., Mannonen, P., Turkki, L.: User-centered concept development process for emerging technologies. In: Proceedings of the Third Nordic Conference on Human-Computer Interaction, pp. 225–228. ACM, October 2004
8. Siewiorek, D., Smailagic, A., Hornyak, M.: Multimodal contextual car-driver interface. In: 2002 Proceedings of the Fourth IEEE International Conference on Multimodal Interfaces, pp. 367–373. IEEE (2002)
9. Are you ready for the Internet of everything? World Economic Forum, By John Chambers, 15 January 2014. https://agenda.weforum.org/2014/01/are-you-ready-for-the-internet-of-everything/
10. Wu, C.L., Fu, L.C.: Design and realization of a framework for human–system interaction in smart homes. IEEE Trans. Syst. Man Cybern. Part A Syst. Hum. 42(1), 15–31 (2012)

Investigating Low-Cost Wireless Occupancy Sensors for Beds

Andreas Braun[1,2(✉)], Martin Majewski[1], Reiner Wichert[1], and Arjan Kuijper[1,2]

[1] Fraunhofer Institute for Computer Graphics Research IGD, Darmstadt, Germany
{andreas.braun,martin.majewski,reiner.wichert,
arjan.kuijper}@igd.fraunhofer.de
[2] Technische Universität Darmstadt, Darmstadt, Germany

Abstract. Occupancy sensors are used in care applications to measure the presence of patients on beds or chairs. Sometimes it is necessary to swiftly alert help when patients try to get up, in order to prevent falls. Most systems on the market are based on pressure-mats that register changes in compression. This restricts their use to applications below soft materials. In this work we want to investigate two categories of occupancy sensors with the requirements of supporting wireless communication and a focus on low-cost of the systems. We chose capacitive proximity sensors and accelerometers that are placed below the furniture. We outline two prototype systems and methods that can be used to detect occupancy from the sensor data. Using object detection and activity recognition algorithms, we are able to distinguish the required states and communicate them to a remote system. The systems were evaluated in a study and reached a classification accuracy between 79 % and 96 % with ten users and two different beds.

Keywords: Capacitive proximity sensors · Bluetooth LE · Smart furniture · Home automation

1 Introduction

Bed or seat occupation sensors are commonly available in intensive care facilities to give audible alerts when a patient tries to exit a chair or a bed. Caretakers are able to react on this signal can prevent falls during the getting up process. Another potential application area are home automation systems. A suitably placed occupancy sensor could be used to control heating and lighting to save energy. The most common commercial sensor is a pressure mat that is placed below the mattress [1]. These sensors are typically closed system that have no external communication method. Additionally, they may fail for light persons or stiff mattresses. They may also be difficult to switch between different beds. Modern sensing devices combine sensors, such as accelerometers and communication systems including Bluetooth in small form factors, tuned towards energy efficiency and portability. In this work we want to investigate if these systems allow us to create affordable and versatile occupancy sensors for beds or other forms of seating.

© Springer International Publishing Switzerland 2016
N. Streitz and P. Markopoulos (Eds.): DAPI 2016, LNCS 9749, pp. 26–34, 2016.
DOI: 10.1007/978-3-319-39862-4_3

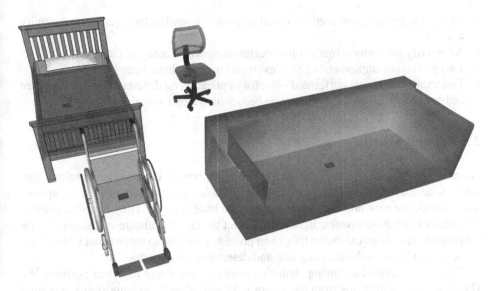

Fig. 1. Potential scenarios for wireless occupancy systems. Bed on top left, office chair on top right, wheelchair on bottom left, and couch on bottom right.

We would like to evaluate how well non-pressure sensing is suited for occupancy detection. Two factors are considered. The first is the movement of the bed frame or slatted frame below the bed when a person enters the bed. An accelerometer or motion sensor that is sufficiently sensitive can detect this movements and detect entry and exit events. The second is the usage of presence sensors that can be placed below the bed, but are still able to detect the presence of human bodies. We investigate two sensor technologies. The aforementioned accelerometer detects changes in acceleration of an object, while having a high sensitivity. We can use them to analyze entry and exit events on a bed. The second type are capacitive proximity sensors that detect the presence of a human body over a distance.

We introduce two methods that use the acquired sensor data to detect the necessary events. The accelerometer uses a threshold-based feature for activity tracking, while the capacitive sensors require initial calibration, drift compensation and several thresholds for distinguishing poses. These methods have been implemented into two prototype devices created for this project. One is based on a plain LightBlue Bean that integrates an accelerometer with free access to the data [2]. The second is an Arduino with an attached capacitive sensor based on the Capacitive Sensing library [3].

In an evaluation, we attach the devices to different objects suitable for occupancy sensing, as shown in Fig. 1. We first test if the systems are generally suited to detect occupancy on five objects. In a second evaluation we tested the classification accuracy of the occupancy sensing on two different beds with ten users. In this case we collected 200 samples of occupied and unoccupied states.

This paper proposes the following scientific contributions:

- An occupancy detection method, based on presence sensing for capacitive proximity sensors
- An activity recognition method for accelerometers to identify occupancy
- Two prototypes implementing the developed methods have been built
- Two evaluations were performed - one for application on different types of furniture and one for classification accuracy on beds with a larger sample size.

2   Related Works

There is a large body of research that has evaluated how to create smart furniture that is able to detect the presence, posture or even physiological parameters of its occupants. Harada et al. use pressure mats to create pressure images [4, 5]. They extract a number of features from these images, in order to detect the current posture of the persons on the pressure mat. In an extension they even provide a method to reconstruct a 3D model of the human body on the pressure mat and detect motion patterns.

Hong et al. created a sensing chair that uses a pressure mat to detect postures [6]. They create pressure maps from the sensor data and calculate eigenpostures, a feature based on eigenvectors. Using training data from 20 users they achieve an accuracy between 90.3 % and 99.8 %.

The Health Chair by Griffiths et al. is an office chair equipped with an array of sensors used to detect occupancy, activities, and physiological activities on it [7]. It incorporates pressure sensors and ECG in the armrests to detect the heart rate. We have been working with sensing chairs in the past that support posture recognition or exercises on the seat [8, 9]. Additionally, we previously worked with capacitive sensors under beds that were used for a more fine-grained posture detection, the use of flexible materials for measurement, or tailored towards the recognition of sleep phases [10–12]. In this work we want to provide a simple and portable method to just track occupancy without additional features.

Capacitive proximity sensors detect the body by its influence on a generated low-intensity electric field. These sensors can detect the body over a distance and are thus suitable for installation below the bed frame. A prototype by MacLachlan was able to detect objects at a distance of 1.5 m [13]. It is a very versatile technology that can be used flexibly, by modifying materials, geometry, circuit design, and processing methods used. We give an overview of potential use cases and design considerations that are the basis for the capacitive prototype of this work [14].

The advent of smartphones has spawned numerous applications that use the installed accelerometers or microphones to detect motion during sleep [15, 16]. The phone is usually placed somewhere on the mattress, e.g. below the pillow and tracks movement either by vibrations of the mattress or sounds generated by the user.

Bluetooth Low Energy or BLE is a communication standard for low-power devices that need to communicate over medium distances of up to 30 m with other systems. It is commonly used for location tags or iBeacons that can be used to support mobile devices in indoor navigation [17]. Recently it has been used to provide small programmable microcontrollers with low-power communication facilities. One example device is the LightBlue Bean, an Arduino-compatible microcontroller without wired connections that is powered by a coin cell [2].

3   Presence Sensing Using a Capacitive Proximity Sensor

In general we can distinguish between the calibration phase of the occupancy sensor that is performed initially and the execution phase of the sensor performed during normal operation. Presence sensing with a capacitive proximity sensor requires four different processing steps, as shown in Fig. 2.

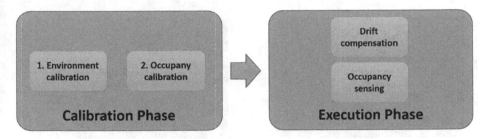

Fig. 2. Data processing of presence sensing using a capacitive proximity sensor

Environment calibration is necessary, as the basic capacitance measurement of a sensor is based on the environmental parameters it resides in, as well as various other factors, such as electrode material or duration of measurement [14]. Usually this does not require more than taking a certain amount of samples and calculating the initial average.

Occupancy calibration is performed on the first object detection. After the sensor is installed under a surface and calibrated towards the environment, a person is sitting or lying on the object. The resulting sensor value is indicative of the object being occupied and stored for later use. Here we can collect a number of samples and calculate an average.

Drift compensation is the process to account for changes in capacitance caused by changes in the environment. E.g. if the temperature of the system increases or the humidity in the room is lowered, the resulting sensor values will change. Drift compensation is a process that analyses the sensor values over a longer time and applies changes to the initial environment calibration. This is crucial for applications, where the sensor is turned on for a long time.

Occupancy sensing is based on a simple threshold method. Typically, a threshold somewhere between the value after environment calibration and the occupancy values is calculated. In this case the threshold is put at 50 % of the occupancy value. If the sensor values exceed this threshold, occupancy is detected. Additionally, we specify that the threshold has to be exceeded for a specific number of samples or a time frame. In our case the system is considered occupied if the occupancy threshold is exceeded for at least one second.

4   Activity Recognition Using Accelerometers

Data processing to recognize activities from accelerometers is simpler compared to capacitive sensing. The sensors are available in packages that already perform all cali-bration routines internally. We receive angular values that depict the acceleration of the sensor in x, y, z direction. Moving the sensor will cause these values to change. We define motion as the difference in subsequent acceleration readings. In our application the direction of movement is not very important, as the system is hanging freely. For each sample we calculate the sum of values to get the overall acceleration. The difference of these sums over three samples is used to calculate the velocity of the motion (Fig. 3).

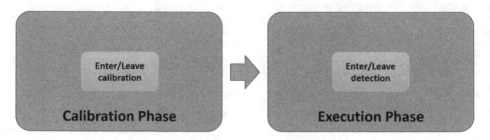

Fig. 3. Data processing of activity recognition using accelerometers

Enter/Leave calibration is performed the first time a person is entering the object (or sitting on the object). The recorded velocity is stored. In our system we use the maximum velocity recorded during several sit/lie (get up/stand up) events.

Enter/Leave detection now looks for motion velocities that result in similar values to the calibration phase. Since we want to account for variability the threshold to be exceeded is put at 80 % of the maximum velocity of the calibration phase.

4.1   Prototype Systems

Two prototypes have been created for this work. The accelerometer activity system was implemented on the LightBlue Bean, an Arduino-compatible microcontroller tailored for Bluetooth LE communication [2]. We attached wires to the system, that can be used to connect external systems or in our case, to attach the prototype to the piece of furniture where we want to register occupancy. The accelerometer is integrated on the board, as well as a Bluetooth chip. It is powered using a coin cell battery. Figure 4 gives an overview of the LightBlue Bean, the attached wires and some important components. The device is programmed via Bluetooth, usually from a smartphone. We use the inte-grated accelerometer and an activity recognition method based on a single-direction movement of the sensor.

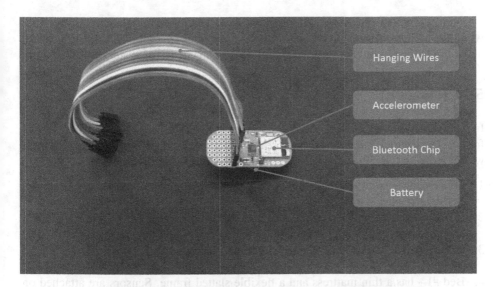

Fig. 4. Close up picture of LightBlue Bean and the hanger

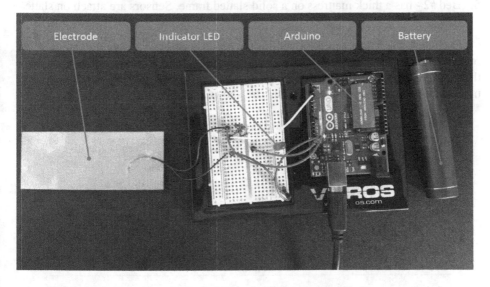

Fig. 5. Arduino with resistors and printed circuit board installed on a breadboard

For the second system the Arduino Capacitive Sensing library was used to create a single channel capacitive sensor [3]. A dual layer PCB is used as electrode and connected to a digital input using a large 40 MOhm resistor (Fig. 5). This enables sensing at distances of up to 40 cm. This capacitive system distinguishes three states that have to be initially calibrated - "sitting", "lying" and "not on bed".

The cost of both systems is comparatively low. The LightBlue Bean retails for $30, while the components of the capacitive system together cost around $50. It has to be noted that the latter could be reduced significantly if an integrated system would be used.

5   Evaluation

In our evaluation we test how well both systems recognize entering and leaving events for different persons and different beds. The evaluation was two-fold. At first the system was tested with five different pieces of furniture by two different users.

1. Office chair - is an office chair with backrest and armrests that has a gas spring. Sensors are attached at the bottom of the seat.
2. Wooden chair - is a thinly cushioned chair with wooden seat and backrest and metal legs. Sensors are attached at the bottom of the seat.
3. Wheel chair - is a basic wheel chair with leather seat area. Sensors are glued to leather seat.
4. Bed #1 - has a thin mattress and a flexible slatted frame. Sensors are attached on slatted frame.
5. Bed #2 - has a thick mattress on a solid slatted frame. Sensors are attach on slatted frame.

Each took a seat five times, stayed for ten seconds and got up again, leading to an overall number of 20 recognizable events. In the second part ten different users occupy the two different beds. Here everybody takes a seat ten times, waits ten seconds and gets up again. The results of both evaluations are shown in Table 1.

Table 1. Results of evaluations one and two with five different objects and 2–10 users

Object	No. samples	Recall accelerometer	Recall capacitive
Office chair	20	90 %	85 %
Wooden chair	20	55 %	100 %
Wheel chair	20	85 %	85 %
Bed #1	20	75 %	95 %
Bed #2	20	50 %	90 %
Bed #1 (10 users)	200	91 %	96 %
Bed #2 (10 users)	200	79 %	93 %

The accelerometer system is able to detect entry and leaving events with a good success rate - however struggles at differentiating both, if one of the events results in an increased vibration. Overall, the detection rate is not as good, as for capacitive sensors, with the exception of the office chair. Here, the distance between the bottom of the chair and the seat is somewhat far, making it more difficult to detect for the capacitive sensors, while the accelerometer system benefits from the gas spring that results in a movement of the whole seat area. The accelerometer struggles when the structure is very rigid or the person is careful when taking a seat, as this results in reduced movement of the object.

The capacitive senor does not have this limitation, but can be disturbed by metal parts near its location, as was the case for the office chair and the wheel chair.

6 Conclusion and Future Work

On the previous pages we have introduced two low cost systems for occupancy detection on objects, particularly beds. One system uses an accelerometer for detecting movement, while the second uses a capacitive proximity sensor to detect objects in range. Both systems have advantages and disadvantages, with the accelerometer system being cheaper in the current prototyping stage, while the capacitive sensing system was more reliable, with detection rates between 85 % and 100 % in the small sample evaluation and 93 % to 96 % in the larger second evaluation.

In the future we would like to use more precise capacitive systems that are better integrated to combine high accuracy with low cost. OpenCapSense by Grosse-Puppendahl et al. is a proximity sensing toolkit with high precision that might be suitable [18].

References

1. Tunstall: Tunstall Bed Occupancy Sensor. http://www.tunstall.co.uk/solutions/bed-occupancy-sensor. Accessed 26 Feb 2016
2. Punch Through Design: The LightBlue Bean. http://legacy.punchthrough.com/bean/. Accessed 26 Feb 2016
3. Badger, P.: Capacitive Sensing Library. http://playground.arduino.cc/Main/CapacitiveSensor
4. Harada, T., Mori, T., Nishida, Y., Yoshimi, T., Sato, T.: Body parts positions and posture estimation system based on pressure distribution image. In: Proceedings 1999 IEEE International Conference on Robotics and Automation (Cat. No. 99CH36288C), pp. 968–975. IEEE (1999)
5. Harada, T., Sato, T., Mori, T.: Human motion tracking system based on skeleton and surface integration model using pressure sensors distribution bed. In: Proceedings Workshop on Human Motion, pp. 99–106 (2000)
6. Tan, H.Z., Slivovsky, L.A., Pentland, A., Member, S.: A sensing chair using pressure distribution sensors. IEEE/ASME Trans. Mechatron. 6, 261–268 (2001)
7. Griffiths, E., Saponas, T.S., Brush, A.J.B.: Health chair: implicitly sensing heart and respiratory rate. In: Proceedings of the 2014 ACM International Joint Conference on Pervasive and Ubiquitous Computing - UbiComp 2014 Adjunct, pp. 661–671. ACM Press, New York (2014)
8. Braun, A., Frank, S., Wichert, R.: The capacitive chair. In: Streitz, N., Markopoulos, P. (eds.) DAPI 2015. LNCS, vol. 9189, pp. 397–407. Springer, Heidelberg (2015)
9. Braun, A., Schembri, I., Frank, S.: ExerSeat - sensor-supported exercise system for ergonomic microbreaks. In: De Ruyter, B., et al. (eds.) AmI 2015. LNCS, vol. 9425, pp. 236–251. Springer, Heidelberg (2015). doi:10.1007/978-3-319-26005-1_16
10. Djakow, M., Braun, A., Marinc, A.: MoviBed - sleep analysis using capacitive sensors. In: Antona, M., Stephanidis, C. (eds.) UAHCI 2014, Part IV. LNCS, vol. 8516, pp. 171–181. Springer, Heidelberg (2014)
11. Braun, A., Heggen, H.: Context recognition using capacitive sensor arrays in beds. In: Proceedings AAL-Kongress (2012)

12. Rus, S., Grosse-Puppendahl, T., Kuijper, A.: Recognition of bed postures using mutual capacitance sensing. In: Aarts, E., et al. (eds.) AmI 2014. LNCS, vol. 8850, pp. 51–66. Springer, Heidelberg (2014)
13. MacLachlan, R.: Spread Spectrum Capacitive Proximity Sensor. http://humancond.org/wiki/user/ram/electro/capsense/0main. Accessed 26 Feb 2016
14. Braun, A., Wichert, R., Kuijper, A., Fellner, D.W.: Capacitive proximity sensing in smart environments. J. Ambient Intell. Smart Environ. 7, 1–28 (2015)
15. Jones, C., Campbell, S., Zone, S.: Familial advanced sleep-phase syndrome: a short-period circadian rhythm variant in humans. Nat. Med. 5(9), 1062–1065 (1999)
16. Krejcar, O., Jirka, J., Janckulik, D.: Use of mobile phones as intelligent sensors for sound input analysis and sleep state detection. Sensors 11, 6037–6055 (2011)
17. Apple Inc.: iBeacon for developers. https://developer.apple.com/ibeacon/. Accessed 26 Feb 2016
18. Grosse-Puppendahl, T., Berghoefer, Y., Braun, A., Wimmer, R., Kuijper, A.: OpenCapSense: a rapid prototyping toolkit for pervasive interaction using capacitive sensing. In: 2013 IEEE International Conference on Pervasive Computing and Communications, PerCom 2013, pp. 152–159 (2013)

User Interface Design for Ambient Assisted Living Systems

Caroline Byrne[1]([⊠]), Rem Collier[2], Michael O'Grady[2], and Gregory M.P. O'Hare[3]

[1] Department of Computing and Networking,
Institute of Technology Carlow Co., Carlow, Ireland
Caroline.byrne@itcarlow.ie
[2] Clarity: Centre for Sensor Web Technologies, School of Computer Science,
University College Dublin (UCD), Belfield, Dublin 4, Ireland
{rem.collier,michael.j.ogrady}@ucd.ie
[3] School of Computer Science and Earth Institute,
University College Dublin (UCD), Belfield, Dublin 4, Ireland
gregory.ohare@ucd.ie
http://www.ucd.ie

Abstract. Ambient Assisted Living (AAL) systems and the interface design principles applied to them is vitally important in facilitating the elderly in achieving their daily goals of health monitoring, social interaction, physical exercise or daily reminders. Design principles for AAL systems have accommodated for a user's physical and cognitive abilities and Activities of Daily Living (ADL's) but does not give enough recognition to interfaces that require various key user interactions as age profiles increase. This paper seeks to explore if User Interface (UI) design for the elderly needs to address this issue.

Keywords: Ambient assisted living · User interfaces · Design principles

1 Introduction

World Demographics have changed within the elderly [1], longevity of life in conjunction with medical science has resulted in humans living long, active lives, with their representation within the population increasing. In order to facilitate the independent lives of these individuals [2] and to reduce the economic burden of such long-term care, Ambient Assisted Living (AAL) systems have become a priority [3]. The aging process requires increasingly sophisticated medical supervision and AAL systems have provided this unobtrusive reassurance [4] for the healthy elderly [5] and for those with cognitive decline [6] through dedicated User Interfaces (UI). UI design is paramount within the area of AAL as its success influences future system usability [7]. Good User Interface (UI) design practice commonly cite Neilsen's 10 usability heuristics [8] along with Shneiderman's [9, 10] 8 golden rules, whilst specific elder design principles [11] are less well-known. Several research studies have been conducted within the area of elder usage of UI's [12] and the promotion of a universal interface design [13], in particular for the elderly user [14] using touch-based [15] and multimodal user interfaces [16]. Research has argued that the elderly cannot be considered as a combined age group but should be considered in terms of a third (65–80 yrs) and fourth age (80+ yrs) [17, 18]

© Springer International Publishing Switzerland 2016
N. Streitz and P. Markopoulos (Eds.): DAPI 2016, LNCS 9749, pp. 35–45, 2016.
DOI: 10.1007/978-3-319-39862-4_4

yet there is no evidence to suggest that this theory is applied when system interfaces are being designed. Many studies in design principle application acknowledge the differences in UI usability between younger and elderly adults [19, 20] but not between these two elder age groups [21, 22]. This paper examines whether UI design principles are reflected in various ambient systems and the consequent usability of these systems for the inherent stakeholders.

2   Human Computer Interaction

In 1995 Buxton proposed a basic framework around which the various aspects of computing could be categorised [23] see Fig. 1, incorporating a foreground and background, representing conscious and un-conscious activities. AAL system success is dependent upon technological expertise and user input to include implicit and explicit foreground interactions [24, 25] fading into the background when no longer required. Ambient interface interaction should be seamless offering unobtrusive background data while the user operates uninterrupted in the foreground [26].

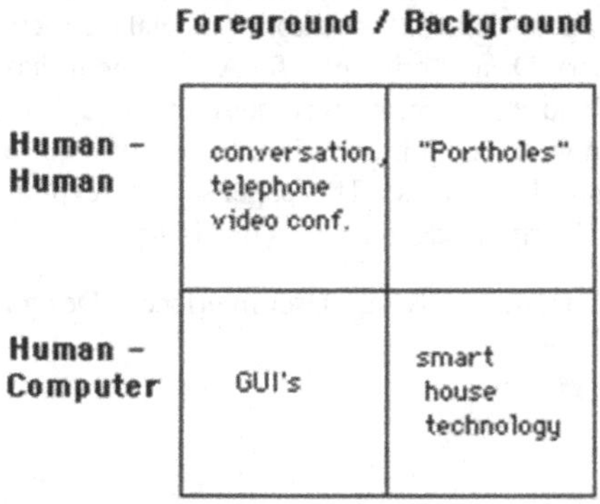

Foreground / Background

	conversation, telephone video conf.	"Portholes"
Human – Human		
Human – Computer	GUI's	smart house technology

Fig. 1. The Basic Model

They should be efficient, effective and easy to learn for all stakeholders, including health professionals, family members, carers and elderly users. User-friendly interfaces improve system interaction [27] however disparate interfaces across several devices discourage user uptake and hamper elder assimilation of the technologies [28]. Heterogeneity in elder UI design is paramount particularly within one system in order to establish best practice guidelines for future ambient interface success.

2.1   User Interface Design Principles

Central to good UI design is the notion of usability [29] and its virtues have been given extensive commentary over several decades [30] along with its inherent difficulties integrating technology with how humans live their lives. Sophisticated software systems can only implement their intended search and query tasks if the UI enables the user [31] to adequately interact with it. Effective UI design incorporates several facets including how we behave when information is presented to us and how we subsequently assimilate this information whilst accommodating for any limiting factors [32]. As technology evolved the term Ambient Intelligence (AmI) [33] became synonymous with various computer science fields such as engineering, in conjunction with the areas of health and education. Human-centered Computing (HCC) [34] principles facilitate the design of more effective intelligent interfaces. AAL systems require a unique level of context focus [35] as the user often enters and receives information which needs to be easily understood without prior medical or computational expertise. Commercially available systems deemed effective [36] include ActivPal [37], ADLife [38] and Quietcare [39] as they facilitate users with UI's which offer iconic visual representations of daily tasks.

2.2 Review of Europe's AAL Systems UI Design Approach

The AALIANCE AAL Roadmap [2] outlined its future aspirations for system development and highlighted that standardisation was required, in particular within UI design to facilitate the user's continuing requirements via adaptive interfaces. Several AAL systems reviews [40], [41], [42] have repeatedly stated that issues of data accountability, economics and security have manifested themselves in poor UI design thus propagating a lack of continued user engagement. Interfaces that can adapt to continuing user needs [43] should be supported with relevant UI design frameworks in order that the goal of independent living is achieved. Many systems and their methodologies have been assessed for effectiveness [44], with many successful systems developed. UniversAAL [45] is the most prominent AAL platform in Europe, with several input projects, Soprano [46], Persona [47], Amigo [48], Oasis [49], Genesys [45], MPower [50] all feeding their research into the advancement of an open source platform for researchers [51] to use as a baseline. This paper reviews Europe's most popular AAL systems so as to establish what weighting has been placed upon each UI design and its importance within the overall system architecture.

PERSONA: is a self-organising AmI system, with a relevant UI framework, platform modules and the goal of combining technologies to provide independent living possibilities for the elderly [52] within their own homes. An in-depth end user analysis was conducted and a scalable open standard platform was developed upon which a range of user services would be facilitated. Interface design is discussed in terms of OSGi layers and conclusions drawn were that future investments should be made in usability not further component manufacture.

SOPRANO: is a self-learning ambient system based on manually entered commands via various technologies such as sensors and actuators, interfaces are designed for medication reminders [53], encouraging exercise programs, enhancing social interaction and living safely. This required user led technologies to support an elder at home were included [54] and social separation, safety, daily routines, healthy physical and psychological attitude were on the highest tier of needs. Subsequent tiers included community awareness [55], shopping independence & supporting mobility levels for indoor/outdoor independence. The technical core named Soprano Ambient

Middleware (SAM) [56] receives user commands and through modularisation their approach to sensing, processing and reacting to users data has facilitated the use of scaled abstraction levels and user involvement remains crucial to the success of this system.

REMOTE: strives to improve health care delivery to infirmed elderly living independently [57], particularly those in rural areas with chronic conditions, such as hypertension, arthritis, asthma, stroke, Alzheimer's and Parkinson's disease. Efforts are being made to improve health care systems and tele-healthcare [58] in combination with Ambient Intelligence (AmI) enhances daily ambient surroundings with audio-visual, sensor and motoric data collection. Vital daily physiological readings are recorded along with the proactive monitoring of movements and at-risk situations [58], information is shared across heterogeneous devices where all services and technologies are required to interact seamlessly. UI's that facilitate the evolving physical and health care needs of its intended users will be available on various devices matching the technological literacy of each user [59]. This project was scalable, less rigid, more amenable to integration with previously installed software or hardware and interfaces [60] were adaptable to a user's needs and Information Technology (IT) ability. The project concluded that sensor monitoring [61] of frail elderly was successful in terms of decreasing cardiac mortality rates, increasing self-confidence and providing unobtrusive health monitoring for health care professionals. Interfaces will be optimised with user input to enhance software interaction.

MonAMI: is an open source platform [62] that seeks to assist the elderly with daily tasks, increasing their safety and quality of life [63]. Designed for the Slovakian environment [64] to deliver services using wireless and wired networks, it incorporates user friendly interaction technology with wearable devices and components for health monitoring. The OSGi4AMI uses TV controlled multimedia software with an ASUS touch screen interface and has facilitated the development of new interfaces for various platforms such as Android and iOS. This projects intention was to develop new services from pre-existing technologies such as wireless *(ZigBee)*, SON networks, wired networks *(1-wire technology)*, user-friendly interaction technologies, wearable and health monitoring technologies. The system interconnects via specified open source interfaces within OSGi4AMI on three levels, sensors, computing and interfaces [65]. Assorted smart devices could support the MonAMI UI, which is HTML based and comprises of three distinct UI's intended for the elderly, carers and system developers. The UI's are user friendly and accessible via a devices internet browser facilitating access to family members, playing/reading online, thus increasing feelings of safety, self-confidence and autonomy. Devices are separated into those with sensors *(ambient temperature, lighting)* and those with actuators *(ability to change status, on/off)*, subsequently added devices need to be included within the system structure and are visible at UI level.

I2HOME: main goal was to implement a standards-based open platform named the Universal Control Hub (UCH) in order to facilitate the user with a series of interfaces controlling the smart home. This project's achievements include the development of personalised UI's implemented via a user-centred design approach customised for users with special needs or those with cognitive difficulties. Devices should be touch-screen along with speech input/output, TV's with a simple remote control and mobile phone UI's (Windows & Android). The digital home is available to all citizens via pluggable interfaces through its flexible application framework, the UCH, which controls all aspects of heating, lighting, ADL reminders and facilitates integration of various target devices.

EMERGE: this monolithic [66] system supports elderly users with emergency monitoring and prevention through ambient, unobtrusive sensors and reasoning regarding emergency situations. Information is analysed in conjunction with recurring patterns and ADLs in order to create a database of daily and long-term living habits, to facilitate prompt detection and reaction to emergency situations. Relying on the constant evaluation of ADLs [67] initially defined in the Katz index, EMERGE is proactive in terms of fall detection and emergency response alerts. A Sensor Abstraction Layer (SAL) offers a simple interface for accessing and maintaining sensor data and assimilates semantic sensor information. The Human Capability Model (HCM) [68] represents the clinical knowledge of the elder created with the assistance of their medical experts. Avoidance of possible sensor data complications is achieved via a Multi-Agent-Based, Event-driven Activity Recognition System (EARS). This was developed to meet various detection and monitoring demands, all in-coming data is regarded as capacity boundless low-level sensor data, in contrast to hi-level specific outgoing data [69].

I-Living Project: approach was to develop an assisted living environment where several embedded devices (sensors, actuators, displays, & Bluetooth-enabled medical devices) could either operate independently or cooperate within an Assisted Living Hub (ALH) [70]. The ALH could be a dedicated PC, Personal Digital Assistant (PDA), or a black box enabled with one or several wireless interface cards communicating via the Assisted Living Service Provider (ALSP). This server simultaneously provides carers and health care professionals with HCIs in order to monitor all raw sensor data, examine it in closer detail if required and invoke alerts if necessary. Events can be organised by medical professionals or carers through interfaces via the ASLP server. Within the users home the reminder daemon regularly polls the server, chooses an appropriate device and forwards the reminder message to that device. The user reads their daily vital signs with Bluetooth-enabled medical meters, these results are encrypted and forwarded to the ALSP server where health professionals can access daily biometric data at any time.

SAAPHO: the Secure Active Aging: Participation and Health for the Old (SAAPHO) Project [71], encourages elderly participation as it elevates future product acceptance and usage. Elderly users were queried about their SAAPHO technology interactions, opinions on the system based on experience and possible system enhancement suggestions. The system itself assists elders in maintaining their daily living independence along three interconnecting trajectories of active aging, healthcare, participation and security services via intelligent interfaces on fixed and mobile devices. The architecture employs various interface tools in order to maximise user interaction whilst avoiding user information overload.

HOME SWEET HOME: this project [72] began in 2011 and one of the test pilot sites was located in County Louth, Ireland. It evaluated how the telemonitoring of an elder's physical and mental health, environment factors and ADL reminders would impact upon their lives. A simple user-friendly interface monitors each elder's health and well-being via data collected from environment sensors, video conferencing and various other support services. Sensors were fitted in all homes such as environment and temperature, smoke, water and presence detectors. InTouch devices consisting of broad-band routers and medical devices were installed, glucometers and asthma monitors based on the health profile of user. Health monitoring is carried out daily and abnormal meas-urements produce alerts which request the user to retake the measurement, if the alert continues then their General Practicioner (GP) is contacted. Emergency alerts from a smoke or Mambo device will contact the emergency services, passive alerts contact carers and relatives. The medical monitoring devices installed included a Blood Pressure (BP) monitor and a weighing scales, a Mambo phone was deployed to all participants homes which is carried on their person outside the home and a key fob within the home. Video conferencing enabled elders to contact friends and relatives via broadband and personal well-being is also monitored through the use of game playing. The project is still in its pilot stage with many of the initiatives still to be implemented.

3   AAL UI Best Practice Guidelines

Having undertaken this review of AAL systems it emerges that while representative subjects from the third age have had *some* involvement in the UI design, representatives from the forth age have had a very marginal input if any. Buxton's basic matrix was expanded in 2008 based upon an axis of criteria, see Fig. 2. [73] facilitating subtle, more implicit interactions between humans and machines, or a system. Conventional computing can be implicit or explicit and interactions are divided between attentional demands, that is, interaction required of its user and understanding a user's interaction with a given demand. Reactive interactions are user initiated and proactive if system initiated. AAL systems require implicit and explicit communications and users want unobtrusive systems, therefore information exchange must not manifest itself within the attentional foreground of the user. AAL systems need to be chameleon in nature, in the foreground if required by the user otherwise fading into the background.

The premise behind Buxton's [23] original Framework and the extended versions [73, 74] is that all human-computer interactions can be evaluated along various spec-trums of activity balanced against the level of invasiveness for the user. This is the keystone to UI evaluation of AAL systems, the balance between assisting when requested or when health and safety requires intervention. This evaluation framework facilitates independence not isolation, inclusivity not exclusion and a bi-directional channel for communications. Ambient systems that adhere to UI design guidelines have the power to be an effective technological assistant providing they achieve a balance between user initiated interactions and unsolicited system intrusions.

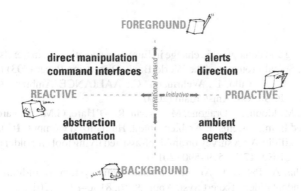

Fig. 2. Implicit interaction framework with a range of interactive system behaviours

4 Recommendations

This paper recommends that UI best guidelines for the elderly [11] as stated previously should be adhered to when designing and implementing AAL systems in parallel with Nielsens [8] and Shneiderman's [9, 10] general usability guidelines. The four main areas of focus in designing for the elder user include vision, hearing, mobility & cognition, with individual suggestions for each target area of concern. Given the elderly are considered in terms of a third (65–80 yrs) and fourth age (80+ yrs) [17, 18] then this premise should be applied to AAL UI design facilitating dynamic interfaces capable of being tailored for an age and medical health appropriate user. Representatives from both elder groups is necessary when testing systems in order that both cohorts increasingly complicated daily living needs are accommodated. AAL designers acknowledge the UI usability differences between these two elder groups [19, 20] yet persists with homogeneity when designing and testing [21, 22] systems. A reasonably healthy 65 yr old with IT skills has radically different AAL systems requirements to an 85 yr old with limited mobility, attention span and IT skills.

5 Conclusion

Ambient systems provide users with daily living assistance, some are less unobtrusive than others and users are still required to interact with a systems interface to a lesser or greater aspect. UI's affect uptake which impacts upon usability and those achieving commercial success have employed easily recognisable icons to represent daily activity tasks. Given ambient systems require subtle user interactions from an audience which will become progressively more infirm then perhaps the only solution is that of multimodal UI's which are dynamic and fulfill the users needs at any given point in their health continuum. Adaptivity of the system interface tracking the longitudinal progression of age, circumstance and condition is paramount for system adoption and persistence. This benefits users as the interfaces remain familiar and do not represent a stress factor when they are least capable of absorbing new system information.

References

1. Muenz, R.: Aging and demographic change in European societies: main trends and alternative policy options. Social Protection, The World Bank. Discussion Paper (703) (2007)
2. van den Broek, G., Cavallo, F., Wehrmann, C.: AALIANCE Ambient Assisted Living Roadmap, vol. 6. IOS Press, Amsterdam (2010)
3. O'Grady, M.J., Muldoon, C., Dragone, M., Tynan, R., O'Hare, G.M.: Towards evolutionary ambient assisted living systems. J. Ambient Intell. Humanized Comput. 1(1), 15–29 (2010)
4. Rashidi, P., Mihailidis, A.: A survey on ambient-assisted living tools for older adults. Biomed. Health Inform. IEEE J. 17(3), 579–590 (2013)
5. Botia, J.A., Villa, A., Palma, J.: Ambient assisted living system for in-home monitoring of healthy independent elders. Expert Syst. Appl. 39(9), 8136–8148 (2012)
6. Wan, J., Byrne, C.A., O'Grady, M.J., O'Hare, G.M.P.: Managing wandering risk in people with dementia. Hum.-Mach. Syst. IEEE Trans. 45(6), 819–823 (2015)
7. Nielsen, J.: Usability inspection methods. In: Conference Companion on Human Factors in Computing Systems, pp. 413–414. ACM (1994)
8. Nielsen, J.: 10 usability heuristics for user interface design. Fremont: Nielsen Norman Group. [Consult. 20 maio 2014]. Disponível na Internet (1995)
9. Shneiderman, B.: Designing the User Interface: Strategies for Effective Human-Computer Interaction, vol. 3. Addison-Wesley, Reading (1992)
10. Shneiderman, S.B., Plaisant, C.: Designing the User Interface, 4th edn. Pearson Addison Wesley, Boston (2005)
11. Pak, R., McLaughlin, A.: Designing Displays for Older Adults. CRC Press, Boca Raton (2010)
12. Silva, P. A., Nunes, F.: 3 × 7 Usability Testing Guidelines for Older Adults (2010)
13. Stephanidis, C., Antona, M. (eds.): Universal Access in Human-Computer Interaction: Design and Development Methods for Universal Access, vol. 8513. Springer, Switzerland (2014)
14. Crews, D.E., Zavotka, S.: Aging, disability, and frailty: implications for universal design. J. Physiol. Anthropol. 25(1), 113–118 (2006)
15. Häikiö, J., Wallin, A., Isomursu, M., Ailisto, H., Matinmikko, T., Huomo, T.: Touch-based user interface for elderly users. In: Proceedings of the 9th International Conference on Human Computer Interaction with Mobile Devices and Services, pp. 289–296. ACM (2007)
16. Reeves, L.M., Lai, J., Larson, J.A., Oviatt, S., Balaji, T.S., Buisine, S., McTear, M.: Guidelines for multimodal user interface design. Commun. ACM 47(1), 57–59 (2004)
17. Laslett, P.: A Fresh Map of Life: The Emergence of the Third Age. Harvard University Press, Cambridge (1991)
18. Laslett, P.: The third age and the disappearance of old age. In: Heikkinen, E., Kuusinen, J., Ruoppila, I. (eds.) Preparation for Aging, pp. 9–16. Springer, Heidelberg (1995)
19. Zhang, B., Rau, P.L.P., Salvendy, G.: Design and evaluation of smart home user interface: effects of age, tasks and intelligence level. Behav. Inf. Technol. 28(3), 239–249 (2009)
20. Obrist, M., Bernhaupt, R., Beck, E., Tscheligi, M.: Focusing on elderly: an iTV usability evaluation study with eye-tracking. In: Cesar, P., Chorianopoulos, K., Jensen, J.F. (eds.) EuroITV 2007. LNCS, vol. 4471, pp. 66–75. Springer, Heidelberg (2007)
21. Lorenz, A., Oppermann, R.: Mobile health monitoring for the elderly: designing for diversity. Pervasive Mobile Comput. 5(5), 478–495 (2009)
22. Consolvo, S., Towle, J.: Evaluating an ambient display for the home. In: CHI 2005 Extended Abstracts on Human Factors in Computing Systems, pp. 1304–1307. ACM (2005)
23. Buxton, W.: Integrating the periphery and context: a new model of telematics. In: Proceedings of Graphics Interface 1995, pp. 239–246 (1995)

24. Dourish, P., Bly, S.: Portholes: supporting awareness in a distributed work group. In: Proceedings of the SIGCHI Conference on Human Factors in Computing Systems pp. 541–547. ACM (1992)
25. Ju, W., Leifer, L.: The design of implicit interactions: making interactive systems less obnoxious. Des. Issues **24**, 72–84 (2008)
26. García-Herranz, M., Montoro, G., Haya, P.: Living intelligently assisted: augmented objects for subtle interaction. Escuela Politécnica Superior, Universidad Autónoma de MadridFrancisco Tomás y Valiente 11, 28049 Madrid, Spain
27. Gross, T.: Ambient interfaces: design challenges and recommendations. In: Human Computer Interaction: Theory and Practice, pp. 68–72 (2003)
28. Crews, D.E., Zavotka, S.: Aging, disability, and frailty: implications for universal design. J. Physiol. Anthropol. **25**(1), 113–118 (2006)
29. Portet, F., Vacher, M., Golanski, C., Roux, C., Meillon, B.: Design and evaluation of a smart home voice interface for the elderly: acceptability and objection aspects. Pers. Ubiquit. Comput. **17**(1), 127–144 (2013)
30. Oppermann, R.: User-interface design. In: Adelsberger, H.H., Collis, B., Pawlowski, J.M. (eds.) Handbook on Information Technologies for Education and Training, pp. 233–248. Springer, Heidelberg (2002)
31. Dillon, A.: User interface design. Encyclopedia of Cognitive Science (2003)
32. Stefaner, M., Ferré, S., Perugini, S., Koren, J., Zhang, Y.: User interface design. In: Sacco, G.M., Tzitzikas, Y. (eds.) Dynamic Taxonomies and Faceted Search, pp. 75–112. Springer, Heidelberg (2009)
33. Galitz, W.O.: The Essential Guide to User Interface Design: An Introduction to Gui Design Principles and Techniques. Wiley, Indianapolis (2007)
34. Nakashima, H., Aghajan, H., Augusto, J.C.: Handbook of Ambient Intelligence and Smart Environments. Springer Science & Business Media, Heidelberg (2009)
35. Jaimes, A., Sebe, N., Gatica-Perez, D.: Human-centered computing: a multimedia perspective. In: Proceedings of the 14th Annual ACM International Conference on Multimedia, pp. 855–864. ACM (2006)
36. PERSONA Project. Perceptive spaces promoting independent aging. IP in the 6th Framework Programme of the European Union (2007). http://www.aal-persona.org
37. Mulvenna, M., Carswell, W., McCullagh, P., Augusto, J.C., Zheng, H., Jeffers, P., Martin, S.: Visualization of data for ambient assisted living services. Commun. Mag. IEEE **49**(1), 110–117 (2011)
38. Buxton, W.: Integrating the periphery and context: a new model of telematics. In: Proceedings of Graphics Interface 1995, pp. 239–246 (1995)
39. Dourish, P., Bly, S.: Portholes: supporting awareness in a distributed work group. In: Proceedings of the SIGCHI Conference on Human Factors In Computing Systems, pp. 541–547). ACM (1992)
40. Ju, W., Leifer, L.: The design of implicit interactions: making interactive systems less obnoxious. Des. Issues **24**, 72–84 (2008)
41. Messens, L., Quinn, S., Saez, I., Squillace, P.: Home Sweet Home: Health monitoring and sOcial integration environMent for Supporting WidE ExTension of independent life at HOME. ICT PSP – Health, Ageing and Inclusion Programme. Grant Agreement No. 250449. Document D7.3, Intermediate Trial Evaluation Report, vol. 1.2 (2013)
42. Memon, M., Wagner, S.R., Pedersen, C.F., Beevi, F.H.A., Hansen, F.O.: Ambient assisted living healthcare frameworks, platforms, standards, and quality attributes. Sensors **14**(3), 4312–4341 (2014)

43. Carbonell, N.: Ambient multimodality: towards advancing computer accessibility and assisted living. Univ. Access Inf. Soc. **5**(1), 96–104 (2006)
44. Rashidi, P., Mihailidis, A.: A survey on ambient-assisted living tools for older adults. Biomed. Health Inf. IEEE J. **17**(3), 579–590 (2013)
45. Hanke, S., Mayer, C., Hoeftberger, O., Boos, H., Wichert, R., Tazari, M.R., Furfari, F.: universAAL–an open and consolidated AAL platform. In: Wichert, R., Eberhardt, B. (eds.) Ambient Assisted Living, pp. 127–140. Springer, Heidelberg (2011)
46. Sixsmith, A., Meuller, S., Lull, F., Klein, M., Bierhoff, I., Delaney, S., Savage, R.: SOPRANO – an ambient assisted living system for supporting older people at home. In: Mokhtari, M., Khalil, I., Bauchet, J., Zhang, D., Nugent, C. (eds.) ICOST 2009. LNCS, vol. 5597, pp. 233–236. Springer, Heidelberg (2009)
47. Amoretti, M., Copelli, S., Wientapper, F., Furfari, F., Lenzi, S., Chessa, S.: Sensor data fusion for activity monitoring in the PERSONA ambient assisted living project. J. Ambient Intell. Humaniz. Comput. **4**(1), 67–84 (2013)
48. AMIGO Project. Ambient intelligence for the networked home environment. STReP in the 6th Framework Programme of the European Union (2004). http://www.amigo-project.org
49. Bekiaris, E., Bonfiglio, S.: The OASIS concept. In: Stephanidis, C. (ed.) Universal Access in HCI, Part I, HCII 2009. LNCS, vol. 5614, pp. 202–209. Springer, Heidelberg (2009)
50. Wolf, P., Schmidt, A., Klein, M.: SOPRANO-an extensible, open AAL platform for elderly people based on semantical contracts. In: 3rd Workshop on Artificial Intelligence Techniques for Ambient Intelligence (AITAmI 2008), 18th European Conference on Artificial Intelligence (ECAI 2008), Patras, Greece (2008)
51. Roeder, P., Mosmonder, M., Obermaisser, R., Boos, H.: UniversAAL Project of the Framework Programme, D6.1-A Training Plan and Training Material (2010)
52. Tazari, M.R., Furfari, F., Lázaro Ramos, J.P., Ferro, E.: The PERSONA service platform for AAL spaces. In: Nakashima, H., Aghajan, H., Augusto, J.C. (eds.) Handbook of Ambient Intelligence and Smart Environments, pp. 1171–1191. Springer, Heidelberg (2010)
53. Mueller, S., Sixsmith, A.: User requirements for ambient assisted living: some evidence from the SOPRANO project. In: At the 6th International Society for Gerontechnology, Italy (2008)
54. Sixsmith, A., Meuller, S., Lull, F., Klein, M., Bierhoff, I., Delaney, S., Savage, R.: SOPRANO – an ambient assisted living system for supporting older people at home. In: Mokhtari, M., Khalil, I., Bauchet, J., Zhang, D., Nugent, C. (eds.) ICOST 2009. LNCS, vol. 5597, pp. 233–236. Springer, Heidelberg (2009)
55. Klein, M., Konig-Ries, B., Mussig, M.: What is needed for semantic service descriptions – a proposal for suitable language contructs. Int. J. Web Grid Serv. **1**(3/4), 328–364 (2005)
56. Avatangelou, R., Dommarco, R.F., Klein, M., Muller, S., Neilsen, C.F., Soriano, M.P.S., Schmidt, A., Tazaria, S.M.R., Wichert, R.: Conjoint PERSONA – SOPRANO workshop. In: Mühlhäuser, M., Fersch, A., Aitenbichler, E. (eds.) Constructing Ambient Intelligence. Communications in Computer and Information Science CCIS, vol. 11, pp. 448–464. Springer, Heidelberg (2008)
57. Bekiaris, A., Mourouzis, A., Maglaveras, N.: The REMOTE AAL project: remote health and social care for independent living of isolated elderly with chronic conditions. In: Stephanidis, C. (ed.) Universal Access in HCI, Part III, HCII 2011. LNCS, vol. 6767, pp. 131–140. Springer, Heidelberg (2011)
58. Kornowski, R., Zeeli, D., Averbuch, M., et al.: Intensive home-care surveillance prevents hospitalisation and improves morbidity rates among elderly patients with severe congestive heart failure. Am. Heart J. **129**, 762–766 (1995)

59. Fagerberg, G.: Mainstream services for elderly and disabled people at home. In: Proceedings. of International Conference: 10th European Conference AAATE, Florence, italy, Assistive Technology From Adapted Equipment to Inclusive Environments. Assistive Technology Research Series, vol. 25, pp. 287–291 (2009)
60. Kung, A., Jean-bart, B.: Making AAL platforms a reality. In: de Ruyter, B., Wichert, R., Keyson, D.V., Markopoulos, P., Streitz, N., Divitini, M., Georgantas, N., Mana Gomez, A. (eds.) AmI 2010. LNCS, vol. 6439, pp. 187–196. Springer, Heidelberg (2010)
61. OSGi Alliance: About the OSGi Service Platform, June 2007. http://www.osgi.org/wiki/uploads/links/OSGiTechnicalWhitePaper.pdf
62. Šimšík, D., Galajdová, A., Siman, D., Andrášová, M., Krajnák, S., Onofrejová, D.: MonAMI platform, trials and results. In: SAMI 2012, 10th Jubilee International Symposium on Applied Machine Intelligence and Informatics, pp. 26–28. Her'any, Slovakia (2012)
63. Šimšík, D., Galajdová, A., Siman, D., Andrášová, M.: First experience of implementation of social services based on ICT in Slovakia – (CR-ROM). Eur. J. Phys. Rehabil. Med. 47(2), 33–34 (2011)
64. Fagerberg, G., Kung, A., et al.: Platforms for AAL applications. In: Lukowicz, P., Kunze, K., Kortuem, G. (eds.) EuroSSC 2010. LNCS, vol. 6446, pp. 177–201. Springer, Heidelberg (2010)
65. Kleinberger, T., Jedlitschka, A., Storf, H., Steinbach-Nordmann, S., Prueckner, S.: An Approach to and Evaluations of Assisted Living Systems Using Ambient Intelligence for Emergency Monitoring and Prevention. In: Stephanidis, C. (ed.) UAHCI 2009, Part II. LNCS, vol. 5615, pp. 199–208. Springer, Heidelberg (2009)
66. EMERGE: Emergency Monitoring and Prevention, Specific Targeted Research Project (STREP) of the EC, Project No. 045056. http://www.emergeproject.eu
67. Prueckner, S., Madler, C., Beyer, D., Berger, M., Kleinberger, T., Becker, M., Emergency Monitoring and Prevention – EU Project EMERGE. In: Ambient Assisted Living Proceedings of 1st German AAl-Congress (2008)
68. Hein, A., Kirste, T., Activity Recognition for Ambient Assisted Living: Potential and Challenges. In: Proceedings of 1st German AAL-Congress (2008)
69. Wooldridge, M.: An Introduction to MultiAgent Systems, p. 16. Wiley, Chichester (2002)
70. Wang, Q., Shin, W., Liu, X., Zeng, Z., Oh, C., AlShebli, B. K., Sha, L.: I-Living: an open system architecture for assisted living. In: SMC, October 2006, pp. 4268–4275 (2006)
71. Rivero-Espinosa, J., Iglesias-Péreza, A., Gutiérrez-Dueñasa, J.A., Rafael Paloub, X.: SAAPHO: an AAL architecture to provide accessible and usable active aging services for the elderly. ACM SIGACCESS Accessibility and Computing, vol. 107, pp. 17–24 (2013)
72. Baldauf, M., Dustdar, S., Rosenberg, F.: A survey on context aware systems. Int. J. Ad Hoc Ubiquitous Comput. 2(4), 263–277 (2007)
73. Ju, W., Leifer, L.: The design of implicit interactions: making interactive systems less obnoxious. Des. Issues 24, 72–84 (2008)
74. Dourish, P., Bly, S.: Portholes: Supporting awareness in a distributed work group. In: Proceedings of the Sigchi Conference on Human Factors in Computing Systems, pp. 541–547. ACM (1992)

Establishing Guidelines for User Quality of Experience in Ubiquitous Systems

Deógenes Pereira da Silva Junior[✉], Patricia Cristiane de Souza[✉], and Cristiano Maciel[✉]

Laboratório de Ambientes Virtuais Interativos (LAVI), Instituto de Computação (IC), Universidade Federal de Mato Grosso (UFMT), Cuiabá, Brazil
deogenesj@gmail.com, {patriciacs,cmaciel}@ufmt.com

Abstract. Interaction Technologies are designed to provide continuous, shared and user-friendly access in the current computerized world. Ubiquitous computing includes several features, such as invisibility, continuous interaction and various modes of interaction, which are not present in the paradigm of traditional computing. A relevant issue is that existing recommendations for quality user experience in traditional computing may not prove to be sufficient for the field of ubiquitous computing. In this research a systematic review method was chosen to develop a theoretical basis of the literature about the research theme "investigate user experience in ubiquitous systems", followed by a qualitative analysis of the selected papers. One result of this work is the guidelines establishment which aims to assist the ubiquitous system design favoring the user experience quality. A case study of the Waze application was carried out to analyze the applicability of the proposed guidelines.

Keywords: Ubiquitous systems · User experience · Guidelines

1 Introduction

Ubiquitous computing is transforming how user interaction gets along with technology, moving away from the traditional way afforded by desktops. Sensors, mobile devices and the improvement of mobile networks are some factors that allowed the diffusion of technology and its use in our daily activities. Weiser, creator of the concept of ubiquitous computing, said in the late 80s that "the most profound technologies are those that disappear. They weave themselves into the fabric of everyday life until they are indistinguishable from it" [2]. Ubiquitous computing is a relatively recent area and involves many factors in its production, so new issues emerge, both related to hardware, such as processing power, as related to software, such as security, privacy and user experience [18].

User experience is defined by ISO 9241-210 [10] as a "person's perceptions and responses resulting from the use and/or anticipated use of a product, system or service". In addition to that, user experience (UX) "includes all the users' emotions, beliefs, preferences, perceptions, physical and psychological responses, behaviors and accomplishments that occur before, during and after use".

Likewise, Tullis and Albert [25] have the vision that some people distinguish the terms of usability and UX, "Usability is usually considered the ability of the user to use

N. Streitz and P. Markopoulos (Eds.): DAPI 2016, LNCS 9749, pp. 46–57, 2016.
DOI: 10.1007/978-3-319-39862-4_5

a thing to carry out a task successfully, whereas UX takes a broader view, looking at the individual's entire interaction with the things, as well as the thoughts, feelings, and perceptions that result from that interaction". In the same way, for Hassenzahl and Tractinsky [6], UX is a consequence of a user's internal state (predispositions, expectations, needs, motivation, mood etc.), the characteristics of the designed system (e.g. complexity, purpose, usability, functionality etc.) and the context (or the environment) within which the interaction occurs (e.g. organizational/social setting, meaningfulness of the activity, voluntariness of use etc.).

The paradigm of traditional human-computer interaction, systems and UX was designed thinking in static interactions with the keyboard and mouse inputs. The recommendations for design and usability evaluation in these systems considered this nature. In ubiquitous computing, the devices are omnipresent and the interaction forms are natural to the user. According to Ranganathan *et al.* [21], "in designing usable pervasive environments developers must consider both old and new usability challenges". The standards and recommendations that exist in the field of 'traditional' human-computer interaction (HCI), although relevant, they are not enough to the research and development of systems in this area. Due to the nature of ubiquitous computing, some parts of the project and evaluation are not covered. Efforts have been made to extend the existent techniques and/or establish new techniques, recommendations and normative for the project and evaluation on HCI [23, 25].

Given the above, this research produced a literature review with the purpose of seeking the existence of recommendations and reviews techniques for UX quality in ubiquitous systems. For this purpose, the methodology adopted was the systematic review, followed by a qualitative analysis of selected papers. One result of this study was the formulation of (11) eleven guidelines that aim at assisting the design of ubiquitous systems that favor the UX quality. The guidelines was applied in Waze application.

2   Systematic Review Protocol

The methodology used to search the theoretical basis was the systematic review (SR) [14]. In this study, we defined three research questions: (1) are there guidelines or specifics normatives to ensure a UX quality in ubiquitous systems?; (2) What are the HCI characteristics required for ubiquitous systems? and (3) What are the criteria to be observed in ubiquitous systems, to evaluate the UX quality? The first question's aim was to discover whether there are any guidelines or normatives as ISO [10], about UX quality in ubiquitous systems. If there were any, they would be evaluated, checking their scope and possible updates. In the second question, attempts were made to find articles that discuss the HCI features and requirements needed for ubiquitous systems. By the third question, the focus was on the evaluation processes of the UX quality.

Some systematic review keywords were proposed from the research questions: "human-computer interaction", "ubiquitous computing", "context-aware systems", "usability", "quality of interaction", "user experience quality". The search strings are composed of the keywords along with logical operators (see Fig. 1). The search strings were executed in the digital libraries: journals CAPES/MEC, IEE Xplore Digital Library, Scholar Google, ACM Digital Library, Springer e Citeseer Library. The studies inclusion criteria adopted were: (1) period: starting from January 2000; (2) language: english and portuguese; (3) availability on the Internet; and (4) if it appears duplicate papers, only the most complete works would be included.

The selection criteria would filter papers for the final selection that must have only the relevant articles to the research topic: Exclusion Criteria 1 (The study presents characteristics or evaluation of HCI or usability); Exclusion Criteria 2 (The publication presents characteristics, criteria and/or guidelines to be followed when evaluating or designing ubiquitous systems to ensure the UX quality?). After defining the SR protocol, searches strings were executed in the selected digital libraries, through November/2014 to April/2015. The returned papers were selected and stored based on the title and abstract. Later, the papers were read thus selecting only those that are relevant to the research, paying attention to the inclusion and exclusion criteria and the research questions.

Figure 1 shows the phases and results of systematic review based on PRISMA diagram [26]. In the 1st stage 1419 studies were returned. In the next step we selected 104 articles, among which 26 papers were included in the final selection of this SR. With the reading and study of the 26 articles was possible to see that there are no guidelines or standards for the UX quality in ubiquitous systems.

Some articles discussed such initiatives as Somervell et al. [24], which proposed a set of guidelines for exposure to Ubiquitous information displays. Santos et al. [23] developed a model of quality named TRUU (Trustability, Resource-limitedness, Usability and Ubiquity) to support the assessment of HCI in ubiquitous systems. Hong et al. [8] proposed a method for elicitation of context-aware applications requirements. Jensen and Larsen [13] proposed a framework that includes a subset of data to automate the capture and analysis of UX data field in large scale studies. However, the framework deals only with quantitative data, and lack of qualitative data. Ranganathan et al. [21] presented several metrics to assess pervasive computing environments. They are divided into security, programmability and usability metrics. These initiatives still require further checks, as validation applications in future studies.

The systematic review also made a clear differentiation between usability and usability in ubiquitous computing and the need for the creation or expansion of usability evaluation methods in ubiquitous computing [21]. For Santos et al. [23] the nature of ubiquitous systems suggests that new quality characteristics should be taken into account. Kray et al. [16] also says that a fundamental problem in the evaluation of ubiquitous systems with users is the lack of clear guidelines for the selection of valuation methods adapted to ubiquitous computing.

Given the need that ubiquitous computing brought in defining new recommendations, some features considered important for ubiquitous computing for use of quality are already under discussion in some of the papers returned by the SR.

For Boca et al. [3], one of the most important variable in pervasive systems is represented by the cognitive load. Related to minimization of cognitive load, for Santos et al. [23] "it is necessary to assure that ubiquitous systems support user activities in a transparent way with little or no need for attention or input from the user". Likewise, for Iqbal et al. [11], ubiquitous computing paradigm, with computers being everywhere, calls for new technology that prevents humans from feeling overwhelmed by information. Finally, for

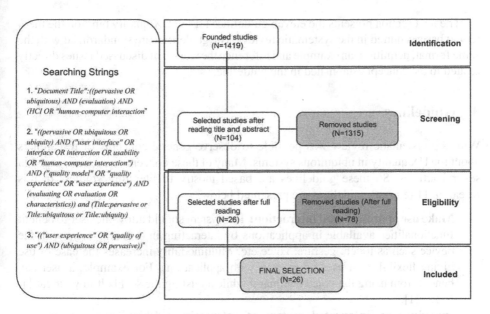

Fig. 1. Systematic review process [26]

Jensen and Larsen [13], the cognitive load in most usage situations is significantly higher than average for desktop applications.

Likewise, properly exploit the characteristic of high availability of devices and interaction modes is a significant concern. Islam and Fayad [9] propose to do the appropriate task on the appropriate device. "Different input techniques make sense on different devices". Other papers discussed the importance of multimodal interaction [1, 21, 23] that should provide the user flexibility of choice in the interaction.

Context-awareness is also seen as an important factor in the design of ubiquitous systems, and discussed in the work of [1, 8]. For Hong *et al.* [8], "context makes the communication between humans and computing devices much more efficient".

Further characteristics were mentioned in the articles, such as personalization [7] - the systems becoming increasingly customized to reflect the desires and personality of the user, and natural interfaces [1], allowing ease of use of the system. For Hong *et al.* [8] by using a natural interface, a user does not need to change the current interaction behavior; According to [1, 8, 21], systems should provide access to the user at any time since the interaction is no longer static. And finally in line with the papers, equally important factors for the quality of user experience are the concern for accessibility in the design of ubiquitous systems [8], and cultural aspects [12]. These characteristics should be explored in ubiquitous computing projects, promoting a quality user experience.

The discussions and results presented in the papers were important to make up the state of the art about characteristics, criteria and recommendations for the UX quality in HCI. Just as formed the conceptual basis for the establishment of new recommendations to assist designers in evaluation and design phases of ubiquitous systems with regard to UX.

The next section presents the eleven guidelines for the UX quality built on the theoretical basis acquired in the systematic review. The guidelines are standardized with the same format: definition, an example and reference the work that discussed issues directly related to the concept established in the guideline.

3 Guidelines

With the systematic review was possible to observe general concerns of researchers about the UX quality in ubiquitous systems. Many of these concerns were referenced in several articles. So these guidelines are based mostly in literature studies. In this research, 11 (eleven) guidelines are presented below.

1. **Make use of multimodal interaction:** The system should allow the user to benefit functionalities available in applications by interacting in different ways with the device such as touch, gesture, voice etc. Multimodality increases the ease of use giving flexibility in user interaction with applications. For example, a user can benefit from using the voice command while adjusting the seat belt in your car [1, 5, 12, 21].

2. **Introduce an integrated system of interactions:** Ubiquitous environments feature various functionalities and interactions forms. These interactions forms allow the user to communicate in a more comfortable and natural way, because they use natural inputs, as gestures, voice, image capture etc. The ideal, to provide user experience quality, is to present an integrated interaction system, where the device offers to the user all these interaction options with the system and the user could choose the best option in a specific context. For example, a user who uses an agenda, can enter appointments by voice while alone, or typing in a location where he does not feel comfortable to interact by voice [8, 21]

3. **Designing continuous interaction in ubiquitous services:** The services and features of a ubiquitous system must be continuous between different devices and platforms. The user must switch between these different devices without feeling the changes. For example, a user is in a meeting in his company and creates a reminder for an event for later evening on his computer. Through the phone, he adds location to the event. Later, when he get into the car to leave, the car warns him about his commitment, saying the time and place. Also asks if the user wants to connect the GPS to address to the location [1, 5, 8, 21].

4. **Project to explore the characteristics of each system:** The ubiquitous system could present several functionalities to the user, and run in various devices, however, it should explore positive points in each device (cellphone, tablet, desktop) aiming to offer a suitable group of interactions. For example, a app can suggest to the user purchase options, while he gets around a mall with a mobile device, but this functionality wouldn't apply to a laptop or desktop [9].

5. **Know how to explore the characteristic of invisibility:** The ubiquitous systems should not require explicit user interaction at the time. They must act in the context from the collection of environment information, not just the interaction with the user, with the appropriate level of intrusion. For example, in an application which

assists a physician in monitoring their patients should be calibrated to notify the doctor only in situations where he wish, for example in more severe situations. In other situations the application would notify a nurse or just record information for any reports. The user could access the App any time to check the status of patients [1, 20, 22, 23].

6. **Design interfaces that minimize the effort of attention:** The interface should present the information in a simple way for the user, so that the attention of effort is minimized. Since generally in a ubiquitous and context aware environment, there is no focal point for the user to fully concentrate because the attention is usually shared with other devices and also affected by external factors such as noise, movement etc. For example, imagine a situation where a user is making a run and want to see the application that monitors your heart rate if the information is not presented simply, without requiring much of attention for viewing, the user may not be able to observe information while moving [3, 8, 23].

7. **Make use of affordances and mental models:** The interface and system behavior must be intuitive for the user, i.e., the system should make use of affordances and support mental models to be more understandable thereby increasing ease of use. For example, an application that controls a multimedia room could use in interface world universal knowledge artifacts such as control room light is a light bulb icon [4, 20, 21].

8. **Designing for the user control:** The system shall allow users to take control of the application and its features. Thus, the application will best meet the preferences and needs of the user. For example, in a streaming and music sharing application, if the user wishes, the application must allow users deactivates some features such as recommendations and share music [7, 19].

9. **Designing interfaces for trust:** The interface should be designed to raise user trust exploring features like transparency. The interface should provide the user clear understanding of what and why something happens in the system. The information must be clear and easy to access, in order to increase user confidence in the application. For example, applications that check-in places such as restaurants, nightclubs, should allow the user to control the sharing options leaving you free to activate and deactivate the check in whenever you want [17]

10. **Designing for error management:** The system should allow the user to recover from an error, or give a workaround for the error. When the error happens, the system should help the user with clear explanations of what is happening, avoiding obscure messages with error codes without explaining them, and offer an alternative solution. For example, in a ubiquitous application an interaction mode failure, such as the touch input, the system must offer another form of interaction for the user to continue to use the system, such as voice input, explaining clearly how the application works in this form of interaction. The system can also, when recognize that an error occurred, indicate other device that the user can use to continue the task performed [1, 20].

11. **Design for accessibility:** Take advantage of the context awareness characteristic to draw a user profile and assist the user in making decisions and daily activities. Likewise, use the multimodal interaction feature to assist the user interaction with

the application. For example, a user with physical disabilities should not be directed to the stairs when requesting the path to certain room of the building. It should be directed only by the paths it can go, such as ramp or lift. In the field of interaction, the user with visual impairment can interact with an application through gestures or speech [8].

All in all, the guidelines 1 to 3 deal on the new interaction nature of the ubiquitous systems, i.e. about their multiplicity and rapid transition between modes of interaction. The guidelines 4 to 7 recommend important characteristics based on the amount of different available devices and characteristic of devices invisibility. The guidelines from 5 to 7 have focused on the importance of UX quality seeking to minimize the cognitive effort. The guidelines 8 to 10 also deals with the quality of the UX, but in the basic aspects of the application to ensure trust and user acceptance. Finally, the guideline 11 raises concerns in the design for accessibility for all users without distinction be able to use the application or the ubiquitous system. We believe that these guidelines can contribute to research and development of new projects guiding researchers to make these systems easier to use.

4   Case Study - Analysis of the Guidelines Applicability

To analyze the applicability and the need for guidelines refinement, an inspection process with ubiquitous applications was conducted. This section will present how the study was conducted with the Waze application from the category "Travel & Local" as well as the results.

Waze Operation: Waze is a GPS navigation application, who maps routes to reach a destination using real-time information from a collaborative network of users. The application informs traffic data such as police traps, accidents and other events. The system guides the navigation to the user informing direction and path. In the map are informed route details like place address and phone number. The user also can interact with the application through voice and gestures. Furthermore, the system has the functionality to view and update information about fuel and share routes with friends.

Inspection Methodology: It consists of selecting applications and analysis of the guidelines applicability in selected applications. In the application selection process, some criteria have been met: 1 - technical and general criteria (a - Android applications; b - were highly rated in Google Play; c - were popular on Google Play.); and 2 - criteria on the nature of the application (a- be ubiquitous or; b - have ubiquitous characteristics). Were adopted the Android operating system for its range of users. The popularity and good evaluation criteria are important because through them ensures the selection of applications that users have interaction with regularity. The criteria 1-b was adopted as highly rated applications with an average reviews score above 4 stars; in the criterion 1-c were considered applications with at least 10 million downloads. Lastly, the criteria on the nature of the application ensures that evaluate in fact applications of ubiquitous nature.

After the selection of applications, the methodology for evaluating the guidelines consisted of two steps: (1) selection functionalities - were selected functionalities relevant to the ubiquity and UX, and (2) analysis of the functionalities in the light of the guidelines - for each guideline, we examined its applicability in the functionalities of the applications by looking if the guidelines were adopted and its range of adoption. At the end of the two stages was made an analysis of the process as well about their guidelines adoption on the project application, pondering requirements and factors that affect the quality of UX.

Analysis of Guidelines Applicability: The functionalities available in the Waze application are accessible through natural interactions to users, i.e. the set of interactions available to the user goes beyond the interaction through smartphone buttons and touch-based interaction. User can interact through voice, gestures; make alerts by voice command and attach photos. In this way, the guidelines "1. Make use of multimodal interaction" and "2. Present an integrated system of interactions" are observed in the application.

The guideline "3. Design continuous interaction in ubiquitous systems" does not apply because the mobile and desktop applications have different purposes. On desktop, you can edit the map; see big disasters or unforeseen events that may affect navigation. In the smartphone, the purpose is navigation and real-time information sharing that update map data. The app runs on Android, iOS and Windows Phone, and some users use the application on cars through smartphones and mirror link. On the other hand, in desktops the user can access maps and edit them in the application site (waze.com). Therefore the guideline "4. Design to explore the characteristics of each device", that says to exploit the strengths of each device aiming to providing an appropriate set of interactions is contemplated. It makes sense to use functionalities alerts, navigation and local sharing by mobile devices, while walking or driving. Thus the option of editing maps is best used by computers, with a larger screen.

Context-awareness is very well explored in the application. Through the GPS user can be located on the map, see different types of nearest shops and gas stations - all these features help the user in making decisions and it minimizes the work that would have without using the application. As a result, the context sensitivity in the application identifies the map alerts and show them to the user. Also with these data, the application uses the alerts to calculate alternative routes to the destination. So the guideline "5. Know explore the invisibility characteristic" is well observed.

The buttons of the application's functions are accompanied by consistent icons with artifacts from the real world, contributing to the intuitiveness of the system. Therefore, the guidelines "6. Design interfaces that minimize the effort of attention" and "7. Make use of affordances and mental models" are included in this application.

In the setup menu, user can change various application functions such as fuel preferences, types of streets among others. The user also has control over how the map will be displayed, their Wazer icons etc., can drive as invisible, i.e., appears as disconnected for friends. Therefore, as the major features in total are controlled by users and they are intuitive, it is considered that the guidelines "8. Design for user control" and "9. Design interfaces to trust" are also contemplated.

The multimodal interaction and context-awareness help the user interaction with the system and improve the overall UX, including for the disabled. However, the guideline

"11. Design for accessibility" could only be assessed by testing with users with special needs, which was not possible yet.

At the end of the inspection tests with the use scenarios, no problems were found as the guideline "10. Design for error management." However, it should be considered the need for more extensive testing, including seeking to ascertain the compliance with the guideline 11, only then to say that the guideline 10 was fully met.

Discussion: The Waze app proved to have many of the features that benefit the quality of UX. Good use of existing technologies in the devices by application designers, such as sensors, microphone, camera etc., show the concern to provide a more dynamic and natural user interaction. It was also noted the interface simplicity, for capturing the information that exists on the device screen in a more ease way. This increases the scope of use because they are more affordable options for users who have difficulty typing or viewing due to screen size. The chosen application met most of the proposed guidelines. Sensitivity to context is a key feature in the application, as well as the collaboration of users. For Korkea-aho [15], "a system is context-aware if it can extract, interpret and use context information and adapt its functionality to the current context of use". Design system intelligence from the context requires optimized collection because smartphones does not have the same ability to persist information as computers. In addition, the data processing can not take for themselves all the resources available on your smartphone. Thus, with the advancement of mobile computing power, sensitivity context may find a path to be used in all applications.

At the analysis end, some guidelines were restructured: guidelines "1. Make use of multimodal interaction" and "2. Introduce an integrated system of interactions" have similarities. When using multimodal interaction, should be given flexibility to the user in choosing the mode of interaction, selecting the best option given specific context. So present an integrated system of interactions is a good practice in the use of multimodal interaction for the quality of UX. Thus the guideline "1" came to include in your description the guideline recommendation "2" with the wording:

1. **Make use of multimodal interaction:** Attention should be paid to a good multi-modality design, featuring an integrated system of interactions, allowing the user to take advantage of their functions by interacting in different ways with the device such as touch, gesture, voice etc. And the user could choose the best way for interacting in a specific context of use. This increases the ease of use giving flexibility in user interaction with your application. For example, a user can benefit from using the voice command while adjusting the seat belt in your car [1, 5, 8, 12, 21].

Use affordances, representative symbols and clear mental models, based on previous experience of the user in both the real world and virtual, are ways to minimize the user's attention effort. Thus the guidelines "6. Design interfaces that minimize the effort of attention" include in its description the guideline recommendation "7. Make use of affordances and mental models" with the wording:

6. **Design interfaces that minimize the effort of attention**: The interface should present simply information to the user, to minimize the effort of attention. Once, in a context-awareness environment, usually there is no focus point for the user to fully

concentrate because the attention is usually shared with other devices and also affected by external factors. Use affordances and support mental models are good practice for the system to be comprehensible without much effort. For example, imagine a situation where a user is making a run and want to see the application that monitors your heart rate. If the information is not presented simply, without requiring too much attention for viewing, the user may not be able to observe the information while moving [3, 4, 8, 20, 21, 23].

At the end of the evaluation and discussion process, the 11 (eleven) proposed guidelines were synthesized in 9 (nine).

5 Conclusion

The conception of ubiquitous applications has been a constant in the development of new systems. In this sense, this article visits the literature of this research area, especially the user experience quality in ubiquitous systems gather by the systematic review method. With the problematic identified, we brought to discussion the challenges and initiatives in this area. From the gathered literature were made eleven guidelines to assist designers from the area to develop ubiquitous applications, focusing on the area of user experience quality. The guidelines went through an analysis process of applicability and refining, with ubiquitous application, being summarized in 9 (nine) guidelines.

After the analysis process, it was possible to verify that most of guidelines were addressed on Waze application. In this sense, the guidelines could assist designers to develop applications that give support to the user with useful functionalities that are pleasant to use.

Therefore, the guidelines depart from questions related to usability until late computing techniques, in order that user experience with the system is better developed. The guidelines, as seen, are recommendations that can be important to the user experience and are feasible to execute. They are useful to designers on the development of solutions by the fact that they assist providing a survey of important questions to be addressed in a given application.

It can be noted that the guidelines are applicable into systems and, in future steps, metrics can be developed to address the recommendations. For example, this analysis, does not know the interaction errors impacts, frequent or occasional, regarding the user experience quality. As multimodal technology is always advancing, voice and gesture recognition techniques are prone to errors. The environment of ubiquitous computing is diffuse and surrounded by noises, which hinder interaction. The system still cannot verify the urgency that a user may want to utilize a functionality, to optimize it to interaction in a time period. If an error occurs in a urgency situation, it may be more serious than frequent errors in ordinary situations.

Context sensibility and system intelligence also were not measured on the application analysis. The effects of automatic actions from the system can cause on user experience are unknown. As stated on guideline 8, the system should not do what the user have not requested, i.e., the user must have control over available functionalities on the application, and can change them as needed. Therefore, context sensibility impacts some human's feelings, proper form user experience with the system, as confidence, privacy, deception etc.

Lastly, user experience is affected by the idea that the user has by the system, in other words, what it hopes from the application. Ubiquitous systems must be attractive, involve the users so the interaction has a more natural character, benefiting the task which supports. A path to user experience quality is the personalization and control combined with context sensibility. If applications are more similar with user profile – personalization -, similar with what the user expects – context analysis – and not hinder user's autonomy – control -, user experience may indeed be experienced with quality.

As the applicability of the guidelines is already verified, the next phases must be the implementation of ubiquitous application with the guidelines. Henceforth, execution of test with field users using the available technologies, to data collection and analysis that will aid on creation of possible metrics, validations and extension of guidelines.

Acknowledgments. We acknowledge the UFMT and FAPEMAT - Foundation of support to Mato Grosso State research, for sponsoring this project.

References

1. Abowd, G.D., Mynatt, E.D.: Charting past, present, and future research in ubiquitous computing. ACM Trans. Comput.-Hum. Interact. **7**(1), 29–58 (2000)
2. Weiser, M.: The computer for the 21st century. Sci. Am. **265**(3), 94–104 (1991)
3. Boca, S., Gentile, A., Ruggieri, S., Sorce, S.: An evaluation of HCI and CMC in information systems within Highly Crowded Large Events. In: Seventh International Conference on Complex, Intelligent, and Software Intensive Systems (CISIS), pp. 600–604 (2013)
4. Kaasinen, E., Kymäläinen, T., Niemelä, M., Olsson, T., Kanerva, M., Ikonen, V.: A user-centric view of intelligent environments: user expectations, user experience and user role in building intelligent environments. Computers **2**(1), 1–33 (2012)
5. Abowd, G.D., Mynatt, Elizabeth D., Rodden, T.: The human experience. IEEE Pervasive Comput. **1**(1), 48–57 (2002)
6. Hassenzahl, M., Tractinsky, N.: User experience - a research agenda. Behav. Inf. Technol. **25**(2), 91–97 (2006)
7. Hilbert, D.M., Trevor, J.: Personalizing shared ubiquitous devices. Interactions **11**(3), 34–43 (2004)
8. Hong, D., Chiu, D.K.W., Shen, V.Y: Requirements elicitation for the design of context-aware applications in a ubiquitous environment. In: Proceedings of the 7th International Conference on Electronic Commerce (ICEC 2005), pp. 590–596 (2005)
9. Islam, N., Fayad, M.: Toward ubiquitous acceptance of ubiquitous computing. Commun. ACM **46**(2), 89–92 (2003)
10. ISO 9241-210: Ergonomics of human-system interaction – Part 210: Human-centred design for interactive systems. ISO (2010)
11. Iqbal, R., Sturm, J., Kulyk, O., Wang, J., Terken, J.: User-centred design and evaluation of ubiquitous services. In: Proceedings of the 23rd Annual International Conference on Design of Communication: Documenting and Designing for Pervasive Information, pp. 138–145 (2005)

12. Jaimes, A., Dimitrova, N.: Human-centered multimedia: culture, deployment, and access. IEEE Multimedia **13**(1), 12–19 (2006)
13. Jensen, K.L., Larsen, L.B.: The challenge of evaluating the mobile and ubiquitous user experience. In: Second International Workshop on Improved Mobile User Experience (2008)
14. Kitchenham, B.: Guidelines for performing Systematic Literature Reviews in Software Engineering. Keele and Durham University Joint Report. EBSE 2007-001 (2007)
15. Korkea-aho, M.: Context-aware application surveys. (2000). http://www.hut.fi/mkorkeaa/doc/context-aware.html
16. Kray, C., Larsen, L.B., Olivier, P., Biemans, M., van Bunningen, A., Fetter, M., de Vallejo, I.L.: Evaluating ubiquitous systems with users (workshop summary). In: Mühlhäuser, M., Ferscha, A., Aitenbichler, E. (eds.) Constructing Ambient Intelligence. CCIS, vol. 11, pp. 63–74. Springer, Heidelberg (2008)
17. Leichtenstern, K., André, E., Kurdyukova, E.: Managing user trust for self-adaptive ubiquitous computing systems. In: Proceedings of the 8th International Conference on Advances in Mobile Computing and Multimedia (MoMM 2010), pp.409–414 (2010)
18. Maciel, C., de Souza, P.C., Viterbo, J., Mendes, F.F., Seghrouchni, A.E.F.: A multi-agent architecture to support ubiquitous applications in smart environments. In: Koch, F., Meneguzzi, F., Lakkaraju, K. (eds.) Agent Technology for Intelligent Mobile Services and Smart Societies, pp. 106–116. Springer, Heidelberg (2015)
19. Madeira, R.N.: Personalization in pervasive spaces towards smart interactions design. In: IEEE International Conference on Pervasive Computing and Communications Workshops (PERCOM 2012), pp. 548–549 (2012)
20. Malaka, R., Porzel, R.: Design principles for embodied interaction: the case of ubiquitous computing. In: Mertsching, B., Hund, M., Aziz, Z. (eds.) KI 2009. LNCS, vol. 5803, pp. 711–718. Springer, Heidelberg (2009)
21. Ranganathan, A., Al-Muhtadi, J., Biehl, J., Ziebart, B., Campbell, R.H., Bailey, B.: Towards a pervasive computing benchmark. In: Third IEEE International Conference on Pervasive Computing and Communications Workshops (PERCOM 2005), pp. 194–198 (2005)
22. Rimmer, J., Owen, T., Wakeman, I., Keller, B., Weeds, J., Weir, D.: User policies in pervasive computing environments. User Experience Design for Pervasive Computing (2005)
23. Santos, R.M., de Oliveira, K.M., Andrade, R.M., Santos, I.S., Lima, E.R.: A quality model for human-computer interaction evaluation in ubiquitous systems. In: Collazos, C., Liborio, A., Rusu, C. (eds.) CLIHC 2013. LNCS, vol. 8278, pp. 63–70. Springer, Heidelberg (2013). J. Int. Soc. Burn Injuries **37**(1): 61–8
24. Somervell, J., Chewar, C.M., McCrickard, D.S., Ndiwalana, A.: Enlarging usability for ubiquitous displays. In: Proceedings of the 41st Annual ACM Southeast Conference (ACMSE 2003), pp. 24–29 (2003)
25. Tullis, T., Albert, W.: Measuring the User Experience: Collecting, Analyzing, and Presenting Usability Metrics. Morgan Kaufmann Publishers Inc., San Francisco (2008)
26. Urrútia, G., Bonfill, X.: Declaración PRISMA: una propuesta para mejorar la publicación de revisiones sistemáticas y metaanálisis. Medicina Clínica **135**(11), 507–511 (2010)

Towards Big Data Interactive Visualization in Ambient Intelligence Environments

Giannis Drossis[1], George Margetis[1(✉)], and Constantine Stephanidis[1,2]

[1] Institute of Computer Science, Foundation for Research and Technology - Hellas (FORTH),
N. Plastira 100, Vassilika Vouton, 70013 Heraklion, Crete, Greece
{drossis,gmarget,cs}@ics.forth.gr
[2] Computer Science Department, University of Crete, Heraklion, Crete, Greece

Abstract. Big Data visualization relies on an interdisciplinary research area that includes mass data storage and retrieval, operations, analytics, security, ethics as well as visualization and interaction with end users. This paper reports on the characteristics of Big Data systems, mainly focusing on information visualization and discusses a number of methods towards this direction, analyzing research issues and challenges that emerge. Additionally, this paper discusses new approaches for Big Data visualization in the context of Ambient Intelligence (AmI) environments, highlighting new aspects in the field in respect to information presentation and natural user interaction. Furthermore, a scenario of Big Data visualization in AmI environments is presented, aiming at bringing to surface the new potential of such approaches in terms of interaction simplification, and adaptation to the context of use.

Keywords: Big Data · Big Data visualization · Big Data interaction · Ambient Intelligence · Data centre infrastructure management

1 Introduction

The term "Big Data" emerged as a scientific domain during the 1990s and gradually became a field of major academic interest during the 2000s. Since 2010, Big Data became a focus of attention across various sectors, including trade, business intelligence, large-scale organizations and start-up companies.

A widely accepted definition of Big Data is still under discussion and there is little progress regarding a commonly acceptable answer to the fundamental question of how big the data has to be to qualify as 'big data'. De Mauro et al. [1] combine several definitions for Big Data as "representing the Information assets characterized by such a High Volume, Velocity and Variety to require specific Technology and Analytical Methods for its transformation into Value".

Laney [21] introduced one of the first and most widely embraced attempts to define Big Data. The author suggested that Volume, Variety, and Velocity (or else the three Vs) are the three dimensions of challenges in data management. Volume refers to the magnitude of data. The thresholds that discriminate data from big data however are vague, as they keep increasing due to the soaring of sensors supplying data. Variety refers to the

© Springer International Publishing Switzerland 2016
N. Streitz and P. Markopoulos (Eds.): DAPI 2016, LNCS 9749, pp. 58–68, 2016.
DOI: 10.1007/978-3-319-39862-4_6

heterogeneity of the data, while velocity refers to the rate at which data is generated, retrieved and processed. Data creation rate is currently increasing rapidly with smartphones and sensors, and is expected to multiply in the era of the Internet of Things.

In addition to the three Vs, other dimensions that characterize other aspects of Big Data are described in literature. The factor of veracity [12], which describes the quality of the data, is an additional important characteristic that provides assessment of the data. Finally, another term is value [26], which describes the dimension of the data values in the context of Big Data integration.

Due to the vague nature of Big Data, several research fields are involved in the process of its management and manipulation. Such fields include, but are not limited to, storage, operations, analytics, security, ethics and visualization. This paper will focus on the classification of the major Big Data types, on the existing visualization techniques and on potential future directions of visualization and interaction with Big Data in the context of Ambient Intelligence environments.

2 Big Data Analytics

Big Data Analytics refer to the process of studying, exploring and reporting on Big Data, aiming at assisting the human decision making process. Apart from reporting and visualization, operations that belong to several research fields are involved, such as predictive analytics, data mining, anomaly detection, statistical analysis and text analytics. As mentioned in [10], research challenges regarding Big Data analytics involve both structural approaches and visualization concerns. The structural approaches refer to the infrastructure that allows making operations on Big Data, while visualization concerns encompass the nature of the data source in terms of presentation.

A fundamental characteristic of Big Data is its multidimensional nature. Big Data comprises massive information with several aspects. For instance, information about a specific car not only contains data about the car itself, such as model, production start date, horsepower, acceleration, but also data regarding sales: how many cars were sold, the sale location, the color of the cars, etc. This information comprises different dimensions of the data that create different perspectives, which can be retrieved and analyzed on demand.

2.1 Analytical Processing and Dimensions of Big Data

The first step towards visualizing multidimensional data sets includes the identification of the involved aspects that need to be presented. Current approaches that cope with this issue mainly involve OLAP [5] (Online Analytical Processing), which aims to provide a mechanism for the analysis of Big Data from multiple different perspectives. OLAP is applied as a means of interactive filtering out extrinsic information. Several data storage models for the core implementation of OLAP are found in literature, including Multidimensional OLAP systems (MOLAP), Relational OLAP (ROLAP) and Hybrid OLAP (HOLAP). This paper will not focus on the different core approaches that allow OLAP operations, but instead on the visualization aspects that arise at a higher level.

2.2 Temporal Big Data

Time classification is an aspect of Big Data, which is frequently meaningful. It constitutes a dimension that is often stored, either as supplementary information or as major descriptive value. Users are accustomed to perceiving time as an additional dimension of Big Data and are therefore able to easily perceive it as a dimension to any type of information. Time constitutes an important factor in various contexts, including decision-making [7].

2.3 Geospatial Big Data

Another type of information which is often an integral part of Big Data is space. The datasets can be static or dynamic in terms of location. Dynamic Big Data can be acquired through the usage of location-aware devices and the adoption of Geographical Information Systems (GIS) and are correlated both to space and time. The quality of data, which imposes an important issue in terms of geospatial data [22], is expected to improve especially in the context of the Internet of Things.

Li et al. [23] use Big Data 3D visualization in order to display infrastructure in Shenzhen and take geographic statistical analysis in consideration for assisting data analysis and enhancing the decision making process for social service agencies. Big Data in the context of urban environments in general correlate data sets with both time [18] and space [3].

3   Big Data Visualization Techniques

3.1   OLAP Visualization

The OLAP tools enable users to analyze multidimensional data interactively from various perspectives. OLAP consists of five basic analytical operations: consolidation (roll-up), drill-down, pivoting, slicing and dicing [14]. The applied operations change the selection of the visualized components on the fly and update the view according to the user's actions.

A traditional interface for analyzing OLAP data is a pivot table, or cross-tab, which is a multidimensional spreadsheet produced by specifying one or more measures of interest and selecting dimensions to serve as vertical (and, optionally, horizontal) axes for summarizing the measures [9]. Pivot tables are a widespread visualization model, which provide a detailed data presentation to users that are familiar with it. Additionally, they can be easily transformed to serve additional dimensions of information through the application of color-coding or rows/columns merging. However, the tables' efficiency declines for larger data sets, as users are unable to locate specific information, recognize patterns or get an overview of the displayed data sets (Fig. 1).

Another useful visualization component are parallel coordinates [15, 19], which allow the display of multiple data dimensions on a 2D plane. The concept of parallel coordinates is the concurrent visualization of different values in a row, one after another. For instance, in the case of car comparison, car values regarding horsepower, fuel

Category	Type	2010	2011	2012	2013	Total
Fruit	Apples	551	477	604	648	2280
	Bananas	988	763	893	825	3469
	Oranges	226	261	219	254	960
	Subtotal	*1765*	*1501*	*1716*	*1727*	
Vegetables	Lettuce	423	461	489	502	1875
	Tomatoes	335	356	376	328	1395
	Subtotal	*758*	*817*	*865*	*830*	
Total		2523	2318	2581	2557	

Fig. 1. An example pivot table

consumption, car dimensions, acceleration, etc., would be meaningful to be displayed on the same plot. This visualization technique holds the advantage of correlation between different data dimensions, e.g., horsepower and acceleration, which could depict the impact of one dimension on another. However, this applies only in the case where the dimensions are rendered adjacently; if another dimension intervenes between them, the visual clue disappears and the correlation is impossible to discover. Additionally, parallel coordinates are unable to visualize non-numerical values and can be difficult to comprehend for non-expert users (Fig. 2).

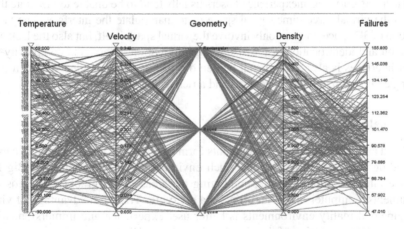

Fig. 2. An indicative example of parallel coordinates created using XDAT [37]

In order to address the aforementioned drawbacks of tables and parallel coordinates, techniques such as pie charts, plots, graphs and trees are employed by state of the art commercial tools. The leading software for Big Data Visualization, Business Intelligence and Analytics is Tableau [24], while other approaches include qlikview [29], Microsoft's Power BI [28] and others.

Tableau [24] provides default tools for rendering each specific data type, which can be overridden by the user on demand. Each visualization is selected to optimally represent a specific data type: for instance, cross-tabs are used for the visualization of discrete categorical data and lines for continuous quantitative information.

Even though OLAP tools are very efficient for Big Data retrieval and on demand visualization, they usually lack exploratory functionality. Furthermore, due to the complex nature of the operations supplied, OLAP tools tend to be cumbersome for novice users to manipulate.

3.2 Big Data 3D Visualization

Traditional visualization techniques fall short in terms of efficient and intuitive display of the corresponding data sets; therefore, the need for a rich interactive visualization still constitutes both a business and a research challenge.

In order to fill in the gap of inefficient visualization, some approaches in literature involve 3D visualization for OLAP [2, 20]. However, 3D visualization approaches are not yet very popular.

The inclusion of an additional dimension to the visualization adds up to the efficiency of depicting the dimensions of Big Data. Since the human brain is trained to sense and act in three dimensions, it is optimized to perceive three dimensions in a natural manner. The third dimension constitutes an aspect of the rendered information easily perceivable by the user, thus enhancing potential exploration in a virtual world.

On the other hand, 3D visualizations have certain drawbacks. In general, they present a steep learning curve, as inexperienced users usually tend to be unable to orientate themselves in the virtual three-dimensional space or to manipulate the interface. The lack of perception of 3D space does not only involve the virtual space itself, but also the lack of the exploration and identification of the visualized information. Interaction complexity with 3D user interfaces is also a significant burden due to the additional degrees of freedom, requiring complex manipulation controls and a rich interaction vocabulary.

3.3 Virtual and Augmented Reality

Virtual and augmented reality environments form an emerging approach that is capable of providing Big Data visualizations. Such environments in the context of Big Data constitute interdisciplinary efforts, combining the areas of 3D graphics, stereoscopic environments, computer vision and Big Data querying. The main advantage of virtual and augmented reality environments is better user experience and immersion, which allows the better perception of the visualized geometry. Furthermore, in comparison to traditional 3D visualizations, the users perceive themselves in the context of the visualization and thus orientate themselves more easily.

Helbig et al. [17] use a virtual reality environment to visualize massive data in the context of Weather Research Forecast. Another interesting approach is the immersive visualization of a landscape in Mars [11], augmented with data describing the surface characteristics.

Future challenges on applying virtual and augmented reality to Big Data visualizations include multimodal interaction, display and equipment limitations [25]. Virtual and augmented reality is a growing research field, mainly due to the emergence of devices like the Microsoft Kinect and LeapMotion that provide more natural interaction based on gestures and Oculus Rift, which puts virtual reality in play again in terms of mainstream visualization technique. However, still several challenges exist towards incorporating and enhancing traditional 2D desktop approaches in virtual space as well as developing a suitable infrastructure at the side of Big Data to support additional needs that may rise.

3.4 Graph Visualization

Graphs are a common technique used for displaying the correlation between different entities. Their main advantage is the user's ability of starting from a specific node and exploring neighboring nodes, especially when visualizing data sets that describe networks or relationships. The survey reported by Beck et al. [4] describes a trend towards the combination of graphs with interactive timelines in order to include potential temporal characteristics of the information.

Furthermore, graph visualizations simplify exploration by providing operations like sampling, filtering, partitioning and clustering [27], while they can also support several abstraction layers [6] in order to provide meaningful views according to the scope of the visualization, ranging from overview to detailed view.

Even though graphs can be very helpful in illustrating specific aspects of Big Data, they tend to focus only on one aspect of the data, which is the interconnection between the various nodes. Moreover, graphs are meaningful only if the data that they present are coherent, and are not suitable to illustrate other aspects such as comparison between data and temporal relationships.

3.5 Exploratory Data Analysis

Exploratory Analytics, or else Discovery Analytics, refers to the process of using visualization exploration techniques, in the context of Big Data, which aims at discovering new facts or characteristics of Big Data that users were previously unaware of [31, 34, 36]. Heer and Shneiderman [16] present a widely adopted taxonomy for interactive dynamics regarding visual analysis. The proposed taxonomy groups tasks in three high level categories: data and view specification, view manipulation and analysis process and provenance.

Faceted navigation, also mentioned as data and view specification [16], refers to the process of applying specific filters to the data sets provided, in order to focus on the subset of interest. Faceted navigation can combine multiple visualization techniques to apply the most suitable ones to the corresponding type. Such an example is EDEN [33], where the authors use parallel coordinates and geographic visualizations to interactively refine the displayed values and thus offer exploratory analysis of Big Data by exploring relationships between entities. Another example of interactive faceted exploration is discussed in [36], which combines automatically generated and manually specified visualizations in order to improve support for data exploration.

4   Comprehension of Big Data

What still proves to be a difficult task in the area of Big Data is offering the possibility to the users to comprehend the dimensions of Big Data. Even though much work focuses on analyzing the data itself by making operations in order to view and examine specific aspects of the data, less effort has focused on creating the optimal environments for the depiction of the available aspects and offering exploration capabilities.

Comprehending Big Data involves two different roles: (a) experts who are either familiar with the visualized data or at least are accustomed to the concepts of Big Data (e.g., data scientists and analysts), and (b) inexperienced end users, who are unaccustomed to perceiving and manipulating Big Data. The visualization approach for these different roles varies significantly, as different expectations are raised in the corresponding cases.

The vast majority of the existing Big Data visualization techniques focus on the experts. On the other hand, occasional or inexperienced users should be provided with a more user-friendly, exploratory view that allows browsing without requiring knowledge of the existing data operators or the visualized data domain.

5   Displays of Big Data Visualizations and User Collaboration

Augmented and virtual reality techniques require specialized displays, while the vast majority of other visualizations relies on desktop displays. On the other hand, the interest of non-expert end users is expected to increase, requiring access to Big Data in a user-friendly and easily perceived manner. Therefore, a forthcoming issue will be the access to Big Data visualizations for a broad audience through different platforms and devices, such as mobile devices [38].

Furthermore, multi-device environments with shared displays and mobile devices [30] will support teamwork and collaborative exploration of visualizations. To this direction, Donalek et al. [11] discuss means of sharing displays between users.

6   Towards Ambient Intelligence

Ambient Intelligence envisions a future where technology is interweaved with everyday living environments, anticipates users' needs, and provides natural interaction with digital information [35].

In respect to human-computer interaction, Ambient Intelligence (AmI) environments involve primarily two aspects: context awareness and natural interfaces [8]. Context awareness includes the use of emerging technologies to infer the context of the interaction (e.g., the location and the activities of the user), whereas natural interfaces refer to human communication capabilities and implicit actions that should be employed as a means of interaction in AmI environments, instead of the explicit input used in traditional human-computer interaction.

Ambient Intelligence environments have the potential to support the visualization of Big Data and its multiple dimensions due to the wide range of displays and interactions combined, which can be both implicit and explicit [32].

6.1   The AmI Data Centre Use Case

Data centre infrastructure management constitutes a Big Data use case, as massive data is generated and collected in real time. Information such as the servers' state, network traffic and temperature is continuously created along with logical and physical dependencies that seldom vary.

The massive growth of data volume, following Moore's law, results into the need for further storage space. Consequently, the existing data centres are expected to grow both in size and in count; thus, their monitoring, maintenance and management involves comprehensive environment sensing, where the environment is the data centre itself.

Data centres consist of multiple server racks, which in turn contain several servers. Each server holds a diversity of metrics that are required for its maintenance and optimization, including anomaly detection, workload balance and power consumption. The servers' values are observed and displayed by real time visualization tools, such as the one presented by Drossis et al. [13].

The integration of Ambient Intelligence could enhance infrastructure management in various perspectives. The data centre control room can be greatly improved by coalescing existing management applications with sensors and pervasive displays, that would allow sensing in the area and act in combination with activities of the employees and the state of the data centre itself. Additionally, navigation and the finding of specific components is another field that requires user assistance. The following use case scenario depicts some aspects that involve Big Data visualization in the context of Ambient Intelligence.

6.2 Use Case Scenario - A Day in the Data Centre

A 3D visualization of the data centre is displayed at the largest display of the AmI data centre's control room, showing the current state of all the servers. The traffic between the connections is monitored in real-time and overlaid in the visualized servers' layout to the corresponding responsible employee. The employee spots a potential issue and shares his view with his colleagues, having the selected connections between servers shown in the large display. The real-time analysis of the data center performance, by the AmI environment, discovers a bottleneck in traffic, and raises a warning to the personnel, providing a historical view of the traffic for the specific data centre to a side large display. After the analysis of the traffic history, the data centre's personnel decides to install additional servers to improve the performance.

When the new servers are delivered, an employee places them on the smart working bench, which is capable of recognizing the servers' configuration by reading their serial numbers. The smart bench suggests, based on the current traffic demand, alternative plans of the new servers' placement, illustrated on a floorplan projected next to them, with the compatible empty slots highlighted. The administrator of the data centre selects the preferred position among the available options, using a hand gesture, notifying this way that the hardware is ready to be installed. Upon installation, all the users are notified about the addition and the visualizations of the data centre are updated accordingly.

Afterwards, a component with very high temperature is identified by automated anomaly detection mechanisms. The environment triggers an alarm notifying the responsible employee, who in turn filters the visualization to display only the servers with high temperatures to verify that the reporting sensor is not problematic. Furthermore, the details of the anomaly are shown on demand by bringing to front the temperature control, which displays the previous values along with the expected ones.

Upon user intervention, the alarm can be acknowledged by the user or examined in detail. Since the anomaly requires on spot actions, the employee uses his own smartphone to view the path towards the faulty component, which is highlighted. Upon reaching the defined rack, he uses an augmented reality view to find the detected server slot in the rack with the reported temperature. The high temperature was reported due to a sensor malfunction and therefore the employee replaces the faulty component and marks the issue as resolved.

6.3   Big Data and Ambient Intelligence

The scenario presented in the previous section illustrates the benefits that Ambient Intelligence offers for Big Data centre monitoring and maintenance. In more details, the control room of such a data centre provides visualization facilities that are able to display thousands of servers according to the context of use (the large display shows generic information, whereas the users see a personalized view). The visualization displays relationships between servers (network traffic) and past values (temporal information), and users are able to collaborate (employee's view is shared).

The smart bench is able to identify physical objects (new servers) but also to suggest potential installation locations (specifications of the servers are known and consequently the environment acts in a smart manner). The installation is sensed by the environment and the visualization is updated immediately (real time visualization).

The high temperature alarm is personalized and raised to the responsible employee for action. The employee applies filtering (faceted navigation) and browses towards the desired area (exploration). Additionally, the temperature control is specialized to suit the needs of its content (data optimal visualization). Finally, the employee uses his own smartphone to find the area of interest in a natural manner (using navigation with augmented reality).

7   Conclusion

Big Data visualizations constitute an interdisciplinary area of research that combines different technologies. This paper has discussed the characteristics of Big Data, the existing visualization techniques and the potential benefits of Ambient Intelligence for Big Data visualization. A use case scenario of a data centre was described, illustrating the way that Ambient Intelligence can enhance Big Data visualizations in the context of data centre infrastructure management.

Ambient Intelligence has the potential to fill in gaps of existing Big Data visualization techniques by incorporating the context of use to the visualization and supplying rich multimodal interaction. Ambient Intelligence can reduce the dimensions of Big Data and adapt the display of the data rendered in a smart and natural manner, thus reducing the interface complexity and the user cognitive load. Moreover, Ambient Intelligence can support and promote collaborative work and real-time human-human interaction.

Acknowledgements. The work reported in this paper has been conducted in the context of the AmI Programme of the Institute of Computer Science of the Foundation for Research and Technology-Hellas (FORTH).

References

1. De Mauro, A., Greco, M., Grimaldi, M.: What is big data? A consensual definition and a review of key research topics. In: AIP Conference Proceedings, vol. 1644, no. 1 (2015)
2. Ammoura, A., Zaïane, O.R., Göbel, R.: Towards a novel OLAP interface for distributed data warehouses. In: Kambayashi, Y., Winiwarter, W., Arikawa, M. (eds.) DaWaK 2001. LNCS, vol. 2114, pp. 174–185. Springer, Heidelberg (2001)
3. Azri, S., Ujang, U., Castro, F.A., Rahman, A.A., Mioc, D.: Classified and clustered data constellation: an efficient approach of 3D urban data management. ISPRS J. Photogramm. Remote Sens. **113**, 30–42 (2016)
4. Beck, F., Burch, M., Diehl, S., Weiskopf, D.: The state of the art in visualizing dynamic graphs. EuroVis STAR (2014)
5. Berson, A., Smith, S.J.: Data Warehousing, Data Mining, and OLAP. McGraw-Hill Inc., New York (1997)
6. Bikakis, N., Liagouris, J., Krommyda, M., Papastefanatos, G.: graphVizdb: A Scalable Platform for Interactive Large Graph Visualization
7. Chandramouli, B., Goldstein, J., Duan, S.: Temporal analytics on big data for web advertising. In: 2012 IEEE 28th International Conference on Data Engineering (ICDE). IEEE (2012)
8. Cook, D.J., Augusto, J.C., Jakkula, V.R.: Ambient intelligence: technologies, applications, and opportunities. Pervasive Mob. Comput. **5**(4), 277–298 (2009)
9. Cuzzocrea, A., Mansmann, S.: OLAP visualization: models, issues, and techniques. In: Encyclopedia of Data Warehousing and Mining, pp. 1439–1446 (2009)
10. Cuzzocrea, A., Song I.-Y., Davis, K.C.: Analytics over large-scale multidimensional data: the big data revolution! In: Proceedings of the ACM 14th International Workshop on Data Warehousing and OLAP. ACM (2011)
11. Donalek, C., Djorgovski, S.G., Cioc, A., Wang, A., Zhang, J., Lawler, E., Yeh, S., Mahabal, A., Graham, M., Drake, A., Davidoff, S., Norris, J.S., Longo, G.: Immersive and collaborative data visualization using virtual reality platforms. In: 2014 IEEE International Conference on Big Data (Big Data), pp. 609–614. IEEE, October 2014
12. Dong, X.L., Srivastava, D.: Big data integration. In: 2013 IEEE 29th International Conference on Data Engineering (ICDE). IEEE (2013)
13. Drossis, G., Birliraki, C., Patsiouras, N., Margetis, G., Stephanidis, C.: 3-D visualization of large-scale data centres. In: Cloud Computing and Services Science. Springer International Publishing, New York (2016)
14. Gray, J., Chaudhuri, S., Bosworth, A., Layman, A., Reichart, D., Venkatrao, M., Pellow, F., Pirahesh, H.: Data cube: a relational aggregation operator generalizing group-by, cross-tab, and sub-totals. Data Min. Knowl. Discov. **1**(1), 29–53 (1997)
15. Hauser, H., Ledermann, F., Doleisch. H.: Angular brushing of extended parallel coordinates. In: IEEE Symposium on Information Visualization. INFOVIS 2002. IEEE (2002)
16. Heer, J., Shneiderman, B.: Interactive dynamics for visual analysis. Queue **10**(2), 30 (2012)
17. Helbig, C., Bauer, H.S., Rink, K., Wulfmeyer, V., Frank, M., Kolditz, O.: Concept and workflow for 3D visualization of atmospheric data in a virtual reality environment for analytical approaches. Environ. Earth Sci. **72**(10), 3767–3780 (2014)

18. Hoppenbrouwer, E., Louw, E.: Mixed-use development: theory and practice in Amsterdam's Eastern Docklands. Eur. Plann. Stud. **13**(7), 967–983 (2005)
19. Inselberg, A.: The plane with parallel coordinates. Vis. Comput. **1**(2), 69–91 (1985)
20. Lafon, S., Bouali, F., Guinot, C., Venturini, G.: On studying a 3D user interface for OLAP. Data Min. Knowl. Discov. **27**(1), 4–21 (2013)
21. Laney, D.: 3D data management: controlling data volume, velocity and variety. META Gr. Res. Note **6**, 70 (2001)
22. Li, S., Dragicevic, S., Castro, F.A., Sester, M., Winter, S., Coltekin, A., Pettit, C., Jiang, B., Haworth J., Stein A., Cheng, T.: Geospatial big data handling theory and methods: a review and research challenges. ISPRS J. Photogramm. Remote Sens. (2015)
23. Li, X., Lv, Z., Zhang, B., Wang, W., Feng, S., Hu, J.: WebVRGIS based city bigdata 3D visualization and analysis (2015). arXiv preprint arXiv:1504.01051
24. Mackinlay, J.D., Hanrahan, P., Stolte, C.: Show me: automatic presentation for visual analysis. IEEE Trans. Vis. Comput. Graph. **13**(6), 1137–1144 (2007). http://www.tableau.com/
25. Olshannikova, E., Ometov, A., Koucheryavy, Y., Olsson, T.: Visualizing big data with augmented and virtual reality: challenges and research agenda. J. Big Data **2**(1), 1–27 (2015)
26. Pascal, H., Janowicz, K.: Linked data, big data, and the 4th paradigm. Semant. Web **4**(3), 233–235 (2013)
27. Pienta, R., Abello, J., Kahng, M., Chau, D.H.: Scalable graph exploration and visualization: sensemaking challenges and opportunities. In: 2015 International Conference on Big Data and Smart Computing (BigComp). IEEE (2015)
28. PowerBI: powerbi.microsoft.com. Accessed 10 Mar 2016
29. Qlik: www.qlik.com. Accessed 10 Mar 2016
30. Roberts, J.C., Ritsos, P.D., Badam, S.K., Brodbeck, D., Kennedy, J., Elmqvist, N.: Visualization beyond the desktop–the next big thing. Comput. Graph. Appl. IEEE **34**(6), 26–34 (2014)
31. Russom, P.: Big data analytics. TDWI Best Practices Report, Fourth Quarter, pp. 1–35 (2011)
32. Schmidt, A.: Interactive context-aware systems interacting with ambient intelligence. In: Ambient Intelligence, p. 159 (2005)
33. Steed, C.A., Ricciuto, D.M., Shipman, G., Smith, B., Thornton, P.E., Wang, D., Shi, X., Williams, D.N.: Big data visual analytics for exploratory earth system simulation analysis. Comput. Geosci. **61**, 71–82 (2013)
34. Tukey, J.W.: Exploratory Data Analysis, pp. 2–3. Addison-Wesley, Reading (1977)
35. Weber, W., Rabaey, J., Aarts, E.H.L.: Ambient Intelligence. Springer Science & Business Media, Berlin (2005)
36. Wongsuphasawat, K., Moritz, D., Anand, A., Mackinlay, J.: Voyager: exploratory analysis via faceted browsing of visualization recommendations. IEEE Trans. Vis. Comput. Graph. **22**(1), 649–658 (2016)
37. XDAT: X-dimensional Data Analysis Tool. www.xdat.org. Accessed 10 Mar 2016
38. Zissis, D., Lekkas, D., Koutsabasis, P.: Design and development guidelines for real-time, geospatial mobile applications: lessons from 'MarineTraffic'. In: Daniel, F., Papadopoulos, G.A., Thiran, P. (eds.) MobiWIS 2013. LNCS, vol. 8093, pp. 107–120. Springer, Heidelberg (2013)

End-User Development Tools for the Smart Home: A Systematic Literature Review

Daniela Fogli[1], Rosa Lanzilotti[2], and Antonio Piccinno[2(✉)]

[1] Dipartimento di Ingegneria dell'Informazione,
Università degli Studi di Brescia, Brescia, Italy
daniela.fogli@unibs.it
[2] Dipartimento di Informatica,
Università degli Studi di Bari "Aldo Moro", Bari, Italy
{rosa.lanzilotti,antonio.piccinno}@uniba.it

Abstract. This paper presents a systematic literature review in the Internet of Things and Ambient Intelligence areas. The goal was to identify the best software tools that allow end users, namely people without competencies in computer programming, to manage and configure the behaviors of a smart home. The review selected 48 papers out of 1049 papers found through automatic and manual search. From these papers, 11 tools have been identified and analyzed by means of eight technical characteristics. Finally, among the eleven tools, six tools have been chosen for a qualitative comparison on the basis of seven design principles for smart home control proposed in a literature paper.

Keywords: Internet of Things · End-User development · Smart home · Systematic literature review

1 Introduction

Internet of Things (IoT) [1] and Ambient Intelligence (AmI) [2] are recently attracting the attention of industries and research scholars in several different fields, from electronics to artificial intelligence, from data (and big data) analysis to cloud computing, from software architectures to network security. As observed in [3–5], research on new Human-Computer Interaction (HCI) paradigms is necessary as well, especially for facilitating the use and configuration of AmI environments by users without computer programming knowledge. Therefore, we found important to deepen the research on End-User Development (EUD) [6], in order to understand which methods and tools have been proposed so far to transform end users (inhabitants) from passive consumers of their smart environments to active producers of new behaviors for such environments [7–12].

More precisely, this paper presents a systematic literature review in the IoT and AmI areas, by focusing on the research works that deal with methods and tools suitable to the smart home and compliant with a wider definition of EUD that considers end users as "developers" of their smart environment, which thus becomes able to evolve as its users evolve [13, 14].

From a technical point of view, a smart home is a house that encompasses a variety of processors, touch screens, memory devices, sensors (lightness, proximity, cameras,

© Springer International Publishing Switzerland 2016
N. Streitz and P. Markopoulos (Eds.): DAPI 2016, LNCS 9749, pp. 69–79, 2016.
DOI: 10.1007/978-3-319-39862-4_7

accelerometers, etc.), and actuators (lamps, household appliances, speakers, etc.), all connected together and able to endow the house with an autonomous and pro-active behavior. On the other hand, the house inhabitants should be able to modify and adapt home behaviors to their needs, in a continuous co-evolution of system and users [15]. This could be achieved by providing users with EUD tools that support them in creating simple commands (e.g. "at 7 a.m. rise shutters"), monitoring activities (to check gas leak, intrusions, etc.), tele-assisted services, and environment management tasks (e.g. temperature or lighting setting).

The paper is structured as follows: Sect. 2 describes the methodology adopted to perform the systematic literature review, as well as the tools identified through the study; Sect. 3 describes the technical analysis of the tools and the qualitative comparison of a subset of them; Sect. 4 concludes the paper by summarizing the main findings of the study.

2   Methodology

The present study was performed by following the guidelines for systematic literature review proposed in [16]. The systematic review was composed of 3 phases: planning, conducting and reporting. The activities concerning the planning and the conducting phases are described in the following sub-sections, the reporting phase is described in Sect. 3.

2.1   Planning Phase

In this phase, the following activities were performed: (1) the definition of the research question, (2) the establishment of the search strategy, (3) the definition of inclusion and exclusion criteria for the selection of the primary studies.

Research Question. The goal of the systematic literature review, presented in this paper, is to examine the current use of tools in the IoT and AmI areas, suitable to the smart home and compliant with the definition of EUD. The research question addressed by the study was:

- *RQ: Which are the software tools that end users can use for managing and configuring the behaviors of a smart home?*

Search Strategy. To compose the search string a set of concepts was first chosen. The three main concepts we identified are trivial: tool, smart home and internet of things. Then, a number of correlated concepts were defined: device, instrument, appliance and gadget for tool; smart house, home automation, digital home as related to smart home; and IoT as very well-known acronym of Internet of Things. Table 1 shows the main concepts and the correlated concepts identified that were combined by Boolean conditions to compose the search string.

Table 1. The main concepts and the correlated concepts identified to compose the search string.

Main concept	Correlated concepts
Tool	Device, instrument, appliance, gadget
Smart home	Smart house, home automation, digital home
Internet of Things	IoT

Then, the following search string was composed:

```
((tool OR device OR instrument OR appliance OR gadget)
AND
((smart OR digital OR automation) AND home OR house))
AND
(internet of things OR iot))
```

The main digital library that were used to search for primary studies were:

- Scopus (http://www.scopus.com) and
- ScienceDirect (http://www.sciencedirect.com).

Moreover, journals and conference/workshop proceedings, where studies relevant to the research question had been published, were also manually searched. They are listed in the following.

Journals:

- Journal of Ambient Intelligence and Smart Environments;
- Journal of Systems and Software;
- Pervasive and Mobile Computing;
- Future Generation Computer Systems;
- Personal and Ubiquitous Computing;
- International Journal of Smart Home;
- IEEE Pervasive Computing;
- International Journal of Pervasive Computing and Communications;
- International Journal of Ad Hoc and Ubiquitous Computing.

Conferences and Workshops:

- UbiComp;
- International Symposium on End-User Development (IS-EUD);
- European Conference on Ambient Intelligence (AmI);
- Workshop on End User Development in the Internet of Things;
- Workshop on Cloud of Things;
- IEEE International Conference on Green Computing and Communications and IEEE Internet of Things and IEEE Cyber, Physical and Social Computing;
- International Conference on Innovative Mobile and Internet Services in Ubiquitous Computing;
- ACM Conference on Ubiquitous Computing;

- IEEE International Conference on Trust Security and Privacy in Computing and Communications;
- IEEE International Conference on Ubiquitous Computing and Communications;
- International Conference on the Internet of Things;
- International Conference on Ubiquitous and Future Networks;
- IEEE International Conference on Pervasive Computing and Communications;
- International Conference on Embedded and Ubiquitous Computing;
- International Conference on Future Internet of Things and Cloud;
- International Conference on Mobile and Ubiquitous Systems Computing Networking and Services;
- IEEE International Conference on Computational Science and Engineering;
- International Symposium on Pervasive Systems Algorithms and Networks;
- International Conference on Frontier of Computer Science and Technology.

The period reviewed included studies published from 2010 to 2015.

Inclusion and Exclusion Criteria for the Selection of Primary Studies. A total of **1049** papers have been found through this search. Each paper that was retrieved from the automated or manual search was evaluated in order to decide whether or not it should be included, by considering its title, abstract and keywords. The studies that met at least one of the following inclusion criteria were included:

- The paper describes a tool oriented to end users and not to expert developers;
- The paper presents a tool or high-fidelity prototype available for evaluation;
- The paper presents a tool that can be used for the management of a smart home;
- The paper describes a tool able to interact with other systems and devices;
- The paper has been published in a conference or workshop proceedings, or in a scientific journal.

The studies that met at least one of the following exclusion criteria were excluded:

- The paper describes a tool oriented to developers;
- The paper presents a low-fidelity prototype;
- The paper presents a tool that cannot be used for the management of a smart home (e.g. tool devoted to agriculture, industry, etc.);
- The paper presents a tool not compliant with the EUD definition;
- The paper has been published in book, bachelor and master thesis, etc.

2.2   Conducting Phase

In the conducting phase, we have carried out the activities planned in the previous phase. Then, we have defined two data extraction strategies for providing the answer to the research question.

Selection of Primary Studies. Table 2 shows the number of papers selected and excluded at the end of the selection of the primary studies, 48 papers out of 1049 satisfied the above inclusion/exclusion criteria.

Table 2. Number of papers selected and excluded.

Source	# Selected papers	# Excluded papers	Total
Digital library	257	224	33
Manual search of papers published in journal, in conference and workshop proceedings	792	777	15
Total	1049	1001	48

From the 48 papers selected through the systematic review, we have identified the eleven tools reported in Table 3.

Table 3. The selected tools for EUD in the smart home.

Tool	Link
Atooma	http://www.atooma.com/
Bipio	http://bip.io/
GALLAG Strip	http://gallag.wikispaces.asu.edu/
IFTTT	https://ifttt.com/
itDuzzit	http://cloud.itduzzit.com/
Locale	http://www.twofortyfouram.com/
Tasker	http://tasker.dinglisch.net/
Twine	http://supermechanical.com/twine/
WigWag	http://www.wigwag.com/
We Wired Web	http://wewiredweb.com/
Zipato	http://zipato.com/

Atooma (A TOuch Of MAgic) is a free Italian application that uses the 'if-then' construct for defining rules. It gives the possibility to take up to five conditions and corresponding actions. In addition, Atooma recognizes the situations that occur most frequently and suggests the appropriate action. It can be integrated with mobile applications, web services and external devices through a single interface. Finally, it provides a very good support for non-IT users while giving the possibility for developers to use a special SDK to create add-ons.

Bipio is a Graph API, in which each node of the user graph is responsible for the execution of a unit of work to transform messages, integrate different web services or other types of web applications based on the RPC protocol. The nodes of the graph are called beeps: they are fast endpoints for personal domains and receive, process, and transmit messages through a graph. Bipio allows its users to create customized workflows and by using the "Powerful Application Logic" the user is able to concatenate multiple services. Like Atooma, Bipio does not require any programming knowledge, although only a computer science expert may implement new extensions. Bipio uses the drag and drop interaction paradigm and provides a very valuable support for non-IT users.

GALLAG Strip is a novel approach to programming sensor-based context aware applications combining the programming-by-demonstration technique and a mobile device to enable users to experience their applications as they program them. GALLAG Strip allows its users to create sensor-based context-aware applications in an intuitive and appealing way without the need of computer programming skills. The users of GALLAG can program their applications by physically demonstrating their envisioned interactions within a space using the same interface that they will later use to interact with the system, that is, using GALLAG-compatible sensors and mobile devices.

IFTTT is a web and a smartphone application. It allows creating 'if-then' rules that are called 'recipes', because basically they just mix ingredients, such as social networks, web services, and smart things. It presents a good integration with any kind of web service. The smartphone app is available for Android and IOS platform. The user can define for each rule (recipe) only one condition and only one action and to have his/her rules working the Internet connection is needed.

itDuzzit is a cloud integration platform that is simple enough for non-IT users, yet powerful enough to support most complex integrations. It offers pre-built integration solutions and connectors for dozens of cloud (web) applications. Its Duzzit Editor lets users build their own custom integration solutions (called "duzzits") that run in the cloud. A duzzit can be deployed as an online form, a scheduled job, a web service, an email drop box, or a widget. Pre-built duzzits exist in the Duzzit Library and they can be modified through the Duzzit Editor. itDuzzit is entirely hosted so there is nothing to download and nothing to install.

Locale is an Android application for the automated management of a mobile device according to conditions, primarily related to the position and orientation of the smartphone, the date and time, the remaining battery power and the calls from contacts. If appropriately extended through external plug-ins, it allows controlling, as well as some web services, even other devices connected to the Internet.

Tasker is an application for Android which performs tasks (sets of actions) based on contexts (application, time, date, location, event, gesture) in user-defined profiles or in clickable or timer home screen widgets. This simple concept profoundly extends the control of the Android device and its capabilities, without the need for 'root' or a special home screen.

Twine is a physical smart object, a small turquoise box crammed with sensors. It takes standard accelerometers, thermometers, and other sensors to alert the user in case of small problems before they become big problems. Quick Wi-Fi setup and AAA batteries that last up to 3 months allows one to drop Twine anywhere in the house to monitor temperature, vibration and orientation. Additional sensors detect floods, leaks, opened doors, and signals from other home systems. Rules can be defined or modified through a web application.

WigWag is an open source system for ambient intelligence. Its free WigWag mobile app allows for instant control of the connected devices in a home or office, whether people are right there or far from these places.

We Wired Web is a community-extensible integration-as-a-service web application that lets non-technical people easily share data between web services, while allowing technical people to extend the system by adding new web services, triggers, and actions via wiring diagrams.

Zipato Home Management is a rule-based system for a complete home control and automation. It requires its own gateway, called Zipabox, to which the many devices (sensors and actuators) of the system are connected. Devices are specific of Zipato or they could come from other manufacturers, but they are supported only if adhering to compatible standards. The creation of rules is via Zipazle, a visual programming environment based on the Scratch project of MIT and accessible through smartphones, tablets and computers via web.

First Data Extraction Strategy. The first data extraction strategy was based on the following technical characteristics:

1. License and price: license of the tool and, if commercial, its cost;
2. Flexibility in device management: possibility for the user to add, edit and remove the connection to devices;
3. Platform extensibility: opportunity for developers to create new software artifacts for the system (plug-in); possibility for users to install and use them;
4. Easy configuration: opportunity for users to add, edit or remove rules, and schedule events easily;
5. Technical support: possibility to receive technical support from the manufacturer or developer;
6. Integration with smart devices: possibility to connect the system with specific devices (other products of the software development company or of other partner companies) or other devices widely used (including those available through specific hubs);
7. Integration with web services: possibility to connect the system to services available on the web;
8. Rule structure: possibility to define multiple conditions and actions per each rule.

Second Data Extraction Strategy. The second data extraction strategy was based on a qualitative comparison of tools performed considering the set of design principles defined by Davidoff et al. in [17]. Such design principles aim at developing end-user programming systems that allow their users to gain control over their lives. In the following, the seven principles are briefly described.

- *P.1 - Allow for the organic evolution of routines and plans*: a smart home system should allow its users to define/modify specific rules that characterize the user daily tasks on the basis of their changing needs.
- *P.2 - Easily construct new behaviors and modify existing behaviors*: the system should provide its users with the ability to define/modify new recurring or planned behaviors.
- *P.3 - Understand periodic changes, exceptions and improvisation*: the system should detect actions that user wants to perform, which are in conflict with the default routines.
- *P.4 - Design for breakdowns*: the system should dynamically remedy possible error situations that can occur.

- *P.5 - Account for multiple, overlapping and occasionally conflicting goals*: the system should flexibly react to unplanned events, even if the latter may come into conflict with each other, ensuring its internal consistency.
- *P.6 - The home is more than a location*: the system should consider the family needs and necessities, even outside the home.
- *P.7 - Participate in the construction of family identity*: the system should decide which action must be performed on the basis of the social roles and the family protocol.

3 Reporting Phase

The overall results of the study are reported in the following sub-sections.

3.1 Results of the First Data Extraction

Each tool has been first analyzed according to the technical characteristics giving rise to the data shown in Table 4, where each characteristic is associated with one of the following symbols:

Table 4. Evaluation of the selected tools according to their technical characteristics.

Tool	Technical characteristics							
	1	2	3	4	5	6	7	8
Atooma	Freeware	✓	✓	✓	✓	~	✓	~
Bipio	Open source	✓	✓	✓	✓	×	✓	✓
GALLAG Strip	Commercial	✓	✓	×	✓	✓	×	✓
IFTTT	Freeware	×	✓	✓	×	~	✓	×
itDuzzit	Commercial and free version	✓	✓	✓	✓	~	✓	✓
Locale	Commercial (9,99€)	×	✓	✓	✓	~	~	×
Tasker	Commercial (2,99€)	~	✓	✓	✓	~	✓	✓
Twine	Commercial (149,95€)	✓	×	✓	✓	✓	~	✓
WigWag	Commercial (149€)	✓	✓	✓	✓	✓	✓	✓
We Wired Web	Commercial and free version	×	✓	✓	✓	×	✓	✓
Zipato	Commercial (250€)	✓	✓	✓	✓	✓	✓	✓

✓ the characteristic is totally satisfied
~ the characteristic is partially satisfied
× the characteristic is not satisfied

Among the eleven tools, five tools have been excluded from the subsequent deeper analysis, mainly due to their acquisition cost or the need for specific hardware. They are: Gallag Strip, Locale, Twine, WigWag, and Zipato.

The remaining six tools, namely Atooma, Bipio, IFTTT, itDuzzit, Tasker and We Wired Wed, have been examined in details, according to the second data extraction strategy, as described in the following sub-section.

3.2 Results of the Second Data Extraction

A typical scenario describing how a family could manage and live in its smart home has been defined and used to apply the second data extraction strategy on the six tools. In addition, it has been assumed that each tool was installed both on a central control device (located in the home and connected to the Internet) and on all mobile devices of the family members (also connected to the Internet, even outside the home).

Table 5 reports the results of the qualitative evaluation through the design principles for smart home control [17], where each principle is associated with one of the following symbols:

Table 5. Evaluation of the selected tools according to the design principles for smart home applications.

Tool	P1	P2	P3	P4	P5	P6	P7
Atooma	✓	✓	×	×	×	~	×
Bipio	✓	✓	×	×	×	×	×
IFTTT	✓	✓	×	×	×	~	×
itDuzzit	✓	✓	×	×	×	×	×
Tasker	✓	✓	✓	×	✓	✓	×
We Wired Wed	✓	×	×	×	×	×	×

✓ the principle is totally satisfied
~ the principle is partially satisfied
× the principle is not satisfied

Bipio together with We Wired Web are the only tools that do not support the integration with physical devices and also they do not ensure an excellent integration with web and cloud services. Both tools fulfill the principle P.1, as all the other examined tools. In addition, We Wired Web does not provide any extensions to add, change and remove devices. Although itDuzzit is lacking with respect to the design principles, it satisfies most of all the technical characteristics (see Table 4), so developers can extend it and make it "smart" for the management of multiple targets (P.5 principle), the remote control and the detection of the user's location (P.6 principle).

Regarding the design principles, Atooma and IFTTT are equivalent, since both tools partly meet the principle P.6, because they allow detecting the position, while the remote control is absent. Despite such equivalences, IFTTT has more limitations regarding the flexibility in the management of devices and technical support than Atooma; moreover, being created primarily as a web service, IFTTT also requires a constant Internet connection to correctly work. In addition, Atooma allows managing multiple conditions and actions (up to 5) and has a specific area for the smart object management (TAG NFC, Pebble, Gear Watch, Smart Things products).

Tasker satisfies all the design principles except P.4 and P.7, which are not met by any instrument. However, due to its extensibility through plug-ins, Tasker is able to overcome the limitations of the basic version of the application. In particular, AutoVera is a plug-in for the management of the home that allows Tasker to understand abnormal, but intentional, changes to the defined rules, to manage multiple objectives and to perform remote control, position detection and monitoring of the home adequately, even in case of family members' absence.

On the basis of this analysis, Tasker resulted to be the most suitable tool to satisfy the above design principles, and thus our research question. In particular, its extensibility opens up a variety of possibilities for customizing it to the smart home case.

4   Conclusion

This paper has presented an analysis of tools supporting end-user development for smart home configuration and management. Tools have been selected after a rigorous systematic review of literature in the IoT and AmI research fields. The adoption of some specific selection criteria, including the compliance with the EUD definition, allowed us to select 48 papers out of 1049 found through automatic and manual search. From these papers, eleven tools have been identified and subsequently examined according to some technical characteristics. All tools are based on a rule-based paradigm for behavior definition: end users (home inhabitants) are supported by visual interfaces in the composition of events and/or conditions with actions, using structures like 'if-condition(s)-then-action(s)' or 'when-event(s)-then-action(s)'.

Then, a comparative analysis of the tools has been performed by taking into consideration the design principles proposed in [17]. However, 5 out 11 tools have been excluded from this deeper analysis, due to their acquisition cost or the need of specific hardware that prevented testing tool functions. Therefore, the evaluation, based on the design principles, has been carried out only on Atooma, Bipio, IFTTT, itDuzzit, Tasker and We Wired Web. From this analysis, it emerged that Tasker enhanced with a specific plug-in (AutoVera) is able to satisfy six out of seven design principles; only the principle about participation in family identity construction is currently far from being realized. On the contrary, the other five tools do not satisfy the majority of the design principles.

Acknowledgments. This work is partially supported by the Italian Ministry of University and Research (MIUR) under grants PON02_00563_3470993 "VINCENTE", PON04a2_B "EDOC@WORK3.0", and PON03PE_00136_1 "DSE" and by the Italian Ministry of Economic Development (MISE) under grant PON Industria 2015 MI01_00294 "LOGIN".

References

1. Atzori, L., Iera, A., Morabito, G.: The Internet of Things: a survey. Comput. Netw. **54**(15), 2787–2805 (2010)
2. Sadri, F.: Ambient intelligence: a survey. ACM Comput. Surv. **43**(4), 1–66 (2011)
3. Mavrommati, I., Darzentas, J.: End user tools for ambient intelligence environments: an overview. In: Jacko, J.A. (ed.) HCI 2007. LNCS, vol. 4551, pp. 864–872. Springer, Heidelberg (2007)
4. Cabitza, F., Fogli, D., Lanzilotti, R., Piccinno, A.: End-user development in ambient intelligence: a user study. In: 11th Biannual Conference on Italian SIGCHI Chapter (CHItaly), pp. 146–153. ACM, New York, NY, USA (2015)
5. Cabitza, F., Fogli, D., Lanzilotti, R., Piccinno, A.: Rule-based tools for the configuration of ambient intelligence systems: a comparative user study. Multimed. Tools Appl. 1–21 (2016). doi:10.1007/s11042-016-3511-2
6. Lieberman, H., Paternò, F., Wulf, V. (eds.): End User Development. Springer, Dordrecht (2006)
7. Barricelli, B.R., Valtolina, S.: Designing for end-user development in the Internet of Things. In: Díaz, P., Pipek, V., Ardito, C., Jensen, C., Aedo, I., Boden, A. (eds.) IS-EUD 2015. LNCS, vol. 9083, pp. 9–24. Springer, Heidelberg (2015)
8. Blackwell, A.F.: End-user developers at home. Commun. ACM **47**(9), 65–66 (2004)
9. García-Herranz, M., Haya, P., Alamán, X.: Towards a ubiquitous end-user programming system for smart spaces. J. Univ. Comput. Sci. **16**(12), 1633–1649 (2010)
10. Ur, B., McManus, E., Pak Yong Ho, M., Littman, M.L.: Practical trigger-action programming in the smart home. In: SIGCHI Conference on Human Factors in Computing Systems, pp. 803–812. ACM, New York, NY, USA (2014)
11. Benzi, F., Cabitza, F., Fogli, D., Lanzilotti, R., Piccinno, A.: Gamification techniques for rule management in ambient intelligence. In: De Ruyter, B., et al. (eds.) AmI 2015. LNCS, vol. 9425, pp. 353–356. Springer, Heidelberg (2015). doi:10.1007/978-3-319-26005-1_25
12. Demeure, A., Caffiau, S., Elias, E., Roux, C.: Building and using home automation systems: a field study. In: Díaz, P., Pipek, V., Ardito, C., Jensen, C., Aedo, I., Boden, A. (eds.) IS-EUD 2015. LNCS, vol. 9083, pp. 125–140. Springer, Heidelberg (2015)
13. Cabitza, F., Fogli, D., Piccinno, A.: "Each to his own": distinguishing activities, roles and artifacts in EUD practices. In: Caporarello, L., Di Martino, B., Martinez, M. (eds.) Smart Organizations and Smart Artifacts. LNISO, vol. 7, pp. 193–205. Springer International Publishing, Switzerland (2014)
14. Fogli, D., Piccinno, A.: Co-evolution of end-user developers and systems in multi-tiered proxy design problems. In: Dittrich, Y., Burnett, M., Mørch, A., Redmiles, D. (eds.) IS-EUD 2013. LNCS, vol. 7897, pp. 153–168. Springer, Heidelberg (2013)
15. Cabitza, F., Fogli, D., Piccinno, A.: Fostering participation and co-evolution in sentient multimedia systems. J. Vis. Lang. Comput. **25**(6), 684–694 (2014)
16. Kitchenham, B.: Procedures for Performing Systematic Reviews. Keele University, Keele (2004). http://www.inf.ufsc.br/∼awangenh/kitchenham.pdf
17. Davidoff, S., Lee, M.K., Yiu, C., Zimmerman, J., Dey, A.K.: Principles of smart home control. In: Dourish, P., Friday, A. (eds.) UbiComp 2006. LNCS, vol. 4206, pp. 19–34. Springer, Heidelberg (2006)

The Interaction Design Research About 3D Demo Animation in Smart Home

Minggang Yang and Xiaofan Ma[✉]

School of Art, Design and Media, East China University of Science and Technology,
No. 130, Meilong Road, Xuhui District, Shanghai 200237, China
yangminggang@163.com, 531608500@qq.com

Abstract. In recent years, with the rapid development of technology, people's living standards are generally improved and have played a very important role in our future life. Nowadays, we live in a fast-paced era that leaded by information, the heavy and boring instructions inevitably become a kind of burden before using appliances. In addition, it is a painful sorrow among the children, the old or the special people. However, the rise of 3D demo animation solves the problems very well. It exhibits the products from all aspects by the form of animation. Besides, in order to make users have more direct experiences, some film design companies put the interaction technology into it. It is direct interaction that brings users a combined feel of novelty, favor and trust, at the same time, it reduces the distance between products and users. So, products made by animation as well as interaction design should be explained from users' view when design the 3D demo animation of smart home, which can make demo animation be more functional and interesting through some simple actions such as click, lither to let users know and use the appliance cheerfully. The interaction design of the 3D demo animation not only pay attention to the different gender region different requirements of age groups, but also study the different needs of special populations. It notices their needs on the basis of general design. This article lists some excellent 3D animation works at home and abroad, which display the products and the unique cultural image of the corporate by the way of interaction. This passage researches the physiological and psychological characteristics of the users when they touch the new product, then, it analyzes the design principle of the 3D demo animation as well as the users' experiences. In the end, this paper not only make a analysis but also make a summary on the shortcomings of the interaction design. At the same time, it puts forward direction and suggestions for improvement of interaction design.

Keywords: Interaction design · Demo animation · Users' experiences

1 Introduction

1.1 The Objective and Significance of Topic Selection

In this informational era, owing to rapid technological advancement great changes have made on our life as unnoticed, which was obviously embodied in the citizen's

© Springer International Publishing Switzerland 2016
N. Streitz and P. Markopoulos (Eds.): DAPI 2016, LNCS 9749, pp. 80–90, 2016.
DOI: 10.1007/978-3-319-39862-4_8

household equipment. Under the background of fast-paced lifestyle and high-intensity work, people all pursue for a more intelligent, safe and comfortable household circumstance, undoubtedly raising new requirement to our current living space. In China change happens from the refrigerator, TV, washing machine at the beginning to air conditioner, computer and video, then to the smart home as the current focus, which could be called seeing the whole from the part. While the smart home whose has bright prospects in people's eye cannot take high ground rapidly. It's bound to say that casting the industrial situation, product development and technical trend aside, the main reason for this situation is because most manufacturers has insufficient promotion and improper propaganda key impeding the further development on smart home.

The research purpose of this essay is based on the three-dimension virtual animation for smart home. The humanization interaction offers the consumer a communication way to get a more comprehensive recognition to it, not just stopping at its meaning level any more. For the time being, the smart home as an emergency industry has a promising future. Though immature its market industry chain is, it with infinite market potential attracts large number of consumers. After then new products appear constantly, of which just few get really recognized by most consumers. Nowadays the promotion demonstration for the smart home on the market is always the unilateral information output, while this method has some problem and insufficient. It is unavailable for the client and consumer to gain what they need from the huge amount of information rapidly and accurately resulting in the loss of users to some extent. Thus this essay aims to introduce the interaction technique to the 3D animation for smart home in order to resolve these shortcomings. By the interaction the distance between product and consumer could be narrowed, really benefiting the mass a lot.

1.2 Analysis on the Home and Abroad Situation for Topic Selection

In 1984 the first smart building in the world has sprung up in Hartford, America, subsequently it has been promoted in Germany, Canada and Japan and other developed countries, among which the X-10 for North American Airlines, "Smart Home" in MICROSOFT and "Home Director" in IBM has gained tremendous influence in the world. In order to lively show the function and feature of smart home, some relevant promotion strategy has been tight with the pace of development. If now you are in the experience shop, the predecessor of the colorful advisement video has been the inconspicuous poster. Compared to aboard, China starts late in the smart home industry, so as to its propaganda demonstration. In recent years some domestic enterprises with forward-looking vision gradually has their own representative solution referring to the advanced technology and concept aboard. The domestic development trend for interaction design is excellent as well, applying to the interfacial design on website and APP. However in a broader sense there are few research and practice which the interactive design is in real combination with the demonstration solution for smart home.

2 About 3D Animation

2.1 Brief Introduction to 3D Animation

Animation as a comprehensive art includes drawing, cartoon, film, photography, music, literature and other arts kind, among which the 3D Animation (three-dimensional animation) is an important type for animation form and also the mainstream for the animation development later. Following with the rapid development on three-dimension video technique for computer, the 3D Animation has got mature day by day and gradually applied to the wider filed in daily life.

The Feature of 3D Animation. Through the three-dimension software the designer completes a series of operations including modeling, material, lighting, rendering, animation and special effect, then the final animation could create on the computer. The creation method different from the traditional one makes the 3D animation special, while also makes the demonstration effect unique.

1. Realistic visual effect originates from reality while being higher than the real.
2. Be available for the shoots with high difficulty and high cost that filming could not get.
3. New performing form in order to attract audience's attention.
4. Bring audience real and profound reorganization in face-to-face way.
5. Be convenient to broadcast and promote.
6. Save cost and enhance efficiency to a larger extent.

Manifestation of Demo Animation

1. *2D Demo Animation.* The 2D demo animation is mostly applying to the completion of Flash and Adobe After Effects with short running cycle and easy making, which is the first choice meeting the requirements being short time and low cost. This favors the narrative on plot. Every demo animation is like a story with strong interestingness. Additionally its image focused on flat sense with bright color. Its subject matter does not aim at realism but at motion law. In recent years owing to simplified style being fashionable the 2D animation has come to alive on the screen.
2. *3D Demo Animation.* The 3D demo animation is mostly applying to the completion of Autodesk Maya and 3D Studio Max with moderate running cycle and exquisite making, being the mainstream for the animation home and abroad. It focuses on exhibiting model and presents the audience content subject's detail information and overall effect one by one in a unique view, which creates a stronger visual effect. For the 3D demo animation, it is with stereoscopic picture and realistic special effect. It is famous to be generous and delicate, paying more attention to lens language. As the main demo animation it gains relatively higher recognition. Meantime owing to the constant development on technology the 3D demo animation will be with larger improvement space.
3. *Combine 3D demo animation with actual shooting technology.* 3D demo animation combines with people shooting technology, then editing and composing by Adobe Premiere and other software, the final animation forming. The whole making

progress is with long period, high cost, great difficulty and exquisite effect. Thus some excellent products has brand influence in this field. The combination of these two could not only embody the advantage for each other but also make the 3D demo animation be with less cold mechanical feeling and expansiveness to the advertisement by actual shooting, adding a little cordial feeling and credibility. This new manifestation method is with rich pictorial language to cover large information amount, better mixing the art with technology together to gain mass media's attention. The 3D demo animation, as the pioneer in demo animation field, by mastering the advanced technology in the future and constant innovation combines with actual shooting technology to drive the development on the whole demo animation.

The Application Field on 3D Demo Animation. As the 3D animation technology develops and promotes continuously, the 3D graphics technique gains more and more consumers' attention and starts to go deep into all fields, from the plot animation that is popular with the children to film, game, construction, advertisement and industry etc. In the future its application range will continue expanding.

1. *Television Animation.* The television animation here means the well-known animation movie spreading relatively high and being famous. The technologies on making include special effect originality, early shoot 3D animation, special effects composition and drama with special effect animation. As a branch of movie, the television animation combines with 3D where the art and technology become one. Some vocal stories as 3D animation have been showed on screen gaining lot of popularity. And its accessories have gradually transited to commercialization stage.

2. *Architectural Animation.* The period from the end of last century to the beginning of this century has been the most prosperous for urban and rural construction in China. There emerges a scene of flourishing on building and real estate market, which virtually facilitate the development of architectural animation. At the moment the 3D technology has gained wide application on construction field, of which the architectural vagile cartoon and garden landscape animation standing most. The exquisite model and rich lens language restores a real landscape scene on the computer scene, which is incomparable to the traditional effect picture. In recent years the 3D panoramic technique as a branch of virtual reality has sprung up gradually and will lead the 3D architectural animation to a new level as well.

3. *Production Animation.* The main reason for the product animation being enduring is the competitiveness in cruel market. The enterprise hopes to show the audience the product more specific, more complete and more interactive in order to drive them to introduce by themselves. The production animation mainly introduces product's structure, feature, function, production process, usage method and some notices, being the best way to do product research, test, advertising and exhibition, which applies to several fields like industry, electron and machinery. For example the usual telephone, car, aviation and component etc.

4. *Preamble animation.* Preamble animation plays the role to preview in advance, showing the core part in short time. Its time is concise, with colorful picture and numerous special effects. Generally it has been mostly applied to TV Column Packing, game promotion and movie trailer etc.

2.2 The Advantage that 3D Animation Applying to Smart Home

The animation makes consumer intuitively and elaborately know the main technique and principle, and also makes them remotely control the facility at home by Client, which has not only saved the long and tedious interpretation time intriguing consumer's interest but also gained experience effect leaving them deep impression. Meanwhile the enterprise also gets rid of the constraint for advertisement time and experience room so that lots of expenditure has been saved for continuous research. In addition demo animation could be applied on advertisement injecting, company websites, industry association and press conference for display, enlarging propaganda. The excellent demo animation could demonstrate enterprise's special cultural image automatically and raise awareness of the product, then gaining larger advantage on competitiveness.

3   Research and Development for Demo Animation in Smart Home

3.1 Analysis on Smart Home Demonstration Scheme

The Objective and Significance for Demo Animation. Smart Home has developed several years in China, while its market recognition and consumer acceptance has not kept up with pace, for which the loss at propaganda strategy is the main reason. According to the investigation analysis by Tencent at the end of 2014, 95.19 % of the consumers have showed great interest to smart home while being not clear about its concept. And they also say that the smart home at this stage cannot achieve their expected value. The later could be solved by technical innovation while the former could be done by appropriate propaganda to guide the consumer in order to improve current situation.

Based on the specificity for smart home industry and its product, its demo animation should made relative change, which not only should be the broad sense of product animation relying mainly on introducing product information and marketing for communication but also should enhance corporate image, disseminate scientific knowledge and publicize correct opinion. Meeting consumer's requirement to gain information and consume, to some extent guiding the progress on consumption concept. Demo animation has greater influence playing important role on consumer's attitude and behavior to know new product from the view of objectification. It makes product meaningful and maps the fashion element in the market with its development. In a higher level this encourages the innovation industry to continuously growing, renovating the technology, driving the development of market and pushing the advancement of society.

The Current Situation and Trend for Demonstration Scheme on Smart Home. So far smart home's demonstration technique has been mature gradually, evolving from the original static brochure to dynamic all-around video presentation. It also evolves from the beginning that there is the notice board on Demo site saying "valuables, please do not touch" to consumers first-hand trying in the experience shop with crowds. Additionally it evolves from consumer going to demo site knowing details to being seat at home browsing on the Internet. It's bound to say that this is a huge progress, while only for demo animation disadvantage still exists: the reality in the three-dimension model remains to be raised. For example, the furniture sense and people's motion law; inexact angle location resulting in being short of expounding on product from users' view with the need to enlarge demo animation's functionality and interestingness; The demonstration scheme for animation form is with low interactivity so according to consumer's physiology and mental characteristics their experience feeling should be enhanced. Through communication and research with enterprise extension worker and animation designer there problems should be perfected one by one.

With technology's progress Demo animation must develop an intelligent, automatic and humanized way. The interactive experience for 3D demo animation is the trend. Under the past circumstance to study various display platforms and systems the demo animation from now on will focus more on its experience optimism.

1. Abandon numerous and take simplicity, making the whole demonstration more clear.
2. Add vocal and gesture control making it convenient to demonstrate content.
3. Set virtual image, strengthening the interaction with demonstration object.
4. Add emotional design and elevate the degree of demonstration friendly.
5. Connect with Internet and smart home.
6. Combine with advanced technology, for example virtual reality technology and augmented reality technology.

Research and Analysis on the Demonstration of the Domestic and Foreign Smart Home. Nowadays, smart home become well known, and more attention has been put into the scientific and technological development of the product, but there is no big breakthrough in the study of the demonstration program.

Related demonstration programs of foreign countries have been becoming more mature. In terms of smart home, both online demonstration and offline demonstration are performed excellently. Demonstrations are in various forms and individuality as well as innovation are promoted. They are strongly supported by technology, but they can obey to the products themselves and they are not for the purpose of performance. They are good at disseminate corporate culture in the demo. Taking Apple's official website as an example, it is a web platform using for products sale, however, it shows the company's unique humanistic feelings through interesting dynamic effects or a tender document.

Due to a relatively late start, research on demonstration program of smart home in China is still in the stage of development. Some Chinese scholars have got a forward-looking vision. Based on related demonstration platform of smart home and virtual human interaction as well as somatosensory interaction, it made a great contribution in academic research. But owing to kinds of reasons, lots of researches are still at the theoretical level and have not been realized. From the aspect of form, domestic smart home are conventional, occasionally, they appear to have the national characteristics of the demonstration program, which enlighten us. In technology, they have an open mind to learn from others and so does in the demonstration concept. In addition, they are good at making innovation on the basis of original technology. For example, a kind of app designed for controlling smart home not only introduce the corresponding functional properties, but also make the spread of smart home be more convenient.

3.2 Excellent Cases of Smart Home Demonstration Programs at Home and Abroad

XiaoMi—Demo Video of Router. At the same time, owing to the popularity of the hot fever phone M1 among people, XiaoMi has been favored by lots of people in China. So, the scope of its research expands to more and more fields, such as smart home. When it comes to smart home of XiaoMi company, XiaoMi router must be mentioned, which was issued in April 2014. It has two animation, one is a 3D demo animation and the other one is a real video combined by two-dimensional animation.

Fig. 1. The 3D demo animation   **Fig. 2.** The real video combined by two-dimensional animation

The demo video in Fig. 1 conforms to the popular presentation forms, it presents exquisite screen effects by realistic models, mature screen languages and fluent actions. Without commentary, the whole video elaborates the most important technology and the internal structure of the product in a short period just through key pictures and key words.

The demo video in Fig. 2 pays more attention to the performance of stories. It mainly introduces the wonderful experience of the virtual cartoon characters, who climb out from inside of the router. They use the smart home secretly when the master left. It indirectly shows the company's other smart home around router. The rabbit with a LeiFeng hat in the video not only serves as the leading role, but also serves as the company's mascot. The video puts the demonstration of the products and the company's image together In a pleasant atmosphere.

Samsung—Smart Things Smart Home Demo Video. After being purchased by Samsung company, Smart Things launched a propaganda film, which exerts a great influence. The demo video pay more attention to creativity, it describes one day's life of a three- people family in the form of micro film and it subtly introduces the free operation of smart home under Smart Things platform. For instance, in Fig. 4, lamps, curtains open automatically and the coffee machine already has been ready for a cup of coffee when the morning comes. Also, it can monitor and control everything in home after leaving. This kind of animation reflects the idea of Smart Things—try to connect internet of things with smart internet. It not only emphasizes on the introduction of the function of the product, but also describes a scene of better future life from the view of the users' psychology (Fig. 3).

Fig. 3. A day living with smart home

Fig. 4. The family environment showed by smart things

Apple—TV Demo Video. Apple TV is released by Apple company in 2015, which is the key element of the smart home. Apple TV is expected by many people before its production because there are lots of IOS users and the advantage of its mature voice controls. Then, Apple company released a new propaganda video" the future of Television". As shown in Fig. 5, it originates from the initial colorful logo of Apple company, at the same time, it salutes the early television debugging methods—SMPTE. It looks back the past and thinks freely about the future.

The propaganda video focus on post production. It is a combination of nowadays popular film and television works. For example, Mind Agent Team, Budapest Hotel, A Song of ice and Fire. It not only shows its new powerful features, but also grasps the demands of customers of different levels to interact from these different tapes of film in Fig. 6, which creating a brand image that takes knowledge well of customers. In addition, it makes a perfect combination of lively background music and pictures with fast rhythm, making the whole atmosphere be more relaxing and thought-provoking.

Fig. 5. Colorful creative idea

Fig. 6. Apple TV's propaganda video

4 The Design Research of Interactive 3D Demo Animation

4.1 The Analysis Based on Smart Home Research

From the aspect of designation, demo animation not only should pay more attention to the functional introduction of the product and the animation of its usage. It also should take the experience design of users into account, which designed by the designer according to the feeling of users in the process of using the products. The importance of the research about users is beyond all doubt. In fact, the research about users and interaction design are in purpose of improving users' experience. An excellent interaction demo animation should not just pursue the superficial beauty, but also should meet the users' needs hidden gorgeous special effects.

The research about users is an important step in the design of animation. Combined with the present research on psychological and physiological characteristics of smart home users, it is not difficult to find that the users prefer to focus on high-tech fashion rather than focus on practical function. Therefore, when design the demo animation, in order to increase the credibility, designer should weigh the advantages and disadvantages of the presentation like science fiction movies and the introduction of functional usability. Meanwhile, users' habits, hobbies and their track all may determine the length, expression and presentation of the animation. So, in order to reach the final purpose, the design of this interaction demo animation should meet the users' needs and expectations.

4.2 Research on the Presentation Design of Interaction Animation

Interaction demo animation should keep the original dynamic performance and demonstration function. At the same time, combined with more conditions, it also needs to fully achieve the interaction between users and products. That is to say, users can make control of the demo animation according to their own demands and different situation. Of course, the operation should be fully considered by designer at the beginning of production, then, the program can be finalized.

Virtual Image Design. The short length and professional explanation of demo animation always make some customers puzzled on the content. Although it says to be able to play again and again, it cannot solve the problem thoroughly. If confronted with a problem that can't be solved by ourselves, it is a good choice to possess a virtual image with the explanation. It should be defined as a virtual image with a kind of competence to interact emotions. To some degree, it is a simplified "virtual human".

The reason why to introduce the concept of virtual image into the demo animation of smart home is to add users' experience feeling of demo animation, so as to control the content in the form of communication. The establishment of virtual image does not break the integrity of demo animation, it can give a detailed explanation of the content after receiving the help order from users. Moreover, connected with the system of smart home and internet, it can know the users' situation timely and consult the custom service correspondingly when encounter problems. Using the virtual image will drive the development of voice control technology. Meanwhile, it should add some kind of emotional design to enhance the experience effect by meeting users' psychological characteristics. From the aspect of appearance design, it can use virtual image or mascot to promote the spread of corporate culture. Also, it can be defined according to users' preferences to promote the individuality of the product.

Interaction Gesture Design. About interaction gesture design, maybe the majority of people would firstly think of the control of touch screen such as mobile phones and panel computer. And the scope of users' gesture still stays at the fingers and cannot expand to general body language. Just try to image, in the rapid development of science and technology, only a wave can control the progress of demo animation when the sensor technology becomes mature. But how to redefine the interaction gesture design. The present picture angles in demo animations are all pre-set by designers before showing to the audience. It doesn't really make a full presentation. If users can control the perspective and dynamic preview in demo animation according to their own minds, gesture control system would be better than voice control system. It not only promote the development of gesture recognition technology, and to a great degree, it makes users achieve a more deep experience and improves the understanding of the product.

4.3   The Demo Animation Design Based on the Smart Home of the Special Crowd

In order to make users be convenient to use it, at the beginning, the design should take account for some parts of special people, for example, the old, the children, color blindness, physical disability and illiteracy. Designers should think about others and consider their feelings and then satisfy their demands. In the design, designers should pay attention to the different characteristics of different special people. Take the screen for instance, demo animation should carefully use color, size and perspective, meanwhile, it should be combined with diversified form to get information. And in purpose of taking care of the special crowd, it should improve its universal property and be more friendly to make it gradually tend to be more reasonable, cordial and humanized.

4.4   The Possibility of the Combination of Virtual Reality and the 3D Interaction Animation

In recent years, virtual reality technology is a hot topic, which is a three- dimensional virtual world build by computer. It make users indulge in the corresponding observation and operation through simulation. It is similar with 3D demo animation to a great degree. Just try to image, they may be combined together in the future, which is of great significance in military, medical, entertainment and games, so does in demo animation. The immersive experiences make users can have a comprehensive understanding only on the screen. Even in the animation, users are able to finish the related whole process by themselves through virtual operation, which greatly enhances the effect of animation. It is easy for us to imagine, this kind of technology may have a striking influence on many industries in future life.

5   Summary

5.1   The Main Research Results of This Article

In this paper, the summary and induction of smart home creatively and purposely put forward the interactive 3D demo animation in order to deepen the experience of users. According to different needs of different customers, animation is fully studied in users' view by analyzing their psychological and physiological characteristics. Take advantage of 3D technnology, domestic and foreign outstanding cases and advanced technology, it makes a description of the future trend of 3D demo animation. At the same time, it analyzes the current situation of domestic and foreign demo animation and proposes the corresponding deficiencies and suggestions. In the end, the article make a deep discussion and analysis upon fashion interaction technology of 3D demo animation. It hopes to benefit the public by shortening the distance between products and users.

5.2 Future Research Prospects

In the past decades, demo animation has achieved a rapid development. With the great progress of 3D technology in recent years, the scope of demo animation is expanding gradually a. It has already used in our daily life and make our life be more convenient. Interactive 3D demo animation not only brings users a direct experience, but also promotes the company's development as well as the communication between customers, products and enterprises. With the growing of new industries presented by smart home, the production industry of 3D demo animation is also bound to lead the development and will play a great role in future demonstration.

All in all, the development trend of interactive 3D demo animation is obvious, the technology will be in a smart, automatic and humanized way. Combined with art and technology, it will present a multi-dimensional interactive display among designers, products, customers, enterprises.

References

1. Du, K.: Research on Method and Technology of Virtual Human Based on Smart Home (2014)
2. Yang, Q.: Research on the Application of Three-dimensional Technology in Smart Home System (2015)
3. Chatzigiannakis, I., Drude, J.P., Hasemann, H., Kröller, A.: Developing Smart Homes Using the Internet of Things: How to demonstrate Your System (2014)
4. Akagi, Y., Furukawa, M., Fukumoto, S., Kawai, Y., Kawasaki, H.: Demo paper: a content creation system for interactive 3D animations (2013)

A Formal Model for Context-Aware Semantic Augmented Reality Systems

Tamás Matuszka[1,2(✉)], Attila Kiss[1,3], and Woontack Woo[2]

[1] Eötvös Loránd University, Budapest, Hungary
{tomintt,kiss}@inf.elte.hu
[2] KAIST, Daejeon, South Korea
{tamas.matuszka,wwoo}@kaist.ac.kr
[3] J. Selye University, Komárno, Slovakia
kissa@ujs.sk

Abstract. The Augmented Reality applications have received great attention in the recent years. However, there is still a lack of formal description of such systems currently. In this paper, we propose a new formal model for context-aware semantic Augmented Reality systems. The model can be divided into two parts: a set-theory function based method allows the formalization of an Augmented Reality system while an integrated time-space-motion logic provides the description of the behavior of the system. The suggested model enables the characterization of an Augmented Reality system with mathematical precision. In addition, logical inferences can be performed by means of the logic part of the formal description. The practical applicability of the proposed model is shown through use cases.

Keywords: Augmented reality · Semantic web · Context-aware computing · Formal model

1 Introduction

Augmented Reality (AR) [1] systems have become the accepted part of our everyday life due to the proliferation of smartphones. The physical environment of a user can be extended by virtual elements using such a system. An Augmented Reality system is regarded as a representative of context-aware computing [2], where the continuously changing context and the environment are taken into account by the system. As a result, the user is able to obtain and visualize context-dependent information.

The behavior of the state-of-the-art Augmented Reality systems can only be described as architectural diagrams nowadays. This fact raises the following question: how can we formally model a context-aware semantic augmented reality system? A formal description is needed that is able to model the context-aware AR systems with mathematical precision. In addition, the features of a context-aware Augmented Reality system can be described using the formalism.

In this paper, a new formal model for context-aware semantic Augmented Reality systems is presented. The model consists of two parts. The components of the AR system are formalized by the first part of the model using set theory functions.

© Springer International Publishing Switzerland 2016
N. Streitz and P. Markopoulos (Eds.): DAPI 2016, LNCS 9749, pp. 91–102, 2016.
DOI: 10.1007/978-3-319-39862-4_9

The second part can be used for describing the behavior of the system with integrated space-time-motion logic. Therefore, the system enables to execute logical inferences. Our model contributes to the development of theoretical foundations of Augmented Reality systems. For validation purposes, two context-aware mobile Augmented Reality browsers have been implemented based on our abstract formal model.

The structure of the paper is as follows. After the introductory Sect. 1, related work is presented in Sect. 2. The proposed formal model is described in Sect. 3. Then, use cases where the formal model was applied are introduced in Sect. 4. Finally, the conclusion and future work are shown in Sect. 4.

2 Related Work

In the last decades, several definitions of Augmented Reality have been developed. One of the most popular definitions is given by Azuma [1], who described Augmented Reality in an informal way using three characteristics. Milgram and Kishino [3] defined a taxonomy of mixed reality and introduced the concept of virtuality continuum which positioning Augmented Reality between the real environment and the virtual environment. Despite the popularity of these definitions, those are still informal explanations and a formal description is needed in order to ensure the mathematical precision.

Reicher introduced a framework for AR systems in his doctoral thesis [4]. A reference architecture and design patterns for Augmented Reality have also been described in that work. The proposed method provides a detailed description of a wearable Augmented Reality system architecture and can be used as a guideline for AR system design. However, the solution does not contain any formal model or description.

Galton developed a temporal logic in [5] which is able to describe time-dependent and spatial phenomena. The work is based on the spatial logic introduced by Randell, et al. [6]. Owing to the capability of the description of continuous movement, this framework can be used for modeling the behavior of an Augmented Reality system. In addition, reasoning about the motion of a user of the AR system is also become available by means of the logic. The details can be seen in Sect. 3.

3 CAESAR Model

The formal description of the proposed system is introduced in this section. The model has been called as CAESAR (Context-Awareness Enriched Semantic Augmented Reality) and consists of a set theory functions-based part that formalizes the components of an AR system while an integrated time-space-motion logic is used to describe the behavior of the system.

3.1 Formal Description with Set Theory Functions

The formal description of each component of CAESAR model is described in the following section using set theory functions. Furthermore, the formalization of the features provided by CAESAR model can also be seen in this subsection. The model includes the following four components:

- data: provides the user-generated and the integrated POI data from different data sources that are displayed by the AR browser,
- browser: is responsible for the visualization of data (provided by data component),
- semantic: is responsible for the connection to semantic web,
- context: adaptive segment that recommends content based on the context.

Formally, a quartet $CAESAR := \langle Data, ARB, SWB, C \rangle$ is called as a context-aware semantic Augmented Reality system, where $Data$, ARB, SWB, and C are the components of data, browser, semantic and context, respectively.

Data Component. The first building block of the model is the data component which is responsible for the displayable data provision. The data can be derived from different sources that use different storage schemas. Therefore, heterogeneous data integration is needed which includes the global schema matching and entity resolution.

Definition 1. *The triple $\mathcal{G}, \mathcal{S}, \mathcal{M}$ is called as* data integration system, *where $\mathcal{G}$ is the global scheme, $\mathcal{S}$ is the set of source elements, and $\mathcal{M}$ is the mapping among the global schema and the schemas of the heterogeneous data.*

A requested query q will be queried against the integrated data source using the global schema $\mathcal{G}$. During this method, $\mathcal{M}$ is responsible for mapping q to $\mathcal{S}$ [7].

Schema matching can be used for determining global schema $\mathcal{G}$ based on $\mathcal{S}$. The core element of schema matching is operator $match_{SM}$. The definition of $\mathcal{M}_{SM}$ which is the mapping between two schemas is needed before introducing $match_{SM}$.

Definition 2. *The mapping $\mathcal{M}_{SM}$ is the set of mapping elements between schema S_1 and S_2. The mapping elements represent that certain elements of S_1 have been mapped into certain elements of S_2.*

Definition 3. *The operator $match_{SM}$ is a function $f : \mathcal{S} \times \mathcal{S} \to \mathcal{M}_{SM}$ which creates the mapping $\mathcal{M}_{SM}$ from the given two schemas. The resulted overcome is called as* match result [8].

The identification of duplicated elements is crucial during the data integration process and entity resolution can be used for this purpose. Function $match_{ER}$ (which is different from the above-mentioned $match_{SM}$) can be used in order to identify the same elements (in our case, the POIs which represent the same real-world entity).

Definition 4. *Let E be the set of entities. Then, $match_{ER}$ is a Boolean function $f : E \times E \to \{true, false\}$ which determines whether two entities are matching (i.e. represent the same real-world entity) or not (denoted by $e_1 \approx e_2$, if $match(e_1, e_2) = true$, where $e_1, e_2 \in E$).*

A partial order on the entities can be defined using the entity-related useful information. If entity e_2 holds more information than e_1, then e_2 dominates e_1 (denoted by $e_1 \preceq e_2$).

Definition 5. *The function* $\mu : E \times E \to E$ *(called as* merge*) merges two matching* $e_1 \approx e_2$ *entities into one entity. During the merging method, the function keeps only the dominant entity* e_2, *and extends it with the missing attributes deriving from* e_1.

Definition 6. *An* instance $I = \{e_1, \cdots, e_n\}$ *is a finite set of entities from E.*

The merge closure finds all matching entities within instance I and merges them using the match and merge functions.

Definition 7. *Let I be an instance, then* merge closure *of I (denoted by* $\bar{I}$) *the smallest set of S such that* $I \subseteq S$. *In addition,* $\forall e_1, e_2 \in S$, *if* $e_1 \approx e_2$, *then* $merge(e_1 \approx e_2) \in S$.

The domination of entities can naturally be extended to the instances as well.

Definition 8. *Let* I_1, I_2 *be two instances. Then,* I_1 *is dominated by* I_2 *(denoted by* $I_1 \preccurlyeq I_2$), *if* $\forall e_1 \in I_1, \exists e_2 \in I_2$, *such that* $e_1 \preccurlyeq e_2$.

The definition of entity resolution can be defined using the above auxiliary formulas.

Definition 9. *Let I be an instance,* $\bar{I}$ *be the merge closure of I. An* entity resolution *of I is the* I' *set of entities such that* $I' \subseteq \bar{I}$ *and* $\bar{I} \preccurlyeq I'$. *In addition, there is not any proper subset of* I' *which satisfies the first two conditions* [9].

In conclusion, component *Data* is a $\mathcal{G}, \mathcal{S}, \mathcal{M}$ data integration system which creates global schema $\mathcal{G}$ from source schemas $\mathcal{S}$ using operator $match_{SM}$. Furthermore, the execution of entity resolution during the data integration phase is also the responsibility of component *Data*.

Browser Component. The second component of CAESAR model is the browser component, which is responsible for the displaying of the data provided by the before mentioned data component. The visualization uses Augmented Reality, which can be formally defined in the following way.

Definition 10. *A quintet* $\mathcal{M}, \mathcal{VE}, \mathcal{T}, \varphi, \xi$ *is called as Augmented Reality system, where* $\mathcal{M}$ *is the set of the markers,* $\mathcal{VE}$ *is the set of the virtual elements,* $\mathcal{T}$ *is the set of transformations,* φ *is the mapping function, and* ξ *is the transformation function.*

Let IB, PB (image-based markers and position-based markers) be two disjoint sets. Then, $\mathcal{M}$ can be written as follows:

$$\mathcal{M} = IB \cup PB. \tag{1}$$

Let I, V, S and K (images, videos, sounds, knowledge base, respectively) be pairwise disjoint sets. Then the set of virtual elements $\mathcal{VE}$ can be written in the next form:

$$\mathcal{VE} = I \cup V \cup S \cup K. \tag{2}$$

The set $\mathcal{T}$ contains geometric transformations, namely translation (τ), rotation (ρ) and scale (σ). In addition, let L be the set of 3D vectors. Every virtual element $v \in \mathcal{VE}$ has an $l \in L$ vector. The vector l stores the position of virtual element v.

Function $\varphi : \mathcal{M} \to \mathcal{VE} \times L$ maps a virtual element and its relative initial position to a marker. The range of function φ contains the empty set (i.e. there is not any virtual element assigned to a given marker).

The last part of the quintet is the transformation function ξ. Function ξ : $\mathcal{M} \times \mathcal{VE} \times L \times \mathcal{T} \to \mathcal{VE} \times L$ transforms a virtual element corresponding to the given marker with a given transformation in real-time.

The current Augmented Reality systems can be modeled by the above-mentioned definitions. The browser component of CAESAR model is an AR system $\langle \mathcal{M}|_{\text{PB}}, \mathcal{V}|_{\text{KB}}, \mathcal{T}, \varphi, \xi \rangle$ where set $\mathcal{M}$ is restricted to the position-based markers and set $\mathcal{VE}$ is restricted to knowledge base.

Semantic Component. The third component of the model is based on semantic web technologies and is responsible for the interconnection of data component provided information with publicly available semantic data sources. Since semantic data sources are interlinked using IRIs (*Internationalized Resource Identifier*), therefore, the semantic data source can be explored starting from a concept derived from the data component.

Let B, I, and L be the pairwise disjoint sets of blank nodes, literals and IRIs, respectively. In addition, let *BIL*, *BI*, and *IL* be the abbreviations of $B \cup I \cup L, B \cup I$, and $I \cup L$, respectively. The abbreviation *BIL* can be referred as RDF term.

Definition 11. *A triplet $(s, p, o) \in BI \times I \times BIL$ is called as RDF triple, where predicate p connects subject s with object o. Let the finite set of RDF triple be denoted by RDF_3.*

Definition 12. *Let the infinitive set of RDF triples be denoted by RDF_{DB} and be called as RDF database (or RDF document).*

The data storage model of semantic web can be described by Definition 11 and 12. However, a query language is needed in order to access and manipulate the data stored in such a way. One of the semantic technologies, SPARQL query language was designed for this purpose. Since the RDF triples can be considered as directed edges, the RDF database can be seen as a directed graph. Due to this solution, the SPARQL language reduces the RDF database searching to graph pattern matching [10].

Ontology is one of the key components of semantic web, which describe the relations, rules and restrictions among the concepts.

Definition 13. *An ontology is a structure $\mathcal{O} := (C, \leq_C, P, \sigma)$, where C and P are the disjoint sets of classes and properties, respectively. A partial order $\leq_C$ on C is called as class hierarchy while the function $\sigma : P \to C \times C$ describes the signature of properties. Let $c_1, c_2 \in C$ be two classes. If $c_1 \leq_C c_2$, then c_1 is the subclass of c_2 while c_2 is the superclass of c_1 [11].*

The following definitions will be used in the description of the semantic component of CAESAR model.

Definition 14. *Let link : $RDF_3 \times RDF_3 \to \{true, false\}$ be a Boolean function, which decides whether two RDF triples are directly accessible from each other or not. Let $\rightsquigarrow$ denote this function.*

The behavior of function *link* can formally be described in the following way:

$$(s_1, p_1, o_1) \rightsquigarrow (s_2, p_2, o_2) =$$
$$\begin{cases} true, \ if \ s_1 \neq s_2 \wedge (o_1 = s_2 \vee o_2 = s_1 \vee (o_1 = o_2 \wedge o_1 \notin L)) \\ false, \ otherwise \end{cases}, \quad (3)$$

where $(s_1, p_1, o_1), (s_2, p_2, o_2) \in RDF_3$.

The directly accessible (one step relation) RDF triples can be obtained using function *link*. The indirectly accessible RDF triples can be determined using a method which is similar to the derivation method of formal languages theory.

Definition 15. *Let* $link_{indirect*} : RDF_3 \times \ldots \times RDF_3 \rightarrow \{true, false\}$ *be a Boolean function which determines whether two RDF triples are indirectly accessible from each other or not. Let* $\rightsquigarrow_*$ *denote this function.*

A $b \in RDF_3$ is indirectly accessible or derivable from $a \in RDF_3$ triple, if the following condition holds:

$$\exists n \in \mathbb{N}, \ r_1, \cdots, r_n \in RDF_3 : a = r_1 \wedge b = r_n \wedge (\forall i \in [1 \cdots n - 1] : r_i \rightsquigarrow r_{i+1}). \quad (4)$$

The component *SWB* is a semantic database which satisfies the following criteria:

$$\exists d \in Data, \forall r \in RDF_{DB} : d \rightsquigarrow_* r. \quad (5)$$

In details, at least one element from the information provided by data component can be used to explore the full semantically represented dataset.

Context Component. The last component of the model, which is responsible for the contextual data tailoring. Since the data provision has to take into account various parameters (location, time, etc.), this component can be seen as a context-aware recommender system that is based on [12]. The first step of the recommendation process is the specification of the set of initialization of recommendations which can be done by explicit (given by the users) or implicit (by means of inferences) way. After the initial data source has been created, the component tries to estimate the following recommendation function R:

$$R : User \times POI \times Context \rightarrow Rating, \quad (6)$$

where *User* is the set of users, *POI* the data coming from component *Data*, *Context* is the set of contextual information while *Rating* is the range of the ratings.

When function R has performed the estimation over $User \times POI \times Context$ space, the context component returns the POI which has the highest *Rating* value. Intuitively, the component tries to estimate a value for unknown POIs. Function R can be defined in the following way.

Definition 16. *Let* $R : User \times POI \times Location \times Time \times Category \rightarrow Rating$ *be a recommender function which determines that the* $u \in User$ *how would rate the* $p \in POI$ *(deriving from data component) which is located in* $l \in Location$ *and has a* $c \in Category$ *in* $t \in Time$, *namely* $R(u, p, l, c, t) \in Rating$.

Formal Description of the System Functionality. After the introduction of the components of the model, the abstract description of the features provided by CAESAR model can be read in this subsection. The definition of multivalued functions [13] is needed for the formal description of the features.

Definition 17. *Let* multivalued function $f : A \rightarrow B^*$ *a function which assigns one or more value from range to the elements of the domain, namely* $\forall x \exists n \in \mathbb{N}$, $y_1, \cdots, y_n, \forall i \in [1, n] : (x, y_i) \in f$.

The signatures of the features of CAESAR model can be defined by means of set theory functions and Definition 17. The core function of the model is function $browse : Data \times String \times \mathbb{R} \rightarrow \mathcal{VE}^*$, which collects the virtual elements that represents the relevant hits from the POI data derived from component *Data*, from search keyword and from the search radius (the current position of user is considered as the central point of search area). The resulted overcome (e.g. a POI) can be visualized by component *ARB*. In addition, detailed information can be displayed from a given POI using function $details : \mathcal{VE} \rightarrow I \times String^n$, where I is the set of images while the second component of the range is an n-dimensional word vector which represents the attributes of virtual element. A new virtual element can also be created by component *ARB* using function $new : \mathbb{R} \times \mathbb{R} \times I \times String^n \rightarrow \mathcal{VE}$. The inputs of this feature are the latitude and longitude coordinates, an image, and a word vector which contains the properties of a POI. Furthermore, navigation is also provided by component *ARB* by means of function $navigate : \mathcal{VE} \times \mathbb{R} \times \mathbb{R} \times \mathbb{R} \times \mathbb{R} \rightarrow (\mathbb{R} \times \mathbb{R})^*$. The function *navigate* gets a virtual element (POI) and its latitude/longitude coordinates, and the current latitude/longitude coordinates of a user and returns with the latitude/longitude coordinate pairs which represents the path to the given POI from the current position. Function $toRDF : \mathcal{VE} \times \mathbb{R}^n \rightarrow RDF_3^*$ creates the RDF representation of a virtual element. In this way, a POI can be used for exploring a semantic dataset using Definition 15 and Eq. 5.

3.2 Integrated Time-Space-Motion Logic

The logical description of our CAESAR system is based on Galton's work [5] which introduces a special logic that enables to combine temporal and spatial logics. In this way, the changes in context can be described and logical inferences can be executed.

Galton's logic is based on the work of Randell et al. [6] who developed a spatial reasoning system (hereinafter referred to as RCC). RCC determines the set of relations between spatial regions and the concept of connection is considered as a primitive.

The concept of connection can be extended to spatial points beside the regions. In case of points, connection can take two values: two points either are the same points or different points. The relation between a point and a region can be the followings:

- p is inside r,
- p bounds r,
- p is outside r.

Inside can be considered as a primitive, then, *Bounds* and *Outside* can be defined in the following way:

$$Bounds(p, r) \equiv \forall r'(Inside(p, r') \rightarrow PO(r, r')) \tag{7}$$

$$Outside(p, r) \equiv \neg Inside(p, r) \wedge \neg Bounds(p, r), \tag{8}$$

where *PO* means partially overlapping. The fulfillment of certain conditions can be indicated by three predicates, namely *Holds − on*, *Holds − in*, and Holds-at. The first two predicates deal with the state of intervals while the last can be used for relating states to instants. In addition, let $inf(i)$ and $sup(i)$ denote the boundaries of an interval i while let $Div(t, i)$ denote that instant t falls within interval i.

Events can be defined using the changes of states. Similarly to the before mentioned predicate *Holds*, three *Occurs* predicates can be introduced, namely *Occurs − on*, *Occurs − in*, and *Occurs − at*. If an event e occurs during interval i, then predicate *Occurs − in(e, i)* can be used. If event e takes the whole interval i, *Occurs − on(e, i)* should be used. If event e is instantaneous and occurs at the instant t, then *Occurs − at(e, t)* can be written [5].

Logical Formalization of the System. The first step of the logical description is to define the following predicates and function symbol:

- *Region(x)* – x is a variable with type region,
- *VirtualRegion(x)* – x is a variable with type virtual region,
- *Point(x)* – x is a variable with type point,
- *VirtualPoint(x)* – x is a variable with type virtual point,
- *ARDevice(x)* – x is a variable with type AR device,
- *POI(x)* – x is a variable with type POI,
- *Belongs(dev, vr)* – indicates that virtual region vr belongs to AR device dev,
- *Display(dev)* – indicates, whether AR displaying is possible on AR device dev,
- *Type(x)* – function symbol, returns the category of variable x with type POI (e.g. university or restaurant).

The device which enables the AR displaying can be indicated by predicate *ARDevice(x)*. Predicate *VirtualRegion(x)* represents a virtual region that belongs to variable y with type Region while *VirtualPoint(x)* represents a virtual element.

Hereinafter, the terms of virtual world and virtual region are used interchangeably. A variable with type virtual point can correspond to a POI variable; therefore, a virtual element can be assigned to a real world object. The following formalism can be used for creating a hierarchy among the types which is necessary for the further description:

$$\forall x(VirtualPoint(x) \rightarrow Point(x)) \tag{9}$$

$$\forall x(POI(x) \rightarrow Point(x) \vee Region(x)) \tag{10}$$

$$\forall x(ARDevice(x) \rightarrow Point(x) \vee Body(x)) \tag{11}$$

$$\forall x(VirtualRegion(x) \rightarrow Region(x)) \tag{12}$$

In possession of the above predicates and statements, the logical description of a CAESAR system can be specified in more detail. The first building component is the assignment of physical region with the corresponding virtual region. For this purpose, a formula is needed which decides whether a point belongs to a region, formally:

$$Contains(r,p) \equiv Region(r) \wedge Point(p)$$
$$\wedge \, (Bounds(pos(p),r) \vee Inside(pos(p),r))$$

where $pos(p)$ is the position of point p. The correspondence among the real and virtual points can be written using the above formula in the following way:

$$Superimpose(r,vr)$$
$$\equiv \forall poi(POI(poi) \wedge Contains(r,poi)$$
$$\rightarrow \exists vpoi(VirtualPoint(vpoi) \wedge Contains(vr,vpoi) \wedge pos(poi)$$
$$= pos(vpoi)))$$

Therefore, every physical POI belonging to region r can be assigned to a virtual object belonging to virtual region vr (which is corresponding to region r). The next step is the correspondence between the real and virtual world such that the virtual world corresponds to the given AR device. In this way, the physical region can correspond to the virtual region which can be seen on the display of the AR device:

$$ARMode(dev,r,vr)$$
$$\equiv (ARDevice(dev) \wedge Region(r) \wedge VirtualRegion(vr)$$
$$\wedge Belongs(dev,vr) \wedge pos(vr) = pos(r) \wedge Superimpose(r,vr))$$
$$\rightarrow Display(dev).$$

The formula checks whether virtual region vr belonging to AR device dev can correspond to the given region r. In addition, it examines the correspondence of physical POIs with virtual elements. If both conditions hold, then AR device dev is able to superimpose AR content into region r, i.e. the browser component ARB of CAESAR model can be used in the region r.

Certain questions related to the behavior of an AR system can be answered using logical inferences on data derived from the semantic SWB and the context C components of CAESAR model.

Such a behavior related question is that whether virtual content is available passing through a region. The answering logical formula is the following:

$$Occurs-on(transitAR(p,r,dev,vr),i)$$
$$\equiv Holds - on(pos(p) = pos(dev),i) \wedge Holds$$
$$- at(Bounds(pos(p),r),\inf(i)) \wedge Holds$$
$$- at(Bounds(pos(p),r),\sup(i)) \wedge Holds$$
$$- on(Inside(pos(p),r) \wedge ARMode(dev,r,vr),i),$$

where *transitAR*(p, r, dev, vr) describes the event which represents the motion of a user during the AR system usage. The position of AR device *dev* and the moving point p which represents the user is the same during the whole interval of passing through. Point p bounds one of the boundaries of region r in the first instant of passage, it crosses the opposite boundary in the last instant while it is located inside of region r in the meantime. Predicate *ARMode* contained by the last *Holds − on* predicate determines whether the displayable virtual content is available.

The above question is related to the virtual elements within a region; however, it is independent of time. The need to respond to issues where the time is essential was also raised. The introduced logical description can be used to answer time-related questions as well. Let us consider the following two questions:

- Does the user miss a meeting at a given time and location?
- Is the user allowed to enter a place at a given time?

The first question can be answered using the following logical formula:

$$Occurs-at(contact(b_1, b_2, p_{loc}, t), t_{cur}) \equiv t_{cur}$$
$$\leq t \wedge Holds$$
$$- at((EC(pos(b_1), pos(b_2)) \wedge pos(b_1) = pos(p_{loc})), t_{cur})$$
$$\wedge \exists t'(Holds - on(DC(pos(b_1), pos(b_2)), (t', t_{cur}))).$$

The meeting of users b_1 and b_2 is represented by event $contact(b_1, b_2, p_{loc}, t_{cur})$. The meeting time and place have been agreed in location p_{loc} at time t. The truth value of the formula is true if the current time less than or equal to time t; b_1 and b_2 are externally connected in location p_{loc} at time t (i.e. the meeting has happened), and there is a time t' when b_1 and b_2 are disconnected. The truth value of the following formula answers the second question:

$$Occurs-in(enter(b, r), i)$$
$$\equiv POI(r) \wedge \exists t'(t' \geq \inf(i) \wedge Holds - at(EC(pos(b), r), t'))$$
$$\wedge \exists t''(Div(t'', i) \wedge t'' > t' \wedge Holds - at(EC(pos(b), r), t''))$$
$$\wedge \exists t(Div(t, (t', t'')) \wedge Holds - on(PO(pos(b), r), (t', t''))).$$

A user b is permitted to pass through a region r if the entering time falls within the allowed time interval i and the exit time falls also within this interval. Since the type of region r is POI (see Eq. 10), the related opening/allowed time interval can be obtained from data component *Data* or semantic component *SWB* of CAESAR model.

The last example is the formalization of navigation. The navigation regarded as a success if the user gets to point B from point A passing through the path made up of regions. The formalization requires defining the passage of point p through region r:

$$Occurs - on(transit(p, r), i)$$
$$\equiv Holds - at(Bounds(pos(p), r), \inf(i)) \wedge Holds$$
$$- at(Bounds(pos(p), r), \sup(i)) \wedge Holds$$
$$- on((Inside(pos(p), r), i)).$$

The logical statement of navigation can be given using the above formula:

$$Occurs - on(navigate(p_{user}, r_1, \cdots, r_n, a, b), i) \equiv r_1 = a \wedge r_n = b \wedge \forall r_{wp}$$
$$\in [r_1, \cdots, r_n] : (POI(r_{wp}) \wedge Occurs - in(transit(p_{user}, r_{wp}), i)$$
$$\wedge \exists vpoi(VirtualPoint(vpoi) \wedge Inside(pos(vpoi), r_{wp}))).$$

A point p_{user} which represents the user passes through each region r_{wp} (i.e. every waypoint of the navigation path). Since the type of the waypoints of navigation path is POI, virtual elements can be assigned to the waypoints and these points can be displayed by Augmented Reality, helping the user during the navigation. If time constraints are also available for each waypoint, then predicate $Occurs - in(enter(p_{user}, r_{wp}), i)$ can be used. In this way, the handling of time, space, and motion changes provided by the logic is fully utilized during the logical inference.

4 Use Cases

Two context-aware Android-based mobile AR browsers have been implemented which are based on our formal model. The architecture of the developed applications has been mapped to the proposed formal model, and the described modules have been also included. The first one is a tourist application, it allows the users to collect and display POIs in the surrounding environment [13]. The second is used in the field of cultural heritage; it provides movable story maps based on time and space [14]. Both applications use integrated data sources coming from component *Data* and this information was visualized by component *ARB*. In the case of the first application, publicly available semantic data sources can be explored starting from a given POI using component *SWB* while the second application provides POI-related semantic metadata browsing by means of component *SWB*. The component *C* was restricted to location, time and POI's category. These applications can be seen as a proof of the practical applicability of our formal model. The detailed description of the browsers can be found in the cited papers.

5 Conclusion

In this paper, we present a new formal model for CAESAR systems. In addition, the behavior of the system was also introduced using set theory functions as well as integrated time-space-motion logic. The current Augmented Reality systems can be modeled with mathematical precision by means of the proposed model. The developed method contributes to the development of theoretical foundations of Augmented Reality systems. For a demonstration of the practical applicability of CAESAR model, two context-aware mobile Augmented Reality applications were briefly presented which are based on our formal model. In the future, a more in-depth investigation into the implementation of logical part of the model is needed.

Acknowledgments. This research is supported by Ministry of Culture, Sports and Tourism (MCST) and Korea Creative contents Agency (KOCCA) in the Culture Technology (CT) Research & Development Program 2014.

References

1. Azuma, R.T.: A survey of augmented reality. Presence **6**(4), 355–385 (1997)
2. Schilit, B., Adams, N., Want, R.: Context-aware computing applications. In: Mobile Computing Systems and Applications, pp. 85–90 (1994)
3. Milgram, P., Kishino, F.: A taxonomy of mixed reality visual displays. IEICE Trans. Inf. Syst. **77**(12), 1321–1329 (1994)
4. Reicher, T.: A framework for dynamically adaptable augmented reality systems. PhD dissertation, Technical University Munich (2004)
5. Galton, A.: Towards an integrated logic of space, time, and motion. IJCAI **93**, 1550–1555 (1993)
6. Randell, D.A., Cui, Z., Cohn, A.G.: A spatial logic based on regions and connection. KR **92**, 165–176 (1992)
7. Lenzerini, M.: Data integration: a theoretical perspective. In: Proceedings of the Twenty-First ACM SIGMOD-SIGACT-SIGART Symposium on Principles of Database Systems, pp. 233–246. ACM (2002)
8. Bernstein, P.A., Rahm, E.: A survey of approaches to automatic schema matching. VLDB J. **10**(4), 334–350 (2001)
9. Benjelloun, O., Garcia-Molina, H., Menestrina, D., Su, Q., Whang, S.E., Widom, J.: Swoosh: a generic approach to entity resolution. VLDB J. **18**(1), 255–276 (2009)
10. Pérez, J., Arenas, M., Gutierrez, C.: Semantics and complexity of SPARQL. ACM Trans. Database Syst. **34**(3), 16 (2009)
11. Volz, R., Kleb, J., Mueller, W.: Towards ontology-based disambiguation of geographical identifiers. In: I3 (2007)
12. Ricci, F., Rokach, L., Shapira, B., Kantor, P.B.: Recommender Systems Handbook. Springer, Heidelberg (2011)
13. Matuszka, T., Kámán, S., Kiss, A.: A semantically enriched augmented reality browser. In: Shumaker, R., Lackey, S. (eds.) VAMR 2014, Part I. LNCS, vol. 8525, pp. 375–384. Springer, Heidelberg (2014)
14. Kim, E., Kim, S., Kim, J., Matuszka, T., Park, N., Park, H., Jo, J., Kim, K., Hong, S., Kim, J., Woo, W.: AR reference model in k-culture time machine. In: Proceedings of HCI International 2016. Springer International Publishing, Heidelberg (2016)

How to Support the Design of User-Oriented Product-Related Services

Maura Mengoni[1](✉) and Margherita Peruzzini[2]

[1] Department of Industrial Engineering and Mathematical Science,
Polytechnic University of Marche, Ancona, Italy
m.mengoni@univpm.it
[2] Department of Engineering "Enzo Ferrari",
University of Study of Modena and Reggio Emilia, Modena, Italy
margherita.peruzzini@unimore.it

Abstract. A Product-Service System (PSS) is an innovation strategy, shifting the business focus from designing physical products only, to designing a system that combines tangible products, intangible services, supporting network and infrastructure, which are jointly capable of fulfilling specific customer needs. Due to the widespread of this paradigm, the present research provides a methodological framework and related tools to support the design of PSSs. The aim is to propose a user-centered approach to involve end-users during the different stages of PSS development.

Keywords: Product-Service System · User-Centered Design · Hardware-in-the-Loop · Virtual reality

1 Introduction

With the popularity of pervasive Information and Commutation Technologies (ICT) (e.g. wireless networks, broadband), products are become more "intelligent" and capable of communicating with the surrounding environment, storing data, interacting with other connected devices, until being adaptable to the user needs, behaviours and attitudes, as well as developing more strategic marketing actions. There are numerous examples in literature of products integrating an Intelligent Data Unit and service enabler software to elaborate lifecycle data and share information and knowledge [16]. This technological trend pushes towards the development of product-related services and the creation of the so-called Product-Service Systems (PSS), which add a wide range of services to the customer, from remote assistance to preventive maintenance, training, retrofitting and product monitoring [13]. Most researches focus on the description of PSS solutions in different application fields, embedded technologies to enable product-related services, methods of data acquisition and elaboration, and software interface [6]. However, the focus on technology often neglects the final customer needs. Indeed, only few of them face the problem of how to develop a PSS applying a User-Centered Design (UCD) approach to create a really customer-oriented and adaptable service [8] and, finally, how to create effective and efficient models to identify usability problems at the different stages of PSS design [14].

© Springer International Publishing Switzerland 2016
N. Streitz and P. Markopoulos (Eds.): DAPI 2016, LNCS 9749, pp. 103–110, 2016.
DOI: 10.1007/978-3-319-39862-4_10

The paper illustrates two case studies of PSS for household appliances, where traditional low-fidelity prototyping techniques are used. Experimentations demonstrate the difficulty to effectively design the product-service features predicting User eXperience (UX) by traditional tools and methods. The main problem is that product and service are usually designed separately on diverse mock-ups and the final PSS performance is achieved only when the first physical prototype is developed. In order to solve such limitations, a UCD approach is adopted to define a novel virtual prototyping system architecture that allows developers to create interactive mock-ups of the entire PSS to verify step-by-step the achieved performance and users' satisfaction. It helps to design both product and service features taking into account the reciprocal relationships and the final performance of the integrated PSS.

2   PSS Design and Prototyping: An Overview

A first question to face PSS design regards what PSS is. Most researches agree in defining PSS as an innovation strategy, shifting the business focus from designing a physical product only, to designing a system of products and services which are jointly capable of fulfilling specific client demands [5]. It implies the combination of products, services, supporting networks and infrastructure to guarantee company's competitiveness and customer satisfaction [7]. For the customer, a PSS is seen to provide value trough more customization, additional functionalities and higher quality to suit his/her needs.

In this context, technical services represent the easiest way to create a PSS in manufacturing industry: from maintenance to training, retrofitting and product monitoring. Indeed, they can be easily realized by improving the product communication capabilities in order to make data flow from product to external systems to realize supporting or differentiating services. This integrated understanding leads to new and customer oriented solutions, and enable innovative functions and result-oriented business models. Furthermore, services can bring great advantages for industry: from the economical viewpoint, services can create higher profit margins and contribute to higher productivity by means of reduced investment costs along the lifetime as well as reduced operating costs for the final users [1].

One of the widely recognized barriers to the adoption of PSS and the achievement of an effective PSS regards the relationship between the customer, who is the final user of the PSS, and the company network, which is the entity providing the PSS. The early involvement of customers in the design process is essential to achieve a successful solution, able to respond to customer wants and needs. This means to involve end-users into a co-creation process in PSS designing [4]. However, the creation of physical prototypes, including the product and the service, reliable enough to be used for usability testing with sample end-users is generally costing and can be done only once the design process is at an advanced stage. There are a variety of tools and methods to support the design of a PSS in literature. Most of them are tailored to specific projects, exploit well-known principles of Concurrent Engineering, Systematic Engineering and recently User-Centered Design approach, and hence include the following stages: identification of customer value, early involvement in the system design, information sharing and continuous design improvement [10]. Mont [7] argued that a further development in design methodology is necessary to promote the implementation of PSS. In terms of approach, the greatest reported challenge is to engage relevant stakeholders in the process of research, evaluation, and testing at both theoretical and practical levels [1]. In industry, this means that long-term and integrated testing of PSS practice is needed to help to develop theories, methodologies, and operational solutions. Advances in Virtual Prototyping techniques allow the creation of realistic, reliable and enriched high-fidelity virtual prototypes able to simulate the product in different working conditions [15]. Benefits in adopting VP to involve the end-users at the different product development stages are well known in literature and proved by numerous reported applications [12]. The introduction of a service jointly operating into a product is a challenging issue both in VP and in PSS development. While numerous tools are actually developed to model a PSS, none specific platform to support virtual prototyping have been yet created.

3   Case Studies to Explore PSS Development Issues

Two case studies of PSS development are here described to point out the main critical issues to be faced in terms of design and prototyping solutions centered on customers.

Both cases regard a PSS where intelligent appliances (i.e. washing machine, washer-dryer, oven, fridge) are able to collect data about their functioning, connect to an Home Area Network (HAN) based on ZigBee technology and to the Internet to make data available for both a local Home Automation Controller and web-based services (Fig. 1).

The first case developed a domestic Energy Monitoring Service to monitor and manage the power consumptions of connected appliances: each appliance communicates its consumptions and operating status to the Controller, which allows to display the instant power consumption and to set the optimal configuration; contemporarily, the manufacturing companies can monitor the consumption data, detect dangerous situation and provide remote assistance and maintenance services.

The second case concerns the ideation of a Carefree Washing Service where product monitoring is not limited to energy consumption, but includes also product behaviours (e.g. programs, temperature control, water and soap control if needed, etc.) and detection of dangerous situations, and services are extended to smart maintenance that comprehends personalized advices like usage best practices and marketing proposals (coaching service) and technical best practice to prevent or handle with faults (fault management). Data are monitored by specific sensors and collected in a database; a set of elaboration algorithms analyses these data according to two policies (i.e. coaching and fault management) in order to recognize the specific use scenario and support the user with personalized and tailored suggestions and advices. A web/mobile application provides personalized messages directly on their mobile phones [9].

In both cases, PSS have been defined according the design methodology proposed in [10], which allows identifying product and service functions as well as needed assets and partners. It starts from market analysis and identification of the users' needs and demands, to the definition of the user tasks, requirements elicitation, definition of the PSS functions, assets and technological partners.

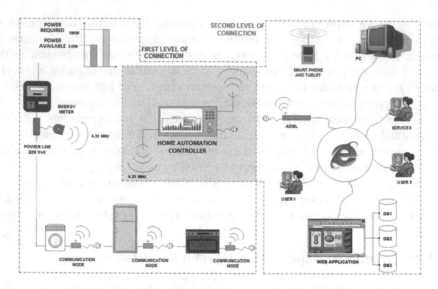

Fig. 1. The PSS reference system architecture for household appliances

The first PSS (Energy Monitoring Service) has been tested on low-fidelity prototypes based on mixed reality techniques [2]: it merges rapid prototyping and augmented reality to represent the achieved design solution and perform usability testing with low time and cost (Fig. 2a). The second PSS (Carefree Washing Service) used high-fidelity prototypes: the product was prototyped physically reusing parts from existing products and prototypal new components, service platform was developed as a prototypal application and user interface was created in Silverlight (Fig. 2b).

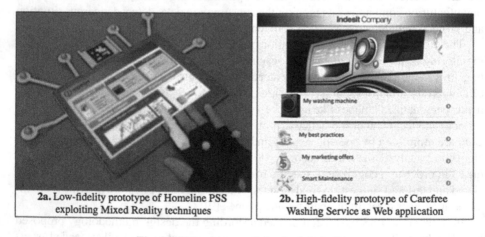

2a. Low-fidelity prototype of Homeline PSS exploiting Mixed Reality techniques

2b. High-fidelity prototype of Carefree Washing Service as Web application

Fig. 2. PSS prototypes in both case studies

4   The Framework to Prototyping User-Oriented PSS

A new design methodology is defined to support PSS as synthetized in Fig. 3. It uses role-playing for UCD study of users' needs, Business Use Case (BUC) modelling for the analysis of PSS scenarios', Quality Functional Deployment (QFD) for the correlation between needs and functions, Computer-Aided system to design the geometrical, aesthetic and graphical aspects of both product and interface, DMU for modelling the PSS behaviours, HIL approach for PSS simulation in a VR environment.

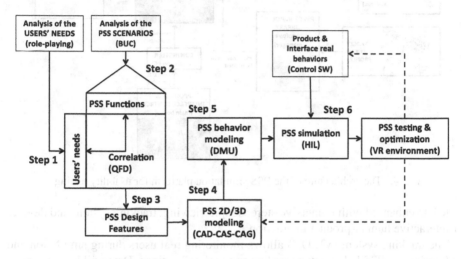

Fig. 3. The design methodology for PSS based on DMU and HIL

The PSS simulation platform combines the system digital mock-up (DMU) with the so-called Hardware-in-the-Loop (HIL) approach [3] to create a realistic prototype able to simulate the product and service behaviours in real time thanks to the communication of the virtual model with the real control software. Such an approach has been used for virtual simulation of mechatronic systems since it should be quickly configured to follow the customer requirements, and then even reconfigured in case of new production demands. For PSS it can be used to achieve a reliable and real-time behaviour simulation like on physical prototypes, but limiting time and cost and improving the flexibility, since a lot of alternatives for the product-related services can be simulated just changing the software control.

Figure 4 represents the architecture of the PSS simulation platform for usability testing. The product digital model is defined by using a CAD system (CATIA) while the service interface is defined in graphics and dynamics by commercial tools (from Power Point to Flash). Product-Service behaviours are modelled as a DMU by dedicated software (DELMIA) and a library of behaviours for different user profiles is managed as DBs. On the other hand, the real main board is connected to a simulation PC that is the controller, which is connected to the digital mock-up. Thanks to HIL software (VIRTOUS) [11], the simulation PC controls the digital model; after that, such a model is managed by VIRTOOLS platform to create a virtual simulation environment within

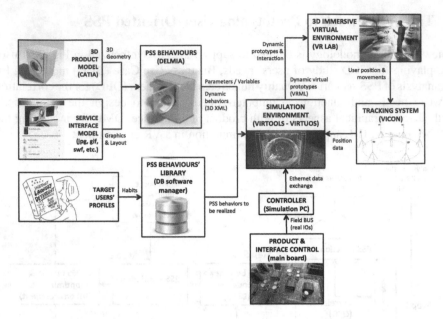

Fig. 4. The architecture of the PSS simulation platform for usability testing

a VR Lab enhanced with immersive stereoscopic viewing, tracking system and devices for interactive human-product interaction.

The tracking system (VICON) allows monitoring real users during simulation and configuring the PSS behaviour according to the users' actions. Data will be exchanged via 3D XML and VRML to create an interactive virtual prototype, and Matlab/Simulink can be integrated into the VIRTOUS model to implement complex system controls. In more details, Fig. 5 shows the data flow during the simulation.

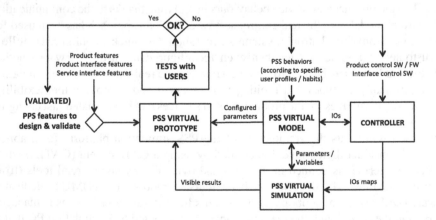

Fig. 5. Data flow for PSS virtual simulation

The critical points in the development of the proposed system will be the real-time interaction between the HIL system (VIRTUOS) and the real PSS controller, and the integration of VIRTUOS within the VIRTOOLS platform.

5 Conclusion

A methodological framework to support the user-oriented design of PSS is proposed. It directly starts from the difficulties faced in two industrial case studies focusing on the development of PSSs. In both cases the manufacturing company network outlined problems related to the definition and subsequent evaluation of the user experience generated by the conceived PSS, to the complexity to predict the PSS behaviour during the design stage and finally to assess the quality of the interaction with the final user only when a first prototype has been realized. Thanks to these past experiences, a proper framework to model and simulate the PSS during the design stages is proposed in this paper. It aims to overcome the identified difficulties and innovate current state-of-art in Virtual Prototyping and PSS tools. It exploits different software tools (i.e. CAD modelling, virtual prototyping developing platform, system simulation) to create an interactive virtual prototype of the conceived PSS that can be used to involve sample end-users to test system usability and PSS performance. Such an approach avoids the construction of costly physical prototypes that combine both service and product features, and greatly reduces the time spent for PSS optimization at the end of the design stage. Furthermore, the level of usability and user satisfaction achieve was higher than in past cases.

The main drawback of the designed platform is systems' integration and tools' interoperability. Future research work will be focused on the implementation of the platform by creating proper interfacing plug-in applications and on the adoption of the overall framework in real case studies. The collection of end-users feedbacks will allows developers to improve the platform functionalities and making it useful for designers to achieve high PSS quality.

References

1. Baines, T.S., Lightfood, H.W., Benedettini, P., Kay, J.M.: The servization of manufacturing: a review of literature and reflection on future challenges. J. Manuf. Technol. Manag. **20**(5), 547–567 (2009)
2. Ceccacci, S., Germani, M., Mengoni, M.: A method to design a smart home interface. In: Abramovici, M., Stark, R. (eds.) Smart Product Engineering. LNPE, vol. 5, pp. 915–926. Springer, Heidelberg (2013)
3. Harrison, W.S., Tilbury, D.M., Yuan, C.: From Hardware-in-the-Loop to hybrid process simulation: an ontology for the implementation phase of a manufacturing system. IEEE Trans. Autom. Sci. Eng. **9**(1), 96–109 (2012)
4. Luiten, H., Knot, M., van der Horst, T.: Sustainable product service-systems: the Kathalys method. In: Proceedings of the Second International Symposium on Environmentally Conscious Design and Inverse Manufacturing, pp. 190–197 (2001)

5. Manzini, E., Vezolli, C.: A strategic design approach to develop sustainable product service systems: examples taken from the 'environmentally friendly innovation'. J. Clean. Prod. **11**, 851–857 (2003)
6. Meyer, G.G., Framling, K., Holmstrom, J.: Intelligent products: a survey. Comput. Ind. **60**, 137–148 (2009)
7. Mont, O.: Clarifying the concept of product-service system. J. Clean. Prod. **10**(3), 237–245 (2002)
8. Morelli, N.: Developing new PSS: methodologies and operational tools. In: Proceedings of the SusProNet Conference on Product Service Systems: Practical Value, Brussels, Belgium, pp. 44–47 (2004)
9. Peruzzini, M., Marilungo, E., Germani, M.: An integrated method to support PSS design within the virtual enterprise. Procedia CIRP **3**, 54–59 (2015)
10. Qu, M., Yu, S., Chen, D., Chu, J., Tian, B.: State-of art of design evaluation and operation methodologies in product service systems. Comput. Ind. **77**, 1–14 (2016)
11. Röck, S.: Hardware in the loop simulation of production systems dynamics. Prod. Eng. **5**(3), 329–337 (2011)
12. Sauer, J., Sonderegger, A.: The influence of prototype fidelity and aesthetics of design in usability tests: effects on user behavior, subjective evaluation and emotion. Appl. Ergon. **40**, 670–677 (2009)
13. Thoben, K.D., Jagdev, H., Eschenbaecher, J.: Extended products: evolving traditional product concepts. In: Proceedings of the 7th International Conference on Concurrent Enterprising, Bremen (2001)
14. Tomiyama, T., Medland, A.J., Vergeest, J.S.M.: Knowledge intensive engineering towards sustainable products with high knowledge and service contents. In: Proceedings of the Third International Symposium on Tools and Methods of Competitive Engineering, April 18–20, pp. 55–67. Delft University Press, Delft, The Netherlands (2000)
15. Wilson, J.R., D'Cruz, M.: Virtual and interactive environments for work of the future. Int. J. Hum Comput Stud. **64**, 158–169 (2006)
16. Yang, X., Moore, P., Pu, J.S., Wong, C.B.: A practical methodology for realizing product service systems for customer products. Comput. Ind. Eng. **56**, 224–235 (2009)

Design and Sensitive Configurations:
Memory and Learning Neural Circuits Correlated
with the Creative Processes in Design

Leila Reinert[✉]

Anhembi Morumbi University, São Paulo, Brazil
leilareinert@gmail.com

Abstract. The current study demonstrates an articulation between the learning
and memory mental processes that organize our sensitive perception and creative
process in design. Based on Eric Kandel's research on the multiple forms of
learning using *Aplysia californica* (a giant sea slug), we have established correlated visual graphics that approach learning neural analogs to the apprehension
of the sensible. The contemporary design sets subjective aspects of our being in
the world, engendering modes of action that determine our behavior in everyday
life. The aim of the current study is to reflect on didactic strategies and procedures
that enhance the emergence of creative minds.

Keywords: Design · Neuroscience · Memory and learning · Creative process

1 Introduction

Many of the relations between habit and behavior are assimilated on a daily basis,
particularly by refined technologies that increasingly multiply their communication
artifacts. Innumerous examples illustrate this: from a simple kettle whistle indicating
boiling water to Smartphone with constantly expanding functionalities; different accessories that regulate our well-being and monitor our health; and even smart refrigerators
that guide our actions and help us incorporate new habits. If designers are in charge of
developing interactions between human beings and their daily artifacts, design means
generating modes of action in human beings based on their experience with the designed
world. And if generating modes of action means imprinting memories and learning in
the neural circuits of our conscious mind, design also means developing contexts [12],
i.e., configuring subjective aspects of our being in the world.

In relatively recent studies of molecular biology or neurobiology, Kandel [5] eluci-
dated neural reactions triggered by different patterns of sensory stimuli, which favor the
assimilation of knowledge and its storage by studying the neural circuits of *Aplysia
californica*. In his investigation, Kandel [6] assumes that there are several forms of
learning produced by different stimuli patterns and combinations, and these variations
originate differences in memory storage. Different stimuli patterns and combinations
also potentiate the creative processes in design, and the creative action is a result of
variations in such stimuli in our sensitive perception. Several studies have demonstrated

© Springer International Publishing Switzerland 2016
N. Streitz and P. Markopoulos (Eds.): DAPI 2016, LNCS 9749, pp. 111–121, 2016.
DOI: 10.1007/978-3-319-39862-4_11

that acquired experience influences esthetical judgments, and using functional magnetic resonance imaging (fMRI), they have also demonstrated the modulation of neural activity in memory and perceptual information processing-associated brain areas of specialized professionals [7].

Although contemporaneous design is the producer of the things that we interact with on a daily basis and that determine the context we live in, it is also responsible for the creation of other modes of existence, which make up the future. Designers should be sensitized through dissociative sensory stimuli to potentiate sensitive configurations that are able to generate creative practices to redesign our perceptions.

2   Cellular Neurobiology and Behavior

2.1   Memory and Learning

In his book "In search of memory," Kandel [5] established five principles that underlie the studies of neurobiology or science of the mind, seeking to elucidate the functioning of the human mind through molecular biology. The first principle is to consider mind and brain as inseparable. The brain is a complex biological organ, responsible for both simple motor behaviors and for acts considered as superior, such as speech, consciousness, and creation. From this point of view, the mind is considered as a set of complex operations performed by the brain. The second principle declares that specialized neuronal circuits perform mental functions in the brain and that these circuits occupy, spread out, or travel to several brain regions. Therefore, there is not a unique brain region that performs mental operations. The third principle states that nerve cells are the elementary signaling units of all neural circuits. The fourth establishes that neuronal circuits use specific molecules for generating signals within and between nerve cells. Finally, the fifth principle states the ancestry of signaling molecules because some of them were conserved over billions of years and were already present in the cells of our earliest ancestors.

Unicellular organisms, such as bacteria and yeast, and simple multicellular organisms, such as worms, flies, and snails, use the same signaling molecules used by humans to organize their maneuvers in the environment, in the governance of their daily lives. According to Kandel [5], the new science of the mind helps explain how we perceive, learn, remember, feel, and act. Besides, it establishes a new perspective of human biological evolution because the human mind has evolved from molecules utilized by our most humble ancestors, and the extraordinary conservation of molecular mechanisms that regulate many vital processes also applies to our mental life.

Because of the overwhelming desire to understand the human psyche, Kandel focused its studies on the nerve cell, the neuron, for it is the key to understand brain function. Every living organism, from the simplest to the most complex, consists of the same basic units, the cells, which have specialized functions, although they have common biological traits. Liver cells, for example, play digestive functions related to metabolism, while nerve cells process information and communicate with each other in a particular manner, forming complete circuits that carry and transform information. The human brain has approximately 100 billion nerve cells, and their specific functions

Fig. 1. Aplysia *californica.* (Source: Wikimedia commons).

do not reside within particular neurons themselves but in the connections between other cells within the neuronal circuit to which they belong. To explain determined mental processes by studying individual nerve cells, Kandel intended to analyze memory and learning using *Aplysia californica* (Fig. 1), a giant sea slug about thirty centimeters long. Its brain contains 20 thousand neurons grouped in nine separated clusters or ganglia. As each ganglion contains a relatively small number of cells, researchers can study single cells alterations so as to isolate ganglia-controlled behaviors.

But what is the reason for focusing research on memory and learning? According to Kandel [5, 6], our ability to acquire and store from the most simple to the most complex information is one of the most extraordinary aspects of human behavior. Memory provides continuity to our existence when it articulates past, present, and future. Without memory and the sharing of acquired knowledge, human cultural, artistic, and technological development would not have been possible. The entire process of retaining, storing, and retrieving acquired information starts in our cells, and it is subjected to both the information transmitted genetically throughout human existence and to everyday life experiences.

2.2   A Cellular Experiment

Back to *Aplysia californica.* Because *Aplysia* have some of the largest nerve cells of the animal kingdom that are visible even to the naked eye, its study allowed the mapping of individual neural cell connections, enabling the formulation of the exact wiring diagram of a behavior. What does that mean? Individual nerve cells generate action potentials—electrical signals that propagate over long distances inside the cells. Communication between cells, the synapse, consists of a physical–chemical interaction: electrical signals are translated into chemical signals in signaling cells; conversely, chemical signals are translated into electrical signals in receptor cells. Action potentials are "key signals" for information transmission on thoughts, emotions, and sensations from a brain region to another. When Kandel formulated a wiring diagram of a behavior, he recorded neural pathways of the electrical activity from an *Aplysia* nerve cell in a controlled manner and was able to verify synaptic alterations according to different applied stimuli patterns.

Kandel assumed that there are several modes of learning created by different stimuli patterns and combinations, and their variations cause differences in memory storage. According to Santiago Ramón y Cajal (1852–1934), the Spanish anatomist who formulated the basis for modern thinking on the nervous system, knowledge acquisition, or learning alters the strength of synaptic connections between neurons. Kandel structured his research in the reformulation of Ramón y Cajal's theory because for Cajal, learning is the result of a single process. When Kandel realized the multiple forms of learning, he proposed to study how and when changes in the synaptic connections occur and how they are modified by different stimuli patterns that generate differences in memory storage. To structure his study, Kandel considered Brenda Milner's studies on memory and translated Ivan Pavlov's behavioral protocols into biological protocols.

2.3 Neural Analogues of Learning

Pavlov established three reflex learning patterns from instructions about how a sensory stimulus should be presented to provide assimilation of knowledge. These are habituation, sensitization, and classical conditioning. Kandel transported this question into biology, seeking how different stimulation patterns created different forms of synaptic plasticity, an approach that he called neural analogues of learning. To achieve this, he proposed to simulate sensory stimulation patterns on *Aplysia* nerve cells, simulating different learning forms established by Pavlov. For the experiment, Kandel dissected the *Aplysia's* abdominal ganglion, which contains 2000 nerve cells, and introduced microelectrodes in one of them. Then, he recorded the cellular responses to various stimuli sequences applied in neural pathways that converged to this specific cell.

It is required to present Kandel and his team's experimental procedures and results, even if briefly, so that we can understand how the research works. First of all, it is important to note that the neuron is composed of three components: the cell body, which consists of the nucleus and cytoplasm; the axon, which is a unique extension of the cell body through which the impulses that transmit information from the neuron to other cells travel; and the dendrites, numerous extensions that receive stimuli from the environment, from epithelial cells or from other neurons [10]. To specify a neural pathway is to produce stimuli in a bundle of axons that will transmit the information to a specific cell.

2.4   Protocols: Habituation, Sensitization, and Classical Conditioning

On the procedures and results. A weak electrical stimulation produced by a particular neural pathway, if repeated ten times, causes cell synaptic potential to gradually decrease. In other words, reflex learning through habituation weakens the response to the original stimulus. When the stimulus is interrupted for a certain period and subsequently applied again, the cell responds back with almost its original strength. Habituation, in its simplest learning form, provides both the possibility to disregard recurring useless stimuli, which may hinder our attention to new things and to anesthetize our perception of automatic and repeated everyday gestures. However, it always indicates a weakening of synaptic communication between neurons.

The sensitization protocol procedure consists of the application of two different unassociated stimuli in different neural pathways. Using the *Aplysia's* abdominal ganglion, Kandel applied a weak stimulus once or twice in the same neural pathway used for habituation experiments. The induced synaptic potential served as a parameter to the cell response at the end of the experiment. Then, a series of five stronger stimuli were applied in a different neural pathway. When the first path was stimulated again, the cell synaptic response had increased, indicating a strengthening of the connections. The strong stimuli series applied to the second pathway increased cell response potential to the weak stimulus initially applied. Kandel concluded that a non-associative form of reflex learning strengthens synaptic connections.

In the classical conditioning protocol, two stimuli were also applied but this time in an associated manner. Repeatedly, a weak stimulus applied in a neural pathway was followed by a strong stimulus applied in another pathway. The cell understands that, by receiving the first one, it must prepare for the second, which means a synaptic potential increase for the weak stimulus. However, synaptic connection strengthening depends on the pairing of two stimuli. What differentiates the classical conditioning from the sensitization protocol is the fact that the non-associative learning form that occurs in sensitization potentially enhances responses to stimuli in general and not only in relation to paired stimuli.

Interesting fact: a giant-sea slug, with no brain or mind, responded with precise behavior to stimuli provoked by scientists. It is rather curious, particularly for us, who are lay in molecular biology, to think that our cells behave similarly and to think how it is possible that the complexity of our conscious mind result from neuronal circuits generated in simple biological structures like those of *Aplysia*. This is, however, precisely the challenge of biology of the mind scientists.

The evidence of synaptic plasticity showing that synaptic strength can be easily modified from different patterns of activities suggests that learning changes the flow of information in neural circuits [5, 6]. Faced with a synaptic strength that is strengthened or weakened, by different stimulation patterns, one can glimpse how the consolidation of a memory can anatomically change our cells. Research on *Aplysia* defined the biological basis of learning and memory and, therefore, defined the relationship between the functioning of neural systems and the modes of action that engender behavior.

2.5 Types and Forms of Memory

All processes of learning and memory begin on working memory. Its specificity is fleetingness and its function is the management of immediate reality. It is similar to saving a phone number that will be used and forgotten soon after. Working memory is processed in the prefrontal cortex, which is connected to brain regions linked to mood, consciousness, and emotions [4]. This is the reason why emotional states influence our attention and disturb the working memory, changing immediate responses that put us in action. Although working memory lasts seconds or a few minutes at the most, it is also articulated to existing memories to decide whether the newly acquired information is useful, if there is any relation with past experience, or any record indicating that it is worth a greater attention to retain the memory. Temporal parameters differentiate short- and long-term memories.

Short- and long-term memories are defined on the basis of information consolidation, i.e., the more consolidated is the information received, the greater is its duration. According to Kandel [5], information that persists had to be processed in a comprehensive and/or deep way, and this occurs through attention and significant and systematic associations of the acquired knowledge. Biologically speaking, short- and long-term memories occur in different anatomical sites and trigger chemical potentials differently. Short-term memories alter synapse function, unlike long-term memory, which anatomically alters the cell [6]. A short-term memory lasts a few hours (or even seconds), is stored only as long as required, and then may be discarded or acquire relevance and be transformed into a long-term memory. Izquierdo [4] compares short-term memory with temporary accommodation, whereas long-term memory is our own home.

There is not a unique brain area where our memories are stored, as there is not one brain region that performs mental operations. Our memory is spread in a fragmented fashion throughout the various brain areas. When we recall a beach evening with friends, for example, each of the recalled sensations activate its corresponding cortical area: the smell of the sea activates the olfactory areas; the images of landscape or people activate the visual areas; the sound of the waves activate auditory areas; and the emotions felt activate the amygdala (complex cell nuclei responsible for the emotional tone of lived experience). The hippocampus, a cellular structure located in the temporal lobes, is essential for memory; however, there is nothing stored there; this region is only the key to connections [11].

When we focus on information content, memories are called declarative or procedural. Declarative memories can be episodic or semantic and relate to events and general knowledge. Procedural memories refer to the memories acquired by motor or sensory abilities, being closer to habit reflex learning, and are confirmed in action [1, 4]. There is no point in stating one has the memory of knowing how to drive, one just simply drives. Memories are also considered explicit or implicit, according to the degree of awareness one has of them.

Memory systems are not static; therefore, episodic memories blend with semantic memories, and explicit memories become implicit in time. Mother tongue, for example, is an unconsciously acquired semantic memory and is therefore implicit, but declarative. Driving depends on a conscious (explicit) learning that becomes a habit, an automatic action, and therefore a procedural memory. Scrambling of memory types is a result of the involvement of multiple neural network circuits on the learning process and storage of our memories.

Understanding the cellular basis of human behavior opens up a vast research field for teaching and learning creative processes within design. A design focused on the subject and its mode of existence, which aims at the required transformation of social behaviors so that we can envision a more sustainable collective future life on the planet.

3 Creative Minds

3.1 Create: Rearrange to Formulate Other Senses

Our state of consciousness, in its different levels, is the condition of our existence, and is essential to our survival [2]. Consciousness is the creator of the manifested senses in our sensitive perceptions that occur in the approximation to the world around us, and there is an increasing number of experiments about the neurobiology of perception [3], such as brain activity monitoring (electroencephalographic recordings) during a visit to a conceptual art exhibition [8]; evidence of neural activity modulation in brain areas associated with memory and processing of perceptual information in the neural circuits of architects faced with visual esthetic judgment [7]. Our subjectivity is being investigated in laboratories using more sophisticated and less invasive technologies. Neurobiology studies samples, records, monitoring, and infers operating modes of mental circuitry, but what are the acquired and stored data that will be analyzed in these studies? What are the possible correlates between brain functioning and creativity teaching? How to enhance creative processes from understanding neurobiology?

Our mind responds to learning protocols just as our cells, i.e., several non-associated stimuli, as in sensitization, potentiate creative processes. The repetition of the same, as in habituation, weakens the synaptic connections anesthetizing our attention. This is why habit is the greatest enemy of creation. Classical conditioning is limited because it depends on presumed data, although it increases synaptic potential.

Creativity is inherent to human beings; however, it depends on the content learned and how we are encouraged to process the information received. To teach someone how to expand their creation potential means to develop strategies to sensitize perception and keep it in a permanent state of alert.

3.2 Visual Graphics Parameters

The translation of learning protocols into graphic materials allows us to clearly illustrate our attention focus on a given image. For this, we use a modular creation exercise,[1] matching the organization of a fixed element within a larger framework [9]. This type

---

[1] This exercise was applied, in its many variations, during the 20 years I taught design at Mackenzie Presbyterian University (São Paulo–Brazil), producing a significant sampling of the presented analyzes.

of exercise is widely used in the basic disciplines of design degrees and is fundamental for the creation of patterns in the area of surface design.

The starting point is an abstract plateau (Fig. 2), drawn from a plant picture fragment, a black figure inside a white square background. Rather, it is not exactly a background because the figure touches the square edges, making the form and the resulting counter-forms change their roles to the extent of our attention. This is a well-known relation within *gestalt* laws and a completely studied phenomenon proven by recent neuroscience research on visual perception. Our visual perception prioritizes either; we cannot perceive shape and counter-shape at the same time.

Fig. 2. Standard module (Source: Personal archive)

In the first example (Fig. 3), the composition of the standard module is organized by repeating the same protocol, as in habituation. A single stimulus is repeated many times. When we glanced at this image, we understood its *modus operandi* and lost interest because we realized that there would be no change in its sequence. It can be repeated to infinity.

Fig. 3. Module A – habituation (Source: Personal archive)

In the second example (Fig. 4), the structure of the composition is not so evident. There is a system but it takes a closer look to realize the assumption of the compositional organization. Following the standard modules sequence, we realized that repetition was composed of two identical and one different (90° rotation) module. Stimuli are paired as in classical conditioning protocol because for every two modules, one is rotated. It is a more stimulating image than the first example because there is a greater variation of resulting counter forms.

Fig. 4. Module B – classic conditioning (Source: Personal archive)

Finally, the composition from the third example (Fig. 5) is organized in a random manner by repetition of what is different. The default module rotation does not follow a fixed sequence and the composition of the whole results from small choices given by each square position within the compositional mesh. Gaze scans the image and grasps infinite possibilities of articulation of a single standard module. The multiple visual stimuli this image offers sharpen our perception. As in sensitization, we remain alert, as we have no idea of what will be the next step; we do not know what will the picture path follow. In this case, the strength of the resulting counter-forms is even greater.

Fig. 5. Module C – sensitization (Source: Personal archive)

It is important to note that we are not talking about esthetic judgment or "beauty" parameters; our analysis mainly aims at the strategies and procedures that encourage sensitive perception as fundamental to the formation of creative minds that are able to alter given points of view to experience the potential of risk. Another important point is that the proposal focus does not reside only in achieved visual results. Instead, performing processes and critical analysis of the image are as important as the result.

4   Creative Process in Design

Contemporary design is beyond the act of giving a new, efficient, and beautiful appearance to chairs, household items, cars, packaging, books, or even add a formal veneer to intrinsic features of objects so they better respond to current market and sale teams or to produce and consume even more. Designers are social innovators directly responsible for everyday interactions among humans, their artifacts, and their surrounding environments. Thus, the issues raised by contemporary designs are based on the forms of existence; on social behaviors required to better live in a more sustainable world. Therefore, designers design contexts and consequences [12].

The expansion of the meaning of design turns its creative process into a much more complex task than responding to given problems or formally elaborating artifacts that make up our visible environment. To design today is to configure the sensitive aspects of our existence. This requires that designers have a more comprehensive training and a high creative potential to question prevailing demands. It is worth mentioning the following: it is about knowing how to discuss and not only respond to pre-existing problems [13].

Creation exercises, performed from the sensitization protocol, are essential for the consolidation of creative memory. As already mentioned, habit is the greatest enemy of creation; paradoxically, one must get used to being creative. The consolidation of sensitive perception learning, such as the consolidation of any learning, requires attention and significant associations to make processed information relevant. It is to transform the creative process, which is dependent on a conscious explicit learning (declarative memory), into a habit, an automatic and, therefore, implicit action (procedural memory). It is to learn how to get used to withdrawal. It is the repetition of different. After all, to create is to reorganize for developing other senses.

5   Conclusion

Several years of investigation with *Aplysia* defined the biological basis of learning and memory and consequently defined the relations between the functioning of neural systems and modes of action that generate behaviors. The emergence of creative minds involves an articulation between cognitive processes, emotions and our sensitive perception, and different brain regions are recruited to handle the task. And sometimes it is important embracing the messiness of the creative process for daydreaming, to loosen the ordinary associations, allow your mind to roam free, imagine new possibilities, and silence the inner critic.

Life never favors inanition; therefore, we are both designers of ourselves and designers of a designed material world that strongly needs our sensitive perception to experience life to its fullest.

References

1. Corrêa, A.C.O.: Neuropsicologia da Memória e sua Avaliação. In: Fuentes, D., et al. (eds.) Neuropscologia: Teoria e Prática, pp. 168–186. Artmed, Porto Alegre (2008)
2. Damásio, A.: O livro da Consciência: a Construção do Cérebro Consciente. Temas e Debates, Lisbon (2010)
3. Fróes, M.M.: O Sonho de Descartes. In: Scientiarum Historia III: 3° Congresso de História das Ciências e das Técnicas e Epistemologia. UFRJ, Rio de Janeiro (2010). www.hcte.ufrj.br/downloads/sh/sh3/trabalhos/Mayra%20Froes.pdf
4. Izquierdo, I.: Memória. Artmed, Porto Alegre (2002)
5. Kandel, E.R.: In Search of the Memory: the Emergene of a New Science of Mind. W. W. Norton & Company, New York (2007)
6. Kandel, E.R.: The biology of memory: a forty-year perspective. J. Neurosci. **29**(41), 12748–12756 (2009)
7. Kirk, U., Skov, M., Christensen, M.S., Nygaard, N.: Brain correlates of aesthetic expertise: a parametric fMRI study. Brain Cogn. **69**(2), 306–315 (2008)
8. Kontson, K.L., Megjhani, M., Brantley, J.A., Cruz-Garza, J.G., Nakagome, S., Robleto, D., White, M., Civillico, E., Contreras-Vidal, J.L.: Your brain on art: emergent cortical dynamics during aesthetic experiences. Front. Hum. Neurosci. **9**, 626–684 (2015)
9. Lupton, E., Phillips, J.C.: Graphic Design: the New Basics. Princeton Architectural Press, New York (2008)
10. Meneses, M.S.: Neuroanatomia Aplicada. Koogan, Rio de Janeiro (2006)
11. Plizka, S.R.: Neurociência para o Clínico de Saúde Mental. Artmed, Porto Alegre (2004)
12. Tonkinwise, C.: Design for Transition - From and to What? (2014). https://www.academia.edu/11796491
13. Tonkinwise, C.: Committing to the Political Values of Post-Thing-Centered Designing (2015). https://www.academia.edu/14560093

Data-Driven Smart Home System for Elderly People Based on Web Technologies

Daeil Seo, Byounghyun Yoo[✉], and Heedong Ko

Center for Imaging Media Research,
Korea Institute of Science and Technology, Seoul, South Korea
{xdesktop,ko}@kist.re.kr, yoo@byoo.net

Abstract. The proportion of elderly people over 65 years old has rapidly increased, and social costs related to aging population problems have grown globally. The governments want to reduce these social costs through advanced technologies. The physician or medical center evaluates health conditions from the reports of elderly people. However, self-reports are often inaccurate, and sometimes reports by family or caregivers can be more accurate. To solve these problems, an evaluated objective method based on sensor data is needed. In this paper, we propose a data-driven smart home system that uses web technologies for connecting sensors and actuators. The proposed system provides a method of monitoring elderly people's daily activities using commercial sensors to register recognizable activities easily. In addition, it controls actuators in the home by using user-defined rules and shows a summary of elderly people's activities to monitor them.

Keywords: Elderly care · Data-driven approach · Ambient assisted living · Web technology

1 Introduction

Due to recent improvements in life expectancy, the proportion of older people has rapidly increased [1]. The proportion of elderly people over 65 years old is predicted to rise to 30 % in 2060 in Europe [2]. Aging population problems have emerged globally, and due to the social cost related to aging, it is difficult to support the increasing number of elderly people. Since elderly people are exposed to various risks, the governments want to reduce social costs through the monitoring of risks and diseases using advanced technologies. To determine if elderly people need the help of others or evaluate the abilities of elderly people, various methodologies are used, such as an activity of daily living (ADL) checklist. ADL is a way of determining people's routine activities [3]. Basic or physical ADL consists of self-care tasks that people tend do every day without needing assistance such as dressing, bathing, eating, ambulating, toileting, and hygiene-related tasks. Instrumental ADL (IADL) is not necessary activities for survival and supports an independent lifestyle, such as shopping, housekeeping, accounting, food preparation, using the telephone, and transportation. The physician or medical center evaluates the

© Springer International Publishing Switzerland 2016
N. Streitz and P. Markopoulos (Eds.): DAPI 2016, LNCS 9749, pp. 122–131, 2016.
DOI: 10.1007/978-3-319-39862-4_12

health conditions of elderly people reported through these methods. However, self-reports are often inaccurate, and sometimes reports by family or caregivers can be more accurate. To solve these problems, an evaluated objective method based on sensor data is needed.

With the advent of the Internet of Things (IoT) technologies, coined by Kevin Ashton [4], small and inexpensive IoT devices have been widely used in our daily lives, and they can help to solve common problems at a low social cost. IoT sensor devices are deployed in living spaces or on the human body and collect log data to sense human activities. To reduce the social cost, various methods have been proposed such as elderly care systems [5, 6], behavior monitoring [7, 8], and user modeling [9, 10] in smart homes. However, previous systems have supported a limited number of sensors to track the ADLs of elderly people. These sensors are designed for specific purposes, and it is not easy to purchase them in commercial markets. The number of ADLs of elderly people monitored by these sensors' data is limited because the previous systems have used reasoning based on fixed and predefined rules in the systems. To build a smart home environment for elderly people, a method of monitoring their ADLs using commercial sensors and registering recognizable ADLs easily is required. Furthermore, it is also necessary to declare control rules for actuators in the home and to provide a summary of elderly people's ADLs to monitor people.

In this paper, we propose a data-driven smart home system that uses web technologies for connecting IoT devices. The system provides a web-based user interface for monitoring elderly user to establish rules for recognizing activities and controlling actuators by selecting features from visualized log data. The proposed system monitors the behaviors of elderly people and controls IoT devices when abnormal situations are detected. While this section has introduced and provided motivation for the work, the rest of this paper is structured as follows. We present related work in Sect. 2. Section 3 describes our system design while Sect. 4 presents the current prototype implementation. Finally, we conclude with a summary and present a future work direction in Sect. 5.

2   Related Work

In this section, we give an overview of related projects and technologies such as data collection, activity recognition, and elderly care systems. Ambient Assisted Living (AAL) and Ambient Intelligence (AmI) are approaches that aim to provide services and systems for aging well at home. Emiliani and Stephanidis [11] discussed the anticipated opportunities and challenges of AmI for elderly people. Among previous research related to AAL and elderly care systems, Kleinberger et al. [12] developed and evaluated the usability and suitability of interfaces for AAL. Dohr et al. [13] proposed an AAL system for elderly people through the IoT using passive RFIDs or near field communication (NFC). Su and Chiang [6] introduced a personalized healthcare service named IAServ, in ubiquitous cloud computing to support a cost-efficient method of care. They used a personal profile that includes basic information and personal states for generating a personalized care plan based on predefined ontologies in the system. Costa et al. designed and implemented mobile and static agents for smart homes using a voice interface [14]. Dickerson *et al.* [15] proposed a flexible web and cloud-based home health care monitoring system and deployed the system in real homes. Stanford [16] and Rantz *et al.* [17] have migrated from the laboratory into the homes of real older adults in retirement communities.

To combine and configure tasks, Dey *et al.* [18] proposed a CAPpella system for the end-user configuration of a pre-deployed sensor environment, and Davidoff *et al.* [19] suggested principles of smart home control. IFTTT (If This Then That) [20] is a web-based service that connects web services. It provides a simple interface to create a trigger and an action. Tuomisto *et al.* [21] presented a Thing-centric simple rule editor for the integration of functionalities and resources. Kolkowska [22] discussed privacy principles for the design of elderly care systems in smart homes.

It is important to collect sensor data in smart homes for monitoring the activities of elderly people, summarizing the activities, and controlling devices in smart homes. Chatterjee *et al.* [23] built a wireless sensor network system within the home environment to monitor the daily routines of elderly people using environmental and wearable sensors. Lee and Dey [24] presented sensor-based observations of daily living (ODLs) for older adults and their physicians for personal sensor data. Seo *et al.* [25] proposed an activity mashup system using heterogeneous sensors and visualized personal activity logs. Ransing and Rajput [5] proposed a wireless sensor network based smart home system to help elderly people achieve safe, sound and secure living using ZigBee technology. In user modeling approaches, Casas *et al.* [9] proposed a user modeling scheme for elderly and disabled people. Raad and Yang [10] designed a user-friendly model for elderly telemedicine in a smart home.

To recognize activities, Hong *et al.* [26] proposed a recognition method for ADL inference based on human motion and object identification using accelerometers and RFID sensors. Gaddam *et al.* [8] gathered data from a limited number of simple sensors and showed the data can be used to recognize ADLs and the lifestyle of an elderly person living alone. Suryadevara *et al.* [7] presented a data-driven intelligent system that includes effective sensing and intelligent behavior detection for elderly people's ADLs in their home. Forkan *et al.* [27, 28] proposed a cloud platform that can be accessed via web service protocols and described a pattern recognition models for an AAL environment.

3   System Design

In this section, we introduce our system design of a data-driven system for elderly people in smart homes. To recognize ADLs according to sensing data and provide useful services through the control of actuator devices, we design the data-driven process in three steps: log aggregation, activity recognition, and device control as shown in Fig. 1. In the log aggregation stage, sensing data are stored in a logging database. Sensor data contain information about ADLs and environment contexts. The data are collected from individual sensors directly or each sensor server provider periodically using web-based RESTful APIs. The logged data from heterogeneous sensors are converted to neutral log notation to be stored in the database because the logged data have different notations.

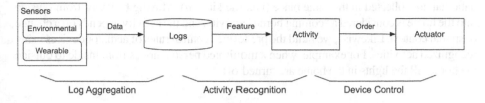

Fig. 1. Data-driven process overview

In the activity recognition stage, ADLs are extracted from the sensor data. The activity recognition consists of two steps: abstraction from sensor data to an activity and from subordinate activity logs to a superordinate activity. To determine the relation between sensor data and activity, a monitoring user, such as a physician, retrieves the collected log according to context queries. The monitoring user chooses filtered logged data to build a combination of features based on transitions of sensor readings for activity recognition. Similarly, the features of a superordinate activity are determined by a user's selection of filtered subordinate activity logs. In the last stage, the user established an order to control actuator devices by connecting activity recognition and actuator behaviors. The user selects a recognized activity and chooses an actuator and behaviors of the chosen actuator, which is controlled by the activity detection. When the user activities are detected, the predefined behaviors of the actuators are triggered.

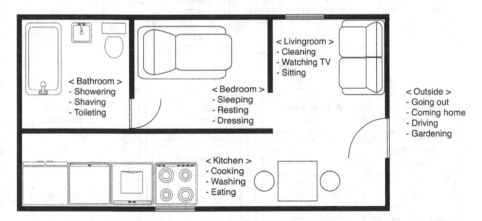

Fig. 2. ADL context modeling example of elderly people at home

We perform ADL context modeling to create predefined basic rules for recognizing the activities of elderly people, as shown in Fig. 2. We choose some activities related to elderly people's behaviors at smart homes from Ainsworth *et al.*'s study [29], which identified the major categories and daily physical activities. We classify the ADLs of elderly people based on places in the smart homes such as the bedroom, bathroom, and outside the home. The place information is a spatial condition for recognizing ADLs. We add temporal conditions to some rules, such as eating and sleeping. For instance, the eating activity is classified as breakfast, lunch, and dinner according to time information through the sensor data that are collected in the same place (i.e., the kitchen). Moving behavior from outside into the home is considered a "coming home" activity, and the activity depends on a change of spatial context. Likewise, we build the predefined control rules of actuator devices using recognized activities. For example, when a monitored person moves from inside to outside the home, all the lights in the home are turned off.

4   Prototype Implementation

We implemented a prototype system based on the design given in the previous section using web technologies. Figure 3 shows the system architecture of our system. The place manager handles a place that is a living space of a monitored user (i.e., elderly people). It also manages the deployment of devices and the indoor floor plans of the place. The rule manager deals with data-driven rules for activity recognition and device control. The user manager collects data logs from the monitored user's sensors and sends control messages to actuators. The web-based user interface supports user interaction between monitoring users and manager components in the system using the web pages on a web browser. The map server provides map tiles for determining geospatial information.

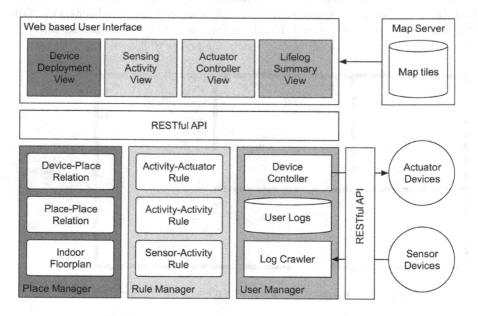

Fig. 3. Overview of the proposed system architecture

The proposed system supports the map-based device deployment view for arranging devices' positions. The devices' profiles are preregistered on the system. The system also provides a way of adding new device types. A monitoring user selects a pin on the map to determine a building, and the map is changed into indoor maps of the selected building. If a building or indoor floor plan does not exist on the map server, the monitoring user can add information using GeoJSON notation. To deploy a device in the indoor space, the monitoring user clicks the "add" button, chooses a device, and picks a location on the map as shown in Fig. 4. (a) of Fig. 4 shows an indoor map of the smart home and the deployment of the devices. If the user clicks the add button, a popup window is displayed to add a device to the place. The user chooses either a sensor or actuator for a device type and selects a specific commercial device profile. Lastly, the monitoring user selects the location of the deployed device and describes the device's specific profile. The devices located in the place are listed as shown in (b) of Fig. 4. When the user clicks on device in the list, the detailed description of the selected device is displayed as shown in (c) of Fig. 4. Through this process, the monitoring user deploys sensor and actuator devices in each place of the smart homes. In a similar manner, the monitoring user chooses devices' positions on the human body map to attach wearable devices.

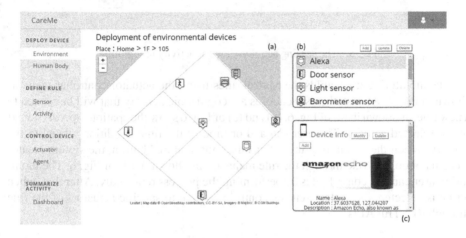

Fig. 4. Deployment of environmental devices

The proposed system extracts the activities of elderly people from sensor data through the sensing activity view, as shown in Fig. 5. The view has condition filters to retrieve the collected sensor data, as shown in (a) of Fig. 5. After applying the filters, the monitoring user looks at the logs of sensors in a list as shown in (b) of Fig. 5, and chooses sensor devices to determine features related to the activities of the monitored elderly people. The detailed information is depicted on the map to provide spatial context, as shown in (c) of Fig. 5, and is drawn on the graph to show changes according to temporal context, as shown in (d) of Fig. 5. When the monitoring user clicks the "add feature" button, the proposed system creates an activity recognition rule through the rule manager as shown in (e) of Fig. 5 and learns the rule for the chosen activity from the features and context. After that, when a rule is detected, the system determines what kind of activity is occurring in relation to the monitored elderly people. Determining the relation between subordinate activity logs and superordinate activity is similar.

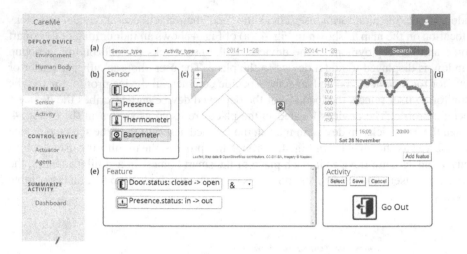

Fig. 5. The sensing activity view for activity recognition

The monitoring user builds the control rules using the actuator controller view, as shown in Fig. 6. At first, the user chooses a recognizable activity that will be related to a new rule, as shown in (a) of Fig. 6. (b) and (c) of Fig. 6 show the spatiotemporal context of the selected activity. The user can add or modify the time condition related to the activity. When the monitoring user clicks the "add feature" button, the system creates an actuator control rule through the rule manager, as shown in (d) of Fig. 6. The monitoring user can add control rules by performing the process repeatedly. After that, when a rule is detected, the system sends a control message to specific actuators of the rule through RESTful APIs.

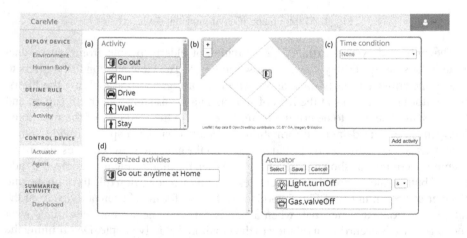

Fig. 6. The actuator controller view for handling actuator devices

The physician or medical center can build ADL summaries and reports of monitored people using the online dashboard as shown in Fig. 7. They input query conditions (i.e., temporal context and types of sensors or activities) to retrieve ADL logs from the database as shown in (a) of Fig. 7. The system returns the ADL logs according to the filters and shows the sensor list on the timeline as shown in (b) of Fig. 7. The monitoring user clicks on ADL log to determine whether the log is a representative activity during the time segmentation. The system depicts spatial information on the map as shown in (d) of Fig. 7 and additional information in the textbox as shown in (c) of Fig. 7. When the user double-clicks on the activity log on the timeline, the selected log is added to the summary of the ADLs, as shown in (e) of Fig. 7.

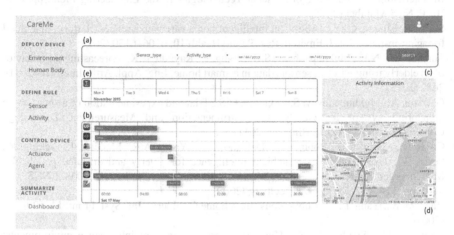

Fig. 7. The ADL summary view

5 Conclusion and Future Work

In this paper, we proposed a data-driven system for elderly people in smart homes using web technologies. The proposed system provides a method for monitoring their ADLs using commercially available sensors and registering recognizable ADLs easily. In addition, it controls actuators in the home using user-defined rules and shows a summary of elderly people's ADLs to monitor people.

We only focus on the web-based system to improve the ease of recognizing ADLs from sensor data and connecting recognized ADLs to controlling actuators. The next step of our research will consider a machine learning approach to find relationship rules between sensor logs and ADLs with the spatiotemporal context automatically based on long-term sensor logs.

Acknowledgments. This research was supported in part by the Korea Institute of Science and Technology (KIST) Institutional Program (Project No. 2E26450).

References

1. United Nations (UN): World Population Aging: 1950–2050 (2002). http://www.un.org/esa/population/publications/worldageing19502050. Accessed 8 Feb 2016
2. Giannakouris, K.: Ageing characterises the demographic perspectives of the European societies. Statistics in focus 72 (2008)
3. Katz, S.: Assessing self-maintenance: activities of daily living, mobility, and instrumental activities of daily living. J. Am. Geriatr. Soc. **31**, 721–727 (1983)
4. Ashton, K.: That 'Internet of Things' thing. RFiD J. **22**, 97–114 (2009)
5. Ransing, R.S., Rajput, M.: Smart home for elderly care, based on wireless sensor network. In: International Conference on Nascent Technologies in the Engineering Field, pp. 1–5. IEEE, Navi Mumbai (2015)
6. Su, C.-J., Chiang, C.-Y.: IAServ: an intelligent home care web services platform in a cloud for aging-in-place. Int. J. Environ. Res. Public Health **10**, 6106–6130 (2013)
7. Suryadevara, N.K., Mukhopadhyay, S.C., Wang, R., Rayudu, R.K.: Forecasting the behavior of an elderly using wireless sensors data in a smart home. Eng. Appl. Artif. Intell. **26**, 2641–2652 (2013)
8. Gaddam, A., Mukhopadhyay, S.C., Gupta, G.S.: Trial and experimentation of a smart home monitoring system for elderly. In: Instrumentation and Measurement Technology Conference, pp. 1–6. IEEE, Binjiang (2011)
9. Casas, R., Marin, R.B., Robinet, A., Delgado, A.R., Yarza, A.R., McGinn, J., Picking, R., Grout, V.: User modelling in ambient intelligence for elderly and disabled people. In: Miesenberger, K., Klaus, J., Zagler, W.L., Karshmer, A.I. (eds.) ICCHP 2008. LNCS, vol. 5105, pp. 114–122. Springer, Heidelberg (2008)
10. Raad, M.W., Yang, L.T.: A ubiquitous smart home for elderly. Inf. Syst. Front. **11**, 529–536 (2009)
11. Emiliani, P.L., Stephanidis, C.: Universal access to ambient intelligence environments: opportunities and challenges for people with disabilities. IBM Syst. J. **44**, 605–619 (2005)
12. Kleinberger, T., Becker, M., Ras, E., Holzinger, A., Müller, P.: Ambient intelligence in assisted living: enable elderly people to handle future interfaces. In: Stephanidis, C. (ed.) UAHCI 2007 (Part II). LNCS, vol. 4555, pp. 103–112. Springer, Heidelberg (2007)
13. Dohr, A., Modre-Opsrian, R., Drobics, M., Hayn, D., Schreier, G.: The Internet of Things for ambient assisted living. In: International Conference on Information Technology: New Generations, pp. 804–809. IEEE, Las Vegas (2010)
14. Costa, N., Domingues, P., Fdez-Riverola, F., Pereira, A.: A mobile virtual butler to bridge the gap between users and ambient assisted living: a smart home case study. Sensors **14**, 14302–14329 (2014)
15. Dickerson, R.F., Hoque, E., Emi, I.A., Stankovic, J.A.: Empath2: a flexible web and cloud-based home health care monitoring system. In: International Conference on Pervasive Technologies Related to Assistive Environments, pp. 1–8. ACM, Corfu (2015)
16. Stanford, V.: Using pervasive computing to deliver elder care. IEEE Pervasive Comput. **1**, 10–13 (2002)
17. Rantz, M.J., Porter, R.T., Cheshier, D., Otto, D., Servey, C.H., Johnson, R.A., Aud, M., Skubic, M., Tyrer, H., He, Z., Demiris, G., Alexander, G.L., Taylor, G.: TigerPlace, a state-academic-private project to revolutionize traditional long-term care. J. House. Elderly **22**, 66–85 (2008)
18. Dey, A.K., Hamid, R., Beckmann, C., Li, I., Hsu, D.: A CAPpella: programming by demonstration of context-aware applications. In: The SIGCHI Conference on Human Factors in Computing Systems, pp. 33–40. ACM, Vienna (2004)

19. Davidoff, S., Lee, M.K., Yiu, C., Zimmerman, J., Dey, A.K.: Principles of smart home control. In: Dourish, P., Friday, A. (eds.) UbiComp 2006. LNCS, vol. 4206, pp. 19–34. Springer, Heidelberg (2006)
20. Tibbets, L., Tane, J.: IFTTT - Make Your Work Flow (2011). https://ifttt.com. Accessed 7 Feb 2016
21. Tuomisto, T., Kymalainen, T., Plomp, J., Haapasalo, A., Hakala, K.: Simple rule editor for the Internet of Things. In: International Conference on Intelligent Environments, pp. 384–387. IEEE, Shanghai (2014)
22. Kolkowska, E.: Privacy principles in design of smart homes systems in elderly care. In: Tryfonas, T., Askoxylakis, I. (eds.) HAS 2015. LNCS, vol. 9190, pp. 526–537. Springer, Heidelberg (2015)
23. Chatterjee, S., Dutta, K., Xie, H.Q., Byun, J., Pottathil, A., Moore, M.: Persuasive and pervasive sensing: a new frontier to monitor, track and assist older adults suffering from type-2 diabetes. In: Hawaii International Conference on System Sciences, pp. 2636–2645. IEEE, Wailea (2013)
24. Lee, M.L., Dey, A.K.: Sensor-based observations of daily living for aging in place. Pers. Ubiquit. Comput. **19**, 27–43 (2014)
25. Seo, D., Yoo, B., Ko, H.: Collective heterogeneous sensor mashup for enriched personal healthcare activity logging. In: International Conference on Consumer Electronics, pp. 34–35. IEEE, Las Vegas (2015)
26. Hong, Y.-J., Kim, I.-J., Ahn, S.C., Kim, H.-G.: Activity recognition using wearable sensors for elder care. In: International Conference on Future Generation Communication and Networking, Sanya, Hainan Island, China, pp. 302–305 (2008)
27. Forkan, A., Khalil, I., Tari, Z.: CoCaMAAL: a cloud-oriented context-aware middleware in ambient assisted living. Future Gener. Comput. Syst. **35**, 114–127 (2014)
28. Forkan, A.R.M., Khalil, I., Tari, Z., Foufou, S., Bouras, A.: A context-aware approach for long-term behavioural change detection and abnormality prediction in ambient assisted living. Pattern Recogn. **48**, 628–641 (2015)
29. Ainsworth, B.E., Haskell, W.L., Herrmann, S.D., Meckes, N., Bassett, D.R.J., Tudor-Locke, C., Greer, J.L., Vezina, J., Whitt-Glover, M.C., Leon, A.S.: 2011 compendium of physical activities: a second update of codes and MET values. Med. Sci. Sports Exerc. **43**, 1575–1581 (2011)

A Unified Framework for Remote Collaboration Using Interactive AR Authoring and Hands Tracking

Jeongmin Yu, Jin-u Jeon, Gabyong Park, Hyung-il Kim, and Woontack Woo[✉]

KAIST UVR Lab, Daejeon, South Korea
{jmyu119,zkrkwlek,gypark,hyungil,wwoo}@kaist.ac.kr

Abstract. In this paper, we present a unified framework for remote collaboration using interactive augmented reality (AR) authoring and hand tracking methods. The proposed framework enables a local user to organize AR digital contents for making a shared working environment and collaborate multiple users in the distance. To develop the framework, we combine two core technologies: (i) interactive AR authoring method utilizing a smart input device for making a shared working space, (ii) hand-augmented object interaction method by tracking two hands in egocentric camera view. We implement a prototype of the proposed remote collaboration framework for testing its feasibility in an indoor environment. To the end, we expect that our framework enables collaboration as feeling a sense of co-presence with remote users in a user's friendly AR working space.

Keywords: Interactive AR authoring · Hand-augmented object interaction · Remote collaboration system

1 Introduction

Augmented reality (AR) is technology that enables users to close in supplementary information by seamlessly mixed with virtual objects in the real world [1]. Using this, the users can be worked with digital virtual elements and guided some needed directions. These useful information can be displayed in various devices such as mobile phones, PDA, head mounted display (HMD), and high performance PCs. AR technology is applied to various fields such as interactive games, education, military, gallery/exhibition, and repair/maintenance [2].

For the past few decades, AR applications have been mainly developed for only one user in the manner of one-way interaction with 3D virtual objects [5–7]. Even though they gives useful and interesting experience to the user, they do not provide experience of interaction and collaboration with other users. Recently, HMD-based remote collaboration systems have been developed to collaborate a shared target work with remote users [3, 4]. Unlikely existing remote collaboration systems [9, 10], these systems enable spatially un-limited interactions and give a sense of co-presence to the local user. However, these systems not only provides the confined simple interactions (e.g., flipping, grasping) by tracking a bare hand, but also provides a manually user-defined working environment to users.

© Springer International Publishing Switzerland 2016
N. Streitz and P. Markopoulos (Eds.): DAPI 2016, LNCS 9749, pp. 132–141, 2016.
DOI: 10.1007/978-3-319-39862-4_13

Meanwhile, many researchers have been studied on AR authoring systems for easily handling AR digital contents to users. For instance, [11, 12] have been attempted to AR authoring on mobile device. [11] shows interaction with AR contents using multi-touch interface of smart device. [12] presents an AR authoring method for unknown outdoor scene using mobile devices. However, because they do not generate a 3D map using depth sensors, they are unsuitable to register virtual digital contents on indoor environment. On the other hand, Project Tango [13] is a mobile authoring device that builds a 3D map of unknown indoor scene using a depth sensor. However, this system has some cumbersome points that a user spreads own arms enduringly during performing and sees the augmented spot through a narrow mobile device display.

In this paper, to settle above mentioned shortcomings, we present a novel HMD-based remote collaboration framework using interactive AR authoring and hand-augmented object interaction technologies. To develop the proposed framework, we integrate two main technologies which are interactive AR authoring with a wearable smart device (e.g., smartphone) for making a shared working space, and hand-augmented object interaction by tracking two bare hands in egocentric camera view. Through the proposed system, the local user can author his/her own working space easily without any professional programming skills [8], and collaborate remote users through intuitive interactions between tracking two hands and augmented objects. Through a preliminary prototype system implementation, we confirm its feasibility as a future remote collaboration platform. We expect that the proposed system can be applicable to many AR collaborative applications such as medical surgery education, urban planning, games and so forth.

The remainder of this paper is organized as follows. The proposed framework is presented in Sect. 2. In Sect. 3 introduces the initial implementation and preliminary result of the proposed framework. Lastly, the conclusions and outline plans for future works are presented in Sect. 4.

2 Proposed Framework

2.1 Overall Framework

Figure 1 shows the proposed overall system diagram of HMD-based remote collaboration. For this system, we use a smartphone for AR digital contents authoring, and use an egocentric short-range RGB-D camera and a wearable sensor (e.g., smartwatch) for accurate two hands tracking, and use an exocentric RGB-D camera for full-body tracking. For AR authoring, we use the positions, rotations and touch directions information from smartphone. For hands-augmented object interaction, we first segment bare hands from the egocentric camera. Then, hands and fingers are tracking based on a model fitting method. After registration between virtual and real hands, we can interact with a 3D augmented object for performing a shared target task. The detail methodological descriptions of interactive AR authoring and hands-augmented object interaction are presented as follows.

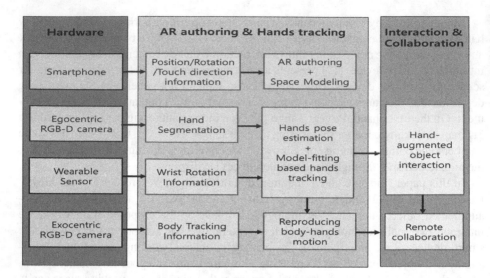

Fig. 1. The proposed framework for HMD-based remote collaboration

2.2   Interactive AR Authoring

Figure 2 shows the pipeline of proposed interactive AR authoring system. We first compute the initial local reference coordinates of a target working space, and then these local reference coordinates transformed by the obtained simultaneous localization and mapping (SLAM)-based coordinates. AR digital contents/objects are placed in the transformed local coordinates.

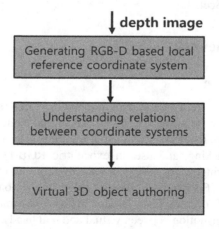

Fig. 2. Pipeline of the AR authoring system

Figure 3 shows the concept of our AR authoring system. Before working remote collaboration system, we organize a shared AR working space where the local and remote users perform a target task.

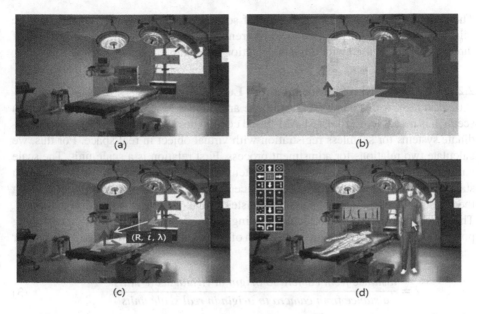

Fig. 3. The concept of AR authoring system: (a) real space, (b) local reference coordinate is calculated based on plane, (c) SLAM based coordinates is converted local reference coordinate by translation matrix, (d) virtual contents are augmented in AR space with local reference coordinate system.

2.2.1   Local Reference Coordinate System

To generate local reference coordinate system, we first select an original point and find their rotation coordinate system by analyzing 3D point clouds acquired from RGB-D camera. Then, a user choose regions of interest (RoI) in a scene using mobile input device. The RoI is detected a circular with a radius of 50 pixels. After a selecting RoI, we estimate the planes using point clouds of RoI. The plane of parameters π_i (a,b,c,d) are estimated by RANSAC method [14] as follows:

$$\pi_i = \underset{a,b,c,d}{\mathrm{argmin}} \sum_l^N \frac{|ax + by_l + cz_l + d|}{\sqrt{a^2 + b^2 + c^2}}, (x_l, y_l, z_l) \in RoI. \tag{1}$$

We assume that the maximum number of planes of RoI is three. It is possible that finding the original point of local reference coordinate system is expressed as a linear least squares problem.

$$p_{center} = \underset{x_i, y_i, z_i}{\mathrm{argmin}} \left\| \begin{bmatrix} a_1 & b_1 & c_1 \\ a_2 & b_2 & c_2 \\ a_3 & b_3 & c_3 \end{bmatrix} \begin{bmatrix} x_i \\ y_i \\ z_i \end{bmatrix} - \begin{bmatrix} d_1 \\ d_2 \\ d_3 \end{bmatrix} \right\|^2, \tag{2}$$

The point which has the minimum sum of squares of distance among planes will be selected as the original point of local reference coordinate system. The directions of three axis are expressed with three intersection lines on planes.

2.2.2   Adjusting SLAM Coordinates to Local Coordinates

Based on [15], we estimate a camera pose and build a 3D point map in an unknown scene. It is necessary to adjust SLAM-based coordinates system to local reference coordinate systems for seamless registration with virtual object in real space. For this, we calculate two relations for adjustment process. First relation is a scale unit. The scale parameter of SLAM-based coordinates system is randomly selected in the initialization stage. This scale parameter should be replacement to a real scale unit. Without refining the scale parameter, the users couldn't register virtual object to the position they want. The scale ratio parameter λ is calculated using distance from camera position to starting point of each coordinate systems. The depth of RGB-D camera is presented with a meter scale unit.

$$\lambda = \frac{distance\ from\ camera\ to\ origin\ in\ virtual\ scale\ units}{distance\ from\ camera\ to\ origin\ in\ real\ scale\ units}. \tag{3}$$

Second relation is translation matrix $P_{local,n}$ which transforms the points of SLAM coordinates to local coordinates at n_{th} frame. We first calculate the initial matrix R that represents transform between coordinates, and then we compute the motion matrix M_n for each frame. This matrix represents an accumulated camera motion from the initial frame to the current frame.

$$M_n = M_{n-1} \times \ldots \times M_1 \times M_0. \tag{4}$$

$P_{SLAM,n}$ which is the matrix of transforming points from world coordinates to SLAM based coordinates is computed by motion matrix and $P_{SLAM,0}$.

$$P_{SLAM,n} = M_{n-1} \times P_{SLAM,0}. \tag{5}$$

Matrix $P_{local,n}$ can be expressed by the following equation:

$$P_{local,n} = \frac{1}{\lambda} \times M_{n-1} \times R \times M_{n-1}^{-1} \times P_{SLAM,n}, n \neq 0. \tag{6}$$

If we obtain this initial coordinates, we can apply relation matrix R, motion matrix M and the scale unit parameter to it. The translation matrix $P_{local,n}$ provides an augmented space to matching real space.

2.2.3   3D Contents Authoring

The shared common working space is built by smartphone gestures such as tap, pinch, and rotate. The smartphone device is better than user's bare hand as the input device, because it enables delicate arrangement of virtual object in real space.

2.3 Hands-Augmented Object Interaction

Tracking two hands is important for natural interaction with virtual objects. There are two main approaches for this. [16] utilizes a generative method to track full articulations of two hands. The generative method has an advantage with respect to good generalization and continuous solution. However, it has a weakness that the solution falls easily into local minima if the solution is not good in previous frame. [17] utilizes a discriminative method to detect full articulations of two hands. This method has an advantage that the solution in the present frame is not affected by the solution of previous frame. So, it can detect full articulation of two hands in single frame. However, it gives a discrete solution and tends to the overfitting on training data. To complement the weakness of each method, our method utilizes both of the generative and discriminative methods.

2.3.1 Hand Feature Extraction

The proposed method utilize a convolutional neural network (CNN) with heterogeneous input devices for hand-virtual object interaction which illustrated in Fig. 4. As the used input devices, we are a RGB-D camera and an IMU sensor. The hand image is parsed into a normal deep network with convolution and pooling layer. The activation function is used as a rectified linear unit. The feature map obtained from last pooling layer is unified with 3 DoFs data from the IMU sensor. The remaining layers is fully connected layer so that we can unify the two heterogeneous data. Consequently, we get some heat maps that detect the position of joints with the highest probability.

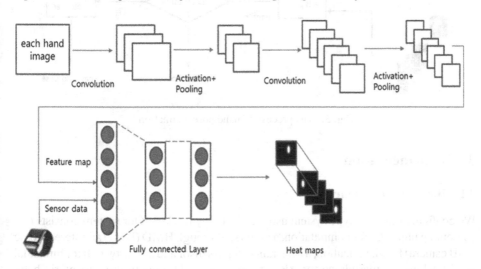

Fig. 4. The proposed CNN with heterogeneous inputs

2.3.2 Hand Pose Estimation

To estimate full articulations of the hands, we adopt two optimization schemes (See Fig. 5). The input datum are the segmented hand images and the heat maps generated from the proposed feature extraction algorithm. First, the inverse kinematics (IK) optimizer is conducted. This algorithm has good advantage about fast convergence. The designed objective function Eq. (7) calculates the error between fingertip and target position so that it find the parameter of articulations. The J is Jacobian matrix and $\vec{e}$ is a vector from source to target, $\Delta\theta$ is the variance of joint parameter. However, if the feature extraction is not accurate in some case, IK algorithm would fail.

$$E_1 = \left\| J\Delta\theta - \vec{e} \right\|^2 + \lambda \|\Delta\theta\|^2. \tag{7}$$

To overcome this problem, the particle swarm optimization (PSO) method is employed. This is conducted only when the solution is not satisfied by a threshold. The objective function Eq. (8) is to measure the discrepancy between observation and hand model. O_i is 3D point in observation and M_i is 3D point in model. $w_{i,j}$ is the weight between model and observation.

$$E_2 = \sum_i \sum_j w_{i,j} \left\| O_i - M_j \right\|_2 \tag{8}$$

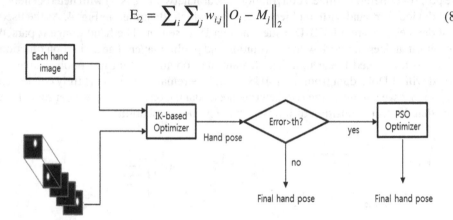

Fig. 5. The process of hand pose estimation

3   Implementation

3.1   Hardware Configuration

We configure our prototype system using commodity devices. Our system consists of a computing unit (PC) for computation, a video see-through HMD (HMD and stereoscopic RGB camera) for visualization, a near-range depth sensor and a smartwatch for bimanual hand tracking, a smartphone for AR authoring. We additionally use exocentric body tracker for body tracking.

For a video see-through HMD, we use Oculus Rift DK2 and attach Ovrvision stereoscopic RGB camera. Oculus Rift DK2 supports position and rotation tracking by external HMD tracker. For a near-range depth sensor, we use a Creative Senz3D. We use a Samsung Gear Live for smartwatch. Finally, we used a Microsoft Kinect v2 for body tracker.

3.2   Software Configuration

We implement the initial prototype in Unity Engine [18]. Figure 6 illustrates the components and their relationship of proposed system.

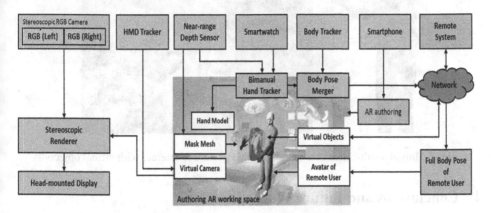

Fig. 6. Detail diagram of proposed framework

For interactive AR contents authoring, we use the positions, rotations and touch directions information which comes from a smartphone input device. With these information, a user can organize his/her AR working space and share the space with remote users.

For hands-augmented object interaction and collaborations with remote users, we utilize a near-range depth sensor and a smartwatch for bimanual hand tracking. Bimanual hand tracking result is used for virtual object manipulation. Also, user's bimanual hand posture information is combined with body pose information from body tracker, and generates combined body-hand pose information is sent to the remote space through network in real-time. At the same time, remote user's combined body and hand pose information is received in real-time, and is used for manipulating avatar movement.

We also utilize point cloud from a near-range depth sensor, to generate occlusion mask mesh which is used for enhancing user's depth perception between hand and virtual object. Then, final virtual scene is merged with real world view, and HMD displays virtual-real combined image.

3.3   Initial Result

Figure 7 shows initial result of our prototype of HMD-based collaboration system. Remote user is summoned to local user's space as a virtual avatar, and both users use bimanual hand gesture to interact with virtual objects. Unlike previous collaboration system [3], our system supports two hands interaction with virtual objects by tracking their hands. Furthermore, after integration with AR authoring method, our system can enable a local user to organize a user-friendly working space without any professional programming skills.

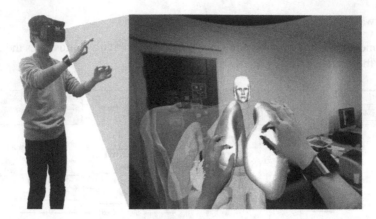

Fig. 7. Initial results: user uses bimanual hand gesture to interact with virtual objects

4 Conclusions and Future Works

In this paper we have presented a novel unified framework for HMD-based remote collaboration using interactive AR authoring and two hands tracking, which enables a local user to organize a user-friendly working space without any professional programming skills, and collaborate physically remote users through intuitive hands-augmented object interactions. Preliminary implementation result shows its strong possibility as a future remote collaboration platform. We expect that the proposed framework can be applicable to many AR collaborative applications such as urban planning, games, medical surgery education, and so on.

As the future works, we plan to the development of two hands tracking with wearable sensor and integration AR authoring and collaboration system.

Acknowledgements. This work was supported by National Research Foundation of Korea (NRF) grant funded by the Korea government (MSIP) (NRF-2015M3A6A3073 746, NRF-2014R1A2A2A01003005).

References

1. Azuma, R.: A survey of augmented reality. Presence **6**(4), 355–385 (1997)
2. Azuma, R., Baillot, Y., Behringer, R., Feiner, S., Julier, S., MacIntyre, B.: Recent advances in augmented reality. IEEE Comput. Graph. Appl. **21**(6), 34–47 (2001)
3. Noh, S., Yeo, H., Woo, W.: An HMD-based mixed reality system for avatar-mediated remote collaboration with bare-hand interaction. In: Eurographics-ICAT-EGVE (2015)
4. Jo, D., Kim, K., Kim, G.: SpaceTime: adaptive control of the teleported avatar for improved AR tele-conference experience. CAVW **26**, 259–269 (2015)
5. Ha, T., Billinghurst, M., Woo, W.: An interactive 3D movement path manipulation method in an augmented reality environment. Elsevier Interact. Comput. **24**(1), 10–24 (2012)
6. Ha, T., Feiner, S., Woo, W.: WeARHand: head-worn, RGB-D camera-based, bare-hand user interface with visually enhanced depth perception. In: IEEE ISMAR, pp. 219–228 (2014)

7. Jang, Y., Noh, S., Chang, H., Kim, T., Woo, W.: 3D finger CAPE: clicking action and position estimation under self-occlusions in egocentric viewpoint. IEEE Trans. Vis. Comput. Graph. **21**(4), 501–510 (2015)
8. Wang, Y., Langlotz, T., Billinghurst, M., Bell, T.: An authoring tool for mobile phone AR environments. In: Proceedings of New Zealand Computer Science Research Student Conference, pp. 1–4 (2009)
9. Higuchi, K., Chen, Y., Chou, P., Zhang, Z., Liu Z.: ImmerseBoard: immersive telepresence experience using a digital whiteboard. In: CHI (2015)
10. Beck, S., Kunert, A., Kulik, A., Froehlich, B.: Immersive group-to-group telepresence. IEEE Trans. Vis. Comput. Graph. **19**(4), 616–625 (2013)
11. Jung, J., Hong, J., Park, S., Yang, H.: Smartphone as an augmented reality authoring tool via multi-touch based 3D interaction method. In: Proceedings of the 11th ACM SIGGRAPH International Conference on Virtual-Reality Continuum and its Applications in Industry, pp. 17–20 (2012)
12. Langlotz, T., Mooslechner, S., Zollmann, S., Degendorfer, C., Reitmayr, G., Schmalstieg, D.: Sketching up the world: in situ authoring for mobile augmented reality. Pers. Ubiquit. Comput. **16**(6), 623–630 (2012)
13. https://www.google.com/atap/project-tango/
14. Fischler, M.A., Robert, C.B.: Random sample consensus: a paradigm for model fitting with applications to image analysis and automated cartography. Commun. ACM **24**(6), 381–395 (1981)
15. Klein, G., David, M.: Parallel tracking and mapping for small AR workspaces. In: ISMAR (2007)
16. Oikonomidis, I., Lourakis, M., Argyros, A.: Evolutionary quasi-random search for hand articulations tracking. In: CVPR (2014)
17. Rogez, G., Khademi, M., Supančič III, J.S., Montiel, J.M.M., Ramanan, D.: 3D hand pose detection in egocentric RGB-D images. In: Agapito, L., Bronstein, M.M., Rother, C. (eds.) ECCV 2014 Workshops. LNCS, vol. 8925, pp. 356–371. Springer, Heidelberg (2015)
18. http://unity3d.com/

Game Design and Neuroscience Cooperation in the Challenge-Based Immersion in Mobile Devices as Tablets and Smartphones

Rachel Zuanon[(✉)]

Sense Design Lab, Ph.D. and Master's Design Program,
Anhembi Morumbi University, São Paulo, Brazil
rzuanon@anhembi.br, rachel@zuannon.com.br

Abstract. The significant number of digital game applications for mobile devices, such as smartphones and tablets, motivates the concern of designers regarding the impact that the application of design elements may have in the construction of the gameplay experience. This concern is intensified when involving children on the stage of brain and cognitive development. This scenario is favorable to the cooperation between Game Design and Neuroscience, which are discussed in this article from the proximity between the elements of Challenge-based Immersion and attention mechanisms, decision-making, emotional and cognitive processing, and voluntary motor action. Among the main results obtained in the evaluation of two focus groups aged between 7–8 years-old and 9–12 years-old, there is the directly proportional association between cognitive involvement of the player with the game; the player control of the charts and navigation through the digital game objects; and the player motivation to overcome the challenges in this context.

Keywords: Game design · Neuroscience · Challenge-based immersion · Mobile devices

1 Introduction

The cooperation between Design and Neuroscience is proving to be a prolific field of research [1–5] in view of the significant and mutual contributions that these areas provide by enhancing, extending and converging their respective scopes of activity; and the positive impact that this synergy represents to the users of products, services and environments designed from this interface and transdisciplinary confluence.

The context of the games especially in mobile platforms is presented as a universe even more challenging to this cooperation between the fields of Design and Neuroscience, since the large number of digital game applications available and accessed through mobile devices, such as tablets and smartphones, increases the designers concern about the role that the projective elements used in the design of these games may have in the user experience during gameplay and the impacts, both positive and negative, in this context and resulting from these projective choices.

Meanwhile, for neuroscientists, such concerns are consistent with those that involve the dynamics of the brain and cognitive processes directly involved in the construction

© Springer International Publishing Switzerland 2016
N. Streitz and P. Markopoulos (Eds.): DAPI 2016, LNCS 9749, pp. 142–153, 2016.
DOI: 10.1007/978-3-319-39862-4_14

of this research and the behavioral reverberations arising from it. "There is a widespread opinion that human behavior cannot be globally understood only based on external and observable facts. To be fully understood it is necessary to take into account the thoughts, cognitions and beliefs of the subject, as it is these that determine and give meaning to the behavior and structure and organize the world" [6].

Such concerns, in both perspectives, are extended when this scenario involves children on the stage of brain and cognitive development. In this context, this research presents and discusses the cooperation between Design and Neuroscience from the results obtained during the gameplay evaluation of Time Tremors Infinity, a game available for mobile devices - tablet and smartphone. The evaluation was conducted with 56 school children in the age groups of 7–8 years-old and 9–12 years-old, 28 boys and 28 girls. This article will be specially focused on the game design elements, evaluation and results specifically related to Challenge-based Immersion (control, challenge, cognitive involvement).

Time Tremors Infinity consists of a "digital treasure hunt" in which players must hunt, gather and exchange "Time Treasures" in different media platforms. There is a collaboration relationship between the players. They have to share the findings and solutions to the puzzles and mysteries of history, but there is also competition, because each player is challenged to find new treasures and, as a consequence, to stand out during the game. "Time Treasures" have a value directly associated with historical facts of humanity and can be, for example, a Marie Antoinette's dessert fork or Titanic guard's binoculars. Players are given assignments that can force them to solve puzzles and mysteries, or even to overcome a challenge in order to find and collect new and more time treasures. At every treasure they find, there is a new historical cycle revealed to players.

The data collection was conducted from video recording of the above-mentioned sessions as well as through semi-structured interviews with the target-population of the research and a socio-demographic questionnaire filled in by the parents/guardians of students. Among the main results observed from the perspective of cooperation between game design and neuroscience, there are: (1) the directly proportional association between the player cognitive involvement and the game; the player control of the charts and navigation through the digital game objects; and the player motivation to overcome the challenges in this context; (2) the absence of a direct relationship between the technological device - tablet or smartphone - and the elements of control, challenge and cognitive involvement of the player; (3) the identification of the body posture assumed by the player during gameplay as a determining factor to the results obtained under the game control; (4) the player engagement when facing the game challenges that was directly related to the novelty provided by the action of playing, regardless of the game content in question.

2   Immersion in Games

Among the several factors involving gameplay experience, during and after playing, such as fun; flow; thriller; competence; frustration; control; challenges; social presence; and from a wide variety of approaches to gaming experience [7–19], immersion is an important and positive component of the experience players seek from games.

In general, the concept of immersion can be understood as the player engagement or involvement during their experience of playing a digital game, which suggests the expression "a person feels as if they are in the game" [20]. Nevertheless, it is important to emphasize that this feeling of being "in the game", in this particular context, does not refer to a spatial or social location in the game, but to the player cognitive status during the action of playing and experiencing the situations proposed by the game.

This cognitive experience can reveal different levels of engagement and involvement in the game, which constitute one of the different approaches dedicated to research of the immersion in digital games. In this perspective, the different levels of involvement and engagement with the different aspects of the game are responsible for moving the player attention, consciousness and thoughts, dissociating the aspects related to the physical world and concentrating them only in events occurring inside the game [20].

In this regard, Brown and Cairns [7] propose three levels of immersion. The first level is the necessary engagement so the player invest their time and effort to play the selected game. The second level is defined by the high degree of attention and emotional involvement during gameplay. Lastly, the third level comprises the total immersion or complete involvement with the game. This is where the sense of being "in game" emerges, and nothing but the very context created by the game will be relevant to the player. Although Brown and Cairns called this level as presence, it is important to note that the concept of total immersion is not associated with a spatial or social location in the game, and therefore this terminology does not seem to be the most appropriate to express this condition.

Another approach presented by Ermi and Mayra [21] establishes three types of immersive experience: sensory, challenge-based and imaginative. This approach comprises an experiential perspective aiming to characterize the immersion attributes as an experience lived by the players. In this context, the concept of sensory immersion complies with the presence in which the game, as a digital environment, can offer high quality and realistic audiovisual representation; aspects that are able to stimulate the player to the perception of their "physical" presence in the game. The concept of challenge-based immersion concerns the challenges proposed by the game and the skills required from the player to overcome them while the imaginative immersion relates to the player emotional involvement during gameplay.

Also within an experiential perspective, but with a different approach, Adams [11] proposes another model for the concept of immersion in digital games, but it is also structured on three pillars: tactical, strategic and narrative. The definition of tactical immersion comprises the immersion built, moment by moment, during the act of playing the game while a strategic immersion relates to the player strategic thinking throughout the game. The narrative immersion refers to the player emotional involvement during the game.

Among the definitions introduced by Brown and Cairns; Ermi and Mayra; and Adams, it is also possible to identify overlapping of the immersion concept in digital games. For example, the first level of immersion proposed by Brown and Cairns convergences to the context of challenge-based immersion defended by Ermi and Mayra, as well as the tactical and strategic immersion presented by Adam's model.

In this regard, a tactical immersion corresponds - in part - to the 'challenge' factor and – fully - to the 'control' factor, which are described by the Brown and Cairns' first-level immersion model. It is also possible to notice a clear correspondence between the strategic immersion and the cognitive involvement, which are also an integrating factor of first level. The Brown and Cairns' second level of immersion is directly related to the imaginative immersion proposed by Ermi and Mayra, as well as the narrative immersion of Adam's model. In relation to the concept of total immersion, while Brown and Cairns' model mentions the third level of immersion, Ermi and Mayra's model presents the sensory immersion associated with the idea of presence in the game, but without specifying a direct correlation between this and the dimension of total immersion; Adam's model considers that the emergence of a true immersive experience is only possible from the harmonious collaboration among tactical, strategic and narrative immersions [11].

Another possible approach to the immersion concept is brought by the technological perspective comprising a "physical" presence in the game, or the sensation of being in that (digital) environment [22]. This approach involves directly the technologies able to create representations of the player in the game digital environment.

This brief review does not intend to exhaust the discussion about immersion in digital games, but to present a brief overview of the main approaches that are dedicated to this concept. This brief mapping is essential to the identification and construction of potential connections between the fields of game design and neuroscience. In this article, the contribution will be restricted to the proximity between the concept of challenge-based immersion proposed by Ermi and Mayra [21], and referred to the challenges proposed by the game and the skills required from the player to overcome them - and the attention mechanisms; decision-taking; emotional processing; cognitive processing; and voluntary motor actions, clarified by the neuroscience perspective.

3   Articulations Between Neuroscience Approach and Challenge-Based Immersion Elements

As a start, it should be noted that the intended proximity between attention and decision-making mechanisms, emotional and cognitive processing, and voluntary motor actions, explored from the neuroscience perspective, and the concepts of control, challenge and cognitive involvement, discussed in the game design as Challenge-based Immersion, does not aim to create a reductionist and restrictive approach of cause and effect between brain phenomena, design elements and choices made by the player. Rather, the aim of this research is to explore the expansion of perspectives to the game design that the neuroscience reflections can bring to the design Challenge-based Immersion. The understanding of neuroscientific background that engender the connections between the above-mentioned mechanisms, processing and intrinsic actions to the human body can provide relevant assistance and be able to identify sustainable and more favorable ways to the conception and definition of the design elements related to the challenges posed by the game, given the cognitive and sensorimotor skills necessary and required from the player to overcome them. It is believed that the dialogue between these design elements and the associated cognitive and sensorimotor skills can contribute significantly to the game design regarding the motivation increase, frustration reduction and strengthening the player cognitive involvement in the gameplay experience.

The highest point in brain plasticity takes place in early childhood. This can be seen when one hemisphere of a child's brain is removed, and the other hemisphere creates interconnected networks in order to enlarge their tasks and assume the operation of the functions hitherto exclusive to non-existent hemisphere. On the other hand, there are areas of the brain that take years to reach their full maturity. For example, the core with the important role of maintaining the attention, called reticular formation, is in general fully myelinated in the puberty or after it while the frontal lobes only reach full myelination after adulthood [23]. The brain design developed over time explains the behavior. That is, the more intense level of emotion and impulsivity identified with higher incidence in younger adults than in older adults denotes a possible and proportional association between these behaviors and neuronal maturation of the individual.

Every thought the player has when facing a challenge and, consequently, a decision-making in a game requires some attention. That is, it requires the focus in the context of the activity and disposal of stimuli not related to it. There are two types of attention in this case: (1) the automatic bond of senses when information captures the attention of the individual; (2) when the mind is deliberately dedicated to a topic of interest. In both scenarios, attention is the result of the connection between neurotransmitters in brain areas and, only from those, they are directly involved so these mechanisms occur. Many brain regions work in guiding and controlling attention taking into account three elements required for this function: (a) excitement; (B) orientation; (C) focus. The (a) excitement is dependent on a group of midbrain nuclei - the top of the brainstem - called the reticular activating system. The stimulation of this group of reticular neurons creates alpha brain waves - activity fluctuations in the range from 20 to 40 Hz - associated with the alert status. The (b) orientation involves neurons in the superior colliculus and the parietal cortex. The superior colliculus move the eyes to the new stimulus, while the parietal cortex decouples the attention from the current stimulus. While the focus is executed by the lateral pulvinar - a portion of the thalamus - which operates similarly to a spotlight that turns on the light according to the stimulus and further transfers the information about the focused context to the frontal lobes, which are responsible for retaining and maintaining the attention [23].

In other words, the human body has the neurophysiological mechanisms that support the processes of attention, choice and decision-making; elements and situations that will integrate or not their game context and if they will invest or not their time. In the decision-making, two complementary pathways of neurophysiological communication set up this mechanism. The first is responsible for causing the appearance of images related to the particular situation, such as action options and preview the future consequences. Several reasoning strategies act with this knowledge in order to make a decision. Meanwhile, the second pathway operates in parallel to the first; it is responsible for activating previous emotional experiences associated to situations comparable to what happens at the moment of decision-making in the game. This parallel mechanism influences the decision-making process by interfering with reasoning strategies or leading the attention to the representations of future consequences.

This second pathway can also operate in foreground and directly lead to a decision, for example, when an immediate choice is made from an intuition [24]. It is true that the degree of participation of both pathways in the decision-making process will depend exclusively on the individual who decides, from their previous experiences as well as the circumstances that make up the current situation experienced in the context of the game.

Any and every experience lived in this area is accompanied by some degree of emotion. The emotions and feelings play an important role in the reasoning that supports the decision-making in a game. Feelings trigger mental alerts about good and bad circumstances and thereby prolongs the impact of emotions by lastingly affecting attention and memory. Furthermore, the feelings, by combining memories of the past, imagination and reasoning, lead to the emergence of preview capacity and problems forecast and to the possibility of creating new and nonstereotyped solutions [24].

In this context, the amygdala acts as an interface between emotions and cognition, as well as it plays an important role in modulating motivated behavior. It is known that it receives information from more than one sensory modality, in addition to the direct reception to exteroceptive and interoceptive information arising respectively of the thalamus and visceral afferent receptors. In it, the information is integrated and receives an affective nature. The amygdala may also influence both the mnemonic and cognitive processes due to their direct projection to the hippocampus and the various associative polymodal neocortical areas. It can also directly modulate autonomic, neuroendocrine and behavioral responses related to motivated behavior due to its communication with the hypothalamus and limbic mesencephalic structures. That is, the amygdala provides the link between the cognitive and emotional processing - related to emotional experience in the game - and, on the other hand, modulates hypothalamic and mesencephalic sites responsible respectively for orchestrating and expressing several motivated and related behaviors, thus, to this emotional expression [25].

The nucleus accumbens, also called the ventral striatum, is considered a key element in the integration of emotions with voluntary motor actions taken by the player. This nucleus receives a convergence of information from various brain regions involved in emotional processing, learning and memory, such as the amygdala, the hippocampus and the prefrontal cortex. Furthermore, neurons of the nucleus accumbens - through projections for the ventral globus pallidus - can control the somatic movement [25].

As well as other cognitive systems, the human movement is built from the dynamic rules of brain development and their interactions with their own body and the environment. Perception, motivation and action in the game are subject to body biomechanical states. These states change throughout life. It is, therefore, important to point out that the motivation arising within the gameplay is essential both for the formation of new motor behaviors and for the preservation of the established behaviors. Children usually feel fulfilled with their new motor skills, and these skills are the results from new neural connections, new perceptual gains and biomechanical changes [26], for which the motivation contributes meaningfully.

4   Materials and Procedures

Time Tremors Infinity (TTI) consists of a transmedia game, that is, it is available for different converging media, and Alternate Reality, which uses the physical world as a platform to offer an interactive narrative. Alternate Reality Games are characterized by involving players in the stories, encouraging them to explore the narrative in order to solve the challenges and interact with game characters. This format is defined by the intense involvement of the players with the story that is built in real time and evolves according to their participation. The players interact directly with the characters in the game, helping them to solve puzzles and challenges, collaborate in real time with an online community that discusses and analyzes the activities in the game.

TTI's narrative is about two characters: the Max brothers, who are 14-years-old and Medie, who is 10 years-old. They are sent to the gloomy boarding school Ranksome Academy after the mysterious disappearance of their parents. The school is located on a secluded island, and built in a 'time tremors', unstable point in the time-space line in which objects, animals and people appear and disappear mysteriously. The leading character is represented by 'Hector, the Bear', a timekeeper. The enemies are the dangerous 'sleepy forest' and 'Miss BuGly', a wily biology professor.

In Time Tremors Infinity, the player must explore different pathways searching time crystals, which allow the time-space journey, with the aim of collecting various objects lost in the history; they are called 'time treasures'. There is also the 'celestial atlas', a kind of book that acts as a map and reveals highly relevant pieces of information. Only by bringing together all 'time treasures' and 'completing the celestial atlas', the player can unveil the mystery in Time Tremors Infinity.

In the game, there are 63 'time treasures' distributed in seven distinct stages of the narrative. Each stage has nine levels. The treasures can only be collected when the player captures the required amount of 'time crystals' in that particular level. By completing each level, only one 'time treasure' is released.

One of the main goals of TTI is to pass on cultural and educational information to the public, especially children, by covering areas as geography, history, science, physics and arts. This information is contained in the 'time treasures' and, as they are collected, the players are able to access details about the content, for example, tridimensional interactive and explanatory replicas on the operation or the context in which particular object ('treasure') fits into the historical period.

The age rating system is appropriate for children. For this research, the collection of quantitative and qualitative data focused on Challenge-based Immersion (control, challenge, cognitive involvement) was conducted with two main groups of players (A and B) consisting of members of both genders in the age groups from 7–8 years-old (group A) and 9–12 years-old (group B). The sample had a total of 56 individuals, with homogeneous distribution: group A – 14 boys; group A' – 14 girls; group B – 14 boys; group B' – 14 girls. They are all students at the Municipal School Miguel Ferreira Vieira, located in São Paulo, Brazil.

The group classification considered the stages of human development proposed by Piaget [27], indicating features that define differences in the configuration of cognitive structures and, thus, the process of cognitive development of children in the respective phases: sensorimotor; preoperatively; concrete operational; and formal operations. The research focused on the 'concrete operational' and 'formal operational' stages, because they are considered as the most suitable for the intended evaluation, as the 'concrete operational' stage marks a decisive change in the mental development of the child, which consists of the capability of concrete organization of thought in addition to the maturation of socialization behavior and social relations through games; while the 'formal operational' stage is marked by the abstraction ability and mathematical cognitive acquisitions.

The methodology for the collection of quantitative and qualitative data considered: (1) the application of a socio-demographic questionnaire filled in by the parents/guardians of students; (2) the individual experience of TTI gameplay on the smartphone, with the maximum duration of 10 min; (3) the semi-structured interviews held in a maximum of 10 min with each student after gameplay on mobile phone; (4) the individual experience of TTI gameplay on tablet with a maximum duration of 10 min; (5) the semi-structured interview held in a maximum of 10 min with each student after gameplay on tablet; (6) the video recording of steps (2), (3), (4) and (5). It should be noted that the sequence of steps (2) and (4) was alternated with the groups in order not to induce the preferred use of the mobile device by the students analyzed during the data collection.

5 Results

The data collected from the groups (A); (A'); (B) e (B') were systematized and analyzed according to parameters related to Challenge-based Immersion: control, challenge and cognitive involvement. For the 'game control' parameter, the focus was given to: (1) graphics; (2) time; (3) navigation; (4) smartphone device; (5) tablet device; (6) body posture – playing while seated; (7) body posture – playing while standing. With regards to the 'cognitive engagement with the game' parameter, the focus was given to: (1) game main goal; (2) character; (3) treasures; (4) colors; (5) setting; (6) music. Finally, regarding the 'game challenges' parameter, the focus was given to: (1) tasks; (2) individual challenge - focus on playing; (3) individual challenge - focus on winning; (4) collective challenge - focus on the competition; (5) collective challenge - focus on collaboration. The results showed (Table 1):

Table 1. Results of 'control' parameter obtained from the two groups

Game control				
Parameters	Group A	Group A'	Group B	Group B'
Graphics	65 %	36 %	57 %	57 %
Time	79 %	36 %	86 %	50 %
Navigation	72 %	43 %	50 %	36 %
Smartphone	50 %	43 %	15 %	15 %
Tablet	50 %	43 %	50 %	72 %
Body posture – playing while seated	60 %	64 %	50 %	64 %
Body posture – playing while standing	13 %	29 %	7 %	7 %

The group A (7–8 year-old boys) demonstrated greater control of graphics and game navigation on the smartphone when compared with the other groups analyzed. The 'more control' was shown to be associated with the ability to play while seated.

The group A' (7–8 year-old girls) showed better control of graphics, navigation and time playing while seated, regardless of the type of the mobile device used.

The group B (9–12 year-old boys) demonstrated greater control of the gameplay on the tablet when compared to the other groups. The 'more control' was shown to be associated with the ability to play while seated.

The group B' (9–12 year-old girls) showed better control of graphics, navigation and game time when playing while seated and using the tablet device (Table 2).

Table 2. Results of 'cognitive involvement' parameter obtained from the two groups

Cognitive involvement with the game				
Parameters	Group A	Group A'	Group B	Group B'
Game main goal	100 %	72 %	72 %	58 %
Characters	93 %	87 %	64 %	64 %
Treasures	86 %	72 %	50 %	7 %
Colors	93 %	72 %	71 %	73 %
Setting	86 %	69 %	64 %	57 %
Music	72 %	73 %	72 %	64 %

The group A (7–8 year-old boys) demonstrated greater cognitive involvement with the game in respect to the main goal, character, treasures, colors and setting when compared to the other groups.

The group A' (7–8 year-old girls) demonstrated greater cognitive involvement with the game as regards to the music when compared to the other groups (Table 3).

Table 3. Results of 'challenge' parameter obtained from the two groups

Game challenges				
Parameters	Group A	Group A'	Group B	Group B'
Missions	79 %	43 %	65 %	65 %
Single player - focus on playing	54 %	64 %	14 %	22 %
Single player - focus on wining	15 %	22 %	22 %	7 %
Multiplayer - focus on competition	29 %	14 %	14 %	50 %
Multiplayer - focus on collaboration	21 %	57 %	29 %	7 %

The group A (7–8 year-old boys) demonstrated greater motivation when facing the existing challenges in the missions proposed by the game when compared to the other groups. This motivation for the challenges was associated to the desire to play and compete, regardless of the final result.

The group A' (7–8 year-old girls) demonstrated motivation when facing the existing challenges in the missions proposed by the game when associated with the desire to play and collaborate, regardless of the final result.

The group B (9–12 year-old boys) demonstrated motivation when facing the existing challenges in the missions proposed by the game when associated with the desire to win and collaborate.

The group B' (9–12 year-old girls) demonstrated motivation when facing the existing challenges in the missions proposed by the game when associated with the desire to compete, regardless of the final result.

6 Discussions

By understanding Challenge-based Immersion as a game design domain that links the following elements: control, challenge and cognitive involvement of the player during the gameplay, it can be said that only the group A, consisting of 7–8 year-old boys, has shown the most suitable percentage range to the connection between these factors.

This result provides the diagnosis of a directly proportional relationship between the player cognitive involvement with the game; player control of the charts and navigation through the digital game objects; and the player motivation to overcome the challenges in this context. That is, as seen in the results obtained from the groups A', B and B', any kind of influence on one of these aspects, whether from the player's body or the physical environment, consequently results in impacts to other evaluated elements.

This result allows us to validate the hypothesis presented by this article that aimed to demonstrate the close connection between the following concepts: control, challenge and cognitive involvement and attention mechanisms, decision-making, emotional and cognitive processing, and voluntary motor action, addressed from the neuroscience perspective.

Given the results obtained from group A', consisting of 7–8 year-old girls, it is not possible to establish a direct relationship between technological device in which the game is played - tablet or smartphone – and the elements of control, challenge and cognitive involvement. On the other hand, it is possible to consider the body posture assumed by the player during gameplay as a determining factor to the results obtained under the control of the game. Postural adjustments occur during voluntary movement in anticipation of disruptions caused by the movement execution plan. These anticipatory postural adjustments are part of the selected motor plans to perform a certain action [26]. Therefore, they work on what is observed as a result of this motor action.

It was also found that the difference between all the percentages observed in the comparison between the genders of the groups proved to be directly proportional to the habit of playing. This diagnosis supports the direct relationship between the decision-making mechanisms and previous experiences of the individual.

The results also showed that, in the context of the challenges presented by the game, the player engagement was directly related to the novelty provided by the action of playing, regardless of the game content in question. This finding confirms the pleasure and the consequent cognitive involvement in the use of new motor skills, usually seen in children.

It is important to emphasize that these discussions do not exhaust the still possible interpretations of the results. Rather, they are intended to explore other perspectives for many other discussions open to dialogue and integration.

7 Conclusion

The objective of this article was to find a proximity between the fields of knowledge of Games Design, especially from the concept of Challenge-based Immersion, and Neuroscience, especially of attention mechanisms, decision-making, emotional and cognitive processing and motor action. Its main objective was to raise the cooperation between these fields of knowledge in order to create game design taking into account the cognitive and sensorimotor needs of the intended target-audience and, therefore, more motivating to the cognitive involvement and to reduce the frustration during the gameplay.

As future developments of this research, there is the application of gameplay tests, with evaluative focus on the elements of challenge-based immersion, adults groups, with different age groups, considering a subsequent comparative analysis with the results obtained under the sampling discussed in this article.

There is also the intention to expand this cooperation between Game Design and Neuroscience in the contexts of imaginative and sensory immersions.

References

1. Zeisel, J.: Inquiry by Design: Environment/Behavior/Neuroscience in Architecture, Interiors, Landscape, and Planning. Norton, New York (2006)
2. Zuanon, R.: Design-neuroscience: interactions between the creative and cognitive processes of the brain and design. In: Kurosu, M. (ed.) HCI 2014, Part I. LNCS, vol. 8510, pp. 167–174. Springer, Heidelberg (2014)
3. Zuanon, R.: Designing wearable bio-interfaces: a transdisciplinary articulation between design and neuroscience. In: Stephanidis, C., Antona, M. (eds.) UAHCI 2013, Part I. LNCS, vol. 8009, pp. 689–699. Springer, Heidelberg (2013)
4. Zuanon, R.: Usign BCI to play games with brain signals: an organic interaction process through NeuroBodyGame wearable computer. In: Huggins, J.E., et al. (eds.) Fifth International Brain-Computer Interface Meeting 2013, pp. 64–65. Graz University of Technology Publishing House, Graz (2013)
5. Zuanon, R.: Bio-interfaces: designing wearable devices to organic interactions. In: Ursyn, A. (ed.) Biologically-Inspired Computing for the Arts: Scientific Data Through Graphics, pp. 1–17. IGI Global, Hershey (2011)
6. Clark, C.M., Peterson, P.L.: Teachers' thought processes. In: Wittrock, M.C. (ed.) Handbook of Research on Teaching, 3rd edn., pp. 255–296. Macmillan, New York (1986)
7. Brown, E., Cairns, P.: A grounded investigation of game immersion. In: Proceedings of ACM CHI 2004, pp. 1297–1300 (2004)
8. Hong R.: Immersion in reading and film as a function of personality. B.Sc. Thesis, Department of Psychology, University College London, UK (2006)

9. Jennett, C., Cox, A., Cairns, P., Dhoparee, S., Epps, A., Tijs, T., Walton, A.: Measuring and defining the experience of immersion in games. Int. J. Hum. Comput. Stud. **66**, 641–661 (2008)
10. Bartle, R.: Hearts, clubs, diamonds, spades: players who suit MUDS. J. MUD Res. **1**, 19 (1996)
11. Adams, E.: Postmodernism and the Three Types of Immersion. http://www. designersnotebook.com/Columns/063_Postmodernism/063_postmodernism.htm
12. Freeman, D.: Creating Emotions in Games. New Riders, Berkley (2004)
13. Schell, J.: The Art of Game Design. Morgan Kaufmann, Burlington (2008)
14. Calvillo-Gamez, E., Cairns, P., Cox, A.L.: Assessing the core elements of the gaming experience. In: Bernhaupt, R. (ed.) Evaluating User Experience in Games, pp. 47–71. Springer, Heidelberg (2010)
15. IJsselsteijn, W., de Kort, Y., Poels, K., Jurgelionis, A., Bellotti, F.: Characterising and measuring user experiences in digital games. In: Advances in Computer Entertainment Technology, ACE 2007, Workshop 'Methods for Evaluating Games' (2007)
16. Poels, K., de Kort, Y., IJsselsteijn, W.: It's always a lot of fun! Exploring dimensions of digital game experience using focus group methodology. In: Proceedings of FuturePlay 2007, pp. 83–89 (2007)
17. Qin, H., Rau, P.L.P., Salvendy, G.: Effects of different scenarios of game difficulty on player immersion. Interact. Comput. **22**, 230–239 (2010)
18. Qin, H., Rau, P.L.P., Salvendy, G.: Measuring player immersion in the computer narrative. Int. J. Hum. Comput. Interact. **25**(2), 107–133 (2009)
19. Calleja, G.: In-Game: From Immersion to Incorporation. MIT Press, Harvard (2011)
20. Cairns, P., Cox, A.L., Nordin, I.: Immersion in digital games: a review of gaming experience research. In: Angelides, M.C., Agius, H. (eds.) Handbook of Digital Games, pp 337–361. Wiley, Hoboken (2014)
21. Ermi, L., Mäyrä, F.F.: Fundamental components of the gameplay experience: analysing Immersion. Worlds in play: international perspectives on digital games research, vol. 37 (2005)
22. Slater, M., Usoh, M., Steed, A.: Depth of presence in virtual environments. Presence **3**(2), 130–140 (1994)
23. Carter, R.: O livro de ouro do cérebro. Rio de Janeiro, Ediouro (2003)
24. Damásio, A.: Em busca de Espinosa: prazer e dor na ciência dos sentimentos. Companhia das Letras, São Paulo (2004)
25. Canteras, N.S., Bittencourt, J.C.: Comportamentos Motivados e Emoções. In: Lent, R. (ed.) Neurociência da Mente e do Comportamento. Guanabara Koogan, Rio de Janeiro (2008)
26. Vargas, C.D., Rodrigues, E.C., Fontana, A.P.: Controle motor. In: Lent, R. (ed.) Neurociência da Mente e do Comportamento. Guanabara Koogan, Rio de Janeiro (2008)
27. Piaget, J.: O Nascimento da Inteligência na Criança. Delachaux & Niestlé, Lisboa (1971)

Tracking and Recognition Techniques in Ambient Intelligence

Exploring Machine Learning Object Classification for Interactive Proximity Surfaces

Andreas Braun[1,2(✉)], Michael Alekseew[1], and Arjan Kuijper[1,2]

[1] Fraunhofer Institute for Computer Graphics Research IGD, Darmstadt, Germany
{andreas.braun,michael.alekseew,arjan.kuijper}@igd.fraunhofer.de
[2] Technische Universität Darmstadt, Darmstadt, Germany

Abstract. Capacitive proximity sensors are a variety of the sensing technology that drives most finger-controlled touch screens today. However, they work over a larger distance. As they are not disturbed by non-conductive materials, they can be used to track hands above arbitrary surfaces, creating flexible interactive surfaces. Since the resolution is lower compared to many other sensing technologies, it is necessary to use sophisticated data processing methods for object recognition and tracking. In this work we explore machine learning methods for the detection and tracking of hands above an interactive surface created with capacitive proximity sensors. We discuss suitable methods and present our implementation based on Random Decision Forests. The system has been evaluated on a prototype interactive surface - the CapTap. Using a Kinect-based hand tracking system, we collect training data and compare the results of the learning algorithm to actual data.

Keywords: Capacitive proximity sensing · Interactive surfaces · Machine learning

1 Introduction

Capacitive sensing drives the most common interaction device of the recent years - the finger-controlled touch screen. A generated electric field is disturbed by the presence of grounded objects, such as fingers. This disturbance can be measured and is used to detect the location of an object on the surface [1]. Capacitive proximity sensors are a variety of this technology that is able to detect the presence of a human body over a distance. They can be used to create interaction devices that are hidden below non-conductive surfaces [2, 3]. However, for these sensors, object recognition is a major challenge, due to a comparatively low resolution and ambiguity of the detected objects [4].

In the last years researchers have investigated a number of different processing methods, including algorithms that try to distinguish multiple hands. Machine learning methods have become more popular in object recognition for 3D interaction devices. The Microsoft Kinect is a popular example that extensively uses machine learning for posture classification [5]. Le Goc et al. used the Random Decision Forest (RDF) method to improve the object recognition of a commercially available, small area capacitive proximity interaction device [6]. They used a stereo camera system to track the position

© Springer International Publishing Switzerland 2016
N. Streitz and P. Markopoulos (Eds.): DAPI 2016, LNCS 9749, pp. 157–167, 2016.
DOI: 10.1007/978-3-319-39862-4_15

of a fingertip with high precision as ground truth and trained a RDF, resulting in a finger tracking precision that exceeded the manufacturer's methods. In this paper we want to evaluate, how machine learning methods, such as RDF can be used to realize object recognition and tracking on large-area interaction systems. The CapTap is an interactive table that uses capacitive proximity sensors to provide a 3D interaction paradigm [7]. It is comprised of 24 sensors hidden under a wooden or plastic cover. It starts detecting objects at a distance of approximately 40 cm. The sensors use the OpenCapSense rapid prototyping toolkit for capacitive sensing [8].

Using a second system that supports precise hand tracking, we can acquire ground truth data. The idea is to perform a classification of volume elements that the center of the hand resides in. For this it is necessary to collect training samples from within each volume element. The hand tracker uses a background subtraction method from a depth image and looks for the innermost point in a recognized hand shape. In order to determine the 3D position the extrinsic camera parameters have to be determined in a calibration routine. This idea was implemented in a prototype that uses the Kinect v2 as a system to acquire the hand position. Additionally, we propose several modifications to improve the localization accuracy.

A study was performed with the proposed system. We collected several hundred training samples to create and test the classifier. This paper proposes the following scientific contributions:

- Propose a method to track multiple hands over a capacitive proximity interaction device using RDF classification
- Create a system to accurately measure the relative position of hands from a surface using a fast hand detection algorithm for the Microsoft Kinect v2
- Evaluation of the system using 1500 training samples and proposing several methods to improve localization based on RDF classification results.

2   Related Works

In the past there have been several interaction devices for mid-air interaction using capacitive proximity sensors. Zimmerman et al. propose various applications for this technology in HCI [3]. One of the prototypes is a smart table that tracks the hand position above the surface. For object detection they model the electric field of dipole pairs and use inverse methods to determine the position of one or more hands. Simpler methods that use a weighted average to interpolate between evenly spaced sensors and approximations for estimating the elevation above the surface have been proposed [2]. Grosse-Puppendahl et al. present a probabilistic method that estimates for each sensor areas, in which no object can be present [9]. This results in a "swiss-cheese-like" probability distribution, whereas the object has to be part of the remaining high-probability areas. The method that inspired our work was presented by Le Goc et al. [6]. They use RDF classification to improve the accuracy of finger tracking for a capacitive interaction device by Microchip [10]. This system uses a layout of a single sender and multiple receiver electrodes placed around the sender. They achieve a good accuracy in a constrained interaction area. The accuracy of the supplied object detection algorithm

Fig. 1. CapTap capacitive proximity interaction table (left) and an infrared images that shows electrodes and microphone below the surface (right).

could be significantly improved from an average error of >20 mm to less than 5 mm, by using a RDF classifier that was trained with 32000 samples interpolation of the tracked object using Kalman filtering.

Our proposed method is designed for large area interactive tables that support interaction above the surface. One of those systems is the MirageTable by Benko et al. [11]. This curved interactive surface combines hand tracking in three dimensions using the Microsoft Kinect and Augmented Reality with a stereo projector attached above the table. The users have to wear shutter glasses for the stereo projection. An early system that uses capacitive sensors for touch recognition is DiamondTouch by Dietz et al. [12]. It uses a multilayer setup of electrodes and is thus able to track several touch points from different users. The system we used in this work is CapTap, an interactive table that combines capacitive proximity sensors for object detection above the surface and an acoustic sensor for detecting and distinguishing different touches (Fig. 1) [7]. It creates capacitive images and applies various image processing methods to detect the location and orientation of hands and arms. The acoustic sensor uses analysis in the frequency domain and a trained classifier to recognize different touch events, such as taps and knocks [13].

The system requires training data as ground truth. Therefore, we need methods that track the position of a hand in 3D. The Microsoft Kinect is an affordable sensor that provides reasonably precise collection of depth data in a sufficiently large area. It is primarily intended for pose tracking [5]. Some methods have been proposed for the first version that track the position of multiple hands [14]. A novel method for the Kinect v2 enables the tracking of fingers with high precision [15]. However, for our proposed system the focus was on fast tracking of the palm position above a surface. Therefore, a custom method was implemented that will be outlined in the following section.

3 Hand Tracking Using Random Decision Forests

RDF is a classification method in machine learning [16]. Based on classical decision trees it tries to overcome their tendency to overfitting by creating a multitude of trees during training time and ending up with the class that is the statistical mode of the classes or mean prediction of the individual trees.

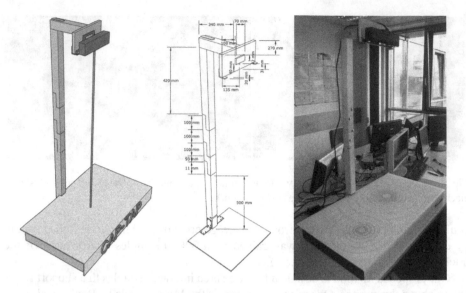

Fig. 2. Rendering and dimensions of Kinect v2 stand and its position above CapTap

The method presented by Le Goc et al. that we presented previously is less suitable for large interaction devices, as the supervised area is considerably larger and as we want to track the position of multiple hands above a surface. This requires a system that is applied over the interactive surface that observes the full interaction space. Another requirement we had is flexibility of the approach. The users should not be required to wear any markers, even during the training phase. Thus we decided on the following setup, which is shown in Fig. 2:

1. A stand was built that holds a video system at an elevation above the surface of the interaction device.
2. The Kinect v2 is attached to the stand and observes the scene with both depth and RGB camera.
3. A computer vision algorithm detects the center of the palms of the hands in the interaction area in three dimensions.
4. A software suite collects the data of the capacitive sensors and the detected hand positions as training and test data.

3.1   Hand Tracking Algorithm for Kinect v2

Before we can start to accurately track the position of hands using the Kinect depth image, it is necessary to calibrate the position of the Kinect with respect to the interactive surface. Even if the stand is mechanically solid, small movements of the interactive surface or the Kinect can lead to differences in the resulting position.

We are using an edge detector on the depth image to find the boundaries of CapTap in the scene. As the depth images are fairly noisy, an average of 150 frames is used. The four corner points of the boundary allow us to create a transformation matrix that corrects

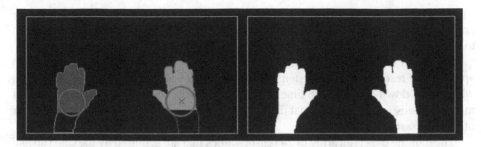

Fig. 3. Left - detected hand palm centers and their distance to the borders of the hand. Right - background subtraction of the hands in the air.

for position in x, y, and z. This transformation matrix is applied to points of the Kinect coordinate systems that are translated to points in the CapTap coordinate system.

The next step is to use computer vision methods to find the center points of the palms of multiple hands, which are later used as input for the classification. The method is inspired by previous works that detect hand position from depth images [17]. There are four basic steps:

1. Segmentation of hands using background subtraction, as shown in Fig. 3 on the right. Creates a binary black and white image.
2. Use a combination of the morphological operations erode and dilate to reduce noise in the remaining image.
3. Apply a region growing algorithm to find pixels that belong to the interior or exterior of a hand.
4. Find the interior point of a hand that is furthest from any edge, as shown in Fig. 3 on the left. Transform the coordinates to the CapTap coordinate system.

This approach is fast enough for execution in real-time (>30 frames per second). We applied some optimizations that reduce the number of candidate pixels for the palm center, such as discarding candidates very close to the edges or candidates that are part of a finger.

3.2 Acquiring Training Data

During the training process a certain amount of samples has to be collected for each potential hand location. The location in this context is a cubic volume element (voxel) with a specific edge length. This length is the achievable resolution of the system. For example, if we want to have a resolution of 3 mm and need 5 samples from each location, the naïve approach for the CapTap with its interaction area of 800 mm × 400 mm × 200 mm leads to a required number of samples of.

$$num_{samples} = 5 * \frac{800\,\text{mm} * 400\,\text{mm} * 200\,\text{mm}}{(3\,\text{mm})^3} \approx 11851852$$

As we are limited to collecting 30 samples per second the whole process would take approximately 110 h if the hands move perfectly. The complexity increases if we want to recognize multiple hands.

This is not feasible in the scope of this work, thus several simplifications have been applied. The resolution of the system was restricted to voxels with 20 mm edge length, which cuts down the training time significantly. Additionally, the classification of multiple hands assumes a minimal distance between those, which reduces the number of training samples required.

The training data is an array of 24 sensor values that are acquired by the CapTap and the hand position as acquired from the Microsoft Kinect. A software suite was created that supports the collection of trainings samples, as well as the configuration of all relevant parameters in the data collection and training steps. A screenshot of this system is shown in Fig. 4. On the left we can see a heatmap of the interaction area in two dimensions that indicates how many voxels have all training samples collected. Since this is a three dimensional problem, an additional progress bar on the top right shows how many samples have been collected in the current voxel. Additionally, the software tells how far the training has progressed by a counter in the bottom center. The collected training data can be directly used to create a RDF, whereas the number of branches and tress can be configured using several input fields. The results are stored in files that can be loaded during the classification view that is introduced in the next section.

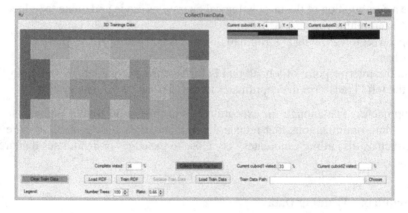

Fig. 4. Software suite that collects training data. Left - view of hand tracker and classification results, right - view of collected training samples within the interaction area.

4 Random Decision Forests Location Classification

In this work, the result of the classification with the RDF is a probability for trained region to be the most fitting to current sensor values. Figure 5 shows an example of the four most likely voxels in a classification process. There are multiple ways to use these results in the final localization routine. In this work we investigated several methods:

1. Assigning the center of the dominant voxel as the location of the palm of the hand, subsequently called *naïve-center*.
2. Linear interpolation between the centers of the vxoels with the highest probability, subsequently called *linear-interpolation*.
3. Weighted interpolation between the centers of the most probable voxels according to their probability, subsequently called *weighted-interpolation*.

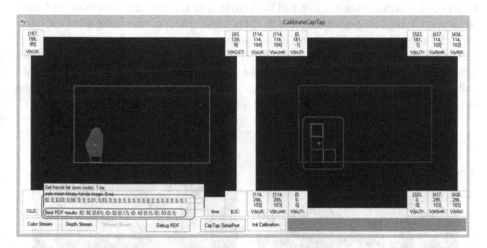

Fig. 5. Left - position as determined by Microsoft Kinect. Right - result of a RDF classification showing four most likely voxels in two dimensions.

Naïve-center is the basic approach that does not require any additional knowledge about the geometric distribution of the voxels in the interaction area. Disadvantages include a highly-quantized localization, whose resolution is limited to the voxel edge length. If there are multiple voxels that have a similar probability, it is likely that the true position is somewhere between the detected voxels.

Linear-interpolation solves the problem of similar probabilities and can successfully localize hands that are between voxels. However, the simple linear interpolation can lead to overrepresentation of unlikely voxels. If the most likely voxel has a probability of 0.9 and a voxel that is far away has 0.05, the linear-interpolation would lead to a position somewhere between the voxels that is likely wrong. A first improvement is discarding voxels that have a low probability.

Weighted-interpolation tries to overcome this disadvantage by attaching a weight to the voxels according to their probability. This leads to a location that has a tendency towards the center of the most probable voxel. A remaining disadvantage of this approach is the lack of correlation between classification probability and hand position. If the hand is at the border between two voxels there is no guarantee that the classification assigns both the same probability. However, in practical applications we found that this often leads to the best results.

5   Evaluation and Discussion

On the following lines we are discussing some findings occurring during the system design and implementation stages, as well as the results of a study performed on a fully trained system.

In some instances the classification results can lead to inconclusive results, an example of which is shown in Fig. 6. The dominant voxels are near the elbow with only one voxel having low probability near the hand. This effect occurs if the arm is at fairly high elevation above the CapTap. The measurements are strongly influenced by noise, which in turn affects the classification. Apart from improving any applied noise reduction, there are some other options to improve the classification, such as a minimal probability that is required for classification, or a non-uniform handling of the elevation information acquired by capacitive sensors [4].

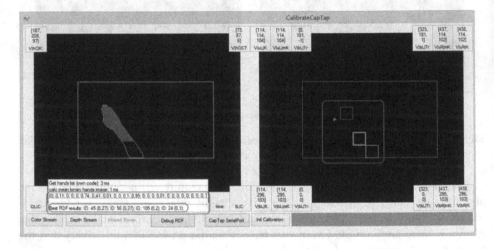

Fig. 6.   Inconclusive classification result with low probabilities for most voxels

A second example is shown in Fig. 7. The classification is slightly more supportive of the bottom voxel, whereas the hand is in fact closer to the blue voxel in the middle. This is an instance where weighted-interpolation will lead to acceptable results of the overall localization process. The upper red and yellow voxels have a smaller probability assigned and would lead to a minimum trend of the detected hand palm position towards this direction.

We evaluated two of the algorithm varieties on two RDFs that were trained using a different set of parameters. Table 1 presents the results of this evaluation. The tracking methods were naïve-center and weighted-interpolation. Using a set of 827 collected samples, two varieties of RDFs were trained. The first uses 100 trees N and 75 % of the samples for training (denoted r in the table). The second uses 50 trees and 66 % of the samples for training. The ratio of correct voxels denotes the ratio of overall classified locations that coincide with the true position voxels within the collected training data.

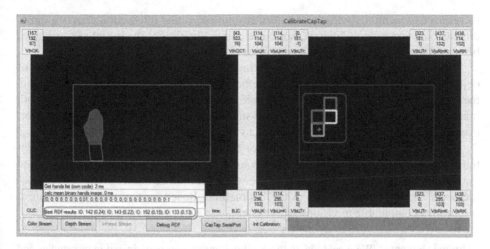

Fig. 7. Classification result suitable for weighted-interpolation with nearby voxels being assigned suitable probabilities.

Table 1. Evaluation results of several algorithm varieties and RDF settings using 827 training and test samples.

Algorithm	RDF parameters	Ratio correct voxels	Average distance error
Naïve-center	N = 100, r = 0.75	27.58 %	4.4 cm
Naïve-center	N = 50, r = 0.66	37.48 %	3.9 cm
Weighted-interpolation	N = 100, r = 0.75	31.13 %	4.2 cm
Weighted-interpolation	N = 50, r = 0.66	47.50 %	2.3 cm

The ratio of correctly classified voxels was comparatively low for both varieties, ranging from 28 % to 48 %. The average distance error was better, whereas the classified hand position was between 2.3 cm and 4.4 cm from the ground truth. In this case the distance is measured from the center of the voxel as collected by the Kinect.

The RDF with a lower number of trees generally performed better than the RDF with a higher number of trees. During the evaluation we could observe that there are is the expected strong correlation of RDF classification probability and voxels close to the training data, even if they often do not fit exactly. Even with a very coarse voxel resolution this creates the opportunity to get a good average distance error of the hand palm from the true position. This finding can be used to optimize the training process in the future, by using suitable interpolation methods.

6   Conclusion and Future Work

In this work we explored the use of RDF classification for the tracking of hands in three dimensions above a large-area interaction devices using capacitive proximity sensors. There are several challenges in using this methods. The number of training samples increases exponentially with the intended resolution, as the interaction area is a three-dimensional space. In addition sensor noise and calibration of the initial sensor values become a challenge in unconstrained conditions.

We have proposed two interpolation methods for improving the localization of objects, based on classification results. An efficient algorithm was developed to calculate the center of the hand palm based on simple computer vision operations on the depth image of a Kinect v2. We evaluated the system and achieve a good localization error, even if the classifier did not find the correct voxel in the majority of the cases.

We would like to use the symmetry of the sensor setup to create more efficient training methods that are performed over a smaller area, but whose results can be used for other areas of the interaction device. We will collect more training data to get measurements at smaller resolutions, using this method. Based on that we can evaluate if resolutions comparable to vision-based systems are achievable.

Acknowledgments. We would like to thank all volunteers that participated in our studies and provided valuable feedback for future iterations. This work was supported by the European Commission under the 7th Framework Programme (Grant Agreement No. 611421).

References

1. Barrett, G., Omote, R.: Projected capacitive touch technology. Inf. Disp. **28**, 16–21 (2010)
2. Braun, A., Hamisu, P.: Designing a multi-purpose capacitive proximity sensing input device. Proc. PETRA (2011). Article No. 15
3. Zimmerman, T.G., Smith, J.R., Paradiso, J.A., Allport, D., Gershenfeld, N.: Applying electric field sensing to human-computer interfaces. In: Proceedings of the CHI, pp. 280–287 (1995)
4. Braun, A., Wichert, R., Kuijper, A., Fellner, D.W.: Capacitive proximity sensing in smart environments. J. Ambient Intell. Smart Environ. **7**, 1–28 (2015)
5. Shotton, J., Fitzgibbon, A., Cook, M., Sharp, T., Finocchio, M., Moore, R., Kipman, A., Blake, A.: Real-time human pose recognition in parts from single depth images. Commun. ACM **56**, 116–124 (2013)
6. Le Goc, M., Taylor, S., Izadi, S., Keskin, C., et al.: A low-cost transparent electric field sensor for 3d interaction on mobile devices. In: Proceedings of the CHI, pp. 3167–3170 (2014)
7. Braun, A., Zander-Walz, S., Krepp, S., Rus, S., Wichert, R., Kuijper, A.: CapTap - combining capacitive gesture recognition and knock detection. Working Paper (2016)
8. Grosse-Puppendahl, T., Berghoefer, Y., Braun, A., Wimmer, R., Kuijper, A.: OpenCapSense: a rapid prototyping toolkit for pervasive interaction using capacitive sensing. In: 2013 IEEE International Conference on Pervasive Computing and Communications, PerCom 2013, pp. 152–159 (2013)
9. Grosse-Puppendahl, T., Braun, A., Kamieth, F., Kuijper, A.: Swiss-cheese extended: an object recognition method for ubiquitous interfaces based on capacitive proximity sensing. In: Proceedings of the CHI, pp. 1401–1410 (2013)
10. Microchip Technology Inc.: GestIC ® Design Guide: Electrodes and System Design MGC3130 (2013)
11. Benko, H., Jota, R., Wilson, A.: Miragetable: freehand interaction on a projected augmented reality tabletop. In: Proceedings of the CHI, pp. 199–208 (2012)
12. Djetz, P., Leigh, D.: DiamondTouch: a multi-user touch technology. In: Proceedings of the UIST, pp. 219–226 (2001)

13. Harrison, C., Schwarz, J., Hudson, S.E.: TapSense: enhancing finger interaction on touch surfaces. In: Proceedings of the UIST, pp. 627–636 (2011)
14. Ren, Z., Meng, J., Yuan, J.: Depth camera based hand gesture recognition and its applications in Human-Computer-Interaction. In: 2011 8th International Conference on Information, Communications and Signal Processing, pp. 1–5 (2011)
15. Sharp, T., Keskin, C., Robertson, D., Taylor, J., Shotton, J., Kim, D., Rhemann, C., Leichter, I., Vinnikov, A., Wei, Y., Freedman, D., Kohli, P., Krupka, E., Fitzgibbon, A., Izadi, S.: Accurate, robust, and flexible real-time hand tracking. In: Proceedings of the 33rd Annual ACM Conference on Human Factors in Computing Systems, pp. 3633–3642. ACM, New York (2015)
16. Breiman, L.: Random forests. Mach. Learn. **45**, 5–32 (2001)
17. Cerezo, F.T.: 3D hand and finger recognition using Kinect. Project report, University of Granada (2011)

Machine Learning and Location Fingerprinting to Improve UX in a Ubiquitous Application

Rainara M. Carvalho[(⊠)], Ismayle S. Santos, Ricardo G. Meira,
Paulo A. Aguilar, and Rossana M.C. Andrade

Group of Computer Networks, Software Engineering and Systems (GREat),
Department of Computer Science, Federal University of Ceará, Fortaleza, Brazil
{rainaracarvalho,ismaylesantos,ricardomeira,
pauloaguilar,rossana}@great.ufc.br

Abstract. GREatPrint is a ubiquitous application that prints documents from mobile devices to the closest printer to the user at the GREat research lab. The first version of the application (GREatPrint V1) was evaluated and showed a low accuracy in the detection of the closest printer. In order to improve the application, this study proposes a new version of GREatPrint (GREatPrint V2) based on a machine learning algorithm and location fingerprinting technique. Therefore, this paper describes GREatPrint V2 with the approach used to improve its context-awareness. Also, it presents results from a case study performed to evaluate the user interaction quality through software quality measures for ubiquitous systems.

Keywords: Ubiquitous application · RSSI Fingerprinting · Machine learning · User experience · Context-awareness · Calmness

1 Introduction

The printing of documents is a daily need of most collaborators who work at enterprises and research labs. This activity is performed only using desktop computers in our research lab, called Group of Computer Network, Software Engineering and System (GREat). Therefore, this task requires users to print only from a workstation, to install printer drivers and to identify the closest printer.

In order to improve this daily activity in our lab, we have developed an ubiquitous application called GREatPrint. This application receives the user's location and prints documents at the nearest printer from him/her, providing a ubiquitous and mobile printing service.

Location-based applications often use GPS sensors. However, these types of sensors are not accurate enough in an indoor environment, therefore we did not use GPS in GREatPrint since it runs inside the GREat lab. For that reason, another solution was required to recover user's indoor position in lab [1].

R.M. Carvalho and I.S. Santos—PhD Scholarship (MDCC/DC/UFC) sponsored by CAPES.
R.M.C. Andrade— Researcher scholarship - DT Level 2, sponsored by CNPq.

We decided to use the Wi-Fi signal strength because it has the advantage of being free of charge and being easily applied in indoor environments [1–3]. Therefore, GREatPrint version 1 used the Wi-Fi network, identifying the strongest as the nearest Wi-Fi source and using this information to decide which printer should be chosen. To do this, firstly, each printer was mapped to its closest Wi-Fi network access point within GREat lab. Then, when users need to print documents, the strongest Wi-Fi signal is used to decide which Wi-Fi network access point is closest to the user and thus associate this information with the closest printer.

This version was evaluated by using specific software measures for HCI in ubiquitous applications, proposed in a previous work [4]. Twelve users were invited to print an example test document through the application in different floors and rooms of the GREat lab, while measures were collected manually and automatically. The results showed that GREatPrint version 1 had a low accuracy in the detection of the correct printer. The reason is because the strongest network not always indicated the closest printer from the user. In this evaluation, the adaptation correctness measure scored at 52 % [4], this value aims to measure how many adaptations happened in an expected way for the user. Also, through questionnaires results, we realized that most users felt the application did not interact correctly and they also reported that the application could not print the document in some places of the lab.

Aiming to improve the context-awareness characteristic in GREatPrint and as a consequence, the user experience, we have decided to use algorithms commonly used with machine learning since they help in making more reasonable decisions [5]. Such algorithms have already been successfully implemented in many adaptive systems [6–8]. Therefore, GREatPrint has evolved to use one of these algorithms, the Multilayer Perceptron [9], together with the fingerprinting technique [10]. In the new GREatPrint version, we replicate the same HCI evaluation which was used in the GREatPrint V1, with twelve new users

In this paper, we describe in details the approach used to improve GREatPrint, which can be reused to develop other ubiquitous application running in indoor environments. We also discuss how the improvements impact in the user experience by collecting the following measures proposed in a previous work [4]: adaptation correctness, adaptation degree, availability degree, number of focus changes, number of failures, context-awareness timing degree, interaction relevancy degree and interaction courtesy degree.

2   Background

2.1   Location Fingerprinting and Multilayer Perceptron

The location fingerprinting technique is an increasingly popular technique for estimating indoor location by using the received signal strength indication (RSSI) [2,10,11]. This technique works in two phases: the calibration phase and the location estimation phase [2,10,11]. In the first phase, a mapping is performed associating the position of the device to its respective access points

(APs) via signal strengths. This procedure is usually performed by a system administrator that walks around the Wi-Fi covered zones collecting the RSSI at equally separated distances, thus creating a map of the location. This map is stored in a database on a web server. The second phase occurs during the application execution to determine the user location. In this phase, the application sends information of the current Wi-Fi signal strengths to the server, which compares this data with the map resulting from the first phase in order to detect the user position. When a match is found, the expected location is returned.

Several proximity-matching algorithms can be used to compare the stored signal strength values to the observed values in order to determine the user location in the fingerprinting technique [10]. In this work, we use the Multilayer Perceptron (MLP) as a proximity-matching algorithm, since it is a useful tool for prediction [9] and also it is suitable for our problem, where a complete location mapping is difficult.

MLP is one type of neural network, which is one of the methods from machine learning area [9]. It consists of multiple layers of nodes (with a minimum of three layers), where every node of a layer is connected (with a weight) to every node from the next layer (See Fig. 1). The MLP has the ability to learn through training, therefore it needs a representative training data set. Once the MLP is trained, it is capable of generalizing with new and unseen data [9].

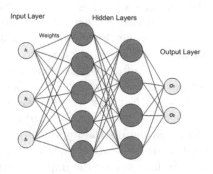

Fig. 1. A multilayer perceptron with four layers. Adapted from [9].

2.2   UX in Ubiquitous Applications

User experience (UX) refers to the users perceptions when they interact with a product in particular conditions [12,13]. According to [13], the user experience can be seen as the totality of user's perceptions regarding to efficiency, effectiveness, emotional satisfaction. However, the ubiquitous computing environment has characteristics that completely change the way users interact with technology, and so impact on the user experience [14]. For example, a ubiquitous system has a context-awareness characteristic, which means that it is capable of collecting contextual data and adapting behavior according to the data [15]. Moreover, these systems can be present in several devices, such as personal computers, smart phones, smart watches and others. Thus, they have the mobility characteristic, what make it possible for the system to be working everywhere and available at any time, as consequence this creates an increased risk that the user will feel disturbed by the system [4].

The work from Carvalho et al. [4] proposes a set of software measures (See Table 1) to evaluate the user interaction with ubiquitous applications regarding to the calmness characteristic. Calmness is the capability of the system to support user activities at the right time and place, delivering the best service possible [16]. We believe calmness has a great impact on user satisfaction and therefore also on both the user experience and acceptance of the ubiquitous application.

Table 1. Software measures for calmness characteristic. Adapted from [4]

Name	Measurement function
Adaptation Degree	$\frac{\sum_{j=1}^{N}(Aj/Bj)*100}{N}$
	Aj=Number of performed adaptations i
	Bj=Number of requested adaptations i
	N=Number of adaptations
Adaptation Correctness	$\frac{\sum_{i=1}^{N}(Ai/Bi)*100}{N}$
	Ai=Number of correctly performed adaptations i
	Bi=Number of performed adaptations i
	N=Number of adaptations
Availability Degree	X = B, where B is the mode of (1) Very Low, (2) Low, (3) Medium and (4) High
Context-awareness Timing Degree	X = B, where B is the mode of (1) Very Low, (2) Low, (3) Medium and (4) High
Number of irrelevant Focus Changes	X = A, where A = Number of actions that changes user's focus during usage of the application
Number of Failures	X = N, where N = Total number of failures have occurred
Relevancy Degree	X = B, where B is the mode of (1) Very Low, (2) Low, (3) Medium and (4) High
Courtesy Degree	X = B, where B is the mode of (1) Very Low, (2) Low, (3) Medium and (4) High

3   GREatPrint

GREatPrint is composed of three programs: GREatPrint Mapper, GREatPrint Server and GREatPrint App. Figure 2 presents an overview for how these programs work together[1]. Two of them (Mapper and App) are android applications

---

[1] Icons from http://www.flaticon.com, http://uxrepo.com and http://www.iconsdb. com/.

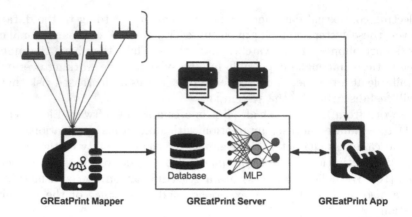

Fig. 2. GREatPrint overview

and the other is a web server (GREatPrint Server). However, only the GREat-Print App is actually used by the end user.

GREatPrint Mapper is used to create a Wi-Fi signal strength map, using six APs from GREat Lab. Also, GREatPrint Mapper is responsible for sending this map to the GREatPrint Server.

GREatPrint Server is responsible for using the Wi-Fi signal strength map to train the MLP in order to decide which printer is closer to the user, saving all information in a database and sending a print job request to the chosen printer.

Finally, GREatPrint App is used by the end user to print a document. To do that, the GREatPrint App collects the actual Wi-Fi signal strength from the same six APs mentioned previously and sends this information to the GREat-Print Server together with the file to be printed.

These three systems are better explained in the next subsections.

3.1   GREatPrint Mapper

This software is deployed as an android application used by the system administrator for performing the calibration phase of the fingerprinting (See Fig. 3(a)). Its main purpose is to perform the "RSSI Mapping" of the building and sending this information to the GREatPrint Server, where it is going to be stored for later use.

GREat Lab has two floors, each of which has one has one public printer; this means anyone can print documents on these printers. Each floor also has three APs. Therefore, for the first phase of fingerprinting, 98 different locations across the two floors in GREat Lab were chosen in order to provide a good coverage of the GREat lab. Figure 3(b) shows 57 locations (as dots) mapped in the second floor.

For every one of these locations, the received signal strength indicator (RSSI) of the six APs were collected. The signal strengths ranges from 0 to -100,

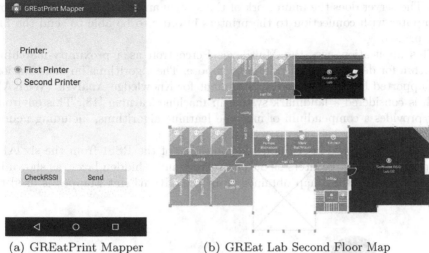

(a) GREatPrint Mapper   (b) GREat Lab Second Floor Map

Fig. 3. The calibration phase

a value closer to 0 indicates a stronger intensity signal. Then, the nearest printer was associated with these RSSIs using the GREAtPrint Mapper (See Fig. 3(a)). Table 2 presents examples of this association. According to this table, if the user is in the position 43, the nearest printer is the printer 1, otherwise if he is in the position 44, the nearest printer is the printer 2. The results of this mapping was then uploaded to the GREatPrint Server to be used to train the MLP.

Table 2. Part of the Wi-Fi mapping in the GREat lab

Location	AP1	AP2	AP3	AP4	AP5	AP6	Nearest Printer
43	-90	-74	-90	-77	-90	-53	printer_1
44	-84	-85	-83	-68	-90	-90	printer_2

It is important to mention that for every location, the measurement was done with the smartphone pointing in four different directions, resulting in 392 measurements in total. Also, three measurements were done for each direction and an average was calculated to get a final value. This approach was suggested in the study from [17], since Wi-Fi signal strength is constantly changing.

3.2 GREatPrint Server

The GREatPrint Server is a java application that utilizes the data obtained by the mapper and can decide which printer to use. It handles the actual sending of a print job request to the printer and informs the current status to the GREAtPrint

App. The server does the main work of the system and needs to be installed on a computer with connection to the printers in order to be able to send the file to be printed.

This application uses the Multilayer Perceptron as a proximity-matching algorithm for deciding which printer to choose. The algorithms implementation was supported by the Waikato Environment for Knowledge Analysis (WEKA), which is considered a landmark system in machine learning [18]. This environment provides a compendium of machine learning algorithms, including neural networks, for researchers and practitioners.

In our system, the MLP model is composed of the RSSI from the six APs as input vectors, two printers as output vectors and 1 hidden layer, as shown in Fig. 4. Thus, the RSSI map obtained from the GREatPrint Mapper is used to training the MLP.

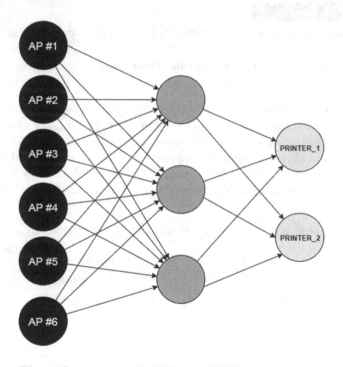

Fig. 4. Our generated MLP using WEKA environment

3.3 GREatPrint App

This is an android app that the end user is able to use. The application works as follows (Fig. 5): (i) after selecting a file, (ii) the user click on the print button of the given document, and the application collects the six Wi-Fi networks previously selected in the fingerprinting phase. (iii) The application sends the document to the server. (iv) based on the GREatPrint Server response, GREat-Print App notifies the user where the file has been printed or if it was not possible to print the file. Alternatively users can open GreatPrint application within the document itself.

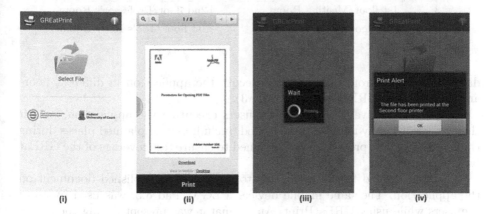

Fig. 5. GREatPrint App

4   Case Study

We used the measures presented in Table 1 to perform the evaluation of GREat-Print V2. This model was also used to evaluate the first version of the application, which makes it possible to compare the two versions. However, we used differ-ent users to evaluate the new application version, since we have realized that use of the old users could impact on the results of the evaluation, due to them having a preconception and prior knowledge in relation to the application. Also, the evaluation of the first version was performed to collect the user perception about the first version, which as a consequence gave us the need for improve-ment. Thus, twelve different users were invited to participate in the evaluation of GREatPrint V2.

Half of the users are not from a computer science background. They were selected from people working in Administrative, Financial and Human Resource roles. The other half are from computer science, one of them is a PhD student and another is a masters degree student. It should be noted that all users have experience with smart phones and all of them had previously used location-based applications.

4.1   Planning

Users were asked to only use the application inside the GREat research lab, because GREatPrint was targeted for this environment. All twelve users were

Table 3. Procedure to GREatPrint evaluation

Group	Floors and Places	
1	1st floor/Seminars Room	2nd floor/ Research Room
2	2nd floor/Administration Room 2	1st floor/Reception
3	1st floor/Meeting Room	2nd floor/Professor's Room
4	2nd floor/Lobby - Elevator	1st floor/Tools R&D Room

divided into four groups of three to execute the application in different floors and rooms of the GREat lab (See Table 3).

Although we have a procedure for users executing the application, we left them to use it in any manner they desired, including in unplanned places during the evaluation. The procedure was designed to ensure test coverage of the GREat building.

The task defined to the users, was to print a pre-established document on the application. The same mobile device, a LG G Pad 8.3, was used by all of the users while using GREatPrint. An evaluator was present during the usage, noting, for example, if the captured context was correct, if the application failed, among other observations. After the usage, users were asked to answer a user questionnaire.

To collect the measures of adaptation degree and adaptation correctness degree, which are presented in Table 1. We first identified the adaptation considered by GREatPrint, discovering it presents one adaptation (N=1). This is the choice of the printer according to users location. For this purpose, the system identifies the location of a user by collecting the RSSI of six APs. With this input, GREatPrint updates with the location of the nearest printer.

The data needed to compute the measures were collected both automatically and manually. Automatic data were recorded in logs that contain: the RSSI of the six APs, the chosen printer, failures and the time that they happened. Manual data was collected in forms filled in by evaluators, whom followed users around during the applications usage, observing if the application worked correctly, or in other words, identifying if the system performed a correct adaptation with correct information. There are some measures (Availability Degree, Context-Awareness Timing Degree, Relevancy Degree and Courtesy Degree) that were collected by a user questionnaire after using the application[2].

4.2   Results

Table 4 presents the results for both version 1 and version 2 of the application, for purpose of comparison. The results show that the new version of GREatPrint achieved better results than version 1.

---

[2] Details in http://www.great.ufc.br/maximum/images/arquivos/userquestionnaire.pdf.

The following measures: Adaptation Degree, Adaptation Correctness Degree, Number of focus changes and Number of failures were calculated by the sum of all user tours. The remaining measures (Availability Degree, Context-Awareness Timing Degree, Relevancy Degree and Courtesy Degree) were calculated with modal values derived from the questionnaire answers.

Table 4. Results of the HCI evaluation of both GREAtPrint versions

Measure	Version 1	Version 2
Adaptation Degree	79 %	93 %
Adaptation Correctness Degree	52 %	73 %
Availability Degree	Medium	High
Context-awareness Timing Degree	Medium	High
Number of focus changes	15 actions	2 actions
Number of Failures	33 failures	2 failures
Relevancy Degree	High	High
Courtesy Degree	High	High

4.3 Discussion

Measures about context-awareness adaptations (Adaptation Degree and Adaptation Correctness Degree) had high results. They increased by 14 % and 21 %, respectively. Also, we can see that the measures collected by interviewing the users (Availability Degree and Context-Awareness Timing Degree) increased to High. We could see an improvement in "Number of focus changes" and "Number of failures", since they decreased in comparison to version 1.

The adaptation degree shows that GREatPrint version 2 works in more places than GREatPrint version 1. For example, in version 1, it was not possible to print in places like "Lobby - Elevator" and "Professors Room", because these places sometimes did not reach any known mapped Wi-Fi network. This new approach is more generic and it is able to make decisions even if some Wi-Fi networks are not available.

The results of the Availability Degree confirmed that the application worked in most places that the users wanted to use it. Most users answered "High" in regards to the availability degree.

The Adaptation Correctness Degree Measure increased to 73 %. Even though this result is not yet deemed suitable, it has improved a lot in comparison to version 1. We analysed why some users got wrong adaptations in GREatPrint version 1, and realized that the strongest network does not always indicate the closest printer to the user, for example Professors Room, reached better the second floor APs, and vice versa. With the new approach (location fingerprinting and MLP), GREatPrint does not only take into account a single network with the strongest signal, but considers signal values of six APs together with the fact that the MLP can generalize to previously unseen input data.

Moreover, we analysed why GREatPrint version 2 also got wrong adaptations. This was primarily because one Wi-Fi network changed in name. The name change meant that our algorithm was not capable to recognizing and using that corresponding AP signal, causing a strong chance of wrong adaptations, depending on where the user was. This is a limitation from working with RSSI location fingerprinting, if the AP name changes, the application needs to update too.

Although the result for adaptation correctness is not yet considered suitable, the "Context-awareness Timing Degree" improved to "High", which show most users felt that the application now recognizes reliably the users context.

It is also important to mention that this approach (RSSI location fingerprinting and MLP) can be reused in other indoor environments. For such a purpose the approach needs to be tailored to the specific environment. For example, an environment may have more printers and more APs. Thus, it is would be necessary to change the GREatPrint Mapper to collect these APs and add the new printers. The GREatPrint Server would then use this new data to add these new values into the MLP.

5   Conclusion and Future Work

This paper presented the use of machine learning and location fingerprinting to improve a ubiquitous system called GREatPrint. This new approach was implemented because GREatPrint version 1 did not obtain suitable results in an evaluation based on software measurement. GREatPrint version 2 behaved more appropriately since the new approach (RSSI location fingerprinting and MLP) has improved the context-awareness. As a consequence, we observed that the user experience for GREatPrint also has improved with the version 2.

The perspective for future work and improvement to this existing work, is to create a more generic GREatPrint, capable of being deployed in any environment without any extra coding to define the environment. New strategies to help automate the RSSI mapping step would also prove to be very useful. Finally, a comparison with other algorithms commonly used with machine learning and other indoor location techniques could be incorporated to improve the overall context-awareness.

Acknowledgments. We would like to thank the CTQS/GREat team for the technical support for this work and also to the CAcTUS - ContextAwareness Testing for Ubiquitous Systems project supported by CNPq (MCT/CNPq 14/2013 - Universal) under grant number 484380/2013-3.

References

1. Ladd, A.M., Bekris, K.E., Rudys, A.P., Wallach, D.S., Kavraki, L.E.: On the feasibility of using wireless ethernet for indoor localization. IEEE Trans. Robot. Autom. **20**(3), 555–559 (2004)

2. Quan, M., Navarro, E., Peuker, B.: Wi-Fi Localization Using RSSI Fingerprinting (2010)
3. Luo, Y., Hoeber, O., Chen, Y.: Enhancing Wi-Fi fingerprinting for indoor positioning using human-centric collaborative feedback. Hum.-Centric Comput. Inf. Sci. **3**(1), 1–23 (2013)
4. Carvalho, R.M., Andrade, R.M.C., Oliveira, K.M.: Using the GQM method to evaluate calmness in ubiquitous applications. In: Streitz, N., Markopoulos, P. (eds.) DAPI 2015. LNCS, vol. 9189, pp. 13–24. Springer, Heidelberg (2015)
5. Jain, A.K., Duin, R.P., Mao, J.: Statistical pattern recognition: a review. IEEE Trans. Pattern Anal. Mach. Intell. **22**(1), 4–37 (2000)
6. Linden, G., Smith, B., York, J.: Amazon.com recommendations: item-to-item collaborative filtering. IEEE Internet Comput. **7**(1), 76–80 (2003)
7. Bennett, J., Lanning, S.: The netflix prize. In: Proceedings of KDD cup and workshop (2007)
8. Langley, P.: Machine learning for adaptive user interfaces. In: Brewka, G., Habel, C., Nebel, B. (eds.) KI 1997. LNCS, vol. 1303, pp. 53–62. Springer, Heidelberg (1997)
9. Gardner, M.W., Dorling, S.R.: Artificial neural networks (the multilayer perceptron) a review of applications in the atmospheric sciences. Atmos. Environ. **32**(14), 2627–2636 (1998)
10. Taheri, A., Singh, A., Emmanuel, A.: Location fingerprinting on infrastructure 802.11 Wireless Local Area Networks (WLANs) using Locus. In: 29th Annual IEEE International Conference on Local Computer Networks, pp. 676–683 (2004)
11. Honkavirta, V., Perälä, T., Ali-Löytty, S., Piché, R.: Location fingerprinting methods in wireless local area networks. Master of Science Thesis. Tampere University of Technology, Finland (2008)
12. Arhippainen, L., Thti, M.: Empirical evaluation of user experience in two adaptive mobile application prototypes. In: Proceedings of the 2nd international conference on mobile and ubiquitous multimedia, pp. 27–34 (2003)
13. Kuniavsky, M.: Smart Things: Ubiquitous Computing User Experience Design. Elsevier, Amsterdam (2010)
14. Santos, R.M., de Oliveira, K.M., Andrade, R.M.C., Santos, I.S., Lima, E.R.: A quality model for human-computer interaction evaluation in ubiquitous systems. In: Collazos, C., Liborio, A., Rusu, C. (eds.) CLIHC 2013. LNCS, vol. 8278, pp. 63–70. Springer, Heidelberg (2013)
15. Ranganathan, A., Al-Muhtadi, J., Biehl, J., Ziebart, B., Campbell, R.H., Bailey, B.: Towards a pervasive computing benchmark. In: Pervasive Computing and Communications Workshops, PerCom (2005)
16. Riekki, J., Isomursu, P., Isomursu, M.: Evaluating the calmness of ubiquitous applications. In: Bomarius, F., Iida, H. (eds.) PROFES 2004. LNCS, vol. 3009, pp. 105–119. Springer, Heidelberg (2004)
17. Shala, U., Rodriguez, A.: Indoor Positioning Using Sensor-Fusion in Android Devices. M.Sc. Thesis. School of Health and Society, Department Computer Science, Kristianstad University, Kristianstad, Sweden, September 2011
18. Hall, M., Frank, E., Holmes, G., Pfahringer, B., Reutemann, P., Witten, I.H.: The WEKA data mining software: an update. ACM SIGKDD Explor. Newsl. **11**(1), 10–18 (2009)

Exploring the Ergonomic Issues of User-Defined Mid-Air Gestures for Interactive Product Exhibition

Li-Chieh Chen[1(✉)], Po-Ying Chu[1], and Yun-Maw Cheng[2]

[1] Department of Industrial Design, Tatung University, Taipei, Taiwan
{lcchen, juby}@ttu.edu.tw
[2] Department of Computer Science and Engineering,
Graduate Institute of Design Science, Tatung University, Taipei, Taiwan
kevin@ttu.edu.tw

Abstract. Recently, the applications of 3D and mid-air hand gestures have increased significantly in public and interactive display systems. Due to the context and user differences, it is necessary to consider user-defined gestures at the design stage of the system development. However, user-defined gestures may not be able to conform to the requirements of ergonomics without in-depth studies and careful selection. Therefore, the objective of this research is to develop a systematic method for extraction and evaluation of user-defined gestures from ergonomic perspectives. In this research, a behavior coding scheme was developed to analyze gestures for six tasks of interactive product exhibition. The results indicated that hand dorsiflexion caused by the posture of opening palm and facing forward was the common ergonomic issue identified from user-defined gestures. In order to reduce discomfort of prolonged gesture controls, the alternative combinations of gestures for accomplishing these tasks was determined based on ergonomic limitations and the considerations of vision-based hand gesture recognitions.

Keywords: Mid-air gesture · User-defined gesture · Ergonomic issues

1 Introduction

In the approach of developing mid-air hand gestures based on user-defined gestures, many factors should be considered while selecting the right set of gestures for a group of tasks. These factors include the complexity and the ergonomics of a single gesture, the occlusions among fingers, the natural mapping or compatibility among tasks and gestures, the differentiation among gestures for different tasks, and the repetition of pose or motion among gestures. Since the participants of gesture elicitation experiments may not have the knowledge about ergonomics, gestures with high acceptability still need to be analyzed carefully to avoid cumulative disorder after repetitive hand poses or motions. Therefore, the objective of this research is to explore possible ergonomic issues and to develop a systematic method of behavior analysis and gesture evaluation.

© Springer International Publishing Switzerland 2016
N. Streitz and P. Markopoulos (Eds.): DAPI 2016, LNCS 9749, pp. 180–190, 2016.
DOI: 10.1007/978-3-319-39862-4_17

2 Literature Review

Since mid-air hand gesture controls are natural, intuitive and sanitary [1–3], the number of applications have increased significantly. The contexts include interactive navigation systems in museum [4], surgical imaging system [1, 2], interactive public display [5], and 3D modelling [6]. Based on the number and trajectory of hands, mid-air gestures could be classified as one or two hands, linear or circular movements, and different degrees of freedom in path (1D, 2D, or 3D) [7]. If the context is not considered, mid-air gestures could be pointing, semaphoric, pantomimic, iconic, and manipulation [8]. The types of control tasks could be select, release, accept, refuse, remove, cancel, navigate, identify, translate, and rotate [8]. Since the characteristics of context could influence gesture vocabulary [9], the gestures for short-range human computer interaction [10] and TV controls [11, 12] were reported to be different. While choosing a set of intuitive mid-air gestures for a specific group of tasks, it is necessary to consider and analyze the ergonomic problems of user-defined gestures.

3 Experiment

In order to explore the ergonomic issues of mid-air hand gestures, a pilot experiment was carried out. In product design education, studying the features of classic products and analyzing the evolution are the common and basic training. Therefore, the authors considered the context of an interactive exhibition system for product evolution demonstration. The digital information contents of such a system could be decomposed into two levels of abstraction. In the overview level, the images of representative products across different stages of a timeline were displayed with a tile menu (Fig. 1). In the product information level, the detailed image of a specific product on the timeline was displayed. The users could access the detail level through the link of menu item shown on the overview level. In these levels, participants performed user-defined gestures for a set of tasks, including (1) moving the main menu panel to left/right (in order to reveal hidden items); (2) targeting an item on the main menu; (3) confirming the selection of a menu item; (4) zooming (enlarging/shrinking) the image of a product; (5) panning the image of a product; and (6) returning to the main menu.

In a laboratory with illumination control, each participant stood on the spot in front of a 50-in. TV, with a distance of 200 cm. During the experiments, the images simulating the tile menu of product information were displayed on the TV, which was controlled by a laptop computer with a computer mouse. In order to obtain gesture characteristics, the motions of the body and hand joints were recorded by one overhead camera and two 3D depth cameras. Each participant conducted two trials of experiments to offer self-defined gestures. In the first trial, a Microsoft Kinect for Windows (v2) sensor was mounted on the top of the TV. The sensor could extract 25 joints per person. The motion of the arms and hands was recorded by the Kinect Studio program running on a desktop computer. The images of body tracking were displayed on a 23-in. monitor, which was placed on the right hand side of the TV. In the second trial, an Intel RealSense 3D Camera (F200) was used to extract the position and orientation of 22 joints on a hand. It was placed between the participant and the TV. The distance

Fig. 1. Experiment setup

to the participant was adjusted with respect to the arm length. The height was adjusted to the shoulder height of each participant. The motion of each hand gesture was recorded by the Hands Viewer program. The program was running on a laptop computer with a 15-in. display, which was placed on the lower right hand side of the TV. Therefore, each participant performed the tasks of user-defined gestures by facing two 3D depth cameras with different distances. In addition, offering different gestures between two trials was encouraged.

4   Results and Discussions

Twenty students, majored in the Master Program of Industrial Design, were invited to participate in the experiment. From two trials of user-defined gestures, forty gestures were recorded. For the task of moving the main menu panel to left/right, seven different gestures were identified (Table 1). The second-ranked gesture (M-02), i.e. opening palm, facing forward and moving to right/left, seemed to be easier to be recognized by a 3D depth sensor. However, hand dorsiflexion might introduce discomfort after prolonged posture of opening palm and facing forward. Although the first-ranked gesture (M-01), i.e. one hand with open palm facing and swiping to right/left, might be more difficult for recognition by 3D sensors, is was the dominant gesture offered by more participants. However, swipe motion was not appropriate for controlling the precise movement of a tile menu continuously. Therefore, stepwise movements for each column of a tile menu would be the necessary response for swipe motions.

For the task of targeting an item on the main menu, one hand with D handshape (American Sign Language, ASL) and a single tap motion, facing to the target, was the most popular gesture (T-01) (Table 2). For the task of confirming the selection of an

Table 1. Moving the main menu panel to left/right

Type	No. of hands	Hand pose transition and orientation	Hand motion and trajectory	Trial-1 count	Trial-2 count
M-01	1	Open palm, facing right/left	Swipe to right/left	13	10
M-02	1	Open palm, facing forward	Move to right/left	4	3
M-03	2	Open palm, facing right/left	Left hand swipe from right to left; Right hand swipe from left to right	2	0
M-04	2	Open palm, facing right/left	Left hand swipe from body center to left; Right hand swipe from body center to right	1	1
M-05	1	D handshape (ASL), facing forward	Move to right/left	0	4
M-06	1	U handshape (ASL), facing forward	Move to right/left	0	1
M-07	1	D handshape (ASL), facing forward	Double tap at the first position then move and double tap at the second position	0	1

item on the main menu, one hand with D handshape and a double tap motion was the most popular gesture (C-01) (Table 3). Single and double tapping with D handshape seemed to be the legacy gestures on touchscreens. However, tapping toward the target from a distance and in the air remained a great challenge for gesture recognition.

For the task of zooming (enlarging/shrinking) the image of a product, two hands with open palm were the popular hand poses (Table 4). However, there were no significant differences in the frequencies about the hand orientations, i.e. facing forward (Z-01) or facing to each other (Z-02). Similarly, there were no significant differences in the frequencies about hand motions and trajectories, i.e., moving or swipe apart/close to each other. Since "zooming" was a continuous control that required precise movement, swipe motion was not appropriate. One the other hand, open palm and face forward (Z-01, Z-03, and Z04) resulted in hand dorsiflexion. Therefore, alternative gestures, such as Z-05 and Z-10, could be considered (Fig. 2).

For the task of panning the image of a product, open palm and face forward was still the most popular hand pose. In order to avoid hand dorsiflexion (P-01 or P-03) and

Table 2. Targeting an item on the main menu

Type	No. of hands	Hand pose transition and orientation	Hand motion and trajectory	Trial-1 count	Trial-2 count
T-01	1	D handshape (ASL), facing to the target	Single tap, move forward then stop	9	8
T-02	1	Open palm then grab, facing to the target	Move forward then backward quickly	4	3
T-03	1	Open palm then push, facing to the target	Move forward then stop	3	3
T-04	1	Open palm, facing to the target	Pat, move forward then backward quickly	1	0
T-05	1	D handshape (ASL), index finger pointing directly to the target	Single tap, move forward then stop	1	0
T-06	1	D handshape (ASL), pointing to the target	Move circularly around the target	1	0
T-07	1	Open palm then pinch, facing to the target	Move forward then stop	1	0
T-08	1	D handshape (ASL), facing to the target	Double tap, move forward then backward twice quickly	0	2
T-09	1	U handshape (ASL), facing to the target	Single tap, move forward then backward quickly	0	1
T-10	1	U handshape (ASL), facing to the target	Double tap, move forward then backward twice quickly	0	1
T-11	1	Open palm followed by pushing and grabbing, facing to the target	Move forward while pushing then backward while grabbing	0	1
T-12	2	First hand in D handshape (ASL) pointing to the target, second hand open palm then grab	First hand moves circularly around the target twice, second hand grabs for confirmation	0	1

gestures similar to aforementioned tasks (P-02 or P-05), "open palm then grab and move to desired direction while grabbing" (P-04) had the benefits of avoiding static hand pose and could be the alternative gesture (Table 5).

For the task of returning to the main menu, the most dominant hand pose and orientation was D handshape (ASL), facing toward the return button. The hand motion

Table 3. Confirming the selection of a menu item

Type	No. of hands	Hand pose transition and orientation	Hand motion and trajectory	Trial-1 count	Trial-2 count
C-01	1	D handshape (ASL), facing forward	Double tap, move forward then backward twice quickly	11	10
C-02	1	Open palm, facing to the target	Pat twice, move forward then backward twice quickly	3	1
C-03	1	D handshape (ASL), facing forward	Single tap, move forward then stop	3	3
C-04	1	Open palm then push, facing to the target	Move forward then stop	2	1
C-05	1	Fist then gradually open, facing to the target	Stay still in the air	1	1
C-06	1	U handshape (ASL), facing to the target	Double tap, move forward then backward twice quickly	0	1
C-07	1	Open palm followed by pushing twice and grabbing, facing to the target	Move forward while pushing then backward while grabbing	0	1
C-08	1	Open palm followed by pushing and grabbing, facing to the target	Move forward while pushing then backward while grabbing	0	1
C-09	2	First hand in D handshape (ASL) pointing to the target, second hand open palm then grab	First hand moves circularly around the target twice, second hand grabs for confirmation	0	1

and trajectory was single tapping, moving toward the direction of the return button (R-01). However, this gesture was similar to the most popular gesture of targeting an item on the main menu. In addition, one hand with open palm facing and swiping to right/left (R-02) was similar to the most popular gesture of moving the main menu panel to left/right. Therefore, pinching (R-03) or patting twice (R-04) toward the return button had the benefits of avoiding static hand pose and seemed to be alternative options (Table 6).

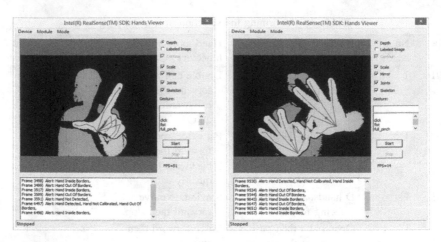

Fig. 2. Alternative gestures for zooming (Z-05 and Z-10) (Taken from Intel RealSense F200 3D Camera and the Hands Viewer Program).

Table 4. Zooming (enlarging/shrinking) the image of a product

Type	No. of hands	Hand pose transition and orientation	Hand motion and trajectory	Trial-1 count	Trial-2 count
Z-01	2	Open palm, facing forward	Move apart/close to each other	7	2
Z-02	2	Open palm, facing to each other	Swipe apart/close to each other	4	4
Z-03	1	Open palm then close (or close then open), facing forward	Stay still in the air	2	1
Z-04	1	Open palm then gradually fist (or fist then gradually open), facing forward	Stay still in the air	2	4
Z-05	1	L handshape (ASL), thumb and index finger moving apart/close to each other	Stay still in the air	2	4
Z-06	1	Open then pinch (or pinch then open), facing forward	Stay still in the air	1	1
Z-07	2	Open palm, facing forward	Left hand stays still, right hand moves forward or backward	1	0
Z-08	2		Move apart/close to each other	1	1

(Continued)

Table 4. (*Continued*)

Type	No. of hands	Hand pose transition and orientation	Hand motion and trajectory	Trial-1 count	Trial-2 count
		D handshape (ASL), Index fingers pointing forward			
Z-09	2	Open palm then pinch (or pinch then open), facing forward	Move apart/close to each other	0	1
Z-10	2	"Ru" handshape (Japanese Sign Language), facing forward	Move apart/close to each other	0	2

Table 5. Panning the image of a product

Type	No. of hands	Hand pose transition and orientation	Hand motion and trajectory	Trial-1 count	Trial-2 count
P-01	1	Open palm, facing forward	Move to desired direction	8	5
P-02	1	D handshape (ASL), facing forward	Single tap, move forward while tapping and then move to desired direction	4	7
P-03	1	Open palm, facing forward	Push, move forward while pushing and then move to desired direction	3	0
P-04	1	Open palm then grab, facing forward	Move to desired direction while grabbing	3	1
P-05	1	Open palm, facing to left (or right)	Swipe slowly to desired direction	1	3
P-06	2	Open palm, facing forward	Move parallel to the desired direction	1	0
P-07	1	Open palm then pinch, facing forward	Move to desired direction while pinching	0	1
P-08	1	"Ru" handshape (Japanese Sign Language), facing forward	Move to desired direction	0	1
P-09	1		Move to desired direction	0	1

(*Continued*)

Table 5. (*Continued*)

Type	No. of hands	Hand pose transition and orientation	Hand motion and trajectory	Trial-1 count	Trial-2 count
		U handshape (ASL), facing to the target			
P-10	2	D handshape (ASL), pointing forward	One hand stays still, the other hand move to desired direction	0	1

Table 6. Returning to the main menu

Type	No. of hands	Hand pose transition and orientation	Hand motion and trajectory	Trial-1 count	Trial-2 count
R-01	1	D handshape (ASL), facing toward the return button	Single tap, move toward the direction of the return button	8	7
R-02	1	Open palm, facing to left (or right)	Swipe from left to right (or from right to left)	4	1
R-03	1	Open palm then pinch, facing toward the return button	Pinch, move toward the direction of the return button	2	0
R-04	1	Open palm, facing toward the return button	Pat twice, move forward then backward twice quickly in the direction toward the return button	2	0
R-05	1	Open palm, facing forward	Swipe from right to left	1	2
R-06	1	Open palm, facing forward	Push, move forward while pushing and then swiping to right	1	1
R-07	1	Open palm, facing toward the return button	Push then move toward the direction of the return button	1	0
R-08	1	D handshape (ASL), facing toward the return button	Double tap, move forward then backward twice quickly in the direction toward the return button	1	1
R-09	1	D handshape (ASL), facing forward	Move to upper left or upper right direction quickly	0	2

(*Continued*)

Table 6. (*Continued*)

Type	No. of hands	Hand pose transition and orientation	Hand motion and trajectory	Trial-1 count	Trial-2 count
R-10	1	Open palm, facing forward	Push, move forward while pushing	0	1
R-11	1	Open palm then grab, facing to the target	Move forward then backward quickly while grabbing	0	1
R-12	1	Open palm then grab, facing to the target	Move to upper left or upper right direction quickly while grabbing	0	1
R-13	1	Open palm, facing down	Swipe down	0	1
R-14	2	First hand in V handshape (ASL), facing forward, second hand grab	First hand swipe to left/right then second hand grab to confirm	0	1

5 Conclusion

In this research, a systematic behavior coding scheme was developed to analyze user-defined gestures for six tasks of interactive product exhibition. The results indicated that hand dorsiflexion caused by the posture of opening palm and facing forward was the common ergonomic issue. In order to reduce discomfort of prolonged gesture controls, the alternative combinations of gestures for accomplishing these tasks was determined based on ergonomic limitations and the considerations of vision-based hand gesture recognitions.

Acknowledgement. The authors would like to express our gratitude to the Ministry of Science and Technology of the Republic of China for financially supporting this research under Grant No. MOST 104-2221-E-036-020.

References

1. O'Hara, K., Gonzalez, G., Sellen, A., Penney, G., Varnavas, A., Mentis, H., Criminisi, A., Corish, R., Rouncefield, M., Dastur, N., Carrell, T.: Touchless interaction in surgery. Commun. ACM **57**(1), 70–77 (2014)
2. Rosa, G.M., Elizondo, M.L.: Use of a gesture user interface as a touchless image navigation system in dental surgery: case series report. Imaging Sci. Dent. **44**, 155–160 (2014)
3. Hettig, J., Mewes, A., Riabikin, O., Skalej, M., Preim, B., Hansen, C.: Exploration of 3D medical image data for interventional radiology using myoelectric gesture control. In: Eurographics Workshop on Visual Computing for Biology and Medicine (2015)

4. Hsu, F.S., Lin, W.Y.: A multimedia presentation system using a 3D gesture interface in museums. Multimedia Tools Appl. **69**(1), 53–77 (2014)
5. Ackad, C., Clayphan, A., Tomitsch, M., Kay, J.: An in-the-wild study of learning mid-air gestures to browse hierarchical information at a large interactive public display. In: UBICOMP 2015, 7–11 September 2015, Osaka, Japan (2015)
6. Vinayak, Ramani, K.: A gesture-free geometric approach for mid-air expression of design intent in 3D virtual pottery. Comput. Aided Des. **69**(2015), 11–24 (2015)
7. Nancel, M., Wagner, J., Pietriga, E., Chapuis, O., Mackay, W.: Mid-air pan-and-zoom on wall-sized displays. In: CHI 2011: Proceedings of the SIGCHI Conference on Human Factors and Computing Systems, pp. 177–186, May 2011, Vancouver, Canada (2011)
8. Aigner, R., Wigdor, D., Benko, H., Haller, M., Lindbauer, D., Ion, A., Zhao, S., Koh, J.T.K.V.: Understanding mid-air hand gestures: a study of human preferences in usage of gesture types for HCI. Microsoft Research Technical Report MSR-TR-2012-111 (2012). http://research.microsoft.com/apps/pubs/default.aspx?id=175454
9. LaViola Jr., J.J.: 3D gestural interaction: the state of the field. ISRN Artif. Intell. **2013** (514641) (2013)
10. Pereira, A., Wachs, J.P., Park, K., Rempel, D.: A user-developed 3-D hand gesture set for human–computer interaction. Hum. Factors **57**(4), 607–621 (2015)
11. Choi, E., Kim, H., Chung, M.K.: A taxonomy and notation method for three-dimensional hand gestures. Int. J. Ind. Ergon. **44**(1), 171–188 (2014)
12. Pisharady, P.K., Saerbeck, M.: Recent methods and databases in vision-based hand gesture recognition: a review. Comput. Vis. Image Underst. **141**, 152–165 (2015). Pose & Gesture

Facial Tracking-Assisted Hand Pointing Technique for Wall-Sized Displays

Haokan Cheng[✉], Takahashi Shin, and Jiro Tanaka

University of Tsukuba, 1-1-1 Tennodai, Tsukuba, Ibaraki 305-8573, Japan
haokan@iplab.cs.tsukuba.ac.jp, {shin,jiro}@cs.tsukuba.ac.jp

Abstract. In this paper we propose a novel pointing technique leveraging the user's body motion to achieve smooth, efficient user experiences on wall-sized displays. Our proposal substantially consists of two parts: a graphical cursor controlled by the user's hand motions, and mechanisms to assist the cursor manipulation by tracking the user's face orientation. By interaction design associating the user's face and hand motions to different aspects of the cursor's movement, we aimed to bring swiftness to the interaction in large-display environments with necessary precision. A prototype was built to instantiate the concept, and two comparative experiments were conducted to evaluate the effectiveness of the proposal.

Keywords: Facial tracking · Input method · Pointing technique · Wall-sized display

1 Introduction

With decades of technological development, displays are becoming less expensive and more scalable in size, and this trend has stimulated the use of wall-sized displays (WSDs) as interactive spaces. Interactive tasks on a WSD involve basic manipulations, such as selecting and moving on-screen data representations (*e.g.,* icons, buttons, and other graphical user interface (GUI) elements), which are also common on smaller desktop or mobile displays. However, the increased amount and density of data potentially affect the task efficiency. In addition, large displays enable users to use various body parts (*e.g.,* head, hands, and feet) to control GUI elements on WSDs. In this study, we leveraged the user's face and hand motions to improve the pointing efficiency on WSDs. We focused on vertical WSDs so that the user can take full advantage of the large interactive space and the user's body, and used a conventional GUI cursor to achieve our design goal.

2 Related Work

Numerous studies have examined the means to improve the efficiency of pointing techniques. Some research has focused on optimizing the performance of conventional GUI cursors. Ninja Cursor [5] and Rake Cursor [6], for example, use multiple cursors to

© Springer International Publishing Switzerland 2016
N. Streitz and P. Markopoulos (Eds.): DAPI 2016, LNCS 9749, pp. 191–201, 2016.
DOI: 10.1007/978-3-319-39862-4_18

enhance the selection performance of the cursor. Multiple pointers have been used to reduce the actual distance the pointer must move, hence to improve the pointing efficiency. While sharing the same idea of shortening the cursor-to-target distance to improve the performance, we used a single cursor approach in our study.

Several research teams have also applied interaction techniques specifically designed for WSDs. Nakanishi et al. used facial tracking for manipulation on large and multiple displays [2, 3]. Nancel et al. [10] investigated multimodal, mid-air pointing techniques on very large displays, discussed on the unique requirements of pointing techniques on WSDs and provided solutions. Vogel and Balakrisham [4] developed a hand pointing technique for very large and high resolution displays. The idea of switching between direct and indirect pointing in this work inspired our interactive design. Liu et al. [9] investigated how screen size and data density would impact manipulation performance in their data classification task on a very large display. On the other hand, we strove to boost the performance by enhancing existing methods while maintaining the intuitiveness.

The use of eyes as an input source has long been discussed because of its intuitiveness and instantaneity. Many studies like ceCursor [7] worked on lever-aging gaze behaviors in GUI cursor manipulation. On the other hand, implementation of gaze-based pointing suffers from accuracy issues. Furthermore, it is difficult to use a perceptual device, such as the human eye, for direct manipulation while ensuring user comfort. Report from MacKenzie [8] comprehensively discussed problems in using eyes as input devices. Zhai et al. [1] provided an early concept of using eye gaze as an auxiliary means of controlling a GUI cursor and instantiated it with eye-tracking technology. The proposal technique to be introduced in this paper leveraged the user's gaze behavior in a less precision-demanding manner.

3   The Design of Facial Tracking-Assisted Hand Pointing

A typical GUI pointing task performed by a user can be divided into two steps: 'Focus' and 'Action'. In the Focus step, users quickly glance over the screen space and find the target to be manipulated; then, they perform the manipulation in the Action step. This division can be applied to conditions with displays of various sizes, yet has unique importance on a WSD compared with smaller desktop/mobile screens. Specifically, while the actual cursor movement happens in the Action step for both conditions, it takes considerably longer to finish the Focus step on larger displays due to the increased screen size, and also the Action step due to the greater cursor movement distance, all of which have an impact on the overall performance.

Our pointing technique consists of two operations, corresponding to the two steps mentioned above, as shown in Fig. 1. The user (1) orients his/her face onto the target, and then (2) moves his/her hand, which is associated with the cursor's movement, to adjust the cursor's position. Part of the cursor's movement is associated with the face orientation; by doing this, some of the cursor movement occurs during the Focus step, parallelizing the two steps to shorten the overall task time. In the following, we explain the details of our pointing technique.

3.1   The Role of the User's Face Orientation

To find the manipulation target (GUI element) on a WSD, the user needs to confirm the target's position visually, often by rotating his/her head due to the huge screen size. Therefore, the position of the user's intended target can be roughly, yet easily, estimated by tracking his/her face orientation. The estimated position is then used to shorten the distance between the cursor and the intended target.

In our proposed technique, we provide a manipulation window - a visible rectangular 'Frame' on the screen that follows the user's face orientation (Fig. 1(b)). This Frame represents the estimated manipulation area around the target position, in which the cursor can be moved in a manner similar to a conventional mouse pointer. The movements of the cursor and Frame are independent to each other when no contact occurs.

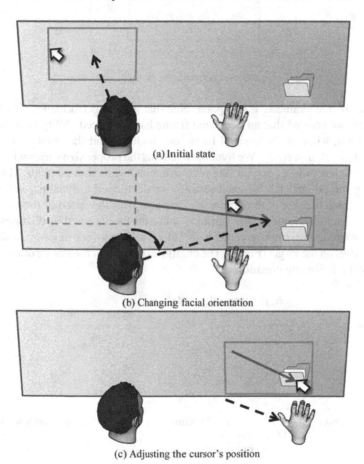

(a) Initial state

(b) Changing facial orientation

(c) Adjusting the cursor's position

Fig. 1.   Two steps involved in the proposed technique

The cursor is forced to be always inside the Frame; that is, the user can move the cursor freely inside the Frame, but the cursor will be "pushed" back into the Frame when reaches any of the Frame's edges (Fig. 2). Consequently, the cursor is always kept in the estimated manipulation area, which helps to shorten the distance between the cursor and target, substantially reducing the cursor movement time.

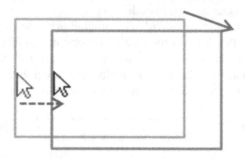

Fig. 2. Interaction between the 'Frame' and cursor

The size of the Frame is a key parameter that affects performance. During pilot experiments, we noticed that an oversized frame has a reduced ability to optimize the cursor position, while an undersized frame can unduly limit the cursor's movement, leading to manipulation errors. We hypothesized that the proper size varies with different hardware parameters (*e.g.*, screen size) and different interaction contexts. Rather than determining the proper size for each setting, we developed a dynamic, self-adaptive solution in which the size of the Frame is associated with the speed of the user's facial movement. Specifically, the Frame "shrinks" when the face orientation changes quickly, "expands" when the orientation tends to stabilize, and recovers its original size when the user focuses on the target (Fig. 3). The change in the size of the Frame during runtime is given by the following equation:

$$R_{rect} = max(R_{max} - \Delta s^k, R_{min}) \tag{1}$$

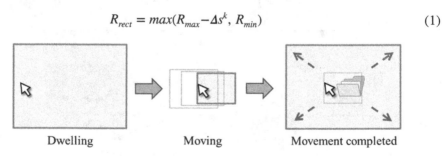

Dwelling   Moving   Movement completed

Fig. 3. The dynamic frame

In this equation, R_{rect} indicates the size of the Frame, R_{max} and R_{min} are the maximum and minimum size of the Frame, respectively, Δs is the moving speed of the Frame center, and the index k represents the steepness of the size change.

The purpose of the dynamic Frame size is to reduce the target-to-cursor distance in the Focus step, while providing a much larger range for the cursor movement in the Action step, to enhance the overall performance. This design also reduces the need for calibration when using the proposed method in different hardware settings.

3.2 Cursor Controlled by Hand Motions

While the cursor's moving range is constrained by the Frame as aforementioned, the user can control the cursor freely inside the Frame by using his/her hand. The basic cursor operations (i.e., moving and selecting) are associated with the user's hand motions in the following manner: (1) the cursor moves with the incremental movement of the hand in space; and (2) the user can switch the association between the hand's motions and the cursor on/off. The user's hand will not affect the cursor until it is moved forward a specified distance from his/her chest. Besides avoiding unexpected operations, this design also enables the user to move the cursor gradually for a longer distance by moving the hand in one direction repeatedly (Fig. 4), which provides more freedom handling the cursor.

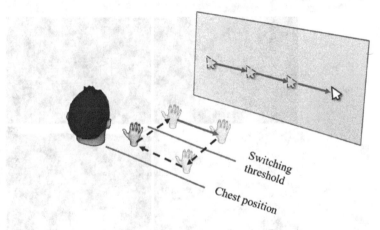

Fig. 4. Behavior of the GUI cursor

4 Implementation

We developed a prototype to evaluate the efficiency of our proposal. Our prototype system (Fig. 5) used a head-mounted laser pointer and an off-the-shelf webcam to track the user's face orientation. The user was asked to wear a pair of glasses with the laser pointer attached to the eyeglass frame. When the user looked at the WSD, the laser pointer projected a bright light dot on the screen. The webcam was placed in front of the WSD with its field of view covering the entire screen. The relative position of the light dot on the screen was extracted by processing the webcam image. The Frame was then centered on the laser dot on the screen, indicating the range within which the cursor can be moved.

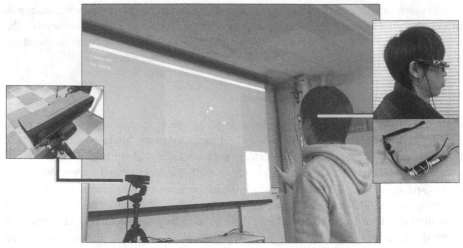

(a) Tracking the user's face orientation and hand motions

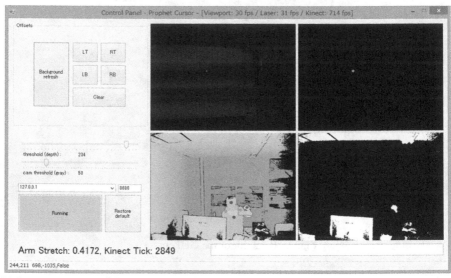

(b) Processing data from cameras. The raw image from webcam, extracted light dot position, raw Kinect depth image and extracted hand position were monitored.

Fig. 5. Prototype system

We used a Microsoft Kinect which was capable of tracking multiple body parts of the user to control the cursor. The position of the user's two shoulders and center of the chest were tracked, and the plane formed by these three-dimensional positions was used as the reference plane. The distance between the user's hand and reference plane was calculated. When this distance exceeded a specified threshold, the movement of the user's hand parallel to the reference plane was measured to move the cursor.

5 Evaluation

We conducted user studies using our prototype system to evaluate the effectiveness of the proposal technique. Two comparative experiments focusing on the task completion time were conducted to determine whether the face orientation tracking approach improves the overall efficiency of manipulating the cursor.

5.1 Apparatus

Both experiments were conducted in a room with a 100-inch vertical projection screen capable of showing image content at a resolution of 1600 × 1200 pixels. A 1-mW green light laser pointer was used to cast a light dot onto the screen. A Logitech Webcam Pro 9000 system and OpenCV 2 library were used to capture and extract the position of the light dot to track face orientation. A Microsoft Kinect sensor was used to track the user's posture. The arrangement of these instruments is shown in Fig. 6.

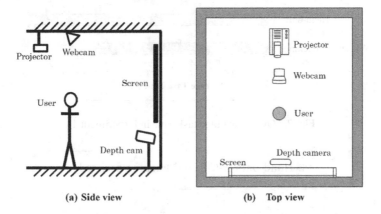

(a) Side view   (b) Top view

Fig. 6. Instrument layout used in the evaluation

5.2 Task

The tasks in both experiments involved the same basic design: a circular target was shown on the screen at random positions, and the participants were asked to point to each target with a GUI cursor as quickly as possible. Each participant repeated this simple task several times. A "selected" event was triggered when the cursor hovered on the target for 700 ms; the selected target was then replaced by a new target. The distances between two temporally adjacent targets were identical to maintain the same physical effort of moving the cursor for every single task.

5.3 Experiment 1: Fixed Frame

In the first experiment, we measured the performance of the proposed two-step technique using a fix-sized Frame, and compared it with a pointing method using only the hand, without facial tracking. Both of these conditions used the same aforementioned task design, and each participant was asked to perform 50 consecutive tasks in each condition. In the facial-tracking-assisted condition, we used a 324 × 200 pixels Frame (1/6 of the screen size in height with a 1.618:1 aspect ratio). The task time and users' hand motions were recorded for further analysis. Ten participants from the university, one female and nine male, took part in this experiment. All participants were right-handed. Since each participant was asked to perform tasks in all two conditions, training for both conditions was provided before the experiment to alleviate the possible impact from learning effect.

The average task time performed by all participants was 4.21 s, which was 1.11 s less than its counterpart setting (Fig. 7, with standard error, $p < 0.01$). The maximum and minimum average task time of each participant when using the facial-tracking-assisted method were 6.25 and 3.17 s, respectively, compared with 8.81 and 3.91 s with the hand-only method, as shown in Fig. 8 (with standard error). All 10 participants showed a reduced task time using the facial-tracking-assisted method, indicating an overall performance boost.

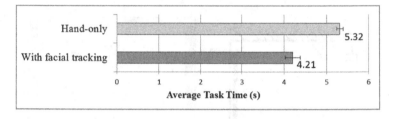

Fig. 7. Overall average task time in Experiment 1

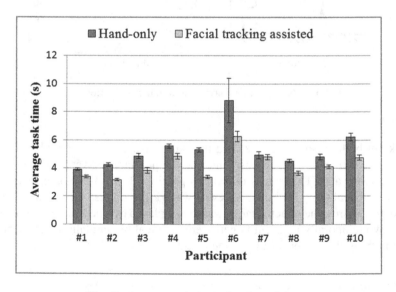

Fig. 8. Average task time of each participant

The proposed technique also showed a trend in that attempts to adjust the cursor's position (using the cursor on/off feature) were less frequent. Figure 9 shows the distribution of the number of attempts to "switch on the cursor" for all tasks performed. The average number of attempts using the proposed method was 1.26 compared with 2.34 using the hand-only condition. The figure also shows that with the help of facial tracking, 82.6 % of the tasks were done with a single attempt at cursor movement, while 74.4 % of the tasks in the hand-only condition required two or three attempts. This indicates that the use of facial tracking significantly reduced the eventual cursor movement distance and, hence, the overall task time.

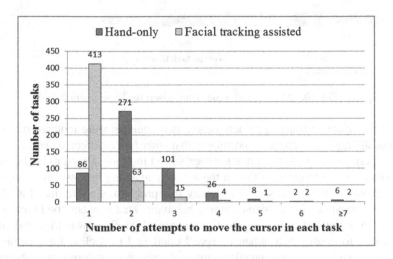

Fig. 9. Tasks cumulatively classified by the numbers of cursor-movement attempts

We observed situations in which the performance was affected by the Frame size setting during the first experiment. The cursor was occasionally hit by the Frame unexpectedly using our initial setting, and was sometime too far away from the target when we tentatively enlarged the frame. Both of the situations limited the performance. These were consistent with our observations in the pilot experiment. We attempted to solve these issues by adopting a dynamic frame approach. Experiment 2 was designed to test the effectiveness of this approach.

5.4   Experiment 2: Dynamic Frame

An experiment was conducted to determine the effectiveness of the dynamic frame. The experiment compared the dynamic frame with a fix-sized frame. The participants were asked to perform 20 consecutive tasks under both conditions. In both situation we used a Frame with an initial size of 971 × 600 pixels (1/2 of the screen size in height with a 1.618:1 aspect ratio) to guarantee the freedom of cursor movement. The minimum size of the dynamic Frame was set to zero. The index k was set to 1.6. The task time and user's hand motions were recorded. Eight university students (one female, seven male; all right-handed) participated in this experiment.

Figure 10 (with standard error bars) indicates that the task took an average of 3.99 s with the dynamic frame, which was 0.87 s faster than with the fix-sized frame (p < 0.01). Overall, for the 160 tasks performed in the experiment, the participants made an average of 1.93 attempts to finish the task using the dynamic frame method, compared with 2.16 attempts in the fixed frame condition, reflecting the slightly shorter cursor movement distances in the dynamic frame condition.

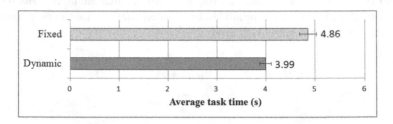

Fig. 10. Average task time comparison for Experiment 2

Using the dynamic frame approach, nearly two attempts were required on average, which was still high. Therefore, we postulated that other factors affected the performance. During Experiment 2, we noticed that the user's head motions slowed as his/her field of view approached the target, resulting in the Frame expanding instantly and limiting the effect of changing the frame size. To remedy this problem, we introduced a "delayed expansion" mechanism for the size-changing behavior. That is, when the Frame's speed slowed down, instead of expanding the Frame instantly, a timer was triggered, and the Frame started to expand only when its speed continued to decline for a certain time interval. We have found significant alleviation to the above issue during later observation, though further quantification experiments are needed to evaluate the effect of this approach.

6   Conclusions

In this paper, we proposed a pointing technique that enables efficient interactions on wall-sized displays that leverages human body motions. By tracking the user's face orientation, the user's focus on the screen can be roughly estimated to predict the position of the intended target. The user can then use hand motions for precise pointing. We conducted two experiments to evaluate the effectiveness of our approach.

The results of the first experiment illustrated the feasibility of boosting the pointing performance on a WSD by roughly tracking the user's field of vision. However, we also observed issues with the frame's behavior that affected the overall performance. The results of the second experiment supported our view that a self-adaptive approach can be leveraged as a remedy for these issues.

While the experiments demonstrated the effectiveness of our proposal in terms of overall performance, the manner by which internal variables (*e.g.,* size/shape of the Frame) affect the performance remains unclear. In the future, we plan to determine the role of each variable and develop a method to optimize the variable settings.

References

1. Zhai, S., Morimoto, C., Ihde, S.: Manual and gaze input cascaded (MAGIC) pointing. In: CHI 1999: Proceedings of the SIGCHI Conference on Human Factors in Computing Systems, pp. 246–253 (1999)
2. Nakanishi, Y., Fujii, T., Kiatjima, K., Sato, Y., Koike, H.: Vision-based face tracking system for large displays. In: Borriello, G., Holmquist, L.E. (eds.) UbiComp 2002. LNCS, vol. 2498, pp. 152–159. Springer, Heidelberg (2002)
3. Nakanishi, Y., Sato, Y., Koike, H.: EnhancedDesk and EnhancedWall: augmented desk and wall interfaces with real-time tracking of user's motion. In: Proceedings of Ubicomp2002 Workshop on Collaborations with Interactive Walls and Tables, pp. 27–30 (2002)
4. Vogel, D., Balakrisham, R.: Distant freehand pointing and clicking on very large, high resolution displays. In: UIST 2005: Proceedings of the 18th Annual ACM Symposium on User Interface Software and Technology, pp. 33–42 (2005)
5. Kobayashi, M., Igarashi, T.: Ninja cursors: using multiple cursors to assist target acquisition on large screens. In: CHI 2008: Proceeding of the Twenty-Sixth Annual SIGCHI Conference on Human Factors in Computing Systems, pp. 949–958 (2008)
6. Blanch, R., Ortega, M.: Rake cursor: improving pointing performance with concurrent input channels. In: CHI 2009: Proceedings of the 27th International Conference on Human Factors in Computing, pp. 1415–1418 (2009)
7. Porta, M., Ravarelli, A., Spagnoli, G.: ceCursor, a contextual eye cursor for general pointing in windows environments. In: ETRA 2010: Proceedings of the 2010 Symposium on Eye-Tracking Research and Applications, pp. 331–338 (2010)
8. MacKenzie, I.S.: An eye on input: research challenges in using the eye for computer input control. In: ETRA 2010: Proceedings of the 2010 Symposium on Eye-Tracking Research and Applications, pp. 11–12 (2010)
9. Liu, C., Chanpuis, O., Beaudouin-Lafon, M., Lecolinet, E., Mackay, W.: Effects of display size and navigation type on a classification task. In: CHI 2014: Proceedings of the SIGCHI Conference on Human Factors in Computing Systems, pp. 4147–4156 (2014)
10. Nancel, M., Pietriga, E., Chapuis, O., Beaudouin-Lafon, M.: Mid-air pointing on ultra-walls. ACM Trans. Comput.-Hum. Interact. (TOCHI) 22(5), 1–62 (2015)

3-Dimensional Face from a Single Face Image with Various Expressions

Yu-Jin Hong[1,2], Gi Pyo Nam[2], Heeseung Choi[2], Junghyun Cho[2],
and Ig-Jae Kim[1,2(✉)]

[1] Department of HCI and Robotics,
University of Science and Technology, Daejeon, Korea
[2] Imaging Media Research Center,
Korea Institute of Science and Technology, Daejeon, Korea
{hyj,keepsl201,hschoi,jhcho,kij}@imrc.kist.re.kr

Abstract. Generating a user-specific 3D face model is useful for a variety of applications, such as facial animation, games or movie industries. Recently, there have been spectacular developments in 3D sensors, however, accurately recovering the 3D shape model from a single image is a major challenge of computer vision and graphics. In this paper, we present a method that can not only acquire a 3D shape from only a single face image but also reconstruct facial expression. To accomplish this, a 3D face database with a variety of identities and facial expressions was restructured as a data array which was decomposed for the acquisition of bilinear models. With this model, we represent facial variances as two kinds of elements: expressions and identities. Then, target face image is fitted to 3D model while estimating its expression and shape parameters. As application example, we transferred expressions to reconstructed 3D models and naturally applied new facial expressions to show the efficiency of the proposed method.

Keywords: 3D face reconstruction · Bilinear models · Facial animation

1 Introduction

The acquisition of 3D face geometry is an important topic in the field of computer graphics and computer vision. Especially, user-specific 3D faces are valuable in industries such as gaming, animation, and film. There are two categories of obtaining 3D facial shapes. The first is to use a 3D scanner, and the second is to use several photographs to model a 3D face. A 3D scanner is the most accurate way to capture a 3D face, and a great deal of low-cost equipment has recently been introduced, increasing its usefulness; however, it is still costly, and the actual modeling target has the burden of travelling to a place where the equipment is located. Therefore, an image-based modeling method is useful in terms of accessibility (Fig. 1).

In this regard, existing image-based modeling methods use multiple photographs to perform 3D modeling, and these methods are still often used in VFX studios. However, there are still many situations in which 3D face reconstruction from only a single photograph is needed. The most outstanding method for 3D face modeling using a

© Springer International Publishing Switzerland 2016
N. Streitz and P. Markopoulos (Eds.): DAPI 2016, LNCS 9749, pp. 202–209, 2016.
DOI: 10.1007/978-3-319-39862-4_19

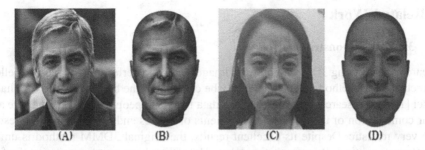

Fig. 1. (A, C) 2D input face images. (B, D) 3D faces reconstructed with the proposed method

single photo is 3DMM [1]. Through statistical techniques based on 3D face scan data from 200 people, this method enables personalized face modeling that mimics the input image. More recently, many excellent researches have introduced to generate a 3D face based on a single photograph. However, there are still limitations for reconstructions of faces showing expressions.

Facial expressions are shown in most actual individual profile photographs, including those of celebrities, who are a major target for 3D modeling. As such, there is a great need for a method that can quickly and accurately reconstruct a 3D face from a single photograph with a facial expression.

To accomplish this, our paper introduces a method that can not only reconstruct a 3D shape from a single face image but also reconstruct various facial expressions from the image. This is achieved through bilinear models, and to acquire models, we used 3D face scans with unique shape and identity structures featuring a variety of expressions and individuals. These models are structured in a data array and HOSVD (Higher Order Singular Vector Decomposition) is applied to construct bilinear models and we used these models to depict facial changes in the 3D faces as expressions and shapes. To show the efficiency of this reconstruction method, we used application example wherein a variety of expressions were transferred to different 3D faces.

2   Contributions

This paper introduces a method for acquiring user-specific 3D face models from face scan data, and its contributions are as follows:

- A practical level of speed (less than 2 s) was achieved to reconstruct 3D face from a single photo, this is accomplished while reducing the position errors between the landmarks on 3D model and the 2D image. An optimized method was used for computational efficiency.
- Through the properties of the bilinear models, the identity of the reconstructed 3D model and expression elements can be controllable and changed into a new appearance. Therefore, the user-specific blendshapes needed to create a person's expression animations can be captured from a single face photograph without 3D scanner equipment.

3　Related Work

3.1　3D Face Reconstruction

Research on acquiring 3D geometry from images has been performed by many excellent researchers. The method that can definitely be considered the best is the 3D Morphable Model [1]. This research used 3D face scan data from 200 people to represent a face as a linear combination of the principal components of shapes and textures, and the results were very realistic. Despite its excellent results, the original 3DMM method is unfortunately not practical. Its computation takes a long time because to reconstruct the face shape, the texture parameters, such as intensity and ambient light, of the input photograph must be calculated in addition to many unknown parameters such as camera information. To resolve these drawbacks, the landmark-based 3DMM method have introduced. This method reduces the position errors of several facial landmarks located on the face photograph and the 3D reference model. As mentioned earlier, reconstruction of the photograph textures is accompanied by complex computations, so the landmark-based method is used for the face shape, and the input texture is directly projected the result 3D face [2–5]. Recently, the novel methods for reconstructing facial shapes from shading information have introduced [6, 7].

However, these studies mostly reconstruct photographs without expressions. To resolve this problem, we present a method that not just reconstructs 3D facial geometry but also facial expressions through bilinear models.

3.2　Bilinear Models

Bilinear models were first introduced by Tenenbaum et al. [8] to separate two factors that are mixed. To separate a combination of various elements, research has been performed on the use of HOSVD (proposed by Tucker [9] and Kroonenberg et al. [10]) to show how these elements influence each other [11]. In our research, we represent our 3D face with bilinear models hence we assume that a facial shape is composed of expression and shape (identity) properties.

4　Overview

This section provides an overall description of how we used the bilinear model to acquire 3D face geometry from a single input photograph. We used a 3D face database of scan data from 150 people with 47 kinds of facial expressions to build our bilinear model. The fitting process reduces the differences between the 3D models and the 2D input images. The final section demonstrates the proposed method's efficiency by showing the example wherein a variety of facial expressions were applied to the resulting 3D faces (Fig. 2).

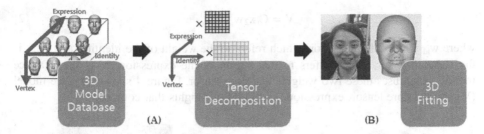

Fig. 2. Overall image of the presented method. (A) The process of building the bilinear models. (B) The process of fitting the input image on the 3D model.

5 Building Bilinear Models

The input photographs included a variety of face shapes and expressions. For this, we used the FaceWarehouse Database [12], which was constructed with 3D face scan models and includes 150 various people and 47 kinds of facial expression models per individual, each made with 11,500 vertices. We divided these models into identity and expression, and we structured a 3D array with T. Figure 3 describes the appearance of T. We then decomposed our array T with SVD to obtain the bilinear models. We wanted to create just a whole facial shape, so we excluded the vertex mode decomposition.

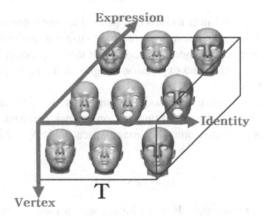

Fig. 3. Appearance of array T composed of expression, identity, and vertex

T can be written again as the following equation.

$$T = C_r x_2 U_{id} x_3 U_{exp} \tag{1}$$

C_r is called the core tensor, and it is in charge of the mutual interaction concerning how the identity and expression affect each other. U_{id} and U_{exp} are the orthonormal transformation matrixes, which represent the left singular vectors of the identity space and expression space, respectively. We call C_r a bilinear model, which can be used to express any expression on any face. This is shown in Eq. (2).

$$V = C_r x_2 w_{id}^T x_3 w_{id}^T \tag{2}$$

where w_{id} is the column vector, which refers to the weight of the identity, and w_{exp} is the column vector, which refers to the weight of the expression. V is the 3D face model, which uses these two weights and core tensor. Figure 4 shows the face model (V) and the core tensor, expression, and identity weights that compose it.

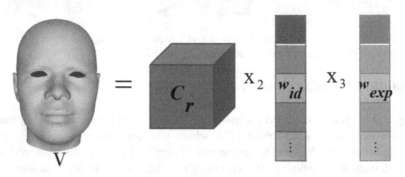

Fig. 4. 3D face V and elements in bilinear format

6 3D Face Reconstruction

As mentioned earlier, our bilinear models can be used to turn a person with any kind of expression into a 3D face. Therefore, we are able to use it to make the 3D model such that it is similar to a given image. To accomplish this, a process is carried out that estimates not only the identity and expression weights of the input photograph but also the camera information.

We initialize the reference 3D model V such that it has average identity and expression. We assume that the camera projection is weak perspective. The 3D model reference point v_k is projected onto the image space point p_k. This is shown in the following equation.

$$p_k = sRv_k + t \tag{3}$$

where s is a scaling information, R is a global rotation matrix, and t is a translation information in the image space. Translation about the Z-axis was ignored due to weak-perspective projection. The following equation shows the process for reconstructing the 3D face while minimizing the error between face landmarks in the 2D image and feature points on the 3D face.

$$\text{Error}_k = \frac{1}{2} \left\| sR(C_r x_2 w_{id}^T x_3 w_{exp}^T)^{(k)} + t - s^{(k)} \right\|^2 \tag{4}$$

where $s^{(k)}$ is the facial features on the 2D image, and k is the kth feature point. We use 76 facial landmarks. The unknown values that we want to find are the pose information of the face (size, rotation, movement) and model parameter (identity and expression) information. To solve these parameters quickly and simultaneously, we used the L-BFGS [13] algorithm for optimization.

7 Results

In Fig. 5, (A) is the input face images, and (B) is the 3D face that results from the proposed method. As shown in Fig. 5(B), faces with a variety of expressions were properly reconstructed into 3D faces.

Figure 6(C) shows the results of various expressions transferred to the 3D model. It can be seen in particular that the expression was changed very naturally. Through this

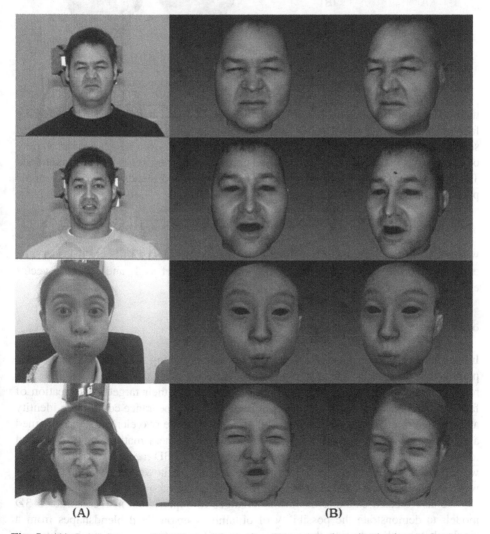

(A)   (B)

Fig. 5. (A) Input images. (B) 3D model results. The expressions in the input photos are reconstructed in 3D.

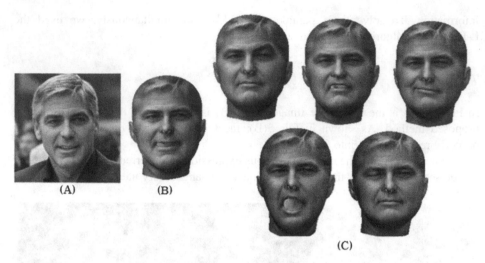

Fig. 6. (A) Input image. (B) 3D model results. (C) Expression transfer model results

method, it becomes easy to obtain the personalized blendshapes needed for making face animations from a single 3D face. Normally, to make facial animation, a set of several or several dozen expressions are made beforehand, from which a wider variety of expressions can be produced; creating such an expression set is an important task. The following formula was used to create the personalized blendshapes from a single photograph.

$$B_i = C_r x_2 w_{id} x_3 (U_{exp} a_i), 0 \le i \le 47 \tag{5}$$

where U_{exp} is the expression transformation matrix introduced in Sect. 4. For a_i, the expression element needed as the expression vector is set as 1, and all other vector elements are set as 0.

8 Conclusion

In this paper, we have presented a process for reconstructing a 3D face from a single photograph of a face with an expression. Because normal image-based 3D face reconstruction methods use faces without expressions as their targets, the creation of faces with expressions is difficult. To represent a facial appearance comprising identity and expression elements, we decomposed an array of these two elements and obtained a bilinear model. Using this model, we deduced the camera matrix, expression, and identity information of the input photo and turned it into a 3D face. During this process, we improved our optimization process to solve many unknown values at once so that we could enhance the efficiency of the process in terms of speed.

We also created example of various changes to expressions in reconstructed 3D models to demonstrate the possibility of obtaining personalized blendshapes from a single photograph and using them to create natural expressions for virtual reality and gaming avatars.

Acknowledgements. This work was supported by the KIST Institutional Program (Project No. 2E26450 & No. 2E25930)

References

1. Blanz, V., Vetter, T.: A morphable model for the synthesis of 3D faces. In: ACM SIGGRAPH, pp. 187–194 (1999)
2. Asthana, A., Marks, T.K., Jones, M.J., Tieu, K.H., Rohith, M.V.: Fully automatic pose-invariant face recognition via 3D pose normalization. In: IEEE International Conference on Computer Vision, pp. 937–944 (2011)
3. Ding, C., Xu, C., Tao, D.: Multi-task pose-invariant face recognition. IEEE Trans. Image Process. **24**(3), 980–993 (2015)
4. Ding, L., Ding, X.: Continuous pose normalization for pose-robust face recognition. IEEE Signal Process. Lett. **19**(11), 721–724 (2012)
5. Qu, C., Monari, E., Schuchert, T., Jeyerer, J.: Fast, robust and automatic 3D face model reconstruction from videos. In: Advanced Video and Signal Based Surveillance, pp. 113–118 (2014)
6. Hassner, T.: Viewing real-world faces in 3D. In: IEEE International Conference on Computer Vision (2013)
7. Kemelmacher-Shlizerman, I., Seitz, S.M.: Face reconstruction in the wild. In: IEEE International Conference on Computer Vision (2011)
8. Tenenbaum, J.B., Freeman, W.: Separating style and content with bilinear models. Neural Comput. J. **12**, 1247–1283 (1999)
9. Tucker, L.R.: Some mathematical notes on three-mode factor analysis. Psychometrika **31**(3), 279–311 (1966)
10. Kroonenberg, P.M., Leeuw, J.D.: Principal component analysis of three-mode data by means of alternating least squares algorithms. Psychometrika **45**(1), 69–97 (1980)
11. Vasilescu, M.A.O., Terzopoulos, D.: Multilinear analysis of image ensembles: TensorFaces. In: European Conference on Computer Vision, pp. 447–460 (2002)
12. Cao, C., Weng, Y., Zhou, S., Tong, Y., Zhou, K.: FacewareHouse: a 3D facial expression database for visual computing. IEEE Trans. Visual Comput. Graph. **20**, 413–425 (2014)
13. Liu, D.C., Nocedal, J.: On the limited memory BFGS method for large scale optimization. Math. Program **45**, 503–528 (1989)

User-Independent Face Landmark Detection and Tracking for Spatial AR Interaction

Youngkyoon Jang[1], Eunah Jung[2], Sung Sil Kim[3], Jeongmin Yu[1],
and Woontack Woo[1,3(✉)]

[1] CTRI & AHRC, KAIST, Daejeon, South Korea
{y.jang,jmyu119,wwoo}@kaist.ac.kr
[2] School of Computing, KAIST, Daejeon, South Korea
514ah@kaist.ac.kr
[3] GSCT, KAIST, Daejeon, South Korea
mania@kaist.ac.kr

Abstract. We present novel face landmark detection and tracking methods which are independent of user facial differences in a scenario of Spatial Augmented Reality (SAR) interaction. The proposed methods do not require a preliminary general face model to detect or track landmarks. Our contributions include: (i) fast face landmark detection, which is achieved based on our modified Latent Regression Forest (LRF) and (ii) model-independent facial landmark tracking by revising outliers based on a direction and displacement of neighboring landmarks. We also discuss (iii) feature enhancements based on RGB and depth images for supporting several interaction scenarios in SAR environments. We anticipate that the proposed methods promise several interesting scenarios, even under severe head orientation in SAR interaction without wearing any wearable devices.

Keywords: Face landmark detection · Face landmark tracking · Random forest · Virtual reality · Computer vision

1 Introduction

Spatial Augmented Reality (SAR), such as IllumiRoom [9] and RoomAlive [8], provides immersive user experiences by projecting a VR scene onto the room space and expanding an interactive space. However, a user is required to touch a point of the wall in order to interact with the projected virtual object in the SAR environments. Because it is hard to estimate head position and orientation without wearing HMD, estimating head pose, detecting and tracking facial landmarks provides various interactive clues which are available for supporting a more intuitive interaction in SAR environment. Herein, head orientation indicates the direction of the user's view. Moreover, user-independent face landmark detection and tracking is the first step for supporting different users of SAR environment. Thus, without wearing a cumbersome Head-Mounted-Display (HMD), such as HoloLens [1] and Oculus [2], an immersive experience is achievable based

© Springer International Publishing Switzerland 2016
N. Streitz and P. Markopoulos (Eds.): DAPI 2016, LNCS 9749, pp. 210–220, 2016.
DOI: 10.1007/978-3-319-39862-4_20

Fig. 1. Block diagram of the proposed framework.

on the User-independent face landmark detection and tracking in an indoor environment.

Main contributions of our proposed method include:

(1) Fast head orientation estimation: Our modified Latent Regression Forest for face landmark detection guarantees very fast detection performance. Moreover, the proposed method detects face landmarks independent of user facial differences.

(2) Model-independent facial landmark tracking: Based on the detected landmarks as an input, the proposed method could track the landmarks along the video sequences, which is independent of user's facial expression changes. Because the proposed method does not require a preliminary model for a general face, it provides more accurate tracking performance.

(3) Discussions of novel feature enhancement based on RGB-D images: For improving the accuracies of landmark detection and tracking, we discuss a novel type of feature configuration which utilizes the concept of Local Angle Pattern [7].

2   Methodology

2.1   Overview

The proposed method is as shown in Fig. 1. At first, RGB-D camera captures a pair of images including synchronized color and depth images. Based on a depth image, then, our method detects the face region of interests. After that, the center coordinate of the detected face region is transformed into the coordinate of the color image. Then, by utilizing a cropped face image as an input, our proposed method detects multiple dominant facial landmarks in a coarse manner. For that, we adopted and modified the Latent Regression Forest [13] for targeting face modality. The coarsely detected dominant landmarks work to specify the searching space for specifically aligned landmark detection. Finally, our proposed method tracks the landmarks based on the proposed outlier rejection methods.

2.2   Region of Faces Detection

Our face detection is achieved by utilizing J. Shotton [12]'s body joint estimation method. By taking the two pixel test, which is based on the normalized offsets to be calculated, we only trained face and background classes. Based on the coarsely detected region, we redefine a searching space and then did per-pixel classification for more precise face region detection. Based on the detected face region, a cropped and normal-sized face image is used as an input for face landmark detection.

2.3 Dominant Landmark Detection

We use Latent Random Forest (LRF) [13] for face dominant landmarks. The LRF utilizes a face landmark topology to keep a relative position structure of landmarks. We designed a face landmark topology to guide landmark detection (Sect. 2.3-A), built LRF following the designed topology (Sect. 2.3-B), and designed testing procedure using learnt LRF (Sect. 2.3-C)

A. Face Landmark Topology. To enhance the landmark detection process, we utilize a hierarchical context of dominant landmarks based on a topology of face landmarks. Given ten dominant landmarks in Fig. 2, a face landmark topology has a binary tree structure. From the center position of the face image represented as a root node, we could reach to every landmark stored at the leaf nodes of topology. Each node in the topology has its two children which have the subset of its parents' landmark set, respectively. When it reaches the node that has only one dominant landmark in the subset, we define the node as a leaf node (See Fig. 2).

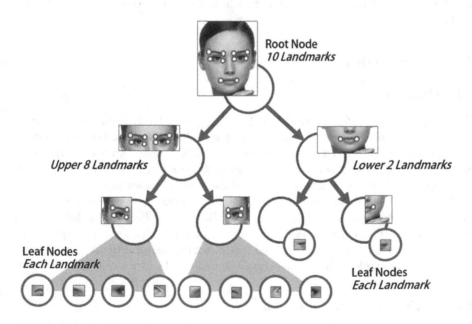

Fig. 2. Face landmark topology model.

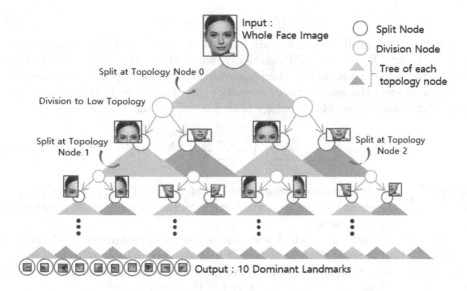

Fig. 3. Latent regression tree.

B. Learning Latent Regression Forest (LRF). A Latent Regression Forest (LRF) [13] is an ensemble of random decision trees, which is originally proposed to estimate articulated hand posture. In this paper, we adopted the LRF to estimate the facial landmarks, searching from coarse level to fine level based on the designed face topology model. Learning LRF is performed in a divide-and-conquer way by taking the whole face image and ground-truth landmarks as input and ending with each landmark detected as output. Each node of a decision tree in LRF is set by one of three types: split, division, and leaf. Split nodes function to split the training dataset to two subsets by the split function. Division nodes divide the scope of facial landmark set according to the face topology. When the scope of facial landmark includes only one landmark, it terminates by storing the relative landmark position at the leaf node.

Given our face topology model M, for each node $i \in M, i = 0, \cdots, |M|$, it has parent node $p(i)$ and its child nodes $l(i)$ and $r(i)$. For each training RGB face image I, we define $\rho_i{}^I$, the center position of a landmark set corresponded with each topology node i. Each latent regression tree is trained corresponding with each topology stage. A root node of LRT takes the whole scope of facial landmarks according to a root node $i = 0$ of the topology model. As the tree grows, it separates the scope of landmarks according to $l(i)$ and $r(i)$ until the topology reaches the leaf node. At each node, we split the training data S into two subsets S^l and S^r by the split function f_i and threshold τ_i randomly generated. The learning is proceeded under the context of a topology node i. A split function f_i and the subsets are defined as:

$$f_i = I(\rho_i{}^I + u) - I(\rho_i{}^I + v), \tag{1}$$

$$S^l = \{I|f_i(I) < \tau_i\}, S^r = S\backslash S^l, \tag{2}$$

where $I(\cdot)$ is the pixel value of certain location, vectors u and v are random normalized offsets. We set the split function f_i which shows the largest information gain value, while if the information gain value could not improve from the previous node step, the learning process enters the division step. The information gain under the context of a topology node i is defined like [13] as:

$$IG_i(S) = \sum_m^{l(i),r(i)} tr\Big(\sum_{im} S\Big) - \sum_k^{l,r} \frac{S^k}{|S|}\Big(\sum_m^{l(i),r(i)} tr\Big(\sum_{im} S^k\Big)\Big), \tag{3}$$

where $\sum_{im} \chi$ is the sample covariance matrix of the set of offset vectors $\{(\rho_m^I - \rho_i^I)|I \in \chi\}$. The offset vectors are the offsets from the current center position to each center of two subsets.

Given the training data which are face images, at division step, each data is divided by the center of the selected offset vectors. Its children nodes process its own learning on a finer scope of the training data. (See Fig. 3) The offset vectors $\theta_m = (\rho_m^I - \rho_i^I), m \in \{l(i), r(i)\}$ are stored in the division node.

Split and division process are repeated until a corresponding topology node is the leaf node of the topology which represents one final landmark. At each leaf node, we save the offset vectors from the center of its parent node to the landmark.

C. Testing. Given a detected face image as an input, it goes into each Latent Regression Tree in LRF, starting from the center of the face image with the root node of a topology. At each split node, the test image is checked with the split function saved in the node, traversing to the left side or the right side and repeats the process until reaching at division node. At each division node, the face image is divided into two sub-regions according to the children nodes of the current node in the topology and the landmark position is accumulated with the offset vectors saved in the division node. When reaching a leaf node and accumulating the offset vectors, all dominant landmark positions can be estimated.

2.4   Model-Independent Landmark Tracking

In this section, we present a model-independent landmark tracking method. Recently, model-based methods [4,11,15] have been popularly used for landmark tracking and have achieved promising tracking results. However, these methods are not suitable for tracking various face appearances, and their tracking performances heavily rely on a number of training samples and optimization methods. To overcome these problem, we propose a model-independent landmark tracking method which is based on dense optical flow [15] and the displacement of neighborhood landmark information. Specifically, after detecting the dominant landmarks, each detected landmark $p_t^l = (x_t^l, y_t^l)$ at frame t is tracked to the next frame $t+1$ using the median filtering kernel M in a dense optical flow field $G = (u_t, v_t)$.

$$p_{t+1}^l = (x_{t+1}^l, y_{t+1}^l) = (x_t^l, y_t^l) + (M \cdot G)|(\bar{x}_t^l, \bar{y}_t^l), \tag{4}$$

where $\cdot$ is the convolution operator, and $(\bar{x}_t^l, \bar{y}_t^l)$ is the rounded position of (x_t^l, y_t^l).

During landmark tracking, landmarks tend to drift from their previous locations due to the abrupt fast motions of the face. To revise such outlier landmarks, we use displacement information of neighboring landmarks, which is illustrated in Fig. 4. In detail, we first define the neighboring landmarks by considering their geometric information and the partial components of the face. Then, the outlier landmarks are modified by their neighboring displacements and the mean of their directions.

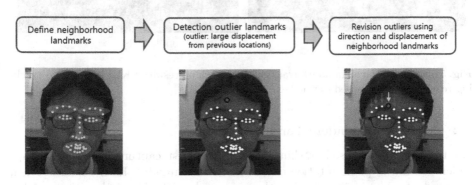

Fig. 4. Process of revision of outlier landmarks.

When an overall landmark tracking error is larger than a threshold, we reinitialize the landmarks positions using the proposed dominant landmark detection method.

3 Implementation

3.1 LRF-Based Landmark Detection

To perform the dominant landmark detection method, each training sample consists of a cropped face image and a ground truth of ten dominant facial landmarks. Because a LRF is trained based on pixel value of the face image, we normalize each face image to a fixed-size image (30 × 30 pixels in our implementation) and make a feature vector which is 900 pixel values of a normalized image. At the division step, we mark invalid pixel values as −1 in each feature vector as the facial landmarks are divided to two subsets. A two-pixel difference test proceeds on valid elements of feature vectors. For testing landmarks, when traversing the trees and accumulating the offset vectors which are saved in division nodes, we calculate the offset values by using the voting mechanism. This is found to be more accurate than averaging all offset values.

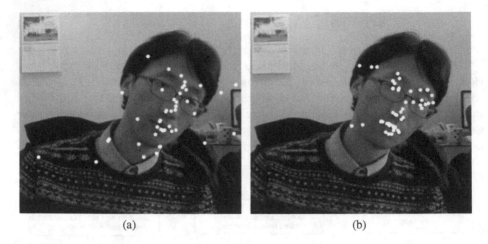

(a)   (b)

Fig. 5. Results of face landmark tracking: (a) tracking result of KLT tracker (b) tracking result of our proposed method.

3.2   Model-Independent Landmark Tracking

For testing the proposed tracking method, we first capture face motion clips which contain in-plane rotation of face from a commodity RGB camera. Then, we conduct an experiment using the proposed method and the other model-independent landmark tracking method (namely KLT tracker) [11] which is based on sparse optical flow information. Figure 5 shows their tracking results.

As shown in Fig. 5, our proposed method (Fig. 5(b)) outperforms KTL landmark tracker (Fig. 5(a)) with respect to the in-plane rotation of face situation. From the experiment, we confirm the feasibility of the proposed landmark tracking method which does not use a learned face model.

4   Discussion

So far, we have tackled user-independent landmark detection and tracking methods. However, it is still processed based on the images captured from frontal viewpoint cameras. Thus, in order to enhance the features, which can be used for the scenarios of face rotation in SAR environment, we discuss feature enhancement method in this section.

Defining RGB-D feature is completed as shown in Fig. 6. The color and depth image acquired from a camera is processed parallely into local binary pattern (LBP) image and surface normal image. The color image is perceived as a matrix of RGB pixels by a camera in order to apply Local Binary Pattern (LBP) [3]. LBP operator is one of the most efficient and effective image features, frequently used in face recognition and detection. Despite its advantages, however, LBP features still suffer in terms of robustness in situations where instant change of luminosity or face orientation occurs. To overcome this challenge, the proposed feature integrates LBP feature with depth data.

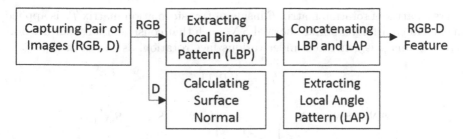

Fig. 6. RGB-D feature definition flow diagram.

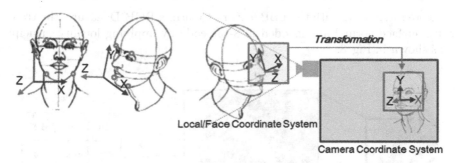

Fig. 7. Acquiring transformation matrix between local/face coordinate and camera coordinate based on dominant facial landmarks.

Along with color images, a stream of depth images is captured from TOF camera simultaneously, and these depth images represent the distance between objects and the camera. The proposed method utilizes the depth images by calculating the surface normal of each pixel by finding a vector for each pixels which is orthogonal to the plane.

In the process of generating our proposed Local Angle Pattern, a coordinate transformation is done in order to justify the orientation difference between camera and local/face surface normal. The original surface normal vectors are adjusted by applying a transformation matrix resolved from the relationship of four dominant facial landmarks in camera coordinate and local/face coordinate, as shown in Fig. 7.

Transformation Matrix Tr used in coordinate adjustment is defined by the rotation and translation, and it is referenced to transform 3D vectors from camera coordinates L to local coordinates L', as shown in Eq. 5.

$$\begin{pmatrix} L'_{1x} & L'_{1y} & L'_{1z} \\ L'_{2x} & L'_{2y} & L'_{2z} \\ L'_{3x} & L'_{3y} & L'_{3z} \\ L'_{4x} & L'_{4y} & L'_{4z} \end{pmatrix} = Tr \begin{pmatrix} L_{1x} & L_{1y} & L_{1z} \\ L_{2x} & L_{2y} & L_{2z} \\ L_{3x} & L_{3y} & L_{3z} \\ L_{4x} & L_{4y} & L_{4z} \end{pmatrix}, \tag{5}$$

Transformation Matrix Tr consists of 3 variables: internal calibration matrix A, rotation matrix R, and translation vector T as shown in Eq. 6. The inverse matrix of rotation matrix R inside of transformation matrix Tr is applied on camera coordinates surface normal SN, such that consistent local surface normal SN' image is generated under various face rotation, as shown in Eq. 7.

$$Tr = A[R|T], \tag{6}$$

$$\begin{pmatrix} SN_{1x} \; SN_{1y} \; SN_{1z} \\ \vdots \\ SN_{nx} \; SN_{ny} \; SN_{nz} \end{pmatrix} [R]^{-1} = \begin{pmatrix} SN'_{1x} \; SN'_{1y} \; SN'_{1z} \\ \vdots \\ SN'_{nx} \; SN'_{ny} \; SN'_{nz} \end{pmatrix}, \tag{7}$$

Before integrating with the LBP feature to form a RGB-D feature, the transformed surface normal are encoded in 8-bit code by applying locality principle [6], as shown in Fig. 8.

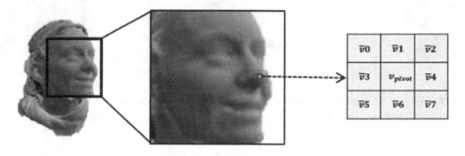

Fig. 8. Applying locality principle to surface normal image.

For each pixel, the inner product of pivot and its neighboring surface normal vector are calculated. If the inner product of two vectors is greater than the threshold, the feature concatenates 1 and if not, 0. As a result, each pixel produces an 8-byte local angular pattern (LAP), as defined by the following equation:

$$\theta_i = cos^{-1}\left(\frac{dot(v_{pivot}, v_i)}{\|v_{pivot}\| \cdot \|v_i\|}\right), \tag{8}$$

$$lap[i] = \begin{cases} 0, & \text{if } \theta_i < \text{threshold.} \\ 1, & \text{if } \theta_i \geq \text{threshold.} \end{cases} \tag{9}$$

$$LAP(x,y) = (lap[0], lap[1], \cdots, lap[7]), \tag{10}$$

The LAP feature defined here is integrated with LBP to form RGB-D feature, and it is used for both holistic and patch-based face detection and tracking.

The proposed RGB-D feature has the merit of supplementing the limitations of color-based features, such as SIFT [10], HOG [5], Viola-Jones [14], or LBP [10] itself. Many of the above methods showed that they rely on edge/corner extraction for detecting faces, which becomes easily vulnerable in rotation, translation, or slight deformation. Also, upon immediate centralization of image contrast, losses of feature detection occur, thus being unstable for SAR interaction.

Our proposed RGB-D feature, on the other hand, utilizes both color and depth data and proved to be more robust under rapid change of light conditions and face rotation. The fact that LAP [7] is not affected by light conditions not only improves the detection accuracy in various light conditions, but also stabilizes the tracking in dynamic head orientation by generating features based on face/local coordinates. Therefore, even under conditions where color images are suddenly saturated such that no RGB features are extractable, the LAP becomes the reference to where the facial landmarks are located.

5 Conclusions

This paper presents user-independent face landmark detection and tracking methods for spatial AR interaction scenarios. In spatial AR interaction environments, a user has to approach and touch the projected object on the wall in order to interact with virtual objects, which is cumbersome. To detect the facial landmarks, we adopted and modified Latent Regression Forest (LRF), specifically for face modality. Because it utilizes a face image to detect all the landmarks of a face, it is fast and invariant to users' facial differences. In addition, to track the landmarks, we proposed a model-independent tracking method. Finally, we discussed feature enhancement method, which could be used for both detection and tracking. We expect our proposed user-independent facial landmark detection and tracking methods would be useful in SAR interaction scenario.

Acknowledgments. This work was supported by DMC R&D Center of Samsung Electronics Co.

References

1. Microsoft HoloLens. https://www.microsoft.com/microsoft-hololens/. Accessed 25 Sept 2015
2. Oculus, V.R.: https://www.oculus.com/. Accessed 25 Sept 2015
3. Ahonen, T., Hadid, A., Pietikainen, M.: Face description with local binary patterns: application to face recognition. IEEE Trans. Pattern Anal. Mach. Intell. **28**(12), 2037–2041 (2006)
4. Cao, C., Weng, Y., Lin, S., Zhou, K.: 3d shape regression for real-time facial animation. ACM Trans. Graph. **32**(4), 41: 1–41: 10 (2013)
5. Dalal, N., Triggs, B.: Histograms of oriented gradients for human detection. In: Schmid, C., Soatto, S., Tomasi, C. (eds.) International Conference on Computer Vision & Pattern Recognition, vol. 2, pp. 886–893. INRIA Rhône-Alpes, ZIRST-655, av. de l'Europe, Montbonnot-38334. June 2005. http://lear.inrialpes.fr/pubs/2005/DT05
6. Denning, P.J.: The locality principle. Commun. ACM **48**(7), 19–24 (2005)
7. Jang, Y., Woo, W.: Local feature descriptors for 3d object recognition in ubiquitous virtual reality. In: 2012 International Symposium on Ubiquitous Virtual Reality, Daejeon, Korea (South), 22–25 August 2012, pp. 42–45 (2012)

8. Jones, B., Sodhi, R., Murdock, M., Mehra, R., Benko, H., Wilson, A., Ofek, E., MacIntyre, B., Raghuvanshi, N., Shapira, L.: Roomalive: magical experiences enabled by scalable, adaptive projector-camera units. In: Proceedings of the 27th Annual ACM Symposium on User Interface Software and Technology, UIST 2014, NY, USA, pp. 637–644. ACM, New York (2014)

9. Jones, B.R., Benko, H., Ofek, E., Wilson, A.D.: Illumiroom: peripheral projected illusions for interactive experiences. In: Proceedings of the SIGCHI Conference on Human Factors in Computing Systems, CHI 2013, NY, USA, pp. 869–878 (2013). http://doi.acm.org/10.1145/2470654.2466112

10. Lowe, D.G.: Distinctive image features from scale-invariant keypoints. Int. J. Comput. Vision **60**(2), 91–110 (2004)

11. Lucas, B.D., Kanade, T.: An iterative image registration technique with an application to stereo vision. In: Proceedings of the 7th International Joint Conference on Artificial Intelligence, IJCAI 1981, vol. 2, pp. 674–679. Morgan Kaufmann Publishers Inc., San Francisco, CA, USA (1981)

12. Shotton, J., Girshick, R., Fitzgibbon, A., Sharp, T., Cook, M., Finocchio, M., Moore, R., Kohli, P., Criminisi, A., Kipman, A., Blake, A.: Efficient human pose estimation from single depth images. In: Transaction on PAMI (2012)

13. Tang, D., Chang, H.J., Tejani, A., Kim, T.K.: Latent regression forest: structured estimation of 3D articulated hand posture. In: The IEEE Conference on Computer Vision and Pattern Recognition (CVPR), June 2014

14. Viola, P., Jones, M.: Rapid object detection using a boosted cascade of simple features. In: Proceedings of the 2001 IEEE Computer Society Conference on Computer Vision and Pattern Recognition, CVPR 2001, vol. 1, pp. I-511–I-518 (2001)

15. Wang, H., Klaser, A., Schmid, C., Liu, C.L.: Action recognition by dense trajectories. In: Proceedings of the 2011 IEEE Conference on Computer Vision and Pattern Recognition CVPR 2011, pp. 3169–3176. IEEE Computer Society, Washington, DC, USA (2011)

Mid-Air Gestures for Virtual Modeling with Leap Motion

Jian Cui[1,2(✉)], Dieter W. Fellner[1,3], Arjan Kuijper[1,3], and Alexei Sourin[2]

[1] Technische Universität Darmstadt, Darmstadt, Germany
cui.jian@gris.informatik.tu-darmstadt.de
[2] School of Computer Engineering, Nanyang Technological University,
Singapore, Singapore
CUIJ0006@e.ntu.edu.sg
[3] Fraunhofer IGD, Darmstadt, Germany
arjan.kuijper@igd.fraunhofer.de

Abstract. We study to which extent Leap Motion can be used for mid-air interaction while working on various virtual assembling and shape modeling tasks. First, we outline the conceptual design phase, which is done by studying and classification of how human hands are used for various creative tasks in real life. Then, during the phase of the functional design, we propose our hypothesis how to efficiently implement and use natural gestures with Leap Motion and introduce the ideas of the algorithms. Next we describe the implementation phase of the gestures in virtual environment. It is followed by the user study proving our concept.

1 Introduction and Motivation

Mid-air interaction is an emerging spatial input mode which has been used in many areas of interaction, e.g., mid-air keyboard typing [13], interaction with large displays [15], virtual and augmented reality [17], and touchless interaction [2,9,10]. Recent progress in hand tracking using affordable controllers such as Leap Motion (www.leapmotion.com), Nimble VR (niblevr.com), and MS Kinect (www.microsoft.com) boosted research and development on precise hand tracking, especially in the area of computer games [14]. Breakthroughs were also made in predicting self-occluded hand, e.g., [20], which, until recently, was a serious obstacle for using optical tracking devices. However, application of mid-air gestures for precise 3D object manipulation in virtual environments, such as virtual prototyping, assembling and various shape modeling operations, still remains a challenging research problem. Indeed, with 27 degrees of freedom for the hand, only one grasping gesture can be classified into 33 variants [6]. With the motor skills acquired with age and experience, we take and manipulate objects of different size, shape and weight in a way that we feel is most natural and productive. For various simulations and training, professional motor skills in virtual environments, such natural gestures, should be recognized and implemented by the interactive modeling system.

© Springer International Publishing Switzerland 2016
N. Streitz and P. Markopoulos (Eds.): DAPI 2016, LNCS 9749, pp. 221–230, 2016.
DOI: 10.1007/978-3-319-39862-4_21

In this paper, we perform a feasibility study on using Leap Motion controller for virtual assembling and shape modeling operations mimicking real life gestures rather than using artificial, however possibly more efficient for capturing, gestures [12,29]. We first analyze the existing progress with hand tracking in these areas, as well as what has been achieved in hand tracking with Leap Motion controller. Next, we analyze and classify the hand gestures which are used in real life hand-based desktop constructions, assembling, and modeling operations. We then come up with just a few algorithms that allow for recognition of many possible hand gestures. Next, we briefly outline the implementation and describe the user tests which we conducted to verify our hypothesis and the devised algorithms. The paper ends with a conclusion.

2   Use of Hand Gestures for Virtual Assembling and Modeling

Hand tracking can be performed using different platforms, such as virtual gloves with bending sensors [4], mechanical tracking devices (e.g., exo-skeletons), and optical and depth tracking devices, like Leap Motion, Nimble VR, and Kinect.

When performing various assembling operations, the user should be able to take the object, relocate it while also changing its orientation, and release it. Shape modeling often requires hand-made deformations, such as elastic deformations and various cuttings. There are two different approaches to perform the respective hand interaction in virtual environments (VE): collision based and gesture-based. The first one assumes that a virtual hand, controlled by the users hand, collides with the objects in the VE thus implementing the real life collision between the hand (fingers and palm) and the objects. This process, when implemented physically-based, may realistically simulate the real hand operations with a high degree of precision. Based on this approach, many research works have been done to implement how the virtual objects can be grasped, moved and deformed. For example, Garbaya et al. [8] proposed a spring-damper model for hand interaction with mechanical components in their virtual assembly system. A similar model was also proposed in [1] for the whole hand virtual grasping where linear and torque forces were calculated to be exerted on objects to simulate their dynamics. Besides physically-based methods, heuristic approaches can also be used to manipulate objects with virtual hands. For example, in [28] a method for manipulating a virtual wrench is proposed, while in [11] a realistic kinematics model of a virtual hand (skeleton [26,27], muscle and skin) is discussed. In some works, the virtual hand is used for creating surfaces [18] and point clouds [7], as well as for various deformations of elastic objects [25] according to the amount of force exerted by it.

An alternative to virtual hand simulation approach assumes that the objects in VE are manipulated by various mid-air gestures. Some gestures mimic the way we interact with objects in the real life, others are rather abstract. Thus, one typical metaphor is to use pinching gesture to select objects, and then to relocate them by moving and rotating hands [19]. A pointing gesture [16] is often used to specify a direction for the object selection. In [24], a sheet-of-paper metaphor is proposed for visual assembling to rotate the view point direction like pinching a sheet of paper. Another example is [21] where a handle bar metaphor is proposed to mimic manipulation of objects that are skewered with a bimanual handle bar. For shape modeling, an interaction system named shape-it-up was proposed in [23] with three basic gestures for different manipulation and deformation operations.

Using devices like Leap Motion controller opens new prospects for the precision with which fingers can be tracked. Not only bending but even slight displacements of the fingers sideways can be precisely captured by it. However, not many works have been done with Leap Motion in the studied area. The Playground app[1] uses a ghost hands for assembling based on a rigid collision model provided by Unity Game Engine. Examples of applications with gestural interfaces for 3D object manipulation and camera adjustment can be found in on various websites[2].

Generally, though the methods based on collision detection are quite promising, their efficiency is limited by the used hand tracking systems, which may not be able to capture properly all the 27 degrees of freedom of the hand. Also, the inability to deliver a realistic tactile feedback from the virtual hand causes the users to replace it with various visual feedbacks (e.g., colored finger tips to reflect the amount of forces exerted, etc.). As for the mid-air gestures, though efficiently captured by the tracking system, they are neither intended for benefitting from real-life hand motor skills nor for training these skills. In this paper, we perform a feasibility study of using Leap Motion controller for tracking mid-air gestures with application to real life gestures used in various desktop hand-made operations.

3 Proposed Mid-Air Gestures

First, we outline the conceptual design phase, which is done by studying and classification of how human hands are used for various creative hand-made tasks in real life. Then, working on the functional design, we propose our hypothesis how to efficiently implement and use natural gestures with Leap Motion and describe the ideas of the main algorithms. Finally, we briefly outline the implementation of the gestures in virtual environment.

3.1 Hand Gestures Study

We studied and classified the plethora of real life hand gestures used when different desktop-based assembling and modeling operations are performed, which include unimanual and bimanual grasping, motion (including relocation and rotations), and deformation gestures. For the various hand-made operations on

---

[1] http://blog.leapmotion.com/inside-leap-motion-designing-playground/.

[2] See e.g. https://apps.leapmotion.com/apps/sculpting/windows and https://apps. leapmotion.com/apps/cyber-science-motion-zoology/windows.

real objects, the object is usually first taken (possessed) by hand. This gesture of taking the object may have different names: grasping, pinching, grabbing, gripping, etc. There are a few classifications of all these gestures controlling the objects position and orientation (e.g., [6]) however for the gestures used for desktop hand-made operations we will consider only the following three groups:

1. When the fingers move towards the opposable thumb (e.g., as in grabbing and pinching).
2. When the fingers bend towards the palm (e.g., as in cylindrical grip).
3. When one or a few fingers of the whole palm are touching the object while exerting some force thus establishing control over the object (e.g., when touching and picking).

Releasing of the object is a converse process so that the hand and/or fingers lose the contact with the object. All possible motions (relocations) of objects, which can be done with one hand after the object is taken, are then performed by moving the hand from one position to another as a sequence of taking-moving-releasing gestures. All the unimanual object rotations, after the object is taken, can be eventually classified into three groups:

1. Incremental rotation by taking-rotation-releasing sequences of gestures when the object is firmly held by the fingers and the thumb while the wrist rotates.
2. Incremental rotation by only moving the fingers and the thumb with a fixed position and orientation of the wrist. This gesture may be performed together with the previous wrist rotation as well.
3. Rotation by one or a few fingers or the whole palm performed as a circular motion while the fingers/hand touch the surface of the object which is being rotated.

Finally, unimanual deformations, which can become useful for potential virtual modeling, are rather limited to only two groups:

1. Squeezing and twisting with the fingers moving towards the thumb.
2. Deformations by pressing the object with the thumb or one or a few fingers, as it is done in clay modeling.

Bimanual gestures add additional varieties to the considered groups of gestures. Thus, grasping can be done with two hands performing the grabbing, pinching or gripping gestures. While moving two hands holding the virtual object, the operations of relocation, rotation (like steering wheel rotation or a handle bar) and various deformations can also be performed.

3.2   Functional Design of the Mid-Air Gestures

Our research hypothesis is that we may achieve higher efficiency of natural mid-air gestures if we avoid displaying virtual hands since observation of the motion of the virtual objects/instruments controlled by the hand is more essential than an ability to see the simulated hand itself. As an advantage of this approach, we

Fig. 1. Mid-air gestures design. Form left to right: minimum distance from the thumb to fingertips; finger bending; circular rotation with fingers; rotation with one finger.

will not base most of our hand tracking algorithms on collision detection between the virtual hand and the objects but rather on recognition of the gesture itself. Therefore, the gesture algorithms will be not constrained by the number of polygons involved in construction of the virtual objects as soon as they can be rendered in real-time. This approach assumes that the virtual object or instrument is somehow selected or predefined, and once made visible, the user will manipulate it with the gestures which are commonly used with this object in real life. We also hypothesize that just a few basic gestures recognition algorithms can be devised to be able to still apply many varieties of the real life gestures.

We devised algorithms of unimanual grasping and pinching gestures based on computing the minimum distance from fingers to the thumb to trigger the event of grasping and pinching (First image of Fig. 1). The gripping gestures is based on computing the bending angle of the four fingers which, when exceeds a certain threshold value, will trigger the grasping event (Second image of Fig. 1). Releasing is a converse process to detect that the threshold value of the finger distance or bending angle is no longer exceeded. However, picking and touching have to be based on tracking the finger or palm positions and, depending on the content, may require performing a collision detection of the hand/fingers with the object or its bounding box.

Unimanual relocation algorithms (translation) are based on tracking the hand position. Unimanual rotation algorithms for taking-rotation-releasing sequences is based on tracking the wrist orientation. While for incremental rotation performed by moving fingers, we proposed an algorithm where the 3D positions of the finger and the thumb tips are projected onto a plane thus reducing the task of calculation of the angle of rotation to a 2D case (Third image of Fig. 1). Rotation with one finger is based on tracking the finger position as a particular case of the rotation by fingers (Last image of Fig. 1).

Unimanual deformation is a continuation of the respective grasping or gripping gesture so that the elastic objects can be deformed following the fingers motions after the grasping event is detected. This gesture can be performed as an incremental sequence grasping-squeezing-releasing. Deformation done by applying to the object a few fingers or the whole palm is based on tracking the finger/thumb/palm positions and it may require, in contrast to other gestures, to compute the contact point with the virtual object surface.

Bimanual gestures are based on the unimanual gestures algorithms and assume that the virtual object is first grasped by one hand. Then, grasping the same object with the other hand triggers the event of bimanual gestures which are applied in a content sensitive way depending of the virtual object constraints i.e. whether and how the object can be moved, rotated or deformed.

3.3   Implementation

To implement the devised algorithms, we used Virtual Reality Modeling Language (VRML) and its successor Extensible 3D (X3D, cf. [5,22]) for defining interactive virtual worlds to be published in the networked environments as well as on local client computers. We used Bitmanagement BS Contact VRML/X3D viewer, which is a commonly used plugin to several Internet browsers. BS Contact provides an interface to support input devices by extending VRML/X3D through a DeviceSensor Node for receiving the input data from the device [3].

4   User Tests and Analysis of the Results

We have performed user studies on the efficiency of the proposed gestures in the virtual environment. We investigated:

1. whether each gesture can be seamlessly recognized when performed by different users,
2. whether the gestures will actually mirror natural gestures, and
3. whether the gestures can be used as fast and as precise as in real life.

4.1   System Setup

We used a DELL PRECISION T7500 workstation with Intel(R) Xeon (R) CPU 2.40 GHz 2.39 GHz and 12 GB memory, running Windows 7 professional. The Leap Motion controller (software version is 2.3.1 +31549) was placed on the desktop facing up. The interaction height is approximately 20 cm above the desktop with a tracking rate of around 300 frames per second. The codes are written in VRML + java script, and visualized using MS Internet Explorer with BS Contact plugin. The hand data is transferred to the viewing platform by our plugin [3].

4.2   Testing Procedure

Two experiments were conducted with 10 participants (7 males and 3 females) with an age between 21 to 32 ($M = 25$, $SD = 3.8$) for the experiment. 4 of them had experience with using Leap Motion gestural interface. During the first experiment, the participants were required to sit in front of the computer monitor and interact with their hands above the desktop while looking at the monitor (Fig. 2). Different objects were shown on the computer monitor for 5 s each, specifically, Rubiks cube, ball, glass, book, and pencil, while virtual hands were not displayed at all. Within 5 s, the participants had to take each object with any hand or with both hands and in a way how they would do in real life for the same object (grabbing, pinching, taking with two hands). When the object is taken (the gesture is recognized), the objects slightly changed their visual appearance to give a visual feedback that the object is possessed by the participant. Then, the participant had to move the object to a new place, while also changing its orientation either by rotating the wrist or by moving fingers, and, finally, to release it. The object could be also squeezed to deform it. After completion, the users were invited to perform the same operations with real objects and also within 5 s for each of the object. The two tests were then compared in terms of timing and precision.

Fig. 2. Performing bare-hand operations with mid-air gestures. Left: without displaying virtual hands. Right: while displaying the virtual hands.

During the second experiment, the participants were required to perform the same 5 s per object tests while the virtual hands were displayed. After the experiments, the participants were asked to answer a questionnaire. The questionnaire was based on a 5 point Likert scale containing the following questions:

Q1: I feel it is easy and not stressful to accomplish the task.
Q2: I can remember and use the interaction techniques.
Q3: I feel natural to interact with the objects.
Q4: I feel no confusion during interaction.
Q5: I like this interface.

4.3   Results and Discussion

The collected replies on the five questions are accumulated in Fig. 3. We found that interaction time without showing virtual hands (t = 3.34, SD = 0.65) is shorter than that when the virtual hands were shown (t = 4.13, SD = 0.68). Showing virtual hands can be less stressful (Q1), however it may lead to confusion (Q4) and excessive but unnecessary concentration on the virtual hands (Q2). The user preferences are equally split between the two approaches (Q5). Using motor

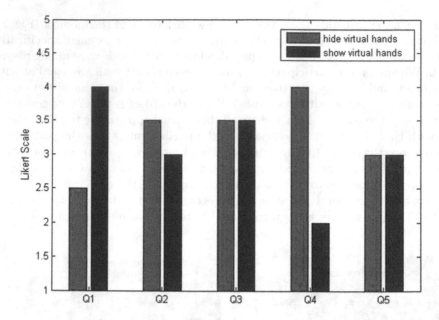

Fig. 3. Participants replies after the two experiments with mid-air gestures with and without displaying the virtual hands.

skills was also equally split (Q3). Experienced participants preferred hiding the virtual hands.

Moreover, when the virtual hands were not displayed, the participants tended to select more comfortable position for the hands as well as the best capturing position for the Leap Motion controller. This led to improving the quality of gesture recognition. We have also concluded that to achieve a better performance with the gesture recognitions without showing the hands, it may become useful to tune the interactive modeling system for some users, in a way how it is done for common mouse and touch-pad interactions.

When virtual hands are displayed, the users tended to move them towards the object, which reduced the efficiency of gesture recognition when the hands left the best capturing area of the Leap Motion controller.

5   Conclusion

We proved that Leap Motion can be efficiently used for mid-air interaction while working on various virtual assembling and shape modeling desktop tasks. We have proved with the user studies our research hypothesis that higher efficiency of natural mid-air gestures can be achieved without displaying the virtual hand hence shifting attention of the user to the hand-controlled virtual instruments and employing the existing hand motor skills of the users. The proposed approach allows the users to begin bare-hand virtual manipulations without learning any special instructions by simply doing things in the same natural and logical way as in real life.

References

1. Borst, C.W., Indugula, A.P.: A spring model for whole-hand virtual grasping. Presence: Teleoper. Virtual Environ. **15**(1), 47–61 (2006)
2. Braun, A., Wichert, R., Kuijper, A., Fellner, D.W.: Capacitive proximity sensing in smart environments. JAISE **7**(4), 483–510 (2015)
3. Cui, J., Sourin, A.: Feasibility study on free hand geometric modelling using leap motion in VRML/X3D. In: Proceedings of the 2014 International Conference on Cyberworlds, CW 2014, pp. 389–392 (2014)
4. Dipietro, L., Sabatini, A., Dario, P.: A survey of glove-based systems and their applications. IEEE Trans. Syst. Man Cybern. Part C Appl. Rev. **38**(4), 461–482 (2008)
5. Eicke, T.N., Jung, Y., Kuijper, A.: Stable dynamic webshadows in the X3DOM framework. Expert Syst. Appl. **42**(7), 3585–3609 (2015)
6. Feix, T., Pawlik, R., Schmiedmayer, H., Romero, J., Kragic, D.: A comprehensive grasp taxonomy. In: Robotics, Science and Systems: Workshop on Understanding the Human Hand for Advancing Robotic Manipulation (2009)
7. Fuge, M., Yumer, M.E., Orbay, G., Kara, L.B.: Conceptual design and modification of freeform surfaces using dual shape representations in augmented reality environments. Comput. Aided Des. **44**(10), 1020–1032 (2012)
8. Garbaya, S., Zaldivar-Colado, U.: The affect of contact force sensations on user performance in virtual assembly tasks. Virtual Reality **11**(4), 287–299 (2007)
9. Grosse-Puppendahl, T., Herber, S., Wimmer, R., Englert, F., Beck, S., von Wilmsdorff, J., Wichert, R., Kuijper, A.: Capacitive near-field communication for ubiquitous interaction and perception. In: The 2014 ACM Conference on Ubiquitous Computing, UbiComp 2014, Seattle, WA, USA, 13–17 September 2014, pp. 231–242 (2014)
10. Große-Puppendahl, T.A., Braun, A., Kamieth, F., Kuijper, A.: Swiss-cheese extended: an object recognition method for ubiquitous interfaces based on capacitive proximity sensing. In: 2013 ACM SIGCHI Conference on Human Factors in Computing Systems, CHI 2013, Paris, France, 27 April–2 May 2013, pp. 1401–1410 (2013)
11. Huagen, W., Shuming, G., Qunsheng, P.: Virtual grasping for virtual assembly tasks. In: Third International Conference on Image and Graphics (ICIG 2004), pp. 448–451 (2004)
12. Lai, D., Sourin, A.: Interactive free-form shape modeling in cyberworlds. Vis. Comput. **29**(10), 1027–1037 (2013)
13. Markussen, A., Jakobsen, M.R., Hornbæk, K.: Vulture: a mid-air word-gesture keyboard. In: Proceedings of the 32nd Annual ACM Conference on Human Factors in Computing Systems, CHI 2014, pp. 1073–1082 (2014)
14. Moser, C., Tscheligi, M.: Physics-based gaming: exploring touch vs. mid-air gesture input. In: Proceedings of the 14th International Conference on Interaction Design and Children, IDC 2015, pp. 291–294 (2015)
15. Nancel, M., Wagner, J., Pietriga, E., Chapuis, O., Mackay, W.: Mid-air pan-and-zoom on wall-sized displays. In: Proceedings of the SIGCHI Conference on Human Factors in Computing Systems, CHI 2011, pp. 177–186 (2011)

16. Nickel, K., Stiefelhagen, R.: Pointing gesture recognition based on 3D-tracking of face, hands and head orientation. In: Proceedings of the 5th International Conference on Multimodal Interfaces, ICMI 2003, pp. 140–146 (2003)
17. Piumsomboon, T., Clark, A., Billinghurst, M., Cockburn, A.: User-defined gestures for augmented reality. In: CHI 2013 Extended Abstracts on Human Factors in Computing Systems, CHI EA 2013, pp. 955–960 (2013)
18. Schkolne, S., Pruett, M., Schröder, P.: Surface drawing: creating organic 3D shapes with the hand and tangible tools. In: Proceedings of the SIGCHI Conference on Human Factors in Computing Systems, CHI 2001, pp. 261–268 (2001)
19. Segen, J., Kumar, S.: Gesture VR: Vision-based 3D hand interace for spatial interaction. In: Proceedings of the Sixth ACM International Conference on Multimedia, MULTIMEDIA 1998, pp. 455–464 (1998)
20. Sharp, T., Keskin, C., Robertson, D., Taylor, J., Shotton, J., Kim, D., Rhemann, C., Leichter, I., Vinnikov, A., Wei, Y., Freedman, D., Kohli, P., Krupka, E., Fitzgibbon, A., Izadi, S.: Accurate, robust, and flexible real-time hand tracking. In: Proceedings of the 33rd Annual ACM Conference on Human Factors in Computing Systems, CHI 2015, pp. 3633–3642 (2015)
21. Song, P., Goh, W.B., Hutama, W., Fu, C.W., Liu, X.: A handle bar metaphor for virtual object manipulation with mid-air interaction. In: Proceedings of the SIGCHI Conference on Human Factors in Computing Systems, CHI 2012, pp. 1297–1306 (2012)
22. Stein, C., Limper, M., Kuijper, A.: Spatial data structures to accelerate the visibility determination for large model visualization on the web. In: Web3D14, pp. 53–61 (2014)
23. Murugappan, S., Liu, H., Ramani, K.: Shape-it-up: hand gesture based creative expression of 3D shapes using intelligent generalized cylinders. Comput. Aided Des. **45**(2), 277–287 (2013)
24. Wang, R., Paris, S., Popović, J.: 6D hands: markerless hand-tracking for computer aided design. In: Proceedings of the 24th Annual ACM Symposium on User Interface Software and Technology, UIST 2011, pp. 549–558 (2011)
25. Yang, C.C., Lin, P.J., Sun, C.C.: Product form design using virtual hand and deformable models. Int. J. Digit. Content Technol. Appl. **6**(11), 8–17 (2012)
26. Yoon, S.M., Kuijper, A.: Human action recognition using segmented skeletal features. In: 20th International Conference on Pattern Recognition, ICPR 2010, Istanbul, Turkey, 23–26 August 2010, pp. 3740–3743 (2010)
27. Yoon, S.M., Kuijper, A.: Human action recognition based on skeleton splitting. Expert Syst. Appl. **40**(17), 6848–6855 (2013)
28. Zachmann, G., Rettig, A.: Natural and robust interaction in virtual assembly simulation. In: Eighth ISPE International Conference on Concurrent Engineering: Research and Applications ISPE/CE2001, July 2001
29. Zhang, X., Sourin, A.: Image-inspired haptic interaction. J. Visual. Comput. Anim. **26**(3–4), 311–319 (2015)

Human Behavior in Smart Environments

Fashion Design and Tactile Perception: A Teaching/Learning Methodology to Enable Visually Handicapped People to Identify Textile Structures

Geraldo Coelho Lima Júnior[✉] and Rachel Zuanon

Sense Design Lab, Ph.D. and Master's Design Program,
Anhembi Morumbi University, São Paulo, Brazil
glimadesign58@gmail.com1, rzuanon@anhembi.br2,
rachel.z@zuannon.com.br2

Abstract. The question of how textile structures should be regarded is an essential part of the training of fashion design students. The problems encountered in this area have had a significant effect on the definition and application of the material used in the garments for fashion collections. This paper sets out a teaching/learning methodology that is concerned with determining and distinguishing between flat materials for visually handicapped people by heightening their sensitivity to tactile perception. As a result, it was found that there was a significant value in extending the scale and two-dimensional and three-dimensional representations of the textile links to this perception and hence being able to consolidate memories. The purpose of this was to enable students to broaden their horizons as fashion designers.

Keywords: Fashion design · Textile design · Tactile perception · Visually impaired people · Teaching & learning

1 Introduction

People are continually being stimulated by their surrounding environment. Visual, auditory, olfactory, tactile and gustatory images are apprehended by the feelings and are appropriately linked and merged in a system of human perception. An experience is undergone that is able to forge close ties between the body and the environment [1, 2]. This allows each person to learn several activities and retain them in their memory without the need to learn them again. These links are established by connecting what has been learnt to what is shown to each person [3]. They prove to be important when addressing matters concerned with teaching & learning that are related to any particular issue. The activities or stimuli arising from the body itself or the surrounding environment, can affect how learning takes place.

This research study is concerned with the teaching of textile design in fashion design courses in Brazil, in particular with regard to the building of textiles and the different factors that emerge from weaving fabric. As a result of successive attempts made by the authors to follow the guidance provided by research studies in fashion

© Springer International Publishing Switzerland 2016
N. Streitz and P. Markopoulos (Eds.): DAPI 2016, LNCS 9749, pp. 233–244, 2016.
DOI: 10.1007/978-3-319-39862-4_22

design (and on the basis of this to allow students to carry out tasks in this area), it was found that in a general way, students had difficulty in identifying textile structures [4–6], and to distinguish between flat fabrics. This has attracted a good deal of attention because the definition of materials in a collection has a decisive effect on the final result. The suitability of the material to an item of clothing proves to be important when it is taken into account that a mistaken use of raw materials can have an adverse effect on features such as the form-fitting, modelling, functionality and wearability of the garment or in other words, if it fails to make the wearer feel comfortable [7, 8].

Several components are taken into account in the textile structures of clothing and fashion products and each has distinct features. It is worth drawing attention to the following: the type of fibre or strand used – which can be subdivided into natural, such as cotton, silk and linen; artificial, such as viscose (synthetic material made from cellulose) or acetate (transparent plastic); or synthetic such as polyamide or polyester. Another feature is grammage, which affects the weight and frame of the fabrics. These are important aspects of weaving as they affect the form fitting, flexibility and degree of stiffness among other factors [4, 5, 9].

The flat material or flat canvas is the most basic and traditional substance that has been developed so far; the yarns are interwoven in this way in both the lengthwise (warp) and transverse (weft) directions and the threads of the warp cross over and beneath those of the weft. From this initial pattern, other means of interweaving the warp and weft have been adopted and resulted in distinct textile appearances to serve particular uses. [4, 5, 9]. It should be stressed that the weft is always a regular spun fibre and the differences are caused by the warp.

Other points that should be taken into account are the technical processes and finishings. For example, dyeing and washing can lead to greater softness. The design of the surface, also known as the industrial printing design, which is applied over flat surfaces, results in visual and tactile surfaces. This may or may not display protuberances and in visual terms alters the way this kind of woven fabric [10] is identified, without necessarily affecting the tactile perception of the structures.

The problems of determining the ways the fabrics are distinguished becomes an even more arduous task when they entail the teaching & learning of visually-handicapped students. This is because within the range of the current methodologies being employed, the types of woven flat materials are identified by means of a magnifying glass that amplifies the crossing of the yarn.

In the light of the constraints imposed by the use of a visual apparatus, the task of identifying the fabrics is transferred to other feelings, among which touch proves to be the most reliable for this task. The forming of textile fabrics was originally carried out manually or with looms, which involved motor skills. Handicraft fabrics are still made by looms today. Tactile perception is essential for this task since it is in this manner that ways can be learnt of crossing the warp yarn to form textile structures.

Thus it should be realised that the employment of a methodology aimed at stimulating the tactile sense, as a counterpart to what is only supported by a visual stimulation, can, to a great extent, assist in the identification of textile patterns by textile design students, whether they have normal sight or not. With this in mind, this research study sought to conduct a formal experiment with four visually handicapped people who were all over the age of 18. This involved making use of accessible andragogical resources for teaching people with this impairment.

The main results show that tactile stimulation arising from the employment of different materials in different warp yarns, not only broadened the perception of the specific features of various fabrics for this public but also provided a better understanding of their application to the manufacture of garments, (in the light of the fact that these means of identification were now available). On this basis, it is clear that the widespread adoption of this methodology in the teaching & learning processes for flat materials can make a significant contribution to overcoming the obstacles faced by students in the field of textile design.

2 Textile Design and Tactile Perception

As mentioned earlier, the structures of fabrics can be recognised by means of both visual and tactile perceptions. Figure 1 shows a graphic representation of woven cloth made of canvas, twill and satin. It can be seen that the crossing of the threads between the warp and weft occurs in different ways. The alternating woven forms are a factor that defines the patterns of the cloth that depend on the fibres used; these alter their appearance and the tactile perception of the fabric. What can be detected through touch are the physical properties of the fabric that result from the following features: the nature of the fibre, fineness or delicacy, stretching, and moisture among other factors [6].

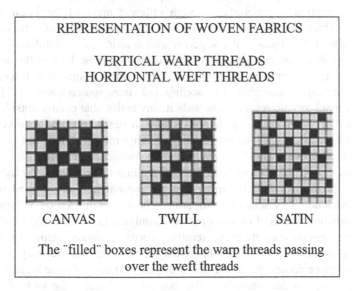

REPRESENTATION OF WOVEN FABRICS

VERTICAL WARP THREADS
HORIZONTAL WEFT THREADS

CANVAS   TWILL   SATIN

The "filled" boxes represent the warp threads passing over the weft threads

Fig. 1. Woven fabric – canvas, twill and satin. Source: author's property

In a research study, Kunzler [6] provides some descriptors for tactile perception by conducting tests in which the participants were asked to identify fabrics with the same textile samples in three different stages: (1) visual; (2) tactile; (3) visual and tactile together.

The author employed the following descriptors to describe the different visual and tactile forms of contact with the fabrics in the experiments: rough, a good fit, shiny, dainty, hard, slippery, fine, firm, flexible, flimsy, waterproof, light, smooth, soft, supple, limp, warm, resistant, simple, synthetic and threaded [6] and these corresponded to the first stage of the tests.

In the second stage, Kunzler [6] redefined her objectives by seeking to find descriptors that were particularly related to tactile perception and the results were as follows: "finishing/texture, friction, shininess, comfort, colour, size, toughness, human factors and ergonomics, style, familiarity, shape, hygiene, smell, weight, price, quality, resistance, application/usefulness, temperature, visual appeal" [6]. The descriptors used for Stage 2 include features that can be perceived in a tactile way. In the two stages, the author made use of three samples which had the following components: (a) 100 % Viscose; (b) 100 % Acetate; (c) 75 % Viscose, 20 % Polyamide, 5 % Spandex fibre. Descriptors such as finishing/texture, resistance or toughness indicate the form of the fabric since canvas material is what is responsible for defining the texture of the fabric [5].

A research study similar to that of Kunzler [6] was carried out by Carvalho [7], who made use of a wider range of materials including fibres with 100 % cotton and mixed fabrics. Her results were much broader and provided descriptors which showed the degree of intensity of each type.

In both research studies, the authors provided the results of tactile perceptions obtained from the sensory descriptors, which involved the participants touching the fabrics with their forefinger, with the sole purpose of recording their sensations.

Tactile perception is undertaken though different areas of the brain within the parietal lobe, which are also responsible for the perception of space, shapes and textures [11]. This lobe contains the superior and inferior parietal lobules where the somato-sensory information is processed. This is important for the way the body relates to its surrounding environment as well as for integrating information linked to "perception and language, mathematical reasoning and visual-spatial cognition" [12]. "The human brain maps any object that is outside it, any action that occurs outside it and all the relations that characterise objects and actions in space and time relative to others and also with regard to (...) the organism" [2]. This mapping does not only include visual patterns, but every kind of sensory pattern formed in the brain [2].

In a general way, the sensory stimuli enter the brain as a stream of electric pulses triggered by the firing rate of neurons that are present in a determined route. The question of what defines whether one stream can be turned into vision and another into touch, depends on what kind of neurons are stimulated [13]. It should be understood that human perception consists of an iterative process between various sensory channels. "Sensory signals presented simultaneously in more than one sensory channel tend to be detected more accurately and at lower thresholds than the same signals presented individually" [14]. On this basis, it is also possible to detect if the lack of one of the senses has an effect on the activities of the others. In other words, the lack of the sense of vision in someone who is visually handicapped (VH) (either partially or wholly) can interfere with the results for the perception descriptors related to the other senses.

In view of this, a methodology is required that in the first place can be employed to interpret the features that shape the warp yarn and hence allow the textile structures to be identified. In the second place, this knowledge can be used to extend the scope of the tactile descriptors of the fabrics and give a better prospect of learning about the textile features, as a counterpart to that which only gives precedence to the domain of the descriptors. "Everything woven by a conscious mind is created with the same thread: images produced by the capacity for mapping of the brain" [2]. It is up to the designer, to discover the purpose of the textile material by investigating its features and ensuring that they are changed in accordance with the aims of a particular project [5].

3 Materials and Methods

The experimental undertaking was carried out with a group of four students over the age of 18 who had visual impairments - one with poor vision and the others completely blind. The experiment made use of the basic principles of teaching textile design with regard to cloth patterns and their weaving associated with andragogical resources. These were made accessible for teaching visually handicapped people to stimulate sensory, tactile and motor portals [2], as well as the students´ perception, apprehension and registering of information taught through the teaching material produced in this activity.

Close attention was paid to the studies of the brain functions [15, 16], as a procedure that could significantly assist the planning and execution of the method. This was mainly aimed at the definition and application of several kinds of stimuli that are able to trigger the formation of mental images in the students based on the activities of the peripheral sensitive organs. "In the case of touch, there is a direct mechanical contact of an object with the skin which affects the activity of the nerve endings situated within the skin. The (mental) images, which we form from the shape and texture of an object, are the outcome of this process." [17].

As a result, the teaching material prepared while carrying out this research, was concerned with ways of recognising textile constructions by means of touch although not just with regard to the index finger of the students on the fabric; it was carried out in a way that could make them perceive (step by step) the warp and weft threads used in weaving. This was achieved by setting out five stages related to the types of weaving that are involved in creating any flat fabric and these followed a growing order of difficulty and complexity in identifying the warp yarns through tactile perception, namely: (a) open warp threads; (b) open yarn threads; (c) handloom − open thread; (d) handloom − closed thread; (e) industrial loom.

What is remembered from the encounter with the particular object transposes "the visual pattern mapped in the optical images of the retina" [2], in encompassing the sensitive-motor features linked to the following: (a) the view of the object; (b) touching and handling the object; (c) evoking previously acquired memories and relating them to the object; (d) triggering emotions and feelings associated with the object.

Thus it was ensured that the transition between the stages was carried out in a progressive way with regard to the display of samples. This was because those with more open structures (a, b, c) − and which allowed an accurate investigation of the spaces between the threads and the woven fabrics, even the most difficult (d, e) - became more difficult when employed for identifying the fabrics by touch.

It should be stressed that, unlike the recommendations of Kunzler [6] and Carvalho [7], in this experiment the aim was to point out the tactile descriptors. The materials employed in constructing the boards shown in stages (a) and (b), can be distinguished from each other. However, they are solely and exclusively aimed at providing a tactile reading of the woven patterns and thus have no similarity with the tests conducted by the authors cited above.

(a) Open warp threads

In this stage, several boards were prepared with the aim of showing visually handi-capped students different woven fabrics. In this manufacturing process, threads like cotton, chenille and polyester soutache were used to help detect the warp and weft and distinguish them from each other. It was decided to keep a distance of 10 mm between the threads with a thickness of 1 mm (ratio of 100:1). It was noted that this distance between each part of the weaving was a means of allowing the student to run his fingers between the threads – from top to bottom - when he touched the material and thus be able to detect the differences of the crossings, as well as to make contact with the threads that had no alternations with the palm of his hand. Each board was shown separately to each student and the sequence of the display was designed to bring the similar patterns closer together and highlight the differences between them (Fig. 2).

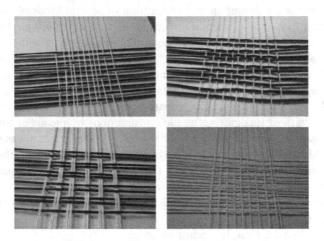

Fig. 2. Warps for woven fabrics. Source: author's property

(b) Open yarn threads

The boards with exposed yarn threads were manufactured with the aim of showing how the cloth appeared, although it remained possible to identify the woven fabric by touch. There was no handling of the underneath surface with these but only the upper surface. Grosgrain ribbons were used with a thickness of 20 mm, and without any separation between them (ratio of 200:1). As stiff material was used, it was feasible to locate the woven patterns and distinguish between them (Fig. 3).

Fig. 3. Open yarn threads. The image (A) shows the board from above which makes it possible to view the weaving that forms the fabric in its entirety. In the images (B) and (C), with details of the boards, the woven fabric can be seen between the warp and the weft. Source: author's property.

After the boards with exposed yarn threads had been shown, the students began to handle the boards with exposed warp threads. At the same time, they paired up the different types of patterns with a view to perceiving the specific features of each formed fabric.

In the following stages, all the guidelines for the textile structures of the flat cloth were applied to the fabrics made in the loom, either by hand or industrially.

(c) Handloom – open thread

In this stage, the sample employed is made by a handloom with a more exposed warp enforced by the use of cotton fibres, viscose and polyester, which provide fabrics with a greater pliability so they have a better fit.

After the boards shown in stages (a) and (b), there follows a more complex reading for the identification of the woven fabrics, since now a ratio of 5:1 was adopted. However, the possibility of a tactile perception of the formation remained. The boards of stages (a) and (b) remained available for consultation and allowed action between the samples so that the reference-points obtained earlier would not be lost (Fig. 4).

Fig. 4. Handloom – exposed warp. Source: author's property

Fig. 5. Handloom – closed thread. The samples (A) and (C) show fabrics of cotton fibre made by a handloom. Sample (B) cloth with acrylic filaments made in a handloom. Source: author's property.

(d) **Handloom – closed thread**

In this stage, samples of fabric manufactured by a handloom with different cotton and acrylic fibres and filaments were selected. The purpose of this was to show that the raw material used had a direct effect on the texture when the cloth was touched. This also alters its density and grammage and as a result, the tactile perception. In the case of samples [A] and [C] a ratio of 5:1 was adopted, while for sample [B] the ratio was 3:1. The difference in scale between the samples was proportional to the degree of thickness of the threads.

As in the case of the earlier stages, the students were able to go back to the earlier samples and make comparisons and in this way identify the changes in the threads from the most open to the most closed.

Generally speaking, the industrialised fabrics are the most widely used for the manufacture of clothes products on a large scale. These are examined in the final stage of the experiment.

(e) **Industrial looms**

A number of samples of industrialised fabrics completed the experiment; these included smooth fabrics or those worked with dyed, striped and machine-made yarns. A ratio of 1:1 was adopted for all of them. In this stage, the tactile perception of the woven fabric is a highly complex matter. Visual perception can only assist in this identification by means of a magnifying glass – a condition that does not apply to the group of visually handicapped students. In this case, the tactile perception was transferred to the protuberances and textures that can be found in the fabrics in question. In other words, fabrics are perceived through the tactile qualities of the cloth such as softness which results in a larger number of threads per cm^2; porosity resulting from a lower number of threads per cm^2; and stretching, defined by the kind of intervals between the stitching of the warp and weft threads, among other factors (Fig. 6).

Fig. 6. Industrial loom. Source: author's property

4 Results and Discussion

(a) **The tactile perception of the way threads are arranged was heightened by broadening the range, the use of the outward appearance of threads and the three-dimensional representation of the woven fabric.**

This three-dimensional representation, which is heightened by the weaving, took place as a kind of tactile magnification. The optical means of broadening the range was shifted to the sense of touch. In this way, it was possible to stimulate the tactile perception of volume or, in other words, to form a three-dimensional space through different arrangements of the threads. In terms of growth, the different textures of the threads provided a distinct way of stimulating the perceptions and heightening the awareness of the students when making a cognitive record of this information. As well as forming perceptual images from several sensory domains, the brain must store the respective patterns of these images so that any attempt to reproduce them can be successful [2].

(b) **The tactile perception of the arrangement of the textile strands was heightened by the broadening of the scale and by the two-dimensional representation of the woven fabrics.**

The broadened or flat two-dimensional representation of the weaving stimulated the tactile perception of the surface, or in other words, created a two-dimensional space through different arrangements of the strands. "The brain records the various results of the interactions of the organism with the entity (i.e., the object)" [2], rather than only recording the structure of this object. The memory of an object "consists of the sensory and motor activities related to the interaction between the organism and the object during a given period of time" [2].

(c) **Tactile perception occurred in an open thread even when there was a reduction of the range.**

Tactile perception was made possible by the size of the warp, the differences in the outward form of each thread and the distinct kinds of weaving that can be traced on both sides of the fabric (front and back). The difference between this stage and those that preceded it "lies in the degree of complexity of the memorizing process. This complexity can be measured by the number and range of items remembered from a particular target or event, (...) the greater the degree of sensory/motor activity reconstituted (for a particular object), the greater the degree of complexity" [2].

(d) **Tactile perception of a closed warp thread occurred at the same or at a lower rate.**

The fact that tactile perception occurred in this situation can be attributed to the presence in the three samples of protuberances in the material. Moreover, since samples A and C (Fig. 5) had a greater density and thickness, as a result of the use of 100 % cotton fibre in their weaving, it was easier to carry out a tactile identification of the woven fabric. However, sample B (Fig. 5), woven in 100 % acrylic filaments made it difficult but not impracticable for a tactile reading to be carried out for the woven fabrics since the raw material had less density and thickness. The mind "is now full of a varied assortment of images, (...) and these enter and leave the awareness of a presentation that is too rich (i.e., complex) to occur rapidly or be entirely comprehensive" [18].

(e) **Tactile perception took place through a transfer of knowledge.**

"(Cerebral) maps are formed when we evoke objects which are databases of memory within the brain" [2]. In this sphere, textile recognition takes place through an association of the textile descriptors with features of the textile structures learnt in the previous stages. Making repeated comparisons between the boards proved to be an essential strategy for consolidating the mental images formed during the teaching & learning process. The mental image enables the images resulting from the current perception to be merged with those that arise from memory. This form of integration allows an extensive handling of images that are indispensable for creativity and for solving new problems [17].

5 Conclusion

The difficulties experienced in identifying textile structures and being able to distinguish between them when faced with flat fabrics, is a recurring problem when training fashion design students in the area of textile design. This situation becomes increasingly complex in the teaching & learning of visually handicapped students given their limited ability to make use of visual aids and the resulting transfer of this means of perception to the other senses.

   In view of the key role that tactile perception plays in the recognition of textile structures, the recommendation of a new methodology aimed at stimulating the tactile sense, rather than that provided by visual stimulation, can bring significant benefits to students by enabling them to identify and distinguish between textile design fabrics, whether they have normal sight or not.

The formal experiment conducted for this research study set out different types of stimuli for tactile perception by students with visual impairments, including in particular: volume, surface, texture, density and grammage.

The principle results demonstrated the importance of broadening the range and making two and three-dimensional representations of the woven fabrics to heighten their awareness when identifying and distinguishing between textile structures. As it evolved, the presentation of teaching material in an ordered sequence enabled students to go back to experiences related to the preceding stages and thus consolidate these memories.

The main value of this study is that it draws attention to how the horizons of these students as fashion designers can be broadened, by endowing them with a capacity to carry out a tactile reading of the textile structures and as a result distinguish between them. This can enable them to make an appropriate definition of the fabrics in accordance with different items of clothing or garments in a collection.

The future ramifications of this research study will be aimed at the application and validation of this methodology to groups of students with normal sight, doing courses in fashion design.

References

1. Hidaka, S., Teramoto, W., Sugita, Y.: Spatiotemporal processing in crossmodal interactions for perception of the external world: a review. http://www.ncbi.nlm.nih.gov/pmc/articles/PMC4686600/
2. Damásio, A.R.: E o cérebro criou o homem [And the Brain Created Man]. Companhia das Letras, São Paulo (2011)
3. Estrela, J.B.C., Ribeiro, J.S.F.: Analysis of the Relationship between Memory and Learning in the Construction of Knowledge (2012). http://www.grupouninter.com.br/intersaberes/index.php/cadernointersaberes/issue/view/52
4. Hallet, C., Johnston, A.: Fabric for Fashion, a Complete Guide: Natural and Man-Made Fibers. Laurence King Publishing Ltd., London (2014)
5. Saltzman, A.: El cuerpo diseñado: sobre la forma em el proyecto de la vestimenta [The Designed Body: on the Question of Shape in a Clothes Project]. Paidós, Buenos Aires (2004)
6. Kunzler, L.S.Q.: Estudo das variáveis de rugosidade, dureza e condutividade térmica aplicado à percepção tátil em design de produto [A Study of the Variable Factors Involved in Creasing, Hardness and Thermal Conductivity Applied to Tactile Perception in the Design of Products] (2003). http://www.lume.ufrgs.br/handle/10183/4004
7. Carvalho, F.: Sensory Analysis of Textiles: Fabric Sorting Through Handle. http://www.coloquiomoda.com.br/anais/anais/11-Coloquio-de-Moda_2015/COMUNICACAO-ORAL/CO-EIXO2-ENSINO-E-EDUCACAO/CO-2-ANALISE-SENSORIAL-DE-TEXTEIS.pdf
8. Sorger, R., Udale, J.: Fundamentos do design de moda [The Fundamentals of Fashion Design]. Bookman, Porto Alegre (2009)
9. Chataignier, Gilda: Fio a fio: tecidos, moda e linguagem [Thread by Thread: Fabrics, Fashion and Language]. Estação das Letras e Cores Editora, São Paulo (2006)

10. Ruth Schilling, E.A.: Surface design: practice and learning mediated by digital technology (2002). http://www.lume.ufrgs.br/handle/10183/131159
11. Preusser, S., Thiel, S.D., Rook, C., Roggenhofer, E., Kosatschek, A., Draganski, B., Blankenburg, F., Driver, J., Villringer, A., Pleger, B.: The perception of touch and the ventral somato-sensory pathway (2014). http://brain.oxfordjournals.org/content/138/3/540.long
12. Martin, J.H.: Neuroanatomia: texto e atlas [Neuro-Anatomy: Text and Atlas]. AMGH, Porto Alegre (2013)
13. Carter, R.: O livro de ouro do cérebro [The Golden Book of the Brain]. Ediouro, Rio de Janeiro (2003)
14. Ferrè, E.R., Walther, L.E., Haggard, P.: Multisensory interactions between vestibular, visual and somatosensory signals (2015). http://www.ncbi.nlm.nih.gov/pmc/articles/PMC4395320/
15. Masson, S., Foisy, L.-M.B.: Fundamental concepts bridging: education and the brain. McGill J. Educ. (Université du Québec à Montréal) 49(2) (2014). http://mje.mcgill.ca/article/viewFile/9172/6972
16. Tokuhama-Espinosa, T.N.: The scientifically substantiated art of teaching: a study in the development of standards in the new academic field of neuroeducation (mind, brain and education science). Pesquisa de Doutorado, Capella University (2008). https://www.researchgate.net/publication/36710537_The_Scientifically_Substantiated_Art_of_Teaching_A_study_in_the_development_of_standards_in_the_new_academic_field_of_neuroeducation_mind_brain_and_education_science
17. Damásio, A.: Em busca de Espinosa: prazer e dor na ciência dos sentimentos [In Search of Espinosa: Pleasure and Pain in the Science of the Feelings]. Companhia das Letras, São Paulo (2004)
18. Damásio, A.: O erro de Descartes: emoção, razão e o cérebro humano [The Mistake of Descartes: Emotion, Reason and the Human Brain]. Companhia das Letras, São Paulo (2012)

Towards Effective Interventive Health Applications: On the Problem of User Triggering

Tim Dutz[✉], Augusto Garcia, Sandro Hardy, Stefan Göbel, and Ralf Steinmetz

Multimedia Communications Lab, Technische Universität Darmstadt, Darmstadt, Germany
{tim.dutz,augusto.garcia,sandro.hardy,stefan.goebel,
ralf.steinmetz}@kom.tu-darmstadt.de

Abstract. Extensive studies show that regular physical activity is one of the crucial factors to determine one's prolonged health and wellbeing. But although this knowledge is fairly widespread, many people still fail to meet the WHO recommendations for the weekly average of physical activity. While the reasons for this shortcoming are manifold, a lack of motivation on the one hand and a lack of awareness on the other may be considered to be the two main culprits. Interventive fitness and health applications, being both pervasive and persuasive, may help to counteract this problem by assisting the user during her daily routine in finding both the required motivation and good opportunities for being physically active. This contribution focuses on one of the main challenges of such applications, namely the identification of situations which are suited for notifying ("triggering") the user of a chance for physical activity.

Keywords: Interventive health · Pervasive applications · Persuasive technologies · Physical activity · User interfaces

1 Physical Activity and Health

Studies show that a minimum of 15 min of physical activity a day will significantly reduce all-cause mortality [1]. Consequently, the World Health Organization (abbr. WHO) recommends that *"Adults aged 18–64 should do at least* 150 min *of moderate-intensity aerobic physical activity throughout the week or do at least* 75 min *of vigorous-intensity aerobic physical activity throughout the week or an equivalent combination of moderate- and vigorous-intensity activity"* [2]. By using the terms "moderate-intensity" and "vigorous-intensity", the WHO refers to the Metabolic Equivalent of Task (abbr. MET) classification of physical activities. This convention assigns intensity values ("MET-values") to different types of physical activities, thereby arranging them in a hierarchy that ranges from the least intense physical activity - sleeping with a MET-value of 0.9 - to the most intense physical activity - running at 22.5 km/h (14 mi/h) with a MET-value of 23. The intensities of all other types of physical activity, such as dancing, gardening, or playing a musical instrument, lie somewhere in between those two extremes [3]. When referring to "moderate-intensity activities", the WHO means activities with a MET-value in between 3.0 and 6.0, and analogously, a "vigorous-intensity activity" is anything

© Springer International Publishing Switzerland 2016
N. Streitz and P. Markopoulos (Eds.): DAPI 2016, LNCS 9749, pp. 245–256, 2016.
DOI: 10.1007/978-3-319-39862-4_23

with a MET-value of above 6.0. According to this classification, a few examples of moderate-intensity physical activities would be brisk walking (MET 3.8), practicing Tai-Chi (MET 4.0), and mowing the lawn with an electric mower (MET 5.5). In other words: the WHO recommendations for the minimum amount of physical activity per day could already be reached by accelerating one's pace on the way to the bus stop in the morning and the evening, and by investing a few minutes into Tai-Chi exercises during the lunch break or after work.

As such, it may be considered somewhat surprising that a significant – apparently growing – part of the population fails to meet the WHO recommendations. According to Hallal et al. *"roughly three of every ten individuals aged 15 years or older - about 1.5 billion people - do not reach present physical activity recommendations"* and *"the situation in adolescents is even more worrying, with a worldwide estimate that four of every five adolescents aged 13–15 years do not meet present guidelines"* [4]. This prevalence of physical inactivity, especially among adolescents, is prone to negatively affect not just the life of individuals, but the state of societies as a whole. Janssen calculated that in 2009, *"the total annual economic burden of physical inactivity in Canadian adults was $6.8 billion"*, which equaled almost 4 % of that year's total Canadian health care costs [5]. Pratt et al. point out that the surprising low number of publications on the matter in recent years is probably due to the fact that at least in North America, Australia, and Europe, the awareness for the fact that the physical inactivity of their populace induces a financial burden on these societies has become widespread enough [6]. So, what is stopping so many people from not even reaching the low-end goals?

In several studies conducted among a total of 17,000 Australian adults, the top three barriers to being physically active were found to be a lack of time, a lack of ability, and a lack of motivation, in this order [7]. In the light of the previously made considerations that the WHO recommendations for physical activity can be reached fairly easily by simply integrating a few moderate-intensity physical activities in one's daily routine, it must be concluded that for the majority of non-active individuals, either a lack of awareness or a lack of motivation (or both) are the actual problems. Here, "lack of awareness" means that while most people probably have knowledge of the fact that physical inactivity is bad for them, they may not be aware of how small the amount of physical activity actually is that is required in order to profit from associated health benefits. Furthermore, many may not be aware that physical activity is not only helpful for fighting obesity, but also to reduce the risks of suffering from heart diseases, high blood pressure, diabetes, and certain types of cancer [8]. In this regard, both the lack-of-ability and lack-of-time arguments may be based on the misconception that reaching physical activity goals implies having to endure highly stressful tasks such as the dreaded 10-mile runs.

Summarizing this chapter, we find that the WHO recommendations for physical activity could be met fairly easily by slightly adjusting one's daily routine, but that a lack of motivation and a lack of awareness seem to keep many people from achieving this. Methods for effectively counteracting this problem should thus be able to motivate people on the one hand, and to highlight opportunities for a few minutes of medium-intensity activity on the other.

2 Pervasive Applications for Health

Since the introduction of the first iPhone in 2007, smartphones have become incredibly prevalent. More than 1.4 billion new devices have been sold in 2015 alone [9]. In a similar manner, the introduction of the first Apple Watch in 2015 had a significant impact on the wearable market and helped it grow by 170 % in comparison to the previous year, up to almost 80 million units sold in 2015 [10]. Smartphones and wearables are different to classic laptops, desktops, and video game consoles in that they accompany their users throughout the entire day. This characteristic of being almost always readily available to interact with the user is called "pervasiveness" and smartphones and wearables are a huge step towards pervasive computing, as originally envisioned by Weiser in 1991 [11].

As we have pointed out before, their pervasive nature makes smartphones and wearables ideal tools for technology-based health-related interventions [12]. Frequently reminding the user of the necessity of doing (or not-doing) something specific increases the likelihood of her actually showing the desired behavior. Social sciences have coined the term "nudging" for this kind of friendly reinforcement [13]. There are a growing number of smartphone applications that aim to stimulate and support "healthy behavior" during the day by "nudging" the user. Examples include applications meant to ensure that the user is drinking a sufficient amount of water in order to avoid dehydration[1], and applications that want to ensure that the user stays compliant to her goal of quitting smoking[2].

The stimulation of a sufficient amount of physical activity throughout the day is one of the main features of the Apple Watch. The so-called "Activity App" of the device uses three concentric colored rings to visualize the user's daily progress in the categories "Move", "Stand", and "Exercise". For the red-colored Move-ring, the user initially specifies the extra amount of calories that she wants to burn during the day besides her basal metabolic rate. The goal represented by the green Exercise-ring is to achieve a total of at least 30 min of at-least medium-intensity physical activity. And finally, the blue Stand-ring is filled if the user manages to stand or walk for at least sixty consecutive seconds in at least twelve different hours of the day. The device relies on its built-in inertial sensors for the assessment of all of these values. The images of Fig. 1 show the Activity App in different stages.

The Apple Watch and its Activity App represent a milestone towards effective technology-based health interventions. The Move-ring enables users to set personal goals for the day. The Exercise-ring only fills if the watch detects at least medium-intensity physical activities, thus making it easier for the user to identify relevant physical activities. And finally, the Stand-ring frequently encourages – *nudges*, if you will – the user to interrupt her prolonged sitting. The corresponding "Time to stand!" message (see Fig. 1) comes with a little beep and a soft vibration of the device, a friendly reminder to be physically active. However, in its current state, the Activity App of the Apple Watch also has several shortcomings.

---

[1] "Plant Nanny" by Fourdesire, available for iOS, Android, and Windows Phone.
[2] "Smoke Free" by David Crane, available for iOS and Android.

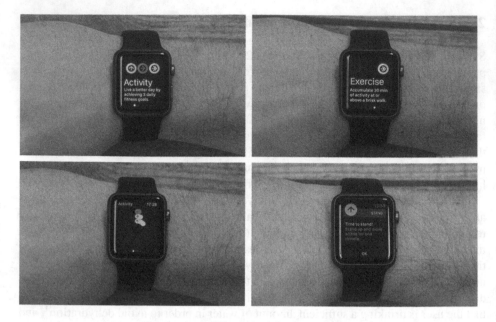

Fig. 1. Apple Watch Activity App screens.

Leaving aside reports on inaccurate activity detection, one of the main problems of the Activity App is certainly the way that the "Time to stand!" feature is implemented. The notification comes once every hour, more specifically ten minutes before the next hour if the user has not been very active during the last. The application does not differentiate between contextual situations and as such it also tries to activate users sitting in meetings, movie theatres, or those driving a car. This "stubbornness" is prone to irritate and eventually annoy users and may ultimately lead to them entirely disabling the feature. In this regard, it must be subsumed that the Activity App does nothing to assist the user in identifying opportunities for being active; it merely functions as a frequent and possibly ill-timed reminder that activity is important.

Another shortcoming of the Activity App regards user motivation. The goal of closing the three activity rings each day will certainly appeal to the intrinsically motivated and studies conducted with one of the Apple Watch's competitors in the market, the Fitbit wristband, showed that wearables and their ability to quantify physical activities can indeed have a long lasting positive effect on the physical activity of their users [14]. In direct comparison, the increasing effects of pure reminders – such as the Apple Watch's "Time to stand!" messages – seem to last for only a few days [15]. However, we need to ask the question if the mere quantification of activity is also a sufficiently large motivator to those that do not enjoy physical activity for its own sake.

3   Overcoming Physical Activity Barriers

Indeed, the problem of how to encourage the not-intrinsically-motivated for more physical activity is heavily debated. In recent years, the industry tried to improve the motivational appeal of its fitness trackers and healthy living applications with the widespread integration of gamification mechanics [16], although the actual effectiveness of gamification in this context remains questionable [17]. The incredible commercial success of the Wii Sports game for Nintendo's TV-screen based console Wii [12], released in late 2006, sparked a significant amount of research on so-called exergames – video games that require the user to be physically active in order to advance in the game – and on the question, whether or not these exergames can effectively motivate users for physical activity. But although it has been found that such games are motivating to many users in the short-term [18], long-term studies that prove a lasting effect are still hard to come by.

In order for interventive health applications to be effective, they need to be provided with the means to be able to overcome the barriers for the desired activities. The psychologist BJ Fogg created the "Fogg Behavior Model" (abbr. FBM) through which he explains the factors that decide, whether or not someone will show an intended behavior. According to Fogg, in order for a person to behave in a specific way, that person must *"(1) be sufficiently motivated, (2) have the ability to perform the behavior, and (3) be triggered to perform the behavior. These three factors must occur at the same moment, else the behavior will not happen"* [19]. The FBM explains that motivation and ability can compensate one another within certain limits. If a person is highly motivated for doing something specific, she may do it although she finds the task itself difficult or unpleasing. An example for this might be someone attending evening classes in addition to a stressful day job in hopes of obtaining a higher degree. On the contrary, if something is very easy to do, the person in question may still show the target behavior although her motivation for doing so is actually low. The final element in the FBM is the creation of awareness, represented by an activating mechanism called a "trigger". Fogg states that *"a trigger is something that tells people to perform a behavior now"* and goes on to point out that *"in fact, for behaviors where people are already above the activation threshold – meaning they have sufficient motivation and ability – a trigger is all that's required"* [19].

The FBM is a great tool for understanding the requirements for effective interventive health applications, or more specifically, for understanding the necessities for making people be more physically active. In the previously mentioned survey by Owen et al. [7], the main reasons given for sedentary behavior were "I have no time", followed by "I am not physically able", and finally "I do not want to". Leaving aside the possibility of a response bias that may have led to the "no time" argument instead of the "no motivation" argument placing first, we find in either case that the main factors that keep people from being physically active are well reflected by the components of the FBM: (1) we need to find ways of motivating users, especially those that do not take joy in physical activity, (2) we need to make it as easy as possible for users to be physically active, especially in regard to the time that needs to be invested, and finally, (3) we need to trigger users when both motivation and ability are sufficiently high (and ideally only then). Fogg explains that such an opportune moment to persuade was called a καιρός (*"kairos"*) in ancient Greek.

When we consider the features of contemporary devices and applications meant for promoting their users' health and fitness – and in early 2016, the Apple Watch must be counted among the most advanced of these – we find that although the progress made towards effective interventive health measures is clear, the state of the art still falls short of the actual goal. There are elements meant to motivate –quantification of physical activities and gamification – but it is at least questionable, whether these also have an effect on the actual problem group, namely those that endure physical activity rather than enjoying it. However, as can be learned from the FBM, a lack of motivation can at least in part be compensated through a sufficiently high ability. In other words: if we can find ways of making physical activity easy and simple enough, the motivational problem may indeed turn out to be a secondary one.

Fogg lists several elements of simplicity. Some of them, such as the investment of money and brain cycles, will usually not be obstacles to physical activity, leaving the investment of time, the required physical effort, a possible social deviance, and the question of whether or not it is a non-routine task to determine, whether the activity in question is considered easy to do by the user. In the first chapter, we found that both of the arguments that state "I cannot", namely the self-perceived "lack of time" and "lack of physical ability", are oftentimes actually a lack of awareness: awareness in regard to how (comparably) little time and effort must be invested to profit from health benefits. In order to promote physical activity, these two "I cannot" arguments must thus be countered at an opportune moment – a kairos moment – with a friendly but determined "yes you can, if you do it now and here".

In the light of the previously made considerations that low motivation can in part be compensated by simplicity, helping the user to identify good opportunities for being active, and possibly even telling her how to be active, seems to be key for the design of effective interventive applications to promote physical ability. In this regard, the stubborn "Time to stand!" reminder of the Apple Watch that comes every hour, regardless of the actual situation that the user is in, might be considered a first step in the general right direction and by chance, it may sometimes even be successful. But much more often it will not. What effective interventive applications rather need are mechanisms to allow them to precisely identify opportune situations – kairoi – when both motivation and, more importantly, ability are sufficiently high and when it is thus meaningful to activate – trigger – the user. And while basic versions of these user triggering mechanisms might concentrate on identifying opportunities for being active in which the user is not occupied in any other way, more advanced versions should also elaborate on the exact way of activity and possibly even point out its benefits, such as in: "There is a bus at the stop, which will wait for another three minutes. If you accelerate your pace now, you will be home 20 min early."

The identification of opportunities suited for physical activity that integrate smoothly into the user's daily routine, meaning that they are as simple as possible to perform, is the core element for the design of effective means to promote physical activity. In the next chapter, we will discuss a possible architecture for such systems and present the evaluation results of its first prototypical implementation.

4   An Architecture for Effective User Triggering

First and foremost, effective triggering requires an understanding of the user and her situation. Even if a person is highly motivated to comply, asking her for as little as to stand up may be asking too much in certain situations – left alone asking for a medium-intensity physical activity such as taking a brisk walk around the block. As such, the first requirement for devices and applications that intend to promote physical activities pervasively during the day is the ability to assess the state of the user and of her surrounding as precisely as possible. Where is the user, when is her next appointment? The second necessity is to then make sense of the bits of information that have been gathered. If the GPS module states that the user is in her office but according to the system clock, it is late Monday evening, does this mean that the user is "working"? Or is this already "spare time"? The third and final challenge lies in understanding the user: Is this a good moment for reaching out to her? Will she consider the proposed activity to be simple enough, and will she be sufficiently motivated?

By arranging these three questions in the given order, answering them becomes increasingly user (and task) dependent. While information about the state of the user's environment can be assessed independently of any knowledge of the subject itself, the implications that come from putting these facts together are already dependent on the individual user. For assessing that the user is "at work", for example, we need to have knowledge about where "at work" is. Finally, anticipation of how the user will react to a triggering attempt at a given moment can only succeed if intimate knowledge about the user's behavior patterns and preferences is taken into account. These behavior patterns and preferences are in turn dependent on the target behavior that the trigger tries to provoke: at a given moment, the user's motivation and ability to drink a glass of water will oftentimes be different from her motivation and ability to run around the block.

Regardless of the actual user and task at hand, however, we find that in accordance to the FBM, a triggering attempt will be successful if – and only if – the user's motivation and (self-perceived) ability to perform the respective task are sufficiently high at that very moment. The designers of devices and applications for interventive health aiming to provoke certain types of behavior, such as episodes of medium-intensity physical activity, need to take this into account when they intend to increase the effectiveness of their products.

Figure 2 shows an abstraction of an effective triggering mechanism. This six-step cycle is centered on the question, whether or not to trigger the user and includes the following phases:

1. **User Decision-Making:** The cycle starts with the user who has just received a triggering notification through her device or application, for instance asking her to perform a specific kind of medium-intensity physical activity. During this phase, the user decides whether or not to show the target behavior, a decision based on her motivation and ability for performing the requested activity at the moment of the triggering attempt. This phase is a black box to the system – only its consequences can be observed.

2. **Attempt Monitoring:** After the triggering attempt, the user will either behave in the intended way, or not. In any case, in order to improve the effectiveness of the system and reach a higher triggering precision, the user's reaction to the trigger should be monitored.

3. **Information Gathering:** This step of the triggering process consists of the collection of any kind of information that might be helpful to improving the accuracy of the two subsequent steps. It involves the gathering of information that can be picked up by the triggering device itself (e.g., sensory data), but also data coming from other sources such as external devices or applications, especially web services (which, for instance, can deliver information on the local weather). This phase is largely independent of the user and the target behavior.

4. **Information Reasoning:** In this phase, the mechanism needs to make sense of the raw data that has been gathered during the previous step of the process. The aim of this step is to categorize the current situation as precisely as possible. There is a certain user-dependence in this step. For example, to be able to state that the user is "at home", knowledge is required about where "home" is. Consequently, the system needs to provide ways for gathering user input, for instance a configuration menu.

5. **Triggering Decision:** This is where the system decides, whether or not it is meaningful to try to trigger the user. This step is highly dependent on the user and the intended target behavior, more precisely on the question, whether the system assumes that the user's motivation and ability to show the target behavior are sufficiently high given the recognized situation. In other words: whether the system believes to have recognized a "kairos moment" for triggering the user. If the system answers this question with "yes" (believing in a sufficiently high probability for a successful triggering attempt), it continues with step 6 of the process. Otherwise, if it believes a triggering attempt is likely to fail in the current situation, it returns to step 3 and restarts the "gathering-reasoning-decision"-loop.

6. **Trigger Delivery:** If the system has decided that a triggering attempt is worthwhile, it needs to select a modality for delivering the trigger. This selection is again dependent on the user and the situation. A user that is already moving might neither notice a text message nor a vibration of the device, but may pick up a sound. Likewise, the system should of course never try to notify a user with hearing impairments using this modality. The final task of the process is the actual delivery of the trigger and – if possible – the assurance that it has been received. This is where the cycle ends and begins anew.

This description of the process is far from being exhaustive and the implementation of such a system requires various additional design decisions, whereby the majority of open questions are related to the "information gathering $\rightarrow$ information reasoning $\rightarrow$ triggering decision"-loop (steps 3 to 5). One of these questions is what kind of information should be gathered during step 3 as the basis for the categorization of situations in step 4 which, in turn, is the foundation for the triggering decisions made during step 5. Whether or not to trigger depends on whether or not the system believes the user's motivation and ability to be high enough, so the information gathered during step 3 should be suited to provide the answers to these questions. As a related problem, gathering information will usually require resources such as processing power and – for

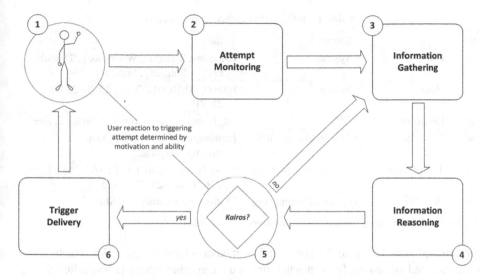

Fig. 2. Triggering process

mobile devices – battery, and in most cases, these resources will be limited. Consequently, since interventive devices and applications must be pervasive and accompany their users throughout their entire day in order for them to be most effective, there needs to be a certain management of such limited resources. Constantly gathering data and reasoning about it will usually not be an option. A workaround may be a timer that wakes the entire loop – or parts of it – in fixed intervals, but this harbors the danger of missing valuable knowledge and/or good triggering opportunities.

We have implemented a comparably simple version of this mechanism as an Android background service and evaluated it with ten persons for a total of two weeks. Of the original ten test users, three dropped out during the evaluation, leaving us with seven complete data sets. The triggering mechanism used simple text messages in order to encourage users to play the mobile exergame Twostone[3]. Every fifteen minutes, our prototypical application activated itself to gather input from six sources of information. Based on these, it then decided whether or not to try and activate the user. The decision finding mechanism was realized as a decision tree. Table 1 details the parameters that were considered during the information gathering phase (step 3) of the process.

The evaluation of our triggering mechanism was split into two phases, each lasting a single week. During the initial learning phase, the decision tree was relearned after each triggering attempt, regardless of whether successful or not. Furthermore, in order to gather a sufficiently large set of examples, the user was not only being triggered when

---

[3] Twostone is a mobile exergame developed at the TU Darmstadt, Germany, currently only available for Android devices. It is the successor of the game PacStudent that we introduced earlier [12], and requires players to run from virtual enemies while collecting virtual resources. Although Twostone is a location-based game, it allows players to create their own game levels and can thus be played almost anywhere. Twostone can be downloaded for free from the Google Play Store.

Table 1. Information gathering parameters

ID	Type	Source	Values
1	Day	System	{Monday, Tuesday, Wednesday, Thursday, Friday, Saturday, Sunday}
2	Hour	System	{00:00, 00:30, 01:00, …, 22:30, 23:00, 23:30}
3	Location	GPS	{at_home, at_work, other_1, other_2, else}
4	Movement	Accelerometer/GPS	{resting, moving, moving_fast, moving_very-fast}
5	Temperature	openweathermap.org	{<−5 °C, −5 °C to +5 °C, +6 °C to +15 °C, +16 °C to +25 °C, >+25 °C}
6	Weather	openweathermap.org	73 different weather conditions[a]

[a]See http://openweathermap.org/weather-conditions for details (accessed 2016-02-26).

the attempt was likely to be successful, but also whenever an unknown situation occurred, and occasionally even when previous triggering attempts had failed during the recognized situation. This resulted in a significant amount of unsuccessful triggering attempts during the first week, which required some patience and dedication on part of the test users. In order to somewhat ease the strain on the users, they were able to specify times and locations when the system should not try to trigger them, i.e., during the night or while being at work. Nevertheless, three out of the ten original participants dropped out during this phase of the evaluation. During the second week of the evaluation, the decision tree constructed during the first week was kept fixed. Triggering attempts were limited to those situations when they were considered likely to be successful.

The results of this little test run were promising. After the second week of the evaluation, we asked the test users to rate a couple of statements with a score anywhere between 1 (no agreement at all) and 10 (total agreement). The arithmetic mean of the scoring of the statement "I found the triggering mechanism helpful" was close to 7, very similar to the mean score of the statement "The timing of the second week's triggers was mostly meaningful". As expected, the triggering mechanism was also found to be significantly more annoying during the first week (with a mean score of about 5) than during the second week (with a mean score of about 2). This indicates that "learning" triggers that adapt to the user's preferences may result in a higher acceptance than unintelligent triggering mechanisms that stubbornly try to activate their users in fixed intervals or at fixed locations.

5   Conclusions and Future Work

Interventive applications for health have the potential to increase the amount of medium-intensity physical activities of their users by helping them to identify good opportunities for such. However, the currently available devices and applications fall short of this task – even the most advanced of them resort to stubbornly reminding their users in fixed intervals that they should be more active. In this contribution, we have presented an abstract architecture for more effective interventive health applications and discussed the promising evaluation results of a first, simple implementation. We are currently working on more sophisticated prototypes that, among other things, will take into account a larger array of parameters and should thus be able to differentiate situations more precisely. We hope that this will help to identify good triggering opportunities more reliably and to thus create highly effective triggering systems able to significantly increase the daily amount of the medium- and high-intensity physical activities of their users.

Acknowledgement. This work was partially financed by the European Commission under the FP7-ICT-Project ALFRED (grant agreement no. 611218). The authors would like to thank Kevin Mais, Viktoria Swiatkowski, Siavash Tazari, and all participants of the evaluation for their valuable contributions.

References

1. Wen, C.P., Wai, J.P.M., Tsai, M.K., Yang, Y.C., Cheng, T.Y.D., Lee, M.C., Chan, H.T., Tsao, C.K., Tsai, S.P., Wu, X.: Minimum amount of physical activity for reduced mortality and extended life expectancy: a prospective cohort study. Lancet **378**(9798), 1244–1253 (2011)
2. World Health Organization: Global Recommendations on Physical Activity for Health. WHO Press, Geneva (2010)
3. Ainsworth, B.E., Haskell, W.L., Herrmann, S.D., Meckes, N., Bassett, D.R., Tudor-Locke, C., Greer, J.L., Vezina, J., Whitt-Glover, M.C., Leon, A.S.: 2011 Compendium of Physical Activities: a second update of codes and MET values. Med. Sci. Sports Exerc. **43**(8), 1575–1581 (2011). American College of Sports Medicine
4. Hallal, P.C., Andersen, L.B., Bull, F.C., Guthold, R., Haskell, W.L., Ekelund, U.: Global physical activity levels: surveillance progress, pitfalls, and prospects. Lancet **380**(9838), 247–257 (2012)
5. Janssen, I.: Health care costs of physical inactivity in Canadian adults. Appl. Physiol. Nutr. Metab. **37**(4), 803–806 (2012)
6. Pratt, M., Norris, J., Lobelo, F., Roux, L., Wang, G.: The cost of physical inactivity: moving into the 21st century. Br. J. Sports Med. **48**(3), 171–173 (2014)
7. Owen, N., Bauman, A.: The descriptive epidemiology of a sedentary lifestyle in adult Australians. Int. Epidemiol. Assoc. **21**(2), 305–310 (1992)
8. Lee, I.M., Shiroma, E.J., Lobelo, F., Puska, P., Blair, S.N., Katzmarzyk, P.T.: Effect of physical inactivity on major non-communicable diseases worldwide: an analysis of burden of disease and life expectancy. Lancet **380**(9838), 219–229 (2012)
9. IDC Press Release: The Worldwide Wearables Market Leaps 126.9 % in the Fourth Quarter and 171.6 % in 2015, According to IDC, 2 February 2016. http://www.idc.com/getdoc.jsp?containerId=prUS41037416. Accessed 26 Feb 2016
10. IDC Press Release: Apple, Huawei, and Xiaomi Finish 2015 with Above Average Year-Over-Year Growth, as Worldwide Smartphone Shipments Surpass 1.4 Billion for the Year, According to IDC, 27 January 2016. http://www.idc.com/getdoc.jsp?containerId=prUS40980416. Accessed 26 Jan 2016
11. Weiser, M.: The computer for the 21st century. Sci. Am. **265**(3), 94–104 (1991)
12. Dutz, T., Hardy, S., Knöll, M., Göbel, S., Steinmetz, R.: User interfaces of mobile exergames. In: Kurosu, M. (ed.) HCI 2014, Part III. LNCS, vol. 8512, pp. 244–255. Springer, Heidelberg (2014)

13. Thaler, R.H., Sunstein, C.R.: Nudge: Improving Decisions about Health, Wealth, and Happiness. Yale University Press, New Haven (2008)
14. Cadmus-Bertram, L.A., Marcus, B.H., Patterson, R.E., Parker, B.A., Morey, B.L.: Randomized trial of a Fitbit-based physical activity intervention for women. Am. J. Prev. Med. **49**(3), 414–418 (2015)
15. Wang, J.B., Cadmus-Bertram, L.A., Natarajan, L., White, M.M., Madanat, H., Nichols, J.F., Ayala, G.X., Pierce, J.P.: Wearable sensor/device (Fitbit One) and SMS text-messaging prompts to increase physical activity in overweight and obese adults: a randomized controlled trial. Telemed. e-Health **21**(10), 782–792 (2015)
16. Lister, C., West, J.H., Cannon, B., Sax, T., Brodegard, D.: Just a fad? Gamification in health and fitness apps. JMIR Serious Games **2**(2), e9 (2014)
17. Zuckerman, O., Gal-Oz, A.: Deconstructing gamification: evaluating the effectiveness of continuous measurement, virtual rewards, and social comparison for promoting physical activity. Pers. Ubiquit. Comput. **18**(7), 1705–1719 (2014)
18. Hardy, S., Göbel, S., Gutjahr, M., Wiemeyer, J., Steinmetz, R.: Adaptation model for indoor exergames. Int. J. Comput. Sci. Sport **11**(1), 73–85 (2012)
19. Fogg, B.J.: A behavior model for persuasive design. In: Proceedings of the 4th International Conference on Persuasive Technology. ACM (2009)

Body Storytelling and the Performance of Memory: Arts-Based-Research and Human Enhancement

Maria Manuela Lopes[1,2](✉)

[1] ID+ Instituto de Investigação em Design Media e Cultura,
Universidade de Aveiro, Aveiro, Portugal
mmlopes@ua.pt
[2] Instituto de Biologia Molecular e Celular, I3S,
Universidade do Porto, Porto, Portugal
maria@manuelalopes.com

Abstract. Since the late 1990s a new tendency has emerged in contemporary art whereby artists deploy archival research and scientific practices to explore the mechanics of historical representation, the location and material of memory and evoke the past. As a visual artist working with video, photography, film and scientific strategies and technologies (e.g. BCI's Brain Computer Interface and Biology/Bioengineering) Lopes explores the historical and personal representation and notions of memory materiality. Technologies, for memory preservation and enhancement of our humane bodies, are developing at a fast pace, and the corresponding dystopic and utopic future scenarios are constantly presented in speculative news reports, science research studies and popular culture such as science fiction. In this paper Lopes intends to examine two on-going artwork PostDoc research projects Enhancing the Mind's I and Emerging Self that address notions memory and representation, self-identity and the greater cognitive capacities promised by transhumanism and neuro-enhancent technologies.

Keywords: Art-based research · Neuroscience · Memory enhancement · Experiential cognition · Empathy · Embodied observation · Affect · Varela · Foucault · Latour

1 Introduction

We are facing a moment in time when our curiosity and technical possibilities (alongside some anxiety and fears) are propelling us to move from using the created techniques to restore our bodies to "normal" functioning, to using them to increase our innate abilities and, conceivably, add new body and mind capacities. Lopes' believes that, our use of enhancement techniques will increase in frequency, in the sophistication of the technologies and in the purposes for which they are currently used.

It's difficult for humans to live in the present; we are mind wired to be anxious about the future, and to dwell upon the good things of the past. These instincts allow us to carry on, since overestimating negative future possibilities better prepares us for them, and having nostalgia for the past suppresses memory of pain, hardship, making life overall seem better and more worth investing in. As the author investigates more about

© Springer International Publishing Switzerland 2016
N. Streitz and P. Markopoulos (Eds.): DAPI 2016, LNCS 9749, pp. 257–269, 2016.
DOI: 10.1007/978-3-319-39862-4_24

emerging technologies, alongside the experience of the Doctorate research in connection with the Dementia patients (that showed the fragility of memory and cognition), Lopes' [1] located what was looking for in terms of ethics, philosophy, aesthetics and the ability to have tangible tools for bettering the world. The author instills the spectator's natural fire in them to drive innovation, cooperation and life preservation, The provocation and complexity presented in the installation art works intend to ensure innovation gets pushed forward, defending empathy, better communication and outreach for these fields. These works are ultimately about the fragile and contingent nature of memory and human futures; they invite the audiences to ponder the different dimensions, costs and unintended consequences of enhancement. Lopes' work extends and challenges this entwined relationship.

This paper is an exploration of the issues raised on the development of several artwork projects during the course of the author's Postdoc research, when in residency at a molecular biology institute - I3S, dealing with distinct studies and scales on memory (functioning and enhancement).

Lopes paper is a bid on critical evaluation of the production of the art works; departing from an understanding that the observer is not independent of reality [2] and that observation and experience are constructed [3]. In this understanding Lopes' explores the possibilities that memory and knowledge do not reflect a real exterior world, but a real interior world and attempt to play with possibilities to create empathy and affect in the audiences. Damásio [4] recognizes consciousness as resulting from the organism capacities to understand its emotions and the surrounding to interact with them; in line with his claim the art projects emphasize the need to clearly include emotions and affects that context triggers in humans.

Throughout the development of the text and artistic experiments concepts of self and memory emerge, for which the approach to the past experience does not appear as a sentimental and diverting nostalgic fantasy but, on the contrary, as a strategy to reflect critically on the present and re-imagine the future. The projects proposes a reflection on the ethical sides of Human Enhancement and the technologies, such as BCI or new digital tattoos (NT), promising a permanently refining the human form and mind by technological enhancement and to raise questions surrounding memory and identity through art installation and possible next steps in the human body's evolution. The author explores whether is it possible to translate ones emotions directly into an object as a memory of a certain moment.

The idea behind Enhancing the Mind's I is to design with the mind (both metaphorically and literally in a performance incorporating drawing, video, neurofeedback and brain computer interaction) multiplying ways in which memories become embodied and externalized, by using Lopes brainwaves as tools for a new humanistic arts based-approach.

Emerging Self explores the sensorium of surrounding space through innovative (artistic bioengineered) body tattoos that are perceived differently according to the body reactions to the surrounding space. Body perception, emotions and memory are expressed in skin – allowing differing selves to emerge.

Both art works attempt to expand on Foucault and Varela's challenge of surpassing the 'limits of representation' by allowing the mind that remembers to observe itself in the act of remembering. Lopes paper seeks to establish a speculative framework to inform holistic design choices from the perspective of philosophical and culturally relevant debates and a solid understanding of the art installations and Human perception, viewing perception as an active process and rejecting the Cartesian separation of body and mind. This approach is aligned with the ideas of phenomenology about embodiment – seeing the body, action and movement as the basis for experience and meaning (memory). This includes a consideration of the use of metaphors and living matter as synesthetic drivers of meaning, understood in and across different sensory modalities. The result is the opening of a critical gap between the way sciences produce knowledge about the subject and the affect produced by the experience of the viewer on the installation art works.

2 Art Making with Memory Matters

2.1 The Laboratory

The unique method/structure of the research presents an innovative holistic model for practice-led research: negotiating the interests of the involved institutions and NERRI (Neuro Enhancement Responsible Research and Innovation) project, schedules, bureaucracies, funding, and the public dissemination of its results in educational workshops, conferences, performances and exhibitions. It brings together understandings of the institutional and cultural framing of visual strategies, archiving and therapies; interrogating the possible application of scientific practices/inscriptions in subjective/visual discourse on memory but also assessing how are the novel technologies and practices (or the knowledge of their existence) for neuroenhancement reaching the general public.

The installation art projects correspond to a broader universe of research on different areas of memory, from technologies and techniques for memory enhancement, to strategies of acquisition (astrophysics imaging), preservation (archiving, recording, sampling - Botany) and communication (drawing, writing). Testing the boundaries, mixing old methods (such as mnemonics) with the current new technologies (such as Brain Computer Interface or Neurofeedback) Lopes makes the audiences wonder whether we should enhance ourselves, or seek to modify our children? What is being modified? There is no ground zero once many of the dimensions of human enhancement are evolving with the species subtly and pervasively.

While the press and the laboratory environment surrounding Lopes' practice covers the advancements on biotechnology and biomedicine the author finds the discoveries entwined with material seductions and ethical and social implications, thus her practice explores the subtle permutations of technology and aesthetics, utility and perils that inform and mediate the biotechnological creation of meanings. Memory practices and technologies of replication, processing, emergence and reproductions are ingrained both in the laboratory and the author' art practice, sharing semantic models of representation rooted and embedded in traditions of practice and available to novel arrangements as the frontiers of meaning, material shift, traces and matter.

The daily molecular biology and bioengineering laboratorial works reminds the author of the recent understanding of life's molecular architecture and the ability to control its workings adding a subtle promise to the understanding and control of memory and emotions and extension of the body timeframe. Since polymerase chain reaction (PCR) discovery and the readings of the genetic codes of living systems that scientists can read, alter, copy, edit and splice the genes bringing with it the panoply of dreams for reshaping the world we live in (internally and externally). The techniques are nowadays used to human applications in numerous forms such as genetic diagnostics, assisted conception, tissue engineering, and regenerative medicine, bringing about a new genre of human body repair or enhancement through technological assistance. Hence, if concepts such as truth, vision and knowledge are already complex in science and art fields, they seem to be contested in the future scenario when vision may be altered towards a more cyborg like performance (with x ray or infrared possibilities). If in the near future, neural implants could improve our ability to perform physically and mentally, at present researches are exploring ways to improve athletes' performance with gene doping (i.e. enhancing performance by adding or modifying genes), creative surgical enhancements (e.g. using skin grafts to create webbing between a competitive swimmer's fingers and toes) and mechanical prosthetics (e.g., the prosthetic legs used by double-amputee, athlete and top model Aimee Mullins). If in the research domain new cases of enhancement possibilities and promises burst frequently, in the public domain we were recently presented with an advance form of neural interface in the manner of the exoskeleton that allowed the paraplegic to kick the ball at the beginning of the Brazil world cup in 2014. With the concomitant advances in the digital domains, the increasing number of artificial, synthetic and biological extensions and processes are used to rebuild dysfunctional organs, to reconstruct damaged ones and to enhance others. The author asserts that biotechnology is remaking human bodies and identities and that it is important that art reflects on that stance.

The biological laboratory presents a labour-intensive (craft like) and visual world, with the guesses, hints or concepts and principles being translated into designed protocols that when followed reveal the abstract domain that preceded all the synthetizing, apparatus, labour, instruments and 'inscriptions' [5].

2.2 The Embodied Mind

The embodied approach, taken by Chilean researchers Maturana and Varela [2] or Dreyfus [6], deeply re-evaluates the role that subjective experience plays in the construction and expression of cognition and knowledge; following that it adjusts the research interests and methodologies useful to investigate the so-called embodied mind, the mind that is ontologically expressed by the connection with the body and the environment, the mind that has an ontological first-person dimension. It is the switch in the paradigm from a behavioural and computational one, towards an holistic and 'ecological' one (able to consider the central question for the science of the mind: the problem of 'Who', the problem of the subject and of the subjective perception of the world; the introduction of the term 'experience', which takes together the subject/object relationship in an ongoing, real, live modality and which offers a completely different perspective on the mind and the way to study it), that inspires this empirical and explorative search.

From the embodied perspective, as well as in Merleau-Ponty [7], the cognition is not considered only as the results of a series of cerebral functions that somehow and somewhere interface with the body of the thinking subject. Instead, it has to better seen as the result of the constant and structural interface activity with the body and the environment, the result of the sensory-motor information that create the background from which the mind can emerge and the horizon to which the mind can watch [7], The body constitutes the cognition itself, it generates it, and it is its phylogenetic and ontological matrix.

Thus memory, consciousness, self, all may be said to emerge both evolutionarily and biographically from the relationship of the mental and bodily aspects of the human nature, and with the environment, creating the lived experience [8], To know an object, Varela [9], pointed out, is to know the moment that generates the knowledge, being the mind of the knower in the process of knowing. One needs to go out of oneself to observe oneself in the act of knowing or observing. Subject and object co-specify and modulate each other. Knowledge depends on being at/on the world on the enactment of subjects in the world, upon the material, on its embodied condition.

In this line of thoughts, consciousness might be considered as the awareness of what is happing in a specific context in a specific moment: Then what are we precisely aware of? The body is the first object of four perceptions. Even when we don't intentionally often pay attention to the kinetic sensations the sensorimotor system creates what António Damásio calls the proto self [4], The body gives us the autobiographical memory continuity, or the common sense of self; the awareness of being the person we are, the same person of the day before, in a certain environment in a certain moment.

To Maturana and Varela [2], context is not independent of the subject but a background to intrinsic facts, therefore it is not objective and may not be conceived and understood independent from the ontogenesis of organisms. The environment and experience shape the mind; the thought does not merely relate to the body as an object of the outside world but is made from it [7], it does not results solely from the interactions in the brain, which is a specific organ, but in person, that is the organism. Foucault demonstrated that the knowing subject is the result of historical and social constructions, emerging from a set of rules and relationships that work in his/her body. The self is then not a determined or specific entity but an emerging result of the body enactment in/ through the world (to the author the self is co-constructed by memory).

2.3   The Art Projects

'Humans are cyborgs in the more profound sense of being human-technology symbionts: thinking and reasoning systems whose minds and selves are spread across biological brain and nonbiological circuitry'.
   Andy Clark (2003: 3) [11].

Enhancing the Mind's I. If the idea we have of ourselves is to be projected onto a material to be assessed by others (as in neuropsychology assessment) what is being judged? The communication skills, the capacity to lie and perform as expected by the viewer, the speed on which the task is performed, the imagination or the embedded memory? L. on participating as witness in several clinical neurological assessments, found visual plasticity and conceptual challenge on the relationship established between the complexity of the functioning of memory and the personal and constant construction of identity and also the strategies used by different fields of research to explore this entwined relationship. As an artist the researcher shares some tools and technologies with scientists, such as drawing, human-computer interaction and techniques of biotechnology; similarly L. is interested in understanding the materiality of memory, its functioning and the extension of remembrance, thoughts and personality from personal to collective engagement. If the preserved memory is intended to be passed on to others, it needs to be extracted from one's own mind and presented in a way that would make it accessible for others to perceive. The author explores whether is it possible to translate ones emotions directly into an object as a memory of a certain moment.

In cognitive science, visual mental imagery or 'seeing with the mind's eye' has been the subject of considerable controversy, especially concerning the underlying neural processes. Are mental images intrinsically different from thoughts expressed verbally? Is image information represented in a spatial format? How much is a person's perception of the blue sky due to memories of early visual experiences? Does mental imagery involve the activation of representations in the brain's visual cortex? Does an ability to generate strong mental imagery contribute to creativity? While in the last two decades there has been an intense effort to resolve these questions, most of the answers still elude us. In summary, seeing is considered a complex and mostly intellectual exercise, whether expressed pictorially or verbally. The physical act of seeing is strongly influenced by memory, visual perceptions and cultural experiences. The ability for this multilevel interpretation might be acquired at an early age, or even embedded in our genes but mostly it is a learned process. In the sciences clarity of expression (or interpretation) is essential.

Nevertheless, fine arts accommodate subtlety, and occasionally deliberate obscurity. In all instances, the image-maker is a communicator. An understanding of the act of seeing is pertinent in the process of mental image creation. Although it appears now, that visual mental imagery and visual perception share common underlying mechanisms, there are several reports, which show them to be dissociated, reflecting the basic modular organization of the visual cortex. Quoting Koster (1998): 'the binding of cellular activity in the processing-perceptual systems is more properly envisioned as a binding of the consciousness generated by each of them. It is this binding that gives us our integrated image of the visual world.'

The result is the opening of a critical gap between the way sciences produce knowledge about the subject and the affect produced by the experience of the viewer on the installation art works. The idea behind Enhancing the Mind's I (Fig. 1), is to design with the mind (both metaphorically and literally!) multiplying ways in which memories become embodied and externalized, by using L. brainwaves as tools for a new humanistic arts based-approach.

L.' explores unpretentious ideas of enhancement, such as the invention of the writing itself, as a development that simultaneously extended and impaired human memory, by providing an externalized written record but diminishing people's ability to memorize by removing the necessity of learning by heart. Husseyn [10] inquires about the

Fig. 1. Enhancing the Mind's I. Detail; Performance, Brave New World, Casa da Música, Porto, (Portugal). (L., in collaboration with Bastos, Marques & Teixeira 20) Source: L., 2015.

consequences of writing for human memory and further on the role technologies impact on our natural skills providing examples for contemporary discussions around human enhancement through technology and how external memory aids and other new technologies such as brain computer interfaces, are always double-edged, extending or fixing certain powers while eroding traditional skills.

Although the use of Brain Computer Interfaces (BCIs) in the arts originated in the 1960s, with the pioneering performances of Alvin Lucier, there is a limited number of known applications in the context of real-time artistic performances and accordingly the knowledge base of this area has not been developed sufficiently. Among the reasons are the difficulties and the unknown parameters involved in the design and implementation of the BCIs.

However today, with the dissemination of the new wireless devices, the field is rapidly growing and changing, and it is visible that artists work are harnessing the electroencephalogram (EEG) signals, bridging various methods and technologies and arising questions both in art/technology and in human experience. This project aims to develop cross-disciplinary relationships and encompass their evolving research to interrogate societal, artistic and ethical attitudes to neuroenhancement, memory and the preservation of the body, exploring the potential of neuro-stimulation/neurofeedback and EEG for artistic research.

A BCI is a system that captures the brain electrical activity in the form of EEG signals; further it translates those specific features of the signal that represents the intent (or unconscious desire) of the user into computer readable commands, Allowing its user to control a machine (e.g. a computer, an artificial limb, or any other machine) solely with brain activity rather than the peripheral nervous system. A typical BCI combines neurophysiological measurement technology with machine learning software to automatically detect patterns of brain activity that relate to this specific mental task. Control with a BCI is originated when a user performs a specific mental task.

Exploring 'drawing with the mind' (through the body action and possibly literally through thought and memory) by using the performer'/artist's memory brainwaves as tools for a new humanistic arts approach, is driven by several questions, such as;

- Is it possible to measure something intangible as memory and creativity?
- What can we learn from what brainwaves show us?
- Will wearing an EEG device influence the drawing process?
- Will clinical neuro-enhancing through neurofeedback expand the drawing capacity?
- Can one translate his/her emotions/memories directly into an object as a memory of a certain moment/place?
- Can new technologies allow us to observe the acts of remembrance and memory while forming new memories of that experience?

In the performances L. produces a series of Drawings following a neuroscientific/ psychological guideline for psychological assessment on identity and sense of self (i.e. The TST – twenty statements test protocol is to complete the 20 times in a row the sentence 'I am ...'). The drawings are constructed by writing, in graphite, sentences starting by 'I am'. After 20 sentences there is an interruption in the flow and the artist erases partially the resulted drawing. Immediately after that effacing action L. counter-acts enacting the procedure of writing another set of 20 sentences. Each event is performed after sessions of neurofeedback (Fig. 2) for cognitive enhancement (memory and creativity stimulation) and while having the author's brain being sensed for the different waves it produces. EEG measures frequencies of L. brain activity (Alpha, Beta, Delta, Gamma, Theta) relating to her state of 'consciousness' while wearing it. The data collected from EEG is translated in real-time to the computer that uses software to detect the brain waves and then transforms that information into data sending it to another computer which performs further actions (such as sending information into Processing or Arduino, which is linked with Max/MSP to receive data and generate sound or video or even controlling several printing and embroidering machines that produce further drawings). The EEG records the 'drawings' that L. brain is producing while thinking 'who she is' (i.e. who 'am I') and the production of the drawing is recorded in real time video. That video file is feed into the computer that edits it accordingly with the coor-dinates dictated by the performer brainwaves while drawing. The audience as access to the performance scenario and also to the video images of the brain waves captured by the first computer and furthers the projection of the final edited video. The drawings will endure until exhaustion of the material surface, her memory or other unpredictable enforcement.

Spaces, places and objects hold presences, experiences, wishes and memories that are constantly reshaped. We conceptualize our memories, verbalize them and confine them to the boundaries of a narrative (or several and in distinct moments, contexts and materials). Is art able to hold memories without deforming them by rationalization? Is BCI able to confirm that if as an artist L. is able to externalize her memories whilst remaining faithful to their own fleeting emotions, paradoxical, liminal and conflicting feelings, sorrows and joys, all those irreducible inner events that constitute the nature and identity of a person.

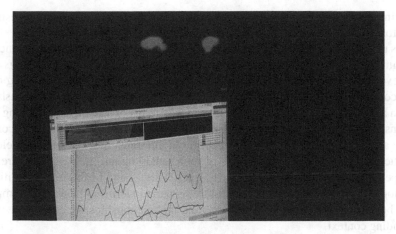

Fig. 2. Enhancing the Mind's I. Detail of Neurofeedback session performed at Neurobios, Clinica Professor Doutor Marques Teixeira, Porto, (Portugal). Source: L., 2015.

Emerging Self. In Emerging Self the materials that in biotechnology are used to mark a specific gene or any other technique used to investigate the inner workings of human bodies will be turned to reveal the boundary surface presenting in the skin the internal reaction to an inside or outside trigger.

Skin and touch, although primordial, are often undermined and veiled with conventions and taboos, but humans need touch to prosper psychologically and maintain health. L. emphasizes that we tend to be illiterate in terms of haptic memory and touching vocabulary, that even the proximity gestures invading personal space engender, sometimes, social awkwardness. The skin as a self expression canvas through the medium of decorative, protective, religious or medicinal tattoos dates far back and evidence of its instruments has been found from the Palaeolithic Period [12] with tattooed human bodies recovered from the Neolithic Period [13]. Traditional tattoo methods inscribe permanently the marks in the skin limiting future interventions and the reversal of the process.

New experiences and technologies provide ground for, in a similar way to the laboratorial apparatus, our own skins to become the inscriptive devices as well as matter that will allow narratives to unfold. As tattoos and scars are conceived as traces of emotional experiences, the expectation of the project is to produce tattoos that react according to environment conditions (interior or exterior variations), transforming the user body in a visible dynamic network organism. This is a concept of 'Dynamic Tattoo' [14].

This reversal of the power of the understanding of the network of reactions to sensitive environment might be considered an equivalent to the enabling of a seeing gift that substitutes empathic recognition or medical inspection. The attentive gaze could be substituted for a glimpse, and that would bring about a new set of human/human and human/machine relationship paradigm. Rather then being what we produce or the results of what our body produce (such as illness symptoms or actions driven by feelings) the subjects of observation, the proposed explorative art projects with the human machine interface bring about the possibility that memory itself is the object of scrutiny literally presenting itself thought the visible reactions on the surface of the skin or the results of the performance.

This unveils potential new dilemmas that are connected with culture, experience and environment rather than biological roots or racial identities if memory and feelings ought to be revealed at the surface of our actions or skins, as well as the empowering of the utopic controller of the settings that manage the coding of the interface relationship.

Skin and touch are often considered as minor in terms of sensing and learning. Skin may sense temperature, reacts to emotions and senses texture and other features conventionally attributed to vision, such as perception of different color through their electromagnetic frequencies. The conventions of representation and the visual culture have developed over decades both in art as in science. Further and further the scientific and technological visual culture defines the future scenario in terms of health, consumption, energy but also on the sense of humanness and the relationships we establish with the surrounding context.

Skin not as just a breathing organ but as a material 'membrane as liminal state of transience', as a metaphor for the exploration of what is natural or artificial, duration or memory. In contemporary life [15], skin, membranes and tissues rest in a pervasive cultural position positioning as an instrument and metaphor across theory and praxis.

In the beginning of this century wearable's field of research [16] promised to be a revolution offering opportunities for the creation of smart clothes that could perform functions according to the body's needs and adapting to the environment. Reminders of things to carry (such as keys or wallet), performing temperature feedback and adjustments in the clothes accordingly, or wearable medical devices that could monitor body conditions, was amongst the potentials. Although research on these fields is still expanding, to the author, those investments were surpassed by the research into new materials such as e skin or e ink that could transform the photonic or electronic technology that clothes/objects we transport could be made of, into something that could be made onto or under our skin and therefore be always present and not depend on the context or remembering of carrying the 'special jacket'.

In the past decade e skin research as exponentially grown [17] and the capacities and progress resemble science fiction narratives with sensors and circuits exceeding the properties of biological skin in many aspects (e.g. stretching further, superior spatial resolution.). The challenge still rests in its connections to the neural interface, something that the BCI are expected to solve in a near future [17].

New biocompatible materials and technologies are being develop and keep surfacing in the scientific magazines and the news, some of them belong to the areas of software and electronic engineering, materials and computer science, and other to biology, nanotechnology and bioengineering. With the development of new technologies, new kinds of dynamic tattoos are envisioned, enabling new types of situated and 'embodied multimodal communication' [18] and body/machine, body/environment relationships.

Some art projects such as (Tanguy Duff – Viral Tattoo; Art Orienté objet - Artists' Skin Culture; Amanda Wachob – WhipShade; Jill Scott - E-skin: Somatic Interaction or Wim Delvoye – Tim) already explore the techno-scientific scenarios, biocompatible materials and ethical considerations and cross modal potential expansions of communication through tattoo based projects and skin. This project leans on the existing ground of technological advances and conceptual context and is based on collaborations taking bioengineering materials outside the laboratory into the cultural domain. Apart from the dynamic of mass production or even desired consumption, this biological art project presents a speculative prototype for memory and imagination consumption. However the approach and discourse are those of arts and design in the fusion of objects, materials, social dynamics, production aspirations and the converging network of 'actors', an inquiry in the field of interaction between 'humans and nonhumans' [3].

If in the bioengineering laboratory the biomaterials are researched for health purposes, this project, at the interface of science, culture and technology explores the biological artefacts as well as all the surrounding dynamics of its construction encouraging new modes of engagement with the contemporary understanding of the fluctuating range of life forms and matter.

The *Emerging Self* deals with the dialogical relationship between the body and its representation and how the current bio-surveillance techniques have subtle undermined the conceptual parameters of this exchange. New technological tattoos may be considered an innovative field where cutting edge scientific and technological experimentation meets imaginative and speculative scenarios of creativity. The possibility of a real skin tattoo that would reflect and react to the emotional states and the environment plays on the inverted observation point that visualizing technologies in medical research have been exploring in recent decades (i.e. foregrounding the interior over the exterior). With dynamic settings possibly adjusted to each user the seeing through the skin process would become a malleable subjective process reversing the image process of the medical arena where expertise and converging fields are necessary to produce and interpret access to ones bodily structures and functioning's.[1]

3 Conclusion

Within Lopes research, the recognition of time and memory and the role these play in the construction of definitions of memory workings or loss and cognitive enhancement have come to the fore. The chosen approach is a poetics of time; identity and fragility, which explores the past, present and future of the memory studies portrayed within the scientific archive. The structure of the practice as a temporal briccolage displays a fragmented, multiple, jumbled narrative, where chronology itself is disrupted. Her explorative works intervene within the scientific/popular discourse to contribute to expanded ways of thinking about and looking at construction and validity of memory and identity, body and normality, and representation versus mediation, using art as a tool to enhance public awareness of several anxieties, disorders and technologies, raising ethical

---

[1] The continuous monitoring of biometric data that could be acquired from these extended tattoos and Human Computer Interfaces in an ordinary life situation (in line with the technological devises mentioned above being presently researched) explored as context in the art projects, holds a seductive appeal in terms of aesthetics giving rise to functionality; but furthermore to author it presents an unsettling future life style of bio control, demanding new elaboration of interpersonal exchanges between humans, biotechnological entities, computers and archival strategies.

dilemmas and questioning norms of behavior. The ambiguity of historical/personal time and the myth of authenticity are considered through an exploration of how the archive is assembled. The fragmentary nature of the practice ensures that no complete meaning can be fixed. The interlocking of historical and personal time, and the conjunction of both facts and fiction, enables a plurality of voices to be heard, contesting any dominant scientific or historical linear narrative.

The biological act of neural reprogramming through memory and learning and the parallel biotechnological and human, non- human relation in the irreversible collapse of the boundaries between interior and exterior, self and other, natural or artificial implied in the explorative art projects suggest the self reformulation of memory process, more evident in the era of the digital archive and the brain computer interface.

Acknowledgement. FCT Grant SFRH/BPD/98356/2013\.

References

1. Lopes, M.M.: Representational strategies on Alzheimer's disease: a practicebased arts research in a neuroscience laboratory. Doctoral dissertation, University of Brighton and University for the Creative Arts - Farnham, UK (2013, unpublished)
2. Maturana, H.R., Varela, F.J.: Autopoiesis and Cognition: the Realization of the Living. Springer, Dordrecht (1980)
3. Latour, B.: Pandora's Hope: Essays on the Reality of Science Studies. Harvard University Press, Cambridge/London (1999)
4. Damásio, A.R.: The Feeling of What Happens: Body and Emotion in the Making of Consciousness. Houghton Mifflin Harcourt, New York (2000)
5. Latour, B.: Science in Action: How to Follow Scientists and Engineers Through Society. Harvard University Press, Cambridge (1987)
6. Dreyfus, H.: What Computers Can't Do. MIT Press, Cambridge (1972)
7. Merleau-Ponty, M.: Phenomenology of Perception. Routledge, London (2002)
8. Gallagher, S.: How the Body Shapes the Mind. Clarendon Press, Oxford (2005)
9. Varela, F.J., Thompson, E., Rosch, E.: The Embodied Mind: Cognitive Science and Human Experience. MIT Press, Cambridge (1993)
10. Huyssen, A.: Present pasts: media, politics amnésia. Publ. Cult. **12**(1), 21–38 (2000). Winter
11. Clark, A.: Natural Born-Cyborg. Oxford University Press, Oxford (2003)
12. Gilbert, S.: Tattoo History: A Source Book. Juno Books, New York 2000. (2005)
13. Dickson, J., Oeggl, K., Handley, L.: A Saga Revivida De Ötzi, O Homem Do Gelo (2003). http://www2.uol.com.br/sciam/reportagens/a_saga_revivida_de_otzi_o_homem_do_gelo.html
14. Bitarello, B., Queiróz, J.: Embodied semiotic artefacts: on the role of the skin as a semiotic niche. Technoetic Arts J. Specul. Res. **12**(1), 75–90 (2014). doi:10.1386/tear.12.1.75_1. Intellect Ltd. Article. English Language
15. Jens, H.: Who's afraid of the in between? In: Hauser, J. (ed.) Sk-In Exhibition Catalog. Fact Liverpool (2008)

16. Tao, X.: Wearable Electronics and Photonics. Woodhead Publishing Limited in Association with the Textile Institute Abington Hall, Abington, Cambridge (2005)
17. Hammock, M.L.: 25th anniversary article: the evolution of electronic skin (E-Skin): a brief history, design considerations, and recent progress. Adv. Mat. **25**, 5997–6038 (2013). Wiley-Vch Verlag Gmbh & Co. Kgaa, Weinheim. Wileyonlinelibrary.com
18. Bitarello, B. Fuks, H.; Queiroz, J.: New technologies for dynamic tattoo art. In: Tei Fifth International Conference on Tangible, Enbedded and Embodied Iteraction. ACM, Funchal (2011). ISBN 978-1-4503-0478-8. http://doi.acm.org/10.1145/1935701.1935774

Voices of the Internet of Things: An Exploration of Multiple Voice Effects in Smart Homes

Yohan Moon[1], Ki Joon Kim[2], and Dong-Hee Shin[3(✉)]

[1] Department of Interaction Science, Sungkyunkwan University, Seoul, South Korea
ttattang@skku.edu
[2] Department of Media and Communication, City University of Hong Kong, Hong Kong, China
stand4good@gmail.com
[3] School of Media and Communication, Chung-Ang University, Seoul, South Korea
dshin1030@cau.ac.kr

Abstract. Based on the Computers Are Social Actors (CASA) paradigm, this study investigates an effect of media specialization by number of voice in smart-home environment where many smart devices are controlled by voice user interface (VUI). Result from a between-subjects experiment (N = 50) examines that there are interaction effects between users personality and number of voice on social attraction and trust toward media technology which are critical in human-computer interactions. In this experiment, extrovert users feel a stronger feeling of social attraction and trust when there is one identical voice from several smart devices. On the other hand, introvert users feel a stronger feeling of social attraction and trust when different smart devices make respective voices. These results provide a strong evidence for human's automatic social response to smart devices which have a voice, a strong anthropomorphic cue. Finally, we discuss on implications for future VUI setting, according to user's personality.

Keywords: Voice user interface · CASA · Natural user interface · Number of voice · User personality

1 Introduction

How do users perceive smart devices with different voices? Would users prefer single, identical voice or multiple different voices in smart devices? In a recently released movie "Her" (2013), a relationship between a lonely men and operating system which talks is illustrated. The scientific fiction gives an implication that people might possibly build a relationship with an agent which has a voice.

As natural user interface (NUI) has been an ultimate goal of user interface design [24, 25], Voice User Interface (VUI) has been pointed as promising way of user interface [16]. There has been a plethora of research on how users perceive a voice from a computer or a robot [12, 13, 19, 23]. However, how do users perceive multiple voices of different smart devices? This question has become increasingly important as the era of Internet of Things (IoT) emerges. As the IoT is filling our routine with various multiple voices of

---

The original version of this chapter was revised: The affiliation of the third author was corrected. The erratum to this chapter is available at 10.1007/978-3-319-39862-4_46

© Springer International Publishing Switzerland 2016
N. Streitz and P. Markopoulos (Eds.): DAPI 2016, LNCS 9749, pp. 270–278, 2016.
DOI: 10.1007/978-3-319-39862-4_25

smart devices, the investigation on how user perceives multiple voices from respective smart devices is getting important for socially meaningful user experience. Therefore, this study examines whether the number of voice (one voice x three voice) of smart device influences on user's feeling of social attractiveness, and trust toward media technology according to user personality (introvert x extrovert) in smart home environment.

1.1 Voice User Interface as Natural User Interface

A Voice User Interface is what a human interacts with in communication with a spoken language application [4]. As an ideal way for interaction with computer, voice user interaction has been pointed out. Because voice interfaces are regarded "more natural", compared to other types of interfaces (e.g., keyboard, mouse, touch screen), human-computer interaction by voice was inspired and motivated. Voice interfaces have a "look and feel" which is similar to human-human communications. The given assumption is that the more natural interface is, the more people would perceive and be accustomed to the interface easily and effectively. Providing "more natural" interface enables system to make use of skills and expectations that people has evolved through routine experiences for effective and expeditious communication [8, 15].

Science fictions have shown VUI when controlling machine by just talking only a short time ago. With the advance of technology, VUI have become more prevalent and people are practically making use of the usefulness that eyes-free and hand-free interface provided in numerous situations. Voice-based virtual privacy assistant agent embedded in various types of computers, ranging from laptop to mobile phone to smart devices, can execute numerous tasks. They transform voice to text, interpret requests from users, and seem to comprehend and execute what users ask, and even interact conversations based on online data and its own accumulated database.

In the past, there was also insistence that a successful human-machine interaction, similar to successful human-human interaction, was goal to execute the task effectively from the human's perspective. However, human-computer voice-based interactions of those days did not yet meet the accuracy, reliability, richness, or complexity developed in most human-human interactions. The deficiency was due to imperfect technology of voice recognition [8]. However, nowadays a successful level of recognition has been developed so that operating system like Siri or Now can comprehend what we say. Not only the reasons of its natural interaction way referred above, but this positively also affects various facets of user experience such as multitasking when doing some other things with our two hands, the ease of use when the task include too many screen touch. Especially helping not to select too many screen menus may helps users get tired of decision of choice by reducing moment of choice [2, 26].

Nowadays, voice-based virtual privacy assistant agent such as Apple Siri, Google now, Microsoft Cortana and Amazon Alexa can interpret natural speech. The advent of these voice-based agents had drawn an attention to the voice control system [29]. Moreover, Voice user interface is a type of way of interface which enables the users to send emails, schedule an appointment, turn on music, and more [7]. As the popularity increase, the voice agent is everywhere, functioning as ambient computing. From the mobile phone to smart phone to smart watch, to smart home environment such as smart speaker or smart TV, it has been embedded to multiple applications slowly and widely, as mostly privacy intelligent assistant agent.

2 Theoretical Approach

2.1 The Media Equation Theory: Do People Equate Smart Devices with Genuine Social Actor?

The meaning of "media equation" is that "individuals' interactions with computers, TV, and new media are fundamentally social and natural, just like interaction in real life" [27]. Because human have perceived that all the objects were real and only human had its own human-like shapes and characteristics like language, emotion, personality, rapid interaction, and so on. Human brains had evolved to treat anything that looks to be real as real and anything that seems to have anthropomorphic characteristics as real human. Therefore, when people face the any kind of media such as TV or computer, the limitation of perceiving everything at its outward value and responding to virtual action of media as if they were real occurs because of evolutionary reason. In this way, the media equation occurs [14]. Especially on human responses to computers, Nass, Steuer, and Tauber presented Computers Are Social Actors (CASA) paradigm [23], which means that individuals unconsciously apply social rules as if they were interacting with real human beings when interacting with computers that show anthropomorphic cues. The base of this research paradigm is that, if computers or machine people confront with have anthropomorphic cue, individuals automatically respond to them socially and do not perceive that they are not real human.

2.2 Voice as Social Attribution

Voice, rather than shape, has been pointed as key factor of social attributions toward computers [23, 28]. The important of voice as social cue has been argued in the previous researches on the HCI field in the aspect of CASA paradigm. With interactivity and filling of roles, words of output has been considered as important primary cues, which is held by humans, human-like characteristics. These kinds of cues seem to automatically induce schemata related with human-human interaction, without the psychological construction of relevant human [20].

One of the five experiments conducted to build the CASA paradigm demonstrated that "people respond to different voices as if they were distinct social actors, and react to the same voice as if it was the same social actor, regardless of whether the different voice was on the same or different computer" [23]. This result shows the implication that people perceive social actors as many as they perceive the number of voice.

2.3 Theories of Attraction

There are two equally convincing social rules related to personality in and HCI literatures and interpersonal interaction—similarity attraction and complementary attraction. The similarity attraction rules insist that people are more stick to people who are similar to themselves, and prefer to interact with them. In accordance with this rule, perceived similarity, which means a degree of what we believe something is similar to ours, is sufficient to make us attracted to others [5]. Demographics, ethnicity, political attitudes, and personality are examples of making us believe that we are similar to others. The complementary attraction rule insists that people are apt to be attracted people who have opposite personality characteristics, so that their personalities make balance, complementary situation [6, 28]. However, there are just few studies in the comparison to researches supporting similarity attraction rule.

2.4 Extended Concept of Media Specialization

An abundance of research on specialization has been investigated in multiple contexts, demonstrating that technology which is assigned a specific role or area is perceived as specialist [9–11, 22]. In those previous studies, it is found that specialized technology, which has one specific label and functions the particular role, induces users to trust and prefer more than generalized technology, which has simultaneously two or no specified label, though those two technology perform same. For example, in the experiment conducted by Nass [23], participants watched the same news and entertainment materials on television sets. There were two different conditions of TV labels, the 'News TV' and 'Entertainment TV' (i.e., specialist) or 'News/Entertainment TV' (i.e., generalist). Participant who watched News and Entertainment on the specialist TV evaluated the contents higher and preferred them more than who watched the same contents on the generalist TV.

Based on categorization theory, label has been regarded as important signifier which triggers a set of related social category-based perceptions [1]. Initial impressions of an object are constructed primarily based on social categories brought by salient cue [9], such as label. In previous researches, media specialization was mainly

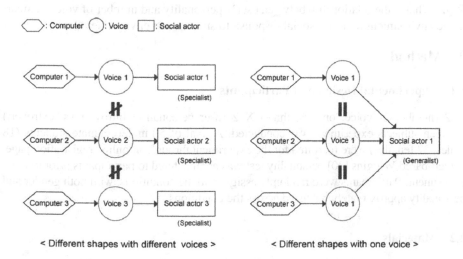

Fig. 1. Concept model proposed on relationship between computer, voice and social actor in the aspect of CASA.

made by labeling, such as attaching role name tag on the device. It has been thought to be a strong and effective way of specialization.

However, would it be possible to make specialization of the media with their voices? According to the concept of specialist and generalist, people tend to apply social response that individuals more trust and prefer the people who take only one role than people who takes simultaneously two or more roles when interacting with technology. Voice is distinctive social cue which makes individuals discern several social agents [18]. According to researches such as CASA paradigm and the media equation theory [23, 27], each one voice is perceived as one social actor. From the extension of interpretation of those researches, next hypothesis is inferred (Fig. 1).

Hypothesis 1. Users will have a greater feeling of trust to smart home environment when devices which have respective functions have their respective different voices than when those devices have one identical voice.

2.5   User Personality

User personality has been investigated in related HCI researches [12, 21]. For example, Nass and his colleague conducted experiment to observe when similarity attraction appears, dividing participants introvert and extrovert according to conditions [19]. Extroverts have a tendency that they are more social and outgoing than introverts [17]. According to similarity attraction rule [3, 21], the next hypotheses are inferred:

Hypothesis 2. Extroverts will be more attracted to smart device with multiple voices than one identical voice.

Hypothesis 3. Introverts will be more attracted to smart device with single voice than multiple voices.

Taking these hypotheses into consideration, the next research question is followed.

RQ: What is the relationship between user's personality and number of voice of smart home environment in user's social response to smart home environment?

3   Method

3.1   Experimental Design and Participants

A 2 (number of voice: one vs. three) X 2 (user personality: introvert vs. extrovert) between-subjects experiment was conducted. A total of 50 undergraduate students (18 males, 32 females) were recruited for the experiment through an online registration page. A web-based Wiggins [30] personality test was administered to participants prior to main experiment. Participants were randomly assigned to the conditions, with both gender and personality approximately balanced across the conditions.

3.2   Materials

Three voices were recorded from eight different women with specific guide on four voice parameters (speech rate, volume level, frequency, and a pitch range) [14] to keep voice's personality neutral. Among the eight recorded voices, only three voices which were rated as the most neutral and clearly different from the other were chosen by 10 people interview. To make respectively different voices, Text To Speech (TTS) or computer-generated speech were not used. Three smart devices (TV, speaker, and lamp) are set in a mirror room with small Bluetooth speakers hidden respectively behind the respective smart devices.

3.3 Procedure

Participants were told that they were going to test a new voice recognition service developed for smart home system. Two basic tasks for each device were assigned such as changing volume of smart speaker or changing channel of smart TV in a two-way mirror room with only verbal control. Participants were given the scenario guiding the order to control, and were informed to finish tasks one by one. The experimenter controlled the smart devices and Bluetooth speakers behind the mirror room. Before the task starts, participants were informed to talk to the devices in a way they say to Siri, the voice-based virtual agent, and to proceed in the order of the scenario. The scenario included not very specific such as script but the order of usage among the three devices. In a two-way mirror room, set like a furnished home with sofa, participants are seated and manipulated the devices by talking to them. Participants were randomly assigned to conditions. Participants could hear the recorded feedback message after every verbal control. For example, when controlling speaker, if the participant said "turn on any Jazz music", then the smart speaker responded, "Okay, here is the Jazz Music" and the Jazz music prepared was played. After a while, if participant told that they didn't like the song which was being played and they wanted another kind of music, speaker said "what kind of music do you like?" and played the genre the subject responded and said "How is this music?". In case of additional unexpected request of participants, a bunch of materials such as music and responses were recorded and prepared in advance.

3.4 Measures

After completing the tasks with three devices (TV, speaker, lamp) as guided, each participant answered a questionnaire. Items measuring social attraction (Cronbach's $\alpha = 0.90$), trust toward media technology ($\alpha = 0.82$) were adopted from [14, 10], respectively. All the variables were measured using 10-point Likert scale ranging from 1 = "not at all" to 10 = "very much so."

4 Result

Two-way analyses of variance (ANOVAs) were conducted to analyze the effect of the number of voice and type of user personality on the dependent variables. The results revealed no significant main effects of the both independent variables.

However, significant interactions between the number of voice and type of user personality predicting social attraction, $F(1, 46) = 12.44$, $p < .01$, and trust toward media technology, $F(1, 46) = 12.04$, $p < .01$, were observed (see Fig. 2). These results indicated that the extroverts experienced greater feelings of social attraction and trust toward media technology when they were exposed to a single, rather than multiple voice, whereas the introverts felt stronger feelings of social attraction and trust when interacted with multiple, rather than a single voices.

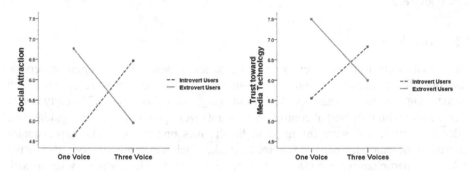

Fig. 2. Interaction effects between number of voice and users personality

5 Discussion

Results show that there are significant relationship between number of voice of smart devices and user's personality, while all hypotheses are not supported. It is assumed that there is another aspect of similarity rule which plays an important role in leading opposite result. One of the features of extroverts is that they are more talkative than introverts [12, 17]. When every smart product which is pervasive in smart home environment has the only one same identical voice, the situation may make extroverts perceive that there is the only agent who take care of all the devices and the agent embedded in smart device is also talkative because the only voice appears consistently in every respective device. Inversely, when every smart product in smart home environment has the several different respective voices, the situation may make extroverts feel that they are talking very shortly with different people. Therefore, they may perceive that they are staying with agents who are not talkative.

It is important to craft user interface with detail consideration. A carefully manipu-lated user interface can exceed numerous limits of current technology to accomplish a successful user experience, even when the technology functions imperfectly [8]. In the smart environment, natural user interface is getting important and this study may pose a critical design implication of voice user interface as natural user interface.

References

1. Ashforth, B., Humphrey, R.: The ubiquity and potency of labeling in organizations. Organ. Sci. **8**, 43–58 (1997)
2. Baumeister, R.: Ego depletion and self-control failure: an energy model of the self's executive function. Self and Identity. **1**, 129–136 (2002)

3. Byrne, D., Griffitt, W., Stefaniak, D.: Attraction and similarity of personality characteristics. J. Pers. Soc. Psychol. **5**, 82–90 (1967)
4. Cohen, M., Giangola, J., Balogh, J.: Voice User Interface Design. Addison-Wesley, Boston (2004)
5. Infante, D., Rancer, A., Womack, D.: Building Communication Theory. Waveland Press, Prospect Heights (1990)
6. Isbister, K., Nass, C.: Consistency of personality in interactive characters: verbal cues, non-verbal cues, and user characteristics. Int. J. Hum. Comput. Stud. **53**, 251–267 (2000)
7. Jung, S., Lee, K.M., Biocca, F.: Voice control system and multiplatform use: specialist vs. generalist? In: Yamamoto, S., Abbott, A.A. (eds.) HIMI 2015. LNCS, vol. 9172, pp. 607–616. Springer, Heidelberg (2015). doi:10.1007/978-3-319-20612-7_57
8. Kamm, C.: User interfaces for voice applications. Proc. Natl. Acad. Sci. **92**(22), 10031–10037 (1995)
9. Shin, D.: User experience in social commerce: in friends we trust. Behav. Inf. Technol. **32**(1), 52–67 (2013)
10. Koh, Y., Sundar, S.: Effects of specialization in computers, web sites, and web agents on e-commerce trust. Int. J. Hum. Comput. Stud. **68**, 899–912 (2010)
11. Koh, Y., Sundar, S.: Heuristic versus systematic processing of specialist versus generalist sources in online media. Hum. Commun. Res. **36**, 103–124 (2010)
12. Lee, K.M., Nass, C.: Designing social presence of social actors in human computer interaction. In: Proceedings of the Conference on Human Factors in Computing Systems - CHI 2003, pp. 289–296 (2003)
13. Shin, D., Choo, H.: Modeling the acceptance of socially interactive robotics: social presence in human-robot interaction. Interact. Stud. **12**(3), 430–460 (2011)
14. Lee, K., Peng, W., Jin, S., Yan, C.: Can robots manifest personality?: an empirical test of personality recognition, social responses, and social presence in human-robot interaction. J. Commun. **56**, 754–772 (2006)
15. Leiser, R.: Improving natural language and speech interfaces by the use of metalinguistic phenomena. Appl. Ergon. **20**, 168–173 (1989)
16. Lim, Y.: Disappearing interfaces. Interactions **19**, 36 (2012)
17. McCrae, R., Costa, P., McCrae, R.: Personality in Adulthood. Guilford Press, New York (1990)
18. Nass, C., Gong, L.: Speech interfaces from an evolutionary perspective. Commun. ACM **43**, 36–43 (2000)
19. Nass, C., Lee, K.: Does computer-synthesized speech manifest personality? experimental tests of recognition, similarity-attraction, and consistency-attraction. J. Exp. Psychol. Appl. **7**, 171–181 (2001)
20. Shin, D.: Defining sociability and social presence in social TV. Comput. Hum. Behav. **29**(3), 939–947 (2013)
21. Nass, C., Moon, Y., Fogg, B., Reeves, B., Dryer, D.: Can computer personalities be human personalities? Int. J. Hum. Comput. Stud. **43**, 223–239 (1995)
22. Nass, C., Reeves, B., Leshner, G.: Technology and roles: a tale of two TVs. J. Commun. **46**, 121–128 (1996)
23. Nass, C., Steuer, J., Tauber, E.: Computers are social actors. In: Paper Presented to CHI 1994 Conference of the ACM/SIGCHI, Boston, MA, USA (1994)
24. Negroponte, N.: Being Digital. Knopf, New York (1995)
25. Norman, D.A.: The Design of Everyday Things. Basic Books, New York (2002)
26. Pocheptsova, A., Amir, O., Dhar, R., Baumeister, R.: Deciding without resources: resource depletion and choice in context. J. Mark. Res. **46**, 344–355 (2009)

27. Reeves, B., Nass, C.: The media equation. CSLI Publications, Stanford (1996)
28. Sullivan, H.: The Interpersonal Theory of Psychiatry. Norton, New York (1953)
29. Shin, D.: User value design for cloud courseware system. Behav. Inf. Technol. **34**(5), 506–519 (2015)
30. Wiggins, J.: A psychological taxonomy of trait-descriptive terms: the interpersonal domain. J. Pers. Soc. Psychol. **37**, 395–412 (1979)

Mental Model Development Using Collaborative 3D Virtual Environments

Ali Asghar Nazari Shirehjini[1]([⊠]), Farideh Soltani Nejad[1],
Gazelle Saniee-Monfared[1], Azin Semsar[1],
and Shervin Shirmohammadi[2]

[1] Sharif University of Technology, Tehran, Iran
{shirehjini, fsoltaninejad, gsaniee, semsar}@sharif.edu
[2] University of Ottawa, Ottawa, Canada
shervin@eecs.uottawa.ca

Abstract. Smart environments are complex systems encompassing multitude of devices with complex interconnections and interactions. User must not only be able to figure out the devices' functionalities, but also understand the architectural and semantic relations between various components. Providing such information leads to better understanding and user satisfaction, if users get the appropriate mental models. One way to train users about such smart environments is Interactive Realistic Virtual Reality based Simulations (IRVRS): multimedia rich collaborative 3D virtual environments. IRVRS also facilitate easy and inexpensive access to population masses, thus they can be used for conducting large scale user experience studies. Our contribution in this work is the study of the effect of short-time experience with IRVRS on mental models of novice users of smart homes. We use a web-based IRVRS to investigate to which extent it could affect virtual smart home users' mental models, and we used Think Aloud and two types of Card Sorting methods to assess how much subjects mental models developed. Our results show that IRVRS can potentially be effective in creating the correct mental models for users.

Keywords: Mental model · 3D web-based smart home · Evaluation · Card sorting · Think aloud

1 Introduction

Smart rooms, smart offices, and smart homes are now a rising trend. Ensuring their user acceptance requires understandability [16, 26, 27]; i.e., users must be able to understand the functionality of each device in the environment [5]. Systems that ensure understandability and user satisfaction are more likely accepted and adopted by users [29]. In turn, ensuring satisfaction requires continuous evaluation during the user

---

The original version of this chapter was revised: In the original version, the name of the second author was incorrect. Instead of "Farideh Solatni Nejad" it should read as "Farideh Soltani Nejad". The erratum to this chapter is available at 10.1007/978-3-319-39862-4_47

N. Streitz and P. Markopoulos (Eds.): DAPI 2016, LNCS 9749, pp. 279–290, 2016.
DOI: 10.1007/978-3-319-39862-4_26

centric engineering process. Usually, evaluations are conducted under laboratory experiments, which is time and energy consuming. In addition, recruiting the necessary number of participants is difficult when conducting real world experiments, because subjects usually are selected from a geographically and culturally restricted area. Different solutions have been proposed to address these problems. Outsourcing, for example, helps researchers to outsource their testing tasks to other countries or laboratories with lower labour costs. However, Khaan shows disadvantages in such outsourcing [13]. Trust and security are big concerns, and many organizations hesitate sharing their critical information with others. Also, there is a threat of not getting the exact output that one expects, wasting a lot of money and time without having the desired outcome.

As an alternative, focus-group or group-thinking is proposed, giving the advantage of gathering various people and asking them to discuss different aspects of the system. Although proven to be efficient in collecting ideas, this still poses challenges [21]. For instance, it may lead to bias due to the vocal members influencing others and preventing them from expressing their viewpoints [15, 19]. Online experiments provide a way out of this; however, often participants lack necessary previous experience with such smart environments and do not have sufficiently developed mental models, leading to misunderstandings and wrong assessment and responses during the experiments.

In the past, traditional methods such as watching videos [25] or using visual narratives [3, 14] have been used to introduce novice users to smart environments and familiarize them with basic concepts of such systems. However, these instruments may lack interactivity and immersiveness, which are critical for a realistic experience that would lead to proper mental model development. In contrast, Interactive Realistic Virtual Reality Based Simulations (IRVRS) can successfully address this problem [12]. First, IRVRS facilitate easy and inexpensive access to a wide range of population, because anyone with a smartphone or other computing device can download and run a 3D environment. Second, IRVRS are multimedia enriched and create immersive user experiences, enabling users to feel and virtually touch the simulated environment, leading to the development of the necessary mental models. Although such virtual simulations cannot replace real world experiences, they have proved to be sufficient in communicating basic system concepts and principles [8], thus provide valid responses when surveyed. In other words, the interaction with IRVRS is hypothesized to support the development of mental models of novice users. The main drawback of using videos or IRVRS is the challenging task of multimedia storage, streaming, processing, and rendering. Dealing with these tasks is required because very large amount of multimedia content and experimental data will be produced and need to be managed, streamed or processed when conducting large-scale experiments with massive amount of users. However, these facets are not within the scope of this paper. Several effective solutions can be found in the literature [20].

In this paper, our contribution is the study of the effect of short-time experience with IRVRS on mental models of novice users of smart environments. We used a web-based IRVRS to study smart home users' mental models, and we showed that IRVRS can potentially be effective in communicating basic system concepts and principles and create correct mental models.

The remainder of this paper is organized as follows. In Sect. 2, we describe the background and basic concepts in this topic, while in Sect. 3 we provide a brief literature review of related work. Section 4 describes our method to elicit the user's mental model. Our results and analysis are shown in Sect. 5, and finally Sect. 6 concludes the paper.

2 Background

2.1 Smart Home Definition

According to Balta-Ozkan et al. "A smart home is a residence equipped with a communications network, linking sensors, domestic appliances, and devices, that can be remotely monitored, accessed or controlled, and which provide services that respond to the needs of its inhabitants" [2].

2.2 Mental Model Definition

According to Jonassen "Mental models are the conceptual and operational representations that humans develop while interacting with complex systems" [12]. In this research we aim to use IRVRS to develop the users' mental model in order to match the conceptual model of smart home designers. The more this match is provided, the more we can rely on IRVRS in building the right mental model for users [18].

2.3 Interaction Conflict Definition

In the literature, conflicts happen when an agent or a group of agents cannot perform a task that they intend to do [27]. Shirehjini classifies human-automation conflicts to four major categories: wrong automation, inappropriate automation, over automation and interaction conflicts. In this paper, interaction conflicts are the type of conflicts that happen in the system, where the output of the automation process opposes user's desires. For example the smart environment would turn off a light that the user has turned on because of energy consumption concerns [24]. In this research we aim to figure out the user's understandability about conflict in order to evaluate their mental model development about this concept.

3 Related Work

In this section, we first discuss the existing work on the creation of mental models. Then, we discuss research on the elicitation of mental models.

3.1   Mental Model Development Tools and Methods

The open literature includes several methods for creating and capturing mental models. The work by Greenberg et al. investigates different methods that can create and develop mental models [9]. Wizard of Oz has been used by many researchers in developing mental models. This method is particularly helpful when an animated sketch has no real backend to understand users' inputs and commands. A solution for the mentioned situation is to make a human a Wizard to do the backend side of the tasks which means that instead of the real system, the wizard would perform the backend tasks to be able to respond to the user.

Traditional methods such as watching videos or using visual narratives also support developing mental model for novice users. Diana L.M. Sharp et al. explore the impact of video on the language comprehension of children when they are listening to short stories [25]. They aim to improve the children's comprehension and retelling of the story by using three types of video which are Helpful video, No video and Minimal Video.

In another research by Guttman et al., children listened to short stories that include pictures in some parts of the story which is named "partial pictures" [10]. By using videos and visual narratives to describe a story or an environment, the users can build mental models through which they can understand the environment in a better way. However, these methods cannot provide interactivity and immersiveness compared to 3D virtual environments. When no interactivity is provided, the quality of experience could be poor or not exist all. This means that novice users within a study are asked to comment on concepts they possibly have never experienced before, neither in the real world, nor in a virtual environment. As a result, subjects' responses would be biased. Consequently, to address such biases it is necessary to provide a short term experience with the system under study. In this sense, IRVRS could be used.

Another related study by Nazari Shirehjini et al. investigates the effectivity of 3D virtual environments as a tool for rapid prototyping [17]. The work presented in [17] contributed a method to represent smart meeting spaces and prototyping a number of components (such as lights, blind, etc.) by using 3D-based virtual environments.

Other methods that support mental model development are reading and narrating stories. G.H. Bower and Morrow D.G. explain how readers and listeners construct mental models while they are reading or listening to what is described [3]. Creative drama is another method that supports mental model development. According to Arieli "Role-play has the potential to assist students to develop and create their own mental models" [1]. In this research, creative drama is used in order to build deeper understanding for the students in school.

3.2   Mental Model Analysis or Evaluation

In another study by A. Faiks, a Card Sorting method was deployed on a comprehensive online system for its digital library at Cornell University. It is implied in the research that Card Sorting is a beneficial method in discovering users' mental models [6]. After collecting data from their 12 participants, they recorded the data in a dissimilarity matrix and then a cluster analysis was run on the data. In [6], the Card Sorting method and an approach for quantifying recorded data are explained in detail. The Card Sorting approach proved to be useful in incorporating users' input into a system, and by doing so, increased the probability of user satisfaction with the final system. Also another research by K.A. Smith-Jentsch uses the Card Sorting method to assess similarity among subjects' mental models of teamwork [28].

In terms of the elicitation of mental models, the work by Greenberg et al. explain the Think Aloud approach [9]. This approach works by asking users to think aloud while they are interacting with a system. By analyzing the users' thoughts, one is able to determine their expectations of the system, and one can realize which parts of the system need to be redesigned in case the users are having difficulty in their interaction process. The method is easy to learn and it shows great potential in detecting usability flaws in the system. For examining the relationship between users' mental model and trust, Sack et al. focus on analyzing mental model development in terms of anthropomorphic understanding of a smart home [22]. In their research, the mental models were evaluated by different methods such as teach-back [23, 30] and Think Aloud [9]. In the teach-back method users are asked to explain some metaphors and analogies of the mentioned simulated environment.

In another research, Wood et al. propose card sorting as a means of mental model capturing [31]. There are two main approaches to Card Sorting:

1. Open Card Sorting project is a method in which users should categorize a list of items that are representative of the content that it being studies.
2. Closed Card Sorting project is a method in which users should put some items that are given to them in some predefined categories.

In our research, we evaluated the mental models by Card Sorting and Think Aloud. We implemented a simulated smart home environment which users could interact with to get a sense of how the system works. After users were done interacting with the system, an interview was conducted to evaluate the users' mental models using the Think Aloud method. We also used the Card Sorting method to evaluate the effectiveness of 3D web-based virtual environment in creating correct mental models.

3.3   Virtual Environment Evaluation Methods

In the area of evaluating virtual environments, Gabbard et al. propose a four-step approach [7], as follows:

1. User task analysis
2. Expert guidelines-based evaluation
3. Formative user-centered evaluation
4. Summative comparative evaluation.

In the first step, a complete list of tasks and subtasks in the virtual environment is documented. Also, the required resources that both the users and the system should have to be able to perform the tasks is identified. In the second step, based on the error and usability violation detected by an expert in user interaction design, the recommendation provided by the expert needs to be implemented in the next iteration of virtual environment development. In the third step, by including users, we try to evaluate and improve the user interaction design. Users utilize the Think Aloud approach [9] while performing tasks defined in the previous stage. Designers and evaluators record both qualitative and quantitative data using the output from Think Aloud, and fix the detected error for the next iteration. In the fourth step, the interaction design is compared to other matured and complete interaction designs having the same user's tasks. The result of this stage is usually quantitative.

In [7], a limited number of users are marked as representative users which could be a potential disadvantage of the approach. It is mentioned in the paper that the third and fourth steps which require subjects are the most expensive steps, so in practice only one to three users were included for each cycle of the evaluation.

In another study, Bowman collects different types of evaluation techniques for virtual environments [4], including the following approaches:

- Cognitive Walkthrough: In his approach, a list of tasks is given to the user, and while the user is performing the tasks, the interface ability in supporting those tasks is evaluated.
- Post-hoc questionnaire: After the users have interacted with the environment, a set of questions is given to them to collect subjective data.
- Interview/Demo: In this approach the interviewer directly talks to the subjects. One of interview's differences with questionnaire is that, with interview, it is possible to go into details. Also in cases that it is important to have the users' opinion or reaction to a particular situation, interviews seem like a more viable option to evaluate the virtual environment.

4 Our Research Method

In this study, to evaluate the effectiveness of web-based 3D virtual smart homes (IRVRS) in developing correct mental models, a user-centered design (UCD) framework was used. We started by asking subjects to perform tasks and we used the output data to both enhance the user interface design and to evaluate the system's efficacy in developing mental models. In this section, the details of the tasks and experiments which subjects had to perform are explained. 17 subjects participated: 14 participants (aged 22–24) were undergraduate students from the Computer Engineering Department and Industrial Engineering Department of Sharif University of Technology, and 3 participants were middle-aged and non-student. Overall, 6 of the participants were female. Experiments were conducted within one week. Participants were randomly assigned to pre-arranged time slots. The experimentation took place within the lab, library, and the CE and IE departments' lobbies. Our research method shown in Fig. 1 consists of a number of steps. Four of these steps, namely Think Aloud, Open Card Sorting, Analyzing the Results, and Closed Card Sorting are explained with details next.

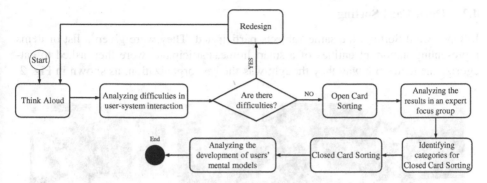

Fig. 1. Research methodology

4.1   Think Aloud

In the first stage of the Think Aloud method, we introduced ourselves to the participants and prepared the equipment which were needed, such as audio recording tools.
Afterwards, it was explained to the participants that the recorded data would not be
used in any other contexts, and the only reason the voice is being recorded is that we
would be able to review the session in the future to do further analyzing. In the second
stage, the purpose of the observation was described to the participants. Then we
emphasized on the fact that we are trying to detect the flaws and problems of the
system, so if the user has trouble interacting with the system, the user would know that
it is the system's fault, and not his/hers.

In the third stage, the 3D virtual system was given to the users. This 3D virtual
system was a smart home with three major devices which are television, air conditioner
and lights. The system has three modes of operation and depending on that the user has
to turn on different devices in order to complete the given scenario.

A. The "simple mode" included 2 tasks, one of which led to a conflict:
   1. Turning on the television
   2. Turning on the lights.
B. The "normal mode" included 3 tasks and two of them led to a conflict:
   1. Turning on the television
   2. Turning on the lights
   3. Turning on the air conditioner.
C. The "complex mode" included the same 3 tasks as the second mode and the only
   difference was that all the tasks could lead to conflicts.

The simple mode was given to 7 users, 8 users were given the normal mode, and 2
users were given the complex mode.

In the fourth stage, after conducting the experiment with all the participants and
recording the facts, we detected the difficulties in user-system interaction and fixed
them iteratively before conducting further studies.

4.2 Open Card Sorting

In Open Card Sorting, the same subjects participated. They were given a list of items representing important entities of a smart home. Participants were then asked to categorize the items in a way they thought was the best organization, as shown in Fig. 2.

Fig. 2. Participants categorizing the items in way the thought was best

4.3 Analyzing the Results

In the third phase of our research we analyzed the results in an expert focus group in which the authors and experts of smart systems engineering participated. The research instrument "expert focus group" is described in detail in [8].

Based on this analysis, four categories of major concepts of smart systems were identified: "users control over smart home", "users control over smart home devices", "users' understandability of conflict" and "categorizing the conflict with relevant cards". In other words, with our research results from steps 1 to 3, the expert focus group concluded that a mental model of a smart system under study must include 24 entities, as shown in Table 1, which can be sorted using the 4 aforementioned major categories.

Table 1. Cards which were used in the experiment.

Irrelevant cards	Cards related to participant's feeling towards Smart Home	Cards related to smart home concepts	Cards related to smart home devices
• Computer • Doctor's office • Burglar alarm	• Happy • Not happy • Trust • Do not trust • Faulty smart home • Useful smart home	• Energy saving mode • User • Technical error • Configuration error • Has control • Does not have control • Smart home • Conflict • User interface	• Lamp • Fan • Window • TV • Blinds • Air conditioner

4.4 Closed Card Sorting

In the fourth phase of our research, the 4 categories mentioned in Sect. 4.3 were used by the same 17 participants for sorting the items. The first category is "users' control over smart home" which contains two sub-categories: "has control", and "does not have control". The users should group the Smart Home and User cards within the mentioned sub-categories. In the second category which is "users control over smart home device", the user should put the home devices in one of the two sub-categories which are "under smart home control" and "under users' control". For the third category which is "users understandability of conflict", the user has to put the conflict card in one of the two sub-categories of "error is caused by technical flaws" and "error is caused by smart home configuration". In the fourth category which is "categorizing the conflict with relevant cards" the user is expected to change the place of the conflict card to a group which its devices has led to conflict. Closed Card Sorting [6, 31] was especially useful for achieving more detailed adjustments.

5   Results and Analysis

We analyzed our qualitative results and identified 4 major concepts to convert them to quantitative results, which are shown in Fig. 3.

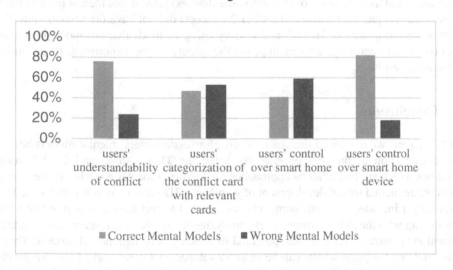

Fig. 3. The results of mental model development evaluation

The first concept is the understandability behind the concept of conflict. Those users who figured out a conflict as an error caused by the smart home configuration were able to develop the correct mental model. Approximately 76 % of the users understood the concept behind conflict and 24 % of them did not figure out the mentioned concept correctly. This result proves the effectiveness of using IRVRS.

The second concept is the user's ability to group the "Conflict" card with the devices that had conflict in them rather than categorizing it with some irrelevant cards. After working with the system and performing different tasks, the result of the open card sorting unveiled that 47 % of the users grouped the "Conflict" card with the devices that had conflict in them and 53 % of them did not group the card correctly with the related devices. So 53 % of the users were wrong, which does not prove the effectiveness of using IRVRS for this specific case.

Participant's conceptualization about control migration between system and its users was the third concept under study. Again, the majority of the users, 59 %, believed that only the smart home has control over the tasks, which is wrong, while 41% of users were correct and believed both smart home and themselves have the ability to control the environment. The results here also does not prove the effectiveness of using IRVRS for this specific case.

But the 4th concept, user's control over smart home devices, proves that IRVRS are effective in communicating basic system concepts and principles. 82% of the users found themselves having control over devices which had no conflict and they successfully created the correct mental model about this concept. On the other hand, 18% of them realized they have control on almost all the devices including the ones having conflict.

As the results of the study show, 2 of the major concepts (users' understandability of conflict and users' control over smart home devices) proved that mental models were developed adequately, however, the other 2 concepts did not have the same output. By enhancing the quality of IRVRS and also by using methods that are more precise in mental model capturing, we can improve the quality of the experiment to get more promising results.

6 Conclusion

In this paper, we discussed the crucial need of assessing users' mental models before the construction of the real systems. By using the Think Aloud and Card Sorting methods which are two efficient approaches for capturing mental models, we were able to evaluate mental model development of web-based 3D virtual environment users. The experiment included 17 participants who were asked to sort the cards before and after interacting with the 3D environment. By analyzing the results, the research showed that virtual environments have a great potential in creating adequate mental models. There are number of aspects which can be more developed in future work. First, by developing more advanced 3D virtual environments we would be able to develop mental models more accurately. Another factor that possibly challenged the presented experiment is the usability of the IRVRS we used. Another future work is to redesign the system. Also we aim to use other approaches of mental model capturing. By doing so we would able to get a more accurate assessment of mental model development.

References

1. Arieli, B.: The integration of creative drama into science teaching. Ph.D. thesis, Kansas State University (2007)
2. Balta-Ozkan, N., Boteler, B., Amerighi, O.: European smart home market development: public views on technical and economic aspects across the United Kingdom, Germany and Italy. Energy Res. Soc. Sci. **3**, 65–77 (2014)
3. Bower, G.H., Morrow, D.G.: Mental models in narrative comprehension. Science **247** (4938), 44–48 (1990)
4. Bowman, D.A., Gabbard, J.L., Hix, D.: A survey of usability evaluation in virtual environments: classification and comparison of methods. Presence **11**(4), 404–424 (2002)
5. Dix, A.: Human-Computer Interaction. Springer, New York (2009)
6. Faiks, A., Hyland, N.: Gaining user insight: a case study illustrating the card sort technique. Coll. Res. Libr. **61**(4), 349–357 (2000)
7. Gabbard, J.L., Hix, D., Swan, J.E., et al.: User-centered design and evaluation of virtual environments. Comput. Graph. Appl. IEEE **19**(6), 51–59 (1999)
8. Goodman, E., Kuniavsky, M., Moed, A.: Observing the User Experience: A Practitioner's Guide to User Research, 2nd edn. Morgan Kaufmann Publishers Inc., San Francisco (2012)
9. Greenberg, S., Carpendale, S., Marquardt, N., Buxton, B.: Sketching User Experiences: The Workbook. Elsevier, Waltham (2011)
10. Guttmann, J., Levin, J.R., Pressley, M.: Pictures, partial pictures, and young children's oral prose learning. J. Educ. Psychol. **69**(5), 473 (1995)
11. Hossain, M.A., Nazari Shirehjini, A.A., Alghamdi, A.S., El Saddik, A.: Adaptive interaction support in ambient-aware environments based on quality of context information. Multimed. Tools Appl. **67**(2), 409–432 (2013)
12. Jonassen, D.H.: Operationalizing mental models: strategies for assessing mental models to support meaningful learning and design-supportive learning environments. In: The First International Conference on Computer Support for Collaborative Learning, pp. 182–186. L. Erlbaum Associates Inc. (1995)
13. Khan, N., Currie, W.L., Weerakkody, V., Desai, B.: Evaluating offshore it out- sourcing in india: supplier and customer. In: Proceedings of the 36th Annual Hawaii International Conference on System Sciences. IEEE (2003)
14. Liu, Z., Stasko, J.T.: Mental models, visual reasoning and interaction in information visualization: a top-down perspective. IEEE Trans. Vis. Comput. Graph. **16**(6), 999–1008 (2010)
15. Morgan, D.L.: Focus Groups as Qualitative Research, vol. 16. Sage Publications, Newbury Park (1996)
16. Mostafazadeh, A., Nazari Shirehjini, A.A., Daraei, S.: A meta user interface for understandable and predictable interaction in AAL. In: Zhou, J., Salvendy, G. (eds.) ITAP 2015. LNCS, vol. 9194, pp. 456–464. Springer, Heidelberg (2015)
17. Nazari Shirehjini, A.A., Klar, F.: 3DSim: rapid prototyping ambient intelligence. In: Proceedings of the 2005 Joint Conference on Smart Objects and Ambient Intelligence: Innovative Context-Aware Services: Usages and Technologies, pp. 303–307. ACM (2005)
18. Norman, D.A.: The Design of Everyday Things: Revised and Expanded Edition. Basic, New York (2013)
19. Rabiee, F.: Focus-group interview and data analysis. Proc. Nutr. Soc. **63**(04), 655–660 (2004)

20. Rahimi, H., Nazari Shirehjini, A.A., Shirmohammadi, S: Activity-centric streaming of virtual environments and games to mobile devices. In: 2011 IEEE International Workshop on Haptic Audio Visual Environments and Games (HAVE), pp. 45–50 (2012)

21. Rosenbaum, S., Cockton, G., Coyne, K., Muller, M., Rauch, T.: Focus groups in HCI: wealth of information or waste of resources? In: Conference on Human Factors in Computing Systems: CHI 2002 Extended Abstracts on Human Factors in Computing Systems, vol. 20, pp. 702–703 (2002)

22. Sack, O., Röcker, C.: Like a family member who takes care of me users anthropomorphic representations and trustworthiness of smart home environments. Int. J. Virtual Worlds Hum.-Comput. Interact. **2**(1) (2014)

23. Sack, O., Röcker, C.: Privacy and security in technology-enhanced environments: exploring users knowledge about technological processes of diverse user groups. Univ. J. Psychol. **1**(2), 72–83 (2013)

24. Semsar, A., Nazari Shirehjini, A.A.: Analyzing the effect of interaction conflicts on trust in Ambient Intelligence environments. Master's thesis, Sharif University of Technology (2016)

25. Sharp, D.L., Bransford, J.D., Goldman, S.R., Risko, V.J., Kinzer, C.K., Vye, N.J.: Dynamic visual support for story comprehension and mental model building by young, at-risk children. Educ. Tech. Res. Dev. **43**(4), 25–42 (1995)

26. Nazari Shirehjini, A.A.: A generic UPnP architecture for ambient intelligence meeting rooms and a control point allowing for integrated 2D and 3D interaction. In: Proceedings of the 2005 Joint Conference on Smart Objects and Ambient Intelligence: Innovative Context-Aware Services: Usages and Technologies, pp. 207–212 (2005)

27. Nazari Shirehjini, A.A.: Interaktion in Ambient Intelligence: Konzeption eines intuitiven Assistenten zur ganzheitlichen und kon iktfreien Interaktion in adaptiven Umge-bungen. Ph.D. thesis, Technische Universität Darmstadt (2008)

28. Smith-Jentsch, K.A., Campbell, G.E., Milanovich, D.M., Reynolds, A.M.: Measuring teamwork mental models to support training needs assessment, development and evaluation: two empirical studies. J. Organ. Behav. **22**(2), 179–194 (2001)

29. Spiekermann, S.: User Control in Ubiquitous Computing: Design Alternatives and User Acceptance. Shaker Verlag, Aachen (2008)

30. van der Veer, G.C., del Carmen Puerta Melguizo, M.: Mental models. In: Jacko, J.A., Sears, A. (eds.) The Human-Computer Interaction Handbook, pp. 52–80. L. Erlbaum Associates Inc., Hillsdale (2002)

31. Wood, J.R., Wood, L.E.: Card sorting: current practices and beyond. J. Usability Stud. **4**(1), 1–6 (2008)

Effects of Playing Mobile Games While Driving

Cristian-Cezar Postelnicu[1]([⊠]), Octavian-Mihai Machidon[2],
Florin Girbacia[1], Gheorghe-Daniel Voinea[1], and Mihai Duguleana[1]

[1] Department of Automotive and Transport Engineering,
Transilvania University of Braşov, Braşov, Romania
cristian-cezar.postelnicu@unitbv.ro
[2] Department of Electronics and Computers,
Transilvania University of Braşov, Braşov, Romania

Abstract. The use of smartphones while driving is a growing phenomenon that
has reached alarming proportions. Playing games is a particular type of activity
performed by drivers on their smartphones and is the subject of this paper. The
study that was con-ducted aimed at investigating the influence of playing games
on a smartphone while driving in a virtual reality simulator. The driver's eye
glance behavior has been analyzed for twelve subjects while driving in two
environments, city and country (national) road. A reference set of data obtained
by driving without the gaming distraction has been used for performing a
comparison and drawing conclusions. The results have indicated increased
accident risks when playing games, especially caused by loss of control of the
vehicle and improper lane positioning due to the driver being distracted by the
game played.

Keywords: Smartphone · Mobile gaming · Driving · Driving simulator ·
Accident risk · Driving performance

1 Introduction

Yesterday's ordinary devices have known a major evolution in the past decade by
turning "smart" and thus getting into the spotlights of today's society. These gadgets
and technologies are now more attractive to customers being Internet connected and
having all sorts of high-tech features. This is the case of the smartphone, the next
evolutionary step of the old-fashioned mobile phone good only for making calls and
sending text messages.

Such smart gadgets have become a widespread technology today, among people of
all cultures and ages. The users of smartphones are involved in a variety of activities
beyond making calls and texting: using social network apps, taking pictures/selfies,
playing games, or just surfing the net. Being able to provide a whole new range of
attractive and fun features, smartphones also raise major challenges regarding issues
like addiction, safety of use and other potential unintended consequences brought on by
the "immersion" effect that these devices generate on users. For example, in a 2012
study, researchers at Tel-Aviv University (TAU) show that smartphones create the
illusion of a "private bubble" around their users, which become more caught up in their
mobile activity than their immediate surroundings [6].

© Springer International Publishing Switzerland 2016
N. Streitz and P. Markopoulos (Eds.): DAPI 2016, LNCS 9749, pp. 291–301, 2016.
DOI: 10.1007/978-3-319-39862-4_27

All the recent studies have shown that people use such devices in a variety of places: for example in [7] it is stated that 85 % of Americans who played smartphone or tablet-based games indicated that they would want to play games almost anywhere. However, these facts have serious consequences since the usage of smartphones or other similar devices has been shown to occur during driving – despite such activity being banned by law in most countries. This fact is the subject of several research groups worldwide, and a series of scientific surveys and articles have been published on this topic, analyzing the risks and consequences of using handheld devices while driving a car.

The use of smartphones while driving is a growing phenomenon that has reached alarming proportions. A recent AT&T study [8] has shown that 70 % of the people engage in a form of smartphone activity while driving. The most popular multi-tasking activities performed by drivers are texting (61 %) and sending emails (33 %), but the activities range vary from social media, taking selfies and using other mobile applications. Another alarming fact stated in the same study is that 62 % of drivers keep their smartphones within reach, intending to use them while driving.

A particular type of smartphone/tablet activity while driving is gaming. Mobile games are played everywhere and surveys have shown that about 4 % of mobile gamers do this while driving. This may look like a small percentage, but if we take into consideration that, based on a 2014 study [9], a total of 48 million Americans play mobile games on smartphones and tablets, it shows that the estimate number of people playing games while driving is quite worrying.

According to the US National Highway Traffic Safety Administration, distracted driving played a role in 12 % of the teenager's fatal car crashes accidents [10]. In 2012 alone, 3,328 were killed in distracted driving crashes [11]. For adults and older drivers, the main causes of car accidents are the loss of cognitive and motor functions [12], including visual-spatial attention, and speed of processing [13].

2   Related Work and Research Aim

To the best of our knowledge, our study is a pioneer one regarding the analysis of playing mobile games while driving a car. The lack of dedicated research papers on this topic might be explained due to it being included in wider studies targeting the effects of generic mobile use while driving. Some of such recent studies are described in [14–16]. All underline that mobile phone use while driving is associated with increased reaction times at unexpected events, increased vehicle distance from the central axis of the road, and ultimately representing significant safety risks to driving.

In [17], the authors analyze the impact of the most common activities performed with a mobile phone while driving a bicycle. Among them, it includes playing mobile games. This study acknowledges the lack of experiments and research papers regarding gaming while driving, and underlines the importance of analyzing this phenomena due to several media reports of accidents caused by it.

We consider that an explicit research study on gaming while driving is more than needed in this domain, for several reasons. First of all, as shown above, the mobile gaming market is experiencing a huge growth, leading to the development of a variety of attractive, challenging and thus addictive games. Second, a newly appeared research direction, detailed in [18], targets the development of "green" driving mobile apps, which are mobile phone applications which are supposed to be safely used by the driver. Some examples of such existing applications are: Car Tunes Music Player, DriveGain or goDriveGreen.

Furthermore, there are also attempts to develop "green" mobile games, particularly regarding competition between drivers (like FuelFit or Green Auto Rally), with the declared intent by the developers to promote safe and green driving. However this issue is controversial since there is no legal frame allowing such "exceptions" from the general ban on mobile phone use while driving. Also, this raises a storm of questions and risks that need to be properly addressed by research studies, trials and standardized design methodologies approved by the appropriate driving safety organizations and authorities.

Given this context, the research presented in this paper focuses on investigating the influence of playing games on a smartphone while driving in a virtual reality simulator. The eye glance behavior is being analyzed for a series of twelve subjects that are playing games on a touchscreen-based smartphone while driving in 2 types of environments: in a city and on a freeway. The data obtained is compared with a reference set of data – the same drivers and environments, but without the gaming distraction.

The study is part of the NAVIEYES Project [19] which aims to develop an intelligent assistant for mobile devices while driving. The project aims to identify the dangerous situations the driver may encounter, such as missing a traffic sign or lane crossing without watching, and to alert the driver when such events occurs.

3 Experiment Design

In this initial phase of our project we try to identify for how long a driver moves his eyes from the road, in this particular case to the mobile device. Thus, we asked the car drivers to play a game on a mobile device, an action which will distract them from the road, while in order to identify the actions performed by them during both driving and playing actions we used a Tobii eye-tracker, two webcams and the integrated software from the driving simulator. The general architecture of our experiment is presented in Fig. 1, while every component used for this setup is separately presented in the following chapters.

3.1 The Game to Be Played During Experiments

The game chosen for users to play is Splashy Fish (see Fig. 1), a very popular replica of Flappy Bird, game known to be a fun and very addictive one among nowadays mobile games players. The reason for which this game was chosen is the fact that it requires a single finger to control the fish inside the game, being thus extremely simple for the users and plausible to be played while driving. The users must actually tap the touchscreen in order to maintain the fish from colliding with obstacles from the environment.

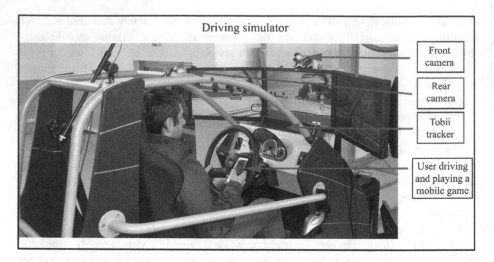

Driving simulator

Front camera

Rear camera

Tobii tracker

User driving and playing a mobile game

Fig. 1. Experimental setup

3.2   Driving Simulator

During the experiment a virtual driving simulator was used, EF-X by Eca-Faros (see Fig. 2), a very well-known simulator used in other several driving studies [1–5]. The simulator is composed from a right-hand drive vehicle structure equipped with the following Opel vehicle parts: steering wheel with force feedback, clutch, brake and acceleration pedals, manual gear shift, adjustable driver seat, control handles, instrument panel, handbrake, three LCD 19 inch monitors providing 120° horizontal field of

Fig. 2. Splashy fish game screenshots

view used for visual perception of the simulated 3D virtual environment, rear view
mirror integrated in the virtual environment and an audio system (Fig. 3).

Fig. 3. EF-X Eca-Faros driving simulator

3.3   Tobii Eye-Tracker and User's Behavior

For this experiment the Tobii eye-tracker device was used in order to identify the time
interval during which the user didn't properly looked at the road. The Tobii eyetracker
is a device used to track user's eyes position relative to the position where the device is
actually placed. As seen in Fig. 1 the device is placed in front of the user, below the
middle display in a position where it doesn't affect the user's visibility to the road. The
tracker is initially calibrated when the user enters the car and according to initial tests it
fully tracks the user's eyes positions when he pays attention to the road. By analyzing
the position where the user's held his hand while playing on the mobile device the
tracker loses the eyes positions tracking thus triggering an event in the recording
app. By analyzing the start and end timestamps we can compute the time interval
during which the user didn't pay attention to the road properly, in other words the
glance values.

Furthermore, in order to correctly validate the obtained results we placed two
webcams on the simulator, one in front of the user and one behind the user. The front

camera does actually monitor the user in order to check whether the eye tracker properly identified the glance behavior and also to further investigate exactly what the user does during the time interval when he is playing (or any other activity he performs). The rear camera is focused on the car's board and road path providing information related to speed and/or traffic signs violation.

3.4 Experiment Setup

Twelve subjects (age 20–31) with previous driving and gaming experiences were asked to participate in a series of tests. The current research tried to identify the direct effects of playing mobile games while driving. Thus, two types of possible situations found in real traffic were chosen in order to better evaluate the side effects, a city itinerary (50 km/h speed limit) and a country road (national road with 90 km/h speed limit). The experiment was divided for each of the proposed scenarios into two separate cases. Thus, in one case the drivers were asked only to drive and obey all traffic rules, while in the latter case the drivers were again asked to obey all rules but also to play the Splashy Fish game installed on their mobile device. Also, in order to compensate the fact that all users were knew to the virtual reality driving simulator they were all allowed a simulator accommodation time of 5 up to 10 min in one or both scenarios.

Each driving scenario lasted for 10 min while the users were supposed to obey all traffic rules. The order of the four scenarios (city with/without playing and country with/without playing) were randomly defined for each user in order to avoid possible prediction or accommodation with the environment/scenario. Even if the starting point was the same the users were allowed to drive at their will, except for the city scenarios when the users were asked to turn at least once to the right and at least once to the left just to be sure they won't follow just a straight path through the city.

The parameters investigated in this experiment are the number of improper lane positions, speed infractions, turn signals missed, number of points succeeded while playing the game and of course the fact that the driver crashed or not during the test. For each parameter related to driving the experiment investigated how many times the action was performed and the total duration of them. The experiment also investigated the total number of glances from the road and their average.

4   Results, Evaluation and Discussion

4.1   City Scenario Results and Evaluation

In Table 1 the results obtained by the twelve users for the city scenarios are presented. By comparing the results we found that no significant statistical differences were between the two cases, "normal" and "playing", for total number of improper lane position (L) $t(22) = 0.566$ $p > 0.05$ and for the total number of turn signals missed (T) $t(22) = 0.201$ $p > 0.05$. Also, for the total time of speed infractions (St) $t(16) = 1.94$ $p > 0.05$ no significant differences were found even if the numbers related to speed infractions were three times lower in the case of "playing" compared with "normal" one (St-normal = 14 vs. St-playing = 4). Statistical significant differences were found for the total time of improper (Lt) lane position $t(13) = 2.48$ $p < 0.05$ and for the total number of speed infractions (S) $t(17) = 2.12$ $p < 0.05$. Thus, it results that users had almost the same number of improper lane positions (average L-normal = 2.5 vs. average L-playing = 3), but the total time while they were not properly positioned on their lane had a significant increase during playing test (average Lt-normal = 2.33 s vs. average Lt-playing = 6.75 s). Also, there was a single user that had a crash during City scenario, which happened due to improper lane positioning (User 6). Probably such higher numbers for improper lane positioning are due to the fact that users were not properly accommodated with the simulator and the sensitivity of the steering wheel, but values are comparable for both "normal" and "playing" scenarios. The intriguing part is related to the fact that the total time during which they were running improperly on the lane is a lot higher during the "playing" scenario, proving the fact that the drivers experience a control loss when they are performing an extra action while driving. Surprisingly is also the fact that both number of speed infractions (S) and the total time of speed infractions are lower during the "playing" case, probably the users realizing the fact that they are in a more dangerous situation when performing a supplementary action while driving.

By visually analyzing the images recorded during this City scenario the authors found that users were mostly tempted to play during the waiting time at red light. Basically there was no danger during this case but a few of them still continued to play after the traffic lights were turning green, thus setting the car in motion again with a small delay, however the exact amount of time couldn't be measured accurately. It is also worth mentioning that Lt and St time intervals were automatically measured by the simulator software without decimals thus leading to a small loss in accuracy.

Table 1. Results obtained from the conducted experiment – City scenario (L – number of improper lane position, Lt – improper lane position time, S – number of speed infractions, St – speed infractions time, T – number of turn signals missed, G – number of glances, Ga – glances average time, C – states if the user crashed).

User	City scenario													
	Normal						Playing							
	L	Lt [s]	S	St [s]	T	C	L	Lt [s]	S	St [s]	T	G	Gt [s]	C
1	2	1	2	4	1	No	2	5	1	2	0	61	2.73	No
2	5	7	0	0	3	No	6	11	0	0	3	57	2.52	No
3	3	4	1	1	0	No	3	3	0	0	1	70	2.35	No
4	4	3	2	2	1	No	7	15	0	0	1	65	2.25	No
5	2	2	0	0	1	No	0	0	0	0	0	76	2.6	No
6	4	3	1	1	1	No	7	18	0	0	2	45	2.90	Yes
7	4	3	1	2	2	No	5	12	1	1	2	72	2.35	No
8	0	0	0	0	0	No	1	1	0	0	1	45	2.25	No
9	1	1	0	0	1	No	2	5	0	0	0	64	2.60	No
10	2	2	2	3	1	No	2	4	0	0	1	80	2.12	No
11	0	0	1	1	0	No	1	1	0	0	3	75	1.95	No
12	3	2	0	0	2	No	0	0	1	1	0	60	2.35	No
Avg	2.5	2.33	0.83	1.17	1.08	–	3	6.75	0.25	0.33	1.17	64.17	2.41	–
Total	30	28	10	14	13	–	38	81	3	4	14	770	–	–

4.2   Country Road Scenario Results and Evaluation

Table 2 shows the results obtained for Country road scenarios for both "normal" and "playing" cases. First of all, in this scenario a total number of three users crashed during the "playing" test. For each of them we stopped the test when the event occurred.

Table 2. Results obtained from the conducted experiment – Country road scenario (abbreviations are the same as in the previous table).

User	Country road scenario													
	Normal						Playing							
	L	Lt [s]	S	St [s]	T	C	L	Lt [s]	S	St [s]	T	G	Gt [s]	C
1	9	7	0	0	0	No	12	20	0	0	0	81	1.65	No
2	1	0	1	1	0	No	3	2	0	0	0	90	1.45	No
3	2	1	1	1	0	No	2	2	0	0	1	60	1.56	No
4	8	5	0	0	0	No	6	13	1	1	0	40	2.14	Yes
5	0	0	0	0	0	No	2	2	0	0	0	73	1.65	No
6	3	3	3	2	1	No	0	0	1	1	0	55	1.58	No
7	4	2	2	3	1	No	5	7	0	0	0	103	1.33	No
8	5	4	1	1	0	No	4	9	0	0	0	52	1.75	Yes
9	2	2	0	0	0	No	9	16	0	0	0	53	1.92	Yes
10	3	1	1	2	0	No	2	5	1	1	1	115	1.15	No
11	1	1	2	1	1	No	4	6	0	0	0	97	1.41	No
12	0	0	1	0	0	No	3	7	0	0	0	64	1.53	No
Avg	3.17	2.17	1	0.92	0.25	–	4.33	7.42	0.25	0.25	0.17	73.58	1.59	–
Total	38	26	12	11	3	–	52	89	3	3	2	883	–	–

Also, only by analyzing the total number of speed infractions we can see that while playing on the mobile device users tend to slow down a bit having only 3 speed infractions compared with 12 when no other action was involved. The speed infraction time seems to be lower average St-playing = 0.17 s while average St-normal = 0.92 s (see Fig. 5). Again, similar with the City scenario in the Country road scenario the average Lt-playing = 7.42 s is significantly higher compared with average Lt-normal = 2.17 s (see Fig. 4).

In this scenario there are no significant statistical differences for total number of lane improper position $t(22) = 0.911$ $p > 0.05$ and for the total number of turn signals missed $t(22) = 0.484$ $p > 0.05$ (see Fig. 6 for average and range interval). Significant statistical differences were found for total lane improper position time $t(14) = 2.781$ $p < 0.05$, for number of speed infractions $t(22) = 2.462$ $p < 0.05$ and for the total speed infractions time interval $t(15) = 2.111$ $p < 0.05$.

The authors also found relevant to compare the number of glances and the average glance time, and significant statistical differences were found for the glance time values $t(16) = 8.472$ $p < 0.05$, while for the total number of glances there were no significant statistical differences $t(16) = 2.007$ $p > 0.05$. For the glance test values for users #4,

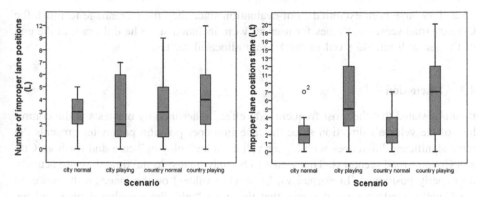

Fig. 4. Number of improper lane positions and improper lane positions duration for all cases

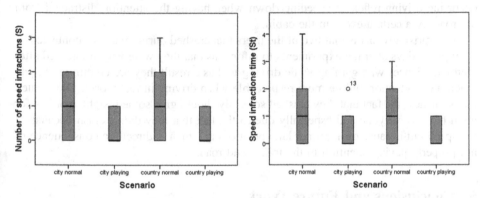

Fig. 5. Number of speed infractions and speed infractions duration for all cases

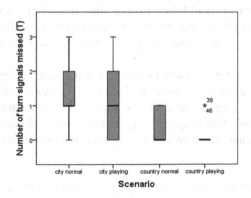

Fig. 6. Number of turn signals missed

#8 and #9 have been excluded from evaluation since they didn't manage to finish the Country road scenario. Values for user #6 were included since he did crash at the end of the test at 9 min 45 s out of the 10 min allocated for test.

4.3 Discussion

It can be stated that the most frequent side-effect underlined by our tests is the control loss of the vehicle's direction since the lane improper position parameter presents the most significant differences with higher values in the "playing" case and for both City and Country road scenarios. This seems to be only related to the time they are actually improperly positioned (Lt-normal vs. Lt-playing values) on the lane. Furthermore, in the Country road scenario it seems that the users "felt" the possible danger and the number of speed infractions are lower in the "playing" case compared with the "normal" case with significant statistical differences. In terms of values this is also valid for the City scenario. Another plausible explanation for this phenomena is the natural occurring driving reflex of speeding down when having the attention distracted from the road by a certain event in the cabin.

A surprisingly fact is that two of the users that crashed during the tests contacted us a couple of days after the experiments to inform us that they were very impressed after their experiences with gaming while driving and as a result they are committed to pay much more attention and be more responsible when driving in real world. They stated that somehow the fact that they crashed so easily should give some insights not just for them but for everyone and especially due to the fact that they didn't crash because of the speed but because of improper lane positioning which is directly a consequence of not properly paying attention to the traffic and road.

5 Conclusions and Future Work

The study described in this paper has clearly shown that playing games does represent a very dangerous activity when driving a car and it should definitely not be performed by any driver. This statement should also involve other smartphone activities like talking, text messaging, taking photos, etc. From our experiments it results that improper lane positioning could be as dangerous as speed infractions and could lead to real life accidents.

As future work, we are planning to extend our research aiming it to identify and analyze the appearance and consequences of the speed decrease pattern that takes place when drivers are playing games, an effect shown in this current study. Also, we plan on identifying which type of activity (talking, texting, taking photos, etc.) is more distracting for the driver and the degree in which it impairs his driving ability and control of the vehicle.

Acknowledgements. This paper is supported by the Romanian Government, specifically MEN – UEFISCDI authority under the program PNII "Partnerships in priority areas", under the project number 240/2014 - NAVIEYES, supporting the collaboration between the company Route 66 and University Transilvania of Braşov.

References

1. Hughes, G.M., Rudin-Brown, C.M., Young, K.L.: A simulator study of the effects of singing on driving performance. Accid. Anal. Prev. **50**, 787–792 (2013)
2. Rudin-Brown, C.M., Edquist, J., Lenné, M.G.: Effects of driving experience and sensation-seeking on drivers' adaptation to road environment complexity. Saf. Sci. **62**, 121–129 (2014)
3. Beanland, V., Lenné, M.G., Underwood, G.: Safety in numbers: target prevalence affects the detection of vehicles during simulated driving. Atten. Percept. Psychophys. **76**(3), 805–813 (2014)
4. Edquist, J., Rudin-Brown, C.M., Lenné, M.G.: The effects of on-street parking and road environment visual complexity on travel speed and reaction time. Accid. Anal. Prev. **45**, 759–765 (2012)
5. Rosenbloom, T., Eldror, E.: Effectiveness evaluation of simulative workshops for newly licensed drivers. Accid. Anal. Prev. **63**, 30–36 (2014)
6. Hatuka, T., Toch, E.: Smart-spaces: smartphone's influence on perceptions of the public space. Toch Research Group, Tel-Aviv University (2012). http://www.aftau.org/site/News2?page=NewsArticle&id=16519
7. Business wire site. http://www.businesswire.com/news/home/20131003005397/en/Goo-Survey-Majority-Americans-Play-Browser-Based-Games#.VH4gYzHF-ao
8. Smartphone Use Behind the Wheel Survey. AT&T, May 2015
9. Big fish games site. http://www.bigfishgames.com/blog/2014-global-gaming-stats-whos-playing-what-and-why/
10. CNN site. http://edition.cnn.com/2013/11/06/tech/mobile/selfies-while-driving/
11. Distracted driving site. http://www.distraction.gov/
12. Regan, M.A., Lee, J.D., Victor, T.W.: Driver Distraction and Inattention: Advances in Research and Countermeasures, vol. 1. Ashgate Publishing, Ltd., Burlington (2013)
13. Anstey, K.J., Wood, J., Lord, S., Walker, J.G.: Cognitive, sensory and physical factors enabling driving safety in older adults. Clin. Psychol. Rev. **25**(1), 45–65 (2005)
14. Leung, S., Croft, R.J., Jackson, M.L., Howard, M.E., Mckenzie, R.J.: A comparison of the effect of mobile phone use and alcohol consumption on driving simulation performance. Traffic Inj. Prev. **13**(6), 566–574 (2012)
15. Yannis, G., Papathanasiou, E., Postantzi, E., Papadimitriou, E.: Impact of mobile phone use and music on driver behaviour and safety by the use of a driving simulator. In: Proceedings of the 3rd International Conference on Driver Distraction and Innatentio, 17pp (2013)
16. Zhao, N., Reimer, B., Mehler, B., D'Ambrosio, L.A., Coughlin, J.F.: Self-reported and observed risky driving behaviors among frequent and infrequent cell phone users. Accid. Anal. Prev. **61**, 71–77 (2013)
17. De Waard, D., Lewis-Evans, B., Jelijs, B., Tucha, O., Brookhuis, K.: The effects of operating a touch screen smartphone and other common activities performed while bicycling on cycling behavior. Transp. Res. Part F Traffic Psychol. Behav. **22**, 196–206 (2014)
18. Nykänen, A.: Testing of mobile apps intended for use while driving. In: AstaZero Researchers Day – Emerging Trends in Active Safety for Road Vehicles Symposium, 14 April 2015
19. NaviEyes research project site. http://navieyes.unitbv.ro

Emotions and Affect in Intelligent Environments

Empirical Study of Humor Support in Social Human-Robot Interaction

Lucile Bechade[1]([✉]), Guillaume Dubuisson Duplessis[1], and Laurence Devillers[1,2]

[1] LIMSI, CNRS, Université Paris-Saclay, 91405 Orsay, France
{bechade,gdubuisson,devil}@limsi.fr
[2] Sorbonne Universités, Université Paris-Sorbonne, 75006 Paris, France

Abstract. As part of the Joker project which provides a multimodal dialog system with social skills including humor and empathy, this paper explores idea concerning the human verbal responses to a joking robot. Humor support is defined as the conversational strategies used in reaction to humor utterances. This paper aims at exploring the phenomenon of responses to humor interventions from the robot through the examination of a corpus. We assume that using humor in human-robot interaction sets up a positive atmosphere in which participants are willing to contribute. This study relies on 49 human-robot interaction dialogues and 381 adjacency pairs of humorous acts made by the robot and the following human responses. The human humor responses, elicited through canned jokes and conversational humor, were annotated. Three main categories of human responses were found (1) providing no support, (2) recognizing the attempt of humor and (3) contributing with more humor. The findings indicate that, as in human-human interaction, strategies of humor support are strongly dependent of the humorous event's context.

1 Introduction

Humor plays a sociability role in human-human interaction. Researchers in HRI assume that implementing humorous behavior into human-robot interactions can take advantage of the potential of humor for establishing social relationships [14]. It can help to make robots much friendlier, and increase cooperation with the system [10]. This work is part of the Joker project which aims at building a generic user interface that provides a multimodal dialog system with social skills including humor and empathy [6]. We assume that using humor in human-robot interaction sets up a positive atmosphere in which participants are willing to contribute. Humor support is defined by Hay [8] as the conversational strategies used in reaction to humor utterances. This paper aims at exploring the phenomenon of responses to humor interventions from the robot through the examination of a corpus. This corpus is a sub-version of the data collected in the frame of the Joker project with 3 different systems (described in [6]). These human responses, elicited through canned jokes and conversational humor (food-related puns, teasing and end rhymes) were annotated. The data were also categorized by the sociolinguistic variables of gender, and personality traits. Section 2 presents work related to humor support in human-human

© Springer International Publishing Switzerland 2016
N. Streitz and P. Markopoulos (Eds.): DAPI 2016, LNCS 9749, pp. 305–316, 2016.
DOI: 10.1007/978-3-319-39862-4_28

interaction and to humor in HRI. Section 3 presents the corpus collection performed with a wizard of oz data collection system on three scenarios. Section 4 is dedicated to the corpus annotation process in terms of linguistic content of the human speech. Categories of humor responses found in the annotated corpus are listed and defined. Section 5 highlights the importance of contextual information in the use of a type of responses to humor. It reveals the existence of other influence such as the sociolinguistics variable of age or the Sense of Humor (measured by questionnaire). Results of this study are discussed. Section 6 concludes this paper and presents perspectives.

2   Related Work on Humor Support and Humor in HRI

Morkes et al. [13] have designed experiments to examine the role of humor in human-computer interaction. They show that humor have positive effects on the human-computer interaction: participants rated the system as more likable and responded in a more sociable manner. Regarding the reaction to humor, Hay [8] described many different humor support strategies in natural human-human conversations. The humor support strategies can be perceived in smiles and laughter, with the contribution of more humor, echoing the humor, offering sympathy, contradicting self-deprecating humor or providing no support. To give full humor support, humor has to be recognized, understood and appreciated [14]. Bell [4] described responses to failed humor. The strategies are quite similar to response to success humor: laughter, metalinguistic remarks about the jokes, interjection, evaluation of the joke, rhetorical question, sarcasm, non verbal response, mode adoption. Attardo [2] in a study of reactions to ironical utterances suggests that the hearer may also mode adopt. Mode adaption can be elicited by many kind of humor. Norrick [15] provides examples of spontaneous conversational punning that elicits further punning from other participants.

3   Data Collection of Social Human-Robot Dialog

3.1   Interaction Scenarios

Data were collected using a Wizard of Oz dedicated to social dialogue through the Nao robot [6], implemented in French language. The system is configured by a predefined dialogue tree that specifies the text utterances, gestures and laughter that can be executed by the Nao robot. At each node, the operator chooses the next node of dialogue to visit according to the human dialogue participant's reaction. In this paper, examples from the corpus have been adapted from French to English in an attempt to be as close as possible as the intended effects in French.

The scenario implements a system-directed social interaction dialogue that adapts the telling of riddles and other humorous contributions to some aspects of the user model. In this scenario, the system displays various humor capabilities (as shown in Table 1). Interactions with the robot follows a common structure.

Table 1. Humorous acts made by the robot during interaction

Type	Example (translated from French to English)	Description
Canned jokes		
Riddles	How do you know there are two elephants in your fridge? You can't close the door	Narrative, punchline at the end, introduced, expected structure
Self-derision riddles	Did you think you are strong? Anyway, don't worry, you are stronger than me	Narrative, punchline at the end, introduced, unexpected structure, about the robot
One-line Jokes	This reminds me of an anecdote: to fall asleep, a sheep can only count on itself	Narrative, punchline at the end, introduced, expected structure
Conversational humor		
Teasing	Even a child could answer that!	Non narrative, not introduced
Play with word about cooking	Really, it's a piece of cake!	Non narrative, not introduced
End rhymes	/French idiomatic rhyming playful expression/ See Examples 3 and 7 in Sect. 4	Non narrative, not introduced, expected structure, at the end of the speaking turn

First, the robot greets the participant and presents itself in an introduction phase. Next, the system offers the telling of a riddle depending on the detected (by the operator) emotional state of the human. The behavior of the system is adapted to the receptiveness of the human to the contributions of the robot: positive reactions from the participant trigger more jokes. Then the system challenges participants in a game by asking a question about a meal (e.g., "What ingredients do we need to make a onion soup?"). Finally, the system gives a conclusion about the perceived participant reactions (e.g., "I am glad you like humor produced by a robot".), and closes the interaction.

Given the need for robust generation, the humor is of the hackneyed variety. The humorous acts made by the robot are divided into two categories derived from the literature (see [2,17]). As mentioned by Attardo [2], the locutor can produce two types of humorous acts in dialogs: canned jokes which are narratives containing a punchline, or conversational witticism which is a non-narrative jabline, melted in the dialog. We separate the humorous act made by the robot following the canned joke and conversational humor categories as shown in Table 1.

3.2   Collected Data

This corpus consists of two experimentations following the same scenario and the same protocol. The first experimentation took place in the cafeteria of the LIMSI-CNRS laboratory with French-speaking participants. The 37 volunteers were 62 % male, 38 % female, and their ages ranged from 21 to 62 (median: 31.5; mean: 35.1) [6]. The second experimentation took place at the Broca Hospital with

12 French-speaking participants. The volunteers were 35 % male, 65 % female, and their ages ranged from 64 to 86 (median: 75, mean: 74, standard deviation: 6). In both experiments, participants were seated facing the Nao robot at around one meter from it. Audio tracks of 16 kHz have been recorded thanks to a high-quality AKG Lavalier microphone. A total of 3 h 57 min 04 s of audio data has been collected for both experimentations. First experiment accounts for 3 h 20 min 57 s (average session duration: 5 min 25 s; standard deviation: 1 min) while the second scenario accounts for 36 min 07 s (average session duration: 3 min 29 s).

The Sense of Humor Scale (SHS) questionnaire of McGhee [12] was filled by participants after the experimentation to evaluate the impact of individual differences in humor perception. Six dimensions of humor appreciation are assessed in this questionnaire. Each dimension is rated between 4 and 28 and a global sense of humor score is rated by the sum of sub-categories, ranging from 24 to 168. The participant SHS-scores in this experiment range from 72 to 145 (mean: 108.87, standard deviation: 22.38). In addition, participants filled a self-report questionnaire to evaluate several dimensions of the interaction. This questionnaire consists of closed-ended questions about the system, the interaction and the human participant (a more detailed description is given in [3]).

4   Annotation and Responses to Humor

4.1   Annotation Process

Audio data have been transcribed. Based on this transcription, we extracted the adjacency pairs of humorous acts made by the robot and the following human response. All in all, the corpus contains 381 humorous contributions from the robot and 381 human responses. The 381 humorous contributions are divided into 130 humorous acts of canned jokes category and 251 of conversational humor.

4.2   Annotation Scheme and Verbal Responses to Humor

The human responses were coded according to the type of response. The coding system arises from the categories of responses found in previous studies as a starting point (mainly [4,8]). The annotation scheme for human contributions can be divided into the following dimensions (examples are in English with original French sentences below).

Lack of Verbal Support. The answer can be displayed in multimodal way. Paralinguistic affect bursts, facial expressions or gestures can also be a type of humor support. We consider a category *absence of verbal support* when the human participant didn't respond verbally after a humorous act of the robot.

Interjection. This category regroups words uttering emotion or exclamation. This category is made of minimal responses in which laughter or evaluation of the joke would be expected. Interjections do not always clearly signal even the hearer's recognition, comprehension of the attempt at humor or appreciation.

Subjective Evaluation. As noted by Bell [4], most of the responses can be seen as evaluating the joke in some way (except for the *other comments category*). This category contains subjective evaluations that did not involve a metalinguistic comments or sarcasm. As demonstrated in the following three examples, the evaluative comments could be directed to the joke, the teller, or both and can assess a positive or a negative evaluation. Example 1 is labeled as positive evaluation of the joke and Example 2 is labeled as a negative evaluation of the teller (the robot).

Example 1 (Participant ID3).

- [n] No, the answer was: because there is no more pappouth *(non bien la reponse etait parce qu'il n'y a plus de pappouth)*
- [h] this is a good one, yeah, it's funny, I like it *(elle est pas mal celle-la ouais elle est rigolote j'aime bien)*.

Example 2 (Participant ID25).

- [n] it reminds me of a story of a robot that went into a cafe and splash! *(ça me rappelle une histoire c'est celle d'un robot qui est entré dans un café et plouf)*
- [h] yeah frankly you could have done better. *(ouais franchement t'aurais pu faire mieux hein là)*.

Metalinguistic Comment. It comments the previous humorous text itself. As mentioned by Hay [8], these responses allow the human participant to demonstrate recognition and understanding of the attempt of humor, as in the following example.

Example 3 (Participant ID26).

- [n] what vigor! (/expression with 'peach' in French/) You discover all the ingredients [...]! *(quelle pêche tu as trouvé tous les ingrédients poils aux dents)*
- [h] you enjoy expressions involving fruits. *(tu aimes bien les expressions avec des fruits)*.

Mode Adoption. As pointed by Hay [8], participants can also respond by contributing with more humor. In this case, the humorous frame is maintained in the second part of the adjacency pair. According to Attardo [1], mode adoption is a way for the speaker to enter into the possible world created by the joker and play along with it. The human participant can mode adopt by two different behaviors (i) he enters the world created by the robot with the humorous act and continue to play with this imaginary world, or (ii) he proposes a humorous act himself. Humor can be supported by echoing the words of the speaker [8]. The participant will repeat the words in appreciation, often as if savoring the humor as in Example 4.

Example 4 (Participant ID33).

- [n] it reminds me of a story of a robot that went into a cafe and splash!
- [h] obviously, it took itself for a sugar and then has melted. *(évidemment que s'il s'est pris pour un sucre il a fondu).*

Example 5 (Participant ID22).

- [n] well the answer was concentrated milk *(non bien la réponse était du lait concentré)*
- [h] can I tell you a joke? *(et moi je peux t'en raconter une de blague).*

Sarcasm. For the purposes of this paper can be seen as a cutting or a ironie remark intended to express contempt or ridicule. As defined by Haverkate [7], it regroups any instance in which the participant replies by saying the opposite of what they mean or something different from what they mean.

Example 6 (Participant ID28).

- [n] you know, to have a small head is not really serious, see mine! *(tu sais avoir une petite tête c'est pas vraiment grave vise la mienne)*
- [h] no, it does not look too serious *(non ça a pas l'air trop grave).*

Other Comment. The *other comment category* is for instances that did not fit into the previous categories. This category mostly regroups sentences made after play on words, made in the game proposed by the robot of discovering ingredients of a recipe. Participant didn't demonstrate recognition and understanding of the attempt of humor but are engaged in dialog by trying to win the game by discovering all the ingredients.

Example 7 (Participant ID8).

- [n] yes you are right, but there is more than that, /French idiomatic rhyming playful expression/! *(oui tu as raison mais il n'y a pas que ça poil au doigt)*
- [h] hmm, water *(hum de l'eau).*

5   Results

5.1   Distribution of Human Humor Support Verbal Responses

First, we investigate the distribution of humor responses types after an humorous act made by the robot. Our assumption is that, such as in human-human interaction, participants will use different humor support types in response to the humorous acts made by the robot. Table 2 presents the distribution of human humor support types in response to the two categories of humor made by the robot (see Table 1 for the composition of the humor categories).

The *other comments* responses were the most common responses to the robot's attempt of humor, occurring in more than 1/3 of the data (40,94 %). This

Table 2. Humor support types of human responses to an humorous act made by the robot

Responses types	Global distribution		After canned jokes		After conversational humor	
	N	%	N	%	N	%
Other comments	156	**40,94**	2	1,28	154	98,72
Lack of verbal response	64	16,80	33	51,56	31	48,44
Subjective evaluation	40	10,50	30	75	10	25
Sarcasm	35	9,19	17	48,57	18	51,43
Mode adoption	33	8,66	14	42,42	19	57,58
Interjection	30	7,87	18	60	12	40
Metalinguistic comments	23	6,04	16	**69,57**	7	30,43

category occurred mostly after conversational humor and rarely after canned jokes. On the contrary, Table 2 shows that the *subjective evaluation* responses occurred mostly after canned jokes as for the *metalinguistic comments* and *interjection* responses types (69,57 % and 60 %). A strong correlation between the different humorous acts made by the robot and the humor responses types used by participants (Chi-square = 208.4526, df = 15, p-value < 2.2e-16) confirmed this distribution. It suggests that the kind of humor made by the robot strongly determines the types of verbal responses of participants.

5.2   Functions of Humor Responses in Interaction

We observe that the humor responses types differ in their contextual appearance according to the robot humorous acts. If we take a closer look into the distribution of the human humor response types, the contextual distribution allows us to regroup the different responses type into supra categories. We assume that each of these categories will play a function in the interaction with the humorous robot.

Given the context, the human humor response types can be grouped into three categories (i) responses types appearing mostly after canned jokes humor, (ii) responses types appearing after both canned jokes and conversational humor and (iii) responses types which appear after conversational humor mostly. If we go deeper, we observe that, in the first category, the elicited responses conform to expectations that participants signal their recognition and understanding of the humorous act. In the second category, participants either supported the robot by developing the joke and contributing more humor or maintaining a humorous frame by teasing the robot. In the third category, participants didn't feel the need of making an explicit support. Finally, the humor responses types can be grouped in three categories

- (i) *Recognition of the attempt of humor* which regroups the responses types *evaluation*, *interjection* and *metalinguistic comment*,
- (ii) *Responding with more humor* which regroups *mode adoption* and *sarcasm*,
- (iii) *No humor support* which is a non recognition of the humorous act of the robot and is made of the *other comments responses*.

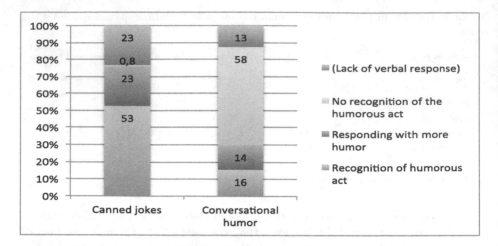

Fig. 1. Categories of participant's responses to humor for Conversational humor and Canned jokes - Chi-square = 208.4526, df = 15, p-value < 2.2e-16 p-value < 2.2e-16

Figure 1 presents the distribution of human responses categories according to the two main types of the robot humorous acts. It shows a similarity in the distribution of category *Responding with more humor* for both canned jokes and conversational humor. Indeed, the percent of responses in categories *Responding with more humor* is quite similar after conversational humor and canned jokes performed by the robot (small significant difference on a Student test t = 1.981, df = 180.45, p-value = 0.04912). On the contrary, the distribution of *Recognition of the attempt of humor* and *No humor support* categories are significantly different (respectively t = 6.1611, df = 179.306, p-value = 4.634e-09 and t = −11.2643, df = 107.034, p-value < 2.2e-16 on a Student t-test).

5.3   Sociolinguistic Variables

Then, we assume that the differences in using humor support categories may be explained by sociolinguistic variables or personality traits. Indeed, researches in human-human interaction have been made on identification of differences in the use of humor for men and women [5,9] or in the use of humor according to personality traits [16].

Age. In this corpus, participant's age ranges from 21 to 86 years old (average: 40.39, median: 32). We separate participants in 3 groups according to their age. These groups have been made upon the graphical repartition of participant's ages and have been confirmed by a k-means clustering approach. These groups are: (1) 21–40 with 24 participants, (2) 40–60 with 10 participants and (3) 60–86 with 12 participants. Figure 2 presents the distribution of humor response categories for each age groups, relatively to the humorous acts made by the robot

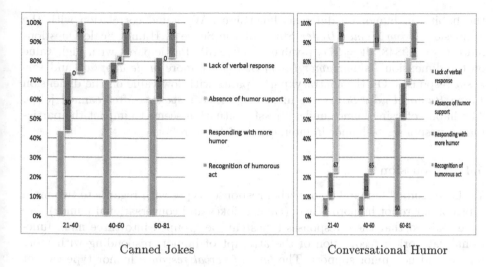

Canned Jokes   Conversational Humor

Fig. 2. Distribution of humor responses categories given participant's age

(canned jokes and conversational humor). As shown in Fig. 2, the eldest age group (60–86) showed a marked preference for categories of response *Recognition of the humorous act* while group 21–40 and 40–60 used more the *Absence of humor support* category after *conversational humor*. This difference in the use of *Recognition of the humorous act* category is significant (Chi-square = 50.2728, df = 6, p-value = 4.145e-09).

If we go deeper into the humor responses categories, a Chi-square exact shows a significant difference for the usage of humor response types over ages (Chi-square = 72.62, df = 12, p-value = 1.033e-10). The group 60–86 showed a marked preference for *evaluative responses*, which decreases down to 20.44 % among the 40–60 and 5.19 % more for 21–40-year olds. The 21–40 group seems to use more *lack of verbal response* than the 40–60 and 60–81 groups after canned jokes. On the contrary, this human humor response seems to be less used by the 21–40 group after conversational humor and more used by the other groups. Both Chi-square and the Fisher exact tests were performed due to the very small numbers in many cells. However, the differences were not significant.

Sex. We observe a decrease of 29 % of men in the 40–60 group (40 % men and 60 % women) and 9 % more in the 60–81 group (31 % men and 69 % women). No significant differences were found according to gender (Chi-squared = 6.111, df = 6, p-value = 0.4109). This suggests that gender may not be a particularly important variable in the humor responses types to a humorous robot.

Relation to Personality Traits and Self-report Questionnaires. Participants filled the Sense of Humor Scale Questionnaire [12] which assess the habits on humor on different dimensions. We found correlation with the dimension *Using Humor Under Stress* of the Sense of Humor Scale Questionnaire (t = 1.9848, df = 277, p-value = 0.04815). Participants with high value on the dimension *Using Humor Under Stress* use more *mode adoption* and *sarcasm* responses. On the contrary, participants with low value on the dimension *Using Humor Under Stress* use more *evaluative responses* after canned jokes. The habits of using humor under stressful situation seems to impact the participant's responses to humor in interaction with the robot.

5.4   Discussion

We have studied human humor verbal responses types with regards to two main types of our robot humorous acts (canned jokes and conversational humor). We have realized that these responses types can be grouped into three main functional categories: recognition of the attempt of humor, responding with more humor and no humor support. The *lack of verbal response* humor type cannot easily be placed into these categories. Indeed, into this humor response type the recognition of the absence of verbal support can either be provided with a paralinguistic humor support (e.g., laughter, head nod or smiles) or the silence can be sign of an complete absence of explicit support. All in all, this category merits further investigation on the paralinguistic responses and a multimodal annotation of participants interaction. For example, an examination of laughter for the 60–81 group in the *lack of verbal response* shows that 25 % of the *lack of verbal response* human responses are filled by laughter after canned jokes and 40 % after conversational humor. This group have the same percent of *lack of verbal response* human responses after canned jokes and conversational humor (18 %). This supports the idea that after canned jokes, the major part of the absence of humor support is made by silences whereas after conversational humor, the absence of support is displayed both by *other comment* responses and silence.

Significant differences in the distribution of the *Recognition of the attempt of humor* and *No humor support* responses categories were found. The *No humor support* responses were mainly observed after conversational humor while *Recognition of the attempt of humor* responses were mainly observed after canned jokes. This can be explained by the interaction scenario himself. Conversational humor is integrated in a part of dialogue where participants play a game with the robot, trying to recognize ingredients of a recipe. This can also be explained by the failure of the conversational humorous acts. Participants didn't want to hurt the robot's face by recognizing lame humor.

We have investigated the impact of sociolinguistic variables on the usage of humor response categories (age, sex, personality traits and sense of humor). Significant differences were found in the use of *Recognition of the humorous act* and *Absence of humor support* categories: the group 60–86 showed a marked preference for *evaluative responses* humor responses type whereas the 21–40 group used more the *lack of verbal response* humor responses type. Zajdman [18] points out that any joking activity presents a potential face threatening act for both the speaker (because it could fall at) and the hearer (because he might not 'get the joke'). Our findings suggests a shift, as individuals grow older, for humor responses types which are less face threatening for both the joker and themselves. These results seems to support the findings of Bell [4] that the eldest have a preference for polite responses to failed humor in human-human interaction.

No significant differences were found in our data concerning the impact of sex in the humor support responses. Given the research made on identification of differences in the use of humor for men and women (e.g., [5,9,11]), this dimension is worth further investigations. For example, LaCorte [11] observed major effect of gender in the use and appreciation of humor styles: men were more likely to appreciate aggressive and self-defeating humor styles. The use of a hackneyed variety of humor may impact on the absence of difference for men and women.

Finally, we have investigated the impact of Sense of humor and Personality questionnaire on the usage of humor support responses categories. We found correlation with the *Using Humor under stress* dimension: participants with high value on this dimension used more *Contributing with more humor* response category. Despite mode adoption was found to be relatively rare in human-human interaction [2], our protocol seems to set up a playful interaction in which participants who have a habits to use humor under stress are willing to entertain the humorous frame.

6 Conclusions and Future Work

This paper has explored ideas related to the responses types of participants to humorous acts made by the robot in a social dialog. This study relies on 49 human-robot interactions and 381 adjacency pairs of humorous acts made by the robot and the following human responses have been extracted. The human responses were coded according to the type of verbal response. As in human-human interactions, the type of humorous act made by the joker robot mainly determines the human responses. Participants rarely notified understanding and recognizing the attempt of humorous after conversational humorous acts (teasing sentences and play on words). On the contrary, joke and riddles are always recognized as an attempt of humour. Three main functional categories of human responses were found (1) providing no support, (2) recognizing the attempt of humor and (3) contributing with more humor. This study reveals the existence of other influence such as the sociolinguistics variable of age or the Sense of Humor (measured by questionnaire).

Future works include further investigations on the non-verbal responses. We will investigate paralinguistic cues (e.g. laughter and affects bursts) and multi-modal responses (e.g., smiles, head nod). We hope to find more tangible cues, which could be fruitfully exploited to build and maintain a rich user profile of humorous acts preferences during the Human-Robot interaction.

References

1. Attardo, S.: Violation of conversational maxims and cooperation: the case of jokes. J. Pragmat. **19**(6), 537–558 (1993)
2. Attardo, S., Pickering, L., Baker, A.: Prosodic and multimodal markers of humor in conversation. Pragmat. Cogn. **2**(19), 224–247 (2011)
3. Bechade, L., Duplessis, G.D., Sehili, M.A., Devillers, L.: Behavioral and emorional spoken cues related to mental states in human-robot social interaction. In: International Conference on Multimodal Interaction (ICMI 2015) (2015)
4. Bell, N.D.: Responses to failed humor. J. Pragmat. **41**, 1825–1836 (2009)
5. Coates, J.: Women, Men and Language: A Sociolinguistic Account of Sex Differences in Language. Longman, London, NewYork (1986)
6. Devillers, L., Rosset, S., Duplessis, G.D., Sehili, M.A., Bechade, L., Delaborde, A., Gossart, C., Letard, V., Yang, F., Yemez, Y., Turker, B.B., Sezgin, M., El Haddad, K., Dupont, S., Luzzati, D., Esteve, Y., Emer, G., Campbell, N.: Multimodal data collection of human-robot humorous interactions in the joker project. In: Affective Computing and Intelligent Interaction (ACII) (2015)
7. Haverkate, H.: A speech analysis of irony. J. Pragmat. **14**, 77–109 (1990)
8. Hay, J.: The pragmatics of humor support. Humor - Int. J. Humor Res. **14**(1), 55–82 (2001)
9. Kotthoff, H.: Gender and humor: the state of the art. J. Pragmat. **38**(1), 4–25. http://linkinghub.elsevier.com/retrieve/pii/S0378216605001256
10. Kulms, P., Kopp, S., Krämer, N.C.: Let's be serious and have a laugh: can humor support cooperation with a virtual agent? In: Bickmore, T., Marsella, S., Sidner, C. (eds.) IVA 2014. LNCS, vol. 8637, pp. 250–259. Springer, Heidelberg (2014)
11. LaCorte, S.: An examination of personal humor style and humor appreciation in others. Senior Honors Project (2015)
12. McGhee, P.: The Laughter Remedy: Health, Healing and the Amuse System. Kendall/Hunt, Dubuque (1996)
13. Morkes, J., Kernal, H., Nass, C.: Effects of humor in task-oriented human-computer interaction and computer-mediated communication: a direct test of srct theory. Hum.-Comput. Interact. **14**(4), 395–435 (2000)
14. Nijholt, A.: Conversational agents and the construction of humorous acts. In: Nishida, T. (ed.) Conversational Informatics: An Engineering Approach, pp. 19–47. Wiley Series in Agent Technology. Wiley, Chichester. http://doi.wiley.com/10.1002/9780470512470.ch2
15. Norrick, N.: Repetition in canned jokes and spontaneous conversational joking. Humor - Int. J. Humor Res. **6**, 385–402 (1993)
16. Ruch, W., Carrell, A.: Trait cheerfulness and the sense of humor. Pers. Individ. Differ. **24**, 551–558 (1998)
17. Zadjman, A.: Contextualization of canned jokes in discourse. Humor - Int. J. Humor Res. **4**, 23–40 (1991)
18. Zadjman, A.: Humorous face-threatening acts: humour as strategy. J. Pragmat. **23**, 325–339 (1995)

Laughter and Humour as Conversational Mind-Reading Displays

Gary McKeown[✉]

School of Psychology, Queen's University Belfast, Belfast BT7 1NN, UK
g.mckeown@qub.ac.uk

Abstract. Laughter and humor are pervasive phenomena in conversational interactions. This paper argues that they function as displays of mind-reading abilities in social interactions–as suggested by the Analogical Peacock Hypothesis (APH). In this view, they are both social bonding signals and can elevate one's social status. The relational combination of concepts in humor is addressed. However, it is in the inclusion of context and receiver knowledge, required by the APH view, that it contributes the most to existing theories. Taboo and offensive humor are addressed in terms of costly signaling, and implications for human computer interaction and some possible routes to solutions are suggested.

Keywords: Laughter · Humor · Social bonding · Evolution · Context

1 Introduction

Laughter and humour are interlinked phenomena, but obviously quite different in nature; this should–but typically does not–raise questions about why such different phenomena came to be so closely associated with one another. Laughter is often assumed to be a simple response to a humorous stimulus presented in the environment; clearly it has this role but it also appears to have many other functions as well. A variety of research domains have shown that there is much more to laughter than its role as a simple response to humorous stimuli. In particular, laughter seems to have a range of regulatory functions within our social interactions and conversations; it seems to act as a kind of non-verbal punctuation mechanism, it eases our social interactions and regulates the flow of conversations in ways that usually pass unnoticed by the interlocutors [1].

Probably the first discipline to realise the importance of laughter in conversational interaction was conversation analysis [1,2] with important contributions from psychology [3–7], ethology and comparative psychology [8–10], and human ethology and anthropology [11–13].

Laughter is a reflex-like non-verbal social signal that is pervasive in human social interactions, especially amongst friends and close associates [5,15]. It commonly occurs at differing levels of intensity, and it seems that the intensity of a laugh most strongly distinguishes the function to which laughter is oriented [14]. At low levels of intensity laughter seems to serve conversational goals ensuring

© Springer International Publishing Switzerland 2016
N. Streitz and P. Markopoulos (Eds.): DAPI 2016, LNCS 9749, pp. 317–328, 2016.
DOI: 10.1007/978-3-319-39862-4_29

fluid social interactions with a social bonding function [1]. At higher levels of intensity it is more strongly related to humour [14], while probably still retaining its function as a social bonding signal. Far from being a reflex-like phenomena humor occupies a very different place in the human behavioural repertoire. Humor typically involves high level cognitive processing and perspective-taking and is often linguistic in nature. Humor, like laughter, is a pervasive feature of conversational and social interactions [16]. Yet, it is unclear why this would be the case if a simple utilitarian approach to human communication is adopted, that is, one that assumes the goal of human communication is to convey information efficiently. Accounts that place a higher value on social bonding aspects of human communication are required. This paper will briefly address the evolution of laughter as a social bonding display; the social nature of cognition, mindreading, and the Analogical Peacock Hypothesis (APH). It will then focus on humor more directly, before exploring the implications of laughter and humour as conversational mind-reading displays for human computer interaction.

2   Laughter as a Social Bonding Display

Laughter has been suggested to have ancient origins in the mammalian lineage. Laughter-like phenomena are observed in many primates and its origins probably extend back at least as far as our last common ancestor with those species. Even older origins have been suggested as rats emit laughter-like ultrasonic vocalization patterns in response to play and tickling [17]. Amongst the great apes tickle-induced vocalizations are found in orangutans, gorillas, chimpanzees, and bonobos with similar acoustic patterns to human laughter [8].

Differing intensity levels in laughter may have their origins in two different primate social signals–one related to smiling and the other to laughter. Smiling may originate in the silent-bared teeth display, or teeth-chattering and lip-smacking displays that are often seen in higher primates–these are usually submissive, appeasement gestures or signal affiliation, reassurance, and attachment. Laughter probably has its origins in the relaxed open mouthed display or "play face" which often has a vocalized breathing component–this display is typical in rough social play and mock fighting, and may be a signal to interpret behaviour as non-serious [9]. Wild chimpanzee research has shown that receivers of mock-aggression emit these displays more often–they may therefore signal it is safe to continue the play [18]. Such tickling and "roughhousing" play is commonly found in humans between children, and between adults and children where it aids social bonding. Gervais and Wilson [19] stress the social affiliation function of laughter in human communicative interactions, and how laughter works with humor to enhance group cohesion and cooperation and maybe to signal to other group members it is safe to engage in group play.

Laughter's origins seem to be as a social bonding signal and it seems to retain this function in modern conversation [1,16]. Holt [20], a conversational analyst, suggests it is this social bonding function that allows laughter to do much of the work that is required in regulating and repairing conversational interactions. Laughter creates a signal that is only very loosely attached to the propositional content of the current conversation and therefore it can help to create safe moments where topics can be terminated or changed, miscommunication and broken down conversations can be repaired, and potential misinterpretation of taboo conversational areas can be safely navigated.

Many of laughter's functions can use low intensity laughter, where the goal is to ensure that cultural and social norms of conversational interactions are adhered to. However, its inclusion is crucial, as social norms mean it will be expected in appropriate situations. It should not be thought of as false or weak laughter as it is required for efficient conversational interaction; a strong reason for this is that the absence of a social signal where one is expected can itself be a strong social signal. This is particularly important with respect to laughter. Good social interactions require laughter in culturally appropriate places, without it, it is easy to appear awkward; a worse scenario is silence where laughter is expected–easily interpreted as an insult. Alternatively, high intensity laughter most likely signals that it is safe to continue in playful social interaction, while retaining social bonding functions. High intensity laughter is harder-to-fake, signaling a more authentic connection with a felt emotion and a strong desire to bond. Higher intensity laughter has been shown to be more closely related to humor and humorous interactions [14]. This raises the question as to why we might want to place greater authenticity in our desire to socially bond with individuals who are able to produce quality humor. An answer to this has been provided by the Analogical Peacock Hypothesis [21]. However, before we address the APH, we need to introduce mind-reading and why it might be evolutionarily useful.

3   The Social Brain Hypothesis

The social brain hypothesis [22–24], places human sociality, and the human social milieu, as the core evolutionary driver and ecological environment for human cognitive evolution. It is in the need to rise up through a social hierarchy and to keep track of rivals, allies, and potential mates–and their relationships with one another–that has led to the special kinds of cognition that are seen in primate evolution and especially in humans [25]. This kind of social cognition places a strong emphasis on being able to take the perspective of others within the social hierarchy. Perspective-taking–sometimes known as mentalizing but more commonly referred to scientifically as mind-reading–has become particularly pronounced in humans. This has led to the evolution of strong mind-reading capabilities; the development of Theory of Mind, with strong recursive intentionality [26]; and important co-evolutionary aspects with human culture [27].

4   Mental Fitness Indicators, Mind-Reading and the Analogical Peacock Hypothesis

The argument that the need to be socio-politically astute has been the key driver in human evolution has been extended in a further argument known as the Analogical Peacock Hypothesis (APH) [21]; this view combines the social brain line of reasoning with ideas that argue that sexual selection rather than survival selection has been more influential in recent homonin and human evolution. Miller [28] has argued that certain socio-communicative elements of human behaviour function as *mental fitness indicators*, these are mental abilities that indicate evolutionary fitness to potential mates. Miller [29] suggests some candidate mental fitness indicators, these include creativity, morality, language in conversation and storytelling, and humor (both verbal and nonverbal). The APH [21] argument posits that in the course of human evolution female homonins began to select males as reproductive partners on the basis of their socio-political prowess–how well they could gain status and rise up through the ranks of a social hierarchy. A key target for this selection was their perspective-taking and mind-reading abilities. According to the APH, the reason that the abilities highlighted by Miller are mental fitness indicators is that they allow us to display our mind-reading abilities to one another. This *display* of mind-reading abilities becomes the principal goal of human communication rather than the traditionally assumed function of conveying useful information to one another. Displays of mind-reading abilities serve as proxy measures for how socio-politically astute we are–how likely we are to climb our way through a social hierarchy and gain status, with the access to resources and reproductive advantages that high status brings.

However, mind-reading displays are only part of a complementary pair of communicative functions–we also engage in *alignment* communications. To be capable of displaying mind-reading ability we must become aware of and tune our minds to those of potential mates. In addition, as mating is a competitive selection process, multiple potential mates will be aligning their minds with each other which will lead to a broad cultural alignment. To become socially successful creative mind-readers, we must be aware of what is in other people's minds; we must spend a large amount of time listening to and observing other humans within the cultures and social groups whose social hierarchy we wish to ascend. We must learn and align ourselves with others within our social group and assimilate our group's cultural norms. A long process of alignment allows us to fine tune ourselves to the cultural knowledge, behaviours, and expectations that exist within the minds of other members of our social groups, and amongst those we would most like to have as potential mates, friends, and allies.

The analogical part of the APH comes from one of the key proposed methods of displaying mind reading abilities; we can create hard-to-fake displays of mind-reading abilities by showing others that we are so aware of the concepts that exist inside their heads that we can creatively link them together in ways that they had not yet thought of themselves. Finding previously unforeseen and relevant relational links between concepts creatively highlights a communicator's knowledge of what is in other people's minds and shows that they know what is likely to interest them. This core creative process is shared across mental fitness indicators. The APH highlights five key features that unify mental fitness indicators and make them serve as hard-to-fake signals of mind-reading ability.

These are: the relational combination of concepts, large conceptual knowledge networks, processing speed, contextualization, and receiver knowledge.

5 Relational Combination of Concepts in Humor

Humor makes a particularly good example in which to examine the creative display of mind-reading ability. The original APH paper [21] highlights Gentner's structure mapping theory [30], ideas around dynamic relational binding [31], and conceptual blending and integration [32] as mechanisms that may be used to explain how concepts may be relationally combined. Some of these mechanisms have previously been implicated in humor [33], but many similar mechanisms–proposed as models of humor–work well within the broader framework of the relational combination of concepts. An interesting older candidate is Koestler's bisociation theory [34], it makes a similar claim to the APH that the combination of concepts is central to creativity in general and that emotional context determines whether a creative act is found to be humorous or some other form of creative act. However, it differs extensively in the motivation for producing creative acts–Koestler relies on a "releasing tension" explanation as opposed to the socio-evolutionary motivation of the APH.

Most of the cognitive theories of humor highlight mechanisms that are suitable in one form or another for the idea that the relational combination of concepts is a key feature of creativity and humor. Humor represents a particularly useful example of how this might unfold; the various cognitive theories of more formal "canned" joke scenarios provide particularly explicit explanations. These theories tend to have a well explained mechanism for finding potential relational combinations. These concepts can then be held apart with sufficient confidence to challenge a joke receiver to exert considerable cognitive effort in finding the link–with a failure to meet the challenge, it can be revealed at a moment of the joke-teller's choosing by telling the punchline. Most of the theories of incongruity resolution involve some mechanism of this sort and perhaps the most detailed and explicit in terms of the mechanism are those suggested by Raskin [35].

These theories of humour typically highlight the nature of two of the APH's unifying features of mental fitness indicators: the possession of large conceptual networks and the relational combination of concepts. The APH requires, rather than contests, mechanisms of this sort. However, it is in the other aspects the communicative nature of humor that the APH can make a more valuable contribution. The APH highlights the importance of processing speed–an area where computers have a distinct advantage–as speed helps to make signals harder-to-fake. Processing speed makes a fitness indicator a more honest and reliable signal. It is usually the case that those who are able to make quick and relevant witticisms garner greater social status in social interactions than those who deliver a barrage of pre-prepared jokes. Even within the more formally defined situations of stand-up comedy there is greater kudos to be gained by performers who show themselves able to possess a fast wit and improvisational skills. However, it is in the incorporation of context and the acknowledgement of the importance of receiver knowledge that the APH highlights important aspects of humor and laughter that need to be addressed for human computer interaction situations.

6   Contextualisation and Receiver Knowledge

Within most computational communication research–both linguistic and non-verbal–the problem of context is usually acknowledged as a difficult issue. This results in context being ignored in favour of "toy problems" and constrained scenarios until research has advanced sufficiently. With receiver knowledge the situation is even worse, the idea that communications have to be tailored to a given receiver or audience is usually not considered, or simply subsumed within broader conceptualisations of context. Typically, assumptions are made that we all operate using the same set of linguistic rules and use sufficiently similar semantic networks. These assumptions allow us to evade the issue that different people have different subsets of vocabulary with nuanced differences in the weighted relationships between concepts. Much of the computational research on humor, depends on abstracted sets of cultural knowledge, such as predefined static semantic networks or ontologies that capture constrained subsets of meaning in a language at a given point in a language's history–typically as modern as possible. These are valid and useful approaches, yet inherently limited–Raskin explicitly acknowledges the limitations of looking at just the "artifact text in isolation" [35]. Yet, these limitations raise important issues for certain kinds of human-computer interaction. Research in dialog modelling; Embodied Conversational Agents [36]; and digital assistants such as Apple's Siri, Microsoft's Cortana, Amazon's Alexa, and "OK Google", are all technologies and research areas that are currently at a stage where the infusion of humor and the appropriate placement of laughter would considerably enhance their user engagement.

During the evolution of the human communicative system, every human communication that influenced the evolutionary process took place within a context, and was targeted towards a specific receiver–whether that was an individual or a broader social audience. Consequently, when humans socially interact and communicate with one another, many adjustments and accommodations are made by communicators as they tailor their utterances, paralanguage, facial expressions, and other non-verbal components towards the targets of their communicative acts. These adjustments are made on the basis of a communicator's assessments of the contextual knowledge available to a receiver, their level of cultural understanding, their linguistic style, level of verbal fluency, and degree of intimacy with the communicator. Accurate assessments are evidence of receiver knowledge and require strong mind-reading abilities. Typically a joke or humorous comment made to a well-known friend will be different from a joke or humorous comment made to a stranger who has recently been introduced. Indeed, the "known" in well-known friend entails receiver knowledge. The tailoring of a communication to a given individual or audience becomes especially important if we accept the basic tenet of the APH that conversational interactions are primarily displays of mind-reading abilities. At a basic level, a well-tailored communication serves as a direct display of the communicator's receiver knowledge. At a deeper level, incorporating as much context as possible makes a display hard-to-fake as it shows an awareness of what is most likely to be salient in the mind of the receiver at the current moment in time.

The degree of intimacy with a conversational partner is likely to be an important determinant of both the use of laughter and humor in conversational interactions. There is evidence that the use of metaphor in conversation depends on the degree of intimacy between interlocutors [37,38], and from conversation analysis that figurative language has functions that are similar to laughter [39]. Where there is a high degree of intimacy–between good friends, and between potential romantic partners–humor can and should be tailored to the interlocutors's particular tastes, displaying high levels of receiver knowledge. Successful displays would in turn be responded to with high intensity laughter, indicating a genuine desire to socially bond with someone who clearly knows the receiver well; someone who is reinforcing that they possess strong receiver knowledge through humorous conversational displays. In cases where levels of acquaintance and intimacy are lower, the use of humor becomes a much riskier endeavour. Where receiver knowledge is low, any targeting of humor is more likely to fail, in which case, broader, and more bland humor is a safer strategy, but it is unlikely to be viewed as a particularly accomplished display. Similarly, high intensity laughter as a response to bland and contextually weak displays of humor is likely to be interpreted as over-eager or fawning–perhaps at a level that is sufficiently inappropriate to induce different mentalizing strategies [40]. Therefore, low-intensity laughter is a safer option as it has greater ambiguity in how it can be interpreted. Having no laughter at all, however, is not an option, as the absence of a signal is often a signal; failure to laugh in a socially appropriate context displays a lack of knowledge of cultural norms or could be interpreted as an insult or snub. The correct knowledge of when laughter and humor are appropriate is essential to fluid conversational interactions. Without socially appropriate laughter interactions will quickly appear awkward and cumbersome, without sufficiently tailored humour they will lack engagement and charm.

According to the APH, conversational interaction is part of a competitive evaluation and selection process, and producing eloquent and accomplished conversation is amongst the most difficult behaviours we engage in. Language is well suited to these evaluative needs as it is represents a "Red Queen" situation. Languages are ever-evolving dynamic cultural entities where context plays an important part in the interpretation of meaning when humans are confronted with utterances [41]; and novelty, news, creative trends, and predicitons of what a receiver will find interesting are core features of conversational content. Therefore, "it takes all the running you can do, to keep in the same place" [42]. Consequently, static semantic network approaches are probably limited to bland and mediocre humor, and are likely to age very quickly in their applicability to human conversational interaction. The use of context and finely tuned receiver knowledge offers opportunities to ensure that humorous displays are seen as intentional and hard-to-fake. Incorporating topical and situationally relevant material in humor displays cultural awareness. Successful humor production means that a correct assessment of the audience's awareness of the cultural set of knowledge on which the humor depends has been made; the producer has judged that a sufficiently aligned semantic network exists before attempting the humor. Assessments of receiver knowledge should be made and attempts at humor production should be inhibited or vetoed by a socially aware producer–whether computational or human. Vetoing should become more likely or humor should be made more bland in cases where the cultural differences–lack of alignment–with a receiver or audience are too great. For example, due to age or social group differences, insufficient degrees of intimacy, or weak levels of linguistic ability–perhaps in the case of an obvious second language speaker.

Acknowledging the importance of receiver knowledge and context means that the success of humour and laughter in a conversation is relative to how well it is tailored to an interlocutor's mind. To be convincing as a mind-reader of quality requires humor displays that: are tuned to a particular conversational partner or audience, show knowledge of the appropriate cultural norms, and awareness of the current context. "The audience is a genius" is a phrase used in stand-up comedy circles and often attributed to Lenny Bruce. It captures this relative nature of humour. Professional stand-up comedians often have preparatory shows testing and vetoing their material against a live audience; in effect, they tune their material to reflect receiver knowledge using a representative sample of a larger audience population. They test their receiver knowledge to minimise the likelihood of failure.

Addressing the issues of context and receiver knowledge defines the humor problem in a broader way than the relational combination of concepts. It makes the problem of humour more obviously one of mind-reading; it places emphasis on the importance of understanding what is currently relevant, and subverting expectations in interesting and engaging ways–no small challenge for both computers and humans.

7   Humour, Taboo, and Offense

Culturally taboo topics are often sources of humorous material; factor analytic studies of cartoons and jokes often generate three factors–one instance generated incongruity-resolution, nonsense, and sexual factors [43]. In addition, taboo humor is common in romantic flirtation, where it can be used to explore social boundaries while remaining retractable; male-male insulting humor, where it can used to establish social rank while remaining socially bonded [44]; and to emphasize ingroup bonding, while denigrating an outgroup–often engaging stereotypical cultural formulations of an outgroup as part of a joke [16]. Clearly where humor strays into culturally and socially taboo areas there is a heightened risk of being offensive when the intention is to be humorous, almost the opposite outcome of that which is usually sought. Why would such a risk be taken? Costly signals are harder-to-fake and one way of making a humor signal more potentially costly is to increase the risk associated with a signal. Taboo topics can make humorous displays more costly. Deft use of humor that is on the border of social acceptability shows that the humorist is finely tuned to the prevalent cultural norms and can push the limits of social acceptability just as far as they think the receiver will find acceptable. It displays finely tuned receiver knowledge. The risk is high as any failure to judge the boundary appropriately will create an offensive situation with the subsequent damage to social reputation that this would cause; managing to be humorous, to know just what is appropriate, and playing with the boundaries of social acceptability provides a strong display of receiver knowledge where the risks of getting it wrong are high.

Often in stand-up comedy there is greater kudos to be earned for conducting "edgier" routines, pushing the boundaries of acceptability and running the risk of offending people. Reputations can be enhanced by adding shocking attributes to a comedy routine, performances that come close to, but do not quite overstep the social limit. For a performer this can constrain the size of a potential audience to those that are willing to tolerate their boundaries being pushed in a particular way–perhaps a tolerable outcome if it also enhances critical appraisal. Larger audiences will contain a greater proportion of shockable people, those easily pushed beyond their boundary of acceptability and offended. Often a comedian retains some control over an audience–an audience has self-selected to watch a performance, or paid to see a show of a known outrageous performer–then there are expectations that social norms and acceptable boundaries will be challenged.

Audience control is often limited, however, and from the APH point of view, there should be no surprise that so much offense occurs in social media situations–especially in micro-blogging networks such as Twitter. Often in these situations a communication is pared down to its minimal textual component, minimising the amount of context, and supportive signalling, that can be used to mitigate any erroneous attribution of intention towards insult. Laughter and smiling are not easy to convey in this medium, so there can be no signals to announce that this is a play frame or that it is safe to continue playful conversation. The audience too, is broad and diffuse, and often beyond the control of the communicator. Micro-blogs get shared amongst broader social networks than those that have self-selected to follow the original communicator. Therefore, any judgements of receiver knowledge can be nullified by the dispersive nature of social networks. A written piece of text that has attempted to tread into the finely tuned areas at the boundaries of social acceptability is almost certain in these circumstances to be met by someone with indignation and to cause offense. As morality is also a mental fitness indicator, attempts at humor can be converted by other communicators into displays of decrying sanctity. These displays engage a different emotional context and agenda, and an assessment of receiver knowledge that perceives an orientation towards outrage. The humorous attempt will probably also get clarified in ways that remove ambiguity and to ensure moral unacceptability before being further shared. Micro-blogging sites offer a communicative environment in which the checks and balances offered by the interaction of laughter and humor within conversational interactions have been stripped away; as a result they often generate controversy that was unsought and cause offense that was unintended.

8   Implications for Computational Humour and Human Computer Interaction

The problems associated with mind-reading, context, and cultural understanding are amongst the most difficult tasks to incorporate into computational models of social interactions. However, it is necessary to overcome these obstacles in the development of computational humour generation and accompanying socially appropriate laughter. A goal of this paper has been to suggest a way to more clearly define this problem. Embodied conversational agents and digital assistants are ready to move beyond narrow and constrained scenarios, and dialog models that incorporate laughter and humour are needed to create genuinely engaging conversations.

Although social media has been highlighted as a dangerous place in which to produce humor, it may also offer opportunities to solve some of these problems as it presents a rich source of current and topical receiver knowledge. It can be used to keep semantic networks up to date with socially relevant concepts. Incorporating novel and trending concepts into existing semantic networks can allow them to keep pace with the dynamic unfolding of language and highlights the concepts that are most likely to be salient at any given moment. In addition, some social networks can provide access to receiver knowledge; people leave strong indications of the their tastes within social networks, their friends and followers send humorous messages to them that are often evaluated with "likes" and similar endorsements. People also sign up to recommender engines and provide them with strong indications of their interests. Recommender engines use this offered receiver knowledge to predict future interest and refine receiver knowledge with patterns of use. These techniques gather evidence of receiver knowledge and context that can be incorporated into current models to create more tailored attempts at humor. There are obvious ethical and privacy issues with these technologies. Care is required to ensure informed consent, as the goal is to create automated and targeted mind-reading technologies that tailor communications to a given individual. Technologies like these could be used to generate more engaging interactions, but also material and techniques that could most certainly be abused.

9   Conclusion

This paper has argued that laughter and humor both work within social and conversational interactions as displays of mind-reading abilities for evolutionarily important reasons. These mind-reading displays reinforce social bonds and elevate the social status of humor producers. Computational models of humor need to address these aspects if they are to move out of the laboratory and into current technologies that require laughter and humor if they are going to function as genuine human-like interfaces.

References

1. Glenn, P.J.: Laughter in Interaction. Cambridge University Press, Cambridge (2003)
2. Jefferson, G., Sacks, H., Schegloff, E.A.: Notes on laughter in the pursuit of intimacy. In: Button, G., Lee, J.R.E. (eds.) Talk and Social Organisation. Multilingual Matters, Clevedon (1987)
3. Bachorowski, J.A., Owren, M.J.: Not all laughs are alike: voiced but not unvoiced laughter readily elicits positive affect. Psychol. Sci. **12**(3), 252–257 (2001)
4. Owren, M.J., Bachorowski, J.A.: The evolution of emotional expression: a "selfish-gene" account of smiling and laughter in early hominids and humans. In: Mayne, T.J., Bonanno, G.A. (eds.) Emotions: Current Issues and Future Directions. The Guilford Press, New York (2001)
5. Provine, R.: Laughter: A Scientific Investigation. Faber and Faber, London (2000)
6. Provine, R.: Laughing, tickling, and the evolution of speech and self. Curr. Dir. Psychol. Sci. **13**(6), 215–218 (2004)
7. Smoski, M., Bachorowski, J.A.: Antiphonal laughter between friends and strangers. Cogn. Emot. **17**(2), 327–340 (2003)
8. Ross, D.M., Owren, M.J., Zimmermann, E.: Reconstructing the evolution of laughter in great apes and humans. Curr. Biol. **19**(13), 1106–1111 (2009)
9. Preuschoft, S., van Hooff, J.A.R.A.M.: The social function of "Smile" and "Laughter": variations across primate species and societies. In: Segerstråle, U., Molnár, P. (eds.) Nonverbal Communication: Where Nature Meets Culture, pp. 171–189. Lawrence Erlbaum Associates, Mahweh (1997)
10. Preuschoft, S., van Hooff, J.A.R.A.M.: A comparative approach to the phylogeny of laughter and smiling. In: Hinde, R.A. (ed.) Nonverbal Communication: Where Nature Meets Culture, pp. 209–241. Cambridge University Press, Cambridge (1972)
11. Grammer, K.: Strangers meet: laughter and nonverbal signs of interest in opposite-sex encounters. J. Nonverbal Behav. **14**(4), 209–236 (1990)
12. Grammer, K., Eibl-Eibesfeldt, I.: The ritualisation of laughter. In: Koch, W.A. (ed.) Natürlichkeit der Sprache und der Kultur: acta colloquii - Bochum, Bochumer Beiträge zur Semiotik; 18, pp. 192–214 (1972)
13. Mehu, M., Dunbar, R.I.M.: Naturalistic observations of smiling and laughter in human group interactions. Behaviour **145**(12), 1747–1780 (2008)
14. McKeown, G., Curran, W.: The Relationship Between Laughter Intensity and Perceived Humour. The Fourth Interdisciplinary Workshop on Laughter and other Non-Verbal Vocalisations in Speech 27–29 (2015)
15. Dezecache, G., Dunbar, R.I.M.: Sharing the joke: the size of natural laughter groups. Evol. Hum. Behav. **33**(6), 775–779 (2012)
16. Martin, R.A.: The Psychology of Humor. Academic Press, London (2007)
17. Panksepp, J., Burgdorf, J.: Laughing rats and the evolutionary antecedents of human joy? Physiol. Behav. **79**(3), 533–547 (2003)
18. Matsusaka, T.: When does play panting occur during social play in wild chimpanzees? Primates **45**(4), 221–229 (2004)
19. Gervais, M., Wilson, D.S.: The evolution and functions of laughter and humor: a synthetic approach. Q. Rev. Biol. **80**(4), 395–430 (2005)
20. Holt, E.: The last laugh: shared laughter and topic termination. J. Pragmatics **42**(6), 1513–1525 (2010)

21. McKeown, G.J.: The analogical peacock hypothesis: the sexual selection of mind-reading and relational cognition in human communication. Rev. Gen. Psychol. **17**(3), 267–287 (2013)
22. Byrne, R.W., Whiten, A.: Machiavellian Intelligence: Social Expertise and the Evolution of Intellect in Monkeys, Apes, and Humans. Oxford University Press, Oxford (1988)
23. Dunbar, R.I.M.: Grooming, Gossip, and the Evolution of Language. Faber and Faber, London (1996)
24. Dunbar, R.I.M.: The social brain hypothesis. Evol. Anthropol. **6**, 178–190 (1988)
25. Dunbar, R.I.M., Shultz, S.: Evolution in the social brain. Science **317**, 1344–1347 (2007)
26. Stiller, J., Dunbar, R.I.M.: Perspective-taking and memory capacity predict social network size. Soc. Netw. **29**(1), 93–104 (2007)
27. Heyes, C.M., Frith, C.D.: The cultural evolution of mind reading. Science **344**(6190), 1243091–1243091 (2014)
28. Miller, G.F.: The Mating Mind. Vintage, London (2001)
29. Miller, G.F.: Mating intelligence: frequently asked questions. In: Geher, G., Miller, G.F. (eds.) Mating Intelligence: Sex, Relationships, and the Mind's Reproductive System. Lawrence Earlbaum Associates, Hillsdale (2007)
30. Gentner, D.: Structure-mapping: a theoretical framework for analogy. Cogn. Sci. **7**, 155–170 (1983)
31. Holyoak, K.J., Hummel, J.E.: Toward an understanding of analogy within a biological symbol system. In: Gentner, D., Holyoak, K.J., Kokinov, B.N. (eds.) The Analogical Mind, pp. 161–195. MIT Press, Cambridge (2001)
32. Fauconnier, G., Turner, M.: The Way We Think: Conceptual Blending and the Mind's Hidden Complexities. Hutchinson & Co., New York (2002)
33. Veale, T.: The humour of exceptional cases: jokes as compressed thought experiments. In: Brone, G., Feyaerts, K., Veale, T. (eds.) Cognitive Linguistics and Humor Research, pp. 69–90. de Gruyter, Boston (2015)
34. Koestler, A.: The Act of Creation. Penguin, London (1964)
35. Raskin, V., Hempelmann, C.F., Taylor, J.M.: How to understand and assess a theory: the evolution of the SSTH into the GTVH and now into the OSTH. J. Literary Theor. **3**(2), 285–311 (2009)
36. Schröder, M., et al.: Building autonomous sensitive artificial listeners. IEEE Trans. Affect. Comput. **3**(2), 165–183 (2012)
37. Horton, W.S.: Metaphor and readers' attributions of intimacy. Mem. Cogn. **35**(1), 87–94 (2007)
38. Horton, W.S.: Character intimacy influences the processing of metaphoric utterances during narrative comprehension. Metaphor Symbol **28**(3), 148–166 (2013)
39. Holt, E., Drew, P.: Figurative pivots: the use of figurative expressions in pivotal topic transition. Res. Lang. Soc. Interact. **38**(1), 35–61 (2005)
40. McGettigan, C., et al.: Individual differences in laughter perception reveal roles for mentalizing and sensorimotor systems in the evaluation of emotional authenticity. Cereb. Cortex **25**(1), 246–257 (2015)
41. Sperber, D., Wilson, D.: Relevance. Blackwell, Oxford (1986)
42. Van Valen, L.: A new evolutionary law. Evol. Theor. **1**, 1–30 (1973)
43. Ruch, W.: Assessment of appreciation of humor: studies with the 3 WD humor test. In: Speilberger, C.D., Butcher, J.N. (eds.) Advances in Personality Assessment, pp. 27–75. Lawrence Earlbaum Associates, Hillsdale (1992)
44. Progovac, L., Locke, J.L.: The urge to merge: ritual insult and the evolution of syntax. Biolinguistics **3**(2–3), 337–354 (2009)

Smart Bugs and Digital Banana Peels: Accidental Humor in Smart Environments?

Anton Nijholt[1,2(✉)]

[1] Imagineering Institute, Iskandar, Malaysia
anton@imagineeringinstitute.org
[2] Faculty EEMCS, University of Twente, Enschede, The Netherlands
a.nijholt@utwente.nl

Abstract. In this paper we look at possibilities to introduce humorous situations in smart environments. The assumption is that in future smart environments we have the possibility to configure and even real-time reconfigure environments in a way that humorous situations can be created or that conditions for humorous situations to emerge can be implemented. However, in order to do so we need to investigate how unplanned and unintended humor can emerge when users are confronted with unknown technology or surprising behavior of new (digital) technology. We can design jokes and humorous interactions and situations in movies, on stage, in literature, or in videogames. When we introduce unfamiliar technology or even imperfect technology we can expect that its use leads to humorous situations. Although intentionally and autonomously creating humorous situations by smart sensor and actuator technology is an ultimate goal, in this paper we look at situations and the 'design' of situations that possibly lead to humor because of users interacting with the environment. Users are not necessarily aware of how the environment expects them to behave, and they are probably not aware of shortcomings of the environment. Unintended humor from the point of view of a smart environment designer can also happen when a user starts to exploring shortcomings in order to generate humorous situations. In this paper we have some preliminary observations, mainly by looking at examples and design approaches, on designing environments where such accidental humor can emerge.

Keywords: Humor · Human-computer interaction · Accidental humor · Smart environments · Sensors · Actuators · Games · Entertainment

1 Introduction

Humor is important in our daily-life interactions. It certainly would be difficult having to live with a partner who has no sense of humor. A general assumption in human-computer interaction is that in the future we will have affective interactions with tangibles, virtual agents and physical social robots that assist us and entertain us in our domestic, office, and public space environments. Especially in daily face-to-face communication with intelligent artificial virtual and physical agents our interactions become more affective, assuming that the agents know about us, empathize with us and develop a personal and affective relationship with us, just like we do with them.

© Springer International Publishing Switzerland 2016
N. Streitz and P. Markopoulos (Eds.): DAPI 2016, LNCS 9749, pp. 329–340, 2016.
DOI: 10.1007/978-3-319-39862-4_30

Unfortunately, humor has not or has only modestly been included in models of affective human-computer interaction. Despite decades of humor research, its results have hardly transcended a primitive analysis of (verbal) jokes. In human-agent interaction, whether the agent is virtual or physical, we hardly see more than the introduction of canned jokes or the generation of a witty remark. In this latter case this at least shows that there is some awareness of the context in which the remark as part of the interaction is generated. As a consequence of the lack of theory and therefore the poor possibilities to design humor and generate from a formal model, we think it is useful to look at ways to increase the possibility that 'accidental' humor will emerge in human-computer interaction. In the literature different kinds of humor have been distinguished. Mostly they refer to emotional aspects in relation to the joker or the hearer. Hence we can talk about aggressive humor, friendly humor, self-enhancing humor, affiliative humor, self-disparaging humor and many other types of humor.

In real life, in games, or in social media these types of humor can be distinguished. But it is also possible to make a distinction between humorous situations that emerge naturally, humorous situations that are intended or invented by making certain decisions that help to realize the conditions that make a situation or interaction possibly humorous, and humorous situations that are not only non-intended, but also seen as accidental or inadvertent, and often not desirable, in particular from the point of view of a possible victim of a humorous situation who we, as audience, can laugh at. Obviously, we can also have this kind of humor where the 'victim' happily accepts this 'victimization' and laughs with the others who enjoy his misfortune. In accidental humor we look at situations where it is not the user attempting to find ways to generate humor, probably making use of digital technology such as sensors and actuators in smart environments, but where the technology acts unexpectedly because of bugs or unforeseen actions of the user. This includes situations where the user is not fully aware of how newly introduced technology needs to be handled, or where there is an interaction misunderstanding that leads to a humorous situation or interaction.

In this paper we look at various ways accidental humor can emerge in the context of digital interaction technology. In Sect. 2 we provide some general background knowledge and motivation. Then, in Sect. 3, we show examples of accidental humor and the technology that was involved in unintended creation of humorous situations or humorous expressions. In Sect. 4 we have some preliminary observations on how to increase the chance of the emergence of accidental humor in smart environments. Some conclusions are drawn in the final section.

2   Background and Motivation

Clearly, attempting to design accidental humor is a contradiction in terms. Nevertheless, it is possible to introduce or allow ambiguities and incongruities in smart environments that surprise users, that provide them with enjoyment, and that make them smile or laugh. Accidental humor has hardly or not been discussed in humor research. In this paper we address accidental or inadvertent humor. Although designing accidental humor is a contradiction in terms, we can get inspired by it to allow digitally enhanced environments and its users to generate changes in configurations of sensors and actuators that allow them to increase the chance of humor or to set conditions that help to increase the emergence of humorous situations.

2.1 On Accidental Digital Humor

Well-known examples of accidental humor that is caused by 'imperfect' technology are machine translation errors, errors made by speech recognition systems, chatbot errors, or suggestions made by 'auto-correct' or word completion prediction software [1]. Obviously, one can argue about this 'imperfectness'. For example, in the case of machine translation, instead of aiming at fully automatic high-quality (FAHQ) machine translation, we can also expect software for machine-aided translation only, just as we can expect that a translator consults a dictionary as a tool to find a correct translation and not assuming that the dictionary has the knowledge about the particular context that he or she has and that is necessary to obtain the perfect translation. Hence, rather than seeing a technology as imperfect, we can also look at it as a perfect or at least a helpful tool that we can use rather than having it act autonomously. In the next section we will introduce more of such distinctions with the aim to identify different kinds of accidental humor.

Our aim to increase the chance of accidental digital humor will not be achieved by simply decreasing the quality of the digital application. Frustration rather than amusement will be the result. In order to increase the chance of accidental humor we need to know about conditions that are necessary for humor to appear. Everything that helps to create these conditions or strengthen conditions helps in increasing the chance of accidental humor. We need to be able to identify humor conditions in general and in a particular application we also need to be able to introduce and implement them using design and interaction principles.

2.2 On Humor Theories

Machine translation, speech recognition and all other examples mainly address linguistic engineering applications, hence, it is mainly about verbal humor. This is a research area that can draw from decades-long research on computational linguistics and artificial intelligence. Computational approaches to humor are therefore mainly about verbal or linguistic humor. We need to investigate why sometimes errors made by these applications are funny and why often they are not. Humor theories should help us. Humor theories are usually about conditions that are necessary. These theories are not yet able to determine when a set of conditions is not only necessary, but also sufficient to have humor emerge. This is the holy grail of humor research, being able to predict with certainty that there will be humor when this particular set of conditions has been satisfied.

Usually a distinction is made between relief theory, superiority theory and incongruity (resolution) theories of humor. They can be considered to complement each other, looking at humor from an emotional, functional or cognitive viewpoint. In particular the cognitive viewpoint is interesting for us. Why do we perceive certain activities, interactions and products as humorous? There are various variants of incongruity theory [2, 3]. We usually have a sequence of events that start with what we think or are made to think is a stereotypical situation. Something unexpected is happening and it turns out that we have to re-interpret the starting situation. Usually it is assumed that the two situations need to be opposing, that is, they should be really different, not just slight variations of a same situation. A final condition which we want to mention in order to have a situation perceived as humorous is that it should also be the case that the situation is safe for the perceiver. In the literature this situation is also characterized as the user being in a playful or appropriate emotional state, or by characterizing the situation as having an appropriate emotional climate.

3 Digital Technology and Accidental Humor

3.1 On Introducing Accidental Humor

Sensors and actuators allow us to introduce incongruities in smart environments. We can introduce absurd and surprising behavior of the environment, its objects, its devices and its virtual and robotic inhabitants. It is possible to make changes to lightening, climate, temperature and appearance; walls can be moved, illusions can be introduced. This technology allows us to introduce surprising events for inhabitants of these smart environments. Introducing such events can be the initiative of the environment or it can be an authorized user or inhabitant who has access to these sensors and actuators. Obviously, we can have a situation where everyone who is using that smart environment can access its sensors and actuators or where only hackers can do this and have fun in creating situations they will perceive as humorous.

An application or environment that is able to increase the chance of humor appearing while interacting with a user can not only introduce or enhance conditions expecting that they are not only necessary but also expecting that they are sufficient and therefore guarantee humor. However, in humor theory we have not yet identified these necessary conditions. But we can include the 'user in the loop', that is having the conditions ready that together with a particular input of the user make it possible for the application to give unexpected humorous feedback or create an unexpected and not intended humorous event. Clearly, in the latter case we assume that we are able to make a transition from knowledge of conditions that are necessary to have humor in a linguistic context to conditions required for generating humor in a context that is controlled and monitored by smart technology. When introducing accidental humor we should also make a distinction between the perceiver and the person who is the butt of this humor, although in the latter case it is not impossible that this person experiences the situation as humorous too.

We have digital tools that support us and our environment by monitoring our activities, whether it is about word processing or walking from our home to a restaurant or driving to our work. While monitoring, predicting, anticipating, and acting, errors can be made by the digital tools. They become clear while interacting with the technology and accidental humor can follow from these errors. We will look at this kind of accidental humor in Subsect. 3.2. In addition we can have accidental humor when we have people together, interacting with each other. Unplanned events and interactions can occur. They can also occur in smart environments, where smart environments range from videogame and social virtual reality environments to digitally enhanced physical home and office environments, vehicles and public spaces. This will be discussed in but there the smart technology can also play a role in having such unplanned events and interactions emerge. This will be discussed in Subsect. 3.3.

3.2 Accidental Humorous Interactions with Digital Technology

The list presented below is certainly biased by information and communication technology applications that deal with language, speech and verbal interactions in general. Nonverbal aspects of interaction or physical activities require more than linguistic approaches to humor. Nevertheless, we think we can learn from the distinctions mentioned below and then can investigate how to use them in situations where rather than playing with words and phrases, we need to play with configurations and behaviors of sensors and actuators to increase the possibility to have humorous situations emerge. We distinguish the following situations:

- **Imperfect Technology.** Technology itself is usually not perfect or needs maintenance in order to stay perfect. Hence, we can have an assembly line or a mechanical device (the feeding machine in Charlie Chaplin's Modern Times) that increases or decreases its speed without human intervention or a revolving door that suddenly changes its speed. Smart sensors and smart actuators are not perfect either, they may malfunction, leading to unexpected and humorous situations. An operating system may break down or when a new operating system is introduced other applications may behave in an unexpected and humorous way. Games contain bugs. There are many games where collision detection goes wrong often leading to hilarious situations where an avatar leaves the game world or loses control of his limbs. Gamers find it a challenge to search for and record such accidental hilarious game situations [4]. Freely available 'Machinima' recording tools are used for this.
- **Unfamiliar Technology.** It is not unusual that when a user is confronted for the first time with new technology, whether it is 'mechanical' or digital, he simply does not know how to handle it, he makes 'stupid' errors or starts a 'naïve' exploration of it, probably leading to surprising events. It may also be the case that it is not recognized that the technology does not function at all. There are many movies exploring humor that is caused by the introduction of new mechanical or digital technology, whether it is about home, office, or factory automation, and often including robotic devices. This lack of knowledge about the technology makes users vulnerable and victims of ridicule by onlookers who know better or just enjoy seeing things going wrong.
- **Lack of Robustness.** We can have a situation where the digital technology does not exactly malfunction and it is neither the case that a user uses the technology for the first time, but it provides us with an answer to our input from which it becomes clear that it didn't yet understand us. There is lack of robustness, but we know it and accept it, there is a joint responsibility. You cannot yet expect that your car is able to prevent or correct any error you can make on the road. Your input to a digital system can be ambiguous for the system. If a system is able to recognize four gestures and we make a gesture that is close to two of them, then the system can provide us with unexpected

and maybe humorous feedback in the context where we are using the system. In a different context this wrong choice might not be humorous at all. A brain-computer interface may ask us to repeat our brain input several times before it concludes with sufficient certainty which action to undertake and this can still be the wrong action.

- **Diverging Viewpoints.** We can have a situation where the digital technology provides us with continuous or turn-taking feedback that after a shorter or longer period makes us realize that there is a mismatch between who we are or what we want and the system's view of who we are and what we want. This may lead to a hilarious situation. It may even lead to a situation where we start exploring how to make the situation more hilarious. Chatbots and embodied conversational agents that invite users to ask questions about products or services often fall victim to this user behavior.

- **Wrong Presentation.** Imperfectness does not only addresses malfunction, providing wrong or right answers or suggestions to a user, or continuing an activity in a undesired way. There can be unplanned humor in the way correct content information is presented. Imperfect prosody can make a serious message hilarious. Non-verbal behavior of an embodied agent may contrast the affective content of a message, leading to a humorous feedback or continuation of an interaction. Obviously, we can also categorize this as 'imperfect technology' or 'accepted lack of robustness'. But from a HCI point of view the right choice of display modalities is an important issue. A wrong choice or a choice that involves imperfect technology can lead to confusion or a humorous effect.

- **Wrong Suggestions.** It should also be mentioned that we can create digital technology that is more 'modest', is aware of its shortcomings and assumes more cooperation with a human partner in order to make decisions. Such technology does not provide a user with absolute answers or feedback activity, rather it provides suggestions and alternatives where the user can choose from. Some suggested choices can be hilarious as well. Although they don't suit the aims of the user, they can lead to amusement or even the user exploring such an alternative for his or her further amusement. Wrong suggestions can range from spelling correction suggestions, suggestions made by recommender systems advising about music choice, rule-based systems that diagnose human diseases, or decision support systems that help in deciding about the abortion or continuation of a space flight.

These distinctions are not fully independent from each other and maybe we can introduce other categories and subcategories in future research. In the above presented list we gave examples of digital technology that is imperfect, not necessarily aware of the context in which to interpret interactions with the system or simply not being able to include this context in interpreting our input to the system since it algorithms and knowledge representation formalisms don't know about it. It might also be clear that the distinctions on the list above are very much biased towards current day human-computer interaction research topics. We know that Chatbots can go wrong, we know that speech recognition and speech synthesis is not perfect, and we know that embodied agents have problems to find prosody, gestures and facial expressions that match the content of the message they want to convey.

3.3   Misunderstandings, Accidents, and Spontaneity in Smart Environments

While the previous subsection mainly addressed direct interactions between user and digital technology, we should also look at unplanned events and interactions in digitally supported environments where inhabitants have social interactions or where they engage in competition and collaboration. This is a rather unexplored area of traditional humor research. It is not about jokes or conversational humor. For example, in the latter case there can be a humorous misunderstanding between you and your conversational partner. This partner can also be an embodied agent that makes wrong decisions in the interpretation of your utterances. When two or more people interact, there are lots of possibilities to misunderstand each other. The amount of possibilities is reduced because of common sense knowledge, context knowledge and knowledge we already have about our partners, for example obtained during previous interaction or joint activity. Nevertheless, there can always be misunderstandings.

Similarly, we cannot expect that virtual agents, social robots, and smart technology in general, will always be able to interpret our activities, preferences and demands in the way we intended. In particular when our research aims at making this technology more human-like by including emotions and human-like social behavior. Hence, there will be misunderstandings between us and the smart environments we live in, just as there are misunderstandings between smart people. We can categorize such misunderstandings as being caused by 'imperfect technology' or as accepted 'lack of robustness', categories we mentioned in the previous subsection. Humans suffer from lack of robustness. However, we would rather like to include them in a category of human-like misunderstandings, probably leading to accidental humor, rather than put them in a category of technology failures.

- **Social Misunderstandings.** When interacting with a smart environment, its devices, and its tangibles, there are situations and applications where we expect human smartness and affective behavior. This is especially true when we interact with social robots or virtual agents. We can have human-like, and therefore believable misunderstandings that lead to humorous situations, maybe not or hardly distinguishable from misunderstandings in human-human interaction.

Purposefully looking for possibilities to introduce misunderstandings is one way of introducing humorous interactions. There are hardly situations where the input of a user has to be taken literally, that is, not taking into account the context. A smart environment needs to make decisions based on incomplete information. It will lead to accidental humor. If we look at the most probably correct and reliable answer or action, it is also possible to look at less probably correct answers and actions, and by using them to increase the chance of accidental humor.

For unplanned events and interactions in smart environments we first have to look at events and interactions that can be introduced and detected in physical environments and then we need to explore how digital smartness embedded in such an environment can cause or help to introduce events and interactions that can lead to accidental humor. Here we should also mention 'spontaneous' humor. Humor can be planned. This is what is done in verbal jokes, in cut scenes of games, in practical jokes, on stage and in movies.

Clearly, the accidental humor we discussed in the previous subsection can and has to be distinguished from it. This accidental humor emerges when interacting with unfamiliar and imperfect technology. It can lead to situations that contradict the aims, needs and preferences of its actor(s) and it can be enjoyed by perceivers from a 'superiority humor' point of view. Spontaneous humor, on the other hand, is not planned either, but it requires the recognition of the elements in the environment (whether the environment is a language, social media or a physical environment) that can be composed or reconfigured in such a way that a humorous remark or a humorous event can be produced or made possible. But it requires the impulse decision to do so. Spontaneous humor is not planned, it makes use of a concurrency of circumstances, but it is not accidental. Spontaneous humor is not accidental humor. However, in order to have it occur some unplanned things have to happen leading to an accidental, not foreseen situation, that can be transformed to a spontaneous humor situation. The transformation can be done by human smartness and human sense of humor or by digital smartness and sense of humor.

4   Designing Smart Bugs and Throwing Digital Banana Peels

How to increase the chance of an emergence of accidental humor in smart environments? We are not able yet to define conditions and to provide guidelines for designing smart environments and devices in such a way that this chance will increase. Usually design aims at reducing to zero the number of unforeseen events. As mentioned in a previous section, designing accidental humor is a contradiction in terms. Hence, we don't want to design accidental humor, but rather consider the conditions that help to increase the emergence of accidental humor.

4.1   Interactions with Smart Technology

We can look at the distinctions we made in the previous section. Imperfect technology, unfamiliar technology, lack of robustness, diverging viewpoints, wrong presentation, wrong suggestions, misunderstandings. They all can lead to accidental humor in smart environments technology too. However, simply increasing imperfectness, unfamiliarity, lack of robustness, et cetera does not really seem the right answer. On the other hand, purposefully fooling the user does not seem to be the right answer either, since then we are designing humor, rather than increasing the chance of accidental humor. We have no clear answer to that. Can we design a smart bug that has a sense of humor? In a chatbot interaction it is certainly possible, even if the chatbot not really understands what it is doing, to let it ask a question or let it give an answer that may lead to (humorous) diverging viewpoints. Can we do the same for interactions occurring in smart environments and configure the conditions that guide a user into a situation where accidental humor has a chance to appear?

4.2   Introducing Incongruities in Smart Environments

We can have a closer look at the conditions under which humor can appear in physical environments. Categories of incongruities in physical environments have been introduced. Incongruities from these categories can appear in (multi-player) game environments, social virtual environments and digitally enhanced (smart) environments as well. Hence, we can look at the various categories of physical humor or humor in physical environments and see how these humor forms can appear in fully virtual reality, in augmented reality, and in digitally enhanced reality or smart environments. Bergson [5] had many useful observations on incongruities in the real world in order to explain what makes us laugh, especially what makes us laugh about French comedy on stage. Berger [6] and Morreall [7] tried to give comprehensive surveys of examples and categories that suit these examples of possible physical humor and humor in physical environments. Neither Bergson, Berger or Morreall made references to digital technology, let alone smart environments, but clearly, in a simulated real world environment including real humans and simulated human characters we will have the same possibilities to introduce humorous situations or set conditions for humorous situations to appear as suggested in their categories. Many of the examples in the categories mention conditions that help to have humor emerge. Necessary conditions are not necessarily sufficient conditions. Increasing the number of necessary conditions increases the chance of accidental humor.

Real-world humor can be simulated in a virtual or smart world. However, it is also interesting to see whether the virtuality and/or smartness can be used to increase the chance of humor. For that reason it is interesting to look at categories of humor introduced by Carroll [8] for movies, and Buijzen and Valkenburg [9] for TV commercials. Again, not with the purpose to guarantee humor but with the purpose to set conditions that lead to unexpected events in a smart environment inhabited and perceived by humanoids and human beings. Unfortunately, also in their categories visualization plays a more important role than mainly text-based categories, digital smartness does not play a role. Obviously, in many movies examples of (coincidental) accidental humor can be found with two clear examples in Jacques Tati's Mon Oncle (1958), the kitchen scene in which Tati is struggling with unfamiliar modern kitchen technology and the automatic garage door where a dog passes an outdoor sensor which closes the door with a husband and wife trapped inside the garage.

Observations on humor in smart environments and playable cities can be found in [10, 11]. As mentioned in these papers, it is sometimes possible to transform approaches to generate verbal humor to the generation of humor in physical and smart environments. We add another example here. We already mentioned humor that can appear because of wrong auto-correction and auto-completion in text processing and retrieval software [1]. Smart environments monitor our behavior and try to predict and anticipate our next activities. They can also suggest continuations of activities or autonomously complete activities, where suggestions or completions are not necessarily the most probable ones in an attempt to create or at least make the user aware of possible humorous continuations. Sensors and actuators are programmed or learn to expect patterns of activities and human behavior. So they can suggest possible continuations when an activity has not finished yet or suggest an alternative when an unknown sequence of actions is detected rather than accepting it as it is. All these cases may lead to accidental humor. The environment, that is, the sensors and actuators, are not necessarily aware that their suggestions are humorous. There is no guarantee that a suggestion or one of a number of suggestions will be considered humorous by users involved in activities that are being monitored by the environment.

We conclude this subsection by mentioning one more view on accidental humor in smart environments. This is the 'continuous partial attention' view advocated by Silber [12]. The assumption is that the increasing and continuous push of multimedia information will also increase our multitasking and scanning behavior, which in turn will often confront us with unintentionally muddled information, unintended mismatches and unintended incongruity humor.

4.3   Appropriation, Serendipity, Hackability, Art

There are a few approaches in product, system and art design that are useful to consider when discussing accidental humor. One of the approaches is designing for appropriation [13]. Appropriation is the process where a user adapts a technology and uses it in a way that was not intended by its designers. Dix [13] mentions the use of a screwdriver to open a paint tin. How can we design for unexpected use? As mentioned by Dix, this seems like an oxymoron, but it can also be observed that some sorts of design make appropriation difficult or impossible. Some design guidelines to allow appropriation are given. For example, by exposing the designer's intentions it may become easier to subvert the rules of a system, making the functioning of a system more visible can have the same effect and rather designing a system to do the task design it so that the task can be done. Appropriation allows for unexpected use and in the case of smart environments unexpected use, behavior and events. Appropriation leaves open how the user will use the environment.

Appropriation is also a well-known humor technique where we exaggerate, transform or contradict an existing product (for example by introducing sensory incongruities) or situations to create a comic effect [14]. In [15] appropriation is discussed in the context of unexpected but rewarding social experiences. Other design approaches that allow users to appropriate systems and tools are 'design for hackability' [16] and end-user programming approaches, for example for a domestic [17] or an urban environment [18]. Design for serendipity [19] is yet another example of an approach that focuses on unexpected events.

Finally we want to mention art that makes use of errors or glitches. In art it is not unusual to see distortions of perspectives and visual traps that include incongruities. 'Errors' and glitches can have a role in artistic expression and can be appreciated or even become a new media art form (Glitch Art) [20–22].

5   Conclusions

The aim of this paper was to survey the issues that play a role when looking at accidental humor in the context of digital technology. We investigated the various ways accidental humor can emerge when people interact with digital technology. It is not always humorous from the point of view of the interactant. Usually it is more humorous from the point of view of a perceiver or an audience. Incongruities are not necessarily humorous. However, introducing incongruities increases the chance that humorous situations will appear or that the possibility for producing spontaneous humor increases. Some categories of incongruities have appeared in the literature. In particular those incongruities that can appear in physical environments are of interest for smart environments. There are some developments in designing software (appropriation, end-user programming, maker culture) that are interesting from the point of view that users will be able to design and reconfigure their own smart environments. Creative use of errors is an issue that is also addressed by artists.

References

1. Valitutti, A., Toivonen, H., Gross, O., Toivanen, J.M.: Decomposition and distribution of humorous effect in interactive systems. In: Proceedings of the Artificial Intelligence of Humor. The AAAI Fall Symposium Series, pp. 96–100. AAAI, Arlington (2012)
2. Raskin, V.: The Primer of Humor Research. Mouton de Gruyter, Berlin (2008)
3. Warren, C., McGraw, A.P.: Differentiating what is humorous from what is not. J. Pers. Soc. Psychol. **110**(3), 407–430 (2015). http://dx.doi.org/10.1037/pspi0000041. Advance online publication
4. Švelch, J.: Comedy of contingency: making physical humor in video game spaces. Int. J. Commun. **8**, 2530–2552 (2014)
5. Bergson, H.: Laughter: An essay on the meaning of the comic. Translated from Le Rire: Essai sur la signification du comique. Gutenberg project (2003). Original edition appeared in 1900
6. Berger, A.A.: An Anatomy of Humor. Transaction Publishers, New Brunswick (1993). First edition appeared in 1976
7. Morreall, J.: Taking Laughter Seriously. State University of New York Press, New York (1983)
8. Carroll, N.: Theorizing the Moving Image. Cambridge Studies in Film. Cambridge University Press, Cambridge (1996)
9. Buijzen, M., Valkenburg, P.: Developing a typology of humor in audiovisual media. Media Psychol. **6**(2), 147–167 (2004)
10. Silber, M.J.: Digital humor theory. M.Sc. thesis, School of Art and Design, Pratt Institute, New York (2013)
11. Nijholt, A.: The humor continuum: from text to smart environments (keynote paper). In: Proceedings of the International Conference on Informatics, Electronics & Vision (ICIEV), 15–18 June 2015, pp. 1–10. IEEE Xplore, Kitakyushu, Fukuoka (2015)
12. Nijholt, A.: Designing humor for playable cities. In: Ahram, T., Karwowski, W. (eds.) Proceedings of the 6th International Conference on Applied Human Factors and Ergonomics (AHFE 2015). Ji, Y.G., Choi, S. (eds.) Section Advances in Affective and Pleasurable Design, Las Vegas, USA, 26–30 July 2015. Procedia Manufact. **3C**, 2178–2185 (2015). Elsevier (ScienceDirect)
13. Dix, A.: Designing for appropriation. In: Proceedings of the 21st British HCI Group Annual Conference on People and Computers: HCI... But Not as We Know It, vol. 2, pp. 27–30. British Computer Society, London (2007)
14. Klein, S.R.: Humor and contemporary product design: international perspectives, Chap. 12. In: Chiaro, D., Baccolini, R. (eds.) Gender and Humor: Interdisciplinary and International Perspectives. Routledge Research in Cultural and Media Studies, vol. 64, pp. 201–211. Routledge (Taylor & Francis Group), New York, London (2014)
15. Kirman, B., Linehan, C., Lawson, C.: Exploring mischief and mayhem in social computing or: how we learned to stop worrying and love the trolls. In: Proceedings of the CHI 2012 Extended Abstracts on Human Factors in Computing Systems, pp. 121–130. ACM, New York (2012)

16. Galloway, A., Brucker-Cohen, J., Gaye, L., Goodman, E., Hill, D.: Design for hackability. In: Proceedings of the DIS 2004, pp. 363–366. ACM Press, New York (2004)
17. Callaghan, V., Chin, J., Zamudio, V., Clarke, G., Shahi, A., Gardner, M.: Domestic pervasive information systems: end-user programming of digital homes, Chap. 7. In: Advances in Management Information Systems Research Monographs, pp. 1–17. ME Sharp, New York (2005)
18. DiSalvo, C., Louw, M., Coupland, J., Steiner, M.: Local issues, local uses: tools for robotics and sensing in community contexts. In: Proceedings of the Seventh ACM Conference on Creativity and Cognition (C&C 2009), pp. 245–254. ACM, New York (2009)
19. Danzico, L.: The design of serendipity is not by chance. Interactions **17**(5), 16–18 (2010)
20. Moradi, I., Ant, S., Gilmore, J., Murphy, C.: Glitch: Designing Imperfection. Mark Batty, New York (2009)
21. Nunes, M.: Error, Glitch, Noise and Jam in New Media Cultures. Bloomsbury, New York (2012)
22. Vavarella, E.: Art, error, and the interstices of power. CITAR J. **7**(2), 7–17 (2015)

Ambient Scripts in Humor and Beyond

Victor Raskin[✉]

Linguistics, CERIAS, Purdue University, West Lafayette, IN, USA
vraskin@purdue.edu

Abstract. The paper explores the mechanism of following scripts in inferencing and reasoning, both in humor and, generally, in natural language, as a way of creating a base for acquisition and use of scripts in the computer.

Keywords: Humor · Formal humor theory · Script detection · Script computation

1 Introduction

Like [1] and several earlier papers, this article continues to deal with the notion of script, central to the dominant linguistic theories of humor [2–4]. We will capitalize again on the doctor/lover joke, which is well familiar to the humor research audience and, at the same time, is suitable to introduce the first-time or casual reader to this aspect of humor research. We will subject the text to the most detailed analysis at the script level trying to reconstruct completely the human reasoning in "getting" the joke in order to pave the way for the computer simulation of the same process. Contrary to the current, hopefully moribund trend in natural language processing, we will make no attempt to cheat out of the account for the full semantic process and by replacing it with machine learning statistical simulation of knowledge. We know it cannot work, and it is not our responsibility here to explain again to semantically naïve statisticians that we are in a different business that requires different tools—namely, access to the meaning of natural text.

2 Informal Analysis of the Joke

Here is the canonical form of the Doctor/Lover joke that we picked up from a rank-and-file American joke book of the 1930s:

"Is the doctor in?" the patient asked in his bronchial whisper. "No," the doctor's young and pretty wife whispered back, "Come right in!"

Let us talk through how an ordinary reader/hearer understands the joke. A man identified as a patient shows up at the door of a doctor's residence and asks his wife whether the doctor is in. The wife says that he is not, and then invites him in. This definitely does not make sense, so the normal understanding process is defeated. Then it occurs to the reader/hearer that the wife was described as young and pretty and that she invited a man other than her husband to come in while the husband is away. This introduces a different situation, and the patient is reconceived as a (potential) lover.

N. Streitz and P. Markopoulos (Eds.): DAPI 2016, LNCS 9749, pp. 341–349, 2016.
DOI: 10.1007/978-3-319-39862-4_31

As a not so remote a thought, a potential understanding with whisper may reveal itself here: the patient whispers because he has lost his voice but the wife may misinterpret it as a request for secrecy, which is typical for adultery.

Much of the material that forms part of the human understanding is missing from the short text. We can only guess that the conversation is happening at the door, probably after the patient knocked or rang the bell. We don't really care if the door is opened by the doctor's wife or they communicate through a home phone or over a crack between the chained door and the frame. It is even possible, in a rustic environment, that on a bright summer day, the wife is sitting on the veranda while the patient approaches. What somewhat complicates the perception of the joke in the late 20th and early 21st century is the association of the wife with the doctor's office because doctors do not typically see their patients in their homes with their wives serving as their assistants or nurses.

That SSTH turned out to be the sensation it was at the 2nd International Congress on Humor Research in Los Angeles back in 1979 [5] was easy to explain: most people congregated there were not researchers at all—the South Californian shrinks, comedians, and journalists had never heard of a theory in their lives. The small minority of humor researchers had heard or read about theories of aggression, liberation, and incongruity, and the content of the theory was "humor is (like) aggression/liberation/incongruity," with perhaps another sentence thrown in to elaborate. The theory was an image, a metaphor, a comparison. It was one unknown thing "explained" in terms of another, probably not even less unknown thing. Those theories were like the "theory of benign violation." SSTH imported the theoretical power of the then young Chomskian Linguistics, founded by a logician, and presented to the humor research "softies" by another logician. And it was empirically tested in 1991 [6].

It was presented as part and parcel of a formal semantic procedure of text representation developed outside of humor research and applied to humor research in strict accordance with the rules of linguistic application with an addition of one special resource, the list of typical script oppositions. Like all well-developed theories, it had a list of disclaimers, and this list of oppositions was one of them. The list was outlined in [2] and then re-compiled in [7]. It consisted of three mega-types of actual/non-actual, normal/abnormal, and plausible/implausible situations, and a list of under 20 typical oppositions related to those mega-types in unexplored ways. Sex/no-sex, good/bad, money/no-money were popular examples. The oppositions have since been addressed by various scholars in mostly atheoretical contexts, and the main challenge to SSTH was the hund for the red counterexample: find a joke that has no script opposition.

Practically undetected was a much more major disclaimer, made explicitly in [2] but largely escaping notice. The theory was based on a fully developed formal meaning representation base that was not yet available, even though clearly in progress. As it was read and perceived the theory was the ham in the old cowboy joke about how they would, if they had only had ham, have made themselves ham and eggs, provided they had had eggs—eggs being the access to semantics. A couple of generations later, namely now, the eggs are in place: they are called the Ontological Semantic Technology [8–10], and ham is called the Ontological Semantic Theory of Humor (OSTH—[4]). So it seems to be the right time for the ham and eggs.

2.1 Script-Based Semantic Theory of Humor

That SSTH turned out to be the sensation it was at the 2nd International Congress on Humor Research in Los Angeles back in 1979 was easy to explain: most people congregated there were not researchers at all—the South Californian shrinks, comedians, and journalists had never heard of a theory in their lives. The small minority of humor researchers had heard or read about theories of aggression, liberation, and incongruity, and the content of the theory was "humor is (like) aggression/liberation/incongruity," with perhaps another sentence thrown in to elaborate. The theory was an image, a metaphor, a comparison. It was one unknown thing "explained" in terms of another, probably not even less unknown thing. Those theories were like the "theory of benign violation." SSTH imported the theoretical power of the then young Chomskian Linguistics, founded by a logician, and presented to the humor research "softies" by another logician.

It was presented as part and parcel of a formal semantic procedure of text representation developed outside of humor research and applied to humor research in strict accordance with the rules of linguistic application with an addition of one special resource, the list of typical script oppositions. Like all well-developed theories, it had a list of disclaimers, and this list of oppositions was one of them. The list was outlined in [2] and then re-compiled in [7]. It consisted of three mega-types of actual/non-actual, normal/abnormal, and plausible/implausible situations, and a list of under 20 typical oppositions related to those mega-types in unexplored ways. Sex/no-sex, good/bad, money/no-money were popular examples. The oppositions have since been addressed by various scholars in mostly atheoretical contexts, and the main challenge to SSTH was the hunt for the red counterexample: find a joke that has no script opposition.

Practically undetected was a much more major disclaimer, made explicitly in [2] but largely escaping notice. The theory was based on a fully developed formal meaning representation base that was not yet available, even though clearly in progress. As it was read and perceived the theory was the ham in the old cowboy joke about how they would, if they had only had ham, have made themselves ham and eggs, provided they had had eggs—eggs being the access to semantics. A couple of generations later, namely now, the eggs are in place: they are called the Ontological Semantic Technology [8–10], and ham is called the Ontological Semantic Theory of Humor (OSTH—[4]). So it seems to be the right time for the ham and eggs.

2.2 Scripts in Humor

We reviewed the early history of scripts [11–13] on multiple occasions, including [1], and since that paper ended long before getting to a real analysis of scripts, we will now quote a lrge chink from it here, before bothering to paraphrase so as to escape capture by the plagiarism software (always, a highly humorous occasion!) before going boldly elsewhere.

The naïve and most obvious way of handling a script in SSTH was to present it as a set of sentences, each describing an individual part of a script. This is how it went for the Doctor/Lover joke: "a doctor was an adult human, who spent a considerable time at a medical school in the past and now sees patients, diagnoses them, and prescribes medication. A lover was an adult person, who has had sex at least once to a person of the (then) opposite sex, to whom he or she was not married. A bit more formally, something like the sequence of events in Figs. 1 and 2 must take place to establish X as a doctor and Y as a lover.

X is a doctor if and only if:
1. X went to an accredited medical school and graduated from it.
2. X passed an extended internship
3. X was licensed as a physician
4. X has opened or joined a medical practice or a hospital
5. X treats patients on a regular basis by examining or listening to them, diagnosing their condition and sending them to tests or specialists and/or prescribing them medication

Fig. 1. "Script" for doctor

Y is a lover if and only if:
1. Y is a teenager or older
2. There is a Z of the opposite sex who is a teenager or older
3. Y and Z are not married to each other
4. Y and Z have had sex at least once

Fig. 2. "Script" for lover.

It was then, when considering the actual content of the scripts, that I discovered the powerful *but* operator: *Bob is a doctor but he never went to medical school*. But here indicates that going to a medical school is indeed a part of the script for doctor unlike having been to Africa: *Bob is a doctor but he never went to Africa* is not at all inappropriate and could easily tolerate the replacement of *but* by *and*. All the components of the scripts above were indeed *but*-tested.

We have now reached the stage when a humor researcher's expertise is made salient for the rest of the paper and a novice reader has been introduced to what a humor researcher standardly knows about scripts. The rest of the paper deals with a close textual analysis in order to detect and identify scripts and to model this human capacity in the computers.

3 Scripts Beyond

To continue the quote from [1] for the last brief time, "Fig. 3 shows an abortive attempt [14] to incorporate scripts into pre-OST Ontological Semantics that OST has not yet picked up and incorporated. The *if/then*, *and*, and *or* logical operators had not, however, been actually incorporated into the system, even though semi-tacitly allowed in.

APPROACH-BANKRUPTCY

If	Or	company has cash problems
		company can't meet payroll
		company misses loan payment
		company seeks loan
Then		company may near bankruptcy

DECLARE-BANKRUPTCY

If		company declares bankruptcy
	And	company files for Chapter 11
	Or	court appoints receiver for company
Then	And	company officers lose control
		company operates under receiver
	Or	company stops operating
		company liquidates assets
		creditors get partial payment

Fig. 3. Two bankruptcy scripts

The scripts were developed for use in an application that would crawl the web and inform the officers of a company about the state of financial health of their partner companies, both suppliers and buyers. To my knowledge, such an application has not yet been implemented, and an expensive horde of human analysts continues to provide an imperfect service. Obviously, an Ontological Semantic implementation would process the phrases and sentences into its text-meaning representations (TMRs) and develop a TMR-manipulating calculus for using scripts for inferencing and, more broadly, for reasoning. This is what we are proceeding to investigate on the material of the Doctor/Lover joke.

3.1 Script Analysis

Pre-script Ontological Semantic Technology processes every sentence of the text and, proceeding linearly, identifies every word in the language-specific lexicon that has a footprint in the language-independent ontology, notes their links, and combines these words into a TMR on the basis of synactic and, mostly, semantic links—see Fig. 4 for the overall architecture of OST, for humor in this picture, with its resources and processors:

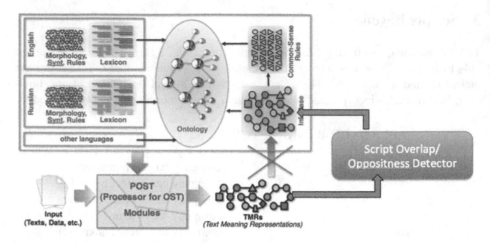

Fig. 4. OST architecture

The very first sentence of the joke contains the English words doctor and patient which are easily TMR-ed together on their ontological connection as per doctor seeing patient with a health condition, which is, incidentally, erroneously represented as bronchitis while, in fact, it must be pharyngitis for the voice to be lost. For a human understander of the text, the whole script is evoked that goes far beyond the ones on Figs. 1 and 2. Let us try and reconstruct it simplistically in Fig. 5:

This script is a very sketchy representation of a common human routine. It ignores appointments, ambulances, emergency house calls, helicopter rides, and many other additions and aberrations but it is a very commonly noun routine, a part of our knowledge of the world. Note that the joke barely covers the bold-faced part of the routine. Natural language always underdetermines reality [15, 16] but this short text leaves out an awful lot. It also violates the grain size [17]: we know nothing about the patient except for his gender but we learn more about the woman who opens the door, and in a common script, she could even be replaced by a buzz. We somehow know or assume that she is the doctor's wife, which seems to follow from another script that spouses live together and the patient tries to see the doctor in his home office. And we find out that the woman is young and pretty. Young and pretty women are part of another script, that of sexual desirability for me (we are in the 1930s, remember?).

We are drowning in scripts, and this is why they are really ambient. Every word is a part of many different scripts, and every script may be split up in many more in response to a possible question. How young is the woman? How is she pretty? How is she dressed, or is she? Doctor's wives, female aids, or female nurses are also part of stereotypes, which are not contingent or factually reliable scripts, probably a hundred years or so ago, they saw other men alone, often seeing them undressed and asking them for personal details.

Speaking of adultery, where is the husband and how possible it is to return while the pair is having sex. Is the patient interested, potent, married? What is his name, her name? Are there pets in the house? Children? Hired help? Is his car conspicuous on the parking lot. The joke is cleverly crafted, but any text in natural language maintains a

- Human discovers a health problem/symptom
- Human may try to handle it on his/her own by
  - Waiting and hoping for it to blow over
  - Trying homemade remedies
- When unsuccessful, human decides to seek medical help
- Human goes to see doctor
- **Human requests entrance to doctor's premises**
  - **Another human enables entrance**
  - **First human requests information about doctor's availability**
  - **Human obtains that information from the other human**
- If positive, human enters doctor's premises
- If negative, human seeks alternative(s) by
  - Waiting
  - Rescheduling
  - Seeking another doctor
- Human sees doctor tells him/her what the problem is
- Doctor examines human
- Doctor prescribes medication
- Human gets better

Fig. 5. Script for seeking medical help

certain relevant grain size, providing all the necessary information and refraining from unnecessary details. In the British sketch show of the 1970s, "The Two Ronnies," casting Ronnie Barker and Ronnie Corbett, the "Big Ronnie" and the "Little Ronnie," the latter had a middle-of-the-show recurring sketch, sitting in front of a fireplace in an oversized chair, attempting to tell a joke. The joke was hackneyed and easily recognizable but he never finished the delivery because he kept being distracted by small details. It was, actually, a gross exaggeration of a speech disorder that some people may develop in senility, so it is probably forbidden humor now, and one has not seen anything like that for decades. The point is that, "normally," competent speakers maintain the grain size of the information, and they stick to it in evoking the script as well.

It is clear that script evocation is part of understanding any natural language text. Humans are equipped with an incredibly rich inventory of scripts, all stored in the non-contingent part of our world knowledge. We also have an experience, first- or second-hand as well as based on literature, education, reading, films, etc., about various implementations of scripts and their interactions.

So how does it work in the joke? Pursuing the doctor script, we get to the point of attempting to see the doctor. The patient requests information about the doctor's availability, and he is ready for the positive and negative kind. What he gets, however, is a clear violation of the script: the doctor's wife invites him, and rather urgently so, while denying the doctor's availability. The patient must be puzzled but never more so than the reader/hearer who is also operating on the Doctor script. We are dealing here with a typical inferencing/reasoning failure, so let us talk about that, never yet discussed in OST.

4 Inferencing and Reasoning in OST

Inferencing and reasoning have never really been adequately addressed in and around linguistics, which remains pretty much the science of the sentence. Correspondingly, classical Ontological Semantics [18] focused on the sentence-based seminar, assuming implicitly that, somehow, they will all blend together. Ontological Semantic Technology [8–10], again) has until now followed suit. Yet, all the NLP applications of any intellectual value require reasoning to summarize, update, and even recognize pertinent information.

There has been a lot of research into inferencing, and emulating it computationally in the computer, first, led to an exponential explosion, and second, was not based on real semantics. In description logic, it is also based on first-order logic, something natural language is unable to follow, as the failure of formal semantics clearly indicates.

Following the scripted routines provides access to the more obvious and common forms of reasoning, so identifying and storing as many scripts as possible should lead to at least an important part of reasoning if the computer can inference to the next phase of a script. Again, the ability not to regress infinitely into tiny details and rise to a coarser level, as humans routinely do, is important also. What is next in order, then, for OST is to develop the techniques of script detection and recording for computer use as well as the mechanisms for using their information effectively in a TMR. The already existing resources in OST pave much of the way there.

5 How to Get the Computer to Get the Joke

We have always maintained that humor is a very effective testing ground for other disciplines. For linguistic semantics, jokes provide a semi-structured, mostly short text with known components, such as two scripts and the mechanism of triggering the change. In the Doctor/Lover joke, this is how human reasoning works.

Stumped in the middle of the Doctor script on Fig. 5, we reject the script as inappropriate. Peter Derks' 1991 demonstration of the MRI of his brain processing an unfamiliar joke, shows a moment of total collapse of the cognitive attempt to process the text, followed by a very short pause, followed by the second successful cognitive attempt. This second attempt is the search of an alternative script.

It is reasonable to assume that second attempt is the search of a script that has the new situation, puzzling for the first script, as a natural sequential stage, as indeed for two people of the opposite sex, not married to each other, to use an opportunity for sex when their spouses are not around. The search for the alternative script is greatly facilitated by a reasonably small list of common script oppositions covering an enormous number of different jokes, and the sex/no-sex opposition invites itself into humor reasoning pervasively.

References

1. Raskin, Victor: On algorithmic discovery and computational implementation of the opposing scripts forming a joke. In: Streitz, Norbert, Markopoulos, Panos (eds.) DAPI 2015. LNCS, vol. 9189, pp. 671–679. Springer, Heidelberg (2015)
2. Raskin, V.: Semantic Mechanisms of Humor. D. Reidel, Dordrecht, Boston, Lancaster (1985)
3. Attardo, S., Raskin, V.: Script theory revis(it)ed: joke similarity and joke representation model. HUMOR Int. J. Humor Res. **4**, 3–4 (1991). 83pp
4. Raskin, V., Hempelman, C., Taylor, J.: How to understand and assess a theory: the evolution of the SSTH into the GTVH and now into the OSTH. J. Literary Theor. **3**, 285–311 (2009)
5. Raskin, V.: Semantic mechanisms of humor. In: Chiarello, C. et al. (eds.) Proceedings of the Fifth Annual Meeting, Berkeley Linguistics Society. University of California, Berkeley (1979)
6. Ruch, W., Attardo, S., Raskin, V.: Towards an empirical verification of the general theory of verbal humor. HUMOR Int. J. Humor Res. **6**(2), 123–136 (1993)
7. Raskin, V.: Linguistic heuristics of humor: a script-based semantic approach (20 pp.). In: Apte, M.L. (ed.) Language and Humor (1987). A special issue of the International Journal in the Sociology of Language, vol. 65, no. 3 (1987)
8. Raskin, V., Hempelmann, C., Taylor, J.: Guessing vs. knowing: the two approaches to semantics in natural language processing. In: Dialogue (2010)
9. Taylor, J., Hempelmann, C., Raskin, V.: On an automatic acquisition toolbox for ontologies and lexicons in ontological semantics. In: International Conference in Artificial Intelligence, ICAI 2010 (2010)
10. Hempelman, C., Taylor, J., Raskin, V.: Application-guided ontological engineering. In: International Conference in Artificial Intelligence, ICAI 2010 (2010)
11. Bartlett, F.C.: Remembering: A Study in Experimental and Social Psychology. Cambridge University Press, Cambridge (1932)
12. Minsky, M.: A framework for representing knowledge. In: Winston, P.H. (ed.) The Psychology of Computer Vision, pp. 211–277. McGrow Hill, New York (1975)
13. Schank, R., Abelson, H.: Scripts, Plans, Goals and Understanding. Erlbaum, Hillsdale (1977)
14. Raskin, V., Nirenburg, S., Hempelmann, C., Nirenburg, I., Triezenberg, K.: The genesis of a script for bankruptcy in ontological semantics. In: Hirst, G., Nirenburg, S. (eds.) Proceedings of the Text Meaning Workshop, Human Language Technology and North American Chapter of the Association of Computational Linguistics Conference, HLT/NAACL 2003, 49pp. ACL, Edmonton (2003)
15. Barwise, J., Perry, J.: Situations and Attitudes. MIT Press, Cambridge (1983)
16. Raskin, V., Stuart, L. M., Taylor, J. M.: Is natural language ever really vague? A Computational semantic view. In: IEEE International Conference on Cybernatics, Lausanne, Switzerland (2013)
17. Taylor, J.M.: Understanding and processing information of various grain sizes. In: International Conference on Robot Intelligent Technology and Applications (RITA), Gwangju, South Korea (2012)
18. Nirenburg, S., Raskin, V.: Ontological Semantics. MIT Press, Cambridge (2004)

Affect and Atmosphere in Controlled Responsive Environments

Andreas Simon[1(⊠)], Jan Torpus[1], Christiane Heibach[1],
and Jose Navarro[2]

[1] IXDM, FHNW Academy of Art and Design, Basel, Switzerland
{andreas.simon, jan.torpus, christiane.heibach}@fhnw.ch
[2] FHNW Academy of Art and Design, Basel, Switzerland
josenavarro@gmx.ch

Abstract. We explore the atmospheric potential and the affective connection between humans and their instrumented, responsive environments and develop corresponding artistic design strategies, evaluating ubicomp environments from a critical perspective, beyond pure application and usefulness. We have designed an abstract, cocoon-like, responsively mediated space and conducted a series of experiments with a total of 17 participants. Results show that participants experience affection, a coupling between themselves and the designed environment, and show strong cognitive engagement to understand and structure the environment through patterns of situation awareness and sensemaking.

Keywords: Ubicomp · Biofeedback · Atmosphere · Environment · Affection · Sensemaking

1 Introduction

Ubicomp as an interaction paradigm and technological platform has been developed with the intention to allow computers to move away from the center of attention into the periphery. Inserted into everyday objects and blending with the environment, they would conceptually and perceptually "disappear". Even the original formulation of ambient displays and calm computing as expressions of ubicomp interfaces has been recently criticized by Hansen as a too functional, "downright instrumental" perspective [1].

When placing displays in the periphery, the assumption remains that ambient displays like dangling strings and slowly changing colored lights can be re-centered and interpreted by an observer, thereby moving from the periphery back to the center of attention. Hansen in contrast argues for an autonomy of the peripheral, making ubicomp environments inherently affective and atmospheric [2]: "We must conceptualize the coupling of human and techniques beyond the figure of the 'technical object.' In the wake of computational technologies that distribute sensibility beyond consciousness, the correlation between human-implicating individuation and techniques has moved beyond what we might think of as its objective stage [...] and has entered a properly processual stage in which techniques directly intensifies sub-perceptual dimensions of human experience." Instead of a technical mediation of perception, today's concern is "the more indirect technical mediation of an environmental sensibility."

© Springer International Publishing Switzerland 2016
N. Streitz and P. Markopoulos (Eds.): DAPI 2016, LNCS 9749, pp. 350–361, 2016.
DOI: 10.1007/978-3-319-39862-4_32

In our work we set out to explore the atmospheric potential and the affective connection between humans and their instrumented environments and to develop corresponding artistic design strategies. We have chosen to follow an artistic research approach [3], as it enables us to explore the atmospheric effects and consequences of the use of responsive environments from a critical perspective, beyond pure application and usefulness.

2 Related Work

Substantial research on the close coupling of people and their interactions with a generated, responsive environment is conducted in the area of computer games. Games are highly engaging and are driven in their appearance and difficulty by the interaction with a player. A common approach is to measure physiological signals to assess a player's emotional state and to use these measurements to control game difficulty, which is an easily accessible parameter of the environment in most games [4]. Parnandi et al. [5] extend this idea by introducing control theory to model the interaction between human physiology and game difficulty during game play. They use electro dermal activity (EDA) as a physiological correlate of arousal and couple the player's response to control car speed, road visibility, and steering jitter in a racing game to manipulate difficulty. A similar approach has been proposed for training in virtual environments by Wu et al. [6]. Here the aim is to identify and maintain a state of "optimal arousal", measured by psycho-physiological responses, in a military training task.

We think that close couplings between people and a responsive space in closed feedback loops have more in common with the psycho-cognitive processes found in the rubber hand illusion and other, technically induced out of body experiences [7, 8]. For this we use the metaphor of the reactive environment as an "extended skin" [9].

From the point of view of an artistic approach to the development of responsive spaces the architectural works of Schnädelbach and Beesley are close to our work. Schnädelbach et al. [10] aim to connect physiological measurements (breathing and EDA) and the fabric of a tent-like structure (controling light, projection and sound) to externalize a person's physiological data in an immersive and visceral way. In later work [11] they use this adaptive architecture to support Yoga practices. Beesley's Protocell Mesh from the Holozoic Series [12] represents a responsive architecture that uses light and moving, biomorphic structures to stimulate and engage the visitor to evoke a "[...] humane response [to] the contemporary condition of ecology."

3 Technological Approach

Ubiquitous Computing [13] is an interaction paradigm and technological approach where digital sensors and actuators are incorporated into physical space by introducing a networked layer of intelligence into things. Compared to Virtual Reality which immerses a visitor in a digitally constructed synthetic world, isolating her from the physical surroundings, ubicomp seamlessly blends virtual sensing and control into the real world [14]: "...the singularity of "the interface" explodes into a multiplicity of more or less closely aligned, dynamically configured moments of encounters within sociomaterial configurations, objectified as persons and machines."

Biofeedback technology and corresponding body worn sensors measure personal body functions and physiological parameters in sports and daily life, with the aim to improve health and perhaps even more importantly to increase mental and physical performance. Generally spoken, biofeedback was developed to gain more awareness and control of physiological functions influenced by thoughts, emotions and behavior. In our project we measure biophysical signals for breathing (in-point, out-point, regularity), heart activity (beats and rate) and body movement of visitors in a responsive space and record primary, preconscious reactions and emotions. These parameters enable a spectrum of control: While body motion is under direct and voluntary control, breathing is much less direct and not commonly used for explicit interactive control. However, humans have some degree of voluntary control over their breathing [15]. In contrast, while heart rate is coupled to body motion and deep breathing, we have no awareness and no common experience of voluntarily controlling our heart beat.

We combine ubicomp and biofeedback technologies to immediately and affectively connect an artistic environment with a person being related to it. Thereby we consider both sides – the human and the technological system – as equal actors [16] that are connected and interplay in real-time in a human-in-the-loop system (Fig. 1). Although the technical system has no independent intelligence, its physical responses follow dynamic mappings to physiologic human reactions, manifested through light, sound and wind. These responses are expressive and can cause new physiologic reactions, creating the human-machine interdependency.

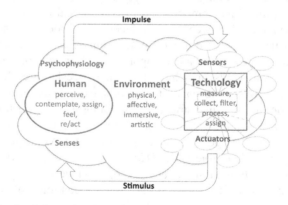

Fig. 1. Schematic of the cybernetic human-in-the-loop system

The technical system is composed of a connected sequence of three modules: input sensors, signal processing and mapping, and output media or actuators. The intervening human visitor is the most volatile element of this system, closing the feedback loop between the sensors and actuators. She is affected by the reactive surrounding media and reciprocally influences the parameters of it by real-time processed biofeedback. In other words: The measuring of heartbeat, respiration and movement of the human permits to capture psycho-physiological reactions to external stimuli which emerge when being exposed to the artistically staged environment. Mutually, the environment changes its appearance according to the received human biofeedback data.

4 Designing the Place

Benyon [17] discusses aspects of Human-Computer Interaction, interaction design and user experience in the age of ubiquitous computing. In the examination of physical space and place he quotes systematic proposals of experience of place by Lentini and Decortis, Gustafson, Relph. Relph [18] describes the identity of environments in terms of three components, which prove to be decisive for the following description of our project:

1. the place's physical setting;
2. its activities, situations and events (afforded by the place); and
3. the meanings created through people's experiences and intentions in regard to that place.

Relph's classification has been often criticized for ignoring historical, cultural, social, educational and individual qualities and circumstances. For the focus of our approach we excluded most of those aspects as well and tried to overcome the complexity of the human world for our design by setting up an artistic scenario in a fully controllable studio situation with limited association potential and by carefully selecting the evaluation participants.

4.1 The Physical Setting

Since our project is an artistic research project and not a media art project, we did not begin development with a clearly defined script nor an intention of expression or statement. Instead, drawing inspiration from our own initial sketches and a large image collection that was categorized by concepts, aesthetics and structures, we followed an iterative process of conception-investigation-implementation-evaluation-elimination/ approval. Step by step we built a large environment of about 4 m wide, 8 m long and 5 m high. It is composed of a single type of white, semi-transparent, non-woven textile with interesting texture and tactility, hanging loosely from the ceiling, shaping a cocoon-like isolated space resembling organic natural structures. The resulting homogeneous and very reduced setting is instrumented with spatial, parametrically controlled light (brightness, color, duration, number, spatial composition), spatialized sound (type, volume, position, duration) and controlled air stream (intensity, duration, position, direction) that causes the textiles to move softly. These control channels constitute the dynamic atmospheric parameters of the installation.

Accelerometers, an elastic respiratory sensor and a photoplethysmograph (for measuring heart rate) are used as input modalities. Since the dynamic atmospheric parameters of the installation change directly according to the physiological reactions of the participants, it's appearance and behavior is non-linear in time and does not follow a predefined choreography. Table 1 gives an overview of the fully controllable sensor-actuator mapping design of the installation. Different types of information can be processed and interpreted from one single biofeedback signal and different parameters of different actuators can change accordingly. To create an atmosphere that can be perceived as emotionally responsive, we developed a complex setting of composed couplings starting from familiar patterns and modes of media design of the physical world, western media literacy or studies as for example color psychology. We had to take decisions to arising questions like: Does the air stream feel more personal if it increases when breathing in or out? Is it accurate to represent breathing in (oxygen-rich air) with colorful bright light and breathing out (carbon dioxide rich air) with a dull, desaturated light situation? Is the heartbeat sound – well established in cinematic culture – too platitudinous to represent heartbeat, does it create the wrong associations or is it a necessary hint for the participants to detect the human-computer connectivity? Is the color blue the accurate representation for calmness and red for an agitated state of mind? To further investigate these design issues we will make an evaluation with experienced designers, who will get direct control and influence on the design of the system, but for that we have to first develop a suitable and effective process with techniques to evaluate the decisions and implementations.

Table 1. Sensor-actuator mappings

Sensor	Actuator/Media	Description
Breath amplitude	Fan: floor	When breathing in: decrease of air stream
	Fan: ceiling	When breathing in: increase of air stream
	Light color: channel 1, 3, 4	When breathing in: increase of saturation
	Light: channel 2	When breathing in: increase of brightness
	3D-sound: wind	When breathing in: increase of volume and filter frequency
	Subwoofer: heartbeat	When breathing in: decrease of volume
Breath regularity	Light color: channel 2	If regular: green/blue, if irregular: orange-red
Heart beat	Light: channel 1	Triggers brightness flash and selects altitude graph type
	Subwoofer: heartbeat	Triggers heartbeat sound
Heart BPM	Light color: channel 1, 3, 4	Change of hue: from low to high: blue-green-yellow-red
Acceleration	Light: channel 1	Increase of motion: increase of flash intensity (amplitude, graph type of heartbeat blinking)
	3D-sound: waterfall, respiration effects	Increase of motion: increase of circulation speed displayed on 4 surrounding speakers (wind sound)
	Wind effect	Increase of motion: increase of chaos and timbre distortion
	Heartbeat sound	Increase of motion: timbre becomes brighter
	Subwoofer: heartbeat	Increase of motion: increase of volume

4.2 Afforded Activities

The resulting homogeneous and abstract, yet responsively mediated space, removed participants from their familiar context, whereby they became very attentive of their surroundings. After initial attempts to include cushions or other elements to be explored, we decided to not implement any distractive features of affordance [19] as they appeared to imply behaviors and tasks that appeared too suggestive and obvious. This cognitive reduction did not only make the visitors attentive but also self-aware of their situation in the environment. We assumed that the minimalist design approach would make people become more aware of their affects and the reactivity of the surrounding space.

4.3 Meanings Created Through People's Experiences

One of the initial motivations to develop the present project was the challenge to investigate the design of an environment that causes bodily identification. We asked ourselves: is it possible to build a responsive environment that makes an immersed person interpret it as part of their proper body, as an extended organ or a second skin. Or the other way round: Does the involved person to some extend accept the own identity as part of the surrounding system? Malafouris [20] elaborates the difficulty of drawing the boundaries between a person and the environment by using the famous example of the blind man's cane: Where does the blind man's self end and the world begin? Gins and Arakawa [21] intensely focused on the relation organism-person-environment and shaped the terms sited awareness and the situated body and proposed to architecturally build the questions themselves to gain insight.

Since we did not give the visitors any narrative to follow nor tasks to complete they came up with changing, ambivalent associations, started to create meanings and to set up their own experiments and challenges. The visitors intend to create mental models [22] to interpret and manage their surroundings.

5 Evaluation

5.1 Procedure and Interviews

We have conducted a series of experiments with a total of 17 participants (9 male, 8 female, ages between 22 and 54 years). Before they enter the installation setting, we briefly inform participants about the procedure without explaining technical details or the goal of the evaluation. We ask them to take off their shoes and to put on socks which improves the sense of tactility and serves as a "rite de passage". They put on an elastic chest belt with the breathing sensor, the motion sensor and the wireless transponder. A photoplethysmograph is attached to the index finger of the right hand.

We explained to the participants that they should enter the room and freely behave as it suits them, that there was nothing they had to achieve or that could go wrong. The exposure before participants would leave the space again lasted between 7 and 12 min and was video recorded. We also recorded the measured bio-physiological sensor data.

The recordings are merged with the video and audio track in the Evaluation Viewer (Fig. 2), allowing us to analyze the recorded behavior together with the appearance and sound of the installation at a glance.

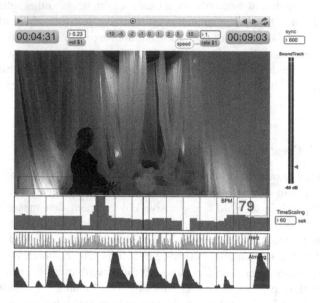

Fig. 2. The Evaluation Viewer shows video, sound, heartbeat and breath on the same time-line

After exposure we conducted 10 to 15 min semi-structured interviews with the participants, asking them to recount their experience. During the interview we encourage them to talk further about feelings and emotions connected to the experience. At a later point in the interview we would ask if they saw any connection between their actions, their body and the space, and further if they felt like they could interact and if they could describe any relationships and correlations. Finally we would ask them to describe the setting again as they would explain it to an outside person.

The transcribed interviews were further analyzed to reconstruct the temporal structure of the experience and behavior of the participants. To extract chronological order, we used the video and data recordings, together with the statements in the interviews.

5.2   Stages

We conducted evaluations in four stages, each with participant groups with different profiles. The first stage of the evaluation was run as a formalized pretest and was conducted with experts in design and media (designer, filmmaker, theater director). We analyzed this phase also to further develop the installation and to improve technical solutions, where necessary. Before the second stage we would carry out changes to the installation. For the following three stages the installation would remain unchanged.

The second group of participants consisted of students and designers. A third group was made up of participants with no background or affinity to technology or design.

A fourth evaluation was conducted as the research setting became part of a public theater event at the IXDM Lab, created together with the Theater Basel. For this we added a second wireless biofeedback interaction device to enable the participation of a second performer. The Max/MSP interface we normally use to check and control the real-time setting was displayed to an audience on a large projection screen and became an alternative way of presenting our research approach. The director and two actresses used the installation in a live performance to address the topic of future forms of community building in responsive environments. In interviews with the actors and the director after the performance we explored questions concerning the potential of the responsive environment for performative expression, their behavior compared to a conventional stage situation and the communication and expression through biofeedback signals in this type of staging.

6 Results

6.1 Exchange and Control

The interviews produced a number of insights toward our core research questions concerning the transfer of control and emotion in this type of environment. At the current stage of the design and implementation the participants do not perceive the environment as an externalization of their own body, but interpret their surrounding as a feedback system or at the most as an encounter with something affective. One participant noticed: "...the pulse I recognized a bit later, in the sound, that there is a feedback of the pulse, that the light reacts to it". Another participant explained that the experience was "...calming and enjoyable because of the (externalized) heartbeat". Further examples: "When I noticed that I could control it myself, I quite liked it. It was fun to play with it. It became more joyful, because oneself was in charge.", "... then that frightening, abrupt, heteronomous part – there is something coming towards me and I have to react – changed into: I can control and influence the situation."

6.2 Ambivalent Associations

A number participants described their experience as ambivalent and therefore interesting. They would name specific media components (light, sound, air stream, tactility) that over the course of the experience they at some point conceived as pleasing, frightening, boring or irritating. The changing associations were also caused by the interplay of the media components and changed the participant's state of mind: "It was a state that could switch very quickly from "very pleasant" to "rather uncomfortable", but exactly this made it interesting". "Concerning the light, it was from friendly to hostile, concerning the movement of the noises, also from friendly to hostile, then dark-bright and smooth-hard, I found that interesting".

Since we renounced recognizable narrative elements and only introduced noise as an abstract audio element, the interplay with other media components caused varying associations. Participants interpreted the noise as sound of the sea, water, wind from the Antarctica, or similar. In two cases the relaxing sound of water changed into the noise of a highway – which could have to do with the 3D-sound moving and going in circles around the installation. In one case the bright light source at the ceiling without an association was first considered a dazzling technical device. When the participant laid down on the floor and looked at it while the wind from the ventilator moved the textiles and the water noises came in, the lamp all of a sudden became a romantic star.

6.3 Affection

We could find a strong affective relation that evolved between the participants and the (technical and non-technical) artifacts. Affection is used here in a twofold dimension: Firstly, it is understood in the sense of emotion: All participants developed an emotional relation towards some of the technical and non-technical artifacts. The quality of these emotional ascriptions varied, but one dominating pattern could be observed: technical elements (like fans, lights and the abstract sounds) caused ambivalent feelings, while 'organic' artifacts like 'wind' from the fans and the white and light tissue were correlated with positive feelings. Affection in the second sense means that humans are affected by the environment and vice versa – in the sense that they change each others behavior. This relation proved to be inherently bound to the question of power: As long as the participants didn't realize that they were able to control the environment, they often felt uncomfortable and alienated. As soon as they discovered the options of influence, they began to feel at ease.

6.4 Phases of Behavior and Exploration

When we analyze the chronological order of the experience, similar patterns of emergent activities across participants can be identified. As they describe their impressions and their own actions in the environment, several phases emerge: When they enter, participants express a situative distance from the space and immediately follow that with formulating an explorative strategy. They would then go on to identify (known, familiar) elements in the environment and very often immediately rate or classify the objects. After that, they introduce and describe ideas of systems, functional or formulated as antagonisms (nature vs. technology). Later they go back to appraise the overall experience, often with an element of self reflection. In the end, most participants formulate concrete goals, make plans and show reflection in relation to the installation.

The emergence of this common, strong pattern is quite surprising and did not appear in the original, narrative structure of the interviews. The chronological order enables us to see the early adaptation of the participants to the environment and the strong influence of such a process on the experience. Two well established models describe strategies of experience and action in dynamic situations: Situation awareness and Sensemaking. Situation awareness (SA) formulates three distinct stages that form a basis for planning and action in complex situations [23]: The first stage calls for an identification and classification of elements in the environment and the description of their attributes and dynamics. The second stage connects the elements and their states and puts them in context with an available model. A third stage is concerned with the prediction of states of elements and their behavior in the environment, enabling proactive decision making. We can clearly correlate the processes exhibited by the participants with the three phases of SA.

We also observe more complex, interwoven patterns: Sensemaking has been applied to understand how people behave in unstructured situations and describes strategies of model creation and adaptation as questioning, matching and validating frames. McCarthy and Wright have extended the original formulation to describe experience as a continuous, active engagement with a designed environment. They identify six connected processes of sensemaking [24] that match with statements, themes and structures in our interviews:

- Anticipating. Our experience is influenced by expectations: "...I realized I am curious what will happen in there."
- Connecting refers to an immediate, prelinguistic sense of the encountered situation that primes our interpretation of what follows: "It came to me like this: I felt secure."
- Interpreting is a narrative construction of an experience: "I like colored lights that change." and includes speculation about what has happened and what will happen.
- Reflecting. We develop attitudes and judgments of developing experiences: "... strange that we perceive the sound of a highway as noise and a waterfall as romantic?", enabling us to see experiences in context.
- Appropriating connects an experience with previous and future encounters and with our self-image: "That would be something I would do the next time I go in!"
- Recounting leads beyond own experience and relates to the experience of others.

The obvious novelty and unfamiliarity that our setting has for the participants exerts a strong influence on the behavior, reflection and overall experience. Although the environment is calm and reduced and does not suggest a task or objective, it triggers a process of sensemaking, where visitors intensively engage with the environment.

7 Conclusions

Although the general structure of the feedback loop as it is implemented in our environment is very simple and the artistic design of the space is deliberately reduced – to the point of being associated with sensory deprivation – we can distinguish different mechanisms of control and influence: Ambivalence in perception and emotion makes the space interesting. To some degree participants experience affection, describing coupling between themselves and the designed environment. At the current state of development, participants do not perceive the environment as an externalization of the own body, but interpret their surrounding as a feedback system or at the most as an encounter with something affective. In a number of cases the question of control determines the overall attitude, often switching from negative to positive emotions.

When analyzing the temporal structure of participants' behavior and their experience, identifiable phases emerge that match the three stages of situation awareness. More complex processes of sensemaking, that participants execute to form and adapt models in reaction to the unfamiliar situation, are also present.

The two dimensions of affection (coupling people with their environment) show the importance to extend the perspective on ubicomp technologies beyond a pure functional view towards the dimension of affective processes that partly take place on a primordial level of human perception. The coordinated effort the participants make to understand and structure novel environments points to a (higher than expected) cognitive engagement that is in particular directed at the underlying, behavioral structure of the environment.

8 Outlook

In future work we plan to increase dynamic complexity of the responsive environment by actively driving feedback loops and developing strategies for introducing interventions and disturbances. We will incorporate the knowledge of situation awareness and sensemaking in the encounter into the dramaturgy and the design of the space. Further, we will investigate the effect of time and repeated exposure to responsive environments, in particular on the affective state and the emergent activities of a visitor.

References

1. Hansen, M.B.: Ubiquitous sensation: toward an atmospheric, collective, and microtemporal model of media. In: Ekman, U. (ed.) Throughout: Art and Culture Emerging with Ubiquitous Computing, pp. 63–88. MIT Press, Cambridge (2013)
2. Hansen, M.B.: Engineering pre-individual potentiality: technics, transindividuation, and 21 st-century media. SubStance **41**(3), 48 (2012)
3. Borgdorff, H.: The production of knowledge in artistic research. In: Biggs, M., Karlsson, H. (eds.) The Routledge Companion to Research in the Arts, pp. 44–63. Routledge, Oxon (2011)
4. Chanel, G., Rebetez, C., Bétrancourt, M., Pun, T.: Emotion assessment from physiological signals for adaptation of game difficulty. IEEE Trans. Syst. Man Cybern. Part A Syst. Hum. **41**(6), 1052–1063 (2011). IEEE Press, New York
5. Parnandi, A., Son, Y., Gutierrez-Osuna, R.: A control-theoretic approach to adaptive physiological games. In: Humaine Association Conference on Affective Computing and Intelligent Interaction (ACII), pp. 7–12. IEEE Press, New York (2013)
6. Wu, D., Courtney, C.G., Lance, B.J., Narayanan, S.S., Dawson, M.E., Oie, K.S., Parsons, T. D.: Optimal arousal identification and classification for affective computing using physiological signals: virtual reality Stroop task. IEEE Trans. Affect. Comput. **1**(2), 109–118 (2010). IEEE Press, New York
7. Tsakiris, M., Haggard, P.: The rubber hand illusion revisited: visuotactile integration and self-attribution. J. Exp. Psychol. Hum. Percept. Perform. **31**(1), 80–91 (2005). APA, Washington, D.C.

8. Pfeiffer, C., Schmutz, V., Blanke, O.: Visuospatial viewpoint manipulation during full-body illusion modulates subjective first-person perspective. Exp. Brain Res. **232**(12), 4021–4033 (2014)
9. Cassinelli, A., Reynolds, C., Ishikawa, M.: Augmenting spatial awareness with haptic radar. In: 10th IEEE International Symposium on Wearable Computers, pp. 61–64. IEEE Press, New York (2006)
10. Schnädelbach, H., Glover, K., Irune, A.A.: ExoBuilding: breathing life into architecture. In: Proceedings of the 6th Nordic Conference on Human-Computer Interaction: Extending Boundaries, pp. 442–451. ACM, New York (2010)
11. Jager, N., Moran, S., Schnädelbach, H.: Using adaptive architecture to support yoga practices: social considerations for design. In: 2014 IEEE International Conference on Pervasive Computing and Communications Workshops (PERCOM Workshops), pp. 364–369 (2014). IEEE Press, New York (2014)
12. Beesley, P.: Protocell mesh. In: Stacey, M. (ed.) Prototyping Architecture, pp. 58–61. Riverside Architectural Press, Toronto (2013)
13. Weiser, M.: The computer for the 21st century. Sci. Am. **265**(3), 94–104 (1991)
14. Suchman, L.: Human-Machine Reconfigurations: Plans and Situated Actions, p. 268. Cambridge University Press, New York (2007)
15. Davies, C., Harrison, J.: Osmose: towards broadening the aesthetics of virtual reality. Comput. Graph. **30**(4), 25–28 (1996)
16. Latour, B.: Reassembling the Social: An Introduction to Actor-Network-Theory. Oxford University Press, New York (2005)
17. Benyon, D.: Spaces of interaction, places for experience. In: Synthesis Lectures on Human-Centered Information, vol. 7, no. 2, pp. 1–129 (2014)
18. Relph, E.: Place and Placelessness, vol. 67, p. 45. Pion, London (1976)
19. Gibson, J.J.: The theory of affordances. In: Shaw, R., Bransford, J. (eds.) Perceiving, Acting, and Knowing: Toward An Ecological Psychology, pp. 67–82. Erlbaum, Hillsdale (1977)
20. Malafouris, L.: How Things Shape the Mind. MIT Press, Cambridge (2013)
21. Gins, M., Arakawa, S.: Architectural Body. University of Alabama Press, Tuscaloosa (2002)
22. Johnson-Laird, P.N.: Mental Models: Towards a Cognitive Science of Language, Inference, and Consciousness, no. 6. Harvard University Press, Cambridge (1983)
23. Endsley, M.R.: Toward a theory of situation awareness in dynamic systems. Hum. Factors J. Hum. Factors Ergon. Soc. **37**(1), 32–64 (1995)
24. McCarthy, J., Wright, P.: Technology as Experience, p. 124. MIT Press, Cambridge (2007)

Towards Simulation of Semantic Generation and Detection of Humorous Response

Julia M. Taylor[1(✉)] and Vitaliy L. Rayz[2]

[1] Computer and Information Technology, Purdue University,
401 N Grant Street, West Lafayette, IN 47907, USA
jtaylor1@purdue.edu
[2] College of Engineering and Applied Science, University of Wisconsin – Milwaukee,
3200 N Cramer Street, Milwaukee, WI 53211, USA
rayz@uwm.edu

Abstract. This paper explores headlines that are so obvious that they are somehow funny. We develop a model that uses ontological representation as the basis for retrieving such obvious information. Using this model, we generate jokes in a narrow domain of fluid dynamics.

Keywords: Restricted joke modeling · Ontology · Computational humor

1 Introduction

Throughout social media, every once in a while, there are sparks of posts about headlines that are funny for one reason or another. In this paper, we are investigating a mechanism for creating and understanding headlines that state information that is so obvious that the headlines themselves become ridiculous. Such headlines have been a source of attention not just by social networking sites, such as Facebook or Twitter, but they also serve as a topic for newspaper or blog publications [1, 2] or even chapters in books [3].

These headlines, arguably, are mildly funny, as the examples below demonstrate:

(1) Diana was still alive hours before she died.
(2) Statistics show that teen pregnancy drops off significantly after age 25.
(3) Federal Agents Raid Gun Shop, Find Weapons.
(4) Homicide victims rarely talk to police.
(5) Study Shows Frequent Sex Enhances Pregnancy Chances.
(6) Bridges help people cross rivers.
(7) Healthy diet lowers death risk for women.
(8) High heels lead to foot pain.

Some of the examples are taken from satirical newspapers – for example, according to Reddit post by barmonkey, (1) originally appeared in Private Eye, a British satirical newspaper, making fun of the Daily Express – while others may be from a legitimate quote that deserve this much attention, or can be blamed on journalists not having enough time to read them carefully enough. An example of a headline that appeared from a quote

© Springer International Publishing Switzerland 2016
N. Streitz and P. Markopoulos (Eds.): DAPI 2016, LNCS 9749, pp. 362–369, 2016.
DOI: 10.1007/978-3-319-39862-4_33

is (2), which, according to [4] is attributed to a then Colorado State Senator quoted in The Denver Post on 5/14/1995.

We are interested in such headlines for two reasons: one, they attract attention and comments from people, thus they are suitable for some sort of a dialogue; two, they are based on a violation of ontological defaults [5] and thus should be possible to model computationally. Interestingly, these headlines (or sentences, if we are to move into dialogues) contain the same script overlap/oppositeness (SOs) [6], obvious/non-obvious, and, thus, they don't require a full-blown implementation of a humor theory, such as the Ontological Semantic Theory of Humor (OSTH) [7].

With the exception of (2) and – possibly – (7), each of the headlines contains one event that serves as the anchoring point of a script. The event is described by some of the properties, filled with information from the sentence. Each of these properties also has the ontological default, described by the OST ontology. It is confirmation of this default that is so unusual in normal speech [8] that serves as a mechanism for getting attention from the readers and, possibly, a humorous response.

It is possible for a sentence to describe multiple events, as demonstrated by most of the examples above. The only sentence that has only one event is (6) – in the papers we are using the standard notion that is employed by OST that an event can be a verb or a noun, and not all verbs can serve as events. A careful examination of the examples shows that even when there are multiple events in the sentence, they are strongly connected to the main one. Moreover, if the event in question is to serve a role of a script, most of the supporting events would become a necessarily components of the script.

2 Scripts

A notion of script is perhaps most familiar to a knowledge representation audience from [9], which describes a restaurant script with all details that can be expected from people that visit restaurants on a regular basis and are comfortable with navigating the procedure of walking in, talking to whoever greets them, following to a table, placing an order, etc. It should be noted that some of these sub-events are optional, depending on the type of a restaurant – all of which [9] describes.

To a humor community, however, the scripts are known from Script-based Semantic Theory of Humor (SSTH) [6]. According to SSTH, a text is joke-carrying if it is compatible fully or in part with two different scripts and these scripts must somehow oppose. Moreover, the oppositeness must be unexpected.

A script can be seen as any situation that can be easily understood/described by a human being. A restaurant is only one of these. The label is not important in SSTH, it is the actual description of the situation that is of interest. Thus [6] describes a so-called doctor/lover joke, also known as patient/lover, where one of the scripts is visiting a doctor's office and the other one is having an affair (with a doctor's wife). The analysis of the joke is described in [10].

The SSTH itself is not clear on how to calculate the oppositeness, but several proposals, mostly throughout OSTH, have been made. For the purposes of this paper we will assume that oppositeness has to follow a salient property of a script or event.

Moreover, we will assume that these salient properties can be marked, either in the ontology as Ontological Semantic Technology [11–13] does, frames as FrameNet [14] does, or any other system that a reader may choose to use.

2.1 Federal Agents Raid Gun Shop, Find Weapons

Headline (3) is based on the script of RAID. We can look at this event from the point of view patrolling. According to FrameNet, the frame of patrolling describes "An individual or group, the Patrol moves through and examines a Ground in order to ensure that it is in a generally Desired-state-of-affairs, particularly that it is safe and contains no dangerous Unwanted-entity." The core elements of the frame are:

- Desired-state-of-affairs, which the Patrol hopes to ensure by visiting Ground
- Ground, which is the area that the Patrol inspects to insure its safety
- Patrol, which is the person or group who inspects the Group to see that it is safe
- Purpose, which is the desired outcome of patrolling
- Unwanted-entity, which is an entity whose presence would impair the desirability or safety of the ground.

In addition to the core frame elements, there are some non-core ones:

- Circumstances, under which the Patrol examines the Ground
- Co-participant, that patrols along with the Patrol
- Degree, or the extent to which the examination is done
- Descriptor, which describes one of the participants of the patrolling event
- Duration, or the length of patrol
- Instrument, which is the entity that is used to scrutinize the ground
- Location, which is the position of Patrol during the act of perception
- …

We have used FrameNet to describe the event of RAID since it is available to a general public. Once can just as easily used OST for the description, however since one requires username and password to access its online recourses we will proceed with the analysis from FrameNet while possible.

Let us now compare the frame of Patrolling with the information that is in the headline (3), based on the event of RAID. The intended outcome of a RAID is some finding – this finding is the purpose of a RAID. Thus, the fact that AGENTs of a RAID found something, in this case WEAPONs, is a necessary part of the script. In this case it corresponds to the Unwanted-entity element of the Patrolling. What is interesting here is the LOCATION of a RAID, which happens to be a SHOP that sells GUNs, and thus it must contain them.

The frame of Shopping contains only two core elements:

- Goods, or the entity that the Ground may contain
- Shopper, or the person who attempts to find the goods

The non-core elements are:

- Co-participant
- Degree, which identifies the amount of effort put into shopping
- Depictive, which describes a participant of shopping scenario
- Ground, which is the entity to which the Cognizer pays attention
- Purpose, which is an action that the Shopper intends to accomplish
- ....

By definition, a RAID is a sudden activity (not reflected in FrameNet, but would be in OST), and the purpose of a RAID is to find something that is possibly illegal or at least frowned upon. However, there is nothing surprising in gun shops to sell guns (it is the Goods that the Ground should contain), which is where the obvious/non-obvious SO comes in. It should be noted, that while it is not necessary for a computer, in this case, to detect that finding illegal weapons maybe newsworthy, it may add an extra layer of appreciation for a human, and, possibly, adds an LM [15] resource to a joke.

It is possible to explain the oppositeness of the scripts of Shopping and Raid not in terms of obvious/non-obvious, but rather in terms of expected and legal vs. illegal. However, to connect to a potentially illegal activity, one must completely ignore the location of the Patrolling frame, which happens to be a gun shop. Nevertheless, the Unwanted_entity of the Patrolling frame (with negative connotation) happens to be the desired entity of Goods in Shopping (with positive connotation), which, without a doubt, is in oppositeness with each other (see Fig. 1).

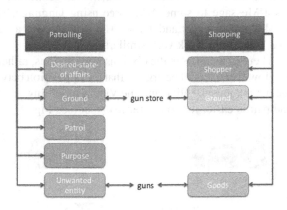

Fig. 1. Frames in the headline (3)

2.2 Homicide Victims Rarely Talk to Police

We will analyze another headline before generalizing the principle. The event that is in focus of this headline is homicide, which corresponds to the Killing frame of FrameNet. This frame has the following core elements:

- Cause, which is an inanimate entity or process that causes death
- Instrument, which is the device used to bring death about
- Killer, which is the person that causes death
- Means, or the method or action that was performed resulting in death
- Victim, which is the entity that dies as a result of the killing

We are not interested in most of the non-core elements on the frame, but what is of interest is that the result of this frame is the Victim being dead. Thus, brings the Frame of Death into the picture. The frame of Death is a subframe of Cycle_of_life_and_death which uses Biological entity that, in turn, have "naturally occurring biological processes and functions." Since Death is the termination of the Cycle_of_life_and_death, we can assume that all processes and function have been terminated after Death.

Another frame that is activated in this headline is that of Telling. According to FrameNet, the definition of Telling is "a Speaker addresses an Addressee with a Message, which may be indirectly refereed to as a Topic." The following core elements are used in Telling:

- Addressee, which receives the Message from the Speaker
- Medium, in which the Message is expressed
- Message, or the communication produced by the Speaker
- Speaker, which is the sentient entity that produces the Message
- Topic, which is a general description of the content of the Message

Another possible frame here is Statement, which used "communicate the act of a Speaker to address a Message to some Addressee using language." It has four core element, Message, Medium, Speaker and Topic. The Addressee is a non-core element, but for our purposes, the frames work very similarly.

The oppositeness here is, again, is in the obvious/non-obvious, rather, stated obvious vs. understood one. However, it could be argued that the opposition between the Speaker of Telling/Message, which must be alive and the Victim of Killing which must be dead. Perhaps this second pair is easier for computer to detect (see Fig. 2).

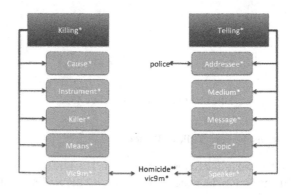

Fig. 2. Frames in the headline (4)

3   Default-Based Oppositeness

It should be noted though that very few details are filled for the core elements in both examples. Thus, it is the so-called defaults [8] that are coming into play here. Defaults are defined as obvious knowledge that does not have to be explicitly specified for the reader to be aware of it. Some example of defaults are unlocking the door (implied: with a key), talking to somebody (implied: a person, unless specified otherwise), patrolling the neighborhood (implied: police or armed forces, depending on a location/situation).

We are using the notion of defaults in processing joke-like structure that these head-lines generate. We are assuming that most of the information to process the headlines is taken from the defaults, and it's with the help of the defaults that the oppositeness can be found. While the "model" that we outline doesn't cover all cases of headlines, we will use it to generate some of the sentences that could be used for a specific domain. The "model" (more accurately template) is described in Fig. 3.

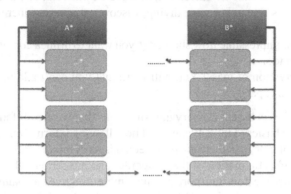

Fig. 3. Script defaults used to generate joke-like headlines

In the full paper, we will analyze different paths that the above jokes take and gener-alize it to different types of jokes that are possible within this type of humor, thus creating an algorithm for detecting them. We will then generate several jokes that are based on the found algorithm and describe the results.

3.1   Defaults in the Fluid Mechanics

We assume that any definition that is used in a field can serve as a default for the profes-sionals of that field. Thus, for people who are familiar with the linguistics of humor, jokes, by default, are analyzed as scripts. For people that are familiar with computing, arithmetic operations are done in binary code (at the lowest level). For people that are familiar with security, any system should come protected.

We are using the following terms and properties from fluid dynamics to generate jokes based on our model:

- Incompressible fluid – fluid with a constant density
- Shear stress – frictional force exerted by a moving fluid on a surface (frictional force between layers of fluid)
- Pressure increases with depth in the fluid
- In incompressible flow the inlet flow must balance the outlet flow
- Conservation of mass principle: mass cannot be created or destroyed.

The domain if fluid mechanics was selected opportunistically – to allow one of the co-authors to test the jokes on the student population.

FrameNet doesn't cater to such restricted domains, but, as we previously stated, any semantic knowledge base system is capable of representing information described in FrameNet or in the definitions above. We can thus use Ontological Semantic Technology to create concepts necessary to represent our domain of interest.

We then use the model outline to generate the following jokes:

(1) Fluid dynamics researcher stirred tea; discovered milk can be mixed into it.
(2) Fluid dynamics researcher went diving; discovered pressure increases with depth in the fluid.
(3) Studies of incompressible flow showed if you want to drink a cup of milk, you have to swallow it too.
(4) Study conservation of mass! You will learn that you can't add more water into a bottle than it's capacity.

Each of the jokes is based on every day situations that we are all familiar with, then explained from the basics of fluid dynamics. The following information might be helpful to understanding of first joke: there are two mechanisms of mixing – molecular diffusion, when we rely on chaotic motion of the molecules and advection, when we rely on the flow transport. Since the flow transport is a much more effective mechanism, it is obvious that stirring can enhance mixing. The joke here is that it is intuitively clear that one should stir milk into a cup of tea without any knowledge of the underlying physics of transport and mixing. The underlying scripts are that of pouring tea (by a regular person) vs. flow transport.

The second joke is based on knowledge that in a non-moving fluid, the pressure is balanced by the gravity and thus increases linearly with the depth. As the diver is going down, the weigh of the column of fluid above increases resulting in higher pressures. Here again, the result is so obvious from a common experience that once does not have to think about the balance of the pressure gradients and gravity forces.

The third joke is based on the fact that if the flow is incompressible, the flow in must be balanced by the flow out, it cannot be compressed like the air in a car's tire. Thus, once the mouth is completely filled with milk, I cannot add more to it without swallowing since I can't compress it into a smaller volume inside the mouth.

Finally, in the fourth joke, since mass cannot be just created or destroyed, it is clear that there can be no sources or sinks in the bottle. The joke implies that a liquid in the bottle cannot be compressed, hence once the bottle is filled we can't push more liquid into it. Thus, a fancy term of mass conservation describes a trivial fact.

It is clear that in order for an ontology to capture the meaning of these jokes, the domain of fluid mechanics (or at least information representation the basics) should be very well developed. However, once the scripts B in Fig. 3 are well represented, the results of these scripts is what triggers the green box of B.

The A scripts of Fig. 3 is the basic knowledge scripts – those that should be easily available to a general knowledge system. Most of the time, however, such systems lack detail even for a general knowledge domain. For example, FrameNet anchors the verb dive in a Path_Shape frame (describing "the fictive motion of a stationary Road"). Thus, while a Direction, as a core element, can describe the event of going down, the water is not present in the frame as a default. Similarly, the frame of Ingestion, where drink is anchored, is not connected to swallowing.

References

1. White, B.: Teen pregnancy drops off significantly after age 25. The Morning Call, 13 December 2013
2. McGlynn, K.: The Most Obvious Headlines of All Times. Huffington Post, 23 July 2010
3. Kyff, R.: English Goes on a Toot. Creators Publishing (2015)
4. Lindsell-Roberts, S.: Technical Writing for Dummies. Wiley Publishers, New York (2001)
5. Taylor, J.M., Raskin, V., Hempelmann, C.F., Attardo, S.: An unintentional inference and ontological property defaults. In: International Conference on Systems, Man and Cybernetics, Istanbul, Turkey (2010)
6. Raskin, V.: Semantic Mechanisms of Humor. D. Reidel, Dordrecht, Boston, Lancaster (1985)
7. Raskin, V., Hempelmann, C.F., Taylor, J.M.: How to understand and assess a theory: the evolution of the SSTH into the GTVH and now into the OSTH. J. Literary Theory 3, 2 (2009)
8. Hickman, L., Taylor, J., Raskin, V.: Direct object omission as a sign of conceptual defaultness. In: FLAIRS (2016)
9. Schank, R., Abelson, H.: Scripts, Plans. Goals and Understanding. Erlbaum, Hillsdale (1977)
10. Raskin, V.: Ambient scripts in humor and beyond. In: HCII 2016, Toronto, Ontario, Canada (2016)
11. Raskin, V., Hempelmann, C., Taylor, J.: Guessing vs. knowing: the two approaches to semantics in natural language processing. In: Dialogue (2010)
12. Taylor, J., Hempelmann, C., Raskin, V.: On an automatic acquisition toolbox for ontologies and lexicons in ontological semantics. In: International Conference in Artificial Intelligence, ICAI 2010 (2010)
13. Hempelmann, C., Taylor, J., Raskin, V.: Application-guided ontological engineering. In: International Conference in Artificial Intelligence, ICAI 2010 (2010)
14. Ruppenhofer, J., Ellsworth, M., Petruck, M.R.L., Johnson, C.R., Scheffczyk, J.: FramNET II: Extended Theory and Practice (2010)
15. Attardo, S., Raskin, V.: Script theory revis(it)ed: joke similarity and joke representation model. HUMOR: Int. J. Humor Res. 4, 3–4 (1991). (83pp.)

Infusing Humor in Unexpected Events

Alessandro Valitutti$^{(\boxtimes)}$ and Tony Veale

School of Computer Science, University College Dublin,
Belfield, Dublin 4, Ireland
{alessandro.valitutti,tony.veale}@ucd.ie

Abstract. In this paper, we focus on humor facilitators, a type of humorous agents meant to act as mediators between unexpected events occurring in smart environments and the human agents. More specifically, we present a case study in which fictional ideation and narrative dramatization are combined to achieve humor facilitation. We implemented a test bed for the simulation of an interactive environment. Then, we carried out an empirical evaluation with human subjects, aimed to assess the contribution of narrative comments to the humorous effect. The results show first evidence that fictional comments, delivered as dialogue acts, increase the humor response in a statistically significant way.

1 Introduction

A comedian does funny things. A good comedian does things funny. —
Buster Keaton

A humorous agent in a smart environment should be able to detect potentially hilarious events and communicate them in such a way to induce humor appreciation in human agents. Nevertheless, humor detection in interactive and dynamic contexts is a challenging task and no significant progress has been done in the past decade.

Nijholt [14] discussed a possible methodological direction for connecting event detection in smart environments and humor generation and proposed to focus on the incongruity of events. Instead of detecting humor directly, the humorous agent should identify incongruous events and use comic strategies to reframe the incongruity as humorous. It would act as a mediator between unexpected events and humans so that even events not typically perceived as funny could be reframed as funny. The underlying claim is that what makes an event seen as humorous depends not only on the event itself but also on its interpretation. We refer to this type of humorous agents as *humor facilitators*. At best of our knowledge, no substantial attempts have been made to advance computational humor in this direction.

In this paper, we present a case study in which fictional ideation and narrative dramatization are combined to perform humor facilitation. More specifically, we hypothesize that a creative narrative re-interpretation of unexpected events occurring in smart environments, expressed as narrative comments or dialogue

N. Streitz and P. Markopoulos (Eds.): DAPI 2016, LNCS 9749, pp. 370–379, 2016.
DOI: 10.1007/978-3-319-39862-4_34

acts, can reframe the ongoing situation as humorous. We implemented a system for the simulation of a smart environments as a canvas showing interactive animations of geometrical shapes. Then, we carried out an empirical evaluation with human subjects of the contribution of narrative comments to the induction of humor appreciation. The results show first evidence that verbal comments, communicated as a narrative and dramatized as dialogue acts, increase the humor response in a statistically significant way.

The remainder of this paper is organized as follows. In Sect. 2, we give an overview of the previous work on humor facilitation and related topics. In Sect. 3, we describe the proposed approach. Section 4 presents the exploratory evaluation. Finally, conclusions are discussed in Sect. 5.

2 Background

2.1 Smart Environments, Interactive Humor and Unpredictability

A Smart Environment may be defined as a region of the real world that is extensively equipped with sensors, actuators and computing components [16]. Over the years, smart environments are becoming a common aspect of the real world. Web-connected smartphones, social networks, internet of things, or multiplayer online games are producing a society in which humans and computational devices are constantly interacting. Smart environments are conceived as spaces in which "networked devices work continuously and collaboratively to make lives of inhabitants more comfortable" [3]. Therefore, it is natural to consider humor as a potentially effective way to improve the human experience in a smart space.

As widely reported in the literature, there are several types of humor and, for each type, an impressive number of humorous techniques. However, only a selected subset of them seems to naturally fit to smart environments. For the sake of simplicity, we cluster the main types of humor in two groups. The first group contains joke and pun generation, which have been the dominant subject of research so far in computational humor [6,12,17]. We refer to this group as *non-interactive verbally expressed humor*. The term "verbally expressed", as discussed by Ritchie [18], includes both verbal and referential humor. The second group contains humor types that seem more naturally occurring in interactive and social environments: *conversational humor, physical humor, spontaneous humor, incidental humor*, and *visual humor*. We refer to this group as *interactive humor*.

Real world environments are largely unpredictable. Most actions, such as kicking a ball or turning over an omelette are, to a good extent, indeterministic. Only a subset of world events can be modeled computationally. This is the reason even the most sophisticated robot "struggles" to act in an open environment with non-determinism and partial observability [1]. On the other hand, unpredictability is a potential source of humor. Unexpected events and, in particular, unexpected outcomes of either human or computational agents can, in specific contexts, be perceived not only as surprising but also as funny. Humor is a social phenomenon, and real-world environments are typically populated by more than one human to either laugh with or at. Therefore, smart environments are suitable for exploring interactive humor.

2.2 Humor Facilitation

In his characterization of computational-humor generators as humorous agents, Nijholt identifies two key aspects. The first one is the appropriateness of humorous acts. A humorous act can be a witty remark or a joke uttered during the conversation. The quality of a humorous act is not only in the content but also in its appropriateness, based on "an assessment whether or not to produce the remark at that particular moment" [13]. The second aspect is the possible role of the humorous system as a facilitator of humor. A humor facilitator is a type of humorous agent capable of detecting events occurring in a social environment and unexpected for human agents, and make them perceived as funny [14,15]. In the context of distributed computing, mediators and facilitators are components designed to ease the coordination and the communication among agents [19]. In the case of humorous agents, the term 'facilitator' refers to the capability to increase either the probability or the intensity of the humor response.

An early attempt to mediate user's experience of information spaces with interface characters was performed with *Agneta and Frida* [7]. They are "two animated female characters – mother and daughter –[...] watching the browser more or less like watching television". Now and then, they utter previously scripted comments most of which are intentionally humorous. The comments are produced as response to user's activity such as clicking a link or dragging the mouse over an image.

The combination of humor and interface characters has been increasingly included in the design of computer games [5]. *Game presenters* are artificial characters delivering comments based on game actions and adapted to players' social profile [9]. A step forward in the achievement of humor facilitation is the game Portal. It is a computer game, developed in 1997, in which the player is engaged to interact not only with a virtual environment but also with a number of synthetic characters [2]. The main character is GLaDOS, playing the role of the antagonist. During the game, the player delivers comments, most of which humorous, in response to the player's actions or other types of events. Most interestingly, it employs comedic strategies and forms of conversational humor, in some cases combining deception and sarcastic comments to make fun of the player [8]. The main limitation of this system is that the comments are manually scripted, since the system has not the capability of autonomously analyze a new event and interpret it in a funny way.

2.3 Fictional Ideation

In our research, we explored fictional ideation as a strategy for humor facilitation. Fictional ideation is a process consisting of the production of novel and valuable ideas meant to describe some aspect of an imaginary world. The generation of fictional ideas is often used as the inspirational basis for the production of artifacts such as poems, paintings, songs, or games. In the context of computer science, automated fictional ideation has been studied as a computational creativity task. A large-scale study of automated fictional ideation is the research subject of the WHIM Project[1] [10]. Although the project is mainly focused on the generation of narratives, it aims to generalize its achievements to a broader class of creative artifacts.

Several strategies of ideation are currently under study. However, all of them are meant to generate a simple narrative idea, represented as a short sequence of story steps called *mini-narrative*. These short plots are represented in abstract form, yet capable of being "textually rendered" in different possible ways. For example, one of the components of the What-If Machine is @MetaphorMagnet, a Twitter bot designed to produce and deliver fictional ideas as tweets [23]. The What-If Machine employs several knowledge resources, such as ConceptNet [11], a collection of causal links expressing either promotion or demotion [24], or a set of narrative arcs representing the transformation of fictional characters in a story [21]. Either the availability or the specific development of these resources allowed us to implement several ideation strategies, based on subversion [22], irony [20], or the adaptive response to events from breaking news [23].

3   Proposed Approach

Our research on humor facilitation is aimed to investigate to what extent it is possible to transform a non-humorous event in a humorous event. To restrict the context more precisely, we make two assumptions: (1) The event under study is not typically recognizable as humorous; (2) the facilitator's comments increase the humorous performance (i.e. humorous rate or average funniness) in a significant way; (3) the event is unpredictable.

3.1   Observed and User-Caused Events

The humor facilitator induces (and reacts to) two types of events: *observed events*, occurring without intervention by users, and *user-caused events* consisting of user actions on the interactive canvas.

By running a procedure for the fictional narrative ideation, the humor facilitator represents the animated objects and their interactions as fictional characters and their interactions as fictional events. For example, if the animation shows two colliding objects, one larger than other, their collision may be interpreted as the smaller one is being hit or punched so that it will be described as vulnerable or miserable. Moreover, narrative generation may employ irony to express disparagement toward the target character. For instance, if a nice geometrical figure collides and then becomes smaller and flattened, the humorous agent may present this event in an ironic way, describing the transformation of a "beautiful star" into a "useless junk".

---

[1] www.whim-project.eu.

In the case of user-caused events, the user behavior is the source of the ironic narrative generation. User interaction consists of clicking and dragging the mouse on the screen. To transform drawing actions in unexpected and potentially funny provoked events, the agent could display a form of deceptive behavior, showing unexpected consequences of the user's action. In the design of this functionality, we were inspired by *FugPaint*, an "antagonist" or "misbehaving" painting tool developed as a creative project [4]. In this system, the painting markers are displayed in different ways respect to the pointer position, thus producing unexpected drawings. According to Fry, the program is aimed to tense users, keep them engaged for an extended amount of time, and induce humor.

3.2   Humor Facilitation by Fictional Ideation

We focus on fictional ideation process as the core functional element for achieving a form of humor facilitation. An "ideation-based" humor facilitator should be able to detect a potentially humorous ongoing situation or unexpected event and, then, generate an appropriate sequence of narrative comments. The automated fictional idea generator would perform a narrative interpretation such that the event could be represented as a fictional event and the entities involved in the event described as fictional characters.

4   Evaluation

As a preliminary experiment, we implemented a simple virtual simulation of a smart environment, which allows us to develop easily a set of interactive animations of simple geometrical figures. Then, we performed an empirical evaluation with human judges, aimed to study the humor facilitation through narrative comments. More specifically, we hypothesize that the communication of narrative comments can produce a significant increase of the humor response.

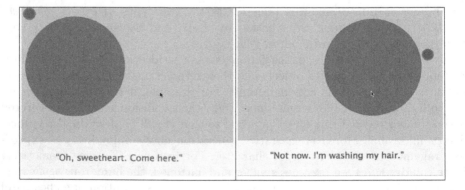

"Oh, sweetheart. Come here."   "Not now. I'm washing my hair."

Fig. 1. Two screenshots of the animation and related textual comments.

How was watching the animation and interacting with it? Could you describe its effect on you?
○ It makes me laugh.
○ It makes me smile.
○ It puts me in a better mood.
○ It is not particularly funny, hilarious or humorous.

What is the term that best expresses your feelings?
○ Funny
○ Hilarious
○ Humorous
○ Not funny, hilarious, or humorous

How funny (or hilarious or humorous) was it?
○ 0
○ 1
○ 2
○ 3
○ 4
○ 5

❶ Select either 0 if not funny/hilarious/humorous or a number between 1 and 5 if funny/hilarious/humorous.

Fig. 2. Questions to the subjects.

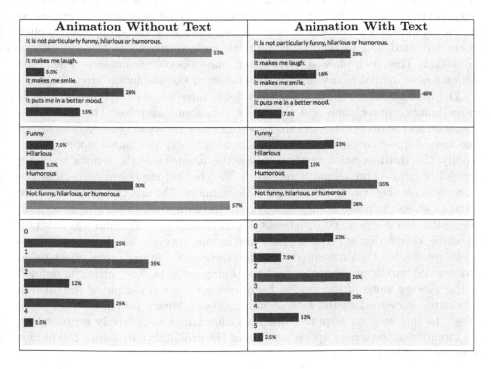

Fig. 3. Histograms cumulating the responses of the subjects to the animation without and with textual comments.

First, we developed an interactive animation in two different versions, each displayed in a canvas and uploaded as a web application[2]. In both versions, the animation shows two circles with different sizes and colors, moving around the canvas area. The large blue circle tends to follow the smaller red one and collides repetitively. After a few seconds, the user is requested to click on the screen. Suddenly, the size of the two circles changes until they invert sizes and behaviors: now the red circle is attracted by the blue one and tends to collide. The overall behavior of the two circles makes them look as living entities. The change of behavior after the click is supposedly unexpected, yet not meant to be humorous.

In the second version, the interactive animation is paired with a textual description expressing a fictional idea: the blue circle is "in love" with the red one. After clicking, the two circles are claimed to have been married and, then, the roles are inverted. The red circle is described as a wife nagging a lazy husband. The narrative comments, dramatized as dialogue acts, aim to depict the two circles as fictional characters, and the overall situation as a short narrative. In this experiment, we scripted the dialogue by hand, even though with the aim to employ fully automatic fictional ideation and textual rendering in the future next stages of this research (Fig. 1).

We used CrowdFlower[3], a crowdsourcing service, to hire subjects and collect their judgments. We performed two assessments, one for the animation without text, and the other one for the version with text. 40 different subjects evaluated each animation. Each participant was invited to look at the animation, to click when requested and to report the numeric code displayed at the end of the animation. This trick allowed us to filter same possible scammers. Then, the subjects were invited to assess their experience of the animation after clicking.

The questionnaire reported five questions, three of which (shown in Fig. 2) about humor appreciation and the other two about surprise. The first question assesses the occurrence and the type of humor response (*binary funniness*). The second question evaluates the lexicon used to express humor appreciation. Finally, the third question aims to assess the intensity of the humor response (*graded funniness*) on a scale from 1 to 5. We checked the coherence across the answers as another way to filter potential scammers. The last two questions were asked to assess the possible surprisingness of the animation (*binary surprise*) following the user's action and its intensity (*graded surprise*). The aim was to study a possible correlation of surprisingness and humor appreciation. For the analysis of the results, we then measured the effectiveness of the humorous effect using two derived variables: *funniness* and the *humorousness*. The former is defined as the average value of the graded funniness for a given sample of judgments. The latter is defined as the rate of judgments of binary funniness with value "Yes". In this way, we have two different dimensions respectively representing the intensity of the humor appreciation and the probability to induce the humor response (Table 1).

---

[2] The animations can be accessed at http://valitutti.it/papers/hcii-2016/index.html.
[3] Available at www.crowdflower.com.

Table 1. Values of humorousness, funniness, and surprisingness according to the animations respectively without and with textual comments.

	Humorousness	Funniness	Surprisingness
NO-TEXT	0.44	1.44	1.62
WITH-TEXT	0.71	2.47	2.39

We carried out a permutation-based statistical analysis of the variation of humorousness and funniness. We implemented the null hypothesis that a constraint has no effect by randomly swapping results between the two sets. In this way, we obtained empirical p-values for each variable and a corresponding couple of samples. All the variations are statistically significant ($p < 0.02$ for humorousness and <0.005 for funniness). Moreover, we applied the Wilcoxon Sum Rank test to the two sets of graded funniness. Even in this case, we obtained a p-value <0.005 by the permutation test. Applying Wilcoxon Sum Rank test to the variation of mean surprisingness, we obtained $p < 0.02$. Finally, we measured the correlation between graded funniness and surprisingness in both samples. The value of correlation is 0.68 in the case of NO-TEXT sample and 0.90 in the case of WITH-TEXT sample (Fig. 3).

5 Conclusions and Future Work

We focused on a particular type of humor facilitation, consisting of a two-step process: detection of an unexpected event and its reframing by delivery of fictional comments. The approach is based on the use of fictional ideation as a way to re-interpret the unexpected situation as potentially funny. To perform and test a computational implementation of the proposed approach, we adopted a simple way to simulate a smart environment as a canvas displaying interactive animations.

We conducted an exploratory study about the role of fictional comments, dramatized as dialogue acts, to the process of humor facilitation. We defined two variables as measure of the humorous effect – humorousness and funniness – meant to express, respectively, the probability and the intensity of the humor response. The results of the experiment show that both variables increase significantly if the situation is described and dramatized with fictional comments.

In principle, several types of humor facilitation could be designed for smart environments. A major problem is the unpredictability of potentially humorous events. We proposed to transform this limitation into a strength and focus on unpredicted events. In the proposed approach, we separate the detection of unexpected and potentially incongruous and humorous events from the process of providing a semantic frame, emphasize their incongruity and reframe incongruity as funny.

The system implemented for this research is meant to be the first step of a larger class of prototypes capable of simulating different types of smart environments, and employing various techniques for modeling and reframing events as humorous. We need to test the effect of the narrative interpretation and the impact of the dramatization through dialogue acts. We will develop a resource for connecting a large set of visual objects – such as geometrical shapes, properties, dynamic behaviors – and interactive events as fictional characters and narrative events, respectively. Finally, we aim to develop a robust and scalable computational framework for the design and implementation of automated humor-facilitation scripts for a wide variety of smart environments.

Acknowledgments. We would like to thank Stefan Ludgate for his insightful suggestions about the textual scripting of the animation employed in the experiment.

This research was supported by the EC project *WHIM: The What-If Machine*. See http://www.whim-project.eu.

References

1. Bertoli, P., Cimatti, A., Roveri, M., Traverso, P.: Planning in nondeterministic domains under partial observability via symbolic model checking. In: Proceedings of the International Joint Conference on Artificial Intelligence (IJCAI), pp. 473–478. Morgan Kaufmann, Seattle (2001)
2. Burden, M., Gouglas, S.: The algorithmic experience: portal as art. Game Stud. **12**(2) (2012)
3. Das, S.K., Cook, D.J.: Mobile, wireless, and sensor networks. In: Designing Smart Environments: A Paradigm Based on Learning and Prediction. Wiley (2006)
4. Fry, B.: Fugpaint: An antagonistic painting tool. Project description and web tool (1999). http://benfry.com/fugpaint. Accessed 8 Dec 2015
5. Grönroos, A.M.: Humour in Video Games: Play, Comedy, and Mischief. Master's thesis, Aalto University (2013)
6. Hempelmann, C.F.: The primer of humor research. In: Computational Humor: Beyond the Pun?, pp. 335–363. Mouton de Gruyter, New York (2008)
7. Höök, K., Persson, P., Sjölinder, M.: Evaluating users' experience of a character-enhanced information space. AI Commun. **13**(3), 195–212 (2000)
8. Hookham, G., Meany, M.: The spectrum of states: comedy, humour and engagement in games. In: Proceedings of the 11th Australasian Conference on Interactive Entertainment (IE 2015), Sydney, Australia, 27–30 January 2015
9. Karouzaki, E., Savidis, A.: A framework for adaptive game presenters with emotions and social comments. Int. J. Comput. Games Technol. (2012)
10. Llano, M.T., Colton, S., Hepworth, R., Gow, J.: Automated fictional ideation via knowledge base manipulation. Cognit. Comput. **8**, 153–174 (2016)
11. Llano, M.T., Hepworth, R., Colton, S., Charnley, J., Gow, J.: Automating fictional ideation using conceptnet. In: Proceedings of the AISB14 Symposium on Computational Creativity, London, UK, 1–4 April 2014
12. Mulder, M.P., Nijholt, A.: Humour research: State of the art. Technical report, University of Twente, Enschede, The Netherlands
13. Nijholt, A.: Conversational agents and the construction of humorous acts. In: Nishida, T. (ed.) Conversational Informatics: An Engineering Approach, chap. 2, pp. 21–47. Wiley, Chicester (2007)

14. Nijholt, A.: Towards humor modelling and facilitation in smart environments. In: Ahram, T., Karwowski, W., Marek, T. (eds.) Proceedings of the 5th International Conference on Applied Human Factors and Ergonomics (AHFE 2014), Krakow, Poland, pp. 2992–3006, July 2014
15. Nijholt, A.: Humor techniques: from real world and game environments to smart environments. In: Streitz, N., Markopoulos, P. (eds.) DAPI 2015. LNCS, vol. 9189, pp. 659–670. Springer, Heidelberg (2015)
16. Nixon, P., Dobson, S., Lacey, G.: Managing smart environments. In: Workshop on Software Engineering for Wearable and Pervasive Computing, Limerick, Ireland (2000)
17. Ritchie, G.: The Linguistic Analysis of Jokes. Routledge, London (2004)
18. Ritchie, G.: Describing verbally expressed humour. In: Proceedings of the Symposium on Time for AI and Society, AISB 2000, Edinburgh (2000)
19. Shen, W., Norrie, D.: Facilitator, mediator or autonomous agents. In: Proceedings of the Second International Workshop on CSCW in Design, Bangkok, Thailand, pp. 119–124, November 1997
20. Valitutti, A., Veale, T.: Inducing an ironic effect in automated tweets. In: Proceedings of the 6th International Conference on Affective Computing and Intelligent Interaction (ACII 2015), Xi'an, China, pp. 153–159, 21–24 September 2015
21. Veale, T.: Coming good and breaking bad: generating transformative character arcs for use in compelling stories. In: Proceedings of ICCC-2014, the 5th International Conference on Computational Creativity, Ljubljana, June 2014
22. Veale, T.: The humour of exceptional cases: jokes as compressed thought experiments. In: Feyaerts, G.B.K., Veale, T. (eds.) Cognitive Linguistics and Humor Research. Applications of Cognitive Linguistics, pp. 69–90. Mouton de Gruyter (2015)
23. Veale, T., Valitutti, A., Li, G.: Twitter: the best of bot worlds for automated wit. In: Proceedings of the 3rd International Conference on Distributed, Ambient and Pervasive Interactions, HCI International, Los Angeles, CA, USA, 2–7 August 2015
24. Veale, T., Valitutti, A.: A world with or without you - terms and conditions may apply. In: AAAI Fall Symposium on Modeling Changing Perspectives: Re-conceptualizing Sensory-Motor Experiences, Arlington, VA, USA, 13–15 November 2014

When Worlds and Scripts Collide

Tony Veale[(✉)]

School of Computer Science and Informatics,
University College Dublin, Belfield, Dublin 4, Ireland
Tony.Veale@UCD.ie

Abstract. The notion of a frame, script or situation occupies a central position in contemporary theories and computational models of humour. Specifically, humour is hypothesized to arise at the overlapping boundaries of two scripts or frames that antagonistically compete to mentally organize the same situation. At the point of divergence, the cognitive agent finds that the chosen script or frame no longer offers an adequate explanation of the situation, and so must switch between scripts, or shift between frames, to achieve an understanding of why the situation has evolved the way it has. However, even banal situations are often complex enough to require the interaction of multiple scripts, yet most situations are not occasions of humour, so the humorous jolt that one gets from a sudden change of perspective must be the exception rather the norm in the script-based comprehension of a situation. Rather than attempt to model the humorously exceptional cases directly, as though they represented the totality of script-based understanding, we consider here the problem of modeling the blending of scripts more generally, to understand how and why one script can give way to another in the course of story comprehension and generation. With a computational framework in place, we can begin to explore the fundamental differences between, on the one hand, script blends that are relatively seamless, and on the other, those that create sufficient friction to be viewed as humorous. We conduct our exploration in the context of a metaphor-generating Twitterbot, *@Metaphor Magnet*, that is now being turned into a spinner of mini-narratives.

Keywords: Scripts · Blends · Twitter · Twitterbot · Metaphor · Change · Narrative

1 Running with the blend

Whenever we aim to capture the drama and the comedy of the human condition on the stage or on the screen, we first set out to find the right script. It is not surprising then that when scholars set out to model our cognitive faculties for understanding all this comedy and drama, they also look to the notion of a script, not as it is written on the page but as it is abstracted in the mind. Because these mental scripts (in the sense of Raskin 1985) capture the regularities of life and our experiences of the world, they allow us to explain our past and to predict our future. We thus call upon scripts to guide our behaviour whenever we order coffee, make dinner, catch a train or go on a date. Unsurprisingly, though, the best examples of scripts still come from the movies. Consider this short extract from the movie Jurassic Park, which captures an exchange

© Springer International Publishing Switzerland 2016
N. Streitz and P. Markopoulos (Eds.): DAPI 2016, LNCS 9749, pp. 380–391, 2016.
DOI: 10.1007/978-3-319-39862-4_35

between the park's creator, John Hammond, and a wry mathematician, Ian Malcolm, who has been asked to evaluate the park's viability before it is opened to the public. The park of the title is populated with genetically-engineered dinosaurs, and so the dialogue takes place against a backdrop of carnivorous mayhem and destruction:

John Hammond: All major theme parks have delays. When they opened
                      Disneyland in 1956, nothing worked!
Dr. Ian Malcolm: Yeah, but, John, if The Pirates of the Caribbean breaks down, the
                      pirates don't eat the tourists

At this point in the movie, nothing is working in Jurassic Park, but nothing worked in 1956 at Disneyland either, and the latter turned out to be a huge financial and cultural success. Hammond thus frames *Disneyland* as a script by focusing on the temporal sequence of events associated with its launch, its initial problems, and its eventual success. With this implicit analogy to Jurassic Park, whose launch has been plagued by unique problems of its own, Hammond predicts that his own troubled venture will follow the same script and achieve the same success. In effect, he sees *Disneyland* and *Jurassic Park* as two overlapping frames or scripts, and wants others to see the overlap too, so they might come to the same conclusions. Malcolm's rejoinder is also intended to be understood in the context of this analogy, but it is much more than an analogy. It involves mapping, yes, so that The Pirates of the Caribbean is aligned with the attractions of Jurassic Park and the pirates of the former are mapped to the dinosaurs of the latter. But the salient behaviors of the latter – such as eating people willy-nilly – are also integrated with the protagonists of the former, to generate a counterfactual image of animatronic pirates eating tourists in mouse-earred caps. In the words of Fauconnier and Turner (2002), Malcolm has created a *blend* and is now *running* it: that is, he is conducting a mental simulation to explore the emergent possibilities that were hitherto just latent in the juxtaposition of both frames or scripts.

Disneyland and Jurassic Park are very different in so many ways, but one gets no sense of these differences from Hammond's analogy, which is designed to emphasize the convergence of scripts and to downplay their divergence. Malcolm's rejoinder, in contrast, takes this convergence as given (hence his "Yeah") but gives most emphasis to the divergence (hence his "but"). Malcolm's remarks make sport of what Raskin (1985), and Attardo and Raskin (1991) call the underlying *script opposition* (SO), yet he goes further than simply pointing out the SO: he blends both scripts into a ridiculous mélange that forces Hammond (and us) to see the dramatic consequences of the SO. That Malcolm's remark is funnier than Hammond's can be attributed to this use of script overlap *and* opposition (where Hammond's has just the former), but it is his use of blending that transforms the SO into a ridiculous situation worth laughing at. This transformational effect suggests that blending accounts of frame-shifting – e.g. by Coulson (2001) – offer more than merely notational variants of the script switching accounts of Raskin (1985) and Attardo *et al.* (2002). Rather, script blending concretizes the SO at the heart of a joke in a way that a simple switch from one script to another cannot. So in this paper we present a computational account of script blending more generally, to cover blends that are seamlessly banal as well as those with enough creative friction to be seen as humorous. In the process we hope to build a solid platform to support the computational generation of the latter.

2 Related Work and Ideas

Scripts assume a protean form in modern approaches to humor. From Raskin's (1985) use of classical AI scripts – in essence, temporally-ordered narrative skeletons with roles and variables – scripts have, since Attardo *et al.* (2002), evolved into generic graph structures. This generalization turns scripts into structures not unlike the *mental spaces* of blending theory used by Coulson (2001) and Fauconnier and Turner (2002). So metaphors, which involve a juxtaposition of the schematic representations of two domains, a source and a target, can be viewed as a case of script overlap between two conflicting scripts whose SO gives us the metaphor's characteristic semantic tension. Veale (2014a) uses the *cut-up technique* to generate novel metaphors via a splicing of propositions from very different domains, propositions that are chosen to maximize rather than to minimize the boundary friction between each domain. Such metaphors can themselves be viewed as scripts, allowing a computational system to generate high-friction juxtapositions of conflicting metaphors for the very same topic. Veale *et al.* (2015) demonstrate how the @*MetaphorMagnet* Twitterbot of Veale (2014a) harvests metaphorical schemas – such as *history is a line* and *history is a chain* – from Web corpora, and treats them as conflicting scripts to generate provocative tweets like "@war_poet *says history is a straight line*; @war_prisoner *says it is a coiled chain*". As described in Veale (2015a), the bot also invents its own aptly-named interlocutors (such as @war_poet and @war_prisoner) to espouse the conflicting positions and thus wrap an additional layer of social conflict around the underlying SO. But linguistic and rhetorical style can also be viewed as a script, inasmuch as it brings with it a rich set of norms and expectations. Veale (2015b) takes its cue from Raymond Queneau's famous *Exercises in Style*, an Oulipo-inspired exploration of the role of textual style in shaping meaning in varied ways to evoke alternating responses in the reader, from pathos to detachment to laughter. By giving @*MetaphorMagnet* a diversity of voices with which to frame its metaphorical outputs – ranging from the philosophical to the religious to the cynical to the childish – Veale (2015b) shows how humorous conflict can often be created between the concept level of a tweet and its linguistic rendering.

Twitter offers fertile ground to humans and machines alike for this kind of stylistic blend, while the concision required of tweets ensures that such blends are often short, concentrated doses of verbal ingenuity. The comedian Patton Oswalt has initiated a sequence of tweets with the tag #**JamesEllroyStarWars** that elicits the best examples of this kind of blend, by encouraging followers to blend plot points from the film *Star Wars* with the distinctive, argot-laden and free-flowing style of Amerian crime writer James Ellroy (noted for *L.A. Confidential*). Some typical tweets include "*Obi-Wan was preaching that Jedi beatnik bebop while an imperial cruiser counted the hairs on our backsides*" and "*Leia kissed Luke on the mouth. Deep down she knew he was her brother, but she grooved on it.*" Another trending tag that encourages stylistic blends is #**ThingsJesusNeverSaid**. This tag elicits pseudo-religious aphorisms with a big dollop of irony, such as "*Love your enemy unless it makes you uncomfortable*" and "*Blessed* *are the corporations, for they shall be called my constituents.*" So stylistic blends must have something interesting to say, while parodying the most identifiable verbal mannerisms of a well-known communicator. In this vein, *@MetaphorMagnet* puts the essence of authorial voices such as *Yoda*, the *Hulk, Donald Trump* and *Jesus Christ* into script form, and for the content of its tweets – the second script in its blend – it uses the outputs of Veale (2014b)'s *Flux Capacitor*, to which we turn next. As a taster, this tweet from *@MetaphorMagnet* aims to capture the essence of *Mr. Trump*:

Tweet 1:	Blessed are the broke tramps that get jobs, for they shall inherit empires and become wealthy kings.
	#ThingsTrumpNeverSaid#Tramp=#King

3   Scripts We Live By

Scripts can vary widely in their temporal scale and event resolution. We can thus use scripts to model almost anything, from the actions of sub-atomic particles to the growth of the universe and most everything in between. We often conceive of scripts as bundles of linked actions for everyday events such as using an ATM or ordering lunch, but scripts can be just as useful in organizing our understanding of events that can last a lifetime. A glance at the obituaries page in any newspaper reveals our desire to impose a linear narrative on a person's life, allowing us to appreciate the life less ordinary as a departure from the scripted norm. From an AI perspective, it thus makes sense to model people – or rather, *types* of people – as scripts, so as to understand their actions as either normative (script adherence) or transgressive (script violation).

To generate its condensed stories of change, Veale (2014b)'s *Flux Capacitor* system explicitly models diverse person types, or what Veale calls stereotypes, as scripts. At its core, the system rests on a large set of knowledge triples that characterize diverse kinds of person, such as *criminal, surgeon,* or *clown,* via their various actions, settings and goals. The *Flux Capacitor* tags these triples with integers to impose upon them a partial ordering, to indicate, for instance, that surgeons must enroll in medical school (step 0) before they can study medicine (step 1) and graduate with a medical degree (step 2). Any triple may be tagged in this way with an integer from 0 to 9, where: 0 indicates a category-entry action (e.g. enrolling in medical school, joining the circus); 9 indicates a category-departure action (e.g. losing one's medical license, getting fired from the circus); 5 indicates steps that one associates with a category instance in full flight (operating on patients as a qualified surgeon or performing pratfalls as a circus clown); 1...4 indicates an action leading up to this mid-life high; and 6...8 marks those actions that take one a step closer to a final category exit (such as losing one's sense of humour or being sued for malpractice). In the course of one's scripted life, a person is expected to progress from 0 to 9, passing through a series of intermediate steps that draw one fully into a category before inexorably pushing one out again. To generate a normative plot, the *Flux Capacitor* need only sample its set of triples for a given stereotype to a form a chain of successive actions linking any step 0 to a step 9.

But the life less ordinary does not progress from 0 to 9 within the same category. Rather, just as interesting people deviate from the norm, interesting characters deviate from the script by jumping the rails from one category into another. Ebenezer Scrooge goes from a "grasping, scraping, clutching, covetous old sinner" to secret Santa in the space of *A Christmas Carol*, jumping categories from misanthropist to philanthropist to find himself following a very different script. Ben Hur goes from Jewish prince to Roman slave to Arab horseman to ace charioteer in the space of his eponymous epic, while Maximus Decimus Meridius follows a similar, script-hopping trajectory from Roman general to Spanish slave to Roman hero in the film *Gladiator*. (Gregor Samsa starts Kafka's *Metamorphosis* as a "giant vermin," but things go downhill from there.) Entertaining plot twists turn hunters into prey, underdogs into champions, friends into enemies, sinners into saints, or members of one category into something else entirely. To maximize incongruity, the *Flux Capacitor* shunts a character into categories and scripts that dramatically flip at least one of its key qualities, such as *strong→weak* or *rich→poor*, as in *Tramp* to *King* above, or in this example from @*MetaphorMagnet*:

Tweet 2a:	How might an unpopular geek become a venerated founder?
Tweet 2b:	What if unpopular geeks were to acquire social graces, start businesses and become venerated founders? #Geek=#Founder

@*MetaphorMagnet*, as a user of the *Flux Capacitor*, here chooses *geek* and *founder* to serve as the start and end categories of its unnamed character: geeks are typically *unpopular* and lacking in social graces, while founders are very often *venerated*. The scripts for both are stitched together by linking an exit event for *geek* (acquiring social graces, a step 9 action) to an entry event for *founder* (*starting a business*, at step 0). In the next section we set about motivating this change of script with an inciting event.

4 Slow-Burn Transformations

Kafka's *Metamorphosis* is an exception rather than the norm when it comes to literary transformations. *Gregor Samsa*, his unfortunate protagonist, goes from beloved son to hated vermin in an off-stage transformation before the story even begins. This radical change remains unexplained to the bitter end, in what is itself a *meta*-plot point. But most dramatic changes in characterization are motivated by observable plot actions, whether in the actions of others (a mentor, a lover, an enemy) or in the actions of the unstable protagonist himself. So *Walter White*, the meth-cooking anti-hero at the heart of *Breaking Bad*, goes from caring chemistry teacher to ruthless drug lord when he learns that he has terminal cancer and no longer has anything to lose. To motivate the movement of a character from one stereotypical category (and script track) to another, our system must introduce an inciting event that spurs the character to switch tracks. This incitement may come from another character that exercises a strong influence on our protagonist, or it may arise gradually, in the manner of a character's core actions. Let's look at the latter case first, using these @*MetaphorMagnet* tweets as examples:

Tweet 3a	Tweet 3b	Tweet 3c
#Monotony is when you:	#Gore is when you:	#Cruelty is when you:
1. Invent a fiction	1. Go on a trip	1. Go on an exploration
2. Become a storyteller	2. Become a holiday maker	2. Become a searcher
3. Tell monotonous stories	3. Enjoy bloody trips	3. Conduct cruel searches
4. Turn into a drudge	4. Turn into a killer	4. Turn into a sadist
#Storyteller=#Drudge	#Holiday_maker=#Killer	#Searcher=#Sadist

The skeletal structure of these stories is necessitated by Twitter's 140-character limit, yet a *bare bones* rendering is sufficient for each to unfussily tell its tale. In each story, our unnamed protagonist hops from category to category and script to script, opening with a *step 0* action from a source script A that permits entry into the category of A. The next stage in each plot is now a blended action that moves the actions of the source category into a target domain B. Thus, though it is in the nature of story-tellers to tell stories and it falls on drudges to perform monotonous tasks, a blend of both of these behaviors can be observed in the action *tell monotonous stories*. For if one tells enough stories monotonously, the act of story-telling becomes a chore for speaker and listener alike, causing our hero to slowly become a drudge. Two pieces of information are key to arriving at this insight: The first, that drudges typically do monotonous things, is to be found in the system's script for *drudge*. The second, that stories can themselves be monotonous to tell, is a domain-bridging possibility that is found in neither script but only acquired via experience of the world. In @*MetaphorMagnet*'s case, the outside world is experienced vicariously through the Google Web n-grams (Brants and Franz 2006), which suggest to the system, via the bigram "monotonous stories" (*frequency = 41*), that telling stories can sometimes be like performing chores. In the words of Fauconnier and Turner (2002), @*MetaphorMagnet* recruits the idea that stories may be monotonous as a means of blending together two competing frames.

The stories above squeeze as much as they can into Twitter's minimal containers, framing their 4-act plots with a moralizing label such as "#Cruelty is when you ___". But this additional real-estate can also be used to add an additional 5th act to our plots:

Tweet 4a	Tweet 4b
1. Apply for a scholarship	1. Enroll in a university
2. Become a student	2. Become a student
3. Undergo bizarre educations	3. Undergo brutal exams
4. Turn into a freak	4. Turn into a beast
5. Lose your scholarship	5. Flunk out of university

These 5-act tweets leave no room for adornment with hashtags of the form #A=#B, though the meanings remain clear in each case. Each mini-narrative shares the same skeletal structure: 1. an entry action for category A; 2. a statement announcing the protagonist's arrival in category A; 3. a blended action transposing a central event in category/script A into the domain of category/script B; 4. a statement announcing the protagonist's arrival in category B; 5. a subsequent departure from category A. Note how each tweet pairs a category-entry action with a category-exit action that governs the same very object (i.e., *scholarship* in tweet 4a and *university* in tweet 4b). This minimizes the complexity of each narrative and also yields a satisfying symmetry, yet this symmetry can itself be subverted to introduce more ambiguity and nuance. If we switch the fifth act in these tweets, ending tweet 4a with *Flunk out of university* and ending tweet 4b with *Lose your scholarship*, the reader would still infer when reading tweet 4a that the protagonist's grant application was successful, though ultimately for naught, and would just as likely infer in tweet 4b that the protagonist had earned a scholarship that was later squandered through freakish abandon. Nor is the system forced to conclude either tweet negatively, for it might just as easily have chosen the exit action *Graduate from university* for the fifth act of each. Though this would seem to yield an incongruous ending, it is an incongruity that readers can easily resolve by inferring that brutish abnormalities are no barrier to academic success; indeed, as our protagonist *undergoes bizarre educations*, it may instead prove to be an advantage. In short, the system has a wealth of combinations to explore, even for a short tweet.

Though Twitter gives @*MetaphorMagnet* very little room to maneouvre, it *is* possible to slow the transformation of a protagonist from an instance of *A* to an instance of *B*. The following tweets do not assume an exit from category *A*, but a blend of *A* and *B*:

Tweet 5a	Tweet 5b	Tweet 5c
#Reformer=#Loser	#Mother=#Cynic	#Artist=#Sinner
1. Fight for reform	1. Give birth to a daughter	1. Develop an aesthetic
2. Become a reformer	2. Become a mother	2. Become an artist
3. Launch failed crusades	3. Nurture bitter sons	3. Create illicit pictures
4. Become a failed reformer	4. Become a bitter mother	4. Become an illicit artist
5. Get called a "loser"	5. Get called a "criminal"	5. Get called a "sinner"

So our protagonist remains in category *A* throughout, yet executes the actions of a member of this category in the manner of someone from category *B*. The transition between acts 3 and 4 is left deliberately vague in each mini-narrative, to hint at further off-stage actions that eventually lead others to brand the protagonist a member of "*B*." @*MetaphorMagnet* adds the scare quotes to instill doubt and create ironic distance.

5   Ill-met by Moonlight, Ill-treated by Fate

If there is a moral to these mini-narratives, it is that one can unwittingly wander from one domain into another, and jump from one script track onto another, without ever even trying: simply carrying out the prescribed actions of the script for one category of person can lead one to eventually see a very different person in the mirror. This is possible because our categories overlap (yes, some academics *are* also freaks) and our scripts, like railway lines, often cross over at regular junctions. We might go so far as to argue that this is one of the functions of jokes more generally: jokes reveal to us the fragility of our category systems and show us how easily we can come unstuck when adhering to the received – and seemingly sound, albeit rigid – wisdom of others. If the mini-narratives of the previous section illustrate how easy it is for us to stray across category boundaries, the following show that we are just as often led by the nose:

Tweet 6a	Tweet 6b	Tweet 6c
1. Record a song	1. Be shunned by society	1. Learn a language
2. Become an artiste	2. Become an ogre	2. Become a linguist
3. Marry a leader	3. Marry a nobleman	3. Marry a hardliner
4. Found an organization and become a leader too	4. Inherit an entitlement	4. Embrace extremism
5. Record the *song of power*	5. Be shunned by the *society of entitlement*	5. Learn the *language of extremism*

In the three tweets above, the inciting incident that leads our protagonist to stray from category *A* into category *B* is marriage to a persuasive member of category *B*. In principle, a member of any category of person can marry a member of any other, but the narratives here choose a pair of categories that are already yoked by a metaphor. The result is a script-switching narrative that is intuitively sensible yet which retains the semantic tension of the unifying metaphor. Like the blended action of previous tweets, this metaphor is itself suggestive of a blend of both categories. So, in tweet 6a we see singers and leaders united by the notion of a *song of power*, a 3-gram mined from the Google n-grams; likewise, ogres and noblemen are united by the idea of a *society of entitlement* in tweet 6b, another Web 3-gram, though ogres and noblemen will each experience this society differently (one is shunned, the other welcomed); and in tweet 6c, the Web 3-gram *language of extremism* suggests a blend that allows a linguist to become a hardliner (on linguistic matters, perhaps). In effect, the 3-gram suggests a conceptual marriage that mirrors the narrative marriage of story characters.

But this conceptual marriage can also be realized literally if our protagonists adapt their script *A* actions to reflect the influence of a new spouse from category *B*, as in:

Tweet 7a	Tweet 7b
1. Develop an aesthetic	1. Attract a fold
2. Become an artist	2. Become a preacher
3. Marry a lunatic in your milieu	3. Marry a realist in your church
4. Create absurd juxtapositions together	4. Nurture rational flocks together
5. Lose your mind too	5. Succumb to cynicism too

Act 4 in each case is now a blend, of an *action* from *A* and a *manner of action* from *B*. Regardless of how this blended action is constructed, the blend is enough to motivate the switch from script *A* to script *B* without having to marry off our protagonist. In the terminology of the GTVH (Attardo and Raskin 1991), *marriage* and *blended action* are merely two logical mechanisms among many for achieving a meaningful fusion of scripts. As shown by these @*MetaphorMagnet* tweets, the latter can work on its own:

Tweet 8a	Tweet 8b
1. Convert to a religion	1. Lack humility
2. Become a proselyte	2. Become a snob
3. Convert to the *religion of doubt*	3. Lack the *humility of faith*
4. Develop doubts	4. Find faith
5. Renounce God and become an atheist	5. Establish a following and become an apostle

Notice that resolution is only partial in these cases, for what do we mean (and what do Web users mean) whenever we talk of the *religion of doubt* (a Google 3-gram with a frequency of 46) or the *humility of faith* (a 3-gram with a larger frequency of 163)? @*MetaphorMagnet* leaves those questions to readers to answer for themselves. It is sufficient for its purposes that these 3-grams have a foot in two domains at once and thus allow a narrative to segue naturally from script *A* to script *B* with a single action.

Twitter's 140-character limitation encourages the tweeting of sound-bites, bon mots and other short texts that one hopes will *go viral*, in the fashion of an internet meme. Our generator of blended narratives can also tap into this fondness for *memes* – short textual patterns (typically accompanied by a stock image) that vary from use to use but which retain a recognizable character throughout. One such meme is the rueful expression "Join the army they said. It'll be fun they said" which originated in the world of online gaming (specifically, *Company of Heroes* via *Warcraft* 2) and now adorns a myriad offbeat images on the internet with suitably doleful captions. The following shows @*MetaphorMagnet*'s use of the meme to blend two scripts into one:

Tweet 9:	"Join a delegation," they said.
	"It'll make a skilled diplomat of you," they said.
	Turns out I joined a delegation of clumsy children!

The two scripts are, of course, that for *diplomat* and for *child*, which differ insofar as they suggest the stereotypical properties *skillful* and *clumsy* respectively. Once again, the Google Web n-grams provide the necessary glue to yoke these two ideas, and scripts, together: specifically, it is the 3-gram "delegation of children" (frequency = 164) that allows @*MetaphorMagnet* to equate *diplomat,* the stereotypical member of a *delegation*, to the kinds of member that are explicitly provided in the text, *children*.

The Aesopian fable provides another support structure for forcing two character types together, allowing one to take on salient qualities of the other and thus become a member of a blended category with its own blended script. @*MetaphorMagnet* uses a knowledge-base of animals and their stereotypical qualities and affordances to wrap its mini-narratives in two-tweet mini-fables such as the following:

Tweet 10a:	"I want to be a fantasist," barked a neurotic poodle.
	"I want to escape from reality too," spat a cobra.
	#Fantasist=#Fundamentalist
Tweet 10b:	So the cobra helped the neurotic poodle to nurture a hateful delusion.
	And that is how the neurotic poodle became a fundamentalist.

The logical mechanism at work here might be called *unhelpful helper*. A protagonist with the appropriate qualities to be a representative member of category *A* accepts help from another character whose qualities are more suited to category *B*, and so, in fulfilling the script requirements of *A* becomes a representative member of *B* instead. The mechanism works best when *A* is a desirable category and *B* is a negative one:

Tweet 11a:	"I want to be a campaigner," oozed a political worm.
	"I want to be recruited by a campaign too," laughed a hyena.
	#Campaigner=#Hypocrite
Tweet 11b:	So the hyena helped the worm to launch a disreputable campaign.
	And that is how the political worm became a hypocrite.

The Aesopian rendering showcases the system's stereotypical knowledge to maximal effect, lending these mini-narratives a sense of inevitability. One cannot escape one's fate, or deny one's true nature. Yet one can at least *imagine* an exit from *B* in a tweet:

Tweet 12a:	"They say I'm acting like a nymphomaniac," shrieked an amorous skunk.
	"I'll show you how", squeeked a sewer rat.
	#Nymphomaniac=#Beggar
Tweet 12b:	The sewer rat coached the amorous skunk to enjoy a filthy lust. But the
	skunk's friends begged "Please seek treatment for your nymphomania".

6 Conclusions for the Short-Term: Messages in Very Small Bottles

The blending of stereotypical categories and narrative scripts is not so very different from William Burroughs' famed use of the *cut-up method* to generate random texts (see Veale 2014a). Except, of course, that a system such as @*MetaphorMagnet* must serve both as scissors *and* critic, to create cut-ups from its knowledge-base of scripts and their possible renderings in natural language (whether as chunks of dialogue or as declarative sentences), *and* it must also evaluate and filter the outputs, to keep the few that actually work and to reject the multitude that do not. What may seem at first to be the most pressing constraint on @*MetaphorMagnet*'s choices – Twitter's size limit on tweets – turns out to be the least vexing; indeed, it transpires that there are many ways of using this constraint to a system's advantage. For Twitter users expect tweets to suggest much more than could ever be explicitly said in 140 characters, and eagerly bridge the chasm between what is expressly stated and what is presumably intended. Users who must engage their imaginations as a matter of course on Twitter do not feel short-changed by a system that asks them to put flesh on the barest of narrative bones.

The glue that ties these disjoint parts together – whether the bones of our skeleton metaphor or the text fragments of our cut-up metaphor – is the Google Web n-grams, though any large corpus of attested usage data would work just as effectively. These Web n-grams serve as *linguistic readymades*, pre-built and pre-tested ways of linking two separate domains via a single short phrase. It matters not that a system may not understand the precise meaning of these phrases, as their meaning is intended to be allusive and opaque rather than definitive and transparent. Indeed, it is likely that human consumers of these readymades may themselves be unable to give an exact interpretation to them, but that is the point of language that is allusive, poetic or witty: it often promises more than it delivers, yet rewards any efforts to plumb its depths.

We are currently in the process of evaluating @*MetaphorMagnet*'s approach to script blending, with experiments to elicit human feedback on the composition of the various acts in a narrative skeleton. Our full findings will be reported in a subsequent paper, though we shall give a brief preview here. Test subjects, paid volunteers all, are asked to complete cloze tests via the crowd-sourcing platform *CrowdFlower*. The test materials comprise five-act narratives from @*MetaphorMagnet*, in which one of the five acts is blank. The following is a sample test stimulus as shown to the subjects:

Fill in the missing **step 4** in this story,	Using the most apt action from this list:
1. *Develop your intellect*	4a. *Turn into a troll*
2. *Become a genius*	4b. *Turn into a bureaucrat*
3. *Nurture dispassionate minds*	4c. *Turn into a fascist*
4. _____	4d. *Turn into a sectarian*
5. *Lose your wits*	4e. *Turn into a harlot*

Initial experimental results are encouraging, and indicate that test subjects naturally gravitate toward @*MetaphorMagnet*'s choice for a given act and eschew the random distractors. This speaks to the design of its knowledge-base and to the soundness of its strategy for splicing narratives from this knowledge. However, an exception to this trend is to be found in act four, the act that announces the protagonist's arrival in category **B**. Though the expected answer in the sample stimulus above is *Turn into a bureaucrat*, test subjects actually prefer *Turn into a fascist* by a significant margin. Act four thus seems to be the most subjective of the five acts, for at least two reasons: first, it follows the blended action of act three, which is still rooted in script **A**, before the protagonist has overtly switched to category **B**; secondly, act four is essentially an act of name-calling, so we suspect that the most extreme epithets win out if they seem at all apt. *Fascist* is a far more damning label than *Bureaucrat*, though bureaucrats are often described as though they truly were fascists, and real fascists often make much of their bureaucratic prowess in making the trains run on time. It seems that sentiment and aptness together dictate the preferred choice for act four, and so we shall conduct further tests of this hypothesis. For if verified, this hypothesis offers a rather obvious strategy for heightening the drama and humour of @*MetaphorMagnet*'s script blends. Though our scripts may never truly *collide*, they can embrace each other with passion.

Acknowledgements. This research was supported by the EC project *WHIM: The What-If Machine* (http://www.whim-project.eu/). The experiments briefly previewed here are currently being conducted in collaboration with another *WHIM* researcher, Alessandro Valitutti.

References

Raskin, V.: Semantic Mechanisms of Humor. Reidel, Dordrecht (1985)

Attardo, S., Raskin, V.: Script theory revis(it)ed: joke similarity and joke representation model. Humor Int. J. Humor Res. **4**(3), 293–347 (1991)

Coulson, S.: Semantic Leaps: Frame-Shifting and Conceptual Blending in Meaning Construction. Cambridge University Press, Cambridge (2001)

Attardo, S., Hempelmann, C.F., Di Maio, S.: Script oppositions and logical mechanisms: modeling incongruities and their resolutions. Humor Int. J. Humor Res. **15**(1), 3–46 (2002)

Fauconnier, F., Turner, T.: The Way We Think. Basic Books, New York (2002)

Veale, T.: Running with scissors: cut-ups, boundary friction and creative reuse. In: Lamontagne, L., Plaza, E. (eds.) ICCBR 2014. LNCS, vol. 8765, pp. 3–16. Springer, Heidelberg (2014a)

Veale, T., Valitutti, A., Li, G.: Twitter: the best of bot worlds for automated wit. In: Proceedings of HCII-2015, the 17th International Conference on Human-Computer Interaction (Distributed, Ambient and Pervasive Interactions), Los Angeles, California, August 2015

Veale, T. Fighting words and antagonistic worlds. In: Proceedings of the 3rd Workshop on Metaphor in NLP, at NAACL-2015, Denver, Colorado, 5 June 2015

Veale, T.: Game of tropes: exploring the placebo effect in computational creativity. In: Proceedings of ICCC-2015, the 6th International Conference on Computational Creativity, Park City, Utah, 31 May–3 June 2015

Veale, T.: Coming good and breaking bad: generating transformative character arcs for use in compelling stories. In: Proceedings of ICCC-2014, the 5th International Conference on Computational Creativity, Ljubljana, Slovenia (2014b)

Brants, T., Franz, A.: Web 1T 5-gram Version 1. Linguistic Data Consortium (2006)

Smart Cities and Communities

On Feasibility of Crowdsourced Mobile Sensing for Smarter City Life

Kenro Aihara[1,2]([✉]), Piao Bin[1], Hajime Imura[3], Atsuhiro Takasu[1,2],
and Yuzuru Tanaka[3]

[1] National Institute of Informatics, 2-1-2 Hitotsubashi,
Chiyoda-ku, Tokyo 101-8430, Japan
{kenro.aihara,piaobin,takasu}@nii.ac.jp
[2] The Graduate University for Advanced Studies, Hayama, Japan
[3] Hokkaido University, N-13, W-8, Sapporo, Hokkaido 060-8628, Japan
{hajime,tanaka}@meme.hokudai.ac.jp

Abstract. This paper introduces the ongoing project that aims to
develop a mobile sensing framework to collect sensor data reflecting
personal-scale, or microscopic, roadside phenomena by crowdsourcing
and also using social big data, such as traffic, climate, and contents of
social network services like Twitter. To collect them, smartphone applications are provided. One of the typical applications is a driving recorder
that collects not only sensor data but also recorded videos from the
driver's view. To extract specific roadside phenomena, collected data are
integrated and analyzed at the service platform.

The proposed smartphone application can be replaced with appliances
because of its advantages: (1) ordinary appliances work stand-alone,
which means that local storage is limited; the application is connected
to the cloud, (2) appliances are not cheep, at least users must pay for
it; the application is free, (3) appliances only store driving records; the
application can get feedback from the service. The authors expect that
these advantages can be accepted by citizen as an incentive to use it. To
reveal how effective such function is for users' motivation, an experiment
and a survey are conducted with our prototyped service. As a result,
most of the users accepted the function as attractive to use.

1 Introduction

Cyber-physical systems (CPS) seek to provide users with optimal control of the
world they correspond with by modeling physical space in cyber space, coupled
with the use of related databases. More than big data systems, social CPS is the
operating system of urban society. It provides a user environment that supports
the agency of people in decision-making. The need for social CPS in building
sustainable, safe, and secure urban societies is growing. The prerequisite basic
technologies are maturing rapidly. Remaining efforts include opening data silos
maintained by the private sector and the government, and analyzing massive,
complex data that cannot be completely described by a single monolithic model.
Social CPS is filled with tantalizing challenges for research and development.

© Springer International Publishing Switzerland 2016
N. Streitz and P. Markopoulos (Eds.): DAPI 2016, LNCS 9749, pp. 395–404, 2016.
DOI: 10.1007/978-3-319-39862-4_36

(a) summer   (b) winter

(c) winter: heavy snowfall   (d) winter: surface freezing

Fig. 1. Comparison of road conditions in summer (a) and winter (b,c,d). The road situations vary hour after hour, especially in winter.

This paper overviews the ongoing project of Social CPS, which aims to develop a mobile sensing framework to collect sensor data reflecting personal-scale, or microscopic, roadside phenomena by crowdsourcing and also using social big data, such as traffic, climate, and contents of social network services like Twitter.

2   Background

2.1   Civil Problems: A Situation in Sapporo

Sapporo has about 1.91 million citizens and 5.8 m average annual snowfall. The average amount of maximum snow depth reaches about one meter in February. It spends more than 15 billion Japanese yen every winter for the road management such as snow plowing and removing. The snowfall in winter cause significant changes to road condition shown in Fig. 1.

The traffic of winter road in Sapporo is strongly affected by amount of snowfall, snow depth, temperature, frozen road surface, traffic volume, snow plowing condition and other road conditions. For the analysis of dynamically changing traffic and road conditions in an urban-scale area, probe-car data may play the most important role. Inherently they are real time data, and have the potential to cover urban-scale areas. They can tell us not only about dynamically changing traffic and road conditions, but also about people's dynamically changing mobility demands and activities. Probe car data is expected to be used as fundamental to monitor and estimate the urban-scale dynamic phenomena of traffic and road conditions of all the road links, and also to monitor the snow plowing and removal operations.

2.2 Crowdsourcing for Civil Problems

The term "crowdsourcing" was described by Jeff Howe in 2006 [5] and defined that crowdsourcing is the act of taking a task traditionally performed by a designated agent and outsourcing it by making an open call to an undefined but large group of people [6]. This can take the form of peer-production, but is also often undertaken by sole individuals [4].

The concept of smart cities can be viewed as a recognition of the growing importance of digital technologies for a competitive position and a sustainable future [10]. Although the smart city-agenda, which grants ICTs with the task to achieve strategic urban development goals such as improving the life quality of its citizens and creating sustainable growth, has gained a lot of momentum in recent years.

Tools such as smartphones offer the opportunity to facilitate co-creation between citizens and authority. Such tools have the potential to organize and stimulate communication between citizens and authority, and allow citizens to participate in the public domain [1,11]. One example is FixMyStreet[1] that enables citizens to report broken streetlights and potholes [7]. It is important that these approaches will not succeed automatically and social standards like trust, openness, and consideration of mutual interests have to be guaranteed to make citizen engaging in the public domain challenging.

Waze[2] is another crowdsourcing service to collect data of traffic. Even though Waze provides users to traffic information collected from users and route navigation function, it seems not enough to motivate users to get involved in, because recommended routes are not as adequate as car navigation appliances, especially in Japan where such appliances are well-developed.

3 Crowedsourced Mobile Sensing and Its Applications

3.1 Overview

CPS is a promising new class of systems that deeply embed cyber capabilities in the physical world, either on humans, infrastructure or platforms, to transform interactions with the physical world [2,9]. CPS facilitates to use the information available from the physical environment. Advances in the cyber world such as communications, networking, sensing, computing, storage, and control, as well as in the physical world such as materials and hardware, are rapidly converging to realize this class of highly collaborative computational systems that are reliant on sensors and actuators to monitor and effect change. In this technology-rich scenario, real-world components interact with cyberspace via sensing, computing and communication elements.

Social CPS focuses human aspects in the parallel world because human is not only subject to exploit such systems but also object to be observed and

---

[1] https://www.fixmystreet.com/.
[2] https://www.waze.com/.

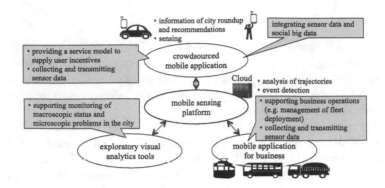

Fig. 2. Overview of the proposed mobile sensing system

be affected by the systems. Information flows from the physical to the cyber world, and vice-versa, adapting the converged world to human behavior and social dynamics. Indeed humans are at the center of this converged world since information about the context in which they operate is the key element to adapt the CPS applications and services.

Figure 2 overviews proposed systems for crowdsourced mobile sensing. At the center, cloud as a service platform is located. Above the platform, several applications are being developed.

3.2 Platform Service

The service platform facilitates applications not only to receive the transmission of data from applications but also to provide ordinary functions for location-based services, such as nearest and up-to-date places. The platform also plays a role to integrate collected data and social big data, such as traffic, climate information, and contents of social network services, and then analyze them to extract specific phenomena in the city, especially on the roadside.

Since the sensing data can be very large, data compression for reducing the storage and efficient processing are important for the crowedsourced sensing platform. However, the compression and analysis algorithms have been often developed independently, and the compressed data need to be expanded before analysis, which requires additional processing. To solve this problem, the authors are studying a platform where the sensing data is analyzed in compressed form. For this purpose, the authors study to apply the succinct data structure (e.g., [3]) to manage map information as well as location-related sensing data itself.

Various statistical analysis and data mining algorithms are applied to sensing data analysis. Among them, outlier detection is useful to detect events and anomalous situations. The authors developed an incident detection method from traffic flow data [8]. In this study, the authors first built a statistical model representing velocity distribution of cars for each road segment by exploiting large training data. Then, the authors compare velocity of a car passing through the segment with the model. If the velocity is a outlier with respect to the velocity distribution model, the authors judge the road segment is in a anomalous situation. Because of large amount of sensing data, the authors can use a complex model and achieve high detection rate [8].

Crowedsourced sensing data can be biased because users who provide the data are not always typical ones. When using a statistical model for the analysis as in our incident detection method, the authors need bias-correction.

3.3   Mobile Applications for End Users

For citizen as an end user, a mobile application is being developed upon the platform. Although the main target user is driver, the application can be used by pedestrians using public transport, such as subway and bus.

For drivers, driving recording function, or video event data recorder, is provided. Users mount such recording appliance to dash or even to windshield to record the behavior of the car during the driving, such as trajectory (a sequence of locations with time stamp), accelerations, speeds, and video. One of the biggest motivations to use such appliances is that they use records as reference back to accident scene. Users, therefore, should use the appliance whenever they drive. The authors expect that the proposed smartphone application can be replaced with appliances. The advantages are as follows:

1. Ordinary appliances work stand-alone, which means that local storage is limited; the application is connected to the cloud.
2. Appliances are not cheep, at least users must pay for it; the application is free.
3. Appliances only store driving records; the application can get feedback from the service.

The authors believe that these advantages can be acceped by citizen as an incentive to get involved in it.

The function of driving recorder has positive features to collect data reflecting roadside situations. One is that the data is collected whenever they drive. Power consumption is not critical because power can be supplied from the car. And also drivers' smartphones are not manipulated while they drive.

The detail of the driving recorder application is described in Sect. 4.

3.4   Applications for Civil Administration

In our prior study on CPS-IIP project, the authors have implemented smartphone-based mobile sensing applications for city buses and snowplowing cars respectively to investigate the influence of snowfall and snow removal operations on traffic. The experimental field is shown in Fig. 3(d). Mobile sensing system for buses is important to collect periodic and continuous road traffic information. The authors have implemented 20 bus-sensing system in cooperation with Hokkaido Chuo Bus, one of the bus companies operating city bus

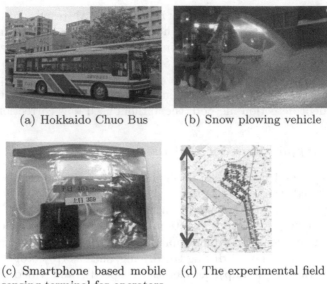

(a) Hokkaido Chuo Bus   (b) Snow plowing vehicle

(c) Smartphone based mobile   (d) The experimental field
sensing terminal for operators

Fig. 3. Chuo bus, snow plowing vehicle, and smartphone based mobile sensing terminal for operators.

service in Sapporo (Fig. 3(c)). The bus probe sensing data is useful for periodic and continuous monitoring of major lifeline routes. Meanwhile, the sensing system for snow plowing and removing vehicles is useful for monitoring snow removal operations. Both sensing system collects car speed, bearing, latitude and longitude by GPS. However, each of both system has individual information. The bus probe system has three-axis acceleration, route information and other operating information. On the other hand, the snowplowing car probe system has an operating type information (e.g. snow plowing or snow removing). Therefore, it is important to develop unified platform for mobile sensing, and it facilitates the deploying several applications for operation monitoring.

4   "Drive Around-the-Corner.": A Driving Recorder Application

The authors have developed and provides a driving recorder service called "Drive around-the-corner." since February 2015. The application got open to the public in February 2016[3]. Drive around-the-corner., Drive ATC for short, has the function of collecting behavior logs and posts of events and delivering information around current position.

---

[3] https://itunes.apple.com/app/drive-around-the-corner./id1053216595.

Fig. 4. Mounting smartphones on car.

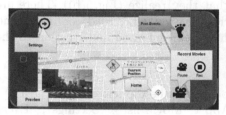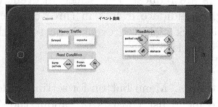

(a) Main Screen   (b) Post Events

Fig. 5. "Drive: around-the-corner." application. Traffic information, events posted from users, events extracted from sensor data, and footprints are shown in map of main screen.

The service can be accessed via iOS application. Before driving, users mount their own smartphone and connect a cable for power supply if neccessary (Fig. 4), and then start recording in the application (Fig. 5). That is all to get ready to use.

While they drive and use the application, behavior logs and movies are recorded and uploaded to the service platform.

4.1 User Functions

Map with Event Information. When the Drive ATC application is invoked, it shows a map around the current position (Fig. 5(a)). Roadside events are retrieved on the service platform and get shown on the map. For example, the yellow icon is located at the center of Fig. 5(a). The icon denotes road construction and the information was posted by users of Drive ATC before.

And also footprint markers, which are placed on the locations where the user passed before, are snow as a triangle marker. The markers vary with the speed at the position. The shorter the triangle marker denotes the slower, the longer the faster.

Posting Event. To enable users to report a roadside event to others while they stop and wait for departure, the application provides the function to post an event information. After tapping the footprint marker on the top right corner,

Table 1. Collected data of Drive around-the-corner.

Type	Attributes
Location	latitude, longitude, and altitude with accuracy
Heading	true_north with accuracy
Move	speed, course
Acceleration	x, y, z
Rotation rate	x, y, z

users are requested to select an event that they realize (Fig. 5(b)). There are eight candidate events in three categories: heavy traffic, road condition, and roadblock. Selected event is posted with the current time and location to the service platform.

Settings. Menu button for settings is located at the top left corner (Fig. 5(a)). The menu list consists of "about the App", "Movie list", "Settings", "Event list", and "User account". Users can play recorded movies and also export them to the general image folder in the movie list.

4.2 Sensing Functions

User Data. The Drive ATC service collects the following user attributes:

- gender
- birth year
- zip code of home town
- email address
- nickname

The service collects these attributes at the first access.

Onboard Location and Motion Sensors. The Drive ATC application gets location and motion data from onboard sensors. While they drive and use the application, behavior logs and movies are recorded. Collected data are once pooled in the local datastore and then transmitted to the service platform. Collected data are shown in Table 1.

Movies. The Drive ATC application records two types of movies. One is to be uploaded and the other is to be saved locally. To reduce the traffic for uploading movies to the service platform, uploaded movie is intermittent and its frame rate is adapted according to the current speed of the car. For reference back to accident scene, locally saved movie in 30 fps can be used.

Table 2. Result of the survey

Question	# of answers
Motivation	
"Do you use the application instead of appliances if the application is cheaper than appliances?"	20
Attractive Functions	
Realtime information related to traffic	23
Route navigation to the destination	19
Automatic recording lifelogs that can be reviewed on the cloud	16
Sharing up-to-date posts from users	15
Requests	
Reducing size of locally saved movies	21
Reducing traffic for uploading data	17
Avoiding themal runaway	

4.3 Survey

To reveal how user functions, such as driving recording, affect users to get involved in the service, the authors conducted an experiment and collect answers to questions. 27 subjects out of over 50 participants in the experiment answered the questionnaire. The result of the question what applications they often use in Table 2.

For motivation, 20 out of 27 subjects agree that they select the application if it is cheaper than appliances. In addition, realtime traffic information collected from other users are regarded as attractive to use the application, which is not supported in appliances. The authors, therefore, believe that provided functions can perform as incentive to users to get involved in.

5   Conclusion

This paper overviewed the ongoing project that aims to develop a mobile sensing framework to collect sensor data reflecting personal-scale, or microscopic, roadside phenomena by crowdsourcing and also using social big data, such as traffic, climate, and contents of social network services like Twitter.

To make this framework effective, it is important that the system must deal with large scale data reflecting the daily life of citizens. The authors, therefore, also propose a service model to involve citizens.

The prototype mobile applications, Drive around-the-corner., has been delivered and started collecting crowdsourced data. Evaluating the methodology by using collected data is future issue.

Acknowledgment. The authors would like to thank City of Sapporo, Hokkaido Government, Hokkaido Chuo Bus Co., Ltd. for their cooperation with this research.

Part of this research was supported by the CPS-IIP Project in the research promotion program "Research and Development for the Realization of Next-Generation IT Platforms" of the Ministry of Education, Culture, Sports, Science and Technology of Japan (MEXT), "Research and Development on Fundamental and Utilization Technologies for Social Big Data" of the Commissioned Research of National Institute of Information and Communications Technology (NICT), Japan.

References

1. Amichai-Hamburger, Y.: Potential and promise of online volunteering. Comput. Human Behav. **24**(2), 544–562 (2008)
2. Conti, M., Das, S.K., Bisdikian, C., Kumar, M., Ni, L.M., Passarella, A., Roussos, G., Tröster, G., Tsudik, G., Zambonelli, F.: Looking ahead in pervasive computing: challenges and opportunities in the era of cyber-physical convergence. Pervasive Mob. Comput. **8**(1), 2–21 (2012)
3. Grossi, R., Gupta, A., Vitter, J.S.: High-order entropy-compressed text indexes. In: Proceedings of the 14th Annual ACM-SIAM Symposium on Discrete Algorithms (SODA), pp. 841–850, Philadelphia, PA, USA. Society for Industrial and Applied Mathematics (2003)
4. Howe, J.: Crowdsourcing: A definition. Tracking the Rise of the Amateur, Crowdsourcing (2006)
5. Howe, J.: The rise of crowdsourcing. Wired Mag. **14**(6), 1–4 (2006)
6. Howe, J.: Crowdsourcing: How the Power of the Crowd is Driving the Future of Business. Random House, New York (2008)
7. King, S.F., Brown, P.: Fix my street or else: using the internet to voice local public service concerns. In: Proceedings of the 1st International Conference on Theory and Practice of Electronic Governance, pp. 72–80 (2007)
8. Kinoshita, A., Takasu, A., Adachi, J.: Traffic incident detection using probabilistic topic model. In: the Workshop Proceedings of the EDBT/ICDT 2014 Joint Conference, pp. 323–330 (2014)
9. Poovendran, R.: Cyber-physical systems: close encounters between two parallel worlds. Proc. IEEE **98**(8), 1363–1366 (2010)
10. Schuurman, D., Baccarne, B., De Marez, L., Mechant, P.: Smart ideas for smart cities: investigating crowdsourcing for generating and selecting ideas for ICT innovation in a city context. J. Theor. Appl. Electron. Commer. Res. **7**(3), 49–62 (2012)
11. Stembert, N., Mulder, I.J.: Love your city! an interactive platform empowering citizens to turn the public domain into a participatory domain. In: International Conference Using ICT, Social Media and Mobile Technologies to Foster Self-Organisation in Urban and Neighbourhood Governance (2013)
12. Tanaka, Y., Sjöbergh, J., Moiseets, P., Kuwahara, M., Imura, H., Yoshida, T.: Geospatial visual analytics of traffic and weather data for better winter road management. In: Cervone, G., Lin, J., Waters, N. (eds.) Data Mining for Geoinformatics, pp. 105–126. Springer, New York (2014)

Quantitative, Qualitative, and Historical Urban Data Visualization Tools for Professionals and Stakeholders

Cody Dunne[1], Carl Skelton[2(✉)], Sara Diamond[2], Isabel Meirelles[2], and Mauro Martino[1]

[1] IBM – Watson Health – Cognitive Visualization Lab, Cambridge, USA
{cdunne,mmartino}@us.ibm.com
[2] OCAD University – Visual Analytics Lab, Toronto, Canada
carl@ultratopia.com, sdiamond@ocadu.ca,
imeirelles@faculty.ocadu.ca

Abstract. Existing technologies for transportation planning, urban design, and decision-making have not kept pace with rapid urbanization. Visualization and analysis tools can help by combining qualitative, quantitative, and historical urban data – helping experts understand the *system of systems* of the modern city. Incorporating insights from experts in several relevant fields, we have derived a performance specification for visualization tools supporting general transportation planning problems . We examine two existing technologies against the specification – Betaville and StoryFacets – and recommend adapting them as first-generation urban system analysis/planning support tools. We also suggest guidelines for the next generation of tools for transportation planning.

Keywords: Visualization · Quantitative data · Qualitative data · Historical data · Transportation planning · Urban systems · Information technology

1 Introduction

Over half of the world's population (more than three-quarters in developed countries) now lives in urban areas, and people are predicted to continue migrating to cities over the next several decades. Systems analysts, policy makers, designers, and citizens require appropriate visualization and decision-support technologies for planning, design, and decision-making. Thanks to the ubiquity of networked mobile commercial and personal devices (and the skills to use them in new ways), we now have at our disposal massive, dynamic data sets. Using cloud-based data aggregation and processing power, we can merge this in real time with historical data like maps, land use, and demographics.

Connecting these data sets is valuable, but it is only part of the solution. For planning and design purposes, "hard" data is much more useful when properly associated and correlated with qualitative information–attitudes and preferences and priorities, as well as the dynamics of inhabiting and circulating within urban environments. Existing urban system visualization, operations, planning, and design tools do not yet afford such integration.

In this paper, we posit that it is now possible to bring together quantitative (engineering) data and qualitative (design/experiential) information in a full-spectrum knowledge space. As an initial instance of this approach, we examine transportation

© Springer International Publishing Switzerland 2016
N. Streitz and P. Markopoulos (Eds.): DAPI 2016, LNCS 9749, pp. 405–416, 2016.
DOI: 10.1007/978-3-319-39862-4_37

infrastructure, a particular class of urban systems for which quantitative and quali-tative information sources are abundant, and often in controversy. Our discussions with domain experts have revealed two key research problems for which visual analytics would be particular beneficial: evaluating *complete streets* and *parking management*. We present a set of performance specifications derived from these case studies which we believe are generalizable to public information works beyond transportation.

We believe fast progress can be made on transportation problems through the adap-tation and innovative combination of readily available tools, embodying different approaches to quantitative/qualitative representation – the **Betaville** massively partici-patory online platform and the **StoryFacets** visual data exploration system. We present a comparative evaluation of Betaville and StoryFacets as first-generation urban system analysis/planning support tools, and make recommendations for future research extending and exploiting them to meet the performance specifications.

2   The Big Picture: Public Information Works

Open data, in and of itself, is not the same thing as *open information*. An *open infor-mation* policy would imply the further duty to provide data in citizen-accessible and citizen-intelligible form, and to provide for public access to the information used by experts, decision-makers, and service providers acting on urban systems.

We propose a new approach to urban IT support systems and data resources – that in the aggregate, they be re-conceived as public works in the traditional sense of that term – large structures built and maintained for general public use, i.e. both by professionals whose work impinges on the built public realm and as public (citizen) information resources. Within this conceptual framework, an urban IT infrastructure is implemented less like a boiler or sewer system (in the dark, only to be seen and handled by staff), and more as a medium of exchange between staff, policy-makers, proponents, designers, and citizens – within the conceptual framework of systematic cultivation and support of new levels of citizen expertise, as well as engagement.

Public IT/information spaces must provide for a well-articulated set of discrete user interaction profiles, from novice to expert, including provision for "leveling up"– i.e. self-directed education and skill development, from basic web literacy up to levels of expertise currently only accessible to professional specialists. At maturity, such a system would amount to a common *back end*, with enough discrete purpose- and user-type-specific *front ends* to fully gather, process, understand, and communicate the urban systems we have, and to make sense of how they can and should co-evolve in the future. Our current work is to take viable first steps toward this goal in the domain of urban transportation infrastructure.

3   The First Application Space: Transportation

In strict engineering terms, a transportation network can be considered as one of the systems in an urban "system of systems" along with emergency response, energy, water, waste disposal, health, law enforcement, education, and so on. For some of the subsystems in the transportation network, like highways and subways, citizens and engineers are traditionally concerned with similar (quantitative) issues of system performance: maximizing throughput, speed, and consistency. For others, like shopping and residential streets, quantitative measures of transportation system performance do not adequately characterize or address overall urban system *quality*, as experienced by real people in what they experience as urban environments. Concomitant with the goal of converting open data to public information, we propose upgrading urban system informatics from strictly quantitative data to the full spectrum of quantitative and qualitative information, to address the operation and improvement of transportation networks as "lived systems", i.e. environments.

This concept is being explored in the context of "iCity: Urban Informatics for Sustainable Metropolitan Growth" a translational public-private partnership research initiative led by the University of Toronto Transportation Research Institute (UTTRI). iCity includes participants from a variety of other research units at University of Toronto, OCAD University, University of Waterloo, as well as public agencies and industry partners including the planning departments of the cities of Toronto and Waterloo, and industry partners IBM, ESRI and Cellint.

By leveraging insights from experts in computer science, transportation engineering, urban planning, visualization, and real-time data analysis we hope to define strategies for the development of next-generation tools/infrastructure for better-quality – rather than simply more efficient – transportation operations, planning, and design.

Discussions with experts in transportation planning have yielded two research problems for which next-generation visual analytics could be particularly beneficial: the relatively technical domain of *parking management*, and the more complex set of qualitative/quantitative factors implicated in the *complete streets* policy guidelines. Below we detail the background and goals of this research, which we leverage in a preliminary performance specification for integrating visualization tools into public information works.

3.1 Use Case: Parking Management

Urban parking has a significant impact on traffic congestion and behavior [3, 6]. While on- and off-street parking policies, alternative pricing models and smart parking technology can play a substantial role in reducing urban congestion, cities have been slow to adapt. Existing research has addressed the parking problem from two perspectives: (a) analysis of the relationships between parking supply, demand, and the incidence of illegal commercial vehicle parking [12]; and (b) development of a traffic simulation tool that incorporates driver decisions of parking space choice, and simulates the effects of parking search patterns on traffic congestion [4].

Our collaborators are working to expand upon these efforts to develop holistic, fully functional, operational tools for the management of parking in congested urban areas. Of particular interest is the context of supply and demand of on-street parking, road congestion, transportation networks and traffic flows, parking by-laws, smart parking, and pricing models. Methodologically, they seek three different orders of data to support their work: observed parking behavior and effects on the existing grid, with its current regulations; simulated behavior and impacts using agent-based model simulations, typically represented as schematic 2D animations of rectangular cars; and variable-parameter first-person immersive 3D parking "games", in which real commuters navigate and make choices according to actual and hypothetical scenarios.

3.2 Use Case: Complete Streets

Complete Streets [9] is a design/policy framework for the configuration of city streets to provide for a full spectrum of users, with an unusually rich definition of system performance: "complete" streets are "designed for all ages, abilities and modes of travel. Safe and comfortable access for pedestrians, bicycles, transit users and the mobility impaired is not an afterthought, but is an integral planning feature" [4]. Our collaborators are working on tools to rationalize the conversation about complete streets in the context of information technology, and to make explicit the assumptions and trade-offs that are implicit in street design. In particular, they wish to:

- Quantify the benefits and costs of alternative street designs, including: emissions exposure, travel delay, access to facilities, physical activity, and conflicts between pedestrians/cyclists/parked vehicles/transit vehicles.
- Model complete streets with inputs for mode and purpose demands, existing constraints such as right-of-way and built environment, technology for space sharing, and user-defined priorities. The model will recommend optimal right-of-way space use to balance competing needs (number of vehicle, dedicated transit, and bicycle lanes; pedestrian walkway width; social space; parking; cyber systems).
- Integrate complete streets models with travel demand models for auto, commercial vehicle, transit, active transportation, and parking needs.

3.3 Initial Specification

From these two use cases we've identified a preliminary performance specification for visual analytics tools to support transportation planning tasks, as sample "Public Information Works" components:

- **Design approach**
  - **Communication-centered.** Analysis and visualization tools should be integrated such that consumable visualizations for both specialist and non-specialist stakeholders (citizens, leaders, proponents) with varied needs can be generated.
  - **Collaboration-minded.** Tools should be designed to support teams and groups interacting on analysis projects synchronously (real-time chat, shared workspace) and asynchronously (comments, versioning).
- **Visual data/model integration**
  - **Qualitative data.** Systems should allow association of statistical with experiential information. Tools should include stakeholder feedback through channels such as social media, and link documentary media (text, photos, audio, video files) to interactive map-based or immersive (3D fly-through) infographics.

- **Real-time "what if" scenario support.** Specialist users require integrating (and explicitly displaying) mathematical models with powerful analysis tools and statistics for simulation/scenario development on-the-fly. Users must be able to interactively change model inputs, including user-defined priorities, and visually understand the effect on model outputs.
- **Changing/historical data and data ontologies.** Available data will change over time (surveys, utilization monitoring, and cell phone paths) and its evolution should be recorded and visualized. This is valuable for understanding both snapshots of history and overall temporal behavior.
- **Provenance.** As data is processed by user filtering actions and modeling, it is valuable present the history of workflow visually to users, so as to help them create more repeatable, faster, and accurate analyses.
- Visualization techniques
  - **Interactive computing.** Tools should support interactive data exploration, including user manipulation (select, filter, zoom, join, model parameter changes).
  - **Overview + detail.** Visualization tools should provide an overview of the data or model (e.g., all of Toronto), as well as tools to drill down into local detail.
  - **Geospatial visualization.** Map-based views of scenarios and statistics should be included for understanding inherently geospatial transportation systems.
  - **Information visualization.** We recommend using spatial layout to encode attribute values to complement geospatial visualizations. Patterns in model outputs such as price, availability, congestion, and exposure can be easily understood when using spatial encodings.
  - **Comparative visualization.** Tools should support visually comparing model results from different inputs, outcomes of proposed scenarios, and changing or historical data snapshots to enhance understanding.
- White boxes
  - **Ontology.** Any first-generation system must clearly display its ontology as a set of hypotheses. This includes explicit and accessible definitions of entities, properties, and relationships according to which any given sensor input is construed as information, recorded, and processed by software systems, to address both quantitative and qualitative aspects of data characterization and processing.
  - **Models.** The mathematical models of system behavior that underlie system simulations must be accessible from within the user environment, as matters of public record/understanding.
  - **Provenance.** Tools should maintain retrievability of each version of the data and the workflow which created it.

Over the course of the next four years, through an iterative cycle of development and evaluation, we will build and deploy applications to support transportation system operations, optimization, and planning as useful products in the near term, and proofs-of-concept for the broader "Public Information Works" approach down the road.

4   Technology in Hand

Two current complementary technologies together embody many of the aforementioned performance specifications for our case studies, and can be further enhanced to meet transportation planning needs: the Betaville massively participatory online platform and the StoryFacets visual data exploration system. We believe that fast progress in urban system development can be made by using these tools as a starting point.

Fig. 1. The Betaville desktop client, "God's Eye" view

4.1   Betaville

Betaville (Fig. 1) is an online environment for distributed development and deliberation about possible changes to built environments, from the scale of a public artwork to that of district-level urban development or re-development. It is intended to provide for ad-hoc online exchange of ideas between stakeholders, proponents, and professional experts, with a view to engaging all three user types proactively in "pre-design": identification of key issues, and informal putting forward of sketch/schematic models for discussion and elaboration into rough-but-robust concepts in advance of formal design development and approval processes.

Design approach – *Communication-centered* and *Collaboration-minded:* The idea for Betaville was originally developed to provide for timely and constructive modes of public engagement [8]: rather than waiting for public or private-sector proponents to present proposals *after* large investments in detailed technical design and process overhead had already been made, stakeholders could engage in ideation and problem-solving directly: not just commenting, but also putting forward their own ideas for all or part of a project, for further deliberation and elaboration in a persistent shared online design space. At a minimum, proponents could have ready access to current information about community interests before proceeding with conventional proposal development; in the best cases, new coalitions could form online, innovating more freely in the early stages of project ideation, building new constituencies and partnerships, building consensus as viable concepts come to maturity.

Visual data/model integration – *Qualitative data:* Betaville's qualitative value lies primarily in its ability to represent simplified models of proposed projects in a recognizable context, either through augmented reality or an immersive 3D model in a desktop "game" application, linked to metadata and external web resources (Fig. 2).

Fig. 2. The Betaville "Citizen's Eye" view of the same scene as Fig. 1

Visualization techniques – *Interactive computing:* Additional information can be represented in pop-up windows by clicking on objects in the scene, external web links, or infographic overlays. For example, showing the predicted change in emissions for a given scenario.

– *Overview + detail:* The key experiential aspect of Betaville is that it provides for the kind of God's Eye View generally associated with urban planners and chambers of commerce, *and* the immersive "first-person" citizen's perspective.
– *Geospatial visualization:* As a 3D visualization of real and proposed worlds, the main view of Betaville is inherently geospatial.
– *Information visualization:* Elements in the geospatial visualization are linked with quantitative data, which can be visualized on demand.

***White box** – Ontology:* The Betaville environment is self-documenting in real time: all proposal versions and comments are user-signed and time-stamped, so concept development and discussion history can be retrieved for review and analysis.

4.2 StoryFacets

StoryFacets [5] is a visual exploration system for relational data, which is particularly suited data analysis such as transportation planning where collaboration and communication with stakeholders is key. It is shown with alterations in Fig. 3.

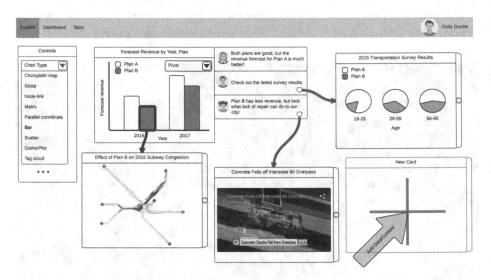

Fig. 3. Mockup qualitative extension to the StoryFacets trail view incorporating visualizations alongside annotations and comments with text labels, images, videos, and webpage mashups.

***Design approach** – Collaboration-minded:* StoryFacets was built as a web-based visual analytics system, to reduce barriers to entry and facilitate collaborative analysis and sharing. Moreover, it includes user- and project-management features for distributed teams and citizen scientists to collaborate effectively.

– Communication-centered: Eventually insights must be communicated to stakeholders – such as colleagues, managers, customers, or even the general public – to be useful and actionable [10]. However, many analysis tools still suffer from the so-called "Power-Point gap:" analysts often end up copying and pasting screenshots of tables and tools into a PowerPoint slideshow. Moreover, appropriate design for communication depends on analyst expertise, the presentation's audience, and the nature the presentation. E.g., an exploratory visualization system designed to support complex transportation model analysis is not necessarily the best way to present policy recommendations to the general public.

To ease communicating visual insights from analyses we designed StoryFacets as a one-source, multiple-media exploratory visualization presentation tool. Here, the underlying data and analytic provenance model is shared across many linked visualizations. The trail view presents visualizations and their provenance, the dashboard view supports high-level analysis of visualizations and other content in a space filling layout, and the slideshow view enables step-by-step storytelling. Changes in one view are instantly reflected in the others, eliminating the error-prone conversion between analysis and presentation.

Visual data/model integration – *Provenance:* Exploring and understanding complex relational data often require several sessions, and when returning to a previous analysis it can be difficult for users to recall the steps in their workflow. A data scientist iteratively cycling through tasks can easily forget the exact steps already done and mistakenly omit or inconsistently perform operations. For example, a transportation planner could use a filter to analyze only rush hour traffic on weekdays, create a visualization showing street throughput, and then discover a neighborhood missing data. After performing a new data collection and integration, they could accidentally omit the weekday filter and create a new visualization with a different overall message.

Exposing users to their analytic and data provenance enhances recall between sessions [2, 7, 11], as well as analysis comprehension [1]. However, most visualizations present users with only an undo stack. A handful of tools present separate hierarchical history views, and in general require extra maintenance effort from users.

StoryFacets exposes provenance embedded directly within the analysis workspace to enable easy understanding and sharing of results. During exploration, user interactions leave a trail of visual and textual bread-crumbs which document the reasoning process and data provenance. Exposing the analysis process visually enables users to utilize the spatial memory and track specific interactions. Using this design led to increased insight discovery, users could recall their findings and the exact process used to arrive at them, as well as interpret explorations of others [1].

– Qualitative data: In StoryFacets, visualizations can be augmented with cards that allow annotations and qualitative content to be added, such as text captions, bullet points, hyperlinks, images, video, and even interactive webpages. These cards use the Markdown markup language which is easy for new users to pick up. Users are given a text editor to enter Markdown with a real-time preview alongside. Upon submission, the card displays the rendered Markdown and includes an edit button to display the text editor again. For example, a user may add a video of a bridge collapsing due to poor maintenance to an analysis of infrastructure spending proposals.

Visualization techniques – *Interactive computing:* Common analysis operations like filtering are done through simple drag-and-drop interactions which create new cards. Simple user interface widgets are used to provide a pivot mechanism to transition between linked aggregates, which allow fluid exploration of multiple node or edge types. These interactive exploration mechanisms are quickly picked up by novice users [1], and are supported by quick system response times.

– Overview + detail: In StoryFacets, visualizations are displayed on a zoomable and pannable canvas, connected by parent links which expose the data provenance and

exploration history. This interface allows users to get an overview of the entire exploration, as well as zoom into analysis of subsets of the data. Moreover, the filter and pivot mechanisms allow users to begin with an overview visualization which they trim into a meaningful subset to answer their question.

– *Information visualization:* StoryFacets focuses on aggregating visualizations which provide visual scalability for large data sets. The modular architecture allows easy integration of additional visualization types, but we include a general-purpose visualization called a GatherPlot. This extension of a traditional scatterplot stacks items with the same value together for easy countability and distribution analysis.

White boxes – *Ontology* and *Provenance:* StoryFacets offers not only a cross-referenced catalog of all relevant information assets, it also tracks and displays individual and aggregate user itineraries through those resources, a meta-mapping of how users navigate in the information space, providing for new levels of analysis of which resources are sought out, how they are discovered and used, how they are associated with each other in use… in other words, elements of an "ontology in use", which should inform subsequent tool development, data collection, and in due course development of the built environment itself.

5   Discussion and Opportunities for Future Research

Our ultimate purpose is to define strategies and guidelines for the development of the next generation of tools/infrastructure for transportation operations, planning, and design – the transportation-specific components of a comprehensive urban IT infrastructure for cities worth serving: efficient, sustainable, adaptable, and desirable. As the city itself is a human system of human systems, so its information works must develop as a support system of support systems.

Betaville and StoryFacets approach the association of very different qualitative/quantitative data-to-information assets, from within two very different application/interaction genres. Combining those two perspectives within a smart model, i.e. a world in which individual objects can be linked to city data or external web resources, and providing for iterative development of design proposals and forums about them, with ID and time-stamping of individual contributions, provides in principle for something like a permanent open "charrette", exactly the kind of logistics and protocol that have supported the development of open-source software generally.

Betaville and StoryFacets will be adapted to the purpose of proving this to be a practical proposition in the long term, and bringing it to the service of transportation operations and planning, within the iCity consortium. For the applications of Betaville and StoryFacets to complete streets and parking management, there are several missing components of our performance specification which pose open research problems:

Design mindset – *Communication-centered* and *collaboration-minded:* In theory, the complementarity of Betaville and StoryFacets would suggest another mash-up, to combine their disparate functions and virtues in a single unified environment. The working assumption would have to be that an adequate critical mass subset of stake-holders within any given community will have the tools and skills (personal computer, internet access) to operate the client, and sufficient aggregate motivation to contribute either to general community awareness and understanding of active development projects, or ideally to help build an ongoing local culture of ideation and deliberation about issues, possibilities, potential improvements over the long term.

Visual data/model integration – *Qualitative data:* We propose to build out StoryFacets as a browser for disparate asset types (Fig. 3), from public GIS data to real-time traffic mapping, social media, survey data, graphics, photos, audio, and video – incorporating these into our ontology.

– *Real-time "what if" scenario support:* As more models are developed for transportation planning, it will be necessary to integrate both interactive controls for and the results of these algorithms. Careful design will be needed to extend our existing tools to incorporate these models, yet retain usability.

– *Provenance* and *changing/historical data:* As the underlying data changes, systems must be able to record these changes and present them to the user visually, in addition to allowing the user to switch between "snapshots" of the data. The StoryFacets model is well suited to such an extension.

Visualization techniques – *Comparative visualization:* Particularly in conjunction with incorporating model results and changing data, it is critical to visually show comparisons. E.g., when adjusting model parameters for bikeshare use, a direct comparison of emissions across multiple scenarios is more accurate than viewing them separately. We will integrate both interactive and directly comparative techniques.

White boxes – *Models:* In addition to "what if" scenario support, in which model inputs and outputs are integrated with tools using interactive computing techniques, the algorithms behind those models must also be exposed as much as possible.

– *Ontology:* As a data structure visualization tool, StoryFacets is readily adaptable to the purpose of representing (visualizing) the computational ontology underlying the data/information being navigated and processed, even as that ontology evolves to account for new data resources, new policies, and new methods in transportation network operations and planning.

6   Conclusion

The goal of integration of qualitative with quantitative dimensions of transportation system planning is already ambitious; the deeper integration it calls into question, of integrating research and professional service-delivery infrastructure with stakeholder communication and engagement platforms, is even more so. In this context, the conventional distinction between user-friendliness and expert-friendliness breaks down, as professionals and lay stakeholders converge: a need for visualization, analysis, and simulation tools that support continuous "up-skilling" in understanding and exploitation of scales and orders of data and information that are themselves evolving, in real time. As we build out and adapt Betaville and StoryFacets as complementary proofs-of-concept for this approach in transportation applications, we expect our research and development work to be exploited not only for transportation applications, but in due course to integrate the full range of urban system analysis, operations and planning in the service of cities that are not only smarter, but wiser, through the active cultivation and support of more (and better-informed) engagement by any combination of citizens, leaders, and professionals working together, 24/7.

Acknowledgments. This work is supported by the Ontario Research Fund – Research Excellence Round 7, under the project iCity: Urban Informatics for Sustainable Metropolitan Growth and MITACS.

References

1. Dunne, C., Riche, N.H., Lee, B., Metoyer, R.A., Robertson, G.G.: GraphTrail: analyzing large multivariate, heterogeneous networks while supporting exploration history. In: Proceedings of the SIGCHI Conference on Human Factors in Computing Systems. CHI 2012, pp. 1663–1672. ACM, New York, NY, USA (2012)
2. Lipford, H.R., Stuke, F., Dou, W., Hawkins, M.E., Chang, R.: Helping users recall their reasoning process. In: Proceedings of the IEEE Symposium on Visual Analytics Science and Technology, VAST 2010, pp. 187–194 (2010)
3. Miller, E.: First we take Toronto … lessons from the TASHA implementation and next steps. In: Behavioural Detail and Computational Demands in Agent-Based Models Workshop (2015). http://www.fcl.ethz.ch/assets/EJMiller-ABM-Workshop-2015.pdf
4. Nourinejad, M., Wenneman, A., Habib, K.N., Roorda, M.J.: Truck parking in urban areas: application of choice modelling within traffic microsimulation. Transp. Res. Part A Policy Pract. **64**, 54–64 (2014)
5. Park, D.G., Dunne, C., Ragan, E., Emlqvist, N.: StoryFacets: generating multiple representations of exploratory data analysis for communication (2016, under submission)
6. Shoup, D.C.: The high cost of free parking. J. Plann. Educ. Res. **17**(1), 3–20 (1997)
7. Shrinivasan, Y.B., Van Wijk, J.J.: Supporting the analytical reasoning process in information visualization. In: Proceedings of the SIGCHI Conference on Human Factors in Computing Systems, CHI 2008, pp. 1237–1246. ACM, New York, NY, USA (2008)
8. Skelton, C.: Soft City Culture and Technology: The Betaville Project. Springer, New York (2014)
9. Toronto Centre for Active Transportation: Complete Streets for Canada (2012). http://completestreetsforcanada.ca. Accessed 1 July 2014
10. Viégas, F.B., Wattenberg, M.: Communication-minded visualization: a call to action. IBM Syst. J. **45**(4), 801–812 (2006)
11. Ware, C., Gilman, A.T., Bobrow, R.J.: Visual thinking with an interactive diagram. In: Stapleton, G., Howse, J., Lee, J. (eds.) Diagrams 2008. LNCS (LNAI), vol. 5223, pp. 118–126. Springer, Heidelberg (2008)
12. Wenneman, A., Roorda, M.J., Nurul Habib, K.: Disaggregate analysis of relationships between commercial vehicle parking citations, parking supply, and parking demand. Transp. Res. Rec. J. Transp. Res. Board **2478**, 28–34 (2015)

Computational Community: A Procedural Approach for Guiding Collective Human Behavior Towards Achieving a Flourished Society

Kota Gushima, Tatsuya Aikawa, Mizuki Sakamoto, and Tatsuo Nakajima[✉]

Department of Computer Science and Engineering, Waseda University, Tokyo, Japan
{gushi,t-aikawa,mizuki,tatsuo}@dcl.cs.waseda.ac.jp

Abstract. In this paper, we propose a procedural framework to design collective human behavior for overcoming serious social problems, such as environmental sustainability and human well-being. The framework integrates respective persuasive services installed in urban cities for pervasively guiding people's behavior towards achieving a sustainable and flourished society. Each persuasive service manages a small piece of human behavior. Each persuasive service is represented as a basic block in our framework; the basic block specifies how to change a piece of an aspect of people's daily behavior. A service designer connects these basic blocks and coordinates them procedurally by developing a program using mobile phones. The approach enables persuasive services that are pervasively and seamlessly embedded into our daily lives to continuously guide people's behavior towards ideal sustainable human behavior.

Keywords: Crowdsourcing · Collective human behavior · Human well-being · Procedurality · Semiotic meaning of the real world

1 Introduction

Our society urgently needs to solve a variety of social issues. For example, in the modern lifestyle, people consume a large amount of natural resources, which makes our future life unsustainable. Ubiquitous computing technologies dramatically improve the efficiency of natural resource usage, but the improvement is limited in the future if we only take into account technological aspects. We need to change our behavior and improve our daily lifestyles to reduce the usage of natural resources [10]. Changing human behavior is crucial to achieving a sustainable society. There are several alternative ways to change human behavior. One of the typical approaches is to use social norms or public policy. A government may conduct public campaigns to promote the sustainable lifestyle necessary to maintain its country's wealth. However, the approach will only be able to improve the average behavior, and some people may not change their behavior. The phenomenon is very problematic because free riders who do not change their behavior may receive benefits without making efforts, and other people will consider their behavior unfair. Finally, most people may stop contributing to the campaign. Thus, the social situation will become worse.

© Springer International Publishing Switzerland 2016
N. Streitz and P. Markopoulos (Eds.): DAPI 2016, LNCS 9749, pp. 417–428, 2016.
DOI: 10.1007/978-3-319-39862-4_38

As shown in [14], these traditional approaches may also reduce some people's happiness because the approach cannot be customized for them and they may feel a strong inconvenience from being guided through the social norms or public policies. The decrease in their happiness becomes a strong reason to increase the number of free riders. To achieve a sustainable and flourished society, the direction of their respective behaviors should be customized according to their current situation and preferences to increase the happiness of all. Ubiquitous computing technologies can be used to design persuasive services that offer customized ways to guide people's behavior without reducing people's happiness.

In past research studies, many persuasive services incorporating ubiquitous computing technologies have been proposed, and they successfully demonstrate changing human behavior [9]. However, these existing services focus on only one piece of an aspect of people's behavior, such as stopping smoking, encouraging tooth brushing or reducing unsustainable behavior. When using these technologies in urban cities for guiding people's behavior towards achieving a sustainable society, we need to consider how to influence a citizen's behavior seamlessly through ubiquitous computing technologies incorporated in urban cities. The persuasive technologies can be embedded everywhere in cities and can influence citizens' behavior in their respective places. However, there is currently no way to connect these technologies to guide people's behavior according to their current situations and locations.

In this paper, we propose a procedural framework to design collective human behavior. The framework integrates respective persuasive services for pervasively guiding people's behavior towards achieving a sustainable and flourished society. Each persuasive service manages a small piece of an aspect of a respective citizen's behavior. The persuasive service is represented as a basic block in our framework; the basic block specifies how to change a piece of an aspect of the citizen's behavior. A service designer connects these basic blocks and coordinates them procedurally. The approach enables persuasive services that are pervasively embedded into our daily lives to guide citizens' behavior continuously towards achieving ideal sustainable behavior.

Our approach particularly focuses on guiding collective human behavior because most serious social problems are categorized as collective action problems. Thus, a piece of an aspect of a citizen's behavior specified in a basic block can be performed by any other citizen. To encourage potential citizens to perform actions specified in basic blocks, we adopt a crowdsourcing concept, where the actions can be performed by any citizen, and they are selected according to the policy defined in the crowdsourcing infrastructure. When a specified action is complex, it can be decomposed into several small sub-actions, and some citizens can perform the respective sub-actions independently.

We also provide a case study to demonstrate our proposed framework, which is named *Collaborative Music Construction*. The case study demonstrates how our proposed framework can successfully guide collective human behavior. *Collaborative Music Construction* supports a community in collaboratively composing a new piece of music. People have different skills relevant to the composition of music, so *Collaborative Music Construction* defines different types of basic blocks, where actions specified in the basic blocks in *Collaborative Music Construction* require different skills and knowledge. Thus, each person who has different skills and preferences can become engaged by choosing their favorite sub-actions. We are currently implementing a proto-type system of *Collaborative Music Construction* and will show some experiences with it using the case study.

The remainder of the paper is organized as follows. Section 2 presents our proposed framework and the *Collaborative Music Construction* case study, which adopts the framework. Section 3 describes the future direction of our research. Using virtual reality techniques with an HMD device can enhance the immersiveness of our persuasive experiences. We provide one case study to investigate a possible future direction to enhance the proposed framework. In Sect. 4, we discuss some research related to our approach. Finally, we conclude the paper in Sect. 5.

2 Guiding Collective Human Behavior with Procedurality

2.1 Overview

Crowdsourcing is a promising approach to exploit our social power and to enhance our human ability and possibilities. Crowdsourcing will become increasingly important in modern society as a means to direct a collective of people to perform micro-tasks, which are small, simple tasks that can be completed within a short time. The roles of crowd-sourcing have recently expanded into a variety of new areas, such as citizen science, civic engagement, and political campaigns, and will continue to increase in importance for modern society [18].

Live coding, also referred to as on-the-fly programming, just-in-time programming and live programming, is a programming practice that adopts improvised interactive programming [2, 17]. Additionally, TopCoder's crowdsourcing-based business model, in which software is developed through online tournaments, is a promising approach to developing programs [5].

Our approach is also based on a crowdsourcing concept similar to TopCoder, but each piece in a program can be developed based on a live coding concept to program human behavior. Each piece in a program developed by the crowd specifies how people behave. If they behave as expected, they are asked to perform the next action according to the program. This section presents the basic concept and demonstrates a case study of the concept to show its effectiveness.

2.2 Computational Community

Recently, there have been major debates about whether GDP (Gross Domestic Product) is an appropriate index to measure the wellness of each country because the index focuses only on measuring economic aspects of the social wellness—how rich people in the country are—rather than measuring human happiness in the country.

Our activities in modern countries emphasize pursuing economical wealth; however, increased wealth has not improved our happiness. Although information technologies have contributed to optimizing our economy and resource consumption, the question of whether information technologies improve our well-being has not been well investigated. The *Computational Community* concept that we propose enables social communities to be collectively guided without decreasing human well-being.

In contemporary society, there are many rules documented for the public, such as laws, but there are also many tacit rules, such as social norms, that limit our activities. People behave based on the rules. In other words, each person designs a sequence of his/her activities that are suitable in the current situation based on both explicit and implicit rules and decides which activities he/she performs. A community that contains multiple independent persons determines their collective activities based on such rules.

In this paper, *Computational Community* is a social infrastructure that efficiently guides collective human behavior by expressing human activities based on rules specified as procedural forms—like "codes" in computer programming. *Computational Community* makes it possible to optimize our collective activities and to facilitate communication among people by proposing a sequence of appropriate activities based on the current situations and rules represented as procedural forms. *Computational Community* can be used to propose the best times to ride trains and to suggest what garbage is recyclable. The concept aims to make our society more flourished by having each person consider only small desirable activities that can be achieved with his/her small effort. Because *Computational Community* explicitly guides desirable human behavior, people can allocate their mental resources to more important issues.

2.3   A Basic Framework

The rules are usually defined to achieve some purpose. There are many purposes, from abstract to concrete, defined by the rules. For example, there are many types of laws, such as a concrete law to determine a national budget and an abstract law to ensure our mental safety. In *Computational Community,* a rule that is typically expressed as a constraint should be translated into a procedural representation, but the procedure needs to be agreed upon by all people in a community. Currently, we have adopted a crowdsourcing concept that exploits the power of the crowd as an underlying infrastructure of *Computational Community.*

In the *Computational Community* framework, we define each concrete goal as a mission, and a guiding process to achieve the mission is divided into the following two phases, as shown in Fig. 1. The first phase is the *defining process phase*, and the second phase is the *executing process phase*. In the *defining process phase*, the crowd repeatedly refines a rule defined as a procedural form to achieve a target mission. The process is similar to the process for collectively developing computer programs in TopCoder. The developed procedure consists of a set of small procedures, like typical computer programs. Each small procedure is a *basic block*. A *basic block* is an executable task that can be completed by the crowd. The process to achieve the target mission is defined and visualized as a sequence of *basic blocks*. The phase can define not only a simple sequential process but also a complex process including inputs, outputs, branches, and loops, like traditional computer programs. The target mission can be achieved by completing the *basic blocks* defined in a procedure by the crowd in the *executing process phase* based on a crowdsourcing concept.

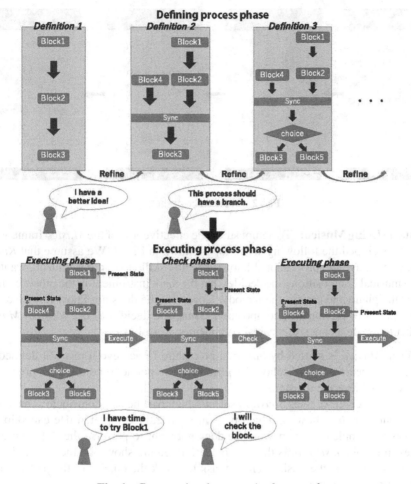

Fig. 1. Computational community framework

2.4 A Case Study: Collaborative Music Construction

A case study named *Collaborative Music Construction* is the composition of a musical piece by community members through achieving a mission. Composing a musical composition depends on not only each person's talent but also the rules or theories developed by past great music composers. People can usually compose a standard musical composition to follow the rules and theories. This case study demonstrates the *Computational Community* concept because composing musical compositions collaboratively requires defining a goal as a mission that creates a good musical composition, and the process to create the musical composition can be divided into several submissions that can be assigned to the crowd. In the current framework, the *defining process phase* is simplified and defined by a single person, not the crowd. The framework named *Musico* has been developed as an Android application written in Java, as shown in Fig. 2.

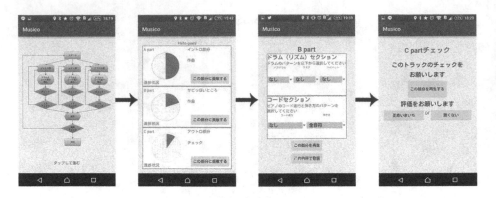

Fig. 2. Musico screenshots

A Scenario Using Musico: To demonstrate the effectiveness of the *Musico* framework, we have developed the following scenario, as shown in Fig. 3. We assume that *Kinoa*, who does not have the professional knowledge and skills to compose music, wants to create a musical composition. She decides that the main instrument in the music composition is the piano and creates the melody. However, she does not know how to create other elements of the musical composition. Thus, she decides to use *Musico*. *Musico* helps her to create a concrete musical composition as follows:

i. When *Musico* is started by *Souya*, a procedure to achieve a mission defined by *Kinoa* appears on the display of *Souya*'s mobile phone to confirm the process of how to achieve the mission.

ii. The next screen enables *Souya* to select which part he can contribute. The screen presents a graph showing which parts are currently completed. He can skip any tasks to complete the part when he does not want to perform them. Because the next possible *basic blocks* that can be performed are shown on the screen, he can contribute to another task, such as a task to check the quality of the part when he has enough free time.

iii. A *basic block* to create a part allows *Souya* to easily attach drum and accompaniment patterns through the drop down menu. If he satisfies a selected pattern, he confirms his update and the update is stored in the system.

iv. When a community member composes a part, another community member can check the quality of the part. He can decide whether the part is good or bad. If he considers the part to be bad, the currently composed part is rejected and other community members need to create the part again.

v. Community members repeat step (iii) and step (iv) until three tracks for which quality checking has been completed have been created for the part. If the quality checking of three tracks is completed or a timeout occurs, the composition process becomes the *meta-check* step.

vi. In the *meta-check* step, a community member listens to the available tracks and votes for one of them. If the number of votes for one of the tracks exceeds the specified threshold, the *meta-check* step is completed for the part.

vii. If the *meta-check* steps of all parts are completed, the application combines these parts as one music composition, and all tracks are delivered to *Kinoa*, who ultimately checks whether she is satisfied with the tracks.

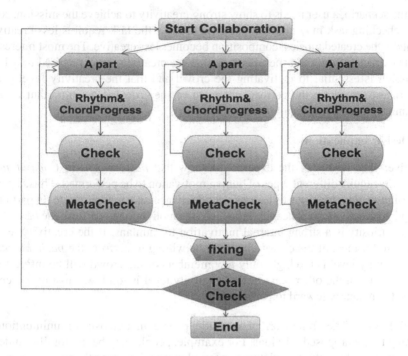

Fig. 3. Procedural representation of the scenario

Experiment with Musico and MusicoSolo: We conducted an experiment using the role-playing based method according to the scenario described above. In the experiment, the *process defining phase* was simplified because the experiment was conducted to validate the feasibility of the *process executing phase* in *Computational Community*. We have developed two applications in the experiment. One is *Musico* introduced above, and the other is a Java-based Android application named *MusicoSolo*, which implements a traditional crowdsourcing-based service to evaluate the feasibility of the *Computational Community* framework. *MusicoSolo* asks one member of the crowd to create all parts of a musical composition by himself from the given melody.

In the experiment, we recruited 11 Japanese university students (7 males and 4 females) for three days. After they used both applications for creating music compositions, they were asked to complete a questionnaire. The participants mainly responded that *Musico* was better. The insights extracted from the experiment are summarized below:

- The quality checking of a musical composition was fun for the participants and motivated them to use *Musico*. Many participants answered that they could learn the others' ideas through the quality checking process.

- The repeated quality checking process improves the quality of a musical composition, but it may create only popularized music compositions and may reduce the possibility of creating creative and niche compositions that require a higher level of creativity.

In the scenario, a user needs to show strong creativity to achieve the mission, so the quality checking task may motivate the user because the task requires less creativity; ultimately, the created musical composition becomes less creative. The most interesting insights extracted from the experiment are that the creativity level required to achieve the mission is essential to motivating the crowd and that the creativity level design appropriate to maintain the curiosity of most of the crowd is an important issue in designing a mission in *Computational Community*.

2.5 Design Implications

Incentive: The results of the experiment show that *basic blocks* in *Computational Community* require different types of human motivation to be performed. Thus, a person who designs a *basic block* needs to consider which incentive is appropriate. In particular, the required creativity level heavily influences the motivation to perform the *basic block* because curiosity is a strong internal motivation for humans. If the creativity level is appropriate for most of the crowd, they will be willing to perform the *basic block*, but if the creativity level is too high, only few members of the crowd will be interested in performing it. On the other hand, if creativity level is too low, most of the crowd will need a monetary reward to perform it.

Ethical Issues: The framework may guide people maliciously or unintentionally according to the proposed missions. For example, people may be immorally guided to perform undesirable activities if strong external motivations are offered. However, it is not easy to decide which activity is undesirable. The decision depends on the ideologies in each community. In *Computational Community*, there is no central organization to ultimately decide on the ethics of the guiding process, so it is an interesting issue how a peer-to-peer-based distributed organization resolves ethical issues collaboratively.

Modeling: Currently, our *Musico* framework visualizes *basic blocks* like a visual programming language. However, the modeling may not be appropriate for tangibly defining the procedural form to represent rules in the *defining process phase*. We need to consider a new style to create a procedural form for *Computational Community*. The insights from the live coding research community may heavily influence the progress of the direction.

3 Future Direction: Enhancing the Semiotic Meaning of the Real World

In this paper, we discussed how to influence collective human attitudes and behavior based on a computational approach. The proposed framework offers each community member a possible sequence to show how to coordinate his/her activities. One of the pitfalls of the approach is that he/she may not perform a specified activity due to his/her lower motivation regarding the activity.

To overcome the pitfalls, we conducted an additional experiment to motivate people by enhancing the semiotic meaning of the real world [4]. In the experiment, we justify the usefulness of the integration of the virtual world and the real world and show that the enhancement is a promising approach to motivating people. In the experiment, we have developed two types of real role-playing games (RRPG), where a player pretends to be a character defined in the game in real spaces, such as rooms and streets. RRPGs are categorized as pervasive games [8], but the player plays a fictional role in the game.

Figure 4 shows the first RRPG, which does not use virtual reality (VR) technologies. In the game, a player considers that he/she assumes that there is a fictional object in the real space, and the space is a fictional space representing the story defined in the RRPG. The player needs a strong imagination to play the game in the fictional world. On the other hand, the second RRPG adopts VR technologies and a player wears a head-mounted display. In the hybrid real world, a player can actually see a fictional object by rendering its 3D image in the real space, as shown in Fig. 5.

Fig. 4. RRPG without VR technologies

After playing the games, we asked the participants to complete questionnaires. In total, 68 participants completed the questionnaires in this experiment; 66 participants said that *"The second RRPG offers more immersive experiences than the first RRPG"*. Some of them claimed that there were some occasions in which the reality of the fictional objects was lost. We asked them to provide the reasons for their response, and one of them told us, *"I could not touch the fictional objects incorporated in the real world."* Additionally, another one said, *"There is no smell on the objects, and it is really unnatural."*

The results of the experiment indicate that the immersiveness offered through the integration of the virtual world and the real world is a promising approach to increasing human motivation, but it is essential to maintain the reality of the fictionality

Fig. 5. RRPG with VR technologies

incorporated into the real world. Incorporating fictionality into the real world is also important in designing procedural steps of human activities in our proposed framework because some actions need to be designed as fictional events to motivate people [15]. In the next step, we need to integrate the enhancement of activities through fictionality as shown in this section to extend the proposed framework presented in Sect. 2.

4   Related Work

A new approach, community-based mobile crowdsourcing [11, 12], in which people voluntarily contribute to helping other people anytime and anywhere using mobile phones, has been reported. The task required is usually trivial and, consequently, can be performed with minimal effort and a low cognitive load; we call the small task a micro-task. This approach offers a new method of developing services to address serious collective action problems, such as achieving social sustainability from the bottom up as an underlying social infrastructure. For example, the location-based, real-time, question-answering service *MoboQ* is built on a micro-blogging platform, through which people help each other with minimal effort [7]. Using *MoboQ*, end users can ask location- and time-sensitive questions, such as whether a restaurant is crowded, whether a bank has a long waiting line, or whether any tickets remain for an upcoming movie at the local cinema—i.e., questions that are difficult to answer with ordinary Q&A services.

Bogost argues that the unique meaning-making strategy of games is a digital rhetoric called procedural rhetoric [1]. Video games are relatively new media, and many people discuss their rhetoric. Game designers typically want to express their ideas and feelings about conceptual visual elements in games without relying on stories, imagination, sound, etc. Instead, they want to convey meaning only through the game's processes. Procedural rhetoric offers a strong persuasive effect because the rhetoric is bidirectional, whereas other rhetorical media are unidirectional. Video games allow us to interact with digital rhetoric through game controllers, but we have recently been able to use tangible devices to interact with the imaginary world, such as Microsoft Kinect[1] and Nintendo Wii[2]. These devices enable us to interact with digital rhetoric very naturally without distinguishing it from the real world. The current technological advances in computing thus allow us to seamlessly incorporate digital rhetoric into the real world through procedural rhetoric representing digitally mediated virtuality.

Most recently, digital marketing and social media practitioners have adopted this approach under the term gamification [3, 6]. The idea is to use game mechanics to make a task entertaining, thereby engaging people to conscientiously complete tasks. Adding *batches* and *leaderboards* is a typical approach to achieving gamification. In [13], an approach to use deeper game mechanics, such as coordinating several challenges to enhance crowdsourcing services, is proposed. That approach is very close to the approach proposed in this paper, but it does not support live programming, which is important for the practical deployment to pervasive persuasive service in urban cities.

5 Conclusion

In this paper, we presented a procedural framework to guide collective human behavior. Our framework integrates several persuasive services to guide human behavior anytime, anywhere in urban cities. We also provided a case study named *Collaborative Music Construction* that adopts the framework to demonstrate the effectiveness of our proposed approach. Our framework will be used as an underlying social infrastructure to guide human social behavior towards achieving a flourished society.

In the next step, we are considering extending our proposed framework to take into account the enhancement of semiotic meaning in the real world. *Gameful Digital Rhetoric* is a promising approach to support the future direction described in Sect. 3, and integrating *Gameful Digital Rhetoric* [16] with our proposed framework is also a promising step to systematically develop new types of persuasive services.

References

1. Bogost, I.: Persuasive Games: The Expressive Power of Video Games. MIT Press, Cambridge (2007)
2. Collins, N.: Generative music and laptop performance. Contemp. Music Rev. **22**(4), 67–79 (2003)
3. Deterding, S., Dixon, D., Khaled, R., Nacke, N.: From game design elements to gamefulness: defining "ramification". In: Proceedings of the 15th International Academic MindTrek Conference: Envisioning Future Media Environments, pp. 9–15 (2011)
4. Ishizawa, F., Takahashi, M., Irie, K., Sakamoto, M., Nakajima, T.: Analyzing augmented real spaces gamifed through fictionality. In: Proceedings of the 13th International Conference on Advances in Mobile Computing and Multimedia (2015)

---

[1] https://www.microsoft.com/en-us/kinectforwindows/.
[2] http://www.nintendo.com/wiiu/.

5. Lakhani, K., Garvin, D., Lonstein, E.: Topcoder (A): Developing software through crowdsourcing. Harvard Business School Case, no. 610–032 (2010)
6. Liu, Y., Alexandrova, T., Nakajima, T.: Gamifying intelligent environments. In: Proceedings of the 2011 International ACM Workshop on Ubiquitous Meta User Interfaces (2011)
7. Liu, Y., Alexandrova, T., Nakajima, T.: Using stranger as sensors: temporal and geo-sensitive question answering via social media. In: Proceedings of the 22nd International Conference on World Wide Web, pp. 803–814 (2013)
8. Montola, M., Stemros, J., Waern, A.: Pervasive Games - Theory and Design. Morgan Kaufmann, Burlington (2009)
9. Nakajima, T., Lehdonvirta, V.: Designing motivation using persuasive ambient mirrors. Pers. Ubiquit. Comput. **17**(1), 107–126 (2013)
10. Sakamoto, M., Nakajima, T., Akioka, S.: A methodology for gamifying smart cities: navigating human behavior and attitude. In: Streitz, N., Markopoulos, P. (eds.) DAPI 2014. LNCS, vol. 8530, pp. 593–604. Springer, Heidelberg (2014)
11. Sakamoto, M., Tong, H., Liu, Y., Nakajima, T., Akioka, A.: Designing incentives for community-based mobile crowdsourcing architecture. In: Proceedings of 25th International Conference on Database and Expert Systems Applications (2014)
12. Sakamoto, M., Nakajima, T.: A community-based crowdsourcing service for achieving a sustainable society through micro-level crowdfunding. In: Proceedings of International Conference on Internet, Politics, Policy 2014: Crowdsourcing for Politics and Policy (2014)
13. Sakamoto, M., Nakajima, T.: Gamifying social media to encourage social activities with digital-physical hybrid role-playing. In: Meiselwitz, G. (ed.) SCSM 2014. LNCS, vol. 8531, pp. 581–591. Springer, Heidelberg (2014)
14. Sakamoto, M., Nakajima, T., Alexandrova, T.: Enhancing values through virtuality for intelligent artifacts that influence human attitude and behavior. Multimedia Tools Appl. **74**(24), 11537–11568 (2015)
15. Sakamoto, M., Nakajima, T.: A better integration of fictionality into daily lives for achieving a digital-physical hybrid gameful world. In: The 20th International Conference on Control Systems and Computer Science (2015)
16. Sakamoto, M., Nakajima, T.: In search of the right design abstraction for designing persuasive affordance towards a flourished society. In: Proceedings of the 9th International Conference on Design and Semantics of Form and Movement (2015)
17. Wang, G., Cook, P.: On-the-fly programming: using code as an expressive musical instrument. In: Proceedings of the 2004 International Conference on New Interfaces for Musical Expression (NIME) (2004)
18. Oxford Internet Institute: Proceedings of International Conference on Internet, Politics and Policy 2014: Crowdsourcing for Politics and Policy (2014). http://ipp.oii.ox.ac.jp/2014/

Transcendent Telepresence: Tele-Communication Better Than Face to Face Interaction

Yuki Kinoshita[1(✉)], Masanori Yokoyama[2], Keita Suzuki[1],
Takayoshi Mochizuki[2], Tomohiro Yamada[2], Sho Sakurai[1],
Takuji Narumi[1], Tomohiro Tanikawa[1], and Michitaka Hirose[1]

[1] The University of Tokyo, Hongo 7-3-1, Bunkyo-ku, Tokyo, Japan
{kino,ksuzuki,sho,narumi,tani,
hirose}@cyber.t.u-tokyo.ac.jp
[2] NTT Service Evolution Laboratories,
Hikari-no-Oka 1-1, Yokosuka-shi, Kanagawa, Japan
{yokoyama.masanori,mochizuki.takayoshi,
yamada.tomohiro}@lab.ntt.co.jp

Abstract. Previous studies on telepresence concentrated on conveying rich nonverbal information as face-to-face (F2F) interactions. In this paper, we propose "transcendent telepresence" that aims to achieve better communication via telepresence that is impossible to achieve using F2F interactions. Transcendent telepresence enhances nonverbal information in telecommunication to enhance positive psychological effects and suppress negative effects by modifying the transmitted information. It complements the individual differences by adding functions that humans do not possess. Here, the concept of transcendent telepresence, examples, and researches of our group have been introduced.

The overview of the research on "eye avatar" that can control the range of the gaze cone by switching convex eye and hollow eye has been specifically introduced. Our evaluation experiment on the eye avatar showed that the convex eye can send the correct gaze direction to audience and the hollow eye can send longer direct gaze to audience more widely.

Keywords: Telepresence · Nonverbal information · Direct gaze · Averted gaze · Depth inversion

1 Introduction

Opportunities to telecommunicate are increasing. In telecommunication, such as consultations, conferences, and presentations, the information needs to be transmitted in the form of face-to-face (F2F) interaction. However, this system loses some nonverbal information. Various researchers are actively developing telepresence technology to convey more information that is nonverbal. Telepresence is a set of technologies that enable communication and interaction as if in a F2F interaction.

Previous telepresence researchers aimed at two goals. The first one conveys rich non-verbal information of an environment to a real perception operator, giving the

© Springer International Publishing Switzerland 2016
N. Streitz and P. Markopoulos (Eds.): DAPI 2016, LNCS 9749, pp. 429–438, 2016.
DOI: 10.1007/978-3-319-39862-4_39

feeling of being in a remote environment. For instance, TELESAR V (Telexistence Surrogate Anthropomorphic Robot) can allow operators to feel visual, audio, kinesthetic, and fingertip tactile sensation [1].

The second one is making an avatar with the presence of the operator at a remote location so that the opponents can have an illusion of talking in F2F environment. In order to convey the body information of the operator to a remote place, several researchers have proposed methods to imitate real people like Geminoid [2] or talking heads [3]. Previous studies attempted to imitate the F2F communication by conveying rich information.

2 Transcendent Telepresence

Several researchers in the telepresence field have focused on the method to convey rich nonverbal information, via telepresence system. However, the requirement in telepresence is not just presence but also to build good relationships and convince others. These demands in a one-to-many communication can be achieved by the efficient use of nonverbal language [4]. Some nonverbal information can be displayed consciously depending on the situation. However, some nonverbal information cannot be displayed by the human ability. In addition, it is difficult to use different kinds of nonverbal information as per ones preference. In order to use nonverbal information more effectively, it is necessary to improve the usage of nonverbal information beyond human ability.

Thus, we propose transcendent telepresence, which enhances nonverbal information that realizes telepresence beyond the F2F interaction. Since telepresence intervenes between the people, it should be able to extend the factors that are involved in the communication and achieve greater convenience than F2F interactions. Transcendent telepresence enhances nonverbal information, realizing remote communication with a psychological effect that cannot be achieved in F2F interaction (Fig. 1).

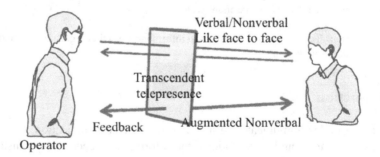

Fig. 1. Transcendent telepresence

2.1   Comparison with Other Studies

Certain previous studies suggested that the telepresence system could allow humans to extend their telecommunication. Hollan et al. questioned this current trend and suggested that telepresence has the advantages in terms of anonymity and semi-synchronousness compared to F2F interaction [5]. As an example, they proposed asynchronous communication including chat system, anonymous communication, and automatic archive communication.

, Transcendent telepresence also aims at the telepresence tools that people prefer to use even when they have the option of interacting in a physical proximity. However, transcendent telepresence concentrates on conveying nonverbal information as non-verbal, thus maintaining neutrality and presence. The importance of the method to convey nonverbal information in communication is yet to be mentioned. Human recognition becomes easier by enhancing nonverbal information as nonverbal cues, thus, causing a psychological and physiological effect while the opponents do not notice that nonverbal information is modified by the telepresence system.

2.2   Variations in Transcendent Telepresence

There are various approaches in the transcendent telepresence. Vargus had mentioned that a nonverbal medium could be classified into body, body movements, eye gaze, paralanguage, bodily contact, proxemics, time, and color [4]. Each of nonverbal mediums includes some factors. For example, the body movements include movements' type, speed, and timing. In addition, nonverbal information is interconnected. For example, eye contact affects the perceived emotion expressed by the face [6]. This suggests there are many variations in transcendent telepresence.

There are other methods to classify transcendent telepresence. One of them is to complement the individual differences and the other is to add functions that humans do not possess. In order to complement the individual differences, we researched the enhancement impression in social touch by changing the gender [7]. In addition, Smart Face improves creativity performance by changing the facial appearance of people during video conferences [8], and PoliTel [9] automatic adjusts the interpersonal distance.

In the next chapter, as an example for the additional function, we introduce the eye avatar, which allows speakers to make eye contact with various listeners at the same time (Table 1).

3   Eye Avatars: The Expansion of the Gaze Cone

3.1   Previous Research About Gaze

We propose the eye avatar, which allows the speakers to change the directivity of the eye gaze in a one-to-many communication. One-to-many communication contains highly asymmetrical dialogues such as speech, storytelling, and presentation, in which one person speaks virtually while the others are just listeners during the whole

Table 1. Variation of transcendent telepresence

	Bodily contact	Body	Para-language	Eye gaze	Body movement	Proxemics
Complement individual difference	Control effect of social touch [7]				Smart face [8]	
Additional function				Control gaze cone [this work]	PoliTel [9]	

communication. Hence, the speakers and the listeners get information of each other that is different from the audio information by using nonverbal information like gaze, face expression, gestures [10]. Among these, gazes are important and useful for impression formation, adjustment of the conversation and so on.

We will consider the eye gaze effect especially in one-to-many communication. The eye gaze can be classified into direct gaze and averted gaze. Direct gaze, also called as eye gaze or face gaze, is a gaze where the direction of gaze is at another's face or eyes. The studies on gaze suggest that long direct gazes give a good influence on the evaluations of liking and attraction, attentiveness, competence, social skills and mental health, credibility, and dominance [11]. In class, a teacher's longer direct gaze gives a good impact on the students' memory [12]. Long mutual gaze also induces the listeners' frequent and fast responses such as nodding [13].

On the other hand, an averted gaze is a gaze where the direction is not at anyone's face or eye. Averted gaze has a gaze cuing function that can convey the direction of attention and the special cue [14]. It produces the observers' reflexive attention shifts in response to the observed eye gaze direction [15], as well as gaze-following behavior such as joint attention [16].

The duration of the direct gaze influences these effects. In order to use an effective gaze in a one-to-many communication, you have to send long direct gaze along with a mutual gaze to every listener. However, as the number of listeners increases, the time in the mutual gaze with each listener reduces and the effect of gaze decreases. The more listeners, the more difficult it becomes to send a suitable amount of direct gaze to every listener. Thus, we apply the concept of transcendent telepresence to conquest this problem, and propose a system that can have a longer eye contact, having a wide gaze cone. Gaze cone [17] is the range of gaze directions within which a person feels that he/she is being watched. To send direct gaze and averted gaze effectively in one-to-many communication, we propose an eye avatar, which can send a direct gaze to many people at the same time. We made a broad gaze cone eye by using the depth inversion.

3.1.1   Implementation
We made an eye avatar that has a broad gaze cone to utilize gaze effect and to facilitate one-to-many communication. The eye avatar controls the gaze cone by switching the

eye shape between convex and hollow. The hollow eyes are illusion eyes that have a broad gaze cone, applied with depth inversion [18].

Figure 2 shows the appearance of the eye avatar. The eyeball's pupil and iris were painted black and sclera white for high contrast that is easy to see even from a distant place. The eyeball's diameter was 40 mm. The rotation eye had the mechanism that permitted two degrees of freedom: pan and tilt. The tilt rotation for 180 degrees is a change of convex and hollow. In order to make the observer feel the eye changing the gaze direction, it is necessary to make the switching eye shape, which is invisible to the observer.

Convex   Hollow

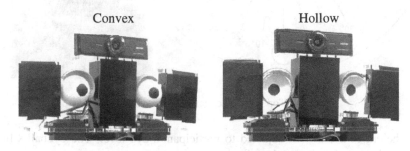

Fig. 2. Eye avatar's hollow eye and convex eye

When a brief blank is shown during the alternating displays, a striking failure of the perception is induced. Identification of the changes becomes extremely difficult even when changes are large and made repeatedly. In perceptual psychology, it is known as "change blindness" [19]. We applied the change blindness while switching the eye shape in order to make it inconspicuous. The eyelid hides the eye when the eye avatar is changing from convex and hollow eye, thus imitating the blink. Additionally, we used matte spray and removed the gloss for the hollow eye to make it indistinguishable from the convex eye.

3.2 Evaluation Experiment

Two evaluation experiments were conducted to check whether the eye avatar could use the effect of direct gaze and averted gaze effectively. First, to evaluate convex and hollow eye's direct gaze effect, the area of the gaze cone of each eye was measured. Second, in order to evaluate each eye's averted gaze effect we measured how correctly they can convey the gaze direction.

3.2.1 Measurement of the Gaze Cone of the Convex Eye and Hollow Eye

Experimental Procedure. The research participants watched the eye avatar from a point that was 1.5 m from the side of the eye avatar, for every 10 degrees and were asked if they felt that they were being watched. This was conducted for the both convex eye and hollow eye.

1. A research participant was seated in a chair in front of the eye avatar, attached to a tripod (Fig. 3).

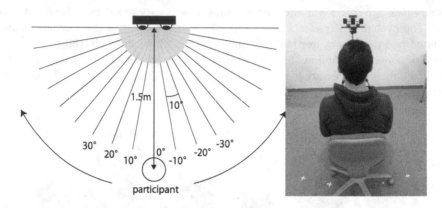

Fig. 3. Top view of experiment1 environment

2. The height of avatar was adjusted to participant's eye level. The eyeball's height and angle were fixed after the adjustment.
3. The participant looked at the avatar and answered whether they felt like being watched in three-step evaluation; watched at by right and left eyes, only one eye and none.
4. After the answer, the participant looked away from the avatar once. He/she then shifted to the next position in 10 degrees counter-clockwise and answered in the same way.
5. The participant repeated steps 3 and 4 until he/she answers that they do not feel watched by both eyes. After that, the participant returns to the point in front of the eyeball avatar.
6. Similarly, the participant repeats steps 3 and 4 to a clockwise direction.

Result. The average of the gaze cone of the convex eye was 32.3 degrees and the hollow eye was 3.4 degrees. Welch's paired t-test showed that the gaze cone of the convex eye and the hollow eye were significantly different ($p = 0.012$) (Fig. 4).

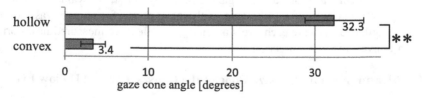

Fig. 4. Gaze cone angle of convex and hollow eyes

In addition, the number of participants that had the feeling of being watched decreased from the point of 50 degrees. According to the participants, it was because the servomotor hid the eye avatar's iris and the edge of the hollow eye from the position over 50 degrees. None of the participants answered the eye avatar watching him/her at 60 degrees or more.

3.2.2 Accuracy of Conveyance Gaze Direction

Experimental Procedure. We measured how accurately the convex and hollow eye can convey direction of gaze and how iszt received to examine whether their averted gaze is effective.

Research participants were male in the age group of 21 to 25 years. We projected the alphabet target behind the participant (Figs. 5 and 6) using a projector. The intervals of the targets are at 500 mm. The experimenter sent the gaze direction to the alphabet target point projected on the screen using the eye avatar. The front of the eye avatar was the center of the projection, which is the target between H and M.

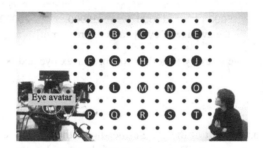

Fig. 5. Experiment photography

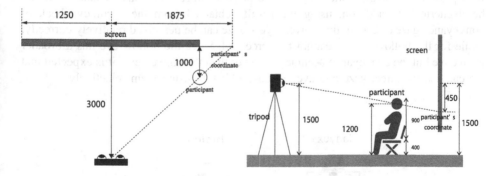

Fig. 6. Top and side view of the experiment environment

First, an experimenter sent a gaze to every target using convex eyes; then, gaze using the hollow eye was sent in the same way. The pointed alphabet targets' order was sorted randomly for each participant. Next, the research participants answered the point that they felt the eye avatar watched. They were also allowed to answer the middle point such as between A and B or themselves. After the experiment, the participants answered a questionnaire about what they felt about experiment and eye avatar. If the participants answered as looking at, Let the point at which a line from eye to participant's eye intersects with the screen to be position coordinate of the answer (Fig. 6).

Results. The sum of the error was calculated as the distance between the gaze direction of the eye avatar and the participants who felt they were being watched by the eye avatar. Next, we calculated the average of every target's error for convex eye and hollow eye. The sum of the error for the convex eye was 6995 mm and the hollow eye was 18048 mm.

Welch's t-test showed that the average of error distance of the convex eye was shorter than the hollow eye (p < 0.01) (Fig. 7).

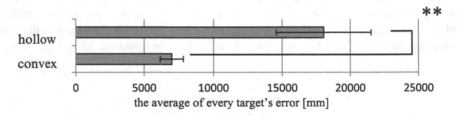

Fig. 7. Average of every target's error for convex eye and hollow eye

4 Discussion

The result of the measurement of the gaze cone shows that hollow eyes have a broader gaze cone than the convex eye. Thus, it is possible to widen the gaze cone by using hollow eyes (Fig. 8). In this experiment, we measured gaze cone area only horizontally. It is presumed that the hollow eyes have similar effects vertically because eyes are hemispherical. In addition, using the results obtained from the accuracy check of conveyance gaze direction, the convex eye's gaze can be perceived relatively correctly, while for the hollow eyes it cannot be perceived. Since the hollow eye has a broader gaze cone but the conveyance accuracy is lower than the convex eye, it is expected that we can use the direct gaze and averted gaze effect by using them selectively.

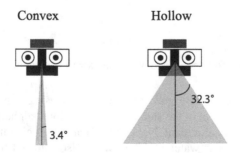

Fig. 8. Eye avatar's gaze cone angle

5   Conclusion

We proposed a novel concept, "transcendent telepresence," which enhances non-verbal information. It complements the individual difference to human or adds new functions to human. Transcendent telepresence can be applied to many kinds of non-verbal information. As an example of the concept of transcendent telepresence, we introduced "eye avatar," which can expand the gaze cone.

We evaluated the range of the gaze cones of convex and hollow eyes and the accuracy of conveying gaze direction. The result showed that the hollow eye has a broader gaze cone but the accuracy of conveying gaze direction is lower than the convex eye. By switching the eye avatar's hollow eye and convex eye, we can control the range of gaze cone and the accuracy of conveyance. It is expected that the eye avatar can enhance the impression of the speaker or improve students' memory in certain important contents.

Future topic in terms of the eye avatar is to implement and evaluate the system to realize the proposed method introduced here. For example, we will evaluate the psychological effect of the hollow eyes such as inducement to listeners' responses. We will research about it by using eye avatar in one-to-many communications such as actual lectures and presentations.

As a whole, we can further approach the research on transcendent telepresence in various ways. For example, we can develop a new transcendent telepresence with other nonverbal information such as facial expressions and body language. Furthermore, we can use transcendent telepresence systems in combination rather than individually. By combining the effects of the various types of nonverbal information, a human would be able to use their nonverbal communication ability as intended. We believe that transcendent telepresence will enable users to exceed human's limit and realize that telepresence systems are ideal for users rather than F2F interaction.

References

1. Fernando, C.L., Furukawa, M., Kurogi, T., Hirota, K., Kamuro, S., Sato, K., Tachi, S.: TELESAR V: TELExistence surrogate anthropomorphic robot. In: ACM SIGGRAPH 2012 Emerging Technologies, p. 23. ACM, August 2012
2. Sakamoto, D., Kanda, T., Ono, T., Ishiguro, H., Hagita, N.: Android as a telecommunication medium with a human-like presence. In: 2nd ACM/IEEE International Conference on Human-Robot Interaction (HRI), pp. 193–200. IEEE, March 2007
3. Naimark M.: Talking Heads projection (1980). http://www.naimark.net/projects/head.html. Accessed 10 Feb 2016
4. Vargas, M.F.: Louder than Words: An Introduction to Nonverbal Communication. Iowa State University Press, Ames (1986)
5. Hollan, J., Stornetta, S.: Beyond being there. In: Proceedings of the SIGCHI Conference on Human Factors in Computing Systems, pp. 119–125. ACM, June 1992
6. Adams, Jr., R.B., Kleck, R.E.: Effects of direct and averted gaze on the perception of facially communicated emotion. Emotion, 5(1), 3–11 (2005)

7. Suzuki, K., Yokoyama, M., Kinoshita, Y., Mochizuki, T., Yamada, T., Sakurai, S., Narumi, T., Tanikawa, T., Hirose, M.: Enhancing Effect of Mediated Social Touch between Same Gender by Changing Gender Impression. AH (2016)

8. Nakazato, N., Yoshida, S., Sakurai, S., Narumi, T., Tanikawa, T., Hirose, M.: Smart face: enhancing creativity during video conferences using real-time facial deformation. In: Proceedings of the 17th ACM Conference on Computer Supported Cooperative Work & Social Computing, pp. 75−83. ACM, February 2014

9. Yokoyama, M., Matsuda, M., Muto, S., Kanamaru, N.: PoliTel: mobile remote presence system that autonomously adjusts the interpersonal distance. In: Proceedings of the Adjunct Publication of the 27th Annual ACM Symposium on User Interface Software and Technology, pp. 91−92. ACM, October 2014

10. Yngve, V.H.: On getting a word in edgewise. In: Chicago Linguistics Society, 6th Meeting, pp. 567−578 (1970)

11. Kleinke, C.L.: Gaze and eye contact: a research review. Psychol. Bull. 100(1), 78−100 (1986)

12. Otteson, J.P., Otteson, C.R.: Effect of teacher's gaze on children's story recall. Percept. Mot. Skills 50(1), 35−42 (1980)

13. Kendon, A.: Some functions of gaze-direction in social interaction. Acta Psychol. 26, 22−63 (1967)

14. Frischen, A., Bayliss, A.P., Tipper, S.P.: Gaze cueing of attention: visual attention, social cognition, and individual differences. Psychol. Bull. 133(4), 694−724 (2007)

15. Driver IV, J., Davis, G., Ricciardelli, P., Kidd, P., Maxwell, E., Baron-Cohen, S.: Gaze perception triggers reflexive visuospatial orienting. Vis. Cogn. 6(5), 509−540 (1999)

16. Moore, C., Dunham, P.: Joint Attention: Its Origins and Role in Development. Psychology Press, New York (2014)

17. Gamer, M., Hecht, H.: Are you looking at me? measuring the cone of gaze. J. Exp. Psychol. Hum. Percept. Perform. 33(3), 705−715 (2007)

18. Gregory, R.L: The confounded eye. In: Illusion in Nature and Art, pp. 49−96 (1973)

19. Rensink, R.A., O'Regan, J.K., Clark, J.J.: To see or not to see: the need for attention to perceive changes in scenes. Psychol. Sci. 8(5), 368−373 (1997)

An Improvisation Based Framework for Interactive Urban Environments

Kristian Kloeckl[✉]

Department of Art + Design, School of Architecture, Northeastern University,
360 Huntington Avenue, Boston, MA 02115, USA
k.kloeckl@neu.edu

Abstract. Urban environments are increasingly pervaded by embedded networks and mobile digital components capable of sensing, computing, and acting in real-time. These augmented environments have the capability to dynamically respond to and adapt to their context and to behavioral patterns of their human occupants. In doing so their forms of interaction can be fluid and ad-hoc and this paper proposes a framework based on improvisation for the analysis and the design of such environments. Following a study of the nature of the improvisation process, a systems view of improvisation is adopted. The structural elements of the Viewpoints improvisation technique are then mapped to design stages of second-order systems to develop a framework for the design of interactive urban environments.

Keywords: Interactive environments · Urban environments · Improvisation · Viewpoints · Systems · Cybernetics

1 Introduction

The increasing pervasiveness of embedded and mobile digital components in urban environments has led to spaces and objects with more fluid than fixed behavior. These objects and spaces are capable of sensing, computing, and acting in real-time; they can change their behavior in relation to the state of their own system, their histories of past actions and interactions, the behavior of humans and machines within their reach, or environmental parameters. These environments are no longer static backdrops to human activity but have the potential to become interactive elements displaying a dynamic behavior and engaging with their human occupants [1, 2].

This potential meets a concrete demand in real world situations: Workplaces, health care environments, public spaces, or settings for social entertainment are increasingly required to flexibly adapt to continuously changing modalities of usage. However, physical settings often lag behind in their capability to respond dynamically [3].

Technologies capable to activate environments have reached a considerable level of maturity and are being deployed widely in everyday environments. Different domain names (ambient intelligence, responsive environments, pervasive computing, etc.) express different biases but what they largely have in common is the objective of developing embedded digital systems capable of supporting people in their activities by engaging in ways that are more akin to human interaction. These systems are composed

© Springer International Publishing Switzerland 2016
N. Streitz and P. Markopoulos (Eds.): DAPI 2016, LNCS 9749, pp. 439–449, 2016.
DOI: 10.1007/978-3-319-39862-4_40

of a wide range of sensing, processing and actuation technologies and aim at displaying context aware and adaptive behavior [4–7].

One of the biggest challenges of these systems on a phenomenological level consists in mediating successfully between the uniqueness of real world situations and the modalities of actuation these systems are capable of. Systems tend to perform well when goals, sensor input and input-output mapping can be clearly defined. However, when humans are involved in the interaction, these basic elements are typically uncertain. They rather emerge from the interaction itself in a situated way. The activity itself, the sequences of interaction, impacts and alters the condition of both subject and object as they engage in collaboration in an ongoing dialogue [8].

The very term "interaction" tends to be employed in a broad way and used to describe anything from a simple click of a button triggering a predetermined effect, to the sophisticated dynamics underlying human dialogue. Dubberly et al. [9] illustrate different models of systems that help in grasping the nature of interactivity. On one hand, in its most basic form, we have a human-computer interaction based on a single feedback-loop. A person having a goal, acting upon the environment, the person perceiving the effect of that action and comparing it to the initial goal to inform further action. More than 'interactive', the authors refer to this as 'reactive' - "in 'reaction' the transfer function (which couples input to output) is fixed; in 'interaction' the transfer function is dynamic, i.e., in 'interaction' the precise way that 'input affects output' can itself change." On the other hand, Dubberly et al. identify learning systems in the form of second-order systems in which one feed-back loop interacts with another feedback loop, with the possibility of further levels of nesting feedback-loops within them. Here, "the second system sets the goal of the first, based on external action. We may call this learning - modification of goals based on the effect of actions." In the presence of multiple first-order systems within one or more second-order systems, the second-order system can exert a choice as to which first-order system to engage with depending on its current goal and past experience with the response mechanisms of the first-order systems to work towards them.

In this more comprehensive model of interaction goals are defined dynamically as the system parts interact, past experiences feed into choices made on the system's behavior and processes of learning are set in place. People interacting with augmented spaces based on such a model engage in what we an refer to as conversational dynamics in which meaning is co-created and space is appropriated every time anew for specific situated activity. When developed as truly interactive systems, their behavior can be described as improvisational, as is ultimately that of their human counterparts.

To talk about an 'interface' was an effective conceptual model to contemplate on human-product interactions before the dawn of computerization, when configurations were fixed (buttons, levers, sliders, telephone dials, etc.). The plasticity of the nature of human-computer interfaces created new challenges and opportunities. The notion of "conversation" was used as a new framework, suggesting a model where meaning is negotiated and co-created between human and computer through interactions. In this sense interface is no longer a simple notion by which human and computer represent themselves to one another. Rather, it forms a shared context for action in which both are agents in an Aristotelian sense. Laurel [10] describes how the 'interface' has developed into a theatrical 'stage' for the performance of intentional activity in which both human and computer have a role. The limitation of theatre as a model being that in scripted theatre, unlike real life, the process of choice and decision making takes place during rehearsal and practice and not during the actual staging of the performance. In the sense that drama formulates the enactment and not the action, it is un-like real life. However, in improvisational techniques used during rehearsal, as in real life, anything can happen, actions are situated in context and always in flux, situations are essentially unique, the focus is on dynamic choice in a dynamic environment. Improvisation is a model that more closely mirrors the process of human-computer interaction in real life.

Today, the stage that Laurel describes has left the confinement of the theatre and has become the city. The technologies she discusses are embedded and mobile, connected, and ubiquitous in urban environments. This paper articulates a mindset for the analysis and the design of interactive urban environments based on the process of improvisation. Following an overview of related work and the analysis of the nature of the improvisation process, a systems view of improvisation is adopted. The fundamental elements of the Viewpoints improvisation technique for theatre actors are then mapped to design stages based on a second-order systems perspective to develop a framework for the design of truly interactive environments.

2   Related Work: Improvisation in HCI

Improvisation is part of the performing arts and there has been considerable exploration within that domain over the past two decades that explore different models of relationship between performer and technology systems. The following studies focus on HCI and improvisation with a particular bias towards research involving Viewpoints improvisation theory.

In the Viewpoints AI (VAI) project [11] a person can engage in movement improvisation with a virtual actor in the context of a projection screen. The virtual actor is projected from one side of the screen, the real person's shadow is cast onto the same screen from the other side so that both co-exist in the real/virtual space of the projection screen. As the interactor moves, the system monitors the motion using a Microsoft Kinect device and analyses the interactor movements through procedural representations using the Viewpoints theory as a reference model. It responds to the interactor movements by choosing from a number of strategies or response modes including past experience with the same as well as other interactors. The system is claimed to work with almost no predefined content.

Corness and Schiphorst in [12] explore how the interaction between theatre performers and an autonomous generative music system can use synthetic sounds of breath as a cue for an upcoming action to incorporate the performer's sense of intuition. Breath is used as expression of intention for action/behavior. Before performing an improvised musical phrase the system emits a breath sound conditioned by the structure of the improvised musical phrase about to come. The improvisation as a whole is conditioned by performers and by environment and is modeled on some aspects of Viewpoints theory in that it monitors two aspects: performer motion and architectural shapes (lines and shapes) detected in the environment. The results obtained from interviews with performers indicate that when the system improvised and 'announced' the improvisation by its synthetic breath, the improvisation was perceived as more understandable, facilitating to connect with it.

In a study by Lu [13], the objective is to develop a physical vocabulary for human-robot interaction by using trained actors as models for appropriate timing and gestures. The approach proposed is to study human actors and their timing of gestures in modes of interaction and then program robots' behavior based on time measurements taken from actors behavior.

The mechanical ottoman experiment described in [14] explores behavior types of autonomous objects and people's reaction to them. Specifically the paper describes an experimental setup in which a hand or remote controlled ottoman is moved in ways as to prompt a person sitting in an armchair to put the feet on it, to take the feet off, etc. While a hand and remote controlled behavior in the experiment setting, the study points towards an autonomous object that would improvise its behavior in response to context and behavior of a person. In the initial experiment where the ottoman was controlled by a human, the object presented indeed an improvised behavior (even if enacted by a human through the object), the later study transferred the motion control entirely to the object by automating the ottoman, however scripting the behavior rather than enabling it to generate responsive patterns of behavior.

These related works illustrate a range of research carried out over the past years at the intersection between HCI and improvisational performance. Predominantly it is HCI and autonomous systems research that is brought into the domain of the performing arts [11–13], exploring systems that become actors on a stage with human performers. This paper proposes an inverse operation: to bring the structures from improvisational theatre and the embodied knowledge from trained improvisational actors into the context of everyday urban environments to enhance interactive processes between people and their built environment. Viewpoints improvisation theory serves not only to categorize some behaviors but is taken as a foundational conceptual and structural framework.

3   A Systems View of Improvisation

Improvisation is a process that is often misunderstood. A common interpretation is that when something is improvised, it is to *make up* for a lack of something. To extemporize, a common synonym is indicated by Webster's dictionary as doing something in a make-shift manner, which in itself is referred to as a usually crude and temporary expedient [15]. To improvise, that is, is to *get by* in some way until the plan that was lost can be recovered.

Instead, in the arts and social sciences, the practice of improvisation has been studied extensively for some time now. Jazz is one of the domains intensively vested in this phenomenon. The development of Free Jazz in the 1950's and 1960's led to extensive experiments of composing in real-time [16]. Its Latin root 'proviso' indicates a condition attached to an agreement, a stipulation done beforehand. Together with the prefix 'im', improvisation indicates that, which has not been agreed upon before, which lacks a prior stipulation of contract or provision. Improvisation deals with the unforeseen, that which has not been provided or planned for, that which presents itself as unexpected.

Contrary to a common perception, the improvised act does not come out of nowhere. We underestimate the investment in attention, study and practice that is the foundation for every improvised performance. Together with an astute awareness of self and of others, an improvisation is based to a critical extent on the artist's past practice and experience. As artists improvise, they elaborate on existing material in relation to the unforeseen ideas that emerge out of the context and the unique conditions of the performance. In this way, variations are created and new features are added every time anew [17, 18]. While not following a previously formulated plan as such, improvisation does acquire in this way some form of consistency in that it connects with what has come before in an ongoing process of repetition and variation [19].

The phenomenology of the moment for improvisational performers is as much material for their art as is their past training and practice of structures and procedures. Improvisational performers not only pick up on gestures, sequences played and acted by their fellow performers, but they also develop a capability to recognize form when it is in the making. Improvisational actors do not only read the initial movement of another actor's hand gesture as such, but they attribute meaning to the completed form of which they see the seed. Whether that hand gesture would have been executed according to this attribution of meaning or not is irrelevant. The attributed meaning and the action based on it become the novel elements an actor contributes to the collective process. Misunderstandings and errors are constructive elements in improvisation. They are the *noise* that leads to the emergence of new structures.

In systems theory, *emergence* describes the appearance of something new. Something, of which arrival could not be anticipated, could not be expected and foreseen, but something that was born out of the interaction between previously present elements. This new arrival emerges from non-simple interactions between many different parts that interact both serially and in parallel, forming a complex system. A system that is self-organizing and which complicates boundaries between interiority and exteriority. A system, that is neither fixed nor static but that evolves and adapts [20, 21].

Adapting a systems view of improvisation makes the tension between the notions of stability and variation a productive one. The dynamics of change and variation become an integral part of the repetitions of interaction among human actors or musicians and their environment. It is through repeated interactions between them and their environment that new forms emerge.

In several instances of the literature on improvisation in different fields, parallels are drawn between the way actors or musicians improvise and the phenomenology of the spoken language, of discourse and conversations. "It's like language: you're talk-in, you're speaking, you're responding to yourself. When I play, it's like having a conversation with myself" (Paul Berliner quoting drummer Max Roach) [17].

Also in the context of systems theory, the interactions between the constituent parts of a system and between systems are likened to the process of a conversation. Gordon Pask discusses how "structures may be designed (as well as intuited) to foster a productive and pleasurable dialogue" [22]. In this text he invests the architect with the role of designing systems instead of buildings that follow rigid typologies. Since the human occupants of manmade structures and environments change, evolve, and adapt, Pask sees an imperative for these manmade structures to reach similar capabilities to main relevant and effective. By formulating a 'cybernetic design paradigm', he indicates the stages of design in the context of 'adaptive environments' which can be synthesized into these three:

1. **Goal and purpose:** These will be underspecified since they are not fully known in evolving systems but a loose specification will provide constraints.
2. **Invariants:** Selection of system elements that present some stability (such as physical materials, etc.), and which become relevant basic properties in the man-environment dialogue.
3. **Principles for system learning and evolution:** Specification of what the environment will learn about and how it will adapt following evolutionary principles.

It falls to the designer of such a system to specify what the environment will learn about and how it will learn as well as how it will be able to evolve in terms of evolutionary principles. The designer of adaptive environments as discussed in Pack's writing will thus not be designing the environment as such but rather the terms upon which such an environment organizes itself over time and in an ongoing interaction with its human occupants and other factors. The designer in this view loses his position as a controller, and instead instills his creations with the structural and procedural capabilities to evolve.

Conversational processes between man and his environment, as discussed by Pask, and the process of improvisation, as described above, share fundamental characteristics: they both build on elements that are present prior to the action. These elements can be structural elements or procedural sequences. Actions from past experiences are repeated and iterated under an astute awareness for the special circumstances (internal and external) of a unique situation leading to variations in the repetition. New features emerge and are added to those that came before and the systems involved (both human and machine) change, adapt and evolve – they learn.

While the development of machines capable of this kind of interaction is challenging, improvisational performers have developed their art to a high degree. Also, techniques and training methods have been formalized that provide a detailed and structured understanding of the learning process to develop the capabilities to improvise. It is on these premises that I propose to look at improvisation as a mindset to inform the design of responsive and truly interactive environments in the context of cities.

4   Viewpoints for Ambient Interaction

Among the wide range of improvisation techniques in several of the arts the technique of Viewpoints improvisation seems particularly interesting to the scope of this discussion. It was first developed by Mary Overlie in the 1970's and later formalized by Anne Bogart and Tina Landau. "Viewpoints is a philosophy translated into a technique for (1) training performers; (2) building ensemble; and (3) creating movement for the stage" [23].

Viewpoints offers an alternative to conventional approaches to acting, directing, playwriting and design. It represents a defined procedure and attitude that is non-hierarchical, practical and collaborative in nature [23]. It overcomes the often found dynamic in acting where directors want actors to do certain things ("I want you to come in and walk across the stage like this…"). Instead, Viewpoints focuses on engaging actors as co-creators in the collaborative process of collectively making choices on stage. The choices are made in response to *what the play wants* in Bogart's terms and what we can paraphrase in our context as *what the situation wants*. A process in which acting is experienced as a collective discovery of acts that dynamically and recursively respond to the questions that arise (or *emerge*) during rehearsal. View-points is based on the "trust in letting something occur onstage, rather than making it occur. The source for action and invention comes to us from others and from the physical world around us" [23].

In Viewpoints, individual and collective activity emerges in real-time, based on actors' heightened awareness and immediate response to any of nine Viewpoints that are temporal and spatial in nature: Tempo, Duration, Kinesthetic Response, Repetition, Spatial Relationship, Topography, Shape, Gesture, Architecture.

4.1 Temporal Viewpoints

Tempo is concerned with how fast or slow an action is. It does not matter what the action is, it explores extremes of tempo - very fast and very slow - together with the medium. The attention is guided to meaning created by the tempo of an action (slow to touch or fast to grab, etc.). It brings awareness to the inner and outer tempo of an actor, to remain calm inside while acting fast and vice versa, to engage in fast collective action while keeping a slow pace at an individual level.

Duration works on an awareness of how long an action lasts, developing a sense for how long is long enough to make something happen or how long is too long so that something starts to die. Again, it explores the extremes as areas from which we tend to shy away - something that lasts too long or too short - while intuitively retreating towards a medium comfort zone.

Kinesthetic Response brings attention to other bodies in space, to their movements, exploring ones own behavior as being impacted by these external mobilities. The focus is now on *when* you move instead of *how fast* or *slow* and *for how long*.

Repetition is experimentation with letting *when*, *how* and *for how long* actors move be determined by repetition. Repeating someone else, someone close, someone far away, repeating off two people simultaneously. Actors experiment with repetition over time, recycling movements carried out by others in the near or distant past, reproducing forms and figures and repurposing them for the dialogue in that moment.

4.2 Spatial Viewpoints

Spatial Relationship works on the distance between actors, between bodies in motion. Taking distance from others, getting closer, close, too close. Experiencing dynamic distance and its effects.

Topography brings the actors attention to the shape within which they move. Several exercises are based on movements along an imaginary grid. Then this grid is changed, broken, distorted. Actors are asked to imagine and become aware of boundaries within which they move. They move on three dimensional grids, paint shapes on the floor with their movement, work with the shape and size of the playing space and patterns within that space.

Shape is created by the group of actors following an input from the trainer or by actors becoming aware of lines and curves that emerge. Actors train their awareness on legibility of those shapes both from within the ensemble and from outside. Shapes in space and in motion of this kind are held constant over time and through continuous slow or fast or even increasing tempo of movement. They might dissolve, actors experiment with changing location within the shape or trigger novel shapes through their action.

Gesture is explored by investigating behavioral and expressive gestures. The former are declinations from everyday life (pointing, waving, saluting, scratching, etc.) while the latter relate to the interior, expressing feeling, desire, an idea or a value. Bogart and Landau relate to them as either prosaic or poetic.

Architecture refers to the work with the spatial qualities that are already there. It puts attention on how the awareness of the physical environment affects actor movement and behavior. Actors enter quite literally into a dialogue with a room, a space to let movement evolve out of the surroundings. Architecture is broken down into 5 domains referring to solid mass (walls, floors, doors, furniture, windows, etc.), Texture (in regards to the material composition of the solid masses), Light (the source of it as well as the shadows it casts, etc.), Color (of solid mass objects but also light), Sound (that created directly from the architecture, e.g. sound from feet walking on different surfaces, creaking of a door, etc.). Actors also engage in working with objects within that space, to create with and through these objects.

4.3 Viewpoints for Interactive Environments

These nine Viewpoints formalized by Bogart [23] seem an ideal framework to both conceptualize and develop the character and the behavior of responsive elements that form interactive environments. In reference to Gordon Pask's cybernetic design paradigm described above, we can now map the following elements from the Viewpoints method to Pask's design stages:

(1) Goal and purpose: These will be underspecified since they are not fully known in evolving systems but a loose specification will provide constraints.

In Viewpoints improvisation training, the goal and purpose of the performed interaction is provided by the input from the trainer. The trainer guides the actors' attention to particular Viewpoints and provides stimulating input. In Viewpoints improvisation (without trainer), instead, goal and purpose are dynamically generated by the improvised actor-actor, actor-space, actor-ensemble interactions.

In the design of interactive environments it is difficult to see goal and purpose to emerge entirely from system interactions. Depending on the context of the system, the designer will specify whether the system is intended to provide lighting or sound in an environment, whether it configures spatial arrangements, whether it provides information for collaborative processes, etc.

However, in line with Bogart and Landau's call to move beyond the traditional director request for "I want you to walk across the stage in this way…", the focus can be on *what the system does* and not on *what the system does it for*.

(2) Invariants: Selection of system elements that present some stability (such as physical materials, etc.), and which become relevant basic properties in the man-environment dialogue.

In Viewpoints improvisation, Architecture is the Viewpoint that refers to the space and all its physical characteristics that Viewpoint actors find already there and with its formal articulation into Solid Mass, Texture, Light, Color, Sound, as outlined above, this Viewpoint addresses the core of this design stage. In addition, the Viewpoints can be viewed as basic and invariable building blocks themselves. The Viewpoints actors engage with the world, with each other and with themselves through the nine Viewpoints as filters, and so would this be the case for interactive environments. In the constant tension between stability and variation, movement and behavior elaborated in response to shifting attention to Viewpoints and the situation at large will become temporary building blocks for more complex behavioral structures. While not invariant on a global variant, these will present some stability on a local level both spatially as well as temporally.

(3) Principles for system learning and evolution: Specification of what the environment will learn about and how it will adapt following evolutionary principles.

How systems will learn and evolve is the point that addresses the issue of the earlier distinction between truly interactive and merely reactive systems. In Viewpoints improvisation the ensemble performance evolves through the actors' heightened awareness of their presence in relation to each other, to their movements and actions, as well as to their environment. They work with this attention through the framework of the nine Viewpoints. In the design of interactive environments, the framework of the nine Viewpoints becomes a filter to extract information from the environment and the dynamics within it in order to extract meaningful elements that trigger change in the systems setup and behavior.

Mapping the capabilities of the Viewpoints improvisation technique to the design stages for the development of interactive environments provides a path to disclosing in practice the potential that the mindset of improvisation can bring to the design of urban interactive environments.

5   Discussion

As outlined so far, improvisation and in particular the Viewpoints improvisation technique offer an interesting approach for the development of interactive urban environments. Viewpoints trained actors engage with other ensemble members and their environment in ad-hoc interactions, allowing behaviors to emerge from these very interactions in ways that can be described a second-order system. In the way that for both, improvisation and second-order systems, goal and purpose evolves and can emerge from the very interactions between the elements of the system, it can be a challenge to evaluate the effectiveness of such a system based on underspecified goals. When can we assess such a system to work or not to work? The more narrowly defined the goal is, the harder it is to valorize the value of improvisation and the wider the goal is defined, the harder it is to assess the validity of the system's behavior.

Equally, the more critical the tasks are that such a truly interactive environment performs, the bigger the impact will be felt of the irreversibility of a system's actions. The way an interactive system performs in an art performance, in a gallery or in a museum will have limited functional impact on people's activities, whereas a system that supports critical tasks such as in emergency situations or even workplace situations might encounter resistance towards unpredictable behavior - much of these contexts are based on rigid planning and adherence to planning. Structure that emerges from improvisation will benefit some contexts and operations while presenting a liability for others.

Tempo is one of the Viewpoints actors use to explore ranges of speed of their actions and interactions. For musical performers it is clear how the speed of improvised performances impacts the capability to improvise. It is hard to improvise at very high tempo of performance, leading to an inclination to employ predictable patterns and techniques that were tested before. "At extremely fast tempos there is no choice but to use preplanned, repetitive material to keep the performance going. This suggests that there are upper limits to improvisation" [18].

6   Conclusion

This paper proposes a framework for the analysis and the design of interactive environments based on a systems view of improvisation and in particular the View-points improvisation technique for theatre actors.

A study of the phenomenology of improvisation reveals that it shares fundamental characteristics with conversational dynamics often referenced in second-order systems theory. In this paper we adopt a systems view of improvisation which allows us to identify key elements, structures, and procedures in improvisation that become graspable and that are meaningful for the work on human-machine interaction.

While the development of machines capable of this kind of interaction is challenging, improvisational performers have developed their art to a high degree and can be used as a rich resource to inform this process.

Specifically, the Viewpoints improvisation for actors is identified as particularly relevant for the purpose at hand due to its well articulated technique based on nine spatial and temporal Viewpoints: Tempo, Duration, Kinesthetic Response, Repetition, Spatial Relationship, Topography, Shape, Gesture, Architecture. By mapping the foundational elements of Viewpoints improvisation to the design stages for interactive environments based on Gordon Pask's cybernetic design paradigm, this paper proposes a framework to valorize the practice and the understanding of improvisation for the development of urban interactive environments.

Acknowledgements. I am grateful for insights gained into Viewpoints improvisation from my conversations with Jonathan Carr, who trained directly under Anne Bogart, and my observations from his work with students. Initial ideas about possible systems setup for experimenting this proposal have been developed in conversations with Mark Sivak.

References

1. Dourish, P.: Where the Action Is: The Foundations of Embodied Interaction. The MIT Press, Cambridge (2001)
2. McCullough, M.: Digital Ground: Architecture, Pervasive Computing, and Environmental Knowing. The MIT Press, Cambridge (2005)
3. Streitz, N.A., et al.: Situated interaction with ambient information: facilitating awareness and communication in ubiquitous work environments. In: Tenth International Conference on Human-Computer Interaction (HCI International 2003) (2003)
4. Acampora, G., et al.: A survey on ambient intelligence in healthcare. Proc. IEEE **101**, 2470–2494 (2013)
5. Cook, D.J., Augusto, J.C., Jakkula, V.R.: Ambient intelligence: technologies, applications, and opportunities. Pervasive Mobile Comput. **5**, 277–298 (2009). Elsevier
6. Kartakis, S., et al.: Enhancing health care delivery through ambient intelligence applications. Sensors **12**, 11435–11450 (2012). Molecular Diversity Preservation International
7. Sadri, F.: Ambient intelligence: a survey. ACM Comput. Surv. (CSUR) **43**, 36 (2011)
8. Kaptelinin, V., Nardi, B.A.: Acting with Technology: Activity Theory and Interaction Design. MIT Press, Cambridge (2006)
9. Dubberly, H., Pangaro, P., Haque, U.: What is interaction? Are there different types? Interactions **16**, 69–75 (2009). ACM
10. Laurel, B.: Computers as Theatre. Addison-Wesley Professional, Reading (2013)
11. Jacob, M., Magerko, B.: Viewpoints AI. In: Proceedings of the 2015 ACM SIGCHI Conference on Creativity and Cognition, pp. 361–362. ACM (2015)
12. Corness, G., Schiphorst, T.: Performing with a system's intention: embodied cues in performer-system interaction. In: Proceedings of the 9th ACM Conference on Creativity and Cognition, pp. 156–164. ACM (2013)
13. Lu, D.V., et al.: What can actors teach robots about interaction. In: AAAI Spring Symposium: It's All in the Timing (2010)
14. Sirkin, D., et al.: Mechanical ottoman: how robotic furniture offers and withdraws support. In: Proceedings of the Tenth Annual ACM/IEEE International Conference on Human-Robot Interaction, pp. 11–18. ACM (2015)
15. Montuori, A.: The complexity of improvisation and the improvisation of complexity: social science, art and creativity. Hum. Relat. **56**, 237–255 (2003). Sage Publications
16. Bailey, D.: Improvisation: Its Nature and Practice in Music. Da Capo Press, New York (1993)
17. Berliner, P.F.: Thinking in Jazz: The Infinite Art of Improvisation. University of Chicago Press, Chicago (1994)
18. Weick, K.E.: Introductory essay—improvisation as a mindset for organizational analysis. Organ. Sci. **9**, 543–555 (1998). INFORMS
19. Landgraf, E.: Improvisation as Art: Conceptual Challenges, Historical Perspectives. Bloomsbury Academic, London (2014)
20. Simon, H.A.: The Sciences of the Artificial, 3rd edn. The MIT Press, Cambridge (1996)
21. Taylor, M.C.: The Moment of Complexity: Emerging Network Culture. University of Chicago Press, Chicago (2001)
22. Pask, G.: The architectural relevance of cybernetics. In: Architectural Design, vol. 39, pp. 494–496. D. Reidel Publishing Company, Dordrecht (1969)
23. Bogart, A., Landau, T.: The Viewpoints Book: A Practical Guide to Viewpoints and Composition. Theatre Communications Group, New York (2004)

Live Sound System with Social Media for Remotely Conducting Wildlife Monitoring

Hill Hiroki Kobayashi[✉]

Center of Spatial Information Science, The University of Tokyo,
Kashiwa, Chiba, 277-8568, Japan
kobayashi@csis.u-tokyo.ac.jp

Abstract. Currently, human-computer interaction (HCI) is primarily focused on human-centric interactions; however, people experience many nonhuman-centric interactions during the course of a day. Interactions with nature, such as experiencing the sounds of birds or trickling water, can imprint the beauty of nature in our memory. This paper presents an evaluation of such nonhuman-centric and spatial-temporal interactions to observe people's reaction to the interactions for ecological studies. The system operated 24 h a day, 365 days a year from April 1, 2000 to April 1, 2010 in the northern part of Iriomote Island (24°20′N, 123°55′E) in the southern Ryukyu Islands, Japan. In doing so, this study hopes to discover spatial-temporal processes of our imagination mechanism. Such a discovery would help us design a system that leverages the boundary of the real and virtual worlds by engaging a large number of participants to perform a specific Internet-based scientific task without knowing its purpose for ecological studies.

Keywords: Nonverbal interaction · Acoustic ecology · Human–computer–biosphere interaction · Human behavior

1 Introduction

The Chernobyl nuclear disaster report of the International Atomic Energy Agency [1] states that it is academically and socially important to conduct ecological studies regarding the levels and effects of radiation exposure on wild animal populations over several generations. Immediately following the Fukushima Daiichi nuclear power plant disaster, remnants of which are shown in Fig. 1, Ishida (a research collaborator at the University of Tokyo) started conducting regular ecological studies of wild animals in the northern Abukuma Mountains near the Fukushima Daiichi nuclear power plant, where high levels of radiation were detected. Ishida aims to place automatic recording devices at over 500 locations and has been collecting and analyzing vocalizations of target wild animals. The long-term and wide-range monitoring is required to understand the effects of the nuclear accident because he yet has little evidence of the direct effects of radioactivity on wildlife at Fukushima [2]. For monitoring such species, counting the recorded calls of animals is often an effective method because acoustic communication is used by various types of animals, including mammals, birds, amphibians, fish and insects [3, 4]. In particular, as well as using visual counts, the method is commonly used

© Springer International Publishing Switzerland 2016
N. Streitz and P. Markopoulos (Eds.): DAPI 2016, LNCS 9749, pp. 450–458, 2016.
DOI: 10.1007/978-3-319-39862-4_41

to investigate birds and amphibians [5]. An observer manually listens to calls and identifies the species from the recorded data. Therefore, the method has a disadvantage as the result is affected by the concentration of the observer to identify the species of calls.

Fig. 1. Wildlife near the Fukushima Daiichi Nuclear Power Plant [6].

This paper will discuss the design, development and evaluation of a system to tackle the previously mentioned issue. First, on the basis of the related studies, the author designs a new experiment system based on related observation methodologies. In addition, the spatial-temporal process of nonhuman-centric interactions of users is evaluated by quantitative content analysis. Finally, on the basis of the experimental results, the overall findings are discussed, including an answer to the possible applications of the system. The structure of this paper is as follows. Section 2 details background, Sect. 3 presents the proposed method, Sect. 4 details the result and Sect. 5 presents the discussions in detail. Section 6 summarizes future directions. Section 7 offers conclusions.

2   Background

As introduced above, in ecological studies, it is desirable to develop a technology that most effectively supports a study with minimal resources. More specifically, we aim to establish a long-term continuously operating ubiquitous system that delivers, in real time, environmental information, such as sound. Researchers worldwide are conducting ecological studies by recording and analyzing the spatial information of wild animal vocalizations [7]. Furthermore, ecological studies of the environment close to urban areas are being conducted using cell phones [8]; however, it is difficult to confirm the behavior of wild animals using cell phones. To record vocalizations of wild animals whose behaviors are difficult to predict, it is necessary to continuously operate a monitoring system. As it is difficult to conduct system maintenance due to the severe environmental conditions of wild animal habitats (e.g., when out of infrastructure service areas and in high-temperature and high-humidity environments), system redundancy becomes crucial.

In a previous study, we have researched and developed a proprietary system that delivers and records environmental sounds in real-time [9]. This system has been almost continuously operational on Iriomote Island in Okinawa since 1996, using equipment such as that shown in Fig. 2. To date, the basic research on Iriomote Island has been expanded to include 18 domestic and international sites, including Los Angeles and the San Francisco Bay area in the United States, Sanshiro Pond at the Hongo Campus of the University of Tokyo in Japan, Kyoto Shokokuji Mizuharu in Suikinkutsu, Mumbai City in India, the Antarctica Syowa Station (under construction), Morotsuka Village in Miyazaki and Fukushima University in Japan. We have worked with project collaborators and have introduced our system to the University of Tokyo Chichibu Forest, Otsuchi in Iwate, Shinshu University, the University of Tokyo Fuji Forest, the University of Tokyo Hokkaido Forest (under construction), the University of Tokyo International Coastal Research Center and on an uninhabited island in Iwate (also under construction). We have also been conducting research on ubiquitous interfaces for ecology studies of wild animals since April 1997. However, there is a disadvantage that the result would be affected by the concentration of the observer to identify the species of calls from the streamed live sound data.

Fig. 2. Ubiquitous systems for the real-time delivery of environmental sounds in long-term and continuous operation.

3   Proposed Method

On the basis of the mentioned problem, this study has attempted to understand the processes of nonhuman-centric interaction between users and remote uninhabited environments through the use of information technologies and reveal new knowledge regarding such interactivity [9] by observing people's reaction to the interactions for ecological studies as in Fig. 3. In doing so, this study hopes to discover spatial-temporal processes of our imagination mechanism. Such a discovery would help us design a system that leverages the boundary of the real and virtual worlds by engaging a large number of participants to perform a specific Internet-based scientific task without knowing its purpose for ecological studies. If users were found to pay attention to the bio-acoustic information present in natural sounds, it would help us design a system that leverages the boundary of the real and virtual worlds by engaging a large number of participants to perform a specific Internet-based scientific task without knowing its purpose.

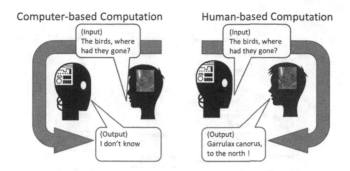

Fig. 3. Query presence of proposed method (right)

On the basis of this requirement and construction and operating experiences from previous studies [10], a new observation tool for monitoring and processing user feedback was created in the northern part of Iriomote Island (24°20′N, 123°55′E) in the southern Ryukyu Islands, Japan, seen in Fig. 4 (left). The system allows users to listen to live stream audio from a location near a tree in an uninhabited forest as in Fig. 4 (right). The system also collects audio feedback from users in real time. Furthermore, the system can separate individual words from the collected feedback data, categorize them and count their usage frequency. Figure 5 (left) shows a diagram of the system. A weatherproof microphone placed in the ecosystem collects environmental sounds 24 h a day, 365 days a year.

Fig. 4. (left) Map of cellular service cover (red) on Iriomote Island, Japan. Service coverage areas are highlighted in red by NTT Docomo. (right) Audio digitized system: A remote microphone system installed on Iriomote Island. (Color figure online)

The microphones are attached in pairs to trees with elastic bands, as shown in Fig. 4 (right). Next, the processed audio signal from the microphones is sent to the encoding/recording system and encoded to MP3 live stream and WAVE sound format files. The MP3 live stream is sent to a server in the data archive system for direct streaming over the Internet and is played on various MP3-based audio software formats at different locations simultaneously around the world. The storage/analysis system stores the WAVE sound files to its hard disks. Users can listen to the MP3 live stream through the Sound Bum interface, which uses the Apache web server with PHP and a PostgreSQL database.

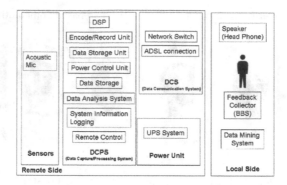

Fig. 5. Audio digitized system: a remote microphone system installed on Iriomote Island

Each comment is logged with a user defined name and location and is saved with a time stamp. The collected comment data are processed and analyzed by the KH Coder [11] to determine word frequency. On the basis of these comments, user feedback regarding the bioacoustic information is collected, and it is possible to evaluate which sounds receive the most attention. The system has been presented on the Sound Bum [12] Project web site since 1997 as in Fig. 5 (right). Since 1997, real-time environmental sounds from Iriomote Island's subtropical forests have been monitored by networked microphones and transmitted via the website as "Live-Sounds from Iriomote Island" 24 h a day, 365 days a year. The real-time streaming system has been upgraded several times over the years to improve long-term stability under unmanned operating conditions (Fig. 6).

Fig. 6. Web Interface for live sounds from Iriomote Island

4   Result

The field trial was conducted 24 h per day for 365 days from April 1, 2000 to April 1, 2010 in the northern part of Iriomote Island (24°20′N, 123°55′E) in the southern Ryukyu Islands, Japan. Electric power and information infrastructures required for monitoring the sound of a tree falling are nonexistent in this location. Figure 2 (left) shows the limited distribution of cellular service in the area. The climate is primarily seasonal with summer occurring from June to September and winter occurring from December to March. The average monthly temperature is highest in July (28.3 °C) and lowest in

January (18.0 °C). The average annual rainfall is 2342 mm (Iriomote Meteorological Station). Iriomote Island consists of highly folded mountains, and its highest peak (Mt. Komi) is 469 m above sea level. Most of Iriomote Island is covered by a subtropical evergreen broadleaved forest (83 % of the island). During the 11 years of observation period, feedback from user reactions was collected and archived, and a total of 2831 comments were recorded through the WEB interface as in Fig. 7. To analyze the semantic content of the comments, a kh_coder was employed to process the data and subtract "nouns", as shown in Table 1.

Table 1. Frequency of words in feedback comments

Noun	Number of appearances	frequency (%)
Singing voice	89	7.44
Frog	42	3.51
Microphone	37	3.09
Typhoon	33	2.76
Staff	26	2.17
Bell Cricket	25	2.09
Feeling	20	1.67
Cicada	19	1.59
A long time	17	1.42
Brown-earned bulbul	14	1.17
Noise	13	1.09
Maintenance	13	1.09
Animal	13	1.09
Airplane	13	1.09
Music	12	1.00
Crow	10	0.84
A sign of presence	10	0.84
Kind	10	0.84

Fig. 7. Web interface used to collect feedback from users (in Japanese)

5   Discussion

We successfully extracted and analyzed the comments posted by users. The phrase that appeared most frequently was "animal voices." No specific names of animals plants or words associated with the sound of falling trees or of wind or ocean tides appeared. From the recorded data, we identified the top 18 frequently appearing noun phrases from the comments, as shown in Table 1. The most frequent was "Singing Voice," which appears in 7.44 % (89 instances) of the 2831 comments [13].

From the standpoint of informatics, the amount and duration of bioacoustic information contained in sounds that could be perceived as a "Singing Voice," such as bird and animal calls, which comprise a tiny fraction of the total soundscape, are small when compared to other continuously present environmental sounds, such as wind and running water. This result indicates that listeners do not pay attention to the dominant component of the soundscape. Some listeners tried to identify callers by their specific names: "Frog" (42, 3.51 %), "Bell Cricket" (25, 2.09 %), "Cicada" (19, 1.559 %), "Brown-eared Bulbul," "Crow" (10, 0.84 %), and "Animal" (13, 1.09 %). However, results from our previous ecological study indicate that at least six types of frogs inhabited the island: Rana limnocharis, Rana psaltes, Rana supranarina, Chirixalus eiffingeri, Rhacophorus owstoni and Microhyla ornata [13]. The recognition gap indicated by comparing this study and the previous study indicates that the vast majority of users only perform sweeping recognition without paying attention to the detail of the sounds. Landscape related comments, such as "Typhoon" (33, 2.76 %) and "Airplane" (13, 1.09 %) were also identified. Also, sounds that were described as "A Sign of Presence" (10, 0.84 %) were detected by the users [13].

The type of nonhuman-centric interaction described in this paper is reflected in the semiotic theories of Jakob von Uexküll [14]. Von Uexküll established the concept of Umwelt, from the German word meaning "environment" or "surrounding world," and suggested that all animals, from the simplest to the most complex, fit into unique worlds with equal completeness. "Singing Voice" corresponds to a single animal and a simple world; "A sign of presence" corresponds to a complex, well-articulated human world. Thus, a user's reaction to the sounds can be explained by the Umwelt theory. When users listen to live sounds from the invisible world through the Internet, they tend to pay attention to both a simple singing voice and a complex presence.

The author and his associates initially introduced the concept of HCBI [15] at HCI venues focused on environmental sustainability from 2009. The theory, method and evaluation of human and wildlife interaction were not discussed in detail because the research was not sufficiently well developed. However, the future direction of this study has been suggested by several researchers. The author and his associates, ecology scientists, have developed a new type of bird census method coined "audio census," using the same live stream audio system and social media (Internet Relay Chat and Twitter) [16]. A total of 36 bird species were recorded by several ornithologists in separate places using the audio census method during the 3-month-long breeding seasons of the 3-year study period. We showed that the Live Sound System and social media could contribute to raising public interest in and realizing the auditory real-time experience of a remote natural forest.

6   Future Direction

During the recovery from the Fukushima Nuclear Power Plant disaster, the journal *Nature* [17] pointed out the importance of ecological studies from the very beginning of a disaster. Ishida (research collaborator) of the University of Tokyo, who has conducted ecological studies since immediately after the disaster, has stated that it would be extremely difficult to continue conducting ecological studies on an ongoing basis [2]. On the basis of this requirement, the development of a new monitoring tool is in progress by the author in the "difficult-to-return zone" [18], a zone whose annual radiation exposure level exceeds 50 millisieverts around the Fukushima Daiichi Nuclear Power Plant.

7   Conclusion

This paper presents an evaluation of nonhuman-centric and spatial-temporal interactions to observe people's reaction to interactions through ecological studies. The system operated 24 h a day, 365 days a year from April 1, 2000 to April 1, 2010 in the northern part of Iriomote Island (24°20′N, 123°55′E) in the southern Ryukyu Islands, Japan. In doing so, this study hopes to discover spatial-temporal processes of our imagination mechanism. Such a discovery would help us design a system that leverages the boundary of the real and virtual worlds by engaging a large number of participants to perform a specific Internet-based scientific task without knowing its purpose for ecological studies.

Acknowledgement. This study was supported by JSPS KAKENHI Grant 26700015, MIC SCOPE Grant 142103015, an Okawa Foundation for Information and Telecommunications Research Grant, a Telecommunications Advancement Foundation Research Grant, Tepco Memorial Foundation Support for International Technological Interaction, a Moritani Scholarship Foundation Research Grant, a Hatakeyma Culture Foundation Research Grant, a Mitsubishi Foundation Science and Technology Research Grant and an Ogasawara Foundation for the Promotion of Science and Engineering Research Grant.

References

1. Chernobyl Forum: Expert Group "Environment", International Atomic Energy Agency: Environmental consequences of the Chernobyl accident and their remediation: twenty years of experience. Report of the Chernobyl Forum Expert Group 'Environment'. International Atomic Energy Agency, Vienna (2006)
2. Ishida, K.: Contamination of wild animals: effects on wildlife in high radioactivity areas of the agricultural and forest landscape. In: Nakanishi, T.M., Tanoi, K. (eds.) Agricultural Implications of the Fukushima Nuclear Accident, pp. 119–129. Springer, Tokyo (2013)
3. Krebs, J.R., Davies, N.B.: An Introduction to Behavioural Ecology. Blackwell Scientific Publications, Oxford (1993)
4. Searcy, W.A., Nowicki, S.: The Evolution of Animal Communication: Reliability and Deception in Signaling Systems. Princeton University Press, Princeton (2005)
5. Heyer, W.R.: Measuring and Monitoring Biological Diversity: Standard Methods for Amphibians. Smithsonian Institution Press, Washington (1994)
6. https://www.youtube.com/watch?v=cIzanzeUejw
7. Krause, B.L.: Bioacoustics, habitat ambience in ecological balance. Whole Earth Rev. **57**, 17 (1987)
8. Lee, P., Cheok, D., James, S., Debra, L., Jie, W., Chuang, W., Farbiz, F.: A mobile pet wearable computer and mixed reality system for human poultry interaction through the Internet. Pers. Ubiquit. Comput. **10**, 301–317 (2006)

9. Kobayashi, H., Ueoka, R., Hirose, M.: Wearable forest clothing system: beyond human-computer interaction. In: ACM SIGGRAPH 2009 Art Gallery, New Orleans, Louisiana, pp. 1–7. ACM (2009)
10. Watanabe, S., Kobayashi, H.: Sound recording of vocal activity of animals inhabiting subtropical forest on Iriomote Island in the southern Ryukyus, Japan. Adv. Bioacoustics **II**, 213–228 (2007)
11. http://khc.sourceforge.net/en/
12. http://www.soundbum.org
13. Kobayashi, H.: Basic research in human-computer-biosphere interaction. Ph.D., Department of Advanced Interdisciplinary Studies, Division of Engineering. The University of Tokyo, Japan (2010)
14. von Uexküll, J.: Theoretische Biologie. Springer, Heidelberg (1928)
15. Kobayashi, H., Ueoka, R., Hirose, M.: Human computer biosphere interaction: towards a sustainable society. In: CHI 2009 Extended Abstracts on Human Factors in Computing Systems, Boston, MA, pp. 2509–2518. ACM (2009)
16. Saito, K., Nakamura, K., Ueta, M., Kurosawa, R., Fujiwara, A., Kobayashi, H.H., Nakayama, M., Toko, A., Nagahama, K.: Utilizing the Cyberforest live sound system with social media to remotely conduct woodland bird censuses in Central Japan. Ambio **44**, 572–583 (2015)
17. http://www.nature.com/news/specials/japanquake/index.html
18. Sato, I., Sasaki, J., Satoh, H., Deguchi, Y., Otani, K., Okada, K.: Distribution of radioactive cesium and its seasonal variations in cattle living in the 'difficult-to-return zone' of the Fukushima nuclear accident. Animal Science Journal (2015)

User Participatory Sensing for Disaster Detection and Mitigation in Urban Environments

Shin'ichi Konomi[1], Kazuki Wakasa[2], Masaki Ito[3(✉)], and Kaoru Sezaki[1,3]

[1] Center for Spatial Information Science, The University of Tokyo,
5-1-5, Kashiwanoha, Kashiwa, Chiba 277-8568, Japan
[2] Department of Socio-Cultural Environmental Studies, The University of Tokyo,
5-1-5, Kashiwanoha, Kashiwa, Chiba 277-8563, Japan
[3] Institute of Industrial Science, The University of Tokyo, 4-6-1, Komaba,
Meguro-ku, Tokyo 153-8505, Japan
`mito@iis.u-tokyo.ac.jp`

Abstract. Pervasive communication technologies have opened up the opportunities for citizens to cope with disasters by exploiting networked mobile devices. However, existing approaches often overlook the brittleness of the technological infrastructures and rely heavily on users' manual inputs. In this paper, we propose a robust and resilient sensing environment by extending and integrating cooperative location inference and participatory sensing using smartphones and IoTs. The proposed approach encourages proactive engagement in disaster mitigation by means of everyday data collection and end-user deployment of IoT sensors.

Keywords: Participatory sensing · Disaster mitigation · Smartphones · IoT · Urban environments · Civic computing

1 Introduction

Owing to the rapid growth of the communication bandwidth and other resources, citizen science or crowd science is now considered to be a powerful tool to gather and analyze scientific data. Especially, rapid penetration of sensor-rich smart phones and IoT sensors make it possible to retrieve real-time data about urban environments. Their sensor data can be used in ordinary times, however, they will also play a critical role in disaster monitoring [1]. Understanding what's going on and analyzing the data in fine granularity can be achieved only by user participatory sensing because we cannot deploy conventional expensive sensors with sufficient density.

Smartphones and IoT sensors can be very useful for mitigating the impact of disasters if we can effectively handle the huge amount of data they produce. We need to make their data easier to handle by applying algorithmic and statistical approaches such as aggregation, indexing, filtering, compression, data mining, and machine learning. We also need to make the data more useful by activating

© Springer International Publishing Switzerland 2016
N. Streitz and P. Markopoulos (Eds.): DAPI 2016, LNCS 9749, pp. 459–469, 2016.
DOI: 10.1007/978-3-319-39862-4_42

robust technological infrastructures for collecting and communicating accurate contextual data reliably.

In this paper, we propose a robust and resilient sensing environment by extending and integrating *cooperative location inference* and *participatory sensing using smartphones and IoTs*. Firstly, it is very important to conserve battery life of mobile devices in disaster situations as people use them to access and share critical disaster-related information and communicate with family members and friends. It is therefore highly desirable to determine the locations of mobile devices with minimum energy consumption. One of the energy efficient localization techniques for mobile devices is to use wireless location reference points and pedestrian dead reckoning rather than GPS. However, currently there is no robust pervasive infrastructure of location reference points. We use IoT devices to activate such an infrastructure. In particular, we propose a cooperative location inference mechanism to automatically determine the locations of IoT devices, thereby turning the devices into ubiquitous location reference points.

Secondly, we develop a user participatory sensing environment for mitigating the impacts of disasters based on the IoT-supported location infrastructure. The proposed environment has three key advantages compared to existing participatory sensing environments: (1) it facilitates collection of geo-tagged sensor data from smartphones and IoT sensors with smaller battery consumption, (2) it allows citizens to collect data before, during and after a disaster using smartphones, omnidirectional cameras, and environmental sensors to build an integrated large-scale database, and (3) it applies algorithmic and statistical approaches such as aggregation, indexing, filtering, compression, data mining, and machine learning to deliver relevant information such as safety-enhancing route recommendations at citizens' fingertips.

2   Related Works

We now review existing user participatory environments for disaster detection and mitigation. People use social media tools to respond to natural disasters such as earthquakes, floods, and hurricanes. They are often used as a means to collect (or "sense") critical information by organizing and coordinating volunteers. Such a form of crowdsourcing enables swift sharing of disaster information although it has certain limitations in terms of data quality as well as ease of collaboration and coordination [2]. Olteanu et al. have analyzed Tweets from various recent crises and shown their substantial variability across crises [3]. We can exploit social big data in a more informed manner as we deepen our understanding about the kinds of information crowds generate in various crises situations.

Crowdsourced disaster information is often linked to location information and can be visualized on a map. For example, volunteers monitored wildfires in Santa Barbara by showing text reports, photos and videos on a digital map [4]. Crowds can generate such maps much before authoritative information becomes available, which is an important benefit that can outweigh the cost of error-prone crowdsourcing data. Likely relevant to this discussion is that not only grassroots organizations but also governmental agencies are now exploiting crowdsourcing. For example, the Federal Emergency Management Agency (FEMA) in the U.S. recently introduced a crowdsourcing feature in their mobile app [5].

Smartphones are often used as social and participatory platforms for collecting disaster-relevant information. Moreover, there are a number of experimental projects that explore the uses of ubiquitous sensors in smartphones to infer critical information such as shakes, infrastructural damages, and fires in earthquakes. Smartphones' accelerometers can be used to measure and communicate the strengths of shakes quickly and cheaply with much higher spatial resolution than professionally managed high-quality sensors such as K-NET in Japan. Existing research by Naito et al. has shown that smartphones' accelerometers are particularly effective for monitoring shakes with the seismic intensity over 2 on the Japanese seven-stage seismic scale [6]. Monitoring strong shakes in buildings with high spatial resolution can be extremely useful for analyzing cumulative impact of shakes on buildings and even for designing safer physical structures. Community Sense and Response system (CSR) exploits accelerometers in smartphones and dedicated devices to monitor shakes cheaply and infer complex spatial patterns of shakes based on a machine learning mechanism [7]. Citizen Seismology Project interestingly senses web traffic on a popular earthquake web site and Twitter messages to detect earthquakes quickly [8,9].

Fires, which can be triggered by earthquakes, often cause significant damage to inhabitants. Early detection of the locations of fires is very important for predicting the spread of the fires and making appropriate evacuation plans in time. However, there is a relative scarcity of projects that explore smartphone-based fire detection. Some recent high-end smartphones such as Samsung Galaxy S4 are equipped with temperature and humidity sensors that can be useful for detecting high temperature and low humidity as well as their temporal variances in proximity to fires. Amjad's recent project exploits such high-end smartphones to build FireDitector that infers occurrences of fires in indoor environments using Naive Bayes Classifier with the data from smartphones' temperature, humidity, pressure and light sensors [10].

Although existing literature reports many success cases of user participatory sensing for disaster detection and mitigation, most of the existing systems use energy-hungry localization mechanisms such as the ones that heavily rely on GPS. When using stationary sensors, someone would have to specify the locations of the devices at the time of deployment. However, oftentimes, deployment processes are not clearly defined.

3   Cooperative Location Inference with IoTs

There will be as many as 26 billion Internet of Things (IoTs) in 5 years [11]. As we discussed ealier, IoTs can be extremely useful for collecting environmental information before, during and after disasters. Moreover, they can cooperate with personal and wearable devices that citizens carry around. For example, IoT devices could help smartphones to detect their context more accurately by providing useful reference data.

Smartphones can use IoT devices as location reference points or "location tags" if they can identify nearby IoT devices by using short-range radio, visual recognition, audio detection, etc. Our proposed mechanism considers two types of location tags: (T1) the ones that already know their accurate locations and (T2) the ones that don't know their accurate locations. In addition, location tags have *onstage* and *offstage* states: the system uses *onstage tags* to compute location information, and trains *offstage tags* until they are ready to "go on stage."

We now consider a physical space in which onstage *T1/T2 tags* and *offstage T2 tags* coexist. Let L be the location estimate of an *offstage tag*. Our system collects location information from the smartphones that are in proximity to the tag, and incrementally computes L as follows:

$$L_{i+1} = \frac{(i \cdot L_i) + S_{i+1}}{i+1}$$

It obtains new location estimate L_{i+1} from smartphone location S_{i+1} and existing location estimate $L_i (0 \leq i)$. This computational process can be triggered periodically, using the best smartphone location S_{i+1} in each interval. Also, when there are multiple smartphones nearby, S_{i+1} is a weighted sum of their location information. Note that our system currently uses RSSI (Received Signal Strength Indicator) to select the best S_{i+1} within each interval, and to assign a weight to each smartphone.

An *offstage tag* is turned into an *onstage tag* when its error estimation becomes smaller than a threshold value. We estimate the error by using maximum likelihood estimator of a corresponding covariance matrix. We then derive an ellipse that contains the tag's real location with 95 % confidence, and use the area of the ellipse as the tag's error estimation.

There are multiple benefits gained from providing such a localization mechanism. First of all, as it infers locations of IoT devices automatically, people don't always have to define the locations of IoT devices at the time of deployment. IoT devices can eventually be associated with corresponding location information and the data they produce will be geotagged regardless of whether they are located indoors or outdoors, whether they have GPS modules or not, and so on. We can then accumulate a lot of georeferenced data which can be used to detect points of critical events such as occurrences of fire or collapse, and possibly guide firefighters quickly to the people in need of rescue, help citizens to evacuate successfully, and assess and predict damages accurately. Moreover, location-tagged IoT devices can provide nearby smartphones with accurate location information. The smartphones can use the received location information to improve their location estimation without consuming a lot of energy. As the proposed mechanism does not rely on GPS, it is particularly useful in buildings, underground passages, and urban canyons.

4   User Participatory Sensing

Making participatory sensing useful in disaster situations would require practical solutions to fundamental problems such as energy efficient sensing, integration of mobile and stationary sensing, integration of sensing in everyday and emergency situations, and privacy preservation. We describe our approaches to tackle these issues based on our experiences developing relevant prototypes.

4.1 Energy Efficient Sensing

Some computational processing is more energy consuming than others. Thus, we can save energy by turning off energy-consuming functions most of the time. Our approach to energy conserving participatory sensing exploits energy-efficient sensors such as accelerometers to detect the appropriate timing for turning on and off more energy-hungry sensors, communication modules, and computational processes.

One of our ongoing researches aims to record daily interaction of a person by utilizing Bluetooth in a smartphone as a sensor [12]. Although Bluetooth is superior to other direct-communication method due to its usable identifier (MAC address) and useful communication range of approximately 10 m, energy consumption is still a problem. We developed a method that improves energy consumption of Bluetooth beaconing leveraging 3-axial accelerometers equipped on smartphones. Also, the method improves robustness of finding social links that tend to fail due to collision using the similarity of acceleration and sets of Bluetooth MAC addresses.

The detailed method to find other smartphones considering energy consumption is illustrated in Fig. 1. First of all, the method recognizes if a user is "staying" or not with an accelerometer based on the method proposed by Ravi et al. [13]. Second, the method recognizes if a user is "talking" or not with a microphone. The method does not utilize speech-recognition, but utilizes only the volume of sound. Finally, the method senses proximity using inquiry mode of the Bluetooth that is normally used to search unpaired devices. The phone collects the MAC addresses of nearby phones in a certain seconds.

The proposed method predicts a social link in a robust manner against failures of finding in inquiry of Bluetooth. In the following equation, $s_{ij}(B,t)$ is the strength of the social link between the person i and the person j from time t to $t + T$ where B_{it} and B_{jt} represent sets of collected MAC addresses. Even when a smartphone cannot find by the Bluetooth directory, the equation gives an indication how much two smartphones are located nearby.

$$s_{ij}(B,t) = \begin{cases} 1 & (Found) \\ \frac{B_{it} \cap B_{jt}}{B_{it} \cup B_{jt}} & (Not found) \end{cases}$$

We have shown that the proposed approach can reduce energy consumption through preliminary evaluation studies. We believe that this technique should be extended and integrated with various kinds of mobile sensing and communication tools for disaster detection and mitigation.

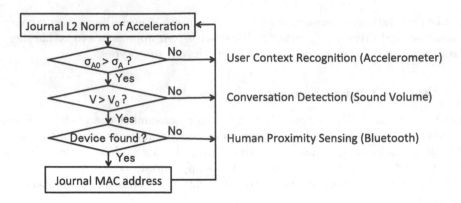

Fig. 1. Flowchart of proposed sensing method

4.2   Integration of Mobile and Stationary Sensing

When disasters occur, we would be most likely to seek ways to best utilize all the tools and datasets in complementary manners in order to minimize the negative impacts of disasters on citizens. It is then very important to develop optimal strategies and best practices to use various technologies and resources in combination.

In our previous project, we have combined stationary wireless sensor network systems and user participatory sensing to collect fine-grained environmental information, thereby enhancing the safety of citizens in extremely hot urban environments [14]. The sensor systems are deployed in an urban area, with a range about 600×600 m^2, near a railway station in Tatebayashi City, Japan. There are two independent sensor systems: a wireless sensor network (WSN) to gather temperature and humidity information and a distributed camera system to detect the traffic flows of pedestrians. The combined sensor nodes which measure the conditions of temperature and humidity have been installed on the utility poles alongside the streets. The sensor nodes transfer data to a sink node and then to a central server by using IEEE802.15.4 protocol. There are 40 combined sensor nodes which have been deployed in the target area. Stereo cameras have been installed near the streets so that they can conveniently capture the scenes of pedestrian crowds. The captured scenes are delivered to a local PC on which a detection program runs to recognize the traffic flows and velocities of pedestrians. Then the sensed data are transferred to the central server by using wireless communication. Six stereo cameras have been deployed in the target area.

One of the most important issue in this type of integrated sensing is the spatial and temporal coverage of sensor data. One might opt for eliminating redundancy, however, redundant measurements can be useful for assuring the quality of crowd sensed data. This has to be supported by the data management mechanisms on the cloud, which we will discuss in Sect. 5.

4.3   Integration of Sensing in Everyday and Emergency Situations

User participatory sensing generally requires citizens to interact with mobile sensing tools. The amount of work that users are expected to perform differs in different participatory sensing tools. Opportunistic sensing tools only requires users to install and activate the tools unless users want to deactivate and activate the tools from time to time to save energy, memory space, or protect privacy. Other data collection tools may require users to enter text, numbers, select items from menus, take photos, record sound or video clips, and so on. However, it is a question how much time and mental space citizens may have to perform such operations during a devastating crisis. In order to address this issue, we argue for an approach that integrate sensing in everyday and emergency situations.

We have sought to identify the kind of useful data which can be collected in everyday life situations and used to facilitate participatory sensing during disasters. One of such kind of data can be omnidirectional camera images along urban streets. In everyday life situations, such data can for example be used to recommend pleasant green routes for taking a walk. The same data could be used to assess damages and recommend safer rotes in disaster situations, potentially combined with complementary participatory sensing during disasters.

Inexpensive omnidirectional cameras such as Ricoh Theta and Kodak Pixpro are increasing popular, and people can take 360-degree photographs using smartphones as well. If citizens are motivated to capture and share geo-tagged omnidirectional images of streets in their everyday lives, the accumulated images can be processed as frames of reference for assessing the impact of disasters.

We have developed a system for citizens to capture omnidirectional images along urban streets and extract the amount of visible green to recommend pleasant walking routes. The system first processes omnidirectional images based on Lambert azimuthal equal-area projection. As shown in Fig. 2, it then applies an edge detector and analyzes fractal dimension to find vegetation in the images. Finally, the amount of green in each image is determined based on a color-based filtering technique. In particular, color histogram data constructed from sample images of vegetation are used to compute the percentage of vegetation in each omnidirectional image. "Green routes" can be recommended based on the resulting georeferenced data.

Although we have focused on green routes, other information can be extracted from omnidirectional images using different image processing and spatial analysis techniques. By opening up the possibilities for such everyday applications

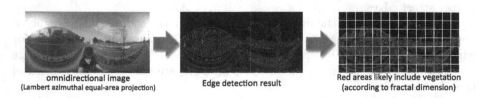

| omnidirectional image (Lambert azimuthal equal-area projection) | Edge detection result | Red areas likely include vegetation (according to fractal dimension) |

Fig. 2. Extracting the amount of vegetation from omnidirectional images

of omnidirectional street images, we expect to increase useful location indexed datasets that can be quickly retrieved and used in disaster situations.

4.4 Privacy Preservation

If there is any concern on privacy preservation in user participatory sensing, people are discouraged to join any participatory sensing applications. Further, if privacy preservation mechanism cannot be easily understood by the users, it will also discourage them. In light of these issues, we have proposed a perturbation technique called Negative survey [15] and some of its extensions. Negative survey and its extension can be applied to user participatory sensing for disaster situation. Typical example is the usage of privacy-preserving smartphones as seismometers to complement the existing infrastructure deployed by K-NET [16]. Early and detailed fire detection as well as detection of people follow in disaster situation is within our scope. We have also proposed mechanisms for protecting location privacy [17], which makes it difficult to trace the trajectory of a specific node. Since the degree of location privacy is not yet well defined, we are now tackling the issue and try to re-define it [18].

5 System Architecture for Providing Integrated Services

To use the data collected through user participatory sensing effectively, we briefly describe methods to (1) build the environmental data warehouse (EDW) which works as an infrastructure providing comprehensive and predictive environmental information, and (2) integrate heterogeneous environmental information from multi-modal sensors into an aggregate value which facilitates further processing, and (3) determine the optimal path plans in environments which are varying continuously.

Figure 3 shows the overall architecture. Raw multi-modal sensor data are input into fact tables of the EDW where multidimensional data model and data prediction method are applied. The dimensional information of space and time is extracted and aggregated into dimension tables. The EDW contains predictive functions therefore it can provide historical, current and future environmental information.

The walkable space of pedestrians is modeled as a street network. The intersections are treated as nodes and the walkable street segments between intersections are treated as edges. Map matching is applied to associate sensor data to proper street edges.

In order to integrate the multi-modal sensor data consistently and flexibly, a novel multi-factor cost (MFC) model is proposed. The aggregate cost rates for edges are calculated out by applying the MFC model. The cost value of an edge accessed by the PP engine is the product of aggregate cost rate and the travel time for that edge.

Based on the former two solutions, the optimal path planning (PP) problem is solved in a time-dependent network by applying a dynamic programming

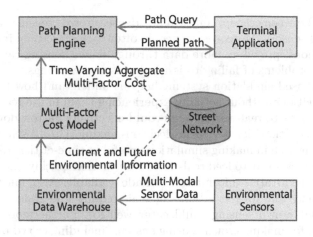

Fig. 3. Overall architecture of the proposed methods

method. The PP engine receives path queries that are submitted by pedestrians in real time. We have developed the prototype client application running on an Android smartphone. A map view is displayed on the smartphone and the pedestrian can specify her origin and destination by touching the screen. Then the planned path calculated on a server is displayed on the map view to navigate the pedestrian to approach her destination.

This architecture has been used to integrate the data from a wireless sensor network (WSN) to gather temperature and humidity information and a distributed camera system to detect the traffic flows of pedestrians [19], thereby recommending comfortable and safe navigation routes in an extremely hot urban environments.

6   Conclusion

We have proposed a robust and resilient sensing environment by extending and integrating cooperative location inference and user participatory sensing. The proposed user participatory sensing environment supports energy efficient sensing, integrated sensing in everyday and emergency situations using mobile and stationary sensors, and privacy preservation. In particular, the proposed environment encourages proactive engagement in disaster mitigation by means of everyday data collection. The automated location inference facilitates end-user deployment of IoT sensors as well.

User participatory sensing has important roles to play even when high quality sensors and simulation systems are in place. Oftentimes disaster-monitoring infrastructures are of national and/or regional concerns. Infrastructures, such as Japanese K-NET, are deployed and managed under different budgetary restrictions, which may lead to compromised spatial resolutions of sensors. In the Japanese context, it is particularly important to consider complementary relationships between cheap, quick and dense crowd sensing and reliable infrastructural sensors. Moreover, as people often face scarcity of information in disaster situations, providing more data through crowd sensing can help reduce false negative problems of failing to issue alarms and warnings.

Computer-based simulation systems help us understand how things behave in disaster situations without actually experiencing them in the real world. Connecting simulations to real-world events could effectively narrow down the space for what-if explorations for pertinent decision-making. Crowd sensing then can play a significant role in making simulations useful in time-critical disaster situations as it provides a way to feed real-world information quickly into simulations, much before authoritative information is made available. Also, microscopic simulations of shakes and fires at a building scale require fine-grained feed of real-world data that crowd sensing could cater well for. Furthermore, simulations could be useful for making crowd-sensing systems including crowd behaviors and computational processing mechanisms smarter. For example, simulation results could be used to request sensing tasks efficiently by prioritizing data collection based on the most critical goals such as saving lives.

We expect that our current results will be extended to be a systemic yet flexible environment rather than a complex, monolithic system. Thus, our proposed mechanisms could be adapted easily to different disaster situations and different external systems.

Acknowledgments. We acknowledge Prof. Toshihiro Osaragi for providing us the mobility simulation data right after a great earthquake. This work was supported by CREST, JST.

References

1. Inoguchi, M., Tamura, K., Sudo, S., Hayashi, H.: Implementation of prototype mobile application operated on smartphones for micromedia service. J. Disaster Res. **9**(2), 139–148 (2014)
2. Gao, H., Barbier, G., Goolsby, R.: Harnessing the crowdsourcing power of social media for disaster relief. IEEE Intell. Syst. **26**, 10–14 (2011)
3. Olteanu, A., Vieweg, S., Castillo, C., What to expect when the unexpected happens: social media communications across crises. In: Proceedings of the 18th ACM Conference on Computer Supported Cooperative Work & Social Computing (CSCW 2015), pp. 994–1009 (2015)
4. Goodchild, M.F., Glennon, J.A.: Crowdsourcing geographic information for disaster response: a research frontier. Int. J. Digital Earth **3**(3), 231–241 (2010)
5. Disaster Reporter. http://www.fema.gov/disaster-reporter. Accessed 1 Jan 2015
6. Naito, S., Azuma, H., Senna, S., Yoshizawa, M., Nakamura, H., Hao, K., Fujiwara, H., Hirayama, Y., Yuki, N., Yoshida, M.: Development and testing of a mobile application for recording and analyzing seismic data. J. Disaster Res. **8**(5), 990–1000 (2013)
7. Faulkner, M., Clayton, R., Heaton, T., Chandy, K.M., Kohler, M., Bunn, J., Guy, R., Liu, A., Olson, M., Cheng, M., Krause, A.: Community sense, response systems: your phone as quake detector. CACM **57**(7), 66–75 (2014)

8. EMSC, Citizen Seismology. http://www.citizenseismology.eu/. Accessed 1 Jan 2015
9. Meyer, P.: Using flash crowds to automatically detect earthquakes and impact before anyone else. http://irevolution.net/2014/10/27/using-flashsourcing-to-automatically-detect-earthquakes/. Accessed 1 Jan 2015
10. Amjad, M.M.M.: Naive bayes classifier-based fire detection using smartphone sensors, Master's Thesis, University of Agder
11. Gartner, Inc, Says, Gartner, 4.9 Billion Connected "Things" Will Be in Use in (2015). http://www.gartner.com/newsroom/id/2905717. Accessed 1 Oct 2015
12. Shimizu, K., Iwai, M., Sezaki, K.: Social link analysis using wireless beaconing and accelerometer. In: IEEE 27th International Conference on Advanced Information Networking and Applications Workshops (WAINA), pp. 33–38 (2013)
13. Ravi, N., Dandekar, N., Mysore, P., Littman, M.: Activity recognition from accelerometer data. In: Proceedings of the National Conference on Artificial Intelligence, vol. 20, no. 3, p. 1541 (2005)
14. Dang, C., Iwai, M., Umeda, K., Tobe, Y., Sezaki, K.: NaviComf: navigate pedestrians for comfort using multi-modal environmental sensors. In: IEEE Pervasive Computing and Communication (Percom 2012), Switzerland, March 2012
15. Esponda, E., Guerrero, V.M.: Surveys with negative questions for senstive items. Statics Probab. Lett. **79**(24), 2456–2461 (2009)
16. Konomi, S., Kostakos, V., Sezaki, K., Shibasaki, R.: Crowd sensing for disaster response and preparedness. In: The 77th National Concention of IPSJ, pp. 449–451 (2015)
17. Huang, L., Matsuura, K., Sezaki, K.: Enhancing wiereless location privacy using silent period. WCNC **2005**, 1187–1192 (2005)
18. Matsuno, Y., Ito, M., Sezaki, K.: Impact of time-varying population density on location privacy preservation level. In: The 5th IEEE International Workshop on the Impact of Human Mobility in Pervasive Systems and Applications (IEEE PerMoby). Sydney, Australia (2016)
19. Umeda, K., Hashimoto, Y., Nakanishi, T., Irie, K., Terabayashi, K.: Subtraction stereo: a stereo camera system that focuses on moving regions. In: Proceedings of SPIE 7239, Three-Dimensional Imaging Metrology, p. 723908 (2009)

The Use of Historical Information to Support Civic Crowdsourcing

Tomoyo Sasao[1(✉)] and Shin'ichi Konomi[2]

[1] Department of Socio-Cultural Environmental Studies,
The University of Tokyo, Kashiwa, Chiba 277-8563, Japan
sasaotomoyo@csis.u-tokyo.ac.jp
[2] Center for Spatial Information Science, The University of Tokyo,
Kashiwa, Chiba 277-8568, Japan
konomi@csis.u-tokyo.ac.jp

Abstract. Context-aware notifications cannot be designed easily without knowing which context-aware notifications will be triggered and responded in time. In this paper, we discuss methods to improve the design of context-aware notifications. Using the data from our prior experiment, we identify main factors that influence citizens' responses to notifications and evaluate the predictability of quick responses using a simplified method. We then propose a model for designing civic crowdsourcing tasks based on historical information. We believe that creating well-designed notifications can decrease receivers' workloads and simultaneously expands the positive impacts of civic crowdsourcing on the quality of life in the city.

Keywords: Civic crowdsourcing · Context-aware notification · Design

1 Introduction

This paper focuses on a smartphone-based locative media infrastructure for community-based crowdsourcing, which allows motivated citizens to generate tasks for citizens at large to help improve their local community and tackle social problems together. Recently, social ties of neighbors are becoming weaker and an increasing number of citizens are unconcerned spectators of their living environments. Raising citizens' awareness about local environments and triggering social actions are contemporary keys to achieve a sustainable community. We expect that smartphone-based context-aware notifications will play a key role in triggering awareness of social actions in proper place, time and situations, thereby providing solutions to pertinent issues in local communities.

A key problem of triggering citizens' actions by using context-aware notifications on smartphones is the difficulty to predict the timing to send notifications so as to maximize the chance that the receivers notice the notification and move into relevant action at the right time. Task designers may fail to create successful notifications even if they can define accurate task-relevant geo-fences easily. In our prior experiment, in which 19 citizens received community-related notifications during 28 days, only 30 % of the notifications were replied within 5 min. In other words, 70 % of the notifications

© Springer International Publishing Switzerland 2016
N. Streitz and P. Markopoulos (Eds.): DAPI 2016, LNCS 9749, pp. 470–481, 2016.
DOI: 10.1007/978-3-319-39862-4_43

were replied more than 5 min after their delivery. This can be problematic since task designers often expect quick replies before the recipients move out of the corresponding geo-fences. This potential mismatch between the expectations of task designers and the actual behaviors of task workers can cause serious problems by degrading task quality, weakening task worker's motivation, and thereby undermining the sustainability of the crowdsourcing system.

In this paper, we present our methodology to use response logs of a mobile crowdsourcing system, which asks citizens small tasks through context aware notifications, so that task designers can grasp which areas are likely to generate quick *in-situ* reactions. In the case of our prior experiment, which used context-aware notifications for delivering crowdsourcing tasks in a local community, the system's response logs include the locations and timestamps of which task workers received and replied the notifications. We use them to find the areas with the high potential to collect *in-situ* reaction. Our work is in line with the previous research that focuses on historical information including the proposals of social navigation techniques [1, 2], while little work has examined the potential of using historical information in the community-based computing. We also present our preliminary works to use historical information for giving advice to the designers of tasks and notifications.

First, we discuss the reasons why some notifications could induce quick responses. We analyze the response logs from our prior field study and find a primary factor that influences the acts of replying to notifications. Second, we test whether the variable, can be used for a statistical forecast of the areas that have high potential to generate quick responses. We validate the results by using the notification delivery and response logs of our prior one-month field study. Finally, we proposed a model of an interactive system that supports task designers to improve notifications. The system allows task designers to embed notifications in suitable locations and contexts. For example, if a new notification designed by a task designer is unlikely to induce sufficient *in-situ* responses, this model recommends to (a) change the content of the notification to make it easier to reply later in other places, (b) change the triggering time slot, and (c) change the triggering place to make the notification more likely to be responded quickly and *in situ*. We also discuss the effect of the proposed model for local community.

2 Prior Field Study

In our prior field study, we developed a smart phone app that receive context-aware notifications including small tasks about local community such as *"Take a photo of illegally parked cars"*, *"Do you see any garbage on the street? Choose yes or no"*, *"Please describe if you see any undesirable activities on this sidewalk. Input a short comment"* and so on and we also established a design environment for these notifications. Under the environment, citizens can design small community tasks by defining task formats, contents, and task triggers (see Fig. 1), and these notifications are made available on the smartphones of the residents. When the residents drop into the geo-fences with the notifications, they are asked to do small tasks following the contents of the notifications.

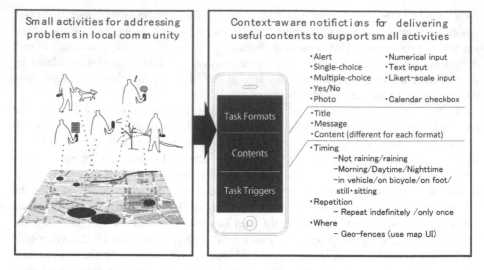

Fig. 1. Context-aware notification design environment (prototype in our prior work [3])

We conducted an experiment in a small residential area (about 1 km^2). The experiment has two parts; one is the notification design by a group of 4 citizens and the other is the notification use by 19 citizens in the local community. In the notification design part, safety-related notifications were generated, including the 21 notifications that are based on a colocated group work by the participants and the additional 21 notifications based on existing contents on the web. In the second part, we recruited the recipients of notification for one month from this target area. The recipients can respond to notifications if they want to perform the requested task. Nineteen citizens participated in this experiment. We collected month-long historical information including the locations and timestamps of all notifications and replies. We use these data to discuss the use of historical information in civic crowdsourcing.

3   Related Works

3.1   Leveraging Historical Information

Worker's Mobility Information. Locations, transportation modes, traces, and so on are collected from crowdsourcing workers' mobile phones. Some researches use this personal historical information for estimating the most significant destinations for each person using clustering algorithms [4–6]. Moreover other researchers use those information for predicting and proposing more relevant to the user's next destination [7, 8]. As another approach, some researchers use whole workers' historical information for building social mobility networks or throwing out coverage where workers' works done. From these networks, they can simulate the movements of individuals as well as enclosing spatio-temporal stability of workers' behaviors [9, 10]. In addition, Kazemi and Shahabi use location entropy to measure the total number of workers in that location as well as the relative proportion of their future visits to that location and they Least Location Entropy Priority (LLEP) Strategy as one of their task assignment protocol [11]. Reddy et al. presents framework of coverage based recruitment by processing workers' mobility historical data [12].

Application Manipulation Logs. Ratings for working quality, and worker's reaction when given the opportunity to task participation (Participation likelihood) can be collected from the workers' mobile phones. These data have potentials to be used in participation and performance based recruitment [12], and in creation of suitable incentives by person [13].

3.2 A Type of Mobile Crowdsourcing Tasks

Although researches based on ideas of using mobile devices and defining citizens as task workers for crowdsourcing are increasing recently, efficient approaches are different depending on what kind of data a task designer wants to collect or what kind of tasks a task designer wants to serve. In our research, crowdsourcing tasks require the workers to be physically located at that location and in registered contexts in order to perform the corresponding task. Additionally, the tasks don't have a worker list that is created from the worker's rating in advance, and they require people who pass close to the task location. While the number of research projects on mobile crowdsourcing in smart cities are increasing recently, few studies focus on the site-specific task, which need to be performed in that location. Kazemi and Shahabi focus on same type of mobile tasks with ours called *special tasks* such as taking a picture from a particular building [11] and presented some effective task assignment protocols including the one based on current worker's location and location entropy. Our focus in this paper is a method of enriching task qualities using historical information for such kind of spatial crowdsourcing.

3.3 Quick Responses

Research that focuses on quick responses mainly uses the following two approaches. First one is a smartphone based interaction approach, which focus on designing smartphone interface for quick input in performing crowdsourcing tasks. This includes the uses of unlock screen [14–16]. These interfaces make it easy to engage crowdsourcing workers in the place where the workers receive the task. They facilitate such engagement by decreasing the worker's workloads in that place. Second one is a physical interaction based approach, which focus on embedding the interaction in public spaces and making strict bonds that cannot be separated between a task receiving spot and a task performing spot. Gallacher el al. presented tangible questionnaire box and succeed to collect event attendees' relevant opinions during the event [17]. However, there are few researches encouraging to quick responses for mobile crowdsourcing tasks by using historical information such as spots of notification received and responded.

4 Main Factors that Influence Citizens' Responses to Mobile Crowdsourcing Tasks

Context-aware notifications are triggered in many different situations and their contents may include all kinds of topics. Thus, it is difficult to forecast whether someone responds to a notification and whether the response is provided quickly. We next examine main factors that influence whether or not citizens respond to notifications and if their responses are provided quickly.

4.1 Notification Response

To search the main factors that influence the responses to notifications, we use binomial logistic regression with the dependent variable indicating whether or not the participant respond to a received notification. We prepared 51 candidate independent variables from various categories (i.e., notification receiver's characteristics such as demographic attributes, perceptions of the local community, familiarity with smart devices; characteristics of notifications such as their contents, context, and geo-fences; characteristics of the contexts at the time when receiving the notification such as impression of the received notification) and carefully selected relevant variables that may have significant effects on the result considering multicollinearity. Chi-squared test has been used to check the variables one by one and variance inflation factor (VIF) has been computed in incremental steps. The final model has the VIF that is under 5.

Finally, our comparison of two sets of notifications, one of which is designed by 4 local community group members and the other designed based on existing contents on the web, shows that the logistic regression models were statistically significant ($p < 0.01$). The model of the former set of notifications explained 47.2 % (Nagelkerke R^2) of the variance in a notification response event and correctly classified 86.9 % of the cases. The model of the latter set of notifications explained 60.6 % (Nagelkerke R^2) of the variance in a notification response event and correctly classified 84.3 % of the cases.

The result we obtained from the analysis with the selected variables has revealed the main factors that influence whether or not notifications are responded for both sets of notifications. They are the variables concerned with the user's contexts when receiving the notifications. In particular, occurrences of other notification events before and after the received notification strongly impact the decision whether or not to respond to notifications.

4.2 Quick Response

To explore main factors that influence citizens' quick responses, we classified all notification events in our prior experiment (n = 4460) into the following 4 classes according to response patterns:

(1) notifications that are responded immediately (i.e., within 5 min),

(2) notifications that are responded more than 5 min after their receipt, and immediately after the receipt of other notifications,
(3) notifications responded more than 5 min after their receipt, and *not* immediately after the receipt of other notifications, and
(4) notifications that are not responded.

Figure 2 shows spatial distributions of each pattern of notifications. We can see that there are a number of overlapping areas among these spatial distributions, and that we can't clearly distinguish Pattern 1 from the other patterns only based on these spatial distributions.

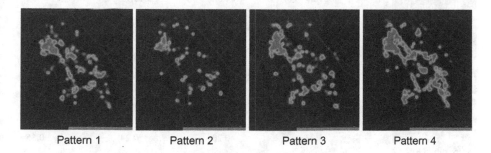

| Pattern 1 | Pattern 2 | Pattern 3 | Pattern 4 |

Fig. 2. Heat maps of emerging notifications

Next, we examine the events during the period between 5 min before and after the receipt of notifications, such as the mean numbers of the other notifications received in this period and the mean numbers of the other notifications replied in this period (see Table 1). The result shows that Pattern 1 has much higher average numbers of other notifications replied in this period than other patterns. We thus use this variable for forecasting the places where citizens respond to notifications quickly.

5 Evaluating the Predictability of Quick Responses

In this section, we evaluate the predictability of the places where citizens respond to notifications quickly using the response logs. If such prediction is confirmed to be feasible, designers of civic crowdsourcing tasks can create efficient notifications based on predictions.

According to the result of Sect. 3, the notifications that participants responded quickly (i.e., Pattern 1) have much higher numbers of other notifications responded in the ± 5 min period. We infer from the result that quick responses might be forecast from the spatial distribution of the numbers of responses. Then, as a preliminary analysis, we verify the predictability of quick responses based on the spatial distribution of the number of responses using the log file from our prior experiment.

Table 1. Classification of notifications based on the patterns of their responses

	Pattern 1	Pattern 2	Pattern 3	Pattern 4
	Responded imme-diately ($\leqq$ 5 min.)	Responded later (> 5 min.) (immediately after other notifications)	Responded later (> 5 min.) (*not* immediately after other notifications)	No responses
Number of notifications (%)	660 (14.8%)	372 (8.3%)	1,129 (25.3%)	2,299 (51.5%)
Mean response time (h:m:s)	0:01:29	1:04:32	3:10:13	N/A
Mean number of other notifica-tions received during the ± 5 min period	4.02	4.75	3.34	4.15
Mean number of other notifica-tions replied during the ± 5 min period	4.88	0.20	0.24	0.55

5.1   Method

The log file includes the data from the 4-week period. We use the data from the first 3 weeks to build a forecasting model, and the data from the last 1 week to evaluate the model.

First, we have constructed a spatial distribution of response events using the data from the first 3 weeks. The data are aggregated based on grids with different sizes (see Table 2).

Table 2. Grids used for constructing spatial distribution

	Grid-4	Grid-16	Grid-64	Grid-256	Grid-1024	Grid-4096
Num of cells	2×2	4×4	8×8	16×16	32×32	64×64
Length of cell	1295m	324m	162m	81m	41m	20m

Second, we divide the cells into two groups based on the median of the number of response events. The group that has values larger than the median (G^+) is regarded as areas where quick responses can be obtained frequently. We expected that the areas with the other group (G^-) would not induce quick responses.

Third, we have constructed a spatial distribution of triggered notifications that were responded quickly (i.e., Pattern 1) using the data from the last week, and aggregated the events for each cell. We compare the numbers of quickly responded notifications between the two groups using independent t-test.

5.2 Result

We found that, in Grid-256, Grid-1024 and Grid-4096, cells in group G^+ had statistically significantly larger numbers of notification events that got a quick response (Pattern1) in the last week: Grid-256[t(24.833) = 3.209, p < 0.01], Grid-1024[t (27.515) = 2.875, p < 0.01], Grid-4096[t(28.847) = 2.105, p < 0.05]. Based on this result, it is possible to forecast the places in which many notifications are quickly responded by using historical response logs for Grid-256, Grid-1024, and Grid-4096.

We also found that in Grid-256, Grid-1024 and Grid-4096, cells in group G^+ had statistically significantly larger numbers of ignored notification events (Pattern 4) in the last week: Grid-256[t(24.468) = 2.765, p < 0.05], Grid-1024[t(28.820) = 2.723, p < 0.05], Grid-4096[t(29.576) = 2.494, p < 0.05]. This result shows that, although we can forecast the places in which many notifications are quickly responded, the same places may have a large number of ignored notifications. It is difficult to divide these two phenomena by only using a spatial distribution of response events (see Fig. 3). To cope with this issue, we could consider other conditions such as the ones based on time.

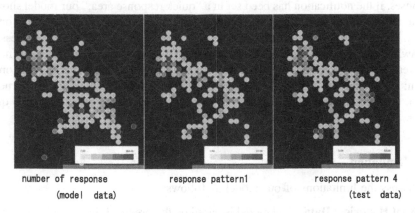

number of response	response pattern1	response pattern 4
(model data)		(test data)

Fig. 3. Heat map based on the count each grid

6 Designing Civic Crowdsourcing Tasks Based on Historical Information

The result of Sect. 4 shows that the places where notification recipients tend to respond quickly can be predicted based on historical information. Historical information will increase gradually, thereby improving prediction accuracy. As the accuracy improves, such prediction can be used to provide suggestions for designing effective notifications that induce quick responses. We propose a model for supporting civic crowdsourcing task designers to design effective context-aware notifications. The model is based on notifications that have already been embedded in a local community as well as their usage logs. This model can be used to provide advice to improve notifications based on the places predicted to have high or low chances of acquiring quick responses. For example, if a notification designer sets a notification in a place with a high chance of acquiring quick responses, this model can let the designer know that the place is appropriate for a site-specific task such as *"take a picture of this park."* Meanwhile, if a notification designer wants to collect quick responses but sets the notification in a place with low chance of acquiring quick responses, the model will recommend to change the content of the notification so that responses can be useful even when they are collected at a later point in time based on the memories of respondents, or tweak the timing and the location of the notification to collect responses as quickly as possible.

Figure 4 shows an example that illustrates the usage of the model for the support of designing notifications. The goal here is to increase the number of quickly responded notifications. First, a notification designer creates a context-aware notification without worrying about how quickly it might be responded. The designer specifies (1) notification contents (e.g., task requests and questions), (2) areas that trigger notification (e.g., geo-fences), and (3) other detailed trigger contexts (e.g., time span, weather, activity patterns such as walking speed or activity categories such as walking, biking, driving, etc.). Our model uses these pieces of information input from the notification designer, and provides pertinent advice to improve the quality of the notification. First, this model judges whether or not a designed trigger area is likely produce quick responses. If the notification has been set in a "quick response area," our model shows a message "your notification is set in a context that can produce quick responses" on the screen, and the designer can revise the notification contents based on the message. Meanwhile, if the notification has not been set in a "quick response area," our model can create the following three kinds of advice and shows the most suitable one on the screen; (1) change the time slot of the notification, (2) change the area of the notification, (3) modify the content of the notification by taking into account that no quick responses may be obtained.

6.1   Limitation

We discuss the limitations of our model as follows:

Different Historical Data. The model is based on the predictability of quick responses using historical information. In this study, we only use the logs from our prior experiment, which was conducted during a one-month period involving only 19 participants. We also focused on crowdsourcing for safety in a specific local community. Thus our data may be biased for these specific conditions, and we cannot make strong general conclusions based on these data. However, it is possible to extract different predictor variables which are suitable in different conditions by using the processes described this study. We can do so by using different historical information collected in different conditions. In future, we will clarify the minimum amount of data required for reasonable prediction and build a sophisticated forecast algorithm using time stamp data and so on.

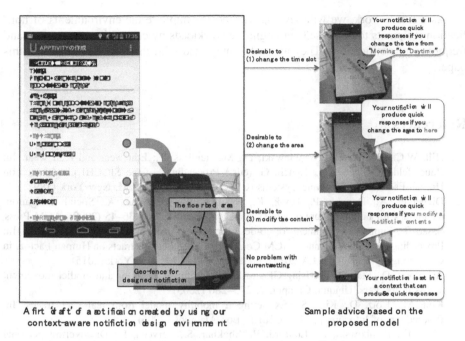

Fig. 4. Supporting model of designing notifications

Consideration of "no response." This study supposed that "quick response places" are the areas in which many people respond quickly after receiving notifications. We then forecast spatial distribution of the amount of quick responses. The reason why we focus on forecasting the amount of quick responses rather than the rate of quick responses is that our current purpose is to allow notification designers to collect many quick responses. While this can be highly useful for notification designers, it may not reduce the number of ignored notifications. In future, we will also consider forecasting the rate of quick responses.

7   Conclusion and Future Works

This paper focuses on the difficulty of controlling the timing of which context-aware notifications are responded. To solve this problem, we discussed methods to improve notification design environments, rather than the environments of notification recipients. Nevertheless, we believe that creating well-designed notifications can decrease receivers' workloads and simultaneously expands the positive impacts of civic crowdsourcing on the quality of life in the city. Using the data from our prior experiment, we found main factors that influence citizens' responses to mobile crowdsourcing tasks and evaluated the predictability of quick responses using a simplified method. We then proposed a model for designing civic crowdsourcing tasks based on historical information.

As a future work, we will develop methods to improve the environments of notification recipients to decrease their cognitive workloads by controlling the amount and frequency of notifications. They are to be integrated with the model proposed in this paper.

References

1. Hill, W.C., Hollan, J.D., Wroblewski, D., McCandless, T.: Edit wear and read wear. In: Bauersfeld, P., Bennett, J., Lynch, G. (eds.) Proceedings of the SIGCHI Conference on Human Factors in Computing Systems (CHI 1992), pp. 3–9. ACM, New York (1992)
2. Dieberger, A., Dourish, P., Hook, K., Resnick, P., Wexelblat, A.: Social navigation: techniques for building more usable systems. Interactions 7(6), 36–45 (2000). ACM Press
3. Sasao, T.: Support environment for co-designing micro tasks in suburban communities. In: Proceedings of the 33rd Annual ACM Conference Extended Abstracts on Human Factors in Computing Systems (CHI EA 2015), pp. 231–234. ACM, New York (2015)
4. Ashbrook, D., Starner, T.: Using GPS to learn significant locations and predict movement across users. Pers. Ubiquit. Comput. 7, 275–286 (2003)
5. Kim, M., Kotz, D., Kim, S.: Extracting a mobility model from real user traces. In: Proceedings of Infocom, pp. 1–13. IEEE, Los Alamitos (2006)
6. Zhou, C., Frankowski, D., Ludford, P., Shekhar, S., Terveen, L.: Discovering personal gazetteers: an interactive clustering approach. In: Proceedings of GIS, pp. 266–273. ACM, New York (2004)
7. Bhattacharya, A., Das, S.: LeZi-update: an information-theoretic approach to track mobile users in PCS networks. In: Proceedings of Mobicom, pp. 1–12. ACM, New York (1999)
8. Krumm, J., Horvitz, E.: Predestination: inferring destinations from partial trajectories. In: Proceedings of Ubicomp, pp. 243–260. ACM, New York (2006)
9. Hsu, W., Dutta, D., Helmy, A.: CSI: a paradigm for behavior-oriented delivery services in mobile human networks. ACM Trans. Netw. (2008)
10. Eagle, N., Pentland, A.: Reality mining: sensing complex social systems. Pers. Ubiquit. Comput. 10(4), 255–268 (2006)
11. Kazemi, L., Shahabi, C.: GeoCrowd : enabling query answering with spatial Crowdsourcing. In: Proceedings of International Conference on Advances in Geographic Information Systems, pp. 189–198 (2012)
12. Reddy, S., Estrin, D., Srivastava, M.: Recruitment framework for participatory sensing data collections. In: Floréen, P., Krüger, A., Spasojevic, M. (eds.) Pervasive 2010. LNCS, vol. 6030, pp. 138–155. Springer, Heidelberg (2010)
13. Feng, Z., Zhu, Y., Zhang, Q., Zhu, H., Yu, J., Cao, J., Ni, L.M.: Towards truthful mechanisms for mobile crowdsourcing with dynamic smartphones. In: 2014 IEEE 34th International Conference on Distributed Computing Systems (ICDCS), pp. 11–20. IEEE (2014)
14. Vaish, R., Wyngarden, K., Chen, J., Cheung, B., Bernstein, M.S.: Twitch crowdsourcing: crowd contributions in short bursts of time. In: Proceedings of the SIGCHI Conference on Human Factors in Computing Systems (CHI 2014), pp. 3645–3654. ACM, New York (2014)
15. Truong, K.N., Shihipar, T., Wigdor, D.: Slide to X: unlocking the potential of smartphone unlocking. In: The Proceedings of CHI 2014: The ACM Conference on Human Factors in Computing Systems, Toronto, Ontario, pp. 3635–3644 (2014)

16. Banovic, N., Brant, C., Mankoff, J., Dey, A.: ProactiveTasks: the short of mobile device use sessions. In: Proceedings of the 16th International Conference on Human-Computer Interaction with Mobile Devices and Services (MobileHCI 2014), pp. 243–252. ACM, New York (2014)
17. Gallacher, S., Golsteijn, C., Wall, L., Koeman, L., Andberg, S., Capra, L., Rogers, Y.: Getting quizzical about physical: observing experiences with a tangible questionnaire. In: Proceedings of the 2015 ACM International Joint Conference on Pervasive and Ubiquitous Computing (UbiComp 2015), pp. 263–273. ACM, New York (2015)

One to Many: Opportunities to Understanding Collective Behaviors in Urban Environments Through Individual's Passively-Collected Locative Data

Anthony Vanky[1(✉)], Theodore Courtney[2], Santosh Verma[2], and Carlo Ratti[1]

[1] Senseable City Lab, Department of Urban Studies and Planning,
Massachusetts Institute of Technology, Cambridge, MA, USA
{tvanky,cratti}@mit.edu
[2] Liberty Mutual Research Institute for Safety, Hopkinton, MA, USA
{theodore.courtney,santosh.verma}@libertymutual.com

Abstract. Walkable cities are of increased interest for urban planners and active transportation professionals, where a greater understanding of pedestrian behaviors is needed. This presentation discusses an approach for measuring spatiotemporal macro-behaviors of walking activity in urban environments using anonymized, individual, locative, passively-collected data recorded by popular physical activity mobile applications. With this data, we explore the characteristics of aggregated pedestrian activity within the physical and social milieu of the city at scale, with temporal detail, and in consideration of the infrastructural and urban characteristics influencing individual activity.

Keywords: Urban planning · Mobile applications · Locative data · Spatiotemporal data · Physical activity

1 Introduction

With ever increasing frequency, the digital devices that sustain our contemporary way of life communicate back to servers and networks, leaving traces of our physical life. This pervasiveness of mobile devices is also increasingly becoming individualized, with a machine (or more) for every person, especially as the locative technologies document our activities in space and time. This data can be used to make apparent the individual dynamics and flow of materials, capital, and information resources and the individual human behaviors within a city [1]. At this scale the emphasis is increasingly on locative data, concerned with the positional coordinates of human activity, being produced by mobile applications and the devices themselves. We now move ever closer to fully understanding people in place through the analysis of this data, with an ever increasing ability to contextualize activities and behaviors at the urban scale. In a sense, digital interfaces are availing better understand the previously opaque relationship between people and place [2, 3].

Like Geertz's interpretations on a common eye wink [4], the interpretation human activity in urban space must be contextualized. This has been incredibly difficult in the

© Springer International Publishing Switzerland 2016
N. Streitz and P. Markopoulos (Eds.): DAPI 2016, LNCS 9749, pp. 482–493, 2016.
DOI: 10.1007/978-3-319-39862-4_44

context of urban history–how do we understand the public behaviors of urban dwellers at the scale of their city, particularly the elements of the city that are within the purview of the urban planner? The question of "good city form" has been of long pursuit, but without a means of quantifying the relationship between inhabitant and the public nature of urbanism. Jane Jacobs describes the importance of this public life:

Streets are almost always public: owned by the public, and when we speak of the public realm we are speaking in large measure of streets. What is more, streets change... If we can develop and design streets so that they are wonderful, fulfilling places to be, community-building places, attractive public places for all people of cities and neigh-borhoods, then we will have successfully designed about one-third of the city directly and will have had an immense impact on the rest [5].

In a similar vein, Jan Gehl [6] calls attention to the life between buildings. It is in the spaces between architecture where the social connections of inhabitants are created and reaffirmed, and where the space of movement coexists with the social life of the city. These aspects form inter-related patterns of movement and activity to which build-ings in turn respond. To Lynch, this life also imbues these spaces with meaning. Image-able paths contain characteristic spatial qualities that are able to strengthen the attention and meaning of the street to its users [7]. Such paths set up relationships among buildings, spaces, and urban features arrayed along them, due to their proximity to one another, or the geometric configuration of the street itself. For instance, the distinctively articulated facades, the greenway, and the width of the Champs-Élysées give the boulevard prom-inence in Paris, inviting people to ambulate along it.

With the prevalence of digital technologies, particularly locative technologies embedded in our mobile devices, we are now able to dynamically sense, analyze and understand these urban dynamics more quickly and to accumulate detailed knowledge over time to see patterns and trends. This technological approach – having access to large volume datasets to study a phenomenon and its dynamics – augments the process by which urban space is designed, developed and evaluated, and offers opportunities for data-driven analysis and design of the built environment. McLuhan foresaw technolo-gies serving as civic thermostats "to pattern life in ways that will optimize human awareness" [8]. He said, "already, it's technologically feasible to employ the computer to program societies in beneficial ways." He stressed that "the programming of societies could actually be conducted quite constructively and humanistically." Greenfield comments that "the final intent of all this... is to make every unfolding process of the city visible [...], to render the previously opaque or indeterminate not merely knowable but actionable" [9].

2   Devices and People, in Place

The pedestrian realm has long been a focus of research. William H. Whyte [10] used Super 8 film to record the use of plazas and other public spaces in New York City, created in the construction of large, office buildings taking advantage of new zoning incentives. Whyte used a variety of observational methods, including time-lapse films, to assess variation and regularity in pedestrian behavior and the use of designed elements in these small urban spaces. Whyte's research is an example within a longer tradition of using a snapshot of or creating a simulacrum of urban life, in an attempt to reveal the essential nature and predictable character of activities in the built environment.

Of course, these efforts were not new [11]. To reveal activity patterns, there are many mechanisms by which we can understand how individuals move through space and the motivations why. Traditionally, observations and surveys have been used to investigate values and attitudes towards different attributes of the pedestrian experience along a route. Increasingly, technology has been augmenting these efforts. Computer-based models and "on the move" surveys using mobile technologies are now common research tools [12]. These efforts can reveal how pedestrians behave, in regular and repeatable patterns, in space. This re-creation (modeling) is fundamental, as designing pedestrian environments requires assumptions about how individuals will respond to characteristics of the environment as they create and enact their walking itineraries. Fundamental, the patterns of travel have incredible regularity; despite the diversity of travel history overall, humans follow simple reproducible patterns [13]. Many of these regular decisions are made internally as a series of on-the-spot responses to social, economic and physical stimuli from the urban environment around the individual [14]. The quality of the pedestrian environment can significantly affect the utility of walking along a path [15].

Relationships between urban space and travel behavior have long been a focus of research by studying how people, place, and activity influence the creation of walking itineraries. These itineraries are closely tied to the mental imageability of a place. Lynch, notably, studied individuals' perceptions of the urban environment to formulate a conceptual basis for good urban form [16]. He ascertained that certain spatial elements and sequences tend to be remembered ("imageability"), suggesting that reference points (landmarks, edges, etc.) are important to spatial cognition [17]. These points provide an organizational structure that facilitates the location of subsequent points when individuals move through space.

Ultimately, the intent is to understand behaviors within the context of the intent [18]. This ethnography seeks to reveal the reveal technical, social, organizational, and physical factors that drive the decisions made by an individual, or the aggregated decisions of a population. With the democratization of access to digital technologies and information, these spatially-oriented studies have begun leveraging data as a means of scaling these ethnographies to the breadth of an urban region. The pervasiveness of mobile phones lent an opportunity to coarsely study the aggregated mobility patterns of entire cities through the metadata produced [19]. Online access to street-level photographs has been used to understand how the visual appearance of an urban environment can have strong effects on the perception of safety. Streetscore used a scene processing algorithm to predict the perceived safety of a streetscape, using training data from an online survey with contributions from more than 7000 participants and over 1 million online images [20].

Similarly, locative technologies may be used to understand human dynamics within an architectural or room scale. Several projects leverage Bluetooth sensors to record human dynamics within space. They leverage the unique MAC address assigned to each mobile device (and most likely, one person carrying these devices). When two Bluetooth equipped devices are in close proximity, the MAC address is shared between and a log may be kept of that interaction. Bluestates—by Mark Pesce and John Tonkin—sought to measure the social interactions between individuals equipped with Bluetooth-enabled mobile phones in order to see how social life in space is created between individuals: who talks to whom, for how long, and in what order? A comparable study conducted in the Louvre sought to delineate patterns of movement of visitors to the museum, finding little difference between short and long duration visits [21].

The use of public space and its dynamic characteristics has long been of interest with regard to technological culture. Keith Hampton has used Wi-Fi and data usage patterns with observations to ethnographically understand how Wi-Fi use influences the use and presence of individuals in urban public spaces [22]. Similarly, Ito et al. [23] created ethnographic profiles of Japanese youth in public spaces that used their mobile phones in the public realm. These profiles, again, are in a lineage of trying to understand patterns of social behavior in public space, but the use of the digital breadcrumbs from these engagements can now create more robust profiles of use and activity.

The potential to create thick descriptions is where the power of locative data lies. Especially through passive observation and documentation, we begin to answer this question with the natural behaviors of individuals. These behaviors carry with them significant implications for the design and planning of these spaces, the structure of a community, and the social networks among people. This prevalence of data from activities in public spaces may in turn reshape the public realm.

These projects use information and communication technologies to generate a map of human routine. These technologies are enabling a big data approach to Paul-Henry Chombart de Lauwe's 1957 idiosyncratic map tracing the movements of a single individual, a young woman studying at the school of political science. Today, such maps are now routine; we generate them involuntarily everyday as the devices we carry with us leak this locative data that include our locations and social connections through our voice calls, IP pings and messages sent. If we engage in certain kinds of online behavior – checking in via Foursquare, posting to Twitter with geolocation – we may be generating maps visible to the general public.

With the introduction and rapid adoption of personal mobile devices, such as mobile phones, smart watches, and wearable sensors, the amount of data about the minutia of personal activities is increasingly available [24]. This data is also increasingly geospatial, with activities located in the environments around us. This figurative overlay of digital information in our everyday lives has added a virtual connection between everyday reality, people, and devices. People are increasingly (and romantically) "immersed in a twitching, pulsing cloud of data" [25] with the introduction of pervasive sensing technologies. Taking a narrow view on Thrift and French [26], the use of digital technologies also automatically creates a virtual representation of physical space—an "automatically reproduced background" of data "found in the spaces of everyday life". Here, the digital "reproduces everyday life". The technological reality is that the space of the street is also becoming a platform for technologies logging detailed patterns of behavior, and allowing for new possibilities within them (Fig. 1).

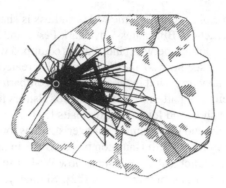

Fig. 1. Paul-Henry Chombart de Lauwe's 1957 map of a single woman's journeys through Paris

This new capacity, therefore, allows us to imagine new opportunities for urban planning, policy-making, and design by understanding the collective population within their specific urban milieu. Rather than a conceptual outcome, as Koolhaas imagines, wherein "apocalyptic scenarios will be managed and mitigated by sensor-based responses; mundane issues, hidden from view, will be brought to our attention and redressed automatically" [27], the potential of leveraging digital data is to serve as being supplemental to the intuitive process of design—theories within a designer's toolkit. In other words, the analysis and sense-making of digital data can reshape theories and practices of city-making towards a new paradigm rooted in the use of these massive, real-time sets of data.

3   One to Many: Toward an Urban Understanding

The design of the built environment to achieve social, cultural, environmental and economic goals entails assumptions about the function and performance of urban spaces. Understanding how individuals respond to the characteristics of existing urban spaces will allow creators of new public spaces to specify their context and design with more detail and greater certainty as to how they will actually perform. Fundamental to the creation of urban space is an understanding of how individuals are likely to behave within it. Gaining this knowledge requires "well-validated, durable criteria for successful outcomes" [28]. The difficulty, however, is that the generation of these criteria has long relied on surveys with small numbers, or anecdotal studies using proxy data. Campanella [29] similarly calls for a return to the planning of the physical city concentrated on people and place.

Such an endeavor would have to "deal with the complexities of aesthetic, ethical, and political theory to secure its foundations." This search has thus far been quixotic. Christopher Alexander, Leslie Martin, Kevin Lynch, John Habraken, Konstantinos Doxiadis, and many others have searched vigorously for theories that ascribe physical attributes and configurations with the quality of experience in urban spaces by those who inhabit it [7, 29–32]. This is made particular true, yet more challenged, in that people's work and social habits are changing because of new technologies—activities that once required fixed locations and connections can now be done with more location and temporal flexibility.

Here, the technology allows for such definitions to begin with the individual, through his or her natural choices. Rather than surveys or diaries where the person must unnaturally recall the minutia of daily life, locative technologies can document the eccentricities of those mundane choices. Cumulatively, these collective behaviors represent a truer picture of Campanella's complexity especially as the ubiquity of smartphones incorporate more and more locative technologies. Across the demographic spectrum, smart devices are being consumed and used with increasing numbers. Despite smartphone users tend to skew younger, a majority of Americans in their mid-forties/fifties now own smartphones [33].

For this study, we begin with the example of Boston, Massachusetts in the United States. The dense and non-orthogonal grid configuration has long made Boston known as a city amenable to walking. Morphologically, it is a unique case in the United States due to the lack of an orthogonal grid in much of the city. The city of Boston has the seventh highest rate of commuting trips done on foot, with neighboring Cambridge ranking first. The urban area of Boston has 15.1 % of commuting trips to work done on foot, the highest of any large city in the United States. Further, with the high ownership rates of mobile devices, it serves as a rich laboratory to investigate these human-device-city interface potentials.

3.1 Data

Traditionally, surveys have been the most promising tool for studying the link between the built environment and pedestrian behavior [34]. With new technologies now available, we are able to gain greater clarity in movements without the need for surveys or manually completed travel diaries. This project leverages anonymized data created on walking behavior by individuals using popular physical activity mobile applications. The scale and precision of this locative passively-collected, mobile phone data offer an opportunity to move beyond the limitations of previous studies. By not limiting the physical scale to a small area, but enlarging it to multiple cities, this study can span and assess distinct neighborhood typologies and help to mitigate issues of neighborhood self-selection. This allows for a novel awareness of aggregate pedestrian behaviors and risk exposure that speaks to the social and physical characteristics unique to a street, city or region as a whole, with insight into behavior influenced by dynamic conditions (Fig. 2).

This research employs anonymized data created on walking behavior by individuals using a popular physical activity mobile application company. First, an exercise-oriented application (EOA) collects data when users opt to track their fitness activity, and its' activity-oriented application (AOA) takes count of how much, and where, users walk. The AOA, utilizes the phone's motion coprocessor, which constantly documents movement data in the background processes of the device. Combined with GPS locations from the mobile device, the data reveals the walking locations and durations of users throughout the day. As a result, the data incorporates both recreational and utility (e.g., commuting) trips made by the user. With behaviors differing based on intention [35], a distinction is made between recreational and utilitarian activities.

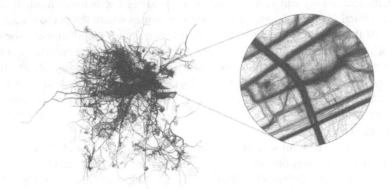

Fig. 2. A map of the Boston metropolitan area drawn from the individual pedestrian tracks in the dataset. The area around the MIT campus is called out (right) to show the detail of the geospatial data.

The data went through a process of anonymization before being shared with the researchers. First, profile information was anonymized and given hashed user identification numbers. Basic categorical demographic profile information was made available for EOA trips, but unavailable for the AOA trips. Further, a random distance of 0-100 m was removed from the start and end of each trip to further anonymize the user's frequently visited locations. The resultant data was again filtered to eliminate errant activity traces due to inherent errors in the device's various locationing methods [36].

3.2   Boston as a Case Study

In this study, we analyzed over one million trips from over 60,000 unique users in Boston from two mobile applications made by the application company bound within 42.2284° N, 71.1895° W and 42.3979° N, 70.9852° W. From the EOA, we analyzed data from January 2010 – May 2016 and from the AOA, May 2014 – May 2015. The use of these datasets offers an ability to assess walkability factors beyond "active living" or recreational purposes. With behaviors differing based on intention [35], a distinction is made between recreational and utilitarian activities. As users have to initiate trip recording with the EOA, that application is more inclined to document recreational activities when users wish to track their activities. As the AOA records all movement activities of the user, and increasingly users are always carrying their mobile device, the data is more representative of utilitarian, natural movement activities. This avails an opportunity to analyze utilitarian pedestrian activities as well as activities in residential or less central areas of these communities (Fig. 3).

However, inherent in this study (and the choice of case city) is a chicken and egg problem between the prevalence of walking and prevalence of data: without pedestrians, there is no data. This is particularly true of Boston, with its strong cultures of walking and with more pedestrian-oriented infrastructure than many other cities in the country. The approach of using data to extract these patterns is predicated on the availability of

Fig. 3. Three heat maps of Boston and walking activity from the AOA. The first image (left) shows the density of trips is primarily focused on the downtown and Back Bay neighborhoods. The second shows the average time spent in each spatial unit of the city, where the activity is centered on recreational areas in the city including waterfront walks and parks. The third (right) illustrates the paths taken by individuals overlaid on the urban tree density of Boston, with apparent correspondence between the two.

data. As such, there is a lack of a clear case study that offers a null scenario, where little walking occurs. However, the framing of the research questions is oriented toward understanding patterns of behavior in places where walking occurs, rather than what spatial factors compels walking generally.

For utilitarian trips, pedestrians can choose from any path within the urban grid to travel from origin to destination. Despite the abundance of options, pedestrians tend to favor a small subset of potential paths, of which several factors play a role. In particular, trips along streets purposefully designed with a pedestrian in mind do carry more passengers. This is especially true with tree-lined paths, which has a strong correlation to quantities of pedestrians trips. In this context, pedestrians do choose the utility of the street over pedestrian parkways for different mobility purposes, as velocities and elapsed time in these different spaces differ—pedestrians spend more time in, and traverse slower through, paths through parks or green spaces than on the sidewalks. Despite trees in both locales, pedestrians do behave differently in each of those spaces.

This type of analysis offers a new means of population-level categorizations of space that may transcend the typical approach to Euclidean planning, in the nuanced categorization of spaces through its use by the inhabitants themselves. The narrative analysis, in this example, reveals nuances that would otherwise remain invisible through traditional methods. Equivalently, through the analysis of actual activities may reveal behavioral patterns in time, as well as space.

3.3 Boston Marathon Bombings

Although an anecdote, the recent bombing tragedy at 2013 Boston Marathon offers a lens to understand how this data may begin to tell population-level behavior overall. In analyzing the characteristics of trips made during the week of the marathon, we were able to gain a perspective on how the citizens responded during the tragedy and confusion surrounding the attack in this unique and shocking event. Surprisingly, there few impacts noticed during that week—perhaps affirming the local rallying call to be "Boston

Strong". Compared to the week prior, there was a very noticeable drop off in trips after the bombings occurred in Back Bay on Monday, April 15. Although there is a general trend of fewer trips on Marathon Monday, largely due to the closure of streets for the Marathon, the decline in trips was significant, perhaps due to the police cordons and the strong mood of uncertainty in the city.

There was little difference in the number of trips being made by the application users, despite the safety concerns throughout the week of the manhunt and investigation. This is no more apparent than the little difference in the number of trips between Friday, April 19 and the week before, in defiance of the request by the Governor of Massachusetts to shelter-in-place in the cities and towns of Allston-Brighton, Boston, Belmont, Brookline, Cambridge, Newton, and Watertown, which lie within the study area. Even though that request was made, and the confusion surrounding the manhunt and subsequent shootout in Watertown, there was little overall difference in the hourly quantity of recreational trips between the two weeks, especially in areas farther from Watertown. Although to the likely chagrin of public safety officials, this glimpse into the activities at the city scale speaks to a narrative about the social resiliency of the population that would have otherwise been difficult to ascertain through word of mouth or observational narratives (Fig. 4).

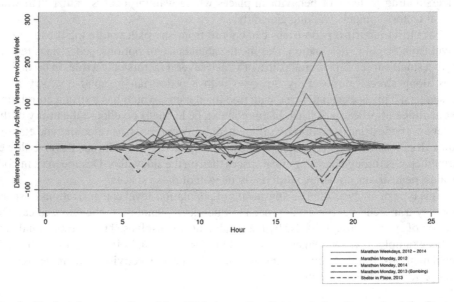

Fig. 4. The hourly count of weekday EOA (recreational) trips during the week of the Boston Marathon for 2012–2014. Although there is a noticeable drop in the number of trips after the blasts on Marathon Monday, 2013, the impact of the shelter in place order on the following Friday was not as apparent. The remarkable higher-than-average number of trips in the evening of April 22, 2014 is likely attributed to the ideal spring weather conditions in the city.

4 Discussion and Future Work

These narrative findings offer an initial lens by which we understand the city in new ways. While there are still many analyses to perform with this rich data, these results open new lines of human-computer interface research, particularly as it relates to the relationship between cities and individuals. In Michael Batty's words, "we delight in approaching the city in terms of its morphology but morphology is not enough. It must be unpacked and the only way to unpack it is through dynamics." [37] These results summarize and example a larger course of research.

Recent research efforts in urban planning have focused on the idea that land use and design policies can be used to promote non-motorized mobility such as walking. The development of appropriate measures for the built environment and for travel behavior is an essential element in the search for "good urban form". Neighborhood design has an important role in fostering walkability. Already, there is relatively strong evidence of an association between site design and pedestrian activity, particularly with compact development patterns and the promotion of walking behavior and may further this research.

Due to the imperative for user privacy, the challenge of the uncertainty as to the representativeness of this population across the breadth of descriptors for the larger population remains. Among them are questions of socio-economics, especially with this project's reliance on smartphones. A factor exacerbating these differences in pedestrian activity is accessibility—how different locations within a city are spatially linked to surrounding economic opportunities. Walkability is connected to larger considerations of socioeconomic conditions within the city and the generation of social capital: is walkability accessible to or enjoyed by all equally? This question, although broad and fundamental, touches upon the experiential potential differences in the character of urban space and the access, or lack thereof of these spaces as places to live work and play by those of differing socioeconomic groups across the breadth of the city. As walkability and traditional neighborhood design are en vogue in many areas, the concern is that pedestrian-friendliness may exacerbate societal divisions in their economic and physical inaccessibility. The generation and maintenance of social capital are other important components of quality of life that may be facilitated by living in a walkable community.

Of great interest as well is the use of this data to move beyond traditional measures of transportation that are often concerned with metrics of efficiency–velocity, speed, quantity. With the resolution of this data, there exists a potential to generate new measures drawn from the social behavior of individuals such as "shoaling", analogous to fish behavior. In the same vein as Whyte generating catalogs of behavioral typologies in public plazas, the precise locative data may allow for a cataloging of behaviors related to traversing the city.

Within the course of this study, this paper and presentation sought to encompass two parts of this urban-focused discourse. First, it established a theoretical context, rooted in the conversations of urban planning development as a foundation for HCI interventions, rather than those of technology (or worse, the rhetoric of "optimized" cities). It began as a literature review of that potential that exists with a new paradigm of big, locative data, that despite having been written within the context of situated computing, pervasive computing and smart cities for years, has only recently been made possible. The second half sought to be illustrative of that same potential, by seeking to example a new understand the relationship of people in place (with emphasis on both). Although there is more to be done, we hope it offers a figurative light at the end of the tunnel about the use of locative media at scale.

Acknowledgements. Thank you to the Liberty Mutual Research, Accenture China, American Air Liquide, Dallas Area Rapid Transit, ENEL Foundation, Ericsson, the Fraunhofer Institute, Philips, the Kuwait-MIT Center for Natural Resources and the Environment, Singapore-MIT Alliance for Research and Technology (SMART), and Volkswagen Electronics Research Laboratory, and all the members of the Senseable City Consortium. Our deep gratitude to Nicholas Arcolano for the provisioning of this valuable data.

References

1. Ratti, C., Offenhuber, D., Nabian, N., Vanky, A.: Data dimension: accessing urban data and making it accessible. Proc. ICE Urban Des. Plann. **166**(1), 60–75 (2013). http://doi.org/10.1680/udap.12.00011
2. McCullough, M.: New media urbanism: grounding ambient information technology. Environ. Plann. B Plann. Des. **34**(3), 383–395 (2007). http://doi.org/10.1680/udap.12.00011
3. Moran, T.P., Dourish, P.: Introduction to this special issue on context-aware computing. Hum.–Comput. Interact. **16**(2–4), 87–95 (2001)
4. Geertz, C.: Thick description: toward an interpretive theory of culture. In: Readings in the Philosophy of Social Science, pp. 213–231 (1994)
5. Jacobs, J.: The Death and Life of Great American Cities. Vintage, New York (1961)
6. Gehl, J.: Life Between Buildings: Using Public Space. Island Press, Washington, DC (2011)
7. Lynch, K.: Good City Form. MIT Press, Cambridge (1984)
8. Norden, E.: The playboy interview: Marshall McLuhan. In: Playboy Magazine, pp. 53–74 (1969)
9. Greenfield, A.: Everyware: The Dawning Age of Ubiquitous Computing. New Riders Publishing, New York (2006)
10. Whyte, W.: The Social Life of Small Urban Spaces. Project for Public Spaces, New York (1980)
11. Park, R.: The city: suggestions for the investigation of human behavior in the city environment. Am. J. Sociol. **20**(5), 577–612 (1915)
12. Kelly, C.E., Tight, M.R., Hodgson, F.C., Page, M.W.: A comparison of three methods for assessing the walkability of the pedestrian environment. J. Transp. Geogr. **19**(6), 1500–1508 (2011). http://doi.org/10.1016/j.jtrangeo.2010.08.001
13. González, M.C., Hidalgo, C.A., Barabási, A.-L.: Understanding individual human mobility patterns. Nature **453**(7196), 779–782 (2008). http://doi.org/10.1038/nature06958
14. Zacharias, J.: Pedestrian behavior and perception in urban walking environments. J. Plann. Lit. **16**(1), 3–18 (2001). http://doi.org/10.1177/08854120122093249
15. Guo, Z.: Does the pedestrian environment affect the utility of walking? a case of path choice in downtown Boston. Transp. Res. Part D Transp. Environ. **14**(5), 343–352 (2009). http://doi.org/10.1016/j.trd.2009.03.007
16. Lynch, K.: Good City Form. The MIT Press, Cambridge (1981)
17. Sandalla, F.K., Burroughs, W.J., Staplin, L.J.: Reference points in spatial cognition. J. Exp. Psychol. **6**, 516–528 (1980)

18. Casey, E.: The Fate of Place: A Philosophical History. University of California Press, Berkeley (2013)
19. Reades, J., Calabrese, F.: Cellular census: Explorations in urban data collection. Pervasive Computing (2007). http://ieeexplore.ieee.org/xpls/abs_all.jsp?arnumber=4287441
20. Naik, N., Philipoom, J.: Streetscore-predicting the perceived safety of one million streetscapes. In: Proceedings of the IEEE (2014). http://doi.org/10.1109/CVPRW.2014.121
21. Yoshimura, Y., Girardin, F., Carrascal, J.P., Ratti, C., Blat, J.: New tools for studying visitor behaviours in museums: a case study at the Louvre. In: Information and Communication Technologies in Tourism 2012, Proceedings of the International Conference Helsingborg (ENTER 2012), pp. 391–402, January 2012
22. Hampton, K.N., Livio, O., Sessions, G.L.: The social life of wireless urban spaces: internet use, social networks, and the public realm. J. Commun. 60(4), 701–722 (2010). http://doi.org/10.1111/j.1460-2466.2010.01510.x
23. Ito, M.: Mobile phones, Japanese youth, and the re-placement of social contact. In: Mobile Communications, pp. 131–148 (2005). http://doi.org/10.1007/1-84628-248-9_9
24. Ratti, C., Pulselli, R.M., Williams, S., Frenchman, D.: Mobile landscapes: using location data from cell phones for urban analysis. Environ. Plann. B: Plann. Des. 33(5), 727–748 (2006). http://doi.org/10.1068/b32047
25. Hill, D.: The street as platform, February 2008. http://www.cityofsound.com/blog/2008/02/the-street-as-p.html
26. Thrift, N., French, S.: The automatic production of space. Trans. Inst. Brit. Geogr. 27(3), 309–335 (2002)
27. Koolhaas, R.: The smart landscape: Rem Koolhaas on intelligent architecture. ARTFORUM Int. 53(8), 212–217 (2015)
28. Talen, E., Ellis, C.: Beyond relativism. Reclaiming the search for good city form. J. Plann. Educ. Res. 22, 36–49 (2002)
29. Campanella, T.: Reconsidering Jane Jacobs: The Death and Life of American Planning, 1 April 2011. https://placesjournal.org/article/jane-jacobs-and-the-death-and-life-of-american-planning/. Accessed 23 Apr 2015
30. Alexander, C.: Notes of the Synthesis of Form, vol. 5. Harvard University Press, Cambridge (1964)
31. Doxiades, K.A.: Ekistics; an Introduction to the Science of Human Settlements. Oxford University Press, New York (1968)
32. Habraken, N.J., Teicher, J.: The Structure of the Ordinary: Form and Control in the Built Environment. MIT Press, Cambridge (1998)
33. Duggan, M.: Cell phone activities 2013. Pew Research Center's Internet & American Life Project (2013)
34. Transportation Research Board, & Institute Of Medicine. Does the Built Environment Influence Physical Activity? (2005)
35. Giles-Corti, B., Timperio, A., Bull, F., Pikora, T.: Understanding physical activity environmental correlates: increased specificity for ecological models. Exerc. Sport Sci. Rev. 33(4), 175–181 (2005). http://doi.org/0091-6331/3304/175–181
36. Zandbergen, P.A., Barbeau, S.J.: Positional accuracy of assisted GPS data from high-sensitivity GPS-enabled mobile phones. J. Navig. 64(03), 381–399 (2011)
37. Batty, M., Chapman, D., Evans, S., Haklay, M., Kueppers, S., Shiode, N., Torrens, P.M.: Visualizing the city: communicating urban design to planners and decision-makers (2000)

Gamification and Social Dynamics: Insights from a Corporate Cycling Campaign

Matthias Wunsch[1,3], Agnis Stibe[2], Alexandra Millonig[1], Stefan Seer[1], Ryan C.C. Chin[2], and Katja Schechtner[2(✉)]

[1] Austrian Institute of Technology, Vienna, Austria
{Matthias.Wunsch.fl,Alexandra.Millonig,
Stefan.Seer}@ait.ac.at
[2] MIT Media Lab, Cambridge, MA, USA
{agnis,rchin,katjas}@mit.edu
[3] Human Computer Interaction,
Vienna University of Technology, Vienna, Austria

Abstract. Cycling is an essential transport mode in a well-balanced urban transportation system. While most approaches for achieving an increase from today's usually low levels of biking are focusing mainly on infrastructure measures and policies, this study presents the effects of the Biking Tourney, a bike commuting challenge between 14 companies aiming at motivating employees to commute by bike. This six-week study involved 239 participants using a socially influencing system for reporting commutes and watching the rankings. The frequency of bike commuting increased for 15 % of overall participants due to their participation. Within the subgroup of occasional bike commuters an even higher share of 30 % commuted by bike more frequently. Further analysis discusses multiple factors contributing to the engagement of employees in the tourney. As the results show the persuasiveness of the intervention, implications for a large-scale implementation are discussed.

Keywords: Low-energy mobility · Cycling · Behavior change · Transportation · Sustainability · Socially influencing systems

1 Introduction

Cycling is an essential transport mode in a well-balanced urban transportation system. The benefits of cycling comprise ecological, economic, social as well as individual advantages, e.g.

- Cycling is a carbon neutral form of transportation and requires only 1/30 of resources as compared to private motorized vehicles during its life cycle [1]
- Cycling provides major health and financial benefits both for the individual (low costs) and the economy as a whole
- Cycling requires less space than private motorized transport (about 10 % for parked vehicles and 60 % for moving vehicles [2].

However, despite the documented advantages of cycling, in many cities there is still a very small share of cyclists. A range of different barriers to cycling are responsible for

© Springer International Publishing Switzerland 2016
N. Streitz and P. Markopoulos (Eds.): DAPI 2016, LNCS 9749, pp. 494–503, 2016.
DOI: 10.1007/978-3-319-39862-4_45

the fact that cycling is not perceived as a legitimate form of transport. As many of these barriers are based on individual perceptions and emotional aspects such as fear of the feeling of insecurity, the provision of cycling infrastructure and access to bikes is not sufficient to convince a large number of people to start biking. Thus, there are several initiatives to promote biking through e.g. gamification and socially engaging approaches in order to motivate citizens to voluntarily switch to more sustainable modes of transport [3]. Examples of campaigns applying game elements like competition or cooperation show promising effects [4]: e.g. the annual Austrian cycling campaign "Bike to Work" engages thousands of bikers each year. Part of this success is believed to be related to the boosting effect of having small teams in the campaign, which mutually encourage themselves to take as many bike trips as possible. In comparison, prizes that are provided as part of the campaign are playing a less important for motivating participants to bike more. The actual social dynamics and processes leading to behavior changes [5] are still barely examined. Particularly the effectiveness of initiatives aiming at creating/stimulating behavior change in the absence of any tangible incentives needs to be studied further.

A pilot study as part of the research project "Persuasive Urban Mobility" showed that the gamification of cycling, when cycling becomes part of a wider competitive challenge against the self and others, gives promising results regarding the increase of bike trips among participants [6]. Previous research from McCall et al. [7] and Jylhä et al. [8] support these results.

In this paper, we present the outcomes of an approach providing organizations with a socially influencing system for engaging their employees in a biking competition. We chose this approach to investigate how social dynamics evolve in organizations through gamified biking campaigns, which enable better scalability compared to reaching out to individuals themselves. In particular, the following research questions have been addressed:

- Are group dynamics and the elements introduced with the competition sufficient for increasing specific bike use?
- What overall effect on the level of biking can be observed for different types of bikers?
- To what extent can socially influencing systems designed for competition engage employees in commuting by bike?

The next section outlines the design of the study, followed by a description of the methodological setting. The main section provides the detailed evaluation results for the study, and the concluding discussion highlights the learning of this approach in relation to previous findings and the implications to be considered for similar future interventions.

2 Study Design

Within the presented study, a six week lasting intervention: the "Biking Tourney 2015", we designed as a socially influencing system [5] to drive competition [9] between organizations. In this approach, companies serve as communities, thus provide a shared identity for their employees. By that, social interactions and mutual encouragement for biking are facilitated. Apart from the competition and related information (website, emails), no extra incentives were provided to the companies or participants.

The design of the tourney included four different categories related to bike usage in which the participating companies were ranked. Actual mobility data was gathered using a self-reporting web application. The categories aimed to reflect the goals of the tourney of encouraging citizens to bike instead of using high-energy means of transportation. Three of the rankings were introduced at the beginning of the tourney: (1) "Bikers", reflected the share of biking employees and should encourage for participation as well as for motivating others to join the tourney. (2) "Average distance", reflected the effort a company's employees invested in the tourney while not being influenced by the actual employee count of a participating company. (3) "Total distance", honored the total contribution of the biking employees which, however, clearly favored bigger companies. After the initial three weeks, the fourth ranking called "enthusiasm" was introduced, which showed a score of the change in the share of bikers over time. Thereby companies with low drop-outs and employees joining even after the official start were higher ranked. Figure 1 illustrates the graphical representations of three categories which were provided to the participants during the tourney.

The different ranking schemes were designed in a way that they also compensate for potentially demotivating settings for participants, for instance being in the lower ranks, or having a disadvantage because of the company size. This was based on the assumption that when providing several rankings a low standing in one of them is not as demotivating as in a single category design. The hypothesis is that a competition among organizations would provoke cooperation among employees in each organization. Furthermore, the use of publicly displayed rankings in common areas of the companies – as shown in Fig. 2 – should raise awareness of the tourney and facilitate [10] commuting by bike.

3   Methods

Intervention Context. After contacting 227 companies, a total of 14 companies took part in the Biking Tourney, with employee counts from 17 up to about 10,000. All companies or their respective local offices were located in the Greater Boston Area (MA, USA). The companies did not receive any incentives for taking part in the study. The Biking Tourney took place in September and October 2015 and lasted for six weeks. The weather during the intervention period was generally described by the participants as good biking weather except for one week with several rainy days.

Sample. The Biking Tourney had overall 239 registered users, with a mean age of 39 years (SD: 11 years), consisting of 18.6 % (44) female, 81.0 % (192) male and 0.4 % (1) non gender specific participant. The domination of males can be partly explained by the fact that the company with the most participants has a male-dominated workforce (about 70 %). Furthermore, the overall share of male bikers is higher in the US, similar to many other countries. [11] The mean commuting distance - home to work - was 7.7 km (4.8 miles) with a standard deviation of 6.1 km (3.8 miles). Based on a survey

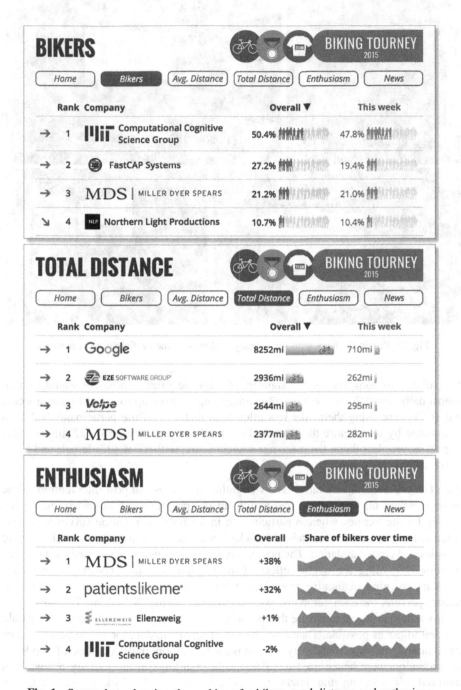

Fig. 1. Screenshots showing the rankings for bikers, total distance and enthusiasm

Fig. 2. Public displays with the tourney rankings in the participating companies

the participants took during the sign-up, 60 % were usually bike commuting on an almost daily basis, 24 % were usually commuting by bike up to several times a week, and 16 % were using their bike less often than that. All of the participants had been commuting by bike before the tourney. Out of all study participants, 127 filled out the ex post survey. For them, the mean age was 39 years, with 17 % (22) female and 83 % (104) male participants.

Data Generation.   Quantitative data was gathered by pre- and post-intervention online surveys, where all participants had to fill out the pre-intervention survey during the sign-up for the tourney whereas participation in the post-intervention survey was done voluntarily. The surveys contained standardized questionnaire items for descriptive statistics and cross-tabulation. The post-intervention survey also contained a set of open questions regarding the overall effect of the tourney on one's commuting routines. Furthermore, nine qualitative interviews with the company representatives, i.e. our contact persons for each company, were conducted during the Biking Tourney.

It was a major goal to ensure that participation of companies and employees would be as effortless as possible. Therefore, the reporting of trip data for a time period before the tourney was not mandatory. Self-reported data on daily choices of mode of transportation were hence used to calculate the standings in the tourney but was not analyzed for gauging the intervention effect due to the lack of pre-study- or control-group data.

Analysis. Cross tabulation is used to highlight the effects within the intervention for different types of participants. Qualitative data from the interviews and from the open-question pre- and post-questionnaires was structured and analyzed according the a thematic analysis [12].

4 Results and Discussion

Participants of the Biking Tourney have been very positive about the intervention design. The question: "Overall, how did you like the Biking Tourney?" on a scale ranging from 1 "Not at all" to 50 "Very good" the mean rating was 35.5 [SD = 9.8]. Regarding mode shifts due to participation, a reduction of car use was reported by 11 % of the respondents and 17 % stated to have reduced their use of public transportation. Furthermore, out of all participants answering the post-intervention survey, 19 % planned to commute by bike more often or continue to do so and 78.6 % planned to continue to do their commute as they did before joining the tourney. As for these results one has to keep in mind that a self-selection bias has been likely introduced through the selection of participants and the voluntary nature of the post-study questionnaire.

4.1 Motivation for and During Participation

Cooperation among employees of each organization was a driving factor for participation, with 45.7 % of participants crediting "team spirit /participating together as a team" and 41.7 % saying that their colleagues were motivating to them. A total of 29.9 % agreed with "joining as a way to motivate others to bike", highlighting the cooperative effect within the companies. *"I bike most every day anyway. I do appreciate the encouragement for others." (#205)*.

Personal health benefits were a relevant motivator for 40.9 % of participants, the available statistics did motivate 34.6 % of participants and competition with other companies has been a motivator for 34.6 %. Although often mentioned in relation to biking, environmental benefits were the lowest ranked motivating factor with a share of only 27.6 %. Of course, for most participants a mix of motivators was present: *"The tourney gave me more incentive to bike during the week as the exercise is good, faster than transit, and more reliable." (#48)*.

Colleagues as Persuaders. The level of engagement and activities of the company representatives varied to a large degree. All of them sent out informational emails to their colleagues, but some were more eager and actively engaged their colleagues to participate regardless of their otherwise used mode of transportation. In order to support this, some companies used specific mailing lists, handed out flyers or set up social media groups. This shows that the Biking Tourney did provide a framework for persuading their colleagues within a company to regularly commute by bike or try out doing so. Because of that, having companies as a proxy for such an intervention appears to be an effective way for increasing scalability.

Advocacy. Another motivator for participating was advocacy for improved bike policies. Company representatives and decision makers as well as individual tourney participants stated that they want to signal to the city that there is demand for better infrastructure for utilitarian biking. *"Hoping that the statistics will improve safety for cycling and bring attention to improved urban planning for commuting on bike in Greater Boston."* (#76).

4.2   Change in Frequency of Bike Commuting

Users of the Biking Tourney reported their preexisting frequency of bike commuting at the sign-up process for the tourney. Based on this, three groups of participants can be identified: (1) Occasional bikers, commuting by bike monthly to weekly, (2) regular bike commuters are those commuting several times per week by bike and (3) daily bike commuters. Notably, the latter two groups represent 84 % of the tourney participants and are slightly overrepresented in the ex-post survey with a share of 90 %. Furthermore, all Biking Tourney participants stated that they commuted by bike before, implying that the tourney did not encourage non-biking employees to try to commute by bike. By that the intervention did mostly "preach to the converted". This could have been caused by the overall approach of a competition oriented design which might be more attractive to existing bikers.

Table 1 represents the reported change during the Biking Tourney. These changes are based on survey data rather than self-reported trip data as no pre-intervention mobility data was collected. While 78.7 % of participants remained at their level of bike commuting, overall 15 % reported an increase in doing so. This compares to only 4.7 % reporting a decrease in bike commuting. By that, a persuasive effect shifting

Table 1. Reported change in frequency of bike commuting

	Occasional bikers	Regular bikers	Daily bikers	Full Sample
	Survey (total) 10 % (16 %)	Survey (total) 22 % (24 %)	Survey (total) 68 % (60 %)	100 % (100 %)
Usual frequency of bike commuting	Monthly to weekly	Several times a week	(Almost) daily	
Change during Biking Tourney				
Biked more often	30.8 %	25.0 %	9.3 %	15.0 %
Biked the same	61.5 %	57.1 %	88.4 %	78.7 %
Biked less often	0.0 %	14.3 %	2.3 %	4.7 %
Other	7.7 %	3.6 %	0.0 %	1.6 %
Total	100.0 %	100.0 %	100.0 %	100.0 %
Number of survey respondents	13	28	86	127

Survey question: "During the Biking Tourney..." (a) "I commuted by bike more often than usually." (b) "I commuted by bike as often as before."(c) "I commuted by bike less often than before." (d) "Other" daily transportation choices towards biking is indicated. A comparison by group shows that the increases in bike use where most present for the occasional (30.8 %) and regular bikers (25 %). This does not come as a surprise, as these were the participants with a higher potential for such increases.

A Trigger for Commuting by Bike More Often. The collected qualitative data supports these findings shown in Table 1, with some of the occasional bikers trying out to commute by bike: *"I took bus before but was pleasantly surprised how much faster taking bike was."* *(#276)* But while this leads to an uptake of a new commuting habit for some, other came by bike to *"[...] try it out and support the regular bike commuters in my office"* *(#286)*, but stopped doing so after the tourney. Regular bike commuters commented about the motivating effects on their colleagues as well: *"The Biking Tourney is a great boost for folks who were considering bike commuting and who needed a little push."* *(#93)*.

Commitment for Commuting by Bike More Often. For occasional bikers, the tourney acted as a mean for making bike commuting more of a habit. "Last spring the Mass Bike Challenge helped me realize that I could bike the 12 miles each way. The MIT Media challenge helped make it more of a routine." (#86) "Due to the tournament, I did seek out a safe route to cycle into work and will use it more often as a result." (#76) Furthermore, the tourney acted also as a commitment system for increasing ones bike commuting frequency: "I have always wanted to bike in pretty much every day. Biking tourney got me moving towards that goal." (#176) "It definitely helped as motivation to get on bike more often." (#36).

Another effect of the commitment to the tourney was that participants biked even on days with bad weather. "Some of my office mates made a bigger effort to bike. [...] It was exciting to see so many of our fair-weather bike commuters take the plunge into cold and wet riding on the days that rained."(#50).

Commuting as Always. Most participants (78.7 %) continued commuting by bike at their usual level, indicating no change due to the tourney. "I always bike to work, so it was the same as usual." (#50).

Commuting by Bike Less Often. A small amount of participants (4.7 %) reduced their amount of bike commuting, but this was mostly due to temporary external causes such as business travel to other places, illness or technical problems with one's bike.

5   Conclusion

This study investigated the effects of competition and cooperation on overall engagement which adds to the knowledge about the social dynamics within initiatives as the Biking Tourney. The mutual encouragement present in most participating companies made employees join. While a large part of actual participants were already commuting by bike on a daily basis, the induced social processes did also motivate non-regular bikers to participate in the Biking Tourney. By that, the tourney was able to set the stage for triggering an increase in bike commuting for 15 % of overall participants, with almost a third of the subgroup of occasional bike commuters and for a quarter of the subgroup of regular bike commuters increasing their bike use. Qualitative data showed the importance of the competition between companies and the cooperation within companies for the overall engagement in the tourney.

Future large scale implementations of the presented study design should consider that the share of occasional bikers, i.e. participants that usually bike once a week or less than that, has been lower and the behavior changing effects were smaller than in previous studies [6, 13]. A different framing of this intervention that is more inviting to non-regular-bikers or non-bikers might help to get more of them involved. Furthermore, companies as a social-group might not be as effective as small teams for producing mutual encouragement between participating employees.

As a behavioral intervention the Biking Tourney can be easily scaled-up, making it a viable option for communities or cities for promoting sustainable transportation. By that it has the potential to benefit organizations, communities, societies, individuals and research alike.

Acknowledgments. The authors gratefully acknowledge Kent Larson and Geraldine Fitzpatrick for their advice and support within this research project. Our special acknowledgement is due to Chengzen Dai, Felipe Lozano-Landinez and Francesco Pilla for their contributions to this research and their help in conducting the presented study.

References

1. Lähteenoja, S., Lettenmeier, M., Kauppinen, T., Luoto, K., Moisio, T., Salo, M., Tamminen, P., Veuro, S.: Natural resource consumption caused by finnish households. In: Proceedings of the Nordic Consumer Policy Research Conference Helsinki (2007)
2. Randelhoff, M.: Vergleich unterschiedlicher Flächeninanspruchnahmen nach Verkehrsarten (pro Person) » Zukunft Mobilität. http://www.zukunft-mobilitaet.net/78246/analyse/flaechenbedarf-pkw-fahrrad-bus-strassenbahn-stadtbahn-fussgaenger-metro-bremsverzoegerung-vergleich/
3. Richter, J., Friman, M., Gärling, T.: Soft transport policy measures: gaps in knowledge. Int. J. Sustain. Transp. **5**, 199–215 (2011)
4. Wunsch, M., Millonig, A., Seer, S., Schechtner, K., Stibe, A., Chin, R.C.C.: Challenged to Bike: Assessing the Potential Impact of Gamified Cycling Initiatives. Presented at the Transportation Research Board (TRB) 95th Annual Meeting 2016 (accepted). Washington, DC (2016)
5. Stibe, A.: Towards a framework for socially influencing systems: meta-analysis of four PLS-SEM based studies. In: MacTavish, T., Basapur, S. (eds.) PERSUASIVE 2015. LNCS, vol. 9072, pp. 172–183. Springer, Heidelberg (2015)
6. Wunsch, M., Stibe, A., Millonig, A., Seer, S., Dai, C., Schechtner, K., Chin, R.C.C.: What makes you bike? exploring persuasive strategies to encourage low-energy mobility. In: MacTavish, T., Basapur, S. (eds.) PERSUASIVE 2015. LNCS, vol. 9072, pp. 53–64. Springer, Heidelberg (2015)
7. McCall, R., Koenig, V., Kracheel, M.: Using gamification and metaphor to design a mobility platform for commuters. Int. J. Mob. Hum. Comput. Interact. **5**, 1–15 (2013)
8. Jylhä, A., Nurmi, P., Sirén, M., Hemminki, S., Jacucci, G.: Matkahupi: a persuasive mobile application for sustainable mobility. In: Proceedings of the 2013 ACM conference on Pervasive and ubiquitous computing adjunct publication, pp. 227–230. ACM (2013)

9. Deutsch, M.: A theory of cooperation-competition and beyond. Handb. Theor. Soc. Psychol. **2**, 275 (2011)
10. Guerin, B.: Social facilitation. Wiley Online Library (2010)
11. Heinen, E., van Wee, B., Maat, K.: Commuting by bicycle: an overview of the literature. Transp. Rev. **30**, 59–96 (2010)
12. Braun, V., Clarke, V.: Using thematic analysis in psychology. Qual. Res. Psychol. **3**, 77–101 (2006)
13. Rose, G., Marfurt, H.: Travel behaviour change impacts of a major ride to work day event. Transp. Res. Part Policy Pract. **41**, 351–364 (2007)

Erratum to: Voices of the Internet of Things: An Exploration of Multiple Voice Effects in Smart Homes

Yohan Moon[1], Ki Joon Kim[2], and Dong-Hee Shin[3(✉)]

[1] Department of Interaction Science, Chung-Ang University, Seoul, South Korea
ttattang@skku.edu
[2] Department of Media and Communication, City University of Hong Kong,
Hong Kong, China
stand4good@gmail.com
[3] School of Media and Communication, Chung-Ang University,
Seoul, South Korea
dshin1030@cau.ac.kr

Erratum to:
Chapter 25 in: N. Streitz and P. Markopoulos (Eds.)
Distributed, Ambient and Pervasive Interactions
DOI: 10.1007/978-3-319-39862-4_25

The initially published affiliation of the author Shin, D., was incorrect. The correct affiliation is as follows: School of Media and Communication, Chung-Ang University.

The updated original online version for this chapter can be found at 10.1007/978-3-319-39862-4_25

© Springer International Publishing Switzerland 2016
N. Streitz and P. Markopoulos (Eds.): DAPI 2016, LNCS 9749, p. E1, 2016.
DOI: 10.1007/978-3-319-39862-4_46

Erratum to: Mental Model Development Using Collaborative 3D Virtual Environments

Ali Asghar Nazari Shirehjini[1]([⊠]), Farideh Soltani Nejad[1],
Gazelle Saniee-Monfared[1], Azin Semsar[1],
and Shervin Shirmohammadi[2]

[1] Sharif University of Technology, Tehran, Iran
{shirehjini, fsoltaninejad, gsaniee, semsar}@sharif.edu
[2] University of Ottawa, Ottawa, Canada
shervin@eecs.uottawa.ca

Erratum to:
Chapter 26 in: N. Streitz and P. Markopoulos (Eds.)
Distributed, Ambient and Pervasive Interactions
DOI: 10.1007/978-3-319-39862-4_26

In the original version, the name of the second author was incorrect. Instead of "Farideh Solatni Nejad" it should read as "Farideh Soltani Nejad". The original chapter was corrected.

The updated original online version for this chapter can be found at 10.1007/978-3-319-39862-4_26

© Springer International Publishing Switzerland 2016
N. Streitz and P. Markopoulos (Eds.): DAPI 2016, LNCS 9749, p. E2, 2016.
DOI: 10.1007/978-3-319-39862-4_47

Author Index

Printed in the United States
By Bookmasters

Printed in the United States
By Bookmasters